To Larry R. Olson,
To the memory of Virginia F. Cox,
and
To our students, who inspired the writing of this text:
Those we have worked with in the past, those we are
currently teaching, and those still to come.

PREFACE

This third edition is based on a personal philosophy that has evolved from the literature in special and general education and from our professional experiences. The teacher effectiveness research in both special and general education provides many exemplary teaching practices that we include in this text. Our professional experiences include teaching both elementary and secondary students in general and special education settings, supervising student teachers, training preservice and in-service teachers, and continuing participation as learners in professional development activities involving effective teaching practices.

The basic philosophy that keeps us actively involved in the profession after more than 30 years is that as teachers, we can "make a difference" in the lives of our students. When the preservice and in-service teachers we work with express concern about not affecting the lives of each of their students to the degree they wish, we remind them of the following story of a young boy walking along the beach. To paraphrase:

> That morning the tide had brought in thousands of starfish and scattered them on the hot, dry, sandy beach. A little boy was walking along the beach, tossing starfish back into the cool, blue water. As he was doing this, an older man approached him. The older man looked at what the young boy was doing and said, "Why are you doing that? Don't you see it's impossible? Look at the thousands of starfish. You can't possibly make a difference." The young boy slowly looked up at the man, picked up another starfish, and threw it back into the water, saying, "It makes a difference to this one." (author unknown)

We hope you continue to find ideas and suggestions in this third edition to make a difference in your students' lives. You have the power to make a difference, for you have chosen to teach.

FEATURES OF THE TEXT

We continue to use an informal, personal tone in writing this third edition. Additionally, we structure and organize the text to include recommendations of teacher effectiveness research, including the following effective teaching practices.

Advance Organizers and Postorganizers

We begin each chapter with an advance organizer by providing an outline that highlights the key topics within the chapter. We close each chapter with discussion questions that challenge you to reflect on your professional practice and to think critically about the chapter content.

Reviewing/Checking for Understanding/Monitoring Progress

Throughout the chapters, we include several checkpoints so that you can monitor your progress as you read. These checkpoints take the form of "Important Points" sections found in the text of each chapter.

Active Involvement

We provide opportunities for you to become actively involved by placing activity sections in each of the chapters. They are interspersed throughout each chapter to give you ample practice. Remember the Chinese proverb: "I hear and I forget, I see and I remember, I do and I understand."

Visual Aids

We include tables, figures, diagrams, photographs, and illustrations throughout the text. We hope you use them to clarify concepts and to increase your interest.

NOTEWORTHY CHANGES

As a result of feedback from reviewers, colleagues, and our students along with input from consumers of the second edition, we have made considerable changes in this edition. As our field is constantly evolving, we have updated information in all of the chapters and reorganized to add clarity. We have included much new information such as detailed lesson plans, more examples that apply to inclusive settings and collaboration among general and special education professionals, more ways to actively involve students, and more suggestions for movement from teacher control and direction to student control.

We expanded information on teaching academic and affective content as we discuss the single-text approach and social skills. Based on our philosophy that special educators must become more adept at adapting materials and communicating with general educators as our students move into inclusive classes, we have also expanded the information in Chapter 4, Instructional Materials, and Chapter 5, Collaborative Consultation and Communication, and emphasized transition.

Based on a literature review of effective practices for teaching students with mild disabilities, we have eliminated the whole-language section to reflect a more balanced approach and combined assessment information in one chapter, as you should diagnose and monitor at the same time. One of our most challenging chapters was Chapter 11, Technology for Teaching and Learning, as it is difficult to keep pace with all the new information.

We believe that our third edition continues to be a text that contains practical, research-based teaching strategies, relates to everyday occurrences in the schools, and describes motivating, experience-based activities. We hope, like the boy and the starfish, "Our ideas and suggestions make a difference to you and your students."

ACKNOWLEDGMENTS

We wish to acknowledge the contributions of everyone who assisted us in the completion of this text. Thanks to Eileen Pracek and Dianne Mathews, who assisted in writing Chapter 11, and to Sara Pankaskie, who wrote Chapter 12. We also wish to thank Debbie Becker, Sharon Dryden, Lauren Hotaling, Amy Kosar, and John Varady for their help in researching and editing the new edition. To Ann Davis, Sheryl Langner, and all the Prentice Hall staff, we express our gratitude for making our dream a reality.

Thank you to our reviewers for their valuable input and suggestions: Martha Cook, University of Alabama; Jean C. Faieta, Edinboro University of Pennsylvania; Jack Hourcade, Boise State University; Robert S. Ristow, St. Ambrose University (IA); and James Yanok, Ohio University.

A special thanks goes to Larry Olson, whose patience with and support of a part-time wife during this process are deeply appreciated. Gratitude and appreciation are given to Chris Platt for his advice, support, and concern during the completion of the text and to Susan Wiehn for her technical assistance.

Without the input of our students at the University of Central Florida and the support and encouragement of our families and friends, we would not have had an opportunity to make a difference in the lives of students with special needs. We are deeply grateful for these many contributions.

CONTENTS

4
Instructional Materials   100

5
Collaborative Consultation and Communication   130

◆ PART 2
INSTRUCTIONAL TECHNIQUES   167

6
The Instructional Cycle   168

PART

FOUNDATIONS FOR INSTRUCTION

1

STUDENTS WITH
SPECIAL NEEDS

The field of special education will grow and change in the 21st century, as schools are restructured to meet the mandate of Goals 2000: Educate America Act (1994). Issues such as student characteristics, cultural diversity, effective teaching strategies, and education reform are being addressed and refined as we begin the new century.

The needs and characteristics of children and adolescents with learning and behavior problems are varied. Being knowledgeable about student characteristics means that you know your students' academic levels, can identify the skills they bring with them to the learning situation, and understand their cultural backgrounds. Children and adolescents with special needs often exhibit problems with academic and social skills that make it difficult for them to meet the demands of school, home, and community.

For optimum learning to occur, it is important that you use effective teaching strategies based on sound research. You must also be aware of the service delivery options that are available for students with special needs. Finally, you need to understand the federal government's education reform strategy, Goals 2000: Educate America Act (1994), and the current emphasis on inclusion of students with disabilities in general education settings.

STUDENT CHARACTERISTICS

Students with special needs often have problems in academic areas, social interactions, motivation, and transition to adult roles. In many school districts, such students are referred to as having learning disabilities (specific learning disabilities), mental disabilities (mental handicaps, mental retardation, educable mental handicaps), or emotional disabilities (emotional disturbance, behavior disorders). Even though educational practice frequently categorizes children and adolescents into these three distinct groups, researchers document many similarities in their characteristics. Wilson, Cone, Bradley, and Reese (1986) found similarities in IQ scores, perceptual-motor performance, and achievement levels of students with learning disabilities and those with emotional disturbances. These researchers also found similarities in the classroom behaviors of students with learning disabilities and those with mental disabilities. On the *Stanford Achievement Test,* Scruggs and Mastropieri (1986) found no differences between the academic performance of 619 primary-aged students with learning disabilities and 863 with behavior disorders. Thus, it appears that there are more similarities than differences among these groups of students.

We group these students together in this text because we feel many of the techniques we share are effective for students with learning disabilities, behavior disorders, or mental disabilities. These students are often categorized as students with mild disabilities. Characteristics that students with special needs may display include:

◆ *Inadequate academic achievement.* Often, such students are two or more years behind their grade-level peers in reading, mathematics, spelling, written expression, and/or oral language skills.
◆ *Inappropriate school behaviors.* Many times, they are physically or verbally aggressive. They are frequently easily frustrated or unable to cope with the demands of the school environment. Other signs of inappropriate school behavior include noncompliance with teacher directions and instructions and lack of teacher-pleasing behaviors, such as being prepared for class, maintaining eye contact, and raising hands.
◆ *Poor attending behaviors.* Students with special needs often have trouble following teacher directions and instructions. They seem to have difficulty attending to the relevant information in a message and are frequently unable to concentrate on an assignment or task.
◆ *Poor memory.* Being unable to remember information from one week to the next or from one day to the next is another characteristic common to many students with special needs. These students frequently have problems remembering spelling words, basic math facts, and two or more directions.
◆ *Inadequate organizational skills.* Students who have special needs may have problems organizing their materials to prepare for an exam or to write a report. Frequently, their desks are cluttered and their materials are lost or misplaced.
◆ *Poor self-concept.* For many students with special needs, school is not a comfortable, rewarding place. Instead, it is a place where they often fail to meet the standards for success.
◆ *Inadequate social skills.* Such students often cannot maintain satisfactory interpersonal relationships, are less socially accepted by peers, and demonstrate impaired communication (pragmatic language) skills. The lack of social skills precludes adequate adjustment not only to the demands of the school environment, but also to the postschool environment. Students with special needs are frequently less accepted and less successful in the world of work due to lack of social skills.

CULTURAL DIVERSITY

Within the population of students with special needs are students who are not members of the

Anglo-American culture. These students are from Native American, Asian, Hispanic (Latino), African-American, or other cultures. The U.S. Bureau of the Census predicts that in the year 2010, children of color will represent the majority of the school population in the states of Florida, New York, and Texas. Students from these groups are disproportionately represented in special education classes. Data from the Office of Civil Rights 1994 Compliance Report revealed that minority students comprised about 34% of the total school age population; 42% of the population of students with mild, moderate, and severe mental disabilities; 34% of the population of students with emotional disabilities; and 33% of the population of students with learning disabilities (McCabe, 1997).

Although students in public schools are from various cultures, the school culture frequently reflects Anglo-American values (Turnbull & Turnbull, 1986). These values, which are often at odds with those of other cultures, include a belief in competition, individual autonomy and independence, an achievement orientation, a future orientation, timeliness, and an informal classroom atmosphere (Briganti, 1989; Grossman, 1990; McGill & Pearce, 1982; Turnbull & Turnbull, 1986).

Competition

School culture tends to promote competition over cooperation (Rivera & Rogers-Adkinson, 1997). However, the Hispanic culture emphasizes working together for the good of the group (Briganti, 1989; Grossman, 1994) and values cooperation over competition (Castaneda, 1976; Grossman, 1994). In the Native American culture, the needs of the family and the tribe are given priority over the needs of individuals (Johnson, 1987). Hispanics or Native Americans may pretend not to know an answer instead of correcting a peer's incorrect answer, as they do not wish to secure individual atten-

tion at the expense of another person (Grossman, 1994). The African-American culture also tends to be social, and it endorses working with others (Grossman, 1994; Hillard, 1980; Rivera & Rogers-Adkinson, 1997).

For many of these students, cooperative learning and peer tutoring are effective strategies (see Chapter 10). These strategies capitalize on students' learning and working with others.

Individual Autonomy and Independence

Anglo-American families tend to promote adultlike behaviors early in their children (Chinn & Plata, 1987), whereas the Hispanic culture often expects children to be dependent on parents and to seek their approval (Rivera & Rogers-Adkinson, 1997). Hispanic and Asian families often feed, dress, and pamper young boys and restrict young girls' independence outside the home (Cartledge, 1996). In the African-American culture, many children are taught to seek approval, guidance, and feedback from others (Grossman, 1994; Hale, 1981). Children who were raised in this manner may find it difficult to form their own opinions and may require assistance to function independently (Grossman, 1994).

Initially, therefore, you may wish to include alternative choices rather than free choices in the curriculum. For example, at the beginning of the school year, Ms. Simons lets students select from three options for free-time activities. By the middle of the school year, she no longer provides options. Instead, students make their own choices for free-time activities.

Timeliness

In the school culture, students are expected to be on time, to complete assignments on time, and to take timed exams. However, many minority cultures view timeliness not as essential, but as secondary to relationships and performance (Briganti, 1989; Zirpoli & Melloy, 1993).

Realizing these differences, Mr. Sams keeps encouraging students to meet important deadlines by listing the days until the assignment is due on the board every morning. He also makes certain to include the appropriate number of items on a timed test so that all students finish the exam within the allotted time.

Achievement Orientation

In the school culture, high achievement is an emphasized goal (Grossman, 1994). Although many Asian-Americans who first immigrated to this country placed a high value on educational achievement (Chan & Kitano, 1987; Kitano, 1987), the culture of more recent Asian immigrants often does not place such a high value on education (Cartledge, 1996). The Hispanic culture endorses the goal of developing children's personalities rather than their highest potential to achieve (Briganti, 1989). Moreover, many Hispanics are taught that it is bad manners to excel over others in a group in an attempt to be recognized for individual achievement (Grossman, 1994). The same is true for Native Americans, who feel that behavior that brings attention to an individual is egotistical (Dillard, 1983). Often, students from diverse cultural groups are pressured by their peers not to achieve in school (Cartledge, 1996; Gollick & Chinn, 1990).

In the African-American culture, the goal of school achievement is frequently integrated into mental, emotional, and physical achievement. Wilson (1989) attributes the success of Project Interface, a preparatory math and science program for black junior high students, to the fact that both the achievement and behavioral needs of the students are considered.

In a successful program of teaching high-risk Native American students, Uthe-Reyno incorporates self-esteem exercises into the curriculum (Uthe-Reyno & McKinnon, 1989). Affective or behavioral objectives are found on the individualized education programs (IEPs) of many special students.

Future Orientation

Many children from diverse cultural groups are more interested in immediate short-term goals (Rivera & Rogers-Adkinson, 1997). Lack of future emphasis promotes the importance of living to the fullest now, instead of delaying for the future. As noted by Turnbull and Turnbull (1986), a lack of emphasis on future goals may result in a reluctance by parents to think about future independent living for their children with special needs.

Realizing this difference, Mr. Hunt has students identify and monitor daily goals before he asks them to monitor monthly goals. At the end of each class period, he has students write whether they met their goal for that day.

Informal Classroom Atmosphere

The informality of the typical school classroom is alien to many students from non-Anglo-American cultures. In the Vietnamese school culture, students are expected to learn by listening, watching, and imitating the teacher (Wei, 1980). Answering questions or speaking up in class is not valued in the Asian culture, which teaches deference toward authority figures (Briganti, 1989; Chinn & Plata, 1987; Grossman, 1994). The Hispanic culture also promotes a formal, respectful relationship with adults (Grossman, 1994). In the Native American culture, youth are taught to value quiet and stillness and to learn by observation (Zirpoli & Melloy, 1993).

Realizing that many of his students may hesitate to answer questions during a group discussion, Mr. Rabinovitch allows students to "pass," as an alternative to answering the question. He also tries to establish a comfortable classroom and to show respect for his students.

Individual Differences

As you can see, some students have problems because their culture is in conflict with the school culture. However, there is an inherent danger of stereotyping when group characteristics are applied to individuals. Obviously, many students do not fit the group descriptions. Students from other cultures frequently adopt the attitudes, behaviors, and values of the school culture and become acculturated. The degree of acculturation depends on such variables as proximity, age, birthplace, and time (Leung, 1989). Immigrants who live in ethnic centers in metropolitan areas have less opportunity to socialize with other ethnic groups, so they tend to retain their ethnic identity longer. Young people usually adapt more readily than older people, and those born in this country usually adapt more readily than do those born in another country. Succeeding generations are less steeped in ethnic traditions than the first generation.

Because of individual differences and the acculturation process, the previous descriptions may not apply to Juan, who is Hispanic, or Latasha, who is African-American. Information concerning cultural differences should be only the first step in your selection of a teaching strategy. As soon as possible, you should begin to collect data and monitor the progress of individual students. For example, Ms. Davis placed Juan with a peer to practice reading basic sight words, to capitalize on the cooperative emphasis of the Hispanic culture. However, monitoring of Juan's progress showed that he was not learning the words. Realizing that peer tutoring was an ineffective strategy for Juan, Ms. Davis initiated another strategy.

 ACTIVITY 1.1

Look back at the section on cultural diversity of students. Discuss how you would use the information about cultural differences in your work with students. (Answers for this and other activities are found in the Instructor's Manual.)

 IMPORTANT POINTS

1. Students with special needs often display one or more of the following characteristics: inadequate academic achievement, inappropriate school behaviors, poor attending behaviors, poor memory, inadequate organizational skills, poor self-concept, and inadequate social skills.
2. The school culture focuses on the values of the Anglo-American culture, even though students come from a variety of cultures.
3. The Anglo-American values, often at odds with those of other cultures, include an emphasis on competition, individual autonomy and independence, timeliness, achievement orientation, future orientation, and an informal classroom atmosphere.
4. Acculturation into the school culture depends on proximity, age, birthplace, and time (Leung, 1989).
5. Cultural factors and individual differences should influence the selection of instructional techniques initially, but then data-based decisions should be made.

EFFECTIVE TEACHING STRATEGIES

In a meta-analysis of over 1,000 research studies, Forness, Kavale, Blum, & Lloyd (1997) identified effective, possibly effective, and ineffective special education interventions. The ineffective strategies included special class placement, perceptual training, the Feingold diet, modality-based instruction, and social skills training. They identified psycholinguistic training, peer tutoring, computer-assisted instruction, stimulant drugs, reduced class size, and psychotropic drugs as possibly effective. Effective strategies included early intervention, formative evaluation, cognitive-behavior modification, direct instruction, behavior modification, reading comprehension instruction, and mnemonic training.

Effective teaching strategies in the field of special education are currently based on two paradigms of the learning process. According to Heshusius (1989), a paradigm represents the "beliefs by which we ultimately think and act" (p. 403). One view is the *reductionist paradigm* (also referred to as scientific, modern empiricism, or Newtonian mechanistic), and the other is the *constructivist paradigm* (also referred to as holistic or social constructivism). In the reductionist paradigm, learners are viewed as learning in a logical, sequential, and externally arranged way (Heshusius, 1989). In the constructivist paradigm, learners are viewed as actively constructing their knowledge through interaction with the physical and social environments (Reid, Kurkjian, & Carruthers, 1994).

Both paradigms influence instructional interactions and generate heated debate in the special education field. For our discussion, we concentrate on a comparison of the two paradigms in regard to their views of the role of the teacher, the role of the student, and their influence on instructional and assessment practices.

Reductionist Paradigm

The reductionist paradigm views the teacher's role as one of providing opportunities for systematic explicit instruction, practice, feedback, and active student involvement in learning (Kimball & Heron, 1988). Effective teachers structure the school day by providing ample instructional time and high task management. They introduce and orient, model and demonstrate, check for understanding, maintain a brisk pace and a high success rate, and monitor seatwork and progress (Englert, Tarrant, & Mariage, 1992). The teacher is in charge of instruction, and knowledge is transmitted from teacher to student. The students frequently are not involved in decision making and often engage in rote learning responses. Through the use of task analysis, the curricu-

lum is separated into components with scope and sequence checklists. Sequential and hierarchical instructional objectives form the basis for curriculum-based measurement and precision teaching assessments as students' weaknesses are identified (Poplin, 1988). The Direct Instruction Model of Engelmann and colleagues is based in the reductionist paradigm (see Chapter 7).

Constructivist Paradigm

In the constructivist paradigm, the teacher's role is more like that of a facilitator as students assume responsibility for their own learning. The effective teacher embeds implicit instruction in meaningful contexts, promotes classroom dialogues, demonstrates responsive instruction, links student's prior knowledge with new knowledge, and establishes classroom learning communities (Englert, Tarrant, & Mariage, 1992). Students often lead discussions, select their own objectives, and learn from other students. They construct their own knowledge through active involvement and integration into their schema. Assessment includes authentic, real-life processes, and errors provide insights not into students' weaknesses but into how students think. Subject areas are taught in authentic contexts (Englert, Tarrant, & Mariage, 1992) and integrated as a whole (Iano, 1989). Reciprocal teaching and much of the literacy-based instruction are examples of curricula that are based in the constructivist paradigm.

Sample Lessons Based on Paradigms

An examination of sample lessons may assist in understanding the effects of the two paradigms on instruction. We begin with a sample lesson from a reductionist viewpoint. Then we present the same lesson based on the constructivist principles, adapted from a lesson presented by Englert, Tarrant, and Mirage (1992). Both lessons are centered around opening morning activities, a beginning routine in many primary inclusive classrooms.

Reductionist-Based

TEACHER: It's time for our morning message. Today is Tuesday. What is today, everyone (hand signal to cue unison response)?

STUDENTS: Tuesday.

TEACHER: Correct. Today is Tuesday. (Teacher writes the sentence on the board.) Let's read our first sentence together. Everyone (signal).

STUDENTS: Today is Tuesday.

TEACHER: Good reading, everyone. Jim, what is happening today?

JIM: We are going on a field trip.

TEACHER: Yes, we are. Where are we going?

SAMANTHA: To the fire station.

TEACHER: Let's say that in a complete sentence, Samantha.

SAMANTHA: We are going to the fire station.

TEACHER: Now that's a complete sentence. (Teacher writes: We are going on a field trip to the fire station.) Everyone, let's read that sentence together (hand signal).

STUDENTS: We are going on a field trip to the fire station.

TEACHER: Good reading, everyone. So where are we going, Sherry?

SHERRY: We are going to the fire station.

TEACHER: Correct. When are we going to the fire station, Kenisha?

Constructivist-Based

TEACHER: Anything special to write about today in our morning message?

JOSH: We are going to the fire station today.

MEGAN: A field trip.

TEACHER: Let's see. (Teacher writes: We are going to the fire station today, a field trip.) Oh! That doesn't sound right. What do you think?

KENISHA: Something's wrong with field trip.

SEBBIE: Maybe it needs a period.

TEACHER: Let's see. (Teacher adds a period before field trip and a capital A.) I added a period so now I need a capital. Let me read it, A field trip. What do you think?

STUDENTS: No.

TEACHER: Maybe, I can say for. (Teacher writes: We are going to the fire station today for a field trip. Teacher reads sentence.) What do you think?

STUDENTS: Yes.

TEACHER: What do you want to say about the field trip?

MEGAN: We leave at 11:00.

ROY: I want to say 11:00 o'clock.

STUDENTS: (Some say, "Yes" and some say, "No.")

TEACHER: Let's vote on adding o'clock. Thumbs up for "Yes." Thumbs down for "No."

 ACTIVITY 1.2

Compare and contrast the different lesson samples based on the two paradigms.

Combining Paradigms for Effective Instructional Practice

Many experts feel that the selection of an effective instructional practice in special education depends on the nature of the task and the individual. Stanovich (1994) states that research indicates explicit instruction grounded in the reductionist paradigm is more effective in teaching basic decoding skills, while implicit instruction grounded in the constructivist paradigm is effective when the focus is on comprehension process or higher-level skills. Howell, Fox, and Morehead (1993) suggest that students who have poor prior knowledge and encounter initial failure on the task may need explicit instruction, whereas students who have good prior knowledge and early success may need implicit instruction.

Current thought in the special education field is that explicit instruction must be integrated in a constructivist framework for students with disabilities. For example, Mercer, Jordan, and Miller (1996) contend that teacher support and direction is needed before students with disabilities may become active, self-motivated learners.

Direct instruction and achievement orientation based in the reductionist model and student selection and open-ended tasks based in the constructivist model seem most effective in improving attitude and achievement in the reading area (Stahl, McKenna, & Pagnucco, 1994). In this text, we incorporate practices based on both paradigms. Chapter 3 contains a discussion of skill and authentic assessments. We

discuss direct instruction procedures, reciprocal teaching, and strategy instruction in Part II.

We include practices from both paradigms in our instructional framework of planning, presentation, independent practice, and evaluation (see Figure 1.1). In this general framework, the teacher, the students, or the combined efforts of the teacher and students may lead to the planning of the lesson. Using a dialogue, the teacher may at first present the lesson and then turn over the lesson presentation to the students; or in classroom communities, the students may learn from one another. In the feedback and evaluation process, the involvement of both the teacher and student is essential. Students may self-evaluate or self-monitor and/or teachers may evaluate and monitor. We discuss the instructional framework in detail in Chapter 6.

Figure 1.1 Instructional Framework

ACTIVITY 1.3

> Reflect on the different practices suggested by the two paradigms. Discuss with a partner when you feel the different practices may be effective.

◇ **IMPORTANT POINTS**

1. In a meta-analysis of over 1,000 research studies, Forness, Kavale, Blum, & Lloyd (1997) identified early intervention, formative evaluation, cognitive-behavior modification, direct instruction, behavior modification, reading comprehension instruction, and mnemonic training as effective strategies.
2. Effective teaching strategies in the field of special education currently are based in either the reductionist or the constructivist paradigms of the learning process.
3. The reductionist paradigm views the teacher as the primary information and decision maker, the student as actively participating in the learning of isolated skills without much input, assessment as leading to sequential and hierarchical instructional objectives, and instruction as fast paced and teacher directed.
4. The constructivist paradigm views the teacher as a facilitator and one of the decision makers, the students as major decision makers as they learn from each other, assessment as occurring in authentic, real-life procedures, and instruction as purposeful and matched to students' interests and experiences.
5. Many special educators feel that both paradigms include practices that are effective for students with special needs, depending on the content and student characteristics.
6. Current thought in the special education field is that explicit instruction must be integrated in a constructivist framework for students with disabilities.
7. Direct instruction and achievement orientation (reductionist model) and student selection and open-ended tasks (constructivist model) are most effective in improving attitude and achievement in the reading area (Stahl, McKenna, & Pagnucco, 1994).

CONTINUUM OF SERVICES

Students with disabilities may be found in a variety of placements and may require a variety of services. These placements and services are typically arranged on a continuum and offer a range of service options to meet the diverse needs of students. The Individuals with Disabilities Education Act Amendments of 1997, PL 105-17, which amended and reauthorized the Individuals with Disabilities Education Act (IDEA), ensures that a continuum of placement alternatives is available for students (Yell & Shriner, 1997). Figure 1.2 illustrates a continuum of services in which a full range of program alternatives is arranged from the most to the least restrictive. When considering educational options for students, it is important to remember that special education services should be flexible and responsive to students' needs, provide access to a variety of services, and offer the support needed for students to achieve their potential (Smith, 1998).

According to the Individuals with Disabilities Education Act (IDEA), schools must place students with disabilities in the least restrictive environment, or LRE. This means that, to the extent appropriate, students with disabilities should be educated with students without disabilities. IDEA further stipulates that special classes, separate schooling, or other removal of students with disabilities from the general educational environment occur only when the nature or severity of the disability is such that education in general education classes with the use of supplementary aids and services cannot be achieved satisfactorily.

Figure 1.2 Continuum of Educational Placements and Services for Students with Disabilities

As you examine Figure 1.2, notice that the model is wide at the bottom and gradually becomes narrower to reflect the number of students served at the different levels. The least restrictive setting is at the bottom and the most restrictive setting is at the top. A greater percentage of students are served in the less restrictive settings (e.g., mild/moderate needs) than in the more restrictive settings (e.g., more intensive needs). Students are moved up in levels only as necessary, and they are moved down to more integrated settings as soon as possible.

Level 1. General education class placement with limited or no supportive services is the most integrated placement. Students may be able to meet the expectations of the general classroom setting with some limited supportive services, or they may not require any supportive services in order to be successful. For example, Ted attends

a general education class with supportive services. His sixth-grade teacher gets suggestions from the special education teacher and then modifies and adapts some of his assignments and instructional materials in math. Kelly attends a general education class without supportive services. She completes the same assignments and meets the same expectations as her classmates.

Level 2. General education class placement with consultation and materials involves the services of a consultant and/or the use of special instructional materials and equipment in order to address the needs of the students. Some students with special needs attend a general class and receive supplementary instructional services. The special education teacher may provide supplementary instruction by teaching in cooperation with the general education teacher (co-teaching) or by teaching small groups of students within the general classroom (in-class or pull-in model). Throughout our textbook, we refer to these services as consultative services. Other students may require the use of special materials or equipment such as large-print books.

Level 3. General education class placement with itinerant services involves generally scheduled visits by an itinerant teacher who travels from school to school to focus on teaching skills to individuals or small groups, providing instructional materials, and offering suggestions to the classroom teacher about specific problems. Some students' problems are not serious enough to warrant a more restrictive placement, and itinerant services are sufficient to support the students' needs.

Level 4. General education class placement with resource room assistance requires students to leave their general education classrooms for instruction by a special education teacher in a resource room or pull-out program. Students spend most of the day in the general education classroom and leave for brief periods of time to work on specific skills, strategies, or content areas. The length of time and frequency of the resource room intervention is determined by the severity of students' problems. For example, Latoya, a tenth grader, is scheduled in general education content classes for most of her school subjects. However, she attends one class in which a special education teacher teaches her strategies in test-taking and note-taking and shows her how to apply them in her content classes. Resource teachers work closely with classroom teachers to keep them informed of their students' progress, share suggestions for instruction and management in the general education classroom, and collaboratively generate solutions to students' problems.

Level 5. Part-time special class, part-time general education class is a placement option in which students are placed in special education classes but are integrated into general classrooms for a considerable amount of time each day (Smith, 1998). The length of time spent in the general education classroom as well as the instructional areas addressed in the general education setting are determined by students' needs. Notice that this level differs from Level 4 because students spend more time in the special class.

Level 6. Full-time special class placement involves providing services to students in full-time special class placements, which may be referred to as self-contained classes. Students who attend these classes may be mainstreamed (placed in general education classrooms with students who do not have disabilities) for part of the school day. However, students attend a special class for most of the day and are included in general education activities minimally (Smith, 1998).

Level 7. Special day school is a placement for students who require more intensive services and thus are enrolled in a special school within the school system. Mark attends a special school where he receives special education services, speech therapy, physical therapy, and counseling.

Level 8. Residential school, and *Level 9.* Hospital/homebound are total care settings and are appropriate for students who receive services outside the school setting. These placements may involve instruction at home or in residential settings, detention centers, or hospitals.

Students with the kinds of learning and behavior problems we address in this text may be served in general education classrooms with or without supportive services or in part-time classes referred to as resource, pull-out, or part-time programs (Levels 1, 2, 3, 4, and 5). In the rest of this text, we do not refer to Levels 6–9. Instead, we concentrate on reporting research, providing examples, and making suggestions for the students with special needs who are being served in the first five levels. They represent over 70% of the population of students with disabilities (U.S. Department of Education, 1996).

NATIONAL EDUCATION REFORM

The current national education reform strategy, Goals 2000: Educate America Act, was signed into law in 1994. It represents a national framework for education reform to improve our systems, policies, standards, and most importantly, outcomes for all students. At the time he signed the law, President Clinton called the initiative a "new and different approach" that would establish "world class" national education standards. He asked school districts at the grassroots level to help achieve these goals. Goals 2000 appears to include students with disabilities in the designation "all children" (see Goal 1). However, some critics fear that these goals ignore the educational needs of students with disabilities and that the emphasis on higher standards has taken the focus away from the needs of students with disabilities who are unable to meet these higher standards.

Many states have operationalized the national goals in their own specific and comprehensive state education reform initiatives. Check with your State Department of Education to examine the education reform initiative that your state has established and that is being implemented in your area, and monitor the impact this initiative is having on students with disabilities. Goals 2000: Educate America Act has as its premise that by the year 2000, the following will occur:

Goal 1: Readiness for school

All children in America will start school ready to learn.

Goal 2: High school completion

The high school graduation rate will increase to at least 90%.

Goal 3: Student achievement and citizenship

American students will leave Grades 4, 8, and 12 having demonstrated competency in challenging subject matter including English, mathematics, science, foreign languages, civics and government, economics, arts, history, and geography.

Goal 4: Teacher education and professional development

The teaching force will have access to programs for the continued improvement of their professional skills.

Goal 5: Science and mathematics

U.S. students will be first in the world in science and mathematics achievement.

Goal 6: Adult literacy and lifelong learning

U.S. students will be literate and will possess the knowledge and skills necessary to compete in a global economy and exercise the rights and responsibilities of citizenship.

Goal 7: Safe, disciplined, and alcohol- and drug-free schools

Every school in America will be free of drugs and the unauthorized presence of firearms and alcohol and will offer a disciplined environment conducive to learning.

Goal 8: Parental participation

Every school will promote parental involvement and participation.

SOURCE: U.S. Senate-House Conference, 1994

 IMPORTANT POINTS

1. Students may receive special education services in a variety of placements, arranged on a continuum from least restrictive to most restrictive.
2. The term least restrictive means that, to the extent appropriate, students who have dis-

abilities should be educated with students who do not have disabilities.

3. Students may receive special education services in general classrooms with limited or no supportive services, through consultative and itinerant services, in resource rooms, in part-time and full-time special classes, in special and residential schools, and in hospital/homebound settings.

4. Goals 2000: Educate America Act (1994) represents a national initiative to improve outcomes for all students and to reform our education systems, policies, and standards.

THE REGULAR EDUCATION INITIATIVE

During the 1980s, many researchers and policymakers advocated for an increase in the extent to which students with mild disabilities were being integrated into general education settings (Biklen & Zollers, 1986; Reynolds, Wang, & Walberg, 1987; Will, 1986). In 1986, Madeline Will, Assistant Secretary of Education, proposed that we place fewer students with disabilities in pull-out programs and instead educate them in general education settings. She advocated a shared responsibility and commitment between general and special education and the use of effective special education techniques beyond the special class setting. It was a call for alignment of programs to achieve better academic outcomes than had been demonstrated by the more traditional, pull-out programs (Zigmond, Jenkins, Fuchs, Deno, Fuchs, Baker, Jenkins, & Coutinho, 1995).

This proposed partnership between general and special education, called the Regular Education Initiative (REI), received mixed reactions from professionals in the field of special education. Proponents suggested a variety of reasons for merging general and special education. These included inadequacy of conventional methods, problems with categorical programs, and the disjointedness of current efforts and programs. Opponents raised a number of concerns, including the ability of students with mild disabilities and other students with special needs to succeed in general classrooms, the ability of general educators to cope with the demands of the proposed initiative, and the effects of what they saw as wholesale mainstreaming. Although many differences regarding REI exist among professionals, points of agreement include (1) dissatisfaction with existing general and special education systems, (2) the need to examine strengths and weaknesses of current practices, (3) the need for reform in education, and (4) the need for general and special educators to work together to develop effective instructional options for diverse student populations.

INCLUSION

One of the major reform issues currently facing the field of education is that of inclusion. The concept of inclusion has as its premise that students with special needs benefit academically and socially by being served alongside normally achieving students as opposed to being separated from them (Banjera & Dailey, 1995). It has become apparent that the number of students with disabilities educated in general classrooms will continue to grow markedly over the next few years (Fuchs & Fuchs, 1994). Proponents of the inclusion movement advocate that the majority of students with disabilities should be included in general classrooms. Although critics of inclusion agree with some of the basic assumptions of the inclusion movement, such as the need for improvements in assessment and instruction and the need for collaboration among special and general education, they disagree with other assumptions, such as the belief that the majority of (if not all) students with disabilities can best be taught in the general classroom.

The topic of inclusion remains a controversial one. In discussing inclusion, it is important to define exactly what is meant (Burnette, 1996, p. 2). Some professionals support full inclusion, the placing of all students with disabilities in general education classrooms, while others favor inclusive schools that welcome students with disabilities, but at the same time, realize that general education placement may not be the best educational option (Burnette, 1996). Still others describe "responsible" inclusion, a school-based education model that is student centered and that bases educational placement and service provisions on the needs of each student (Vaughn & Schumm, 1995).

Most models advocating full inclusion include the following:

1. All students attend the school to which they would go if they had no disability.
2. A natural proportion (i.e., representative of the school district at large) of students with disabilities occurs at any school site.
3. A zero-rejection policy exists, so that no student is excluded on the basis of type or extent of disability.
4. Placements are age and grade appropriate, with no self-contained special education classes operative at the school site.

5. Cooperative learning and peer instruction methods receive significant use in general instruction at the school site.
6. Special education supports are provided within the context of the general education class and in other integrated environments (Sailor, 1991, p. 10).

The issue of full inclusion versus a continuum of service options was discussed at the annual conference of the Council for Exceptional Children (CEC) in 1993, resulting in the adoption of the policy statement that appears in Figure 1.3. The CEC policy statement calls for a continuum of services but supports inclusion as a meaningful goal. Implications for schools include obtaining the support and technical assistance necessary to serve an increasingly diverse student population in inclusive settings, and facilitating collaboration among families, educators, businesses, and agencies to prepare students for membership in inclusive communities (Platt & Olson, 1997).

The Working Forum on Inclusive Schools (1994), a consortium of 10 national education

Figure 1.3   CEC Policy on Inclusive Schools and Community Settings

The Council for Exceptional Children (CEC) believes all children, youth, and young adults with disabilities are entitled to a free and appropriate education and/or services that lead to an adult life characterized by satisfying relations with others, independent living, productive engagement in the community, and participation in society at large.

To achieve such outcomes, there must exist for all children, youth, and young adults a rich variety of early intervention, educational, and vocational program options and experiences.

Access to these programs and experiences should be based on individual educational need and desired outcomes.

Furthermore, students and their families or guardians, as members of the planning team, may recommend the placement, curriculum option, and the exit document to be pursued.

CEC believes that a continuum of services must be available for all children, youth, and young adults.

CEC also believes that the concept of inclusion is a meaningful goal to be pursued in our schools and communities.

In addition, CEC believes children, youth, and young adults with disabilities should be served whenever possible in general education classrooms in inclusive neighborhood schools and community settings.

Such settings should be strengthened and supported by an infusion of specially trained personnel and other appropriate supportive practices according to the individual needs of the child.

NOTE: From "CEC Policy Manual," 1997, Chapter 3, Special Education in the Schools, Section Three, Professional Policies, Part 1, p. 4. Reston, VA: The Council for Exceptional Children. Reprinted by permission.

associations, identified 12 characteristics of inclusive schools:

1. A sense of community (e.g., all students belong and can learn in the mainstream of the school and community).
2. Leadership (e.g., principals should involve faculty in planning and decision making).
3. High standards (e.g., all students are given the opportunity to achieve high educational standards and outcomes).
4. Collaboration and cooperation (e.g., there is an emphasis on collaborative arrangements and support networks among students and staff).
5. Changing roles and responsibilities (e.g., roles of school professionals change, and everyone becomes an active participant in the learning process).
6. An array of services (e.g., varied school/community services are available, all coordinated with the educational staff).
7. Partnerships with parents (e.g., parents are full partners in the education of their children).
8. Flexible learning environments (e.g., flexible groupings and developmentally appropriate experiences are provided to meet students' needs).
9. Strategies based on research (e.g., practices include cooperative learning, curriculum adaptation, peer tutoring, direct instruction, reciprocal teaching, social skills instruction, computer-assisted instruction, study skills training, and mastery learning).
10. New forms of accountability (e.g., there is less emphasis on standardized tests and more on assessment to monitor progress toward goals).
11. Access (e.g., adaptations, modifications, and assistive technology ensure access).
12. Continuing professional development (e.g., staff members continue to improve their knowledge and skills).

Many professionals agree on the value of integrating students with disabilities into general education classroom settings. There is disagreement, however, as to how inclusion is implemented. Many educators believe that inclusion is most effective when the integration of students with disabilities is combined with a broader restructuring that includes multiaged classrooms (Irmsher, 1996). Others recommend guidelines for "responsible" inclusion: "(1) the student and family are considered first; (2) teachers choose to participate in inclusion classrooms; (3) adequate resources are provided; (4) models are developed and implemented at the school-based level; (5) a continuum of services is maintained; (6) the service delivery model is continuously evaluated; and (7) ongoing professional development is provided" (Vaughn & Schumm, 1995, p. 264).

Research on the achievement outcomes of students with disabilities underscores the need to improve services to students no matter where they are provided (Wagner, Blackorby, & Hebbler, 1993). As the debate over how best to meet the needs of students with disabilities continues,

◆ **ACTIVITY 1.4**

Part 1. Prepare a set of questions about inclusion. Interview a general education teacher, a special education teacher, one of your professors, a principal, a parent of a child or adolescent who does not have a disability, or the superintendent of schools in your area. Share your responses in class.

Part 2. Form two panels, one with members who will speak in favor of inclusion and the other with members who will speak against it. Arrange to have a debate in class.

we urge you to evaluate the effects of separate programming and integrated settings on student achievement.

PROFESSIONAL COMMITMENT

The primary international organization that represents the special education field is the Council for Exceptional Children (CEC). The mission of CEC is to improve educational outcomes for individuals with exceptionalities. The following was adopted by the CEC Delegate Assembly in April 1995:

> CEC, a nonprofit association, accomplishes its mission, which is carried out in support of special education professionals and others working on behalf of individuals with exceptionalities, by advocating for appropriate governmental policies, by setting professional standards, by providing continuing professional development, by advocating for newly and historically underserved individuals with exceptionalities, and by helping professionals achieve the conditions and resources necessary for effective professional practice (Council for Exceptional Children, 1995, p. 1).

Members of the special education profession are responsible for upholding and advancing certain principles, called the CEC Code of Ethics, adopted by the CEC Delegate Assembly in April 1983. Special education professionals are committed to developing the highest educational and quality of life potential of individuals with exceptionalities. A career in special education carries with it many professional responsibilities that are stated in the CEC Code of Ethics.

1. Special education professionals promote and maintain a high level of competence and integrity in practicing their profession.
2. Special education professionals engage in professional activities which benefit exceptional individuals, their families, other colleagues, students, or research subjects.
3. Special education professionals exercise objective professional judgment in the practice of their profession.
4. Special education professionals strive to advance their knowledge and skills regarding the education of individuals with exceptionalities.
5. Special education professionals work within the standards and policies of their profession.
6. Special education professionals seek to uphold and improve where necessary the laws, regulations, and policies governing the delivery of special education and related services and the practice of their profession.
7. Special education professionals do not condone nor participate in unethical or illegal acts, or violate professional standards adopted by the Delegate Assembly of CEC (Council for Exceptional Children, 1983, p. 8).

With your acceptance of these responsibilities, you make a commitment to students with exceptionalities, their families, and the teaching profession. Your behavior and conduct as a professional can help you view teaching as important and worthwhile. We hope you will give careful thought to that professional commitment.

WHAT WE BELIEVE

Our text is centered around four beliefs:

1. There are generic, research-based instructional techniques that all teachers of students with special needs should know how to apply and evaluate.
2. These generic, research-based techniques may be used in the teaching of various content areas and for various ages and levels of students with mild disabilities.
3. In the 21st century, special educators will need to modify curriculum and adapt instruction as they work in collaborative partnerships with general educators, administrators, families, and other school professionals

to meet the needs of students in increasingly diverse and inclusive classes.

4. As external partnerships become more critical to the success of students prior to entering school, during school, and in postschool situations, special educators will need a varied repertoire of collaborative skills to initiate and maintain these relationships.

Currently, many texts focus on math, reading, and other content areas. Instead, we thoroughly discuss research-based instructional techniques and apply them, with examples, to various content areas, levels, and settings. We believe that in most inclusive settings, special educators will be responsible for modifying curriculum and adapting instruction, while relying on general educators for their expertise in curriculum areas. We believe our text fulfills the need of pre-service and in-service teachers to have a solid foundation in effective generic methodologies.

 IMPORTANT POINTS

1. The Regular Education Initiative (REI) is a movement to place fewer students with disabilities in pull-out programs and to educate them in general education settings instead.

2. Points of agreement about REI among professionals in the field include (1) dissatisfaction with existing general and special education systems; (2) the need to examine strengths and weaknesses of current practices; (3) the need for reform in education; and (4) the need for general and special educators to work together to develop effective instructional options for diverse student populations.

3. The concept of inclusion has as its premise that students with special needs benefit academically and socially by being served alongside normally achieving students as opposed to being separated from them.

4. The Working Forum on Inclusive Schools identified 12 characteristics of inclusive schools: a sense of community, leadership, high standards, collaboration and cooperation, changing roles and responsibilities, an array of services, partnerships with parents, flexible learning environments, research-based strategies, new forms of accountability, access, and continuing professional development.

5. The Council for Exceptional Children adopted a policy that calls for a continuum of services; supports inclusion as a meaningful goal; and requires the support of schools, communities, colleges, and universities.

6. A career in special education carries with it many professional responsibilities that are stated in the CEC Code of Ethics.

7. In this text, we focus on research-based instructional techniques that may be used for teaching in various content areas for various levels of students. These techniques can be used by special educators to modify curriculum and adapt instruction as they work in partnership with general educators to meet students' needs.

◆ **DISCUSSION QUESTIONS**

1. Discuss with a partner the implications of Goals 2000: Educate America Act on children and adolescents with disabilities.

2. Examine the Code of Ethics adopted by the Council for Exceptional Children. Reflect on what the code means to you as a member of the special education teaching profession.

3. Discuss some of the common characteristics of students with special needs. Relate the characteristics to students with disabilities whom you have taught or worked with previously.

2

BEGINNING-OF-
THE-YEAR
PLANNING

The procedures teachers follow and the decisions they make prior to and during the first week of school establish the climate and set the tone for the rest of the school year. "It is impossible to overemphasize the importance of getting the school year off to a good beginning" (Callahan, Clark, & Kellough, 1998, p. 192). Best (1990) suggests that planning, preparation, and flexibility are important for success on the first day of school. In observations of teachers at the beginning of the year, Moskowitz and Hayman (1976) found that the first day was crucial in setting the stage for the rest of the year. In a study of how effective teachers performed during the first weeks of school, Emmer, Evertson, and Anderson (1980) found that effective teachers (a) managed time well by using a consistent daily schedule of activities; (b) established clear rules and procedures; (c) monitored progress effectively; (d) described objectives clearly; (e) had a variety of effective materials on hand; (f) gave clear, specific directions for activities; and (g) designed activities with an obvious purpose. Similarly, Polloway and Patton (1997) confirmed the critical importance of classroom organization and management (cited in the effective teaching research and in the research regarding the initial problems of beginning teachers). It would appear that taking a proactive approach at the start of the school year, quickly establishing systems and routines, and clearly communicating expectations to students would minimize the likelihood of problems later in the year. In this chapter, we focus on what you should do prior to and during the first week of school as you set up your classroom, orient your students, review individualized education programs (IEPs), develop goals and objectives for students, establish rules, plan, and schedule.

SETTING UP THE CLASSROOM

Due to the varied and complex demands placed upon special education teachers (e.g., implementing the goals and objectives of IEPs, planning appropriate learning activities, adapting instruction, and modifying materials), many tasks must be accomplished before the start of the academic year. Careful attention to these tasks eases the transitions students experience as they return to school. One of the challenges teachers face as they begin the year is setting up and organizing the classroom environment. The topic of classroom organization has taken on more significance with the inclusive education movement (Polloway & Patton, 1997). Greater emphasis is being placed on cooperative learning, and on the co-teaching of classes by general and special educators (Bauwens & Hourcade, 1994). Teachers must consider seating arrangements that are conducive to cooperative learning and peer tutoring, and yet minimize distractions and promote on-task behavior; activities and materials that help students master IEP goals and objectives; and instructional arrangements that promote student participation and academic achievement.

Physical Arrangement

Although the design of a classroom is secondary to instructional methodology and curriculum, evidence indicates that the physical setting may influence student behavior and attitudes (Good & Brophy, 1987; Evertson, Emmer, Clements, & Worsham, 1994). Furthermore, the physical arrangement of the classroom may affect the teacher's ability to implement each student's IEP (Walker, 1981). You may be working with students who have difficulty learning, attending, remembering, getting along, and being organized. For example, Ms. Henderson found that Marcy had a difficult time concentrating and attending, so she set up an office space in her classroom. This space provides Marcy with an area to go to when she needs a place that is free from distractions.

The physical arrangement of the classroom communicates important information to students about how they are expected to interact with each other and with the teacher and about how they are expected to complete tasks (Rosenfield, Lambert, & Black, 1985). The physical setting does not teach; however, it can facilitate the occurrence of certain student behaviors (Weinstein, 1981). For example, if you want students to interact in solving a problem, facilitate interaction by seating students at a table as opposed to seating them at individual desks in rows.

Additionally, not all students need the same physical setting (Polloway & Patton, 1997; Polloway, Patton, Payne, & Payne, 1989). Weinstein (1981) reports the results of four investigations examining the influence of the physical environment on young children. The following general principles emerged from the studies: (a) classrooms should contain options for students (e.g., quiet work areas, group interaction areas, and whole-class discussion areas); (b) interest areas should be clearly defined; (c) areas should be located within easy access of any external requirements (e.g., water, electrical outlets, quiet); (d) incompatible activities should be separated (e.g., creative dramatics and listening centers); (e) areas should be clearly labeled and easy to see; (f) aisles and pathways should be clear and should not pass through work areas; (g) large, open spaces that may invite inappropriate physical activities should be avoided; (h) the teacher's desk should be located out of the way to encourage the teacher's movement around the room; and (i) instructional materials should be accessible and easily retrieved. According to this research, adherence to these principles for organizing the physical environment should positively affect the ways students acquire and express information in the classroom.

Some of the physical variables that affect the way classrooms are organized are the size of the room, the number of electrical outlets, and the storage needs; the acoustics (D'Alonzo, D'Alonzo, & Mauser, 1979); the furniture (Lewis & Doorlag, 1991); the equipment; the type of facility (e.g., portable building, classroom within the school, general education classroom); and whether the classroom has to be shared with another teacher. Arrange seating to avoid overcrowding and to provide for adequate personal space. The following general suggestions will help you get started in setting up and organizing your setting.

Learning Centers and Resource Materials

Learning centers may be developed that include activities to accommodate many different levels of functioning and interest and to provide the opportunity for students to work independently with materials on their own levels (see Chapter 4). Specific areas of the classroom may be designated as free-time areas. Here, you may include activities that are both enjoyable and educational, such as completing a puzzle, solving math problems with a calculator, reading a book, playing a game, or using the computer to visit a Web site or preview a CD-ROM. Books and other reading materials may be set up in the classroom within easy reach of students. It is helpful to assemble reading materials that you know are of interest to your students, such as mysteries, sports and adventure stories, magazines, newspapers, books with accompanying tapes, stories that students have written, predictable books (see Chapter 4), and series books (e.g., the Sweet Valley High series, Pascal, 1983–1989).

Furniture and Supplies

When teachers' desks are put off to the side, in the back, or out of the central area of the class, teachers tend to sit at them less, are more mobile, and circulate more freely around the room to monitor student progress. This helps to elim-inate a long line by the side of the desk as students seek assistance. In addition, by circulating, teachers can use proximity control to keep students on task, actively involved, and alert. By moving around the room to check on students, teachers can become proactive—able to anticipate and prevent problems before they occur—instead of having to react after something has happened. In situations in which teachers float from class to class or co-teach in a general education setting, they may set up their supplies in a desk in that classroom or in a work area off to the side of the room. It is important for special education teachers to have a designated area, materials, and supplies in a co-taught classroom, first, to support their instructional efforts and second, to affirm the important contribution they make in the general education setting.

Equipment and Storage Space

Prior to the start of the school year, you should select and set up the equipment you will need, whether you are teaching in a resource/pullout classroom or in an inclusive classroom. The classroom should have both desks and tables, so that individual work, group work, peer tutoring, and cooperative learning may take place. Allocate specific areas of the room for the storage of audiocassettes, videodiscs, videotapes, CD-ROMs, computer software, manipulatives, periodicals, newspapers, magazines, games, transparencies, and other resource materials. Carefully label these areas so that teachers, students, substitutes, and teaching assistants can find equipment and supplies.

Teachers who are not assigned to one classroom but float from classroom to classroom or co-teach (such as when special and general education teachers work together to teach students jointly in general education settings) may need to set up equipment and supplies on a cart to make their materials mobile, or they may have designated areas within each general education classroom in which they teach. Some teachers use file boxes to organize and store their instructional materials, student folders, games, tape recorders, and manipulatives. For example, Mrs. Nestrada uses a three-tiered cart with two boxes on each shelf to teach six different classes. Although she stores additional materials elsewhere, the cart enables her to keep the most essential materials with her to use in her classes.

In some classrooms, teachers are faced with the dilemma of inadequate storage space for students' materials. There may be more students than desks. In these cases, bookshelves that have sections or cubbyholes may be used for students to store materials, such as pencils, crayons, workbooks, paperback books, journals, notebooks, and textbooks. If shelves are not available, plastic dishpans may accommodate workbooks, books, and papers.

In secondary classrooms, students do not usually have desks in which to store materials. They may be seated at chairs with arms that are used as the writing surface or they may sit at tables. Teachers often set up folders in which they keep student work and sometimes code the folders by color for each class period. Students usually store their books in lockers and are responsible for bringing them to class. Therefore, storage of students' materials may not be a problem in secondary classrooms.

Instructional Materials and Files

Prior to the first week of school, teachers should organize instructional materials so that they are readily available for students to use. When appropriate, they should be visible to students. For example, store games in see-through plastic containers so that students can find and retrieve them easily. Set up a system so that students know what materials they can use and how to access them. Callahan, Clark, and Kellough (1998) recommend arranging materials so that they are located in places that require minimal foot traffic and in a way that avoids having to line up for them.

Additionally, before the school year begins, teachers should organize their files and set them up so that they are easily accessible. For example, many commercial cassette tape and worksheet programs are available to teach listening skills, phonics, and math. Set up a file with folders labeled with the name and number of each lesson from one of these programs. Store worksheets that correspond to each lesson in the folders for easy retrieval at a later date. Use a shoe box for the accompanying audiotapes. Insert index cards between tapes in the box with the appropriate name and number of each lesson written on them. By preparing such files ahead of time, you avoid having to find tapes and prepare worksheets each day before class. With this type of organization, it is possible to teach students to use the file independently to retrieve each day's lesson.

Student Variables

Student variables that affect classroom organization include the number of students in the class, their age and grade levels, their learning levels, cultural and language differences, and related problems students have (mobility, language, behavior, etc.). You may, therefore, arrange the room to accommodate students who are working at various levels and who are focusing on different content and skills by including learning centers, computers, a variety of instructional grouping arrangements, and modified curriculum materials written for several different grade levels. For example, Heron and Harris (1987) suggest that verbal communication moves across, not around, tables. Therefore, they recommend that a student with low verbal skills be seated across from a student with high verbal skills to maximize the reception of verbal messages and nonverbal cues (that is, facial expressions and gestures).

Consider cultural differences in setting up the classroom. Kitano (1987) states that few Asian Americans participate freely in group discussions. This fact is important to know as you plan your instructional activities so that you do not mistake limited participation for lack of ability.

Students from cultures that are people-oriented or that endorse working together for the good of the group may benefit from cooperative learning activities, group projects, and other collaborative activities. For example, Lewis and Doorlag (1991) report that the Native American culture emphasizes cooperation and group achievement and that Native American students may show a preference towards actions as opposed to words. Teachers may want to consider using physical arrangements and activities to complement various cultural preferences by including tables, peer tutoring areas, and activity areas.

Bulletin Boards

Bulletin boards may be used in elementary and secondary settings as instructional tools, as a means of communicating information, and as visual displays. Hayes (1985) suggests four types of bulletin boards: decorative, motivational, instructional, and manipulative. Hannah (1982) recommends a fifth category—informational. A sixth type of bulletin board displays students' work.

Decorative bulletin boards are typically designed to brighten and improve the appearance of a classroom. An example of a decorative bulletin board is one that says "Hello" or "Welcome" in several different languages. This may encourage students to share more of their native language and perhaps some customs with the rest of the class. Middle school, junior high, and high school students enjoy the use of posters on bulletin boards. Teachers may also purchase decorative posters with themes that are of interest to adolescents.

Motivational bulletin boards are used to recognize student effort and progress. For example, teachers may post charts and graphs showing student progress in mastering a particular

skill. Some teachers like to post student goals or progress toward a specific goal. Motivational bulletin boards may be effective when students try to advance their own scores or progress. For example, Mr. Reczek posts a point system on the bulletin board in his middle school class. In this way, the students are able to view their progress in terms of points earned. Adolescents are often motivated by posters and art work with catchy phrases. To motivate her high school students to work in teams on group projects, Ms. Michelson puts up a poster that reads, "Together—not even the sky is the limit!"

Instructional bulletin boards may be subject or task specific. They may be related to the curriculum and used for instruction. When Ms. Stewart posts the steps to an error-monitoring strategy (Schumaker, Nolan, & Deshler, 1985) and teaches it to her students directly from the bulletin board, that is task specific. Later, the bulletin board serves as a cue to students as they practice using the strategy, because it is constantly available as a reference.

Manipulative bulletin boards may be thought of as an enlarged version of a worksheet to be completed by actually attaching things (Hayes, 1985). For example, in Ms. Hall's elementary classroom, students are asked to pin a leaf containing a word with a specific vowel sound to a tree that has the same vowel sound printed on it. Students in middle school or junior high may enjoy tracking the progress of a rocket on a map of the world to show its location.

Informational bulletin boards are used to convey information to students. They can be used for announcements, for current events, or for communication among students. Teachers may also post the dates of tests and deadlines for projects. For both elementary and secondary students, one of the most effective uses of informational bulletin boards is to post the classroom rules and consequences.

Work display bulletin boards are used to display samples of students' work. These should be a regular part of the classroom and should be updated and changed frequently. Students may enjoy displaying their spelling tests, math papers, stories, themes, and products they have developed at learning centers. Special education teachers involved in consulting or co-teaching with general classroom teachers may set up instructional or manipulative bulletin boards in the general education classroom. Teachers who float from class to class may carry a small bulletin board with them.

In preparing bulletin boards, Callahan, Clark, and Kellough (1998) recommend the following guidelines:

◆ Keep it simple.
◆ Focus on one main idea, concept, topic, or theme.
◆ Use illustrations to accent topics.
◆ Use short, concise captions.
◆ Consider gender and ethnic equity.

◆ **ACTIVITY 2.1**

Collect pictures of men, women, adolescents, and children who represent a variety of cultural backgrounds and who are engaged in both common and unusual activities. Decide how you would use these pictures to construct either a decorative or an instructional bulletin board. (Answers for this and other activities are found in the Instructor's Manual.)

Grading and Record-keeping Procedures

At the beginning of the school year, decide how you are going to grade student work, monitor progress, and keep records of student performance, and how you will communicate these procedures to your students. Do this verbally, in writing, as part of the classroom rules, or in all three ways.

Grading

Grading is the most common system used to communicate student evaluation (Bigge, 1988). Grading students with disabilities is particularly perplexing in inclusive settings. In a grading survey, 368 general education teachers rated pass-fail grades and checklists as appropriate for students with disabilities (Bursuck, Polloway, Plante, Epstein, Jayanthi, & McConeghy, 1996). Both general educators (Bursuck et al., 1996) and secondary students (Munk & Bursuck, 1997) felt that grade adaptations only for students with disabilities were unfair.

As a special education teacher, you may be responsible for assigning grades, you may not assign grades at all, or you may assign grades in collaboration with the classroom teacher. Bursuck and others (1996) found that 50% of the general educators in their survey assumed complete responsibility for grading, whereas 40% shared grading with special educators.

General techniques such as assigning multiple grades, contracting for grades, basing grades on a variety of assignments, factoring in growth rate, and establishing criteria for grades have been found to be effective in grading students with special needs (Bigge, 1988; Butler, Magliocca, Torres, & Lee, 1984; Gersten, Vaughn, & Brengelman, 1996; Munk & Bursuck, 1997; Tiedt & Tiedt, 1986). Mehring (1995) suggests the addition of written narratives about students' academic and behavioral performances to quantitative scores on the standard report card.

Multiple Grades. Many assignments may be evaluated with multiple grades. For example, you may assign two grades for a report—one for content and one for mechanics. Giving two grades takes into consideration the ideas (content) as separate from the mechanical aspects (punctuation, spelling, grammar), which present stumbling blocks for many students with special needs. General education teachers and secondary students feel the assigning of separate grades for effort and product is a helpful adaptation for students with special needs (Munk & Bursuck, 1997).

Contracting for Grades. Contracting with students for grades based on a certain level of proficiency on IEP objectives is another suggestion (Polloway, Epstein, Bursuck, Roderique, McConeghy, & Jayanthi, 1994). In this grading procedure, you discuss short-term objectives with the students and agree on the level of proficiency to be reached by the end of each grading period. Reaching the goal level results in a higher grade than not reaching it. If you select 80% as the mastery goal, then 80% should translate to the letter grade A.

Basing Grades on a Variety of Assignments. You may want to assign grades based on a variety of assignments, as opposed to just an exam. Additionally, you may give more weight to reports and homework scores than exam scores for the final grade.

Factoring in Growth Rate. Grading based on improvement is another adaptation that is effective for students with disabilities (Polloway, Epstein, Bursuck, Roderique, McConeghy, & Jayanthi, 1994). One of the authors based students' spelling grades, in part, on the increase in the number of words spelled correctly from the Monday pretest to the final spelling test on Friday. For example, both Jim and Jan earned an A grade. Jim, who improved by 10 words from the spelling pretest to the posttest, earned extra points, which boosted his 85% to an A grade. Jan, who improved by only one word, earned an A, as she scored 100% on the posttest.

Establishing Criteria for Grades. In addition to percentages, always make your criteria clear for the grades you give (Tiedt & Tiedt, 1986). For example, may an A paper have spelling errors?

Discuss with the students the characteristics of outstanding work, average work, and poor work, and show them examples. For example, Mr. Lucas teaches students how to take notes so that they can improve their performance in history class. As part of his teaching procedure, he shows them examples of good and poor notes. He specifies his criteria for grading notes for the content (key points of the lecture) and the technique (accurate use of a note-taking strategy).

One of the most troublesome questions for you as a teacher is whether students with special needs should fail in classes for which you have the responsibility of assigning grades. Special education teachers are supposed to provide students with an appropriate education plan. If a student is failing, the teacher should ask questions like, Did I design an appropriate education plan? Is there something else I might do? Should I add other incentives? We feel that students should not fail in a special education setting if they truly have been provided with an individualized education program.

Record Keeping

Record keeping consists of collecting and keeping information and data for instructional and/or administrative purposes (Polloway & Patton, 1997). Teachers should keep careful, written records on a daily basis regarding student performance. Record-keeping systems may be designed prior to the start of the school year. Charts, graphs, checklists, and other forms may be developed to accompany the activities and materials that students will use in the classroom. In some classes, the record-keeping system is visible to everyone, as in Mrs. Murphy's fourth grade, where the names of the books each student has read are posted. In other cases, the record-keeping system is kept in folders, as in Mr. Russo's high school class, where math students are concentrating on probability. A checklist containing math vocabulary and rules is stapled inside each student's folder, where it is updated on a daily basis.

Teachers may develop other record-keeping systems by recording the date and score for computer activities, audiotape lessons, learning center activities, and drill and practice activities; progress toward mastering specific skills; attendance records; and scores on tests, homework, projects, and other assignments. These records may be kept in a written record book or an electronic record book (such as a computer software program, either commercially produced or teacher-developed using a spreadsheet) (Callahan, Clark, & Kellough, 1998).

Students may be responsible for some of their own record keeping. Mercer and Mercer (1993) suggest using self-correction tapes to provide feedback to students about their math seatwork. After using such tapes, students may fill out their math record for the day (see Figure 2.1). This record keeping on the part of students provides them with immediate awareness of their performance and may lead to application of strategies to improve that performance.

Whatever record-keeping procedures you develop, be sure they reflect the instructional objectives and level of performance designated for each student in each area of the academic and social skills curriculum. Records of student performance in pull-out and inclusive settings may be used to plan, modify, and evaluate instruction and to motivate students to greater achievement.

 ACTIVITY 2.2

Work with a partner to devise a way of keeping records for an individual student in a pull-out classroom and a way for keeping records for a small group of students in an inclusive classroom.

 IMPORTANT POINTS

1. The procedures teachers follow at the beginning of the school year set the stage for the rest of the year.
2. One of the challenges teachers face as they begin the year is setting up and organizing the classroom environment.
3. Considerations in setting up the classroom environment include attention to (a) the physical arrangement of the classroom, (b) equipment and storage space, (c) instructional materials and files, (d) student variables, and (e) bulletin boards.
4. Bulletin boards may be decorative, motivational, instructional, manipulative, or informational, or they may display student work.
5. Effective grading techniques include assigning multiple grades, contracting for grades, basing grades on a variety of assignments, and establishing criteria for grades.
6. Record-keeping procedures include the use of charts, graphs, and checklists to record student progress on computer, audiotape, and learning center activities and may be kept in a written or electronic record book.

Name ____Julie_____

Today I listened to tape ____#7_____

My first score was ____12/15_____

My score after corrections was ____15/15_____

Figure 2.1 Math Record

INSTRUCTIONAL AND MANAGEMENT DECISIONS

Part of beginning-year planning involves making decisions about how to manage the learning environment effectively. Two important decisions that may ensure a successful start to the school year include attention to instructional grouping arrangements and establishment of management procedures.

Instructional Grouping Arrangements

Instruction may be provided in a variety of ways: large groups, small groups, one-to-one, with peers, or independently. Individualization of instruction may be achieved by using any of these instructional arrangements. As Christenson, Thurlow, and Ysseldyke (1987) point out, individualization does not limit the grouping arrangement to situations in which a student works alone or in a one-to-one arrangement with a teacher. Individualization refers to "helping students succeed, to achieve a high percentage of correct responses and to become confident in his/her competence" (p. 6).

Factors influencing decisions about how to provide instruction include (a) the characteristics and needs of the students, (b) the type of learning planned—whether the teacher is teaching a skill for the first time (i.e., acquisition learning) or students are practicing and maintaining a skill that has already been taught (i.e., fluency and maintenance learning), (c) the task or activity (i.e., steps in long division, job interviewing, building a model of the digestive system, or writing in journals), and (d) the types of instructional methodology that are available. Callahan, Clark, and Kellough (1998) recommend that you consider the types of instructional methodology that are available, including:

◆ Cooperative learning
◆ Debates
◆ Games
◆ Laboratory experiments
◆ Multimedia
◆ Problem solving
◆ Peer tutoring
◆ Simulations

◆ Textbooks
◆ Learning centers
◆ Computer-assisted instruction
◆ Demonstrations
◆ Guest speakers
◆ Lecture/presentations
◆ Panel discussions
◆ Questioning
◆ Role playing
◆ Telecommunication
◆ Think-pair-share
◆ Co-teaching

Teachers should choose instructional arrangements that meet students' needs as documented in their IEPs and that address cultural and linguistic diversity.

Large-Group Instruction

There are many opportunities for using large-group instruction. For example, use large-group instruction to introduce a strategy for taking notes. Lewis and Doorlag (1999) suggest providing guided practice for the whole class at once. Have the students practice taking notes by watching a videotape, while you circulate around the room to monitor use of the note-taking strategy. Other appropriate uses of whole-class instruction include the viewing of multimedia presentations or videotapes, large-group discussions of content area subjects, and demonstrations. Fister and Kemp (1995) recommend the use of the Ask, Pause, Call technique during presentations to large groups. The teacher *asks* a question, *pauses* to allow students to process the question and formulate a response, and then *calls* on someone.

Large-group instruction is used extensively in general education classroom settings. Experience in large groups may be helpful to students as they make the transition from special to general education settings (Bos & Vaughn, 1998). In addition, special education teachers who co-teach in inclusive classrooms may share with classroom teachers the responsibility for providing instruction to the whole class. Be aware that when using large-group instruction, not all of the students will learn all of the content you present. You still need to think about individual student needs. Dyck, Sundbye, and Pemberton (1997) use an Interactive Lesson Planning Model to determine the topic of a lesson, the content of the lesson, and what parts of the content can be learned by all, most, or some of the students given their varied levels and skills. This planning model, particularly useful for co-teachers, serves as a basis for differentiating activities, objectives, and assessments for students.

When providing instruction to the entire group, many teachers arrange the desks in rows. This may be appropriate when you are lecturing and making presentations through directive teaching and using the overhead projector or when you are showing slides or videotapes. When utilizing this type of arrangement, it is helpful to move around the room and to direct comments and questions to students seated in the back of the room (Weinstein, 1981). Cegelka (1995) emphasizes the importance of arranging the desks so that all students can see the whole-group instructional area and yet not face areas that could distract them, such as learning center activity areas, windows, or doors.

Small-Group Instruction

Small-group instruction is appropriate when teachers present different material to different students (Lewis & Doorlag, 1999). Small groups are frequently used in acquisition learning to teach a specific skill (Polloway, Patton, Payne, & Payne, 1989). Groups should be flexible: Sondra, Tim, Rahji, and Bertha may be grouped together for instruction in math but be members of other groups for spelling. If Bertha progresses more rapidly than the others, she is moved to another, more appropriate group.

Small-group instruction usually consists of groups of two to five students. It is used when teachers want to work closely with students and provide frequent feedback (Bos & Vaughn, 1994). Small groups may also be used in cooperative teaching situations to divide the class into different skill groups. Brophy and Good (1986) suggest the use of small groups in classes that are highly heterogeneous. Small groups are often used in general education classes because of the heterogeneity of the population and thus would work well in inclusive settings. Students may be grouped for reading, math, spelling, or other academic skills.

Small-group arrangements are particularly effective for teaching academic skills. Reading is frequently taught in small groups. Small-group arrangements are also useful for cooperative learning activities (activities in which students work together and teach each other); role playing; and for drill, practice, and review. A detailed description of cooperative learning is provided in Chapter 10.

Weinstein (1981) suggests that teachers arrange the seating within groups so that group leaders are accessible to all members of the group and less vocal students are seated across from the more vocal leaders. For this reason, you should consider having some tables in your classroom to facilitate group work. When working with a group, some teachers prefer to seat students in a semicircle facing them in order to provide optimum feedback and attention; there is support for this grouping arrangement for low-achieving students in the area of mathematics (Carnine, Silbert, & Kameenui, 1997). Small-group instruction may be appealing to students who have language differences because they may feel more comfortable asking for clarification in a small group and because they may have more opportunity to participate.

Small-group arrangements also facilitate maintenance learning, providing students with opportunities to practice or extend a skill that was presented through direct instruction. Group projects, such as interviewing someone, writing an article for the school newspaper, or developing a budget, may be assigned to groups as extension activities to prompt maintenance and generalization of skills taught.

One-to-One Instruction

Working on a one-to-one basis with the teacher allows students to ask questions, receive corrective feedback, and interact directly with the teacher. Individual instruction is appropriate for students who are working on acquisition learning, having difficulty learning in a small-group setting, or needing assistance with specific aspects of assignments (Polloway, Patton, Payne, & Payne, 1989). The disadvantage of this arrangement is that the teacher's time and attention can be focused on only one student at a time.

Teachers using one-to-one instruction must plan for the rest of the class, perhaps by including cooperative learning activities and peer tutoring. Some teachers utilize the skills of paraprofessionals or volunteers to provide one-to-one instruction to students. Other teachers ask paraprofessionals or volunteers to monitor the rest of the class while they work with individual students. Some co-teaching arrangements are conducive to one-to-one instruction. While one teacher works with most of the class, the co-teacher assists other students on a one-to-one basis (see Chapter 5 for other suggestions). Teachers may want to set up tables or desks away from the rest of the class for one-to-one instruction.

Peer Tutoring

In peer tutoring, one student receives instruction from another under supervision of the teacher. Peer tutoring is effective for fluency and maintenance learning, such as practicing math facts and spelling words. Tutors may also check answers to end-of-chapter questions, provide positive reinforcement and corrective feedback, and teach or reteach specific skills to other students who need extra help. When instruction is provided through tutorial arrangements, you may want to arrange areas in the classroom for peer tutors by putting two desks together or by providing small tables set aside from the rest of the class. Peer tutoring is often combined with other instructional options, such as large- and small-group arrangements. A detailed description of peer tutoring is provided in Chapter 10.

Independent Learning

Students may work independently when they have acquired a skill and need opportunities for practice. Independent practice may include completing an activity at a learning center, using the language master, viewing a multimedia presentation, playing a game, or using self-correcting materials. It is helpful to include a self-correcting component in independent work. The independent learning arrangement does not require the teacher's presence, so teachers should select activities that students can complete with minimal assistance (Bos & Vaughn, 1994). Thus, while some students are engaged in independent work, others work individually or in small groups with the teacher.

Classrooms may be set up to contain individual work areas, perhaps even study carrels, where students can work quietly and independently. Students may also work independently at a table, desk, study carrel, or computer workstation. The challenge for teachers is to place the individual work areas away from the more active areas of the classroom.

There are a variety of ways to arrange the classroom for instruction. You may use any of the previously described arrangements or a combination of one or more of them. It depends upon your instructional purpose(s) and the needs and characteristics of your students. Flexible grouping arrangements allow you to individualize instruction in a variety of ways. Figure 2.2 contains examples of possible arrangements for large- and small-group instruction. Notice how these groupings may be used effectively in both pull-out and inclusive classrooms, and how they allow the teacher to move around the room to provide instruction, reinforce student engagement, and monitor progress.

Desks in rows

Desks in a horseshoe

Desks in clusters

Desks in circles

Figure 2.2 Large- and Small-Group Instructional Arrangements

ACTIVITY 2.3

Choose an elementary, middle, or high school setting and prepare a sketch of a classroom. Assume that you will have students who are involved in both acquisition learning, and fluency and maintenance learning. Be sure to include evidence of the instructional arrangements (large-group, small-group, one-to-one, peer tutoring, and independent learning) you would use, as well as ideas from the section of the chapter called, "Environmental Variables" (learning centers, free-time areas, etc.).

 IMPORTANT POINTS

1. An important decision that may ensure a successful start to the school year includes attention to instructional grouping arrangements.
2. Instruction may be provided in a variety of ways: large groups, small groups, one-to-one, with peers, or independently.
3. Factors influencing decisions about how to provide instruction include attention to the characteristics and needs of the students, the type of learning planned (e.g., acquisition or maintenance), the activity, and the types of instructional methodology that are available.
4. Large-group instruction is appropriate for guided practice activities, the viewing of multimedia presentations or videotapes, large-group discussion of content area subjects, and demonstrations.
5. Small-group instruction is used to present different material to different students and is effective for acquisition learning, teaching of academic skills, cooperative learning activities, role playing, drill, practice, review, and maintenance and generalization of skills.

6. Arrangements in which teachers and students work together on a one-to-one basis are appropriate for students who are working on skills that differ from those of the rest of the class and for those who are working on acquisition learning, having difficulty in a small-group setting, or needing assistance with specific aspects of assignments.
7. Peer tutoring is effective for fluency and maintenance learning, monitoring progress, providing feedback, and teaching and reteaching specific skills to students who need extra help.
8. Independent learning is appropriate when students have acquired a skill and need opportunities for practice.

Management Decisions

Many potential behavior problems may be prevented by the selection of appropriate and motivational materials, the presentation of organized and motivational lessons, the active involvement of the students, and the implementation of structured routines. These techniques are discussed elsewhere, so we do not repeat them here. Unfortunately, not all behavior problems can be prevented or resolved with only these instructional decisions. You must also make wise decisions concerning management options. Some of these decisions center around establishing a classroom rule system.

You will notice as you are reading this section that many of the suggestions are very teacher-directed, even though we urge the use of student input in formulating the rules and the selection of choice strategies. Eventually, we feel that self-management should replace teacher-direction, but this is a gradual process. (Self-management strategies are discussed in Chapters 3 and 8.)

Selecting Rules

Rules are evidenced everywhere. In society, there are formal rules, or laws, and informal rules, or social codes. Formal laws help maintain order, so, unlike in the days of the old West, disputes are not resolved by meeting on Main Street at high noon. Social codes are informal rules that vary from culture to culture.

Rules let students know what you expect. Students react differently during independent seatwork in a class where the teacher expects talking in a low voice than in a class where the teacher expects total silence. Two effective ways for you to identify class rules are to make a list of your behavioral expectations ahead of time and to ask if there are any schoolwide rules (Sprick, 1985). An examination of the list of schoolwide rules will let you know what behaviors administrators and other teachers feel are necessary for maintaining order.

Once you define your expectations, you should establish rules. Following are some guidelines:

1. ***Allow the students to give input concerning the rules.*** Helping to select rules gives students a sense of being a part of the decision-making process and often makes them feel more responsible for following the rules. Sprick (1981) suggests that if you want students to design their own rules, you should post temporary rules for the first 3 or 4 days, until students become familiar with the routines.

2. ***Base rules on acceptable behaviors.*** In deciding on the rules, keep in mind the behaviors that are expected in the general classroom setting. It may be acceptable for a student to complete work standing at a table in a resource room setting, but this behavior may be totally unacceptable in an inclusive setting. In many school districts, there are certain rules that all students are expected to follow. If this is the case, incorporate these rules into your system. Other considerations for deciding which behaviors to include in rules are to select those that promote the ease of functioning as a classroom community.

3. ***State rules positively.*** Positive rules lead to a positive atmosphere in the classroom and clue the students into appropriate behavior. "Speak politely to others by saying *thank you* and *please*" is a much better rule than, "Don't shout at others." The first rule suggests an appropriate behavior, while the latter just warns the students not to shout.

4. ***Select only about five or six rules.*** A rule cannot be invented for every slight infraction that may happen in the class. The more rules you have, the more difficult it is to enforce them consistently (Jensen, Sloan, & Young, 1988).

5. ***Select rules for both academic and social behaviors.*** Rules usually deal with academic behaviors, such as "Complete all assignments," or social behaviors, such as "Keep hands and feet to yourself." Often academic rules will prevent inappropriate social and affective behaviors. If Joan is completing math, she cannot be hitting Sean.

6. ***Relate rules to specific behaviors, but be general enough to cover many classes of that behavior.*** A rule such as "Be kind to others" is general; it can cover many classes of behaviors, including "Say nice things to other students" and "Keep your hands to yourself." Thus, the use of a general rule reduces the number of rules needed. However, students may not understand what is meant by the rule if no specific behavior is identified. This problem may be solved by listing examples of specific behaviors next to the rule or by discussing and role-playing specific behaviors.

7. ***Change rules when necessary.*** If being unprepared for class is a problem for your third-period class, this behavior should become the focus of a new rule. If students are completing all work, it may be time to remove the rule that deals with completing all assignments. This does not mean that students no longer have to complete the work; rather, since everyone is remembering it, a written rule is no longer necessary.

8. ***Relate rules to IEP objectives.*** For many students with special needs, social behavior as well as academic objectives are written in the IEP. These objectives may be added to the rules for each individual student as individual goals or, if many students have similar objectives, may become part of the group list of rules.

9. ***Consider cultural differences.*** In some cultures, student involvement in class is often vocal, exuberant, and physical, so students may be on task even though they are not sitting quietly in their seats. You may want to incorporate such factors into rule selection. For example, "Finish all assignments" may be a better rule than "Work quietly at your seat."

 ACTIVITY 2.4

> Work with a partner and list five or six rules you might use in your class.

Teaching Rules

Once rules are selected, the next step is to teach and discuss them frequently. Particularly at the beginning of the school year, the class rules should be discussed, demonstrated, and, for younger children, practiced. Adding a rationale to an explanation of the rules during the discussion is particularly effective for older students, who often are motivated if reasons for having rules are discussed (Morgan & Jenson, 1988).

The following techniques, adapted from Direct Instruction procedures (Engelmann & Carnine, 1982), are suggested for teaching rules. They include defining or describing the relevant attributes of the behavior, modeling examples and nonexamples, and asking students to discriminate between them (Morgan & Jenson, 1988). For example, with the stay-on-task rule, define for the students what "stay on task" means (e.g., "Stay on task means you write or listen or read when you work"). Next, give positive examples (e.g., "When you are doing a math paper, you are on task if you are writing down the problems, figuring out the answers, or thinking about how to solve the problem") and negative or nonexamples (e.g., "You are not on task if you are looking out the window, thinking about lunch, or talking to a friend"). Then model examples and nonexamples of on-task behaviors and ask the students to identify and explain why the behavior is an example or a nonexample of on-task behavior. In response to this question, a student may say, "You are on task because you are looking at the math book," or "You are not on task because you are looking around the room." Next, have students model the appropriate or inappropriate behavior and have others identify whether the students are displaying on-task behaviors. During this role-play activity, the students are not only practicing the rule, but also learning to evaluate behaviors.

Post the rules in the room or in individual notebooks to help students remember them. Many adolescents write the rules on a sheet of paper to keep in their notebooks. One creative student teacher incorporated the rules into a class constitution to parody the United States Constitution.

Prompting Rules

Having rules does not mean students will automatically follow them immediately. Students often need prompts to internalize or perform behaviors independently (Rosenshine, 1990). Prompts are ways to remind students to follow the rules. For example, verbal prompts such as "Remember, raise your hand," or visual prompts, such as a finger over the lips, usually prevent talk-outs. The visual prompt of standing near the whispering students often stops off-task behavior. Other prompts include sharing expectations, peer modeling, positive repetition, and issuing either warning or choice statements.

Sharing Expectations. Sharing expectations is a way to explain to students what rules are in effect or what behaviors you expect for that particular activity (Sprick, 1985). Rules often vary, depending on whether the activity is to be completed by individuals or by small groups. Stating behavior rules at the beginning of a lesson is especially effective for students with problem behaviors (Borg & Ascione, 1982; Emmer, Evertson, Clement, & Worsham, 1994).

An example of sharing expectations about behaviors appears in these sample instructions given to secondary students: "Today, we begin our study of the Roman Empire. As we discuss the beginning of Roman civilization, please remember to listen to others' ideas without interruptions, to copy the notes from the board, and to participate in the discussion." With many elementary students, you must share your expectations before academic and nonacademic activities. For example, "Bernice, remember, when we stand in line, we keep our hands to ourselves, we face the door, and we do not talk."

Peer Modeling. Peer modeling may also serve as a prompt for following rules (Alberto & Troutman, 1995). To use peer modeling, praise students who are following the rule by identifying specific behaviors (e.g., "Good, Jason, you are standing quietly in line") and ignore the student who is not (e.g., ignore Rashonda). Then, when the student displays the appropriate behavior, praise him or her (e.g., "Good, Rashonda, that's the way to stand quietly in line").

Positive Repetition. Positive repetition is similar to peer modeling in that you first tune in to positive behaviors of the students who are following the rules. At the same time, however, you repeat the directions or instructions you gave (Canter, 1986). For example, if Jane, a middle school student, is refusing to follow your directions to take out her sentence writing book and turn to page 45, ignore Jane and say to Ramone, "Thank you, Ramone. I can see you have your sentence writing book out. I appreciate your turning to page 45, Towanda. This side of the room is ready to begin."

Praising other students instead of tuning in to the inappropriate behavior of a student is difficult even for seasoned teachers. The natural reaction to this type of situation is to focus on the deviant behavior immediately, instead of praising the students who are following the rules. Deviant behaviors can make teachers fearful that their authority is being questioned and that they are losing control. Yet being positive as a first step is frequently sufficient to stop inappropriate behavior. In addition, praising teaches students that teacher attention, often a powerful motivator (Alberto & Troutman, 1999), may be secured through appropriate behaviors instead of inappropriate behaviors.

Grossman (1994) states that students from the African-American culture often behave aggressively and assertively, but these behaviors do not lead to more deviant ones. He further finds that teachers often intervene when no intervention is necessary.

Issuing Warning Statements and Choice Statements. We recommend the use of warning statements and choice statements only after you have tried to change the behavior by positively attending to the appropriate behaviors of other students. If, after praising others, you find that a student is still not following the rule, you may want to use a warning or a choice statement. A warning statement alerts the student to the rule infraction. For example, "You are forgetting our rule to listen to others, Sam. This is a warning," lets Sam know that he needs to display appropriate behavior immediately. Warning statements are often used with younger children.

With a choice statement, you present the appropriate behavior that relates to the rule and some sort of unpleasant option to the student, for example, "Sally, you are breaking Rule 4. Either remember to raise your hand (rule) or leave the group (option). It is your choice."

Once you issue a choice statement, give the student an opportunity to think about the choice. Move out of the student's vicinity to avoid a direct confrontation and continue with other activities. That way, a student can save face and even mumble nasty things out of your hearing range (or, at least, you can pretend not to hear them). Be certain always to acknowledge an appropriate choice in some way, such as "I see you've made a good choice, Sally. Thank you."

An advantage of the use of choice statements is that they place responsibility for the actions with the student. In the previous example, if Sally comes back and blames you for her problems, an appropriate reply is "No, Sally, I gave you a choice and you decided to leave the group." Choice statements help students with special needs realize that they are responsible for their own behaviors. Choice statements are also effective with students from various cultural backgrounds. Grossman (1994) suggests nonauthoritarian methods when disciplining Hispanic adolescents who, because of the patriarchal nature of their culture, may have problems taking commands from female teachers.

In issuing choice or warning statements, you should remain calm and speak in a quiet, firm voice. Lower your voice at the end of a warning statement. Be aware of nonverbal behaviors, such as eye contact. When issuing a warning statement, many teachers point a finger at the student, which is a clue to the student that he or she is upsetting the teacher. Hands resting at the side convey an air of confidence.

Colvin, Ainge, and Nelson (1997) suggest that teachers give students a list of options privately when they break a rule. With this strategy, teachers focus students' attention on ways to solve the problem, instead of focusing on noncompliance. For example, options for Sally, who is not raising her hand, may include: "Sally, talking out is not appropriate. You may raise your hand when you need help, go on to the next problem until I can help you, or reread the directions."

The type of prompt given depends on the type of behavior, the time of the year, and the cultural background of the student. It is not possible to administer a choice statement for behav-

iors that are physically detrimental to a particular student, other students, the teacher, or school property. Samantha cannot be given a choice if she is hitting Jim. You must stop her immediately and send her to the time-out area or refer her to the dean of students or the principal. Frequently, more prompts are given at the beginning of the year until students become familiar with the rules. Public critique of behavior may cause discomfort for many Asian and Arabic students,

 ACTIVITY 2.5

Three people are needed to participate in this activity. One will be the teacher, another the student, and the third will be the observer. Be sure to change roles so that each person has a chance to be the teacher, the student, and the observer. The observer is to evaluate the teacher's use of a choice statement by marking an *X* under *yes* or *no* for each statement on the following checklist. The student is telling the teacher that he is not going to do his math (disobeying the rule to follow teacher directions) and is trying to involve the teacher in a confrontation. The teacher should use a choice statement.

Observer Checklist   **Yes**   **No**

1. Did the teacher remain calm?
2. Did the teacher speak in a firm, quiet voice?
3. Did the teacher maintain eye contact?
4. Did the teacher use her or his hands appropriately?
5. Did the teacher state the appropriate behavior and the option in the choice statement?
6. Did the teacher repeat the choice idea by saying, "It is your choice" or "It is your decision"?
7. Did the teacher give the student some time to think about it?
8. Did the teacher acknowledge selection of the appropriate choice?

who feel such comments bring shame to them and their families (McIntyre, 1998).

Enforcing Rules

The next step is to decide what you are going to do when students follow rules and when they do not. You may want to use specific praise or positive attention intermittently to call attention to students who are following the rules, and then award certificates or free time at the end of the week based on particular criteria.

Specific praise statements identify the praiseworthy aspects of students' behaviors. When using a specific praise statement, include a description of the specific behavior the student is demonstrating and the student's name, for example, "I like the way you are working quietly, Terri" for the young student and "That was a good decision when you ignored Hugo's remark, Josh." For many adolescents, positive public praise from a teacher is unpleasant or embarrassing, as they don't want to be singled out from their peers (Sprick, 1985). Thus, you may want to praise adolescents in private or praise the group effort instead of individuals. This is also true for many Native Americans, who prefer quiet, private, specific praise (Pepper, 1986).

Specific praise and positive attention may be interwoven into your daily routine; neither is time consuming. Attending to the student with a raised hand and ignoring the one shouting out requires no extra time. Stopping at secondary students' desks to compliment them for staying on task during independent practice activities is appropriate for students who enjoy being praised or singled out for teacher attention in private (Sprick, 1985). Specific praise and positive attention are particularly effective for Latino students, whose culture typically endorses a dependency on the approval of others (Grossman, 1984).

What are your options when, even after prompting, a student continues to break the rules? Usually, the options are (a) withholding something the student likes or (b) presenting the student with something he or she doesn't like. Many teachers withhold points, privileges, or free time from students who do not follow the rules; others write referrals or require students to eat lunch alone. Canter (1979) recommends a hierarchy of consequences, such as writing the student's name on the board for the first rule infraction, withdrawing 5 minutes of recess time for the next, and referring the student to the principal for the third. He further states that a severe rule infraction (such as a fight) warrants an immediate severe punishment, such as referral to the principal.

Whatever consequence you use, remember to remain calm and follow through. Some students try to talk teachers out of the consequence, such as "Oh, Mr. Jones, please don't send me to the principal's office. I'll do my work now." A teacher who does not follow through at this time is teaching students that they can wait to do their work until the teacher threatens to take them to the office, and then they can talk the teacher out of taking them there. You need to follow through with the consequence, or your effort becomes just a threat.

In addition to following through with consequences, consistency is a prime consideration in enforcing rules. If "Raise your hand to speak" is a rule, then all students should have to follow it. Be careful not to fall into the trap of giving attention to a student who is shouting out because that student happens to be blurting out the correct answer. Consistency allows students to learn that there are expectations in your class accompanied by rewards for following them and consequences for not complying.

Finally, remember to provide appropriate feedback. For example, Mr. Anderson gave his secondary students the following feedback at the end of fifth period: "Most of today's class went well. All of you followed directions, copying the notes from the board, but I had to prompt you not to interrupt when someone was talking. Let's work on this during tomorrow's class."

IMPORTANT POINTS

1. Guidelines for establishing rules are to incorporate student input, base rules on acceptable behaviors, state rules positively, select only about five or six rules, relate rules to both academic and social behaviors, make rules specific, change rules when necessary, relate rules to IEP objectives, and consider cultural differences.
2. Teaching rules requires defining or describing the important attributes of the behavior, modeling examples and nonexamples, and asking students to discriminate between them.
3. Prompts are used to remind students to follow the rules.
4. Prompts include sharing expectations, peer modeling, positive repetition, and issuing warning or choice statements.
5. In sharing expectations, teachers should praise appropriate behavior, ignore a student displaying inappropriate behavior, and eventually praise that student once the behavior changes.
6. In peer modeling, teachers should praise appropriate behavior, ignore a student displaying inappropriate behavior, and eventually praise that student once the behavior changes.
7. In positive repetition, teachers should praise the appropriate behaviors by calling attention to the instructions students are following.
8. Specific praise and positive repetition may be used for students who follow the rules. Withholding privileges or presenting something unpleasant may be used for students who do not follow the rules.
9. Teachers must be consistent in enforcing rules and following through when students do not follow rules.

PLANNING

Planning guides teachers—for a year, a nine-week term, a day, or a lesson. It requires identification of goals and objectives, materials, instructional strategies, learner needs, and evaluation. "Thoughtful and thorough planning is vital for effective teaching to occur" (Callahan, Clark, & Kellough, 1998, p. 82). Effective planning is a "source of confidence, security, and direction for the teacher" (Florida Performance Measurement System, 1984, p. 3). Similar to the saying, "It's not the mountains ahead that wear you down, but the grain of sand in your shoe," lack of planning may be your downfall.

Resources for planning include curriculum guides, textbooks, and individualized education programs. Many school districts and state departments of education produce curriculum guides that present the scope and sequence of skills for instruction, so that all competencies are covered without repetition. The curriculum for exceptional students may consist of a modification of the general education curriculum or alternative strands (Goldstein, 1986). Textbooks and curriculum programs such as the *Reading Mastery* series (Englemann & Bruner, 1988), *Corrective Reading Program* (Englemann, Becker, Hanner, & Johnson, 1980), and *Learning Strategies* curriculum (Alley & Deshler, 1979; Deshler & Schumaker, 1986) present teachers with guides to follow. The teacher's manuals for *Reading Mastery, Corrective Reading Program,* and *Learning Strategies* curricula are structured so that teachers are told specifically what to say and what correction procedures to use. Many general classroom materials have accompanying teacher's manuals that identify objectives, activities, and even questions for teachers to ask.

Individualized Education Program

Teachers in special education have an advantage in planning, due to the requirements of the Individualized Education Program (IEP).

With the passage of PL 94-142 in 1975, the development of an Individualized Education Program for students with disabilities became a requirement. In 1990, the Individuals with Disabilities Education Act (IDEA) added the requirement that plans for transition services be made part of the IEP no later than age 16. The Amendments of 1997, PL 105-17, amended and reauthorized the Individuals with Disabilities Education Act. The new amendments changed the age from 16 to 14 for developing a statement of transition service needs. This change emphasizes the importance of early planning and preparation by students, parents/families, and teachers. Students' IEPs should reflect the courses that relate to their desired postschool outcomes, such as business and technology courses for a student interested in computer-related employment, and should contain content that addresses postschool desires and needs. For a thorough discussion of transition from school to work and community living and a description of the Transition Individualized Educational Plan (TIEP), see Chapter 12.

The IEP is a written plan, developed in consultation with the student's parents and other professionals, based upon information gathered from assessment (Blackhurst & Berdine, 1993). It is a road map for special education instruction, because it tells where students are going and how they are going to get there. It describes what the student needs and what will be done to address those needs.

One of the essential tasks at the beginning of the year is to become thoroughly familiar with each student's Individualized Education Program (IEP). IEP forms vary by state, school district, and sometimes by category within the same district. But all must contain the following (Figure 2.3):

1. The student's present level of educational performance
2. Annual goals that the student is expected to attain by the end of the year

3. Short-term objectives, which are the intermediate steps leading to the attainment of the annual goal
4. A description of special education and related services
5. The amount of time the student spends in a general education program
6. Projected dates for initiation and duration of special services
7. Evaluation procedures and schedules for determining mastery of short-term objectives at least on an annual basis
8. Needed transition services (from school to work or postsecondary education)

A list of materials and techniques to reach the short-term objectives often appears on the IEP, though it is not required by law.

Present Level of Performance and Annual Goals

The student's present level of educational performance and the annual goals are usually based on results from both formal and informal measures, whereas the short-term objectives are usually identified through informal measures. Formal assessment measures contain specific rules for administration, scoring, and interpretation. They are usually based on a comparison with the performance of students of the same age and grade level (that is, they are norm referenced). Informal measures do not contain rigid rules for administration, scoring, and interpretation. They may consist of inventories, observations, or criterion-referenced tests. Chapter 3 presents a detailed description of informal assessment. In examining the sample IEP in Figure 2.3, notice that both formal tests, such as the *Peabody Individual Achievement Test—Revised* (Markwardt, 1989), and informal measures, such as the *BRIGANCE Comprehensive Inventory of Basic Skills, Revised* (Brigance, 1999), were administered to determine the current level of educational performance and annual goals. Turnbull, Strickland, and Brantly (1982) state that there should be three or four goals for each subject area needing remediation and that these goals should be

Individualized Education Program

Student Information

Name: _Jimmy Smith_

School: _Enterprise Elementary School_

Date: _12/9/99_

Chronological Age: _12 yrs. 2 mos._

Date of Birth: _10/5/87_

Grade: _6_

Parent Notification (if not attending meeting) ————			
Type of			
Date	Attempt	By Whom	Results

Present Level of Educational Performance

Area	Source	Date	Scores
Reading Recognition	PIAT-R, WRAT-R	11/1/99, 10/25/99	5.9, 6.0
Reading Comprehension	PIAT-R, Brigance	11/1/99, 11/5/99	2.0, 2.0
Math	WRAT-R	10/25/99	2.0
Addition—Whole numbers	Probe	11/5/99	10 correct/5 wrong in 1 min.
Subtraction facts (0–9)	Probe	11/5/99	8 correct/5 wrong in 1 min.
Vocab (context clues)	Brigance	11/5/99	1.0

Special Education and Related Services

Program or Service	Amount of Time per Week	Projected Initiation Date	Anticipated Duration	Person Responsible
Varying Exceptionalities Resource	5 hours a week	12/10/99	12 months	VE teacher

IEP Developers' Signature/Title

Eve Peabody-teacher

Lorna Smith-parent

Steve Palladino-LEA Rep.

IEP Date _12/9/99_

IEP Review Date _12/9/00_

Regular Education Hours _25 hours a week_

Annual Goal: _Improve math skills to level commensurate with ability_

Short-term Objectives/ Evaluation Criteria	Evaluation Method	Date Initiated	Date Completed
Calculate subtraction facts/70 cc, 2 ce per min. for 3 days	Teacher-designed probe	1/15/00	
Add two digits plus two digits with regrouping/80% for 3 days	Teacher-designed probe	12/10/99	

Annual Goal: _Improve reading comprehension to level commensurate with ability_

Short-term Objectives/ Evaluation Criteria	Evaluation Method	Date Initiated	Date Completed
Paraphrase main idea of paragraph/95% for 3 sessions	Teacher observation	12/10/99	
Identify the meaning of two new words a week/100%	Checklist	12/10/99	

Figure 2.3 Sample IEP

broad enough to take a year or more to accomplish. Examples of annual goals appropriate for students with special needs are:

1. Master basic computation facts at the first-grade level.
2. Read the 220 Dolch words.
3. Apply note-taking techniques in content area classrooms.
4. Solve math problems commensurate with ability.
5. Become compliant with teacher's requests.

Many school districts require the identification of two short-term objectives for each annual goal.

Short-term Objectives

Informal measures, such as the *BRIGANCE Comprehensive Inventory of Basic Skills, Revised* (Brigance, 1999), and curriculum-based measures may be used to identify and evaluate the attainment of short-term objectives. According to Turnbull, Strickland, and Brantly (1982), PL 94-142, now IDEA, requires that short-term objectives be stated in instructional or behavioral terms. For example, "Lucy is hyperactive" is not written in behavioral terms, whereas "Lucy got out of her seat 32 times during her 25-minute music class" is written in behavioral terms. A behavioral objective includes four components: the learner, the target behavior, the condition, and the criterion.

The target behavior identifies what the learner is asked to do. It should be observable and specific so it can be measured. Following are some sample target behaviors frequently found in the IEPs of students with special needs. Notice that the target behaviors are observable and measurable.

1. Write the answers to subtraction facts.
2. Rephrase the main idea of a paragraph.
3. State two expectations of an employer.
4. Add a column of three one-digit numbers.
5. Name three types of mollusks.
6. Follow teacher's requests.

The condition of a behavioral objective usually relates the circumstances under which the behavior will occur. It frequently tells when or how. Following are examples of conditions:

1. Given a worksheet . . .
2. When asked to begin . . .
3. Without use of a dictionary . . .
4. Given 10 completed checks . . .
5. Using a calculator . . .

The criterion of a behavioral objective describes the minimum level of performance for mastery of the target behavior. The criterion may be expressed in terms of the following:

1. Accuracy—90%, or 15 correct.
2. Rate—15 correct in 1 minute.
3. Time—10 minutes.

Academic behaviors are usually measured in terms of accuracy or rate.

To ensure mastery of an objective, an overlearning measure is frequently suggested (Alberto & Troutman, 1999). The overlearning measure requires that the student perform this behavior more than one time. Examples of overlearning include the following:

1. three days
2. four sessions
3. five attempts
4. three times
5. four trials

Now, putting all four components of a behavioral objective together along with the overlearning measure, the following represent examples of behavioral objectives appropriate for students with special needs:

1. Upon request, Jerome will apply the steps of a test-taking strategy to a practice test within 40 minutes for three sessions.
2. Without prompting, Matt will write the subjects and verbs of sentences with 90% accuracy on three assignments.
3. When asked, Penny will read a passage at 150 correct words per minute with two or fewer errors for three days.

4. Given amounts, dates, and receipts, Melissa will complete, in writing, 10 blank checks with 95% accuracy for four sessions.
5. When asked to begin, Zita will say the names of the states and their capitals within three minutes for three trials.
6. Without prompting, Joe will begin the teacher's assignment within two minutes for three sessions.

In most cases, these components do not all appear in one short-term objective on an IEP. Instead, they are described in various sections of the IEP. For example, the behavioral objective of "Given a teacher-designed probe of 40 addition problems, Jimmy will add two digits plus two digits, with regrouping, with 80% accuracy, for three days" is found in various sections of Jimmy's IEP (see Figure 2.3). The identification of the learner (student's name) is located on the first line of the IEP. The target behavior, "add two digits plus two digits, with regrouping," is listed under the short-term objective/evaluation criteria column. The criterion and overlearning measure, "80% accuracy, for three days," appears in the same column. The condition, "given a teacher-designed test of 40 addition problems," appears in the evaluation method column as a teacher-designed probe.

Because special education teachers are assuming more responsibility for instruction in the general education classroom in consultative and co-teaching roles, IEPs need to be modified to reflect these roles. Short-term objectives can be written for instruction that is delivered in inclusive settings. Table 2.1 provides examples in reading, study skills, and social skills. Notice how more emphasis is placed on the roles of the teachers and where each objective will be accomplished.

Description of Services
Special education and related services appropriate for each student must be included in the IEP. Special education services include di-

rect and indirect services. Direct services are those provided by a special education teacher to the student, while indirect services are those provided by a special education teacher to the general education teacher. Special education teachers may provide these indirect services by helping classroom teachers identify effective instructional techniques and adapt materials. Related services, provided by specialists, include counseling, social work, adapted physical education, psychological testing, and transportation. The roles, responsibilities, and amount of time allocated for special education and related services must be clearly stated in the IEP.

Initiation and Duration of Services
The projected dates for the initiation and duration of services must be indicated on the IEP. For example, Figure 2.3 shows that Jimmy will spend one hour a day in a varying exceptionalities class, beginning 12/10/99 (initiation of services), for 12 months (duration of services).

Evaluation Procedures
Progress toward goals and objectives may be assessed by using the IEP as a tool to monitor students' progress. Teachers must specify the method, the criteria for acceptable performance, and the schedule for evaluation. When teachers use IEPs as working plans for their students, they can truly monitor their students' mastery of objectives.

Weekly and Daily Plans

In addition to the IEP, which is mandated by law, weekly planning is required by many school principals. Often, teachers turn in plan books on Friday for the principal's approval of the next week's lessons. Teachers usually write plans for the week in a plan book. They typically include times, names of texts or materials, and page numbers. Sometimes, special education teachers record information such as the levels

Table 2.1 Sample IEP Objectives for Cooperative Teaching

Area: Reading fluency and comprehension
Objective: Given a trade book, the student will:

What	*Who*	*How*	*When*	*Where*
Read fluently 75 wpm, no errors for 3 days	General Education Reading Specialist	Cooperative Training (Team Teach)	2 × week 45 minutes	General Education Class
Comprehend main ideas and details with 90% accuracy	General Education Reading Specialist	Cooperative Teaching (Compl. Instruct.)	5 × week 1 hour	General Education Class
Respond orally to comprehension questions with meaningful sentences at various levels of Bloom's Taxonomy	General Education Speech/Language Specialist	Cooperative Teaching (Team Teach)	3 × week 30 minutes	General Education Class

Area: Study skills in history
Objective: Given strategy instruction, student will:

What	*Who*	*How*	*When*	*Where*
Take notes with 90% accuracy that include 90% of key points	General/Special Education	Cooperative Teaching (Complementary Instruction)	3 × week 50 minutes	General Education Class

Area: Interaction with peers
Objective: Given small group cooperative learning activities, student will:

What	*Who*	*How*	*When*	*Where*
Initiate conversation with one or more peers for 3 consecutive lessons	General Education Speech/Language Specialist	Cooperative Teaching (Supported Learning)	2 × week	General Education Class

NOTE: From "IEPs for Cooperative Teaching: Developing Legal and Useful Documents," by J. Bauwens and L. Korinek, 1993, *Intervention in School and Clinic, 28,* p. 305. Copyright 1993 by PRO-ED, Inc. Reprinted by permission.

of the students in each of the curriculum materials used in the class, the groups to which they are assigned, the names of students receiving related services, and the names of students and the subjects they are assigned to in general classroom settings.

Weekly plan books do not provide teachers with specifics about presenting lessons and do not have sufficient space to add much detail, which may be a problem if there are 10 students working on different objectives. Therefore, in addition to using a weekly plan book,

resource teachers and teachers who co-teach with classroom teachers in general education classrooms need to use an additional planning format to enable them to be aware of their objectives, procedures, materials, and evaluation methods for each lesson. Figure 2.4, which contains an example of a lesson about the rainforest, includes the essential parts of a lesson. Please see Chapter 6 for a detailed discussion of lesson planning and presentation.

Subject:
Science (1:45–2:30)—"The Rainforest"

Objective:
After instruction, the students will write in their journals three facts about the rainforest, with 95% accuracy, for 2 days.

Procedures:
1. Introduce the lesson by asking students if they can describe a rainforest.
2. Read *A Day in the Rainforest*.
3. Discuss the story with the students.
4. Have the students generate words from the story that describe how it feels to be in the rainforest.
5. Write their suggestions on an overhead transparency.
6. Give a 10-minute presentation on life in the rainforest.
7. Have students name things that live in the rainforest.
8. Write these on an overhead transparency.
9. Have students write in their rainforest journals three facts about the rainforest that they learned in the lesson.
10. To close the lesson, have the students share one fact that they have written about the rainforest.

Materials:
1. The book, *A Day in the Rainforest*
2. Overhead projector, transparencies, and pen
3. Journals

Evaluation:
Students will be evaluated by checking their journals to be sure that they wrote three accurate facts about rainforests.

Figure 2.4 A Lesson from a Science Unit

 ACTIVITY 2.6

Concetta, a sixth grader, has been recommended for placement in a resource setting to work on spelling. Based on the following information, identify Concetta's present level of educational performance and write one annual goal and two short-term objectives for the IEP. Be sure to include evaluation procedures to determine how each short-term objective will be measured.

On the *Peabody Individualized Achievement Test—Revised,* Concetta had difficulty spelling words and scored on a third-grade level on the spelling subtest. When her misspellings were examined, it appeared that she had the most difficulty with vowel combinations such as *ea* and silent letters such as *gh* as in *high*. On an informal measure (a criterion-referenced test), Concetta again performed more like a third grader in spelling. An error analysis of her responses revealed that she had problems with the *ea, oa,* and *ei* combinations. She also misspelled words that contained *gh, ph,* and *ght.*

 IMPORTANT POINTS

1. Resources for planning include curriculum guides, textbooks, and Individualized Education Programs (IEPs).
2. An Individualized Education Program (IEP) is a written plan of instruction for the student, mandated by PL 94-142 (amended in 1990 to the Individuals with Disabilities Education Act and amended and reauthorized in 1997 as PL 105-17). It is the road map for special education instruction.
3. PL 105-17 amended and reauthorized the Individuals with Disabilities Education Act and changed the age from 16 to 14 for developing a statement of transition service needs.
4. The components of an IEP describe (a) the student's present level of educational performance, (b) annual goals, (c) short-term objectives, (d) special education and related services, (e) the amount of time spent in general education, (f) projected dates for

initiation and duration of services, (g) evaluation procedures for determining mastery of each short-term objective, and (h) a description of needed transition services.

5. Information from both formal and informal assessment becomes part of an IEP.
6. In addition to the IEP, planning may include using a weekly plan book and designing specific lesson plans that include objectives, procedures, materials, and evaluation procedures.

SCHEDULING

Scheduling is an essential part of effective teaching for special education teachers. Schedules provide structure and organization and allow teachers to accomplish the goals and objectives that they have planned for their students. Students with learning problems can benefit from the routine that systematic scheduling provides (Mercer & Mercer, 1993). Teachers should let students know what activities they are to accomplish and when they should complete them. Thus, the use of systematic scheduling may increase self-directedness and independence among students by eliminating the need to check with the teacher about each assignment.

General Scheduling Guidelines

Polloway, Patton, Payne, and Payne (1989) underscore the importance of daily schedules as the foundation for learning in classrooms. Following are some of the general scheduling guidelines suggested by Gallagher (1988):

1. Provide each student with a daily schedule.
2. Alternate highly preferred and less preferred activities.
3. Provide time cues.
4. Require students to complete one assignment before they begin another.
5. Include feedback on a student's daily schedule.

It is important to provide students with a daily schedule so that they are aware of what is expected of them. Students should complete their activities in the order assigned. A difficult task should be followed by a less difficult and more highly preferred task to ensure completion of the first task. For example, Jeff dislikes doing written math problems but loves practicing his math facts with some teacher-made games in the math center. His schedule indicates that as soon as he completes his written work and makes any necessary corrections, he can go to the math center.

For students who have problems managing their time, it is helpful to provide time cues. Most daily schedules are developed with the times of the activities listed on the schedules. Some teachers draw clock faces on schedules for young students to remind them when they should complete the activity. Other teachers set kitchen timers to cue students to start the next assignment. Students with learning or behavior problems may have difficulty finishing their work and staying with a task until it is completed. Daily schedules may provide a means of focusing attention on one task at a time until it is completed.

It is important to let your students know how well they are performing the activities planned for them on their daily schedules. In writing directly on your students' schedules, you may note reinforcing comments, grades, progress towards mastering an objective, and happy faces. Alternatively, you may provide verbal and written comments in their folders or on their work. Other suggestions for teachers to follow in scheduling include:

1. Group students by level, interests, and needs.
2. Schedule opportunities for active involvement, cooperative learning, independent work, guided practice, teacher-directed instruction, and peer tutoring.
3. Stress goals and objectives.
4. Emphasize the connection between what is done in the special education setting and its applications to general education classes.

5. Visit general education classrooms, consult with teachers, and meet with other members of the educational team (counselors, school psychologists, administrators, teachers, paraprofessionals, and other specialists).

Special education teachers vary in the amount of time they spend providing direct services (working with students) and indirect services (working with other professionals). Some also plan time for assessment of students as part of their schedule. Your assigned roles and responsibilities affect your schedule and the schedules of your students.

Scheduling in Elementary Schools

As teachers develop schedules in elementary schools, they should utilize the following information in making instructional decisions: (a) each student's needs, which can be prioritized and taken from the IEP; (b) the amount of time the student is supposed to work in the special education setting; (c) the amount of time the student is scheduled in other settings; and (d) the schedules of general classroom teachers.

Consultative Services and Cooperative Teaching

Many students who have special needs are capable of functioning in inclusive settings with modifications and adjustments made by their teachers. These modifications and adjustments are accomplished through collaborative consultation between special and general educators. Special education teachers provide indirect services by participating on school-based assistance teams and by helping general classroom teachers modify the curriculum, develop and adapt materials, and assess students' academic and social behavior. Chapter 5 provides a detailed description of collaborative consultation.

At other times, special education teachers are called upon to provide direct services in the general education classroom. These services may involve co-teaching, that is, working with classroom teachers to co-teach students in inclusive classrooms. When both special and general education teachers share the responsibility for providing instruction, they should plan schedules together.

Resource/Pull-Out Programs

Scheduling in the elementary resource/pull-out program can be time consuming and challenging because students usually participate in multiple settings with several different teachers. Scheduling is typically accomplished in cooperation with general classroom teachers and others (such as speech/language pathologist, counselor, etc.). Students attend the pull-out program for part of the day to work on specific academic and social behaviors identified in their IEPs and spend the rest of the time receiving instruction in the general education classroom and/or in various related services. Because students attend pull-out programs for varying amounts of time, teachers are faced with many challenges in scheduling students for instruction. For example:

1. Students may range in age from 6 to 14.
2. Students may have varied and specific needs.
3. Students may be functioning on many different levels.
4. General classroom teachers may have preferred times for sending students to the pull-out program.
5. Communication with many general classroom teachers may be difficult and time consuming.
6. Locating materials appropriate for many levels, ages, and interests may be challenging.

Despite the difficulties in scheduling students in a resource program, special education teachers may develop effective schedules by following a few guidelines:

1. Collect the schedules of all teachers who have students with mild disabilities assigned to their classrooms.

2. List the academic and social skill areas with which students need help.
3. Group students by area of need, making an effort to keep primary and intermediate students separated.
4. Plan individual and group times to keep class size reasonable and instruction workable.
5. Revise the original schedule until it works.

In addition to providing direct services to students in a resource program, you will also need to consult with general classroom teachers. This is important because of the responsibility for students that is shared between special and general education teachers and because you will want to reintegrate your students into the general education classroom to the extent that is appropriate. This requires close communication and collaboration. Table 2.2 provides an example of an elementary resource program schedule.

Scheduling in Secondary Schools

At the secondary level (middle school, junior high school, and high school), special education teachers may serve as consulting teachers and co-teachers in general classrooms or they may provide instruction in a resource program.

Consultative Services and Cooperative Teaching

Special education teachers at the secondary level fulfill the roles of consulting teachers the same way that elementary special education teachers do. Services to students with special needs may be both direct and indirect. However, secondary schools are usually larger, which means there are more teachers to work with, more schedules to work around, and more subject area classes to deal with. Special education teachers may co-teach with classroom teachers in general education classrooms. For example, Mr. Jessup teaches an outlining strategy to a science class to help the students organize the content Mrs. Lange

presents in science. He also works with her in adapting some of the material in the textbook. Table 2.3 provides an example of a middle school teacher's block schedule. Notice that the teacher works with students in and out of general education classes, co-teaches and consults with classroom teachers, plans, and conducts assessment.

Resource/Pull-Out Programs

Students at the secondary level may attend resource/pull-out programs for assistance in academic skills, social skills, job-seeking skills, learning strategies, and leisure skills (Schumaker & Deshler, 1988). Resource teachers at the secondary level are responsible for providing direct services to students and may also be responsible for assessment of students. In addition, they may have consulting responsibilities, such as working with teachers to adapt materials and instruction. They often work with guidance counselors to schedule students into their classes and into select general education classes.

Secondary schools operate with fixed class periods that are approximately 50 minutes long. Good and Brophy (1984) suggest that the first 8 minutes of class be used for review, the next 20 minutes for teacher presentation and guided practice, and the next 15 minutes for independent practice.

Mrs. Hefter uses the first 5 minutes of class for attendance, general directions, orientation to the day's activities, and a brief review. She spends the next 20 minutes teaching her students how to monitor errors in their written work and providing guided practice. Then the students spend 15 minutes in independent practice with feedback. The next 10 minutes are allocated to addressing pressing individual student needs, such as clarification of an assignment from a general education class, organization of notes and materials from a content area classroom, or a quick review for a test or report from a general education classroom.

Table 2.2   Elementary Resource Schedule (One Week)

	Monday	*Tuesday*	*Wednesday*	*Thursday*	*Friday*
8:00–8:30	Problem-solving committee meeting	Consult with classroom teachers	Consult with classroom teachers	Consult with classroom teachers	Consult with classroom teachers
8:30–9:30	Work with 1st, 2nd, and 3rd grade students (Teacher-directed instruction in reading)	(Learning Centers)	(Teacher-directed instruction in comprehension)	(Process writing)	(Teacher-directed instruction in comprehension)
9:30–10:30	Work with 4th and 5th grade students (Listening)	(Comprehension monitoring)	(Summarization)	(Comprehension monitoring)	(Paraphrasing)
10:30–11:15	Co-teach in 3rd grade	Co-teach in 4th grade	Co-teach in 5th grade	Co-teach in 1st grade	Co-teach in 2nd grade
11:15–12:00	Assessment	Adapt materials	Assessment	Adapt materials	Assessment
12:00–12:30	Lunch	Lunch	Lunch	Lunch	Lunch
12:30–1:00	Work with 4th and 5th grade students in math (Small group)	(Small group)	(Computer)	(Learning center)	(Small group)
1:00–1:30	Work with 2nd and 3rd grade students in language arts (Small group)	Games	(Small group and self-correcting materials)	(Computers)	(Small group)
1:30–2:30	Assist in general classrooms on "as needed" basis in content area subjects (science, social studies, health)				
2:30–3:00	Planning/ Consulting				
3:00	Dismissal	Dismissal	Dismissal	Dismissal	Dismissal

These final few minutes of class are also spent giving a post organizer, such as previewing the next day's class schedule, reinforcing work completed, reporting progress toward class or individual student goals, and announcing schedule changes. By scheduling this way, Mrs. Hefter has effectively utilized all of the class time and met her objectives and curricular responsibilities while providing time for individual student needs (Table 2.4).

Table 2.3 Middle School Teachers Block Schedule—Consultative Services in General Education Classrooms

	Monday	Tuesday	Wednesday	Thursday	Friday
First Period 9:00–10:32	Language Arts (7th Grade)	Language Arts (7th Grade)	Language Arts (7th Grade)	Language Arts (7th Grade)	Language Arts (7th Grade)
Second Period 10:36–11:46	Co-Teach Social Studies (8th Grade)	Co-Teach Social Studies (8th Grade)	Co-Teach Social Studies (8th Grade)	Co-Teach Social Studies (8th Grade)	Co-Teach Social Studies (8th Grade)
Second Period (Continued) 11:46–12:23	Lunch	Lunch	Lunch	Lunch	Lunch
Third Period 12:27–1:55	Adapt Materials for Content Teachers	Adapt Materials for Content Teachers	Adapt Materials for Content Teachers	Adapt Materials for Content Teachers	Evaluate and Select Software Programs
Fourth Period 1:59–3:20	Learning Strategies (7th Grade)	Learning Strategies (7th Grade)	Learning Strategies (7th Grade)	Learning Strategies (7th Grade)	Learning Strategies (7th Grade)
3:20	Dismissal	Dismissal	Dismissal	Dismissal	Dismissal

Table 2.4 Secondary Schedule—Learning Strategies Class (One Class Period)

8:00–8:05	• Take attendance. • Announce next week's exam schedule. • Explain activities for class period.
8:05–8:25	• Review previous lesson in error-monitoring. • Teach students how to detect and correct punctuation errors in paragraphs. • Use overhead projector and handouts (cue cards). • Have students take turns practicing on overhead projector and orally as a group.
8:25–8:40	• Hand out paragraph worksheets. • Have students work independently to detect and correct punctuation errors. • Circulate to monitor and check work.
8:40–8:50	• Check with students on regular class assignments, homework, etc. • Recap day's activities and preview tomorrow's lesson on detecting and correcting spelling errors.
8:50	• Dismissal

Mr. Fletcher, who teaches employability skills in a high school, uses the first 5 minutes of class to explain the day's schedule to students. The schedule is posted on the wall of the classroom. He spends the next 15 minutes of class providing direct instruction to students. The next 20 minutes are devoted to small groups, where students work cooperatively to complete assignments. The final 10 minutes of class are used for whole-class discussion, in which students report the results of their group work.

Many secondary teachers of exceptional students use a folder system. Students come into their classrooms, get their folders, and examine the schedule in the folder. This gives them a preview of the activities for the class period. While some students are receiving teacher-directed instruction, others complete work in their folders or work with a partner or a small group. Some teachers rotate students in and out of learning centers or cooperative learning activities. When not involved with other instruction, the teacher circulates around the room, providing instruction to individuals and groups, monitoring progress, and giving feedback and reinforcement. Notice that both Mrs. Hefter and Mr. Fletcher incorporate elements from the instructional framework introduced in Chapter 1 into their teaching: (a) presentation, (b) guided practice, (c) feedback, (d) independent practice, and (e) evaluation.

Like resource program teachers at the elementary level, resource teachers at the secondary level wear many hats. They must fulfill consulting responsibilities with general classroom teachers, be curriculum and materials specialists, have knowledge of secondary diploma options and the courses students must have to graduate, possess good public relations skills, and be prepared to help students make the transition from school to work and community living.

Students with special needs may receive instruction in math, English, science, and other subjects from a special education teacher in a resource setting. Materials are available to present the same subject matter that is covered in a general education class, but with less emphasis on reading. This is done by modifying the format of the materials and the assignments to be completed. Therefore, students with special needs may take a class called Oceanography, which parallels the class that other students take, but they complete it using modified texts and adapted curriculum materials.

Students Who Need More Time

Despite all your efforts at scheduling, you will find that it is next to impossible to plan one schedule and expect it to work for all students. Some students need more time than others to complete assignments. This becomes problematic in inclusive classrooms, as the same students always seem to be the last to finish or may not finish at all. For students who show a willingness to work hard but who need more time because of a learning problem, limited English proficiency, or other factors, we recommend the following strategies adapted from Callahan, Clark, and Kellough (1998) in combination with our own ideas.

1. Learn as much about the student as you can.
2. Adjust your instruction to the student's preferred learning style.
3. Use all modalities when you teach.
4. Help the student learn content in small, sequential steps with frequent checks for understanding.
5. Use frequent positive reinforcement (verbal and written).
6. Check readability level of materials.
7. Adapt instruction and modify materials if needed.
8. Maximize the use of cooperative learning, peer tutoring, role play, and hands-on activities.
9. Be less concerned about the quantity of content coverage and more concerned with

the student's understanding of the content that is covered.
10. Teach study skills, strategies, and survival skills (such as listening strategies, test-taking strategies, teacher-pleasing and class participation skills, and time-management skills).
11. Pair the student with a classroom buddy for support.

Efficient Use of Time

The National Committee on Excellence in Education (1983) included efficient use of time as one of its five primary recommendations for improved schools. In observation of 230 elementary students who were mildly handicapped, Rich and Ross (1989) found that noninstructional time such as transitions, wait time, free time, snacks, and housekeeping accounted for almost 3 hours of the school day. An examination of 52 high school programs for students with learning or mental disabilities indicated that the students spent an average of 24% of their time in nonacademic activities (Rieth, Polsgrove, Okolo, Bahr, & Eckert, 1987). Since research shows that time spent in academic learning tasks increases achievement, you should schedule the day to maximize student involvement in direct learning activities. As a teacher, you can control the time dimensions of housekeeping, transition, and allocated time by the way you schedule.

Housekeeping Time
Housekeeping time is the time spent in performing such routine chores as taking attendance, collecting homework assignments, and writing on the board. If they are well organized, these activities make a class run smoothly. If they are not managed correctly, these activities can cause behavior problems and loss of valuable teaching time. Housekeeping questions that need to be solved include the ways students are to turn in work, sharpen pencils, and get

permission for restroom breaks and drinks. If you spend time planning routines, you will spend less time on housekeeping activities during class, thus maximizing instructional time.

Transition Time

Transition time involves changing from one activity to another or from one setting to another. Again, valuable teaching time may be lost without smooth transitions. For young students, role-playing transition times, such as moving from the desk to the reading group, is helpful. Posted schedules make both secondary and elementary students aware of subject changes. Teachers who circulate throughout the room to answer questions and monitor students' behavior promote more on-task behavior during transition times (Englert & Thomas, 1982). Frequently, much time is lost in transition from the general education classroom to the resource setting. Incentives are often necessary to motivate students to arrive on time. Extra points, public posting of the names of on-time students, and on-time clubs with special privileges are effective solutions for late arrivals.

Allocated Time

Allocated time is the amount of time assigned to various instructional activities (such as reading groups and independent work) and noninstructional activities (like completion of IEPs and consultations with classroom teachers). Effective schools allocate more of their time to learning tasks than ineffective schools do (Thurlow, Christenson, & Ysseldyke, 1987).

Sargent (1981) collected data for 60 days from 30 resource teachers serving students with mild disabilities in 5 different states and found that most of the time was allocated to and spent on direct instruction (51.48%) and preparing for instruction (16.38%). A number of studies found that time spent in teacher-directed instruction is the best single predictor of achievement (Leinhardt, Zigmond, & Cooley, 1981; Sindelar, Smith, Harriman, Hale, & Wilson,

1986; Stallings, 1980). Achievement is low when students are assigned a lot of seatwork to do totally independently (Medley, 1979) or are taught with curriculum packages (Squires, Huitt, & Segars, 1983). In fact, time spent in independent instructional activities, such as silent reading, was unrelated to achievement for elementary students with mental or learning disabilities (Sindelar, Smith, Harriman, Hale, & Wilson, 1986). Secondary and elementary students achieve more when at least 50% of the school day is spent in direct instruction (Stallings, 1980). Thus, you need to schedule your day so that most of the time is allocated to teacher-directed instruction.

 ACTIVITY 2.7

Brainstorm with three other people to develop more time-saving ideas dealing with housekeeping time, transition time, and allocated time.

 IMPORTANT POINTS

1. Gallagher (1988) provides guidelines for teachers to use in scheduling: (a) provide each student with a daily schedule, (b) alternate highly preferred and less preferred activities, (c) provide time cues, (d) require students to complete one assignment before starting another, and (e) include feedback on a student's daily schedule.

2. Other considerations in scheduling include (a) group students by level, interests, and needs; (b) provide opportunities for active involvement, cooperative learning, independent work, guided practice, teacher-directed instruction, and peer tutoring; (c) stress goals and objectives; (d) emphasize the connection between special and general settings; and (e) allot time for consultative work.

3. Consultative services at the elementary and secondary level may include indirect services (working with teachers) and direct services (working with students) in the inclusive setting.

4. Tips for scheduling in the elementary school include (a) identifying student needs, (b) attending to the amount of time that students should spend in general and special education, and (c) examining the schedules of classroom teachers.

5. Resource program scheduling at the elementary level requires attention to general classroom schedules, the needs of students, grouping arrangements, and flexibility.

6. Secondary schools operate with fixed class periods that include review, teacher presentation, controlled practice, and independent practice.

7. For students who need more time to complete assignments, teach using all modalities; check frequently for understanding; use positive reinforcement; adapt instruction and modify materials; use cooperative learning, peer tutoring, role playing, and hands-on activities; focus on understanding of content; teach study skills, strategies, and survival skills; and pair with a classroom buddy for support.

8. Housekeeping time is the time spent taking attendance, passing out papers, and writing on the board.

9. Transition time is the time spent changing from one activity or setting to another.

10. Allocated time refers to the amount of time assigned to various instructional activities, such as group work, independent work, completion of IEPs, and consultative services. Most of the teachers' time should be allocated to direct instruction.

FIRST-WEEK BAG OF TRICKS

It is important to get to know your students during the first week of school. To build rap-port and contribute to effective classroom management, you should learn your students' names quickly. The first week of school is the ideal time to orient students to the class schedule, grading procedures, and classroom rules. It is the optimal time to establish the operating guidelines of the class, communicate expectations, and establish structure and routines.

Getting-to-Know-You Activities

There are a variety of ways teachers may get to know their students at the beginning of the school year. Following are several ideas that may help teachers of students with special needs at the elementary and secondary levels. The activities are appropriate in both special and general education settings.

Autobiographical and Biographical Activities

It is important to get to know your students quickly at the beginning of the school year and to develop a sense of community within your classroom. The following suggestions may get you started.

Self-Report Forms. You may use autobiographical report forms to find out about students and involve them in a writing exercise. Following is a sample of fill-in statements that you may include. Adapt the items for different age groups.

My name is _____ .

I am _____ years old.

My birthday is on _____ .

My favorite television show is _____
_____ .

In my free time, I like to _____
_____ .

My favorite thing to do after school is _____
_____ .

One thing I can do well is _____
_____ .

My favorite sport, game, or activity is _____
_____ .

This year, I am looking forward to _____
_____ .

Interviews. Secondary students, in particular, enjoy interviewing another student in the class to collect biographical information. Give the students 10 to 15 minutes to talk with a partner. Have the students develop two headlines that can be put up on a bulletin board. One headline should be a school-related achievement and the other a personal accomplishment. Then have the students present their information. For example, Manny Owens introduced another senior, Jerard Collins, with the school-related headline "Collins Makes Honor Roll at End of Junior Year" and the personal headline "High School Senior Lands Summer Job at McDonald's."

Life Lines. Many students enjoy constructing a life line, or time line, of their personal and school-related activities. Have the students draw a horizontal line and write in major events along the line. (This is also an excellent sequencing activity.) Have the students begin with the time of their birth and continue to the present. Let the students present their life lines orally in class or transfer them to a bulletin board.

This Is Your Life Scrapbook. Students may create a *This Is Your Life* scrapbook to tell about themselves. Using construction paper, markers, photographs, and magazines, students make a large book to describe themselves to the rest of the class. They may include such topics as their hobbies; interests; goals; families; favorite music group, sports hero, movie star; and greatest accomplishment. Scrapbooks may be made with 12-by-18-inch pieces of construction paper as the pages and wallpaper as the cover. Young students may call this book *All About Me* and draw pictures of themselves, their families, pets, things they like and dislike, favorite food, and what they want to be when they grow up.

Games

After students introduce themselves to the rest of the class, collect cards on which the students have written introductions. As you read what it says on each card, such as hobbies and favorite food, let the rest of the class guess which student is being described. You may also include a card for yourself.

Incorporate the first and last names of students into reading, writing, and spelling activities during the first week of school. Show the students flash cards during reading to see if they can say each student's name. In writing lessons, include practice exercises with sentences, paragraphs, or short stories about students in the class. Use a fill-in-the-blank format during a writing lesson. For spelling, ask students to alphabetize the names of the students in the class (first or last names) and to spell them. Adjust these activities for different age groups.

Classbuilding

Classbuilding has been suggested as an effective way to develop students' willingness to participate in cooperative behavior (Johnson, Johnson, & Maruyama, 1983; Kagan, 1992) and an excellent way for students to become acquainted. Graves and Bradley (1997) describe three classbuilding activities, Vanity Plates, Line Ups, and Corners, that we suggest you use during the first day or week of school as a getting-to-know-you activity.

Vanity Plates. Give each student a sheet of oak tag the size of a license plate and ask them to create a vanity plate that gives important information about themselves using letters, numbers, pictures, and other symbols. After creating their vanity plates, have the students share them with the class.

Line Ups. Have students form a line based on a response to a topic. For younger students, it could be the month and day of their birthday; for older students, opinions about a controversial political figure. For the birthday example, students born closest to the beginning of January line up first and the students born closest to the end of the year would be last. Next, one half of the line steps forward and turns toward the other half of the line so that the two sections of the line are face to face. Have students pair up with the student opposite them and discuss the topic for about one to two minutes. For the political figure example, students who favor the politician would line up at one end, and those opposed would line up at the other end. Next, fold the line and have the students engage in a discussion about the politician. Then a new topic can be announced and new lines formed.

Corners. The teacher asks the students to make a choice after giving them four alternatives, such as favorite season of the year or favorite choice among four authors, music groups, or movies. Students move to the corner of the room that represents that choice and then discuss with one another the reasons for their choices.

Graves and Bradley (1997) recommend these classbuilding activities for the first day of school and throughout the year. These may be effective as getting-to-know-you activities in inclusive settings as students are reintegrated into general education classrooms.

Orientation Activities

The first week of school is the ideal time to orient students to the operating procedures of the classroom. Many teachers develop and introduce students to organization and transition activities at this time.

Organization Activities

Organization activities help students manage their responsibilities. It is helpful to develop a class calendar to help students manage and remember special occasions and deadlines. You may record special school events, deadlines, student birthdays, field trips, report cards, parent-teacher conferences, and other important dates on the calendar. Encourage the students to suggest calendar entries. Reproduce individual copies of the calendar and distribute them. To add a multicultural element to this activity, you may want to recognize Martin Luther King, Jr.'s birthday in January, Black History Month in February, the Chinese New Year in February, Constitution Day in Puerto Rico in July, American Indian Week in November, or others (Mack, 1988).

In elementary classrooms you frequently select a very important person (VIP), student of the week, or student assistant to the teacher. You may involve students in establishing the procedures for this selection, such as names in a hat or alphabetical order. In addition, during the first week of school, you may discuss the need to share the classroom responsibilities (passing out and collecting work, emptying the trash, being the line leader, etc.). You may assign responsibilities from the first day of school and develop a bulletin board displaying the assignments.

Transition Activities

Transition activities are short, motivating, interesting activities used in both special and general education settings during 10-minute time slots just before lunch, between classes or other assignments, or just before dismissal. They may include a variety of impromptu activities, such as the following:

1. Play a game by asking students questions about the subject matter that they have just completed. A variation of this is to have the students make up the questions.
2. Conduct activities with students following directions by writing or doing.
3. Make up the first line of a story and let each student add another.
4. Have students make an entry in their journals.

ACTIVITY 2.8

Develop the following first-week activities.
1. A detailed schedule for the first day of school (elementary or secondary).
2. Two bulletin board ideas for an elementary classroom and two for a secondary classroom. Be sure to indicate what types of bulletin boards they are (e.g., informational).
3. Two getting-to-know-you activities for an elementary classroom and two for a secondary classroom.
4. Develop a sample first-week checklist appropriate for your setting.

◇ **IMPORTANT POINTS**

1. Effective methods for getting to know your students at the beginning of the year include autobiographical, biographical, or class-building activities and games.
2. Autobiographical and biographical activities include completing self-report forms, interviewing other students, constructing time lines, and making scrapbooks.
3. Suggested classbuilding activities include games like vanity plates, line ups, and corners.
4. Games include identifying from clues which student is being described and using students' names in reading, writing, and spelling activities.
5. Organization activities help students manage their responsibilities.
6. Transition activities are motivating, impromptu, brief activities used before lunch, between classes, and at the end of the day.

◆ **DISCUSSION QUESTIONS**

1. A parent of a student in a general education class questions how a student with disabilities who is included in that class can receive a grade of A. How would you explain this to the parent?
2. Discuss when you would use the following instructional arrangements in your classroom: large group, small group, one-to-one, peer tutoring, and independent learning.
3. Defend the statement, "Thoughtful and thorough planning is essential for effective teaching and learning to occur."

INFORMAL
ASSESSMENT

According to Salvia and Ysseldyke (1988), informal assessment is "any assessment that involves collection of data by anything other than a standardized test" (p. 26). In the special education field, we use different types of informal assessment. Criterion-referenced tests, precision teaching, curriculum-based measurement, and error analysis all suggest systematic data collection procedures. These assessments have a history of use in the field of special education.

The informal assessments of portfolios, interviews, and checklists have less systematic data collection procedures. Portfolios are often identified as authentic assessments. Authentic assessments are based on the constructivist paradigm with its emphasis on "assessing real-life processes and accomplishments" (Heshusius, 1989, p. 412). Teachers are encouraged to adapt and develop their own techniques for data collection. The authentic assessment approach is fairly new to the special education field, and the effectiveness is still uncertain, even though it is being implemented in a growing number of large-scale assessment programs at district and state levels. Fuchs and Fuchs (1996) recommend a framework for integrating curriculum-based measurement and more authentic assessment in the special education field. However, they caution that such a system still requires a vast amount of research and development.

In this chapter we discuss the various informal assessments. Teachers may use these data collection procedures to plan programs for students and to monitor their effectiveness. We conclude the chapter with ways to involve students in data collection procedures.

CRITERION-REFERENCED TESTS

Criterion-referenced tests (CRTs) measure the extent to which a student has mastered a skill or task based on an established criterion (Mercer, 1987). Unlike formal tests, which compare a student's performance to that of other students, a criterion-referenced test compares the student's performance to some expected mastery level.

You may either design a criterion-referenced test or select a commercial one. Commercially produced CRTs may assess many subject areas or a single one. For example, the *BRIGANCE* diagnostic inventories (Brigance, 1981, 1983, 1999) are multiskill batteries that contain subtests measuring skills in areas such as reading, math, employability, life skills, and spelling. Single-subject criterion-referenced tests available commercially include the *Standardized Reading Inventory (SRI)* (Newcomer, 1986), which measures only reading skills. Commercially produced CRTs are available for preschool through secondary populations of students with special needs in academic and vocational areas.

Authors of CRTs typically consult curriculum scope and sequence lists for the selection of the items. For example, Brigance (1983) states that his test items are the direct result of checking the scope and sequence of the most recently published texts of several widely used series. The scope identifies the breadth of the subject matter, and the sequence identifies the sequential arrangement of the subject matter.

For example, the scope of the math curriculum for kindergarten through eighth grade, no matter the particular math series, usually includes math readiness (e.g., recognizing numerals), number facts (e.g., reciting basic facts, such as $4 + 6$), whole numbers (e.g., adding two-digit numbers with regrouping), fractions and mixed numbers (e.g., adding fractions), decimals (e.g., reading decimals), percents (e.g., converting percents to decimals), measurement (e.g., telling time to the hour, recognizing dif-

ferent coins), metrics (e.g., reading Celsius temperature), and geometry (e.g., recognizing squares) (Brigance, 1981, 1983, 1999).

In the sequence, math readiness skills such as rote counting are taught before basic facts, which are taught before fractions. There is also a sequence of skills within each area. For example, subtraction problems that do not require regrouping (e.g., $87 - 14$) are taught before those that require regrouping (e.g., $87 - 19$).

Steps

Although teachers may design criterion-referenced tests, it is much easier to select commercial ones. Therefore, we concentrate on the use of commercial CRTs here. We recommend the following steps: (1) select the test, (2) administer the test, (3) select the expected level of mastery, (4) identify objectives, and (5) monitor progress.

Select the Test

A basic knowledge of the curriculum scope and sequence for various grade levels can help you in test selection. For example, if you are selecting reading tests to assess a first grader's reading performance, you are not likely to select a reading test that measures comprehension of colloquial and figurative expressions, because this skill is usually introduced much later. Instead, tests that measure basic sight vocabulary, initial consonant sounds, and short vowels are more appropriate, because these skills are introduced in the primary-grade reading curriculum. Most series have a scope and sequence that you can check for the various grade levels. Additionally, many school districts identify minimum student performance standards, or curriculum frameworks for students with disabilities. For example, in one language arts curriculum, middle school students are expected to demonstrate literal and inferential reading comprehension (Florida Department of Education, 1994).

It is also helpful to discuss a student's problem with the general education teacher. For example, if Mr. Gonzalez, Jim's second-grade teacher, tells you that Jim has problems telling time, you should, as a first step, select a criterion-referenced test that measures math skills, especially one that contains items dealing with measurement of time.

 ACTIVITY 3.1

> Susan is a sixth grader. Ms. Jones and you have decided to test her math skills because she is failing in the basic math class. Ms. Jones reports that Susan seems to miss problems dealing with the calculation of fractions. Examine the scope and sequence of a sixth-grade math text and identify some skills that you might select for testing.
>   (Answers for this and other activities are found in the Instructor's Manual.)

Administer the Test

You do not have to follow the directions for administration of a criterion-referenced test exactly. However, many of the commercially prepared instruments provide guidelines for where to start and stop testing and general directions and procedures for easy and quick administration. Additionally, you may make adaptations during the testing process. For example, if you wish to hear Latasha's thoughts as she solves the math problems, you may ask her to think aloud as she writes the answers.

Select the Expected Level of Mastery

There are no absolutes for selection of a mastery criterion. For profitable academic learning, students should maintain an accuracy level of 80% during lesson presentation and between 90% and 100% during independent practice (Christenson, Thurlow, & Ysseldyke, 1987). Some CRTs, such as the *BRIGANCE* inventories, suggest mastery levels.

Identify the Objectives

Mastery levels assist in the identification of objectives. For example, if you expected Sharon to score 80% on a reading comprehension test but she scored only 60%, you should target reading comprehension for remediation. Furthermore, you should examine the specific questions that Sharon missed. Did she miss questions that required her to order and sequence events, or did she miss questions that required her to remember significant details? This analysis results in the short-term objective of "When presented with numerous 200-word passages and four questions requiring recall of significant details, Sharon will orally answer three out of four questions correctly for at least three passages."

Monitor Progress

Usually, teachers monitor mastery of the objectives at the end of the year using the same CRT. The results of this posttest are often recorded on the IEP.

Sample Plan

We have presented the steps for using a CRT, but to help you better understand the process, we relate Consuela's experience to each of the steps.

1. *Discuss the student's problem with the general education teacher.* In a conference, Consuela's fifth-grade teacher indicates that Consuela has problems reading words with silent letters and two or more syllables.
2. *Check the curriculum scope and sequence of the subject area and grade level.* A check of the reading scope and sequence from Consuela's classroom text shows that silent letters, prefixes, suffixes, and syllabication are word analysis skills that students should master by fifth grade.
3. *Select a CRT.* Select a CRT that measures the skills identified by the teacher and the curriculum scope and sequence. In this instance, *The BRIGANCE Comprehensive Inventory of Basic Skills—Revised* (CIBS-R) (Brigance,

1999) is an appropriate selection because it measures all of these skills.

4. *Administer the CRT.* Administer the following tests from the *BRIGANCE:* (a) phonetic irregularities to check silent letters, (b) suffixes, (c) prefixes, and (d) division of words into syllables.

5. *Decide on a criterion of mastery.* Select between 90–100% to constitute mastery.

6. *Compare the student's performance to the mastery level.* Consuela reached the established criterion on phonetic irregularities (silent vowels) only. She did not reach mastery on the tests dealing with reading suffixes and prefixes, nor was she able to apply the rules for syllabication.

7. *Identify short-term objectives for initial instruction:* (a) Presented with a list of 50 words, Consuela will read words containing the suffixes *-ous, -ment, -ation, -ward,* and *-ist* and the prefixes *de-, mis-,* and *fore-* with 90% accuracy and (b) presented with a list of two-syllable words, Consuela will apply the syllabication rules dealing with like consonants between

two vowels (*bot\tom*) and unlike consonants between two vowels (*con\form*) to divide the words with 90% accuracy.

8. *Monitor progress.* Administer the same tests to Consuela and record her scores. Often, this is done at the end of the year, but it may be done whenever you feel Consuela has reached the short-term objective.

  IMPORTANT POINTS

1. Criterion-referenced tests (CRTs) measure the extent to which a student has mastered a skill or task based on an established criterion.

2. The items on a CRT are often based on curriculum scope (the skills or content taught at various grade levels) and sequence (the order in which the skills are taught) from many texts.

3. In selecting a CRT, special education teachers often consult the general education teacher and a curriculum scope and sequence.

4. Christenson, Thurlow, and Ysseldyke (1987) recommend a mastery level between 90% and 100% during independent practice.

5. The student's performance is compared to the criterion for acceptable performance (mastery) to arrive at a short-term objective.

6. The same test is administered before and after instruction (pre and post) to monitor student progress.

ACTIVITY 3.2

Write a short-term objective in reading based on the following performance on a test of phonograms.

The criterion for acceptable performance is 90%. Correct = +. Error = −.

The teacher asks the student to read the common phonograms:

1. ail	+	9. ell	+
2. ble	−	10. est	−
3. ing	+	11. all	−
4. tion	−	12. ack	−
5. ter	−	13. op	−
6. ick	+	14. ock	−
7. et	+	15. ill	−
8. ide	+		

PRECISION TEACHING

Precision teaching is a precise and systematic way to measure student performance in academic skills at both the elementary and secondary levels. While precision teaching is not a specific teaching strategy, it helps you decide on and evaluate the effectiveness of instructional strategies.

Using rate of response, precision teaching emphasizes direct and continuous measurement of behavior (West, Young, & Spooner, 1990). Rate is the number of behavior movements divided by the number of minutes observed. In precision teaching, the average number of correct and incorrect responses per minute is calculated. The underlying principle is that a skill is mastered only if it can be performed both accurately and quickly. A student who is able to take notes at 30 words a minute will be more successful in an inclusive setting than one who is just as accurate in writing words but can transcribe only 10 words a minute.

A time limit of 1 minute is specified for measuring most academic skills, although the time limit may vary according to the amount of curriculum measured and student characteristics. For example, 3 minutes may be used when addition, subtraction, multiplication, and division facts are measured at once, compared with 1 minute when measuring addition facts alone. Fifteen seconds may be used for students who are highly distractible and cannot focus on a task for 1 minute (Binder, Haughton, & Eyk, 1990).

◆ ACTIVITY 3.3

Try an experiment. Time yourself for 15 seconds and, with your usual writing hand, write the numbers 1 through 9 as fast as you can, starting with 1 again when you reach 9. How did you do? Can the numbers be read? Count how many numbers you wrote by counting each digit. You probably found this skill to be both accurate and fluent. Now, reverse hands and do the same task for 15 seconds. How are your numbers this time? They can probably be read, but how many digits did you write in the 15 seconds? Unless you are ambidextrous, you probably wrote more digits the first time. If a professor told you that you could take notes with your nonwriting hand only, your accuracy would be somewhat affected, but your fluency would be more affected, and you would miss many notes.

Steps

To use precision teaching, follow these steps: (a) pinpoint the behavior to be taught, (b) design or select a probe, (c) take a baseline, (d) select an aim, (e) decide whether the skill is appropriate, (f) write an objective, (g) decide on an intervention, (h) teach and test, (i) graph scores, and (j) monitor progress. These steps will lead to planning and monitoring decisions.

Pinpoint the Behavior

Pinpointing is choosing a behavior to change. Just as in criterion-referenced assessment, a curriculum scope and sequence may assist you in the selection of the behavior. In precision teaching, each behavior is counted, so the behavior must be repeatable and observable, and it must have a beginning and end (White & Haring, 1980). The skill of reading initial consonant clusters is appropriate to pinpoint. This skill is repeatable, as words requiring initial consonant clusters may be read again and again. It is observable, as you may listen while the student reads. Finally, each initial consonant cluster has a beginning and an end. It is also a skill found in a reading curriculum scope and sequence. Other appropriate pinpointed behaviors are spelling words, writing letters, and saying letter sounds.

"Betty is intelligent" is not an appropriate behavior for pinpointing, as it does not meet the three requirements. How is intelligence repeated? How do you observe intelligence? Where does it begin and end?

ACTIVITY 3.4

Mark *no* by all of the following descriptors that cannot be measured using precision teaching. Then change them so that precision teaching can be used.

1. Counting money.
2. Answering questions at the end of a chapter.
3. Sam has a learning disability.

Design a Probe

Once the skill is pinpointed, you can either design an informal test, called a probe, or use a commercial one. Commercial probes may be secured from the following sources:

◆ Clearinghouse/Information Center Bureau of Instructional Support and Community Services, Division of Public Schools and Community Education, 325 West Gaines St., Suite 614, Tallahassee, FL 32399-0400

◆ West Regional Resource Center, University of Oregon, Eugene, OR 97403-1268. (http://interact.uoregon.edu/WRRC/wrrc.html)

If you plan to design your own probe, you should follow certain guidelines. First, allow a standardized count in order to assess the skill accurately. To ensure a standardized count, the student must have freedom and opportunity to move (White & Haring, 1980). To allow the student freedom to move, design the probe so that you do not place physical constraints on the student. For example, if you use flash cards to test basic sight words, you are probably interfering with how fast the student can read the words, because the student's performance depends, in part, on how quickly you manipulate the cards. Thus, changes in performance during assessment may be due to your dexterity in presenting the flash cards. You are less likely to interfere with a student's freedom to move if you use a typed list instead of flash cards.

Opportunity to move requires that students never run out of problems to complete. White and Haring (1980) recommend that the probe contain more items than any student can possibly finish within the allotted time. (Remember, a 1-minute time limit is usually imposed.) They argue that an overabundance of items allows for a more accurate picture of the student's performance, because it avoids ceiling effects. This is particularly important when you use precision teaching to evaluate the effectiveness of instructional planning. For example, if there

were 12 problems on the probe on Monday and Sam answered all 12 correctly and then there were 20 problems on the probe on Tuesday and Sam answered all 20 correctly, you might conclude that Sam made progress when comparing his raw scores of 12 and 20. However, in reality, Sam's performance on Monday was limited by the number of opportunities he had to show his knowledge. In addition, inclusion of more items than a student can possibly finish within the particular time prevents rote memorization of the answers (Howell & Morehead, 1987).

Having more items on a probe than students can possibly finish does not mean including 140 different words or math facts. Ten words or 10 facts may be repeated 14 times to reach 140, or 2 words or facts may be repeated 70 times. See Table 3.1 for an example of a sight word probe. Notice that even though there are 100 total words on the sample probe, there are only 20 different words, and each word is repeated 5 times. Thus, a student is actually being assessed on 20 words, not 100.

Once you have decided the content of the probe, you should identify the input and output channels for measurement (Hefferan & Diviaio, 1989). Input channels are the ways in which a student receives the information. In a school setting, input channels are usually visual or auditory. The student either sees the information when reading a text or hears the information when listening to the teacher read the text. Output channels are the ways in which a student expresses information. In a school setting, this is often with an oral or written response; for example, the student either says the answer to a math question or writes the answer.

The input and output measures may vary for any task; for example, you may test a student's addition skills by presenting a worksheet of addition problems. This is a visual (*see*) input as the student looks at the problems on the worksheet. However, you can change this input to an auditory (*hear*) one simply by reading the problems from the worksheet instead of giving the

Table 3.1 Sight Word Probe

about	after	be	five	its	must	seven	there	(8)
well	sleep	call	from	him	let	old	around	(16)
upon	after	ask	cold	why	five	must	there	(24)
around	from	let	sleep	cold	why	about	its	(32)
seven	well	be	him	call	old	upon	ask	(40)
after	about	its	five	be	around	well	there	(48)
seven	must	old	let	him	from	call	sleep	(54)
call	about	must	upon	from	seven	after	why	(62)
him	upon	why	ask	cold	be	there	let	(70)
sleep	ask	let	well	five	around	cold	its	(78)
old	about	seven	him	ask	must	from	why	(86)
call	sleep	upon	let	after	be	around	there	(94)
well	old	five	its	about	seven			(100)

paper to the student. In the same way, the output measure can be either a *say* response, if the student responds by orally telling you the answer, or a *write* response, if the student responds by writing the answer.

When designing a probe, you should select the channels that are used most often to perform the skill in the classroom. For instance, in inclusive elementary classrooms, reading instruction usually involves students taking turns reading selections orally during reading groups, so the channels of see and say are appropriate for measuring reading skills at this level. However, the channels of see and write are probably more appropriate at the secondary level, where reading in the content areas often consists of students reading silently and then answering questions. In both elementary and secondary classes, math instruction typically involves paper-and-pencil performance, so see and write are appropriate channels for measuring math skills.

The identification of the input and output channels leads to decisions concerning how to teach. For example, if Juan performs better on a hear/say spelling probe than on a hear/write one, you may suggest to Ms. Mueller, his second-grade teacher, that she allow Juan to spell the words orally to a volunteer in the back of the class during the traditional Friday spelling test. The last information to record on the probe is the cumulative score for each row of problems (see Table 3.1).

Take a Baseline

To take a baseline, you administer the same probe for at least three times without teaching. For most academic skills, this administration takes a minute. It is a good idea to tell the student that it is impossible to finish all of the problems but to do them as quickly as possible. If the student hesitates for more than 2 seconds on any item, tell the student to proceed to the next item. It is also important to stress to the student to be as accurate as possible. Leung (1987) notes that many Asian students, in particular, sacrifice accuracy for speed, because speed is reinforced in most Asian cultures.

Since the probe always contains more problems than a student can complete within the time frame, it is permissible to change the starting point during each session. For example, if Latoya finishes the last problem in the second row during the first baseline session, have her begin the second baseline session with the first problem in the third row. By doing this, you may expose her to all of the problems during the baseline, and you may use the same sheet.

Alternatively, you may wish to staple a transparency to the probe sheet and instruct students to write with nonpermanent pens. That way, you still may use the same sheet repeatedly. A squirt bottle filled with water and a cloth makes the transparency easy to clean.

For accurate timings, you may use a stopwatch or a cassette tape that has recorded time signals (Hefferan & Diviaio, 1989). For example, a bell sound on the tape may signal the start of the timing, followed by a minute of soft music, followed by a bell sound to stop the timing. Follow this sequence with a 15-second interval of silence and then repeat the sequence (bell, soft music, bell, silence, bell, soft music, etc.). This way, you can place a total of 5 to 10 minutes of 1-minute timings on one tape.

If the probe does not require a written student response, as in the area of reading, mark the student's errors on a follow-along sheet, which is just a copy of the student's probe. Again, to conserve paper, laminate the follow-along sheet or staple a transparency to it.

Select an Aim

Just as in criterion-referenced assessment, you select a mastery level, which shows that the student has learned the skill for automatic application to different situations and is ready to proceed to a different skill. Remember, in criterion-referenced assessment, you select the expected level of mastery in terms of a percentage score (e.g., Consuela was to demonstrate mastery of suffixes with 90% accuracy). In precision teaching, the mastery level is expressed in terms of an aim, which consists of correct responses (cc) and error responses (ce) per minute (a rate measure), with an overlearning component (more than one session). A sample precision teaching aim is 80 correct responses and 2 error responses (80 cc/2 ce) per minute for three sessions.

Before discussing the different techniques for calculating an aim, we need to describe the scoring procedures. You score items differently following precision teaching procedures than you do normally. For example, to score math problems, you count each digit in the answer instead of the whole answer. To score reading you frequently count sounds, letters, or words, and to score spelling, you count letters. Traditional scoring of the problem $25 + 42 = 67$ results in only one correct answer, whereas in precision teaching you count each digit to record a score of two correct answers. Conversely, traditional scoring of the problem $25 + 42 = 87$ results in one wrong answer, but in precision teaching the score is one correct (the 7) and one wrong (the 8). Moreover, unlike traditional scoring, which counts all items, items on a probe are scored only as far as the student progresses. Thus, a student who finishes only 10 of 50 problems on a probe is not penalized for failing to complete all 50 problems. Only the 10 completed problems are scored. Skipped problems are usually counted as errors only to where the student finished.

You may calculate a precision teaching aim by using performance standards, peer assessment, student baseline, or the adult/child proportional formula (Eaton, 1978; Haring & Gentry, 1976; Koorland, Keel, & Ueberhorst, 1990). Whichever technique you use, correct responses are calculated and incorrect responses are ignored. Traditionally, two or less per minute is often selected as an appropriate error score (Koorland, Keel, & Ueberhorst, 1990). The Precision Teaching Project in the Great Falls Public Schools (1981) (see Table 3.2) suggests performance standards. These standards are based on the performance of students who have demonstrated mastery of the skill. These standards are based on the performance of students who have demonstrated mastery of the skill and are reported as the number correct within 1 minute. Table 3.3 describes the calculation of an aim using the various procedures.

Remember, the idea of an aim is to set a mastery criterion so that the student generalizes the skill at various times and in various settings. You are hoping that when the student reaches the aim of 80 correct and 2 incorrect digits a

Table 3.2 Suggested Performance Standards

Pinpoint	Standard
Reading	
See/Say Isolated Sounds	60–80 sounds/min.
See/Say Phonetic Words	60–80 words/min.
Think/Say Alphabet (forward or backward)	400+ letter/min.
See/Say Letter Names	80–100 letters/min.
See/Say Sight Words	80–100 words/min.
See/Say Words in Context (oral reading)	200+ words/min.
See/Say Words in Context (silent reading)	400+ words/min.
Think/Say Ideas or Facts	15–30 ideas/min.
Spelling	
Hear/Write Dictated Words	80–100 letters/min.
Hear/Write Dictated Words	15–25 words/min.
Math	
See/Write Numbers Random	100–120 digits/min.
Think/Write Numbers (0–9 serial)	120–160 digits/min.
See/Say Numbers	80–100/min.
Think/Say Numbers in Sequence (count by's)	150–200+/min.
See/Write Math Facts	70–90 digits/min.

NOTE. Adapted from the *Great Falls Precision Teaching Project Training Manual* (p. 43), Great Falls Public Schools, Great Falls, Montana.

 ACTIVITY 3.5

Practice setting an aim for Damion, a seventh grader, for the pinpointed behavior of see/say science vocabulary words such as centimeter, volume, and cylinder.

1. Use the performance standards found in Table 3.2. (Select the one that is closest to the pinpoint of see/say science words in isolation.)
2. Use a peer performance standard: Jason, 60 science vocabulary words a minute; Sally, 70 science vocabulary words a minute; Jenni, 92 science vocabulary words a minute.
3. Use student baseline scores: Monday, 30 correct words a minute; Tuesday, 35 correct; Wednesday, 20 correct.
4. Use the adult-to-child proportional formula: The student said 40 alphabet letters in 15 seconds. The adult said 80 alphabet letters in 15 seconds and read 120 science vocabulary words.

minute on an addition probe, he or she will be able to add at home or during the math class on Friday. If you find that a student meets the aim but then forgets the skill 2 days later, you probably did not set an appropriate mastery level.

Determine the Appropriateness of the Skill

As a general rule, a student must have at least five correct responses (cc), and not reach the aim for two of the three sessions of baseline (White & Haring, 1976) for a skill to be considered appropriate. If the student makes fewer than five correct responses, the skill is probably too difficult. If the student reaches the aim, the skill is too easy.

When the student makes fewer than five correct responses, you may either slice back or step down on the curriculum scope and sequence

(White & Haring, 1980). To slice back, simply cut the curriculum into smaller pieces; for example, use a probe of 0 through 4 multiplication facts to replace the probe of 0 through 9 multiplication facts. To step down, select an easier skill in the curriculum scope and sequence. For example, the student still does poorly on 0 through 4 multiplication facts, so the teacher decides to assess the student's knowledge of addition facts, an easier skill. You should take another baseline if you change the amount of curriculum or the skill.

The rule of five correct responses for selection of an appropriate skill is not absolute. White (1980) reports that some students with no correct responses during the baseline still learn the skill once instruction begins. Teachers of students with speech and language problems have told us that their students are able to progress much faster and maintain interest

Table 3.3   Calculation of Aims for the Pinpoint of See/Say Words in Fifth-Grade Reader

PERFORMANCE STANDARD

Procedures	*Examples*
1. Find the skill in the performance standards most like the one on the probe. Look under the *Pinpoint* heading.	The pinpoint of See/Say words in fifth-grade reader is most like the See/Say words in context (oral reading).
2. Select the suggested standard under the *Standard* heading.	It is 200+ words/min. So student's aim is 200 cc/2 ce per minute.

PEER ASSESSMENT

Procedures	*Examples*
1. Administer the probe for 1 minute to three students who perform the skill appropriately.	Peter: 100 words correct in 1 minute. Rosa: 150 words correct in 1 minute. Amy: 134 words correct in 1 minute.
2. Find the average of the peers' scores.	100 + 150 + 134 = 384 384 ÷ 3 = 128 cc So student's aim is 128 cc/2 ce per minute.

STUDENT BASELINE

Procedures	*Examples*
1. Administer the probe for 1 minute to student for 3 days.	Student scored the following words correct on the three days of baseline: Monday: 50 cc Tuesday: 60 cc Wednesday: 40 cc
2. Find the average of the three baseline assessments.	50 + 60 + 40 = 150 ÷ 3 = 50
3. Take the average score times 2.	50 (average score) × 2 = 100 So student's aim is 100 cc/2 ce per minute.

when they score at least 15 or more correct responses during the baseline.

If you don't seem to be able to apply the rule of five correct responses to the performance of a particular student, begin teaching and monitoring the student's progress. If the student makes little progress, the skill is probably too difficult and you should either slice back or step down the curriculum.

Identify the Objective

The objective consists of the input and output channels, the pinpointed behavior, and the aim. For example, Consuela will see/say (input/output channels) initial consonant clusters in words (pinpointed behavior) at 70 cc and 2 ce per minute for 3 consecutive sessions (aim).

Decide on an Intervention

Although precision teaching may be used with any intervention, guidelines for the selection of a strategy are linked to the learning stages of acquisition, fluency, and maintenance or proficiency. Usually, anyone who learns a new skill, whether driving a car or recalling multiplication facts, proceeds through these three stages. In the first stage, acquisition, the driver attempts to keep the car in the correct lane between the middle line and the shoulder, while the math student tries to answer problems such as 4 + 5 accurately. Modeling, immediate feedback, questioning, and direct instruction are effective strategies for the acquisition stage.

The next stage in the learning hierarchy is fluency. The fluency stage occurs when the stu-

ADULT/CHILD PROPORTIONAL FORMULA

Procedures	*Examples*
1. Select a tool skill. *Math:* Writing and counting digits. *Reading:* Saying the alphabet. *Written Expression:* Writing the alphabet.	Since the pinpoint involves reading, I selected the tool skill of saying the alphabet.
2. Administer the tool skill probe of the alphabet letters placed in random order for 15 seconds to the student to arrive at the Student Tool Skill Rate.	Student read 50 letters correctly in 15 seconds.
3. Convert the score from 15 seconds to 1 minute (number per 15 seconds × 4 = number per minute).	50 letters in 15 seconds converts to 200 letters in 1 minute (50 per 15 seconds × 4 = 200 letters per minute) (Student Tool Skill Rate).
4. Administer the tool skill probe of the alphabet letters placed in random order for 15 seconds to an adult to arrive at the Adult Tool Skill Rate.	The adult read 100 letters in 15 seconds.
5. Convert the score from 15 seconds to 1 minute (number per 15 seconds × 4 = number per minute).	100 letters in 15 seconds converts to 400 letters in 1 minute. (100 per 15 seconds × 4 = 400 letters per minute) (Adult Tool Skill Rate).
6. Administer the regular student probe of "See/Say words in fifth-grade passage" to adult to arrive at the Adult Task Performance Rate.	The adult read 300 words a minute on the regular student probe (Adult Task Performance Rate).

7. Insert scores into the adult/child proportional formula of

$$\frac{\text{Student Aim (to be solved)}}{\text{Student Tool Skill Rate}} = \frac{\text{Adult Task Performance Rate}}{\text{Adult Tool Skill Rate}}$$

$$\frac{x}{200} = \frac{300}{400}$$

8. Solve equation to arrive at student's aim.

$200 \times 300 \div 400 = x$
$200 \times 300 = 60{,}000$
$60{,}000 \div 400 = 150$
So student's aim is 150 cc/2 ce per minute on the regular student probe.

dent is making few errors and is concentrating on pace or speed instead. At this stage, the driver is no longer worried about keeping the car on the road in the proper lane (accuracy) but is attempting to drive more than 10 miles an hour (fluency) while remaining in the proper lane. The math student is trying to answer 4 + 5 before a second passes. Flash cards, drill activities, and reinforcements are frequently recommended for this stage (Haring & Eaton, 1978).

The final stage, maintenance or proficiency, is reached when the aim (both cc and ce) has been obtained. The teaching strategy is to move to another skill because the student has mastered the content. Now, the driver drives on the freeway at the speed limit and the math student adds accurately and quickly. Table 3.4 presents a summary of the decision-making procedures involved in determining the appropriateness of the skill, identifying the learning stage, and deciding on the intervention.

It is possible that a student will proceed through all stages once you begin teaching. For example, Mrs. Corso started teaching Jason addition facts using modeling as Jason was in the

Table 3.4 Decision Making with Precision Teaching

Is the skill appropriate?	Why?	What is the learning stage?	Why?	What is the teaching intervention?
Yes	5 or more are correct Aim not met	Acquisition	5 to 19 correct in a minute	Direct teaching Give immediate feedback
Yes	5 or more are correct Aim not met	Fluency	20 or more correct and 10 or fewer wrong in a minute	Drill and practice Use reinforcers
No (too easy)	Aim reached	Maintenance	Reached mastery level	Go on. Take baseline on the new skill in the scope and sequence.
No (too hard)	Less than 5 correct	Preacquisition	Scored less than 5	Slice back or step down

◆ **ACTIVITY 3.6**

Look at the results of Jan's baseline performance in each of the following skill areas. Then determine the skills to select for instruction, the learning stage, short-term objective, and an intervention for each. Explain the reasons for your answers. The first one is done for you.

See/Say Consonant Sounds

Session 1: 60 cc, 2 ce

Session 2: 65 cc, 3 ce

Session 3: 70 cc, 1 ce (This skill is too easy; Jan reached the mastery level of 60–80 sounds per minute as suggested on the performance standards of "See/Say Isolated Sounds." Since the skill is not appropriate for instruction, no short-term objective should be identified. The learning stage is maintenance because the aim is reached, so move the student to the next skill.)

See/Say Short Vowels

Session 1: 20 cc, 10 ce

Session 2: 24 cc, 7 ce

Session 3: 20 cc, 12 ce

See/Say Long Vowels

Session 1: 4 cc, 10 ce

Session 2: 7 cc, 12 ce

Session 3: 8 cc, 14 ce

acquisition stage. Once Jason reached the fluency stage, she changed to using flash cards.

Teach and Test

Each day, after instruction is completed, you administer the same probe to monitor the effectiveness of the intervention. As previously stated, some teachers become concerned that using the same probe to measure a student's progress allows the student to memorize the answers, but this is easily avoided by requiring the student to start with different problems on the probe.

Graph the Scores

Once you record a raw score, you must convert it into a count per minute (rate) for display on a semilogarithmic chart or graph. In a semilogarithmic graph, the distances between the lines are adjusted proportionally. Proponents of this type of graph argue that a change from 10 to 20 is the same proportionally as a change from 20 to 40; both are a doubling.

Many teachers graph data on a standard celeration chart (SCC) (Lindsley, 1990). Other teachers use adaptations of the SCC, such as the ABC–5 chart (Figure 3.1). We explain how to chart data using the ABC–5 graph. The vertical lines on the ABC–5 graph are called day lines (Hefferan & Diviaio, 1989). You can chart behaviors from Sunday through Saturday for 11 weeks, or 77 days. The short, dark marks at the

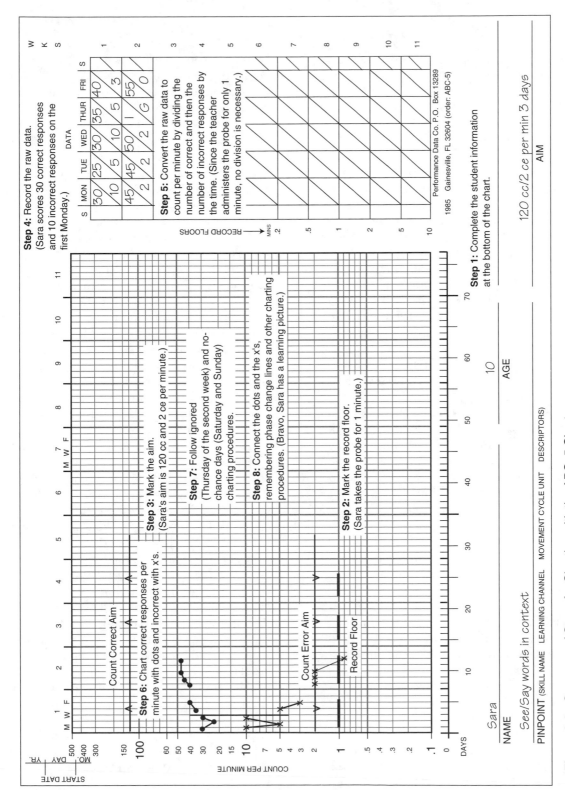

Figure 3.1 Summary of Steps for Charting with the ABC–5 Chart

71

top of the chart are Sunday lines, an easy way to locate the beginning of the week. The horizontal lines are often referred to as number lines (Hefferan & Diviaio, 1989).

On the ABC–5 graph, we are able to count from 0.1 to 500 counts per minute. The graph is rarely marked above 300, because few behaviors may be accomplished at more than 300 counts a minute. Notice that there is a one-to-one correspondence between the numbers 0.1 through 10. However, from 10 to 100, the numbers proceed 10, 15, 20, and then skip in increments of 10 until 100. The count continues 100, 150, 200, 300, 400, and 500. Therefore, to chart counts between 10 and 500, you must estimate.

You are probably wondering why it is necessary to have a count of 0.1 or 0.2 on the graph. Remember, only rate is recorded on the graph, so to record a score of two items missed during a 10-minute probe, you must divide the 2 by the 10, which results in 0.2 incorrect responses per minute.

Steps for charting include (1) complete the student information, (2) mark the record floor, (3) mark the aim, (4) record the raw data, (5) convert the raw data to counts per minute, (6) chart correct and incorrect responses per minute, (7) identify ignored and no-chance days, and (8) connect data points.

1. *Complete the student information.* Identify the name and age of the student, the pinpointed behavior, and the aims at the bottom of the graph.
2. *Mark the record floor.* The record floor identifies the amount of time that you administer a probe. Record floor figures are found on the right side of the graph. Notice that with the ABC–5 graph, you can administer a probe from 0.2 minutes, or 12 seconds, to 10 minutes. Mark the record floor by drawing a horizontal line through each week at the appropriate minutes.
3. *Mark the aim.* Mark the aim on the graph by finding the acceptable performance criteria of

correct and error responses per minute on the count lines. The count correct part of the aim is frequently marked with a horizontal line and arrows pointing upward. The count error part of the aim is frequently marked with a horizontal line and arrows pointing downward.

4. *Record the raw data.* Enter the raw scores in the data boxes at the right of the ABC–5 graph. Enter the correct raw data at the top and the error raw data at the bottom for each day that assessment occurred.
5. *Convert the raw data to counts per minute.* Before you record data on the graph, you must convert each raw score to a count per minute, dividing the score by the number of minutes. Thus, to record a student's score of 3 incorrect responses in 5 minutes, you would first divide 3 by 5, then locate 0.6 on the chart. To show a 0 count, mark the data point just below the record floor. A count of 1 always falls on the record floor line.
6. *Chart correct and incorrect responses per minute.* Use a dot (.) to mark the correct responses per minute and an *x* to mark the incorrect responses per minute. To mark the correct responses on the chart, locate the first day you administered the probe on the day lines. Then locate the count on the number lines. Follow the lines until they intersect and place a dot at the intersection. Follow the same procedures to chart incorrect responses, only place an *x* at the intersection.
7. *Identify ignored and no-chance days.* Before you connect any of the data points, consider no-chance days and ignored days. No-chance days are days when you do not have an opportunity to assess the student, such as over the weekend or during an absence. Ignored days are days when you have an opportunity to assess the student but decide not to. Code IG for ignored and NC for no-chance in the raw data boxes. Do not connect data across no-chance days, but do connect across ignored days. For example, if the student was absent on Tuesday, the picture would look like this:

If the student was present on Tuesday but you decided to ignore data collection and did not administer a probe, the picture would look like this:

If there are many no-chance days, frequent absences may be the reason the student is not progressing. If there are many ignored days, the student may not be progressing due to the infrequency of data collection.

8. *Connect data points.* Connect the correct data points and then connect the error data points. Do not connect data across no-chance days or phase change lines. Phase change lines (vertical lines) denote whenever something is changed, for example, a change in intervention, pinpointed behavior, or mastery aim. Always draw a phase change line between the last session of baseline and the first day of intervention to note that teaching has started.

Once you have connected all the data points, you will have a learning picture. Figure 3.1 presents a pictorial summary of all the charting procedures.

Monitor Progress

Now that you have charted the data, it is time to decide whether the intervention plan is effective and whether the student is making progress. You can do this subjectively, by eyeballing the data, or objectively, by comparing

◆ ACTIVITY 3.7

Chart the following data from a precision teaching assessment on a semilogarithmic graph.

Behavior: See/write addition facts with sums 0–18.

Aim: 80 cc, 2 ce.

Observation time: 1 minute.

Baseline:

Monday—10 cc, 10 ce.

Tuesday—15 cc, 10 ce.

Wednesday—5 cc, 15 ce.

Intervention:

Thursday—20 cc, 10 ce.

Friday—20 cc, 8 ce.

Monday—24 cc, 8 ce.

Tuesday—Ignored.

Wednesday—30 cc, 0 ce.

the data to an expected level of progress (White & Haring, 1976) or an actual level of progress (Fuchs, Fuchs, & Hamlett, 1989).

Subjective Evaluation

Subjective evaluation requires an examination of the direction of the correct data points (correct responses) and error data points (incorrect responses) and a comparison of the student's performance during the baseline and intervention. Effective learning pictures have in common that the correct data points are moving up toward the count correct aim, the error data points are moving down toward the count error aim, and both are improvements on the baseline. In Figure 3.2, we show effective learning pictures.

In each of these examples (A–D), during intervention, the correct data points are moving

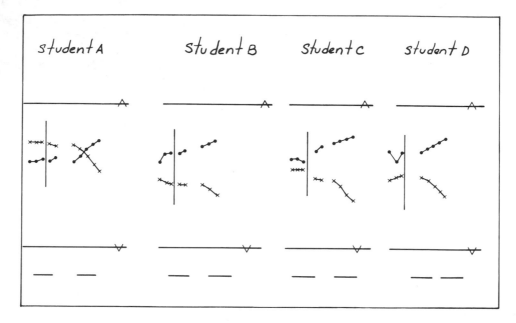

Figure 3.2 Effective Learning Pictures

up toward the correct aim and the error data points are moving down toward the error aim. Student C displays a common pattern. There is a quick gain once instruction begins. This gain is apparent when you compare the last data point of the baseline with the first one of intervention. Student A displays the best learning picture. This student had more incorrect responses than correct during the baseline and more correct responses than incorrect during the intervention. Thus, the intervention was very effective, as it resulted in a picture totally different from the baseline. When you see such pictures, you should continue with the intervention, because they indicate the intervention is working and the student is progressing (Hefferan & Diviaio, 1989).

In ineffective learning pictures, the correct data points and error data points are moving away from the aims or are stagnant (Hefferan & Diviaio, 1989). Often, a comparison with the baseline shows that there is not much difference in progress. Figure 3.3 displays some ineffective

learning pictures. Student A is not progressing, because the correct data points have flattened out. When you see three consecutive sessions of flat data, it is an ineffective picture. Student B is not progressing either, because correct responses are decreasing and incorrect responses are increasing. Note, too, that for Student B, incorrect responses remain higher than correct responses during the intervention. If you consider the intervention data only, you may think that Student C's picture is effective, because the correct data points are ascending and the error data points are descending; however, when you look closer, you see the correct data points are lower and the error data points are higher than they were at baseline. In Student D's picture, the error data points are decreasing, but so are the count correct data points. When you see pictures like these, you should change your intervention or make other program changes (e.g., take multiple timings and average the score or change the goal), because the student is not making adequate progress.

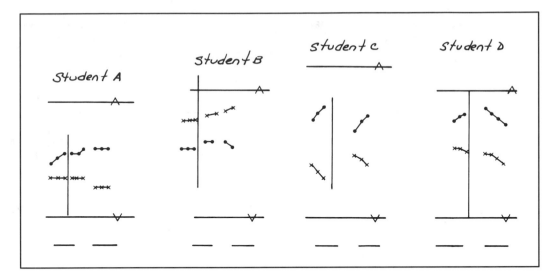

Figure 3.3 Ineffective Learning Pictures

Sometimes, the data do not present a clear picture of progress, especially when there is much fluctuation. In these cases, an objective evaluation is much more effective.

Objective Evaluation

In objective evaluation of a student's progress, you analyze data trends and make changes based on certain decision rules. These decision rules differ, depending on whether you specify an *expected* rate of student change or you examine the *actual* rate of student change. When you use a decision rule based on an expected rate of student change, you need both an aim and a date for achieving the aim. For example, you state that Otis should learn his basic multiplication facts at the rate of 80 cc (correct responses) and 2 ce (incorrect responses) a minute, and that he should accomplish this by the end of the first 9 weeks (the grading period). To tell whether Otis is progressing fast enough to meet your expectations, draw a trend, or celeration, line using aimline procedures (see Figure 3.4). A decision rule states that you should change the intervention or make other changes when a student scores three consecutive data points be-

low the celeration line (White & Haring, 1980; White & Liberty, 1976). The reason for a change is that the student is not progressing as fast as you expected and will not meet the aim within the time available. For example, Otis is not learning the basic multiplication facts rapidly enough to be able to reach your expected aim of 80 cc and 2 ce per minute within 9 weeks, so it is necessary to change the intervention, take multiple timings and average the score, or change the goal.

Some students progress more rapidly than expected. What if Otis learned the basic multiplication facts at 80 cc and 2 ce within 3 weeks instead of 9 weeks? Your expectations of his rate of change were inaccurate and you have lost valuable teaching time. When you measure actual rate of student change, you do not have a preconceived date or aim in mind; instead, you rely on student behavior (the number of correct responses per minute during intervention) to evaluate performance. To measure student change based on a student's actual rate, use the quarter-intersect method to draw the celeration line (Haring, Lovitt, Eaton, & Hansen, 1978; White & Haring, 1980). White

1. Select an aim rate for the student to master the aim, and mark it on the graph.

2. Select a date for the student to master the aim, and draw a line through the aim rate. Circle where they intersect; this is the end mark.

3. Record the baseline data on the graph.

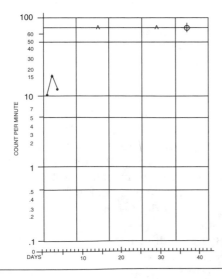

4. Find the mid-day during the baseline (the mid-day comes in the middle of three baseline sessions), and draw a vertical line through it.

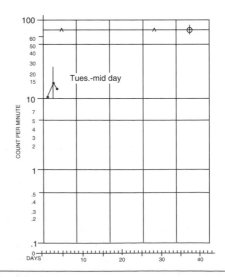

Figure 3.4 Steps for Drawing a Celeration Line Using Aimline Procedures

5. Find the mid-rate during the baseline (the middle count) by ranking the data points in order. If data points are the same, select that number. Draw a horizontal line through it.

6. Put a circle where the lines intersect. This is the start mark, where the celeration line begins.

7. Connect the start mark with the end mark. The celeration line connects the two points.

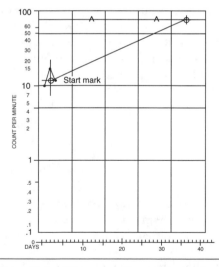

8. Chart the counts per minute during the intervention.

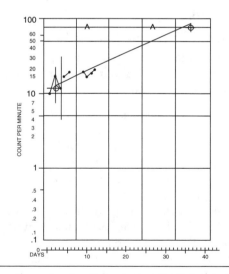

Decision Rule: If there are three consecutive data points below the celeration line, change the intervention, do multiple timings, change the goal or make other changes.

and Haring (1980) recommend that teachers draw celeration lines using the quarter-intersect method every 7 days to evaluate progress and that they change their instruction if the new celeration line based on student correct responses is flat or decreasing. Wesson (1987) recommends evaluating progress using the quarter-intersect method every 2 weeks. In Figure 3.5, we present steps for drawing a celeration line for 7 days of intervention data using the quarter-intersect method and some decision-making rules.

Fuchs, Fuchs, and Hamlett (1989) found that teachers who used the decision rules based on the level of *actual* student performance produced more achievement gains than did a control group of teachers who monitored progress with end-of-unit math tests, unsystematic observations, and workbook and worksheet performances. However, teachers who used decision rules based on *expected* student performance did not produce more achievement gains than did the control group.

Sample Plan

Now that we have discussed all of the steps to precision teaching separately, we bring the steps together to write an instructional program for Rosa, a ninth grader.

1. *Pinpoint a behavior.* After a discussion with the general classroom teacher, you determine that Rosa is having problems simplifying fractions to lowest terms.
2. *Select a probe, input and output channels, a time, and scoring procedures.* Your probe includes 40 different problems, like 4/12 and 8/20. Each of the problems is repeated once, for a total of 80 problems. You decide to administer the probe to Rosa for 1 minute using the see/write channels, because Rosa is expected to perform the skill in an inclusive setting as a paper-and-pencil task. You score each digit of the answer (e.g., 1/4 counts as two digits) only to

where Rosa stops, but you count skipped problems as errors.
3. *Take a baseline.* Administer the probe to Rosa three times without any teaching. She scores 10 cc (count correct) and 5 ce (count error) responses on Day 1, 10 cc and 10 ce on Day 2, and 15 cc and 9 ce on Day 3.
4. *Select a mastery aim.* You check the pinpoint on the performance standard chart (Table 3.2) and try to find a skill that is most like this skill. In this case, the pinpoint of simplifying fractions to lowest terms is most like "See/Write Math Facts" with an aim of 70–90 correct digits per minute for 3 sessions.
5. *Determine the appropriateness of the pinpoint.* After examining the baseline scores and the selected aim, you conclude that this skill is appropriate for Rosa, because she has at least five correct responses and has not reached her aim.
6. *Write a short-term objective.* The objective is "Presented with an 80-item probe, Rosa will see/write fractions to lowest terms at 80 cc and 2 ce per minute for 3 consecutive days."
7. *Select the intervention.* Since Rosa is in the acquisition stage (she scored 5–19 correct responses), you plan to use modeling of the simplification procedures as a teaching intervention. Once Rosa moves into the fluency stage, you plan to use drill activities and provide positive reinforcement.
8. *Begin teaching and testing.* Instruct Rosa using modeling and then administer the same probe that was administered in baseline.
9. *Graph scores.* Either Rosa or you may graph her score each time she takes the probe. Remember the graphing procedures.
10. *Monitor progress.* Using either the aimline or quarter-intersect procedures, decide whether Rosa is making progress. If she is, continue with the same intervention. If she is not, change the intervention, take multiple timings and average the scores, or change the goal.

◆ **ACTIVITY 3.8**

Examine the two students' charts below and tell whether you would plan to make changes based on the learning pictures. Try using both objective and subjective evaluation.

◇ **IMPORTANT POINTS**

1. In precision teaching, behaviors that are repeatable and observable and that have a beginning and end are pinpointed.
2. Probes designed by teachers should not interfere with a student's opportunity or freedom to respond and are administered for three days without any intervention to collect baseline data.
3. The mastery aim may be based on performance standards, peer assessment, student baseline, or the adult-to-child proportional formula.
4. From the baseline data, appropriateness of the skill (at least five correct responses and aim not met), learning stage (acquisition, fluency, or maintenance), and instructional strategies are decided.
5. The acquisition stage requires a score between 5 and 19 correct; the fluency stage, 20 or more correct and 10 or fewer errors; at the maintenance stage, the aim is met.
6. In subjective evaluation, a learning picture is effective when the correct data points are moving up to the count correct aim, the error data points are moving down to the count error aim, and both are improvements over the baseline.
7. Objective evaluation requires the drawing of celeration lines based on either the expected rate of student change or the actual rate of student change.
8. To determine the expected rate of student change, teachers identify both an aim and a date for reaching the aim and draw a celeration line using aimline procedures.
9. A decision rule states that a change is needed when a student scores three consecutive data points below the celeration line for the expected rate of change.
10. To determine the actual rate of student change, teachers draw a celeration line

1. Take intervention data for 7 days.

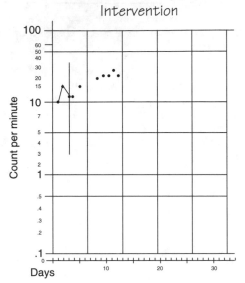

2. Divide the seven data points evenly.

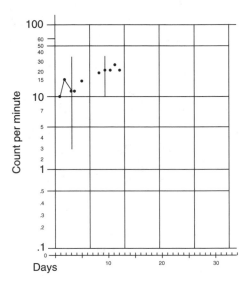

3. Mark the first three points as side A and the last three as side B.

4. Find the mid-rate and the mid-day of side A.

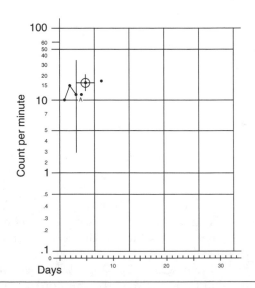

Figure 3.5 Steps for Drawing a Celeration Line Using the Quarter-Intersect Method

5. Find the mid-rate and the mid-day of side B.

6. Connect the two sides with a celeration line.

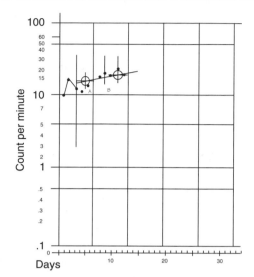

Decision Rules
(a) Continue the intervention with an increasing celeration line.
(b) Change the intervention with a flat celeration line.
* (c) Change the intervention with a decreasing celeration line.

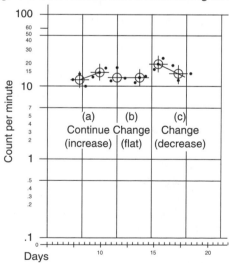

*Instead of changing the intervention you may take multiple timings and calculate an average or change the goal.

every few days using the quarter-intersect method.

11. Decision rules state that a change is needed when a celeration line for the actual rate of change is flat or decreasing.

12. Teachers may change the intervention, take multiple timings, or select a different goal when a student is not progressing.

CURRICULUM-BASED MEASUREMENT

Curriculum-based measurement (CBM) is a measurement and evaluation system developed at the University of Minnesota Institute for Research on Learning Disabilities by Deno, Fuchs, Mirkin, and their colleagues (Deno, 1985). Curriculum-based measurement is a type of curriculum-based assessment (Fuchs, Fuchs, & Hamlett, 1989). CBM is a fluency-based model that considers accuracy and time. In addition to the fluency-based model of CBM, other curriculum-based assessment models include the criterion-referenced models of Blankenship and Idol and colleagues, and the accuracy model of Gickling and colleagues (Marston, 1989).

All of the curriculum-based assessment models employ brief, frequent assessment based on the student's classroom curriculum and provide teachers with a technique for monitoring progress (Frisby, 1987). Thus, if the school district has adopted a specific reading series, material for assessment is selected from the series texts. This ensures that students are assessed on skills that have been or will be taught. The matching of assessment and instructional materials is also recommended for students with cultural and linguistic differences. Such students often perform better when they are tested on material that is presented in the classroom (Fradd & Hallman, 1983; Hoffer, 1983; Sugai, Maheady, & Skouge, 1989).

We select the fluency-based model of CBM for further discussion as it specifies techniques for the creation, administration, and scoring of measurement samples and for monitoring progress. In addition, the systematic procedures of the model demonstrate technical adequacy (Deno & Fuchs, 1987; Fuchs & Deno, 1991; Marston, 1989). According to researchers (Deno, Mirkin, & Chiang, 1982; Marston & Magnusson, 1985), the simple curriculum-based measurement of a 1-minute sampling of words read correctly from a basal reader correlates highly with performance on many standardized reading tests.

Like precision teaching, CBM uses frequent, direct measurement of academic performance in reading, math, spelling, and the writing curriculum. However, CBM focuses on general outcomes measured over time, whereas precision teaching involves mastery measurement of subskills of the curriculum (Fuchs & Deno, 1991). For example, in the area of spelling, precision teaching may involve measuring a student's knowledge of spelling words with silent *e* (e.g., hate, ride), a skill found in the scope and sequence of the second-grade spelling curriculum, whereas CBM involves measuring a student's knowledge of all spelling words, including those with silent *e*, from the second-grade spelling curriculum.

Thus, the test items in the precision teaching example include only those words spelled with a silent *e*, and students practice spelling other words only after they have mastered the silent *e* spelling pattern. In contrast, the test items in the CBM example include alternate test forms of 20 words randomly selected from the 400 words in the second-grade curriculum. The 20 words of each test represent multiple skills (e.g., some words may have the silent *e* spelling pattern; other words, the short *e* spelling pattern). These skills remain constant across the year. Thus, CBM is measuring student performance across the entire yearlong curriculum. Fuchs and Deno (1991) note that this general outcome approach to assessment is more attuned to holistic and integrated learning outcomes.

To date, CBM procedures have been designed for reading, math, spelling, and written expression. For each subject, we discuss the administration and scoring procedures, instructional standards, and mastery standards. Instructional standards often determine the grade level of the materials appropriate for instruction. Mastery standards identify the goals students must reach to show that they have learned the information.

Fuchs and Shin (1989) caution that further research is needed as to the technical adequacy of the determination of instructional and mastery standards. Therefore, this information serves as a guideline. Many school districts are establishing their own instructional and mastery standards for CBM measures.

Reading

Of the reading measures created by Deno and colleagues, the most efficacious, easiest, and best researched is the oral reading fluency measure (Deno, Marston, Mirkin, Lowry, Sindelar, & Jenkins, 1982; Deno, Mirkin, & Chiang, 1982; Deno, Mirkin, & Wesson, 1984). In the assessment of reading performance, the oral reading fluency measure compares favorably with comprehension measures, although there is not a perfect relationship (Tindal & Marston, 1990).

Procedures

To measure a student's oral reading fluency, ask the student to read three passages, each for 1 minute, from various reading texts. These passages should be approximately 100 words in length for young students and 300 words in length for older students. Select one passage from the beginning, one from the middle, and one from the end of various grade-level texts. Be careful to select prose paragraphs without much dialogue or many proper nouns or unusual words (Deno, Mirkin, & Wesson, 1984).

To begin the assessment process, instruct the student to read the passage as quickly as possible. If the student hesitates on a word for more than 2 seconds, say the word and tell the student to go on. Time the selection for only 1-minute (Salvia & Hughes, 1990). While the student is reading each passage, mark the student responses on a follow-along sheet. Count the words read correctly and incorrectly by the student through the last word read for each passage, and rank the number to find the median scores. Words misread (e.g., *house* for *horse*), words omitted (e.g., leaving out *horse*), words reversed (e.g., *was* for *saw*), and phrases reversed (e.g., *the beautiful, wild horse* for *the wild, beautiful horse*) are counted as errors. Misread proper nouns, self-corrections, and insertions (e.g., adding the word *the* to the phrase *the wild "the" dark horse* instead of *the wild, dark horse*) are not counted as errors (Tindal & Marston, 1990). Continue testing with different graded paragraphs until the student reaches an instructional standard, so you will know which reading materials are appropriate for the student.

Instructional Standards

Various instructional standards for reading have been suggested in the special education literature. Marston and Magnusson (1985) suggest instructional standards of about 11 to 20 words per minute (wpm) for first and second graders, and about 41 to 50 wpm for third through sixth graders. Deno, Mirkin, and Wesson (1984) suggest a range of 10 to 30 wpm correct with no more than seven errors for first and second graders, and 30 to 60 wpm correct with no more than seven errors for third through sixth graders.

Mastery Standards

Fuchs and Shinn (1989) recommend the establishment of local norms for determining mastery standards. Others recommend a mastery criterion of 50 to 70 wpm correct for first and second graders and 70 to 100 wpm correct for third through sixth graders (Marston, Dement, Allen, & Allen, 1992). Each year from 1981 to 1990, Hasbrouck and Tindal (1992) collected normative data for oral reading fluency from 7,000 to 9,000 general education and special education students in Grades 2 through 5 in five midwestern and western states. They identified different standards for various times of the year (fall, winter, and spring), different grade levels (second through fifth), and different percentiles (25th percentile, 50th percentile, and 75th percentile). They recommend the use of scores from the 25th percentile to depict typical progress in the reading fluency of low-performing students. We selected the 25th percentile scores established in the spring, as many teachers use spring dates for their annual goals.

The recommended mastery standards are 65 words per minute (wpm) for Grade 2, 87 wpm for Grade 3, 92 wpm for Grade 4, and 100 wpm for Grade 5. For information about the other percentiles and fall and winter scores, please see the original article in TEACHING Exceptional Children, 1992, volume 24, number 3.

Spelling

Spelling measures typically include 20 words. Lists are randomly selected from either the spelling series used in the district or from basal readers (Deno, Mirkin, & Wesson, 1984; Marston & Magnusson, 1985).

Procedures

Begin by dictating words for 2 minutes, directing the student to write as many letters of each word as he or she can. Give about 10 seconds to spell each word and do not present any new words in the last 3 seconds of the test (Deno & Fuchs, 1987).

Score the test by counting the number of correct letter sequences within the 2-minute sample. Counting correctly spelled words by letter sequences usually results in one more count than the number of letters; for example, the word *agent* consists of six possible correct letter sequences: one before *a*, because the student knew where to start (beginning to $a = +1$); one from *a* to *g* ($+2$); one from *g* to *e* ($+3$); one

from *e* to *n* ($+4$); one from *n* to *t* ($+5$); and one after *t*, because the student knew where to end (*t* to end $+6$) (White & Haring, 1976). Thus, *agent* is marked in the following manner: ^{+1}a $^{+2}g\ ^{+3}e\ ^{+4}n\ ^{+5}t^{+6}$. Continue testing the student with spelling lists from different grade levels until the instructional standard is reached and the correct grade level material is selected.

Instructional Standards

Fuchs and Shinn (1989) recommend 20–39 correct letter sequences for students in Grades 1 and 2. They suggest 40–59 correct letter sequences for Grades 3 through 6.

Mastery Standards

Deno, Mirkin, and Wesson (1984) recommend the following mastery standards for spelling: 60–80 correct letter sequences in 2 minutes for students in Grades 1 and 2, and 80–140 correct letter sequences for students in Grades 3 and 4.

Math

Curriculum-based measurement for math consists of multiple tests of the types of problems found in the year's curriculum (Fuchs, Fuchs, Hamlett, & Stecker, 1991). Thus, you are measuring a student's performance on the entire math curriculum over time.

Procedures

You administer the various 25-item tests, directing the students to proceed as quickly as possible. As in precision teaching, score the sample by counting each correct digit. Fuchs, Fuchs, Hamlett, and Whinnery (1991) recommend a test time of 1 minute for Grade 1, 1.5 minutes for Grades 2 and 3, 3 minutes for Grade 4, 4 minutes for Grade 5, and 5 minutes for Grade 6. Others recommend a 2-minute time limit (Shinn, 1989).

Instructional Standards

In their *MBSP* (*Monitoring Basic Skills Progress*) software package, Fuchs, Hamlett, and Fuchs

(1990) recommend the following cutoff scores for placement of students in grade-level texts: a score of 11 or fewer correct digits for placement in a first-grade math text, between 12 and 22 digits correct for placement in a second-grade text, between 23 and 30 digits correct for placement in a third-grade text, between 31 and 46 digits correct for placement in a fourth-grade text, between 32 and 60 digits correct for placement in a fifth-grade text, and more than 60 digits correct for placement in a sixth-grade text. Again, these are just guidelines.

Mastery Standards

Fuchs, Hamlett, and Fuchs (1990) suggest a weekly increase of one digit correct to help select a possible mastery standard. Finally, they suggest that students may wish to self-select their mastery standards. Fuchs, Bahr, and Rieth (1989) found that high school students with learning disabilities outperformed their peers when they selected their own goals (mastery standards) on math tasks.

Written Expression

CBM measures for written expression consist of three story starters or topic sentences (Deno, Marston, & Mirkin, 1982). An example of a story starter is, "The score was tied. As the soccer ball rolled in front of my feet, I . . . ." An example of a topic sentence is, "He went shopping at Marshall Field's."

Procedures

You may either read or write the story starter or topic sentence for the student. Administer the three story starters or topic sentences at one sitting or at three sittings. Give the student 3 minutes to complete the stories, then count the number of words in each story. Do not count numbers (Deno & Fuchs, 1987).

Determining what constitutes a word is a teacher decision. Salvia and Hughes (1990) suggest considering grade level and linguistic backgrounds in scoring words. They recommend counting misspelled words as words for older students (e.g., *summer* spelled *sumar*) and counting any letter sequence that can be identified as a word for younger students (e.g., *summer* spelled as *sum*). For children whose first language is not English, they suggest counting word sequences that are acceptable translations of the native language.

Counting the number of words written demonstrates sensitivity to student growth in written expression (Marston, Fuchs, & Deno, 1985). The measure also effectively differentiates general education students from special education students (Shinn & Marston, 1985) and is highly correlated with teacher judgments of the quality of written expression at the elementary grade levels (Deno, Marston, & Mirkin, 1982).

Instructional Standards

There are no specific instructional standards for written expression, so the instructional standard is the student's median score. Thus, if Jennifer writes 19 words on the first story starter, 13 words on the second, and 16 words on the third, her instructional standard is 16 words in 3 minutes.

Mastery Standards

Suggested mastery standards are 14.7 words in 3 minutes for first graders, 27.8 words for second graders, 36.6 words for third graders, 40.9 words for fourth graders, 49.1 words for fifth graders, and 53.3 words for sixth graders (Deno, Mirkin, & Wesson, 1984).

Steps

Now that we have discussed the assessment procedures, we identify the steps you may follow to use CBM for planning and monitoring of student progress. Examples in the area of reading follow the discussion of each step. However, these same steps may be followed for spelling, math, and written expression. Remember, these are just guidelines.

Select Classroom Materials for Measurement Samples

Remember, passages are usually approximately 100 words in length for young students and 300 words in length for older. Chances are that you will need more than one grade-level text.

EXAMPLE: Mr. Smith decides to test Manu's reading performance using three passages from the Houghton-Mifflin third-grade text (this is the series used in Manu's inclusive third-grade class). He also decides to select three passages from the second-grade text.

Administer the Measurement Samples and Compare Scores to the Instructional Standard to Select Appropriate Materials

Now is the time to select an instructional standard. After considering the errors of mispronunciations, omissions, and reversals, you rank order the scores for each text. Then you compare the median score to the instructional standard and select the instructional material.

EXAMPLE: Based on the school district's instructional standards, Mr. Smith selected a standard of 31 wpm with no more than 7 errors. He then instructed Manu to read the third-grade passages as quickly as possible for a minute each. Following the guidelines for determining reading performance, Mr. Smith found that Manu's median reading score was 10 correct words and 17 errors. This score was below the instructional standard, so Mr. Smith then administered selections from the second-grade reader. Manu read 25 wpm correctly with only 2 errors on the first passage of the second-grade text, 35 wpm correctly with only 3 errors on the second passage, and 30 wpm correctly with 2 errors on the third passage. A ranking of the number of words per minute correct (25, 30, 31) resulted in a median score of 30 wpm correct. Mr. Smith felt this median

performance was close enough to the 31 wpm instructional standard to place Manu in the second-grade text, especially since he made minimal errors.

Write an Annual Goal and Short-Term Objectives

Deno, Mirkin, and Wesson (1984) recommend that teachers compare the instructional and mastery standards along with the IEP review date to write an annual goal and short-term objectives. Fuchs, Fuchs, and Hamlett (1989) recommend that teachers or students select ambitious mastery goals for the best results.

EXAMPLE: (a) *Select a mastery standard.* Mr. Smith, with Manu's input, selected the mastery standard of 87 words per minute. He also wanted Manu to make less than 7 errors. This was an ambitious goal for Manu. Based on this information, Mr. Smith wrote the following annual goal: "When placed in Reader 2 of the Houghton-Mifflin series, Manu will increase his reading from an instructional standard of 30 wpm correct to a mastery standard of 87 wpm correct, with no more than 7 errors, by the next IEP review."

(b) *Subtract the instructional standard from the mastery standard.* In Manu's case, this is 87 wpm correct − 30 wpm correct = 57 wpm correct.

(c) *Check to see when the IEP is to be reviewed and divide the difference between the instructional standard and the mastery standard by the weeks before the next IEP review.* Manu's IEP is scheduled for review in 10 weeks. For Manu, the difference of 57 wpm divided by 10 weeks equals a gain of about 6 wpm a week.

Mr. Smith identified this short-term objective, "Every week, when presented with a random selection from the Houghton-Mifflin second-grade reader, Manu will read aloud with an average increase of 6 wpm correct with no more than 7 errors."

Teach and Test

During teaching and testing, assess the student at least twice a week (Fuchs, Fuchs, & Hamlett, 1989). Use parallel assessment forms. Do not allow the student to practice the material before assessment.

Wesson (1987) suggests that teachers select 10 pages from the beginning, middle, and end of each assigned text for measuring reading progress. The text and 30 slips of paper with page numbers written on each slip are then placed in a container. Old ice cream tubs, such as those from Baskin Robbins, are ideal for storing the materials. A student randomly selects a slip of paper, turns to the page number in the assigned text, reads the passage, and initials the back. Once a student has read and initialed the slip three times, he or she can no longer use that page as a measure of reading progress.

EXAMPLE: Mr. Smith instructed Manu from the second-grade text and selected parallel passages for monitoring Manu's progress. He assessed Manu twice a week with 1-minute samples.

Graph the Scores

Data is charted on an equal interval graph. An equal interval graph is a linear graph in which the distance between lines occupies equal space; that is, the distance between 5 and 10 is the same as the distance between 10 and 15 and between 15 and 20. It's probably the graph that you used in school. Fuchs, Hamlett, and Fuchs (1990) have designed a software program, *MBSP: Monitoring Basic Skills Progress,* which contains graded reading passages, spelling lists, and arithmetic probes. Students enter responses on the computer, and the computer graphs the data.

EXAMPLE: Mr. Smith helps Manu chart his scores on an equal interval chart. They chart the results twice a week.

Evaluate Progress

Fuchs, Fuchs, and Hamlett (1989) recommend that teachers consider both the expected (aimline using aimline procedures) and actual rate of student change (regression line using quarter-intersect procedures) to evaluate intervention effectiveness. Their software program, *Monitoring Basic Skills Progress* (Fuchs, Hamlett, & Fuchs, 1990), displays aimlines and regression lines. The program also communicates the appropriate decision. Additionally, the software conducts a skills analysis of students' responses to the test items (Fuchs, Fuchs, Hamlett, & Whinnery, 1991). Allinder (1996) found that special educators who knew the measurement systems and the software, scheduled frequent assessments, examined students' graphs, implemented decision rules, and had adequate planning time produced more significant math gains. See Figure 3.6 for a sample of the decision rules used to evaluate progress.

EXAMPLE: Based on the decision rules, Mr. Smith finds that Manu is making good progress.

 ACTIVITY 3.9

You have decided to assess the written expression performance of Latoya, a sixth grader, who has a mild disability. Describe the steps you would follow in planning and monitoring using curriculum-based measurement.

 IMPORTANT POINTS

1. Curriculum-based measurement uses classroom materials for assessment, measures performance using fluency, and compares a student's score with suggested instructional and mastery standards or criteria.

(a) Change the intervention or goal if the regression line is lower than the aimline.*

(b) Raise the goal if the regression line is steeper than the aimline.

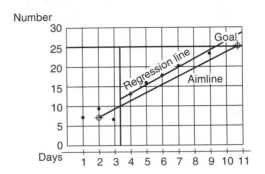

(c) Continue with the intervention if both celeration lines are the same.

The aimline is drawn using aimline procedures and the regression line is drawn using quarter-intersect procedures.

Figure 3.6 CBM Decision Rules

2. The oral reading fluency measure requires a student to read passages for 1 minute from various reading texts to determine the instructional reading level (the grade level for instruction).

3. The spelling measure requires students to write as many spelling words as they can in 2 minutes and is scored by counting letter sequences.

4. In math assessment, sample problems from the whole-years math curriculum are selected and scored by counting the number of digits correct.

5. In written expression assessment, students are given three story starters or three topic sentences and instructed to write a story for each within three minutes.

6. Once the students are assessed, the teacher compares scores to instructional standards to select appropriate grade-level materials.

7. The teacher then selects mastery standards and writes IEP goals and short-term objectives based on suggested guidelines.

8. Decision rules are based on a comparison of expected rate of student change (an aim-

line) and the actual rate of change (a regression line).

9. Decision rules state that teachers should change their intervention when a regression line is lower than the aimline or when a regression line is steeper than the aimline.

10. Critical components of CBM include measurement frequency, goal ambitiousness, compliance with decision rules, and adequate planning time (Allinder, 1996).

ERROR ANALYSIS

Errors help you to focus instruction. For example, if you find that Paul correctly calculates all facts except those involving the basic addition facts of 9 (i.e., 9 + 1 through 9 + 9), you know you must teach just these addition facts. Errors also provide insights into how students think and reason (Heshusius, 1989). Error analysis may be combined with all informal assessments. For example, you may record and analyze errors whether you use CRT, PT, or CBM procedures.

Before using error analysis, you should consider language differences. Many experts argue that language differences, especially those dealing with phonemes, or sounds, should be of concern only if they impair meaning (Ortiz & Polyzoi, 1989; Saville-Troike, 1976). For example, if a Hispanic student reads *easy* as "iysi" or an African-American student reads *they* as "dey," but each understands the content of the message, you should note these substitutions as language differences and not reading errors. Remember, varieties of English are equally effective and valid forms of communication (Grossman, 1994).

Some common language differences found in Black English include omission of the *s* suffix (e.g., "The girl play" or "I have two penny"), the use of *be* as a main verb (e.g., "He be busy"), and the deletion of contracted forms of *is* and *are* (e.g.,

"He here" or "They here") (Gollnick & Chin, 1990; Washington & Miller-Jones, 1989). Spanish speakers often omit the *s* suffix, (e.g., "four bell" for "four bells"), trill the *r* when two *r*'s are together (e.g., "sorrrrel for sorrel"), and pronounce the following sounds the same: *sh* and *ch, s* and *z, n* and *ng, b* and *v, d* and *th, y* and *j, t* and unvoiced *th*, unvoiced *th* and *s*. Native Americans rarely use final consonants; omit articles *a, an,* and *the;* and have difficulty with prepositions (e.g., "get on car" for "get in the car") (Gollnick & Chinn, 1990; Walker, 1987). Many Asian-Americans have difficulty pronouncing *sh, ch, r, x, l,* and *j* (Chan, 1987; Chinn & Plata, 1987).

Reading

In the *Qualitative Reading Inventory*, Leslie and Caldwell (1990) discuss the following decoding errors: (a) omissions (the student omits words when reading), (b) substitutions (the student substitutes a similar word that often makes sense in the sentence), (c) insertions (the student adds words), and (d) reversals (the student reverses letters or phrases). Leslie and Caldwell do not count repetitions (repeating a word or phrase when reading), hesitations (pausing longer at some words when reading), or omissions of punctuation (e.g., not pausing at the end of a sentence) as errors because scoring is unreliable for such factors, and repetitions and hesitations do not alter the text's meaning. In another common error, called an aided word, the teacher supplies the word for the students (Mercer & Mercer, 1998).

Reading comprehension errors frequently include mistakes in text-explicit, text-implicit, and script-implicit comprehension (Pearson & Johnson, 1978). Table 3.5 contains examples that measure each of these areas of comprehension.

Text-explicit comprehension, also termed *literal comprehension,* requires the reader to recall information specifically found in a selection. When you ask students to identify the main characters, or actions of the main characters, or to sequence events, or recall significant details, you are checking text-explicit comprehension. Question 1 in Table 3.5 is an example, because students should find the answer directly in the first sentence of the paragraph.

Text-implicit comprehension, also referred to as *inferential comprehension* (Tindal & Marston, 1990), requires the reader to interact with information that is implied. It is not found directly from any one source in the passage. Forming opinions, predicting the next event in a story, and identifying the influence of the setting on the actions of the main character in a story are examples of text-implicit comprehension. Question 2 in Table 3.5 checks this type of comprehension, because the reader must assimilate the information from more than one sentence.

In script-implicit comprehension questions, the reader must use the information from the text and provide additional personal information (Tindal & Marston, 1990). Undoubtedly, a person who is not familiar with the sport of basketball will not answer Question 3 correctly. This type of comprehension question is gener-

ally difficult for students who lack the necessary background experiences.

Spelling

Common spelling errors include omission of silent letters (e.g., clim for climb) and sounded letters (e.g., cimb for climb), phonetic substitutions (e.g., clime for climb), letter reversals (e.g., cilmb for climb), addition of letters (e.g., climbe for climb), words with apostrophes (e.g., possessives and contractions), and rule overgeneralizations (e.g., add an *s* for plurals such as deers for deer) (Evans, Evans, & Mercer, 1986; Salvia & Hughes, 1990). Spelling is often a problem area for many students with disabilities.

Math

Roberts (1968) identified the following math error categories: (a) wrong operation (the student selects one operation, such as subtraction, when another operation, such as addition, should have been selected), (b) obvious computational error (the student incorrectly recalls a basic number fact $7 + 8 = 16$, instead of 15), (c) defective algorithm (the student employs

Table 3.5 Sample Comprehension Errors

A student reads the following paragraph:

There were 25 seconds left in the championship basketball game. The winner of the game would be high school state champion. The score was tied 98 to 98, but no one could believe that the Tigers were in contention. After all, the tallest player of the team was only 6′5″, the height of the shortest player of the opposition team, the Braves. But the Tigers had been deadly on the 3-point plays and had not missed a free throw.

After reading the paragraph, the student responded to the following sample questions:

1. How much time was left in the game? *Answer:* Twenty-five minutes. (text-explicit error)
2. What was the main idea of the paragraph? *Answer:* There was only a little time left in the game. (text-implicit error)
3. Why is height such an advantage when playing basketball? *Answer:* I don't know. (script-implicit error)

the correct operation and knows the basic number facts but does not use the correct process or procedure, such as $112 - 46 = 76$, in which the student forgot to regroup in the tens place), and (d) random response (the student answers incorrectly without any apparent relationship between problem solving and the problem). Enright (1983) adds placement errors, which occur when students do not align parts of problems correctly, such as alignment of decimals. Cohen and Spencimer (1998) summarized the following word problem errors: difficulty in reading and understanding language and vocabulary, identifying relevant and irrelevant information, using all the steps for solving a problem, and performing the correct mathematical operations.

Procedures

We recommend the following steps for analyzing errors: (a) after scoring the items, list the student errors (e.g., on the addition fact worksheet, Jan is missing $9 + 8$, $7 + 8$, $6 + 8$); (b) make a hypothesis as to the error pattern (e.g., computational error, basic addition facts,

especially the 8 facts); (c) test the hypothesis by examining the correct problems to see if any have the same pattern (e.g., Jan calculated $6 + 4$, $5 + 6$, and $9 + 2$ correctly, so none of the correct ones involved the basic addition facts of 8); (d) if not correct, redo the hypothesis (e.g., steps a–c again); and (e) teach correction of the error (e.g., Jan needs to be retaught the basic addition facts of 8). Sometimes, asking the student to think out loud helps in error analysis.

PORTFOLIO ASSESSMENT

Portfolios are "purposeful, collaborative, and self-reflective collections of student work" generated during the instructional process (McRobbie, 1992). Many states, such as California, Michigan, Pennsylvania, and Vermont, incorporate portfolios into their general education assessment procedures (Kerka, 1995; McRobbie, 1992; Wolf, 1989). Moreover, software programs such as the Portfolio Assessment Kit (1996), the Electronic Portfolio (1996), and The Grady Profile (1995) are now available to help teachers and students organize and monitor portfolios.

◆ **ACTIVITY 3.10**

Identify the following error patterns.

C = correct; X = incorrect (The student's incorrect responses are in parentheses.)

Reading Words

1. for	X (far)	4. man	C	
2. was	X (w)	5. fit	C	
3. of	X (off)	6. top	C	

Math Problems

1.	36	2.	29	3.	47	4.	55
	+19		+68		+16		+79
	55 C		97 C		63 C		(34) X

5.	26	6.	45	7.	26
	+87		+65		+13
	(13) X		(20) X		39 C

Spelling Words

1. might	X (mit)	4. flop	C	
2. rain	C	5. mine	X (min)	
3. run	C	6. sky	X (ski)	

An examination of the literature finds the following advantages and disadvantages of portfolio assessment (Bietau, 1995; Carpenter, Ray, & Bloom, 1995; Kerka, 1995; Rivera, 1995; Schutt & McCabe, 1994; Wesson & King, 1996). Advantages include (a) a variety of ways to measure progress and to demonstrate what learners can or cannot do, (b) the incorporation of student ownership and self-reflection, (c) the measurement of both process and product, (d) the linkage to real-life situations, and (e) the emphasis on students' strengths. Disadvantages include (a) the amount of time required, (b) the lack of reliable scoring procedures, (c) the lack of empirical evidence of effectiveness, (d) cost efficacy, and (e) subjective assessment.

An examination of current literature in the special education field shows that portfolio assessment is receiving more attention as an alternative assessment for students with disabilities (Cohen & Spencimer, 1998; Howell, Fox, & Morehead, 1993; Rueda & Garcia, 1997; Wesson & King, 1996). Currently, the use of portfolio assessment does not have much of an empirical basis. However, a study by Rueda and Garcia (1997) involving special educators, bilingual teachers, and school psychologists found that portfolio assessment can lead to specific instructional recommendations and identification of students' strengths when compared to more traditional assessment. You should couple portfolio assessment with other assessments discussed in this chapter because of the lack of an empirical basis.

Although there are no typical portfolios, common characteristics include: (a) a range of work over time, (b) teacher-assigned work (teachers often determine the number and type of pieces), (c) student-selected work, (d) a student introduction of why a particular piece of work was selected, and (e) a student summary of what was learned from the selection and reflections on compiling the portfolio (McRobbie, 1992; Wolf, 1989). We identify the following steps in creating a student portfolio:

(a) plan the focus (Valencia, 1990), (b) select the content (Valencia, 1990), (c) select the times for adding materials (Jongsma, 1989), (d) design scoring procedures (Popham, 1997; Goodrich, 1996–97), (e) teach students to self-assess and reflect, and (f) arrange periodic conferences (Miller, 1995).

Plan the Focus

To prevent the portfolio from becoming a hodgepodge of papers, Valencia (1990) suggests that the teacher provide a focus. The focus should center on the key goals of instruction. McRobbie (1992) recommends general goals and specific subject-area goals. For example, a general goal is for students to reflect on their work, whereas a specific subject-area goal in language arts is for students to show progress in summarizing a story theme. Cohen and Spencimer (1998) recommend a focus on academic progress and student's self-understanding for middle-school students and a focus on career planning and graduation requirements for secondary students. Wesson and King (1996) suggest that affective behaviors are also appropriate for the portfolio focus. We recommend that the students or the teacher select the goals or short-term objectives on each student's IEP as the major focus.

Select the Content

Portfolios may contain, among other items, samples of students' work selected by the teacher and student (Flood & Lapp, 1989; Valencia, 1990), teachers' observation notes (Flood & Lapp, 1989), students' periodic self-evaluations (Flood & Lapp, 1989; Valencia, 1990), progress notes written by the student and teacher (Valencia, 1990), pictures or videotapes of a student's project (Wesson & King, 1996), a student-generated list of books and genres read each month (Flood & Lapp, 1989), and community service projects (Cohen & Spencimer, 1998). Wesson and King (1996) report that videotapes, instructor observations, self-observations, and home progress reports serve as content for a behavior portfolio. The key is selecting a variety of materials to depict a student's progress (Jongsma, 1989). You may wish to include originals, copies, or summaries of the materials. For example, the student-generated monthly lists of books could be summarized into one list. McRobbie (1992) also suggests that students organize the portfolio with a table of contents, a letter of introduction that explains its organization, dates on all examples, a short explanation of the selection of each piece of work, and references.

Select Times for Adding Materials

Wolf (1989) schedules monthly student checks for his eighth-grade students. At this time, the students remove some papers and keep those that best exemplify their progress. Schutt and McCabe (1994) suggest that students with learning disabilities keep two portfolios: a short-term one for works in progress and a long-term one for final products.

Design Scoring Procedures

Rubrics are scoring guides that are frequently used in portfolio and other authentic assessments. They have three features, which are referred to with different terms depending on the source: (a) criteria, evaluative criteria, or standards; (b) levels of quality or performance; and (c) quality definitions or indicators (Anderson & Reilly, 1995; Kerka, 1995; Marzano, Pickering, & McTighe, 1993; Popham, 1997). For our discussion, we will refer to these three features as criteria, levels, and indicators. Criteria describes the major components that need to be present. For example, criteria for a language arts portfolio may include neatness, mechanics, clarity, organization, and vocabulary. Popham (1997) recommends using only three to five criteria.

Levels identify the degree to which the performance meets the criteria, for example, highly

acceptable, acceptable, or not acceptable. Goodrich (1996–97) suggests that teachers use terms like, "Yes, Yes but, No but, No" to assist students in the understanding of levels. Indicators identify the specific requirements for each level and criteria. For example, an indicator for the criteria of mechanics and the level of highly acceptable may be that the student has written a paper with no spelling errors, total subject and verb agreement, no grammar errors, and complex sentence structures.

Analytic and holistic scoring strategies are another feature of a rubric. An analytic scoring rubric is often used for diagnostic purposes, is specific, is frequently in matrix form, and designates a score for each criteria (Marzano, Pickering, & McTighe, 1993). A holistic rubric promotes an overall impression of a student's performance, is broad and general, is frequently in hierarchical form, and designates one score for the product (Marzano, Pickering, & McTighe, 1997). You may use either or both scoring strategies.

Rubrics make teacher expectations clear, show students how to reach the expectations, and assist students to evaluate quality (Goodrich, 1996–97). Table 3.6 presents a partial scoring rubric with the various features identified. Using the sample holistic math rubric, Jimmy may score a 4 or Competent on his entire math portfolio. Using the sample analytic math rubric, Jimmy may score a 3 or Highly Acceptable in problem solving and a 2 or Acceptable in communication.

Teach Students to Self-Assess and Reflect

Often, students are directed to self-assess and reflect in portfolios. Students with disabilities have problems with this type of metacognitive task (see Chapter 8). To assist a student in self-reflection, you may identify questions for the students to answer and then model your answer to these questions. For example, Mr. Jordan identifies three questions: (1) What is characteristic about this new piece of work I

Table 3.6 Partially Completed Sample Rubric for Math Portfolio

---

SAMPLE HOLISTIC MATH RUBRIC

Superior Performance (6)

Task accomplished in an exceptional manner, superior **problem-solving** skills, apparent knowledge of **underlying concepts** throughout the task, rigorously employed and innovative **appropriate strategies,** logical and thorough **reasoning,** accurate **computations, directions** followed, and responses **communicated** clearly and effectively.

Proficient Performance (5)

Task accomplished in a proficient manner, effective **problem-solving** skills, apparent knowledge of **underlying concepts,** employed **appropriate strategies,** logical **reasoning,** accurate **computations, directions** followed, and responses **communicated** effectively.

Competent Performance (4)

Task accomplished in a competent manner, satisfactory **problem-solving** skills, frequent apparent knowledge of **underlying concepts,** frequently employed **appropriate strategies,** mostly accurate **computations, directions** followed, and responses **communicated** reasonably well.

SAMPLE ANALYTIC MATH RUBRIC

POINTS

	Highly Acceptable (3)	Acceptable (2)	Not Acceptable (1)
Problem Solving	Superior reasoning in problem solving; Answers justified; Valid conclusions drawn; Reasonable predictions made	Satisfactory reasoning in problem solving; Most answers justified; Conclusions usually valid; Usually reasonable predictions	Very limited reasoning in problem solving; Answers often not justified; Many conclusions invalid; Predictions generally unreasonable
Communication	Clear and consistent language, including terminology and symbolism to communicate the problem-solving approach	Generally appropriate language, including terminology to communicate the problem-solving approach in a satisfactory way	Limited language, including terminology to communicate the problem-solving approach in a marginal way

---

underline = levels

bold = criteria

regular print = sample indicators

Adapted from http://www.ebe.on.ca?DEPART/RESEAR/RUBRIC.HTM, January 1998

---

am including in my portfolio? (2) What has changed between my old work and my new work? (3) What remains to be done? He then presents two pieces of his own work and models out loud his answer to the questions before he asks the students to do the same with their works.

Arrange Periodic Conferences

Regular sessions for portfolio discussions between teachers and students should be scheduled throughout the year (Farr, 1989; Valencia, 1990). Wesson and King (1996) suggest monthly reviews and a check of one portfolio a week. During a conference, you should discuss a student's progress (Valencia, 1990), plans for inclusion of other pieces for the portfolio (Valencia, 1990), and the student's thoughts about the portfolio. Ask such questions as, "What is your favorite thing?" "Why did you organize the portfolio the way you did?" (Farr, 1989). Asking these types of questions assists students in self-reflection.

INTERVIEWS

Another type of informal assessment includes interviews in which students are asked to share their thought processes. It is important to establish rapport and provide a safe, secure environment, where students can risk being wrong without penalty. An interview may proceed in the following manner. First, you instruct the student, "Kari, Please complete these problems (e.g., 85 + 19, 67 + 18, 34 + 17) out loud so I can hear how you figure them out." As Kari is calculating the problems, she replies, "Well, 85 plus 19 means to add. Five plus 9 is 14, and 8 plus 1 is 9. So the answer is 9-1-4 [nine, one, four]." She proceeds with similar explanations and mistakes in the other two problems.

In analyzing Kari's thought processes and her answers, you find that she knows that *plus* means to add and she knows the addition facts. She also knows to begin in the ones column, but she does not know place value and the regrouping process, nor does she monitor her computation by checking to see whether the answer of 914 makes sense.

Sometimes, interviews are accompanied by recommended questions for the teacher to ask the student, as in the following spelling interview (Baskwill & Whitman, 1988). To measure spelling using this procedure, select a list of 20 words from either the spelling or reading text that the student is using in the inclusive setting.

To introduce the task in a nonthreatening manner, tell the student that you are really looking for a better way to teach spelling and that it doesn't matter how many mistakes the student makes. Next, give the words in isolation. Then give the same words in context. Add definitions if the student requests them.

Sit down with the student and go over the list together, asking such questions of the student as, "Which words do you think you spelled correctly?" "Which ones aren't you sure about?" "Why did you decide on this particular spelling?" "How else could you have tried to spell this word?" "If this word is incorrect, how could you find the correct spelling?" (Baskwill & Whitman, 1988). Remember that with the interviewing technique, assess both error patterns and strategies.

CHECKLISTS

The use of checklists may provide insight into the ways in which students approach tasks and the types of errors they make. You may also use checklists to gain information concerning any subject area, to find out about interests, or to monitor a student's progress in an inclusive setting. Checklist items are frequently phrased positively to assess what a student can do instead of emphasizing the problems. You may complete checklists using work samples (see Figure 3.7) or during observations. You may

Figure 3.7 A Student's Work Sample

use the checklist found in Figure 3.8 to evaluate written expression as this teacher did in evaluating the work sample in Figure 3.7. Questions for the checklist were compiled from our own experiences and suggestions from Tindal and Marston (1990), Rhodes and Dudley-Marling (1988), and Schumaker and Sheldon (1985). Students may also use self-assessment checklists to monitor their work. For example, you may have students answer whether they identified the relevant information, selected the correct steps, calculated the problems correctly, and verified their results as they solved word problems.

A way to use checklists as communication devices for inclusive settings is to ask the general education teacher to monitor specific behaviors during the class and to have the students return the checklist to you. Behavior and academic achievement items are often included on checklists. Some checklists even have a place for the students or teachers to write in homework assignments (see Figure 3.9). Many special education teachers include the return of checklists among their classroom rules and provide consequences for return and nonreturn of checklists.

---

1. Is the student able to write a topic sentence?
   Yes.
2. Is the student able to write supporting sentences?
   Yes, rest of sentences relate to topic.
3. Does the student use descriptive words?
   No, limited adjectives—"point, great."
4. Is the student able to use a variety of sentences (simple, compound, complex)? *No, all simple.*
5. Does the student use dialogue? *None used.*
6. Are there many mistakes in grammar? *None.*
7. Is the story organized?
   Yes, it begins with a topic sentence and has details and a closing.
8. Are there many spelling errors?
   Yes, 10 out of 40 words.

Figure 3.8   Scoring of the Student's Work Sample in Figure 3.7

 ACTIVITY 3.11

Design a checklist for students to use to help them reflect on the content of their portfolios.

| | Periods | | | | | | | | | | |
| | First | | Second | | Third | | Fourth | | Fifth | | Sixth | |
	Y	N	Y	N	Y	N	Y	N	Y	N	Y	N
Came on time	✓			✓								
Brought supplies	✓			✓								
Followed directions	✓		✓									
Completed work	✓		✓									
Grade on assignment	B		C (*late work*)									
Teacher initials	*gEO*		*JMP*									
Homework assigned	*None*		*Page 91, 1–22*									

Figure 3.9   Teacher Monitoring

INVOLVING STUDENTS IN DATA COLLECTION

Student involvement in data collection increases motivation and makes them feel more responsible for their own learning, plus it often saves teacher time. If you decide to incorporate precision teaching or CBM procedures, teach students to grade their own probes and to chart the results in order to promote active student participation in the learning process. Research shows that self-graphing maintains students' performance at high levels (McDougal & Brady, 1998; Trammel, Schloss, & Alper, 1994).

Wesson (1987) suggests setting up a measurement station in the class to involve the students. Place all materials, such as pencils or pens, a stopwatch with an audible beep, a tape recorder, assessment materials (probes or texts), direction sheets, answer sheets, and graphs, at the center. It is best to file the answer sheets, graphs, probes, and texts in a box for easy access. The direction sheet should contain step-by-step directions, explaining how to use any equipment. For example, Bott (1990) in giving directions for collecting oral reading samples, tells the students to "find the cassette tape labeled with your name, rewind it to the beginning, and press the record and play buttons down at the same time" (p. 287) to assist students in using a tape recorder. You may arrange the probes and texts according to subject areas. Schedule the students at the measurement station and assign them to the assessment materials based on their IEP objectives. Have the students proceed to the center, select the required assessment materials identified on their schedules, follow the assessment procedures, chart the information, and return all materials to their proper places.

Goodrich (1996–97) suggests that students help create scoring rubrics. She recommends that teachers show and discuss examples of good and poor work. From these examples, students list criteria, levels, and indicators. She then suggests they use the rubrics for peer and self-assessment. For example, eighth-grade students in cooperative groups identified the following criteria for their language arts portfolios: neatness, range of characteristics, effectiveness of story, use of unusual vocabulary, and sharpness of ideas and arguments. They then added the levels of "Yes; Yes, but; and Not Quite." They next defined indicators of a "Yes" level for neatness to include minimal erasures on the paper, straight margins, page numbers, proper heading, and legible handwriting. Lastly, they defined the other indicators.

Diaries and logs are other ways for students to participate in their evaluation (Baskwill & Whitman, 1988). Students may identify a list of writing skills they have mastered under "Things I Can Do in Writing" in their writing diaries (Calkins, 1986; Graves & Stuart, 1985). These lists are updated monthly. In learning logs, students enter what they have learned in any subject area. The students date and compile the logs in a notebook. Logs indicate whether students can describe what they have learned, relate isolated ideas, and recognize relevant information (Baskwill & Whitman, 1988). For example, at the end of each day, Ms. Anderson has her students write one thing they learned and how they felt about the day in their logs.

Self-monitoring of academic and social behaviors is another way to involve students in data collection. McDougall and Brady (1998) found that self-monitoring along with other self-management strategies increased math performance and engaged time of students with disabilities in inclusive settings. Students with moderate disabilities self-monitored daily activities with a personal calendar and increased the percentage of responsibilities met (Flores, Schloss, & Alper, 1995). To teach students with special needs to monitor their own progress in an inclusive setting, use the following steps compiled from those suggested by many practitioners (Anderson-Inman, 1986; Frith & Armstrong, 1986; Hughes, Ruhl, & Peterson, 1988; Olson, 1982; Osborne, Kosiewicz, Crumley, & Lee, 1987).

1. *Define the behavior for monitoring.* Behaviors selected for self-monitoring should be easily identified as having occurred or not occurred. Try to select skills or behaviors that result in a permanent product, so that students have something visual to refer to. Behaviors such as turning in homework assignments, raising hand to speak, writing headings on papers, and bringing paper and pencil to class are appropriate for self-monitoring.

2. *Teach students to discriminate the behavior.* Model examples and nonexamples of the behaviors and then ask students to discriminate between them. For example, if you want students to discriminate between appropriate and inappropriate comments during discussion in history class, model appropriate and inappropriate comments and ask the students to discriminate between them.

3. *Design the form for data collection.* On the form, be sure to include the behaviors, dates, and key for coding. See Figure 3.10 for an example of a form. This form was used with secondary students to count how often history homework was turned in on time.

4. *Demonstrate how to record using the form.* Model how to record on the form and explain the scoring code.

5. *Use a time routine.* Scheduling a specific time for students to complete the forms increases the chances that students will remember to monitor the behaviors when you are not around. Schedule the time for monitoring as close to the completion of the task as possible.

6. *Use teacher reliability checks.* A reliability check is easier if the student is monitoring a paper-and-pencil type of task, which leaves a permanent record. For example, a quick check of the general education teacher's grade book will let you know whether the student is correctly monitoring the turning in of history homework on time. Many times, teachers reward students when their counts match. Actually, checking the use of the form is more important than checking accuracy. After all, the objective is for students to monitor their own progress.

7. *Introduce self-monitoring in one inclusive class setting first, and then generalize to others.* Anderson-Inman (1986) reports that allowing students to decide when and where to use the self-monitoring form makes them feel more committed to using it. Perhaps next a secondary student may want to monitor the turning in of math homework on time.

Figure 3.10 Student Monitoring

ACTIVITY 3.12

Identify three ways to involve students with special needs in data collection at either the elementary or secondary level.

 IMPORTANT POINTS

1. Language differences should be considered as errors only if they impair meaning.
2. In reading, decoding errors include omissions, substitutions, insertions, reversals, and nonresponses, whereas comprehension errors include problems with text-explicit, text-implicit, and script-implicit comprehension.
3. Common spelling errors include omission of silent letters and sounded letters, phonetic substitutions, letter reversals, addition of letters, words with apostrophes, and rule overgeneralizations.
4. Math errors include wrong operation, obvious computational error, defective algorithm, random response, and word problems.
5. The following steps are recommended for analyzing errors: (a) list the student errors; (b) make a hypothesis as to the error pattern; (c) test the hypothesis by examining the incorrect problems to see if any of these have the same pattern; (d) if not correct, redo the hypothesis; and (e) teach correction of the error.
6. Portfolio assessment is the collection of samples of the physical ongoing evidence of a student's progress.
7. Teachers must make decisions concerning the focus, the content, the scoring, the teaching of students to self-assess and reflect, the times for adding materials, and the arranging of periodic conferences.

8. Rubrics are scoring guides that include the three features of criteria (e.g., mechanics), levels (e.g., highly acceptable), and indicators (e.g., no spelling errors).
9. In interview assessment, students are often asked to share their thought processes.
10. Teachers may use checklists to gain information concerning subject areas, to identify students' strengths and interests, and to monitor behaviors in inclusive settings.
11. Students may be involved in collecting, scoring, and charting probes; in designing rubrics; and in compiling diaries and logs.
12. To initiate student involvement in monitoring their own behaviors, teachers should define the behavior, teach students to discriminate the behavior, design the form for data collection, demonstrate how to use the form, use a time routine, use reliability checks, and introduce the monitoring gradually.

 ACTIVITY 3.13

As a summary activity for the entire chapter, compare CRT, PT, CBM, and portfolio assessments. Categories for comparison may include administration (individual, group, etc.), content (curriculum scope and sequence, classroom text, etc.), mastery measure (rate, percent, etc.), uses (to identify objectives, goals, etc.), and assessment (skills, interests, etc.).

◆ **DISCUSSION QUESTIONS**

1. Discuss some of the difficulties encountered in establishing and maintaining a monitoring system. Brainstorm some solutions.
2. Discuss ways to involve students with special needs at both elementary and secondary levels in data collection procedures.
3. Present the pros and cons of using CBM compared to portfolio assessment.

INSTRUCTIONAL
MATERIALS

The instructional materials you use are the nuts and bolts of your instructional program, the vehicles through which instruction is delivered. If your students are to achieve success in the classroom, the materials they use must produce appropriate learning outcomes, motivate them, and hold their interest. Teachers play a key role in instructional decision making (Gollnick, Sadker, & Sadker, 1982). In school districts where state-adopted textbooks and materials are used, teachers should be adept at modifying and adapting materials. Udvari-Solner (1997) recommends that general and special education teachers collaborate to design adaptations and accommodations as part of the curriculum. In districts where teachers are given choices in the selection process, they should be skilled in the selection, analysis, and development of materials. In this chapter, we focus on the use of commercial and teacher-made materials and present ways to select, analyze, adapt, and develop instructional materials.

SELECTING INSTRUCTIONAL MATERIALS

The selection of appropriate instructional materials and activities is part of the process of individualizing instruction for students. Many commercially produced instructional materials are available for use with students who have special needs. The suggestions in this section and throughout the chapter are appropriate for teachers to use with students with special needs who are receiving instruction in general education inclusive classrooms as well as in pull-out programs.

Factors Influencing the Selection of Instructional Materials

Remember to exercise care in your selection of instructional materials. Attention to individual learner needs, interest and motivation levels of materials, opportunities for social interaction, and diversity increases the probability of success with commercially produced instructional materials.

Student Needs

In choosing materials, you should consider the fact that you will work with students who have a wide variety of needs, abilities, and individual differences and you will be addressing these needs, abilities, and differences in general education and special class settings. A survey of more than 30,000 teachers underscores the need for materials that address learner characteristics by calling for instructional materials that are adaptable to a variety of disabilities; include supplements like manipulatives, games, and visuals; have varied entry levels; and allow for monitoring of student progress. We add to this our recommendation that materials be developmentally, culturally, linguistically, age, and interest appropriate for students.

Motivation and Interest

Motivation is an important factor to consider when you select materials for your students. Materials that are age appropriate, interesting, appealing, and related to real life are likely to be used by your students, particularly when you have given consideration to cultural backgrounds, gender, and interests. For example, some students benefit from using high-interest, low-level vocabulary materials that are age and interest appropriate. Secondary students are often motivated by functional materials that relate to real life.

Many elementary students enjoy reading themselves or listening to others read commercial materials called predictable books (see Table 4.1). According to Rhodes and Dudley-Marling (1988), "books are predictable when they enable students to quickly and easily predict what the author's going to say and how the author's going to say it based upon their knowledge of the world" (p. 88). Rhodes (1981) has identified the characteristics that make books predictable: (a) a match between the content and the reader's experiences; (b) rhythmical, repetitive patterns; and (c) familiar, well-known stories. You may select books with characters, cultural backgrounds, and themes your students can easily relate to. You can choose books with repetitive patterns, such as *Alexander and the Terrible, Horrible, No Good, Very Bad Day* (Viorst, 1972), and books with which most of your students may be familiar, such as tall tales or folktales. You may include many of the typical American folktales, such as *Paul Bunyan, A Tall Tale* (Kellogg, 1984), and tales from other countries, such as the Asian legend *A Song of Stars* (Birdseye, 1990) and the Chinese tale *The Empty Pot* (Demi, 1990).

Social Interaction

Teachers may use instructional materials, both commercial and teacher-made, to foster social interactions through peer tutoring, learning center activities, role playing, group projects, and cooperative learning activities. Interpersonal skills are important for school and community adjustment (Lovitt & Harris, 1987; Schloss & Schloss, 1987; Schloss, Schloss, & Harris, 1984; Schloss & Sedlak, 1986). For example, Joe and Mike, high school juniors, have been working with instructional materials that emphasize job-seeking skills. In addition to providing them with skills in finding and securing employment, the materials have given them valuable socialization experiences through role-playing the employability activities.

Diversity

Instructional materials may be used to help students recognize and celebrate the diversity and variety that exists among individuals and to

Table 4.1   Predictable Books

Aardema, V. (1981). *Bringing the rain to Kapiti Plain,* New York: Dial.
Ahlberg, J., & Ahlberg, A. (1978). *Each peach pear plum.* New York: Scholastic.
Barrett, J. (1980). *Animals should definitely not act like people.* New York: Atheneum.
Bishop, C., & Wiese, K. (1938). *The five Chinese brothers.* New York: Coward, McCann & Geoghegan.
Brand, O., (1970). *When I first came to this land.* New York: Putman's Sons.
Burke, C. L., & Harste, J. C. (1983). *All kinds of cats.* Worthington, OH: School Book Fairs.
Carle, E. (1969). *The very hungry caterpillar.* Cleveland: Collins World.
Christian, M. B. (1973). *Nothing much happened today.* Reading, MA: Addison-Wesley.
de Paola, T. (1981). *Now one foot, now the other.* New York: Putnam's Sons.
Dodd, L. (1985). *Hairy Maclary.* Milwaukee, WI: Gareth Stevens.
Durrell, J. (1985). *Mouse tails.* New York: Crown.
Galdone, P. (1985). *Cat goes fiddle-i-fee.* New York: Clarion.
Hines, A. (1984). *Come to the meadow.* New York: Clarion.
Hoguet, S. R. (1983). *I unpacked my grandmother's trunk.* New York: Dutton.
Kalan, R. (1981). *Jump, frog, jump!* New York: Greenwillow.
Leydenfrost, R. (1970). *The snake that sneezed!* New York: Putnam's Sons.
Lobel, A. (1984). *The rose in my garden.* New York: Greenwillow.
O'Neill, M. (1961). *Hailstones and halibut bones.* Garden City, NY: Doubleday.
Perme, D. (1982). *Joshua James likes trucks.* Chicago: Children's Press.
Plume, I. (1980). *The Bremen town musicians.* Garden City, NY: Doubleday.
Satchwell, J. (1984). *Odd one out.* New York: Random House.
Singer, M. (1981). *Will you take me to town on strawberry day?* New York: Harper & Row.
Thomas, P. (1971). *"Stand back" said the elephant, "I'm going to sneeze!"* New York: Lothrop, Lee & Shepard.
Viorst, J. (1972). *Alexander and the terrible, horrible, no good, very bad day.* New York: Atheneum.
Williams, B. (1974). *Albert's toothache.* New York: Dutton.

share information about people from different cultural backgrounds. "Students' contextual, linguistic, and gender characteristics influence how they learn" (Winzer & Mazurek, 1998, p. 327). As you select materials, make sure that all groups are represented. Underrepresentation in instructional materials appears to occur most often for minority groups, women, people with disabilities, and older individuals (Gollnick & Chinn, 1990).

In Mr. Rizzati's English class, students read and discuss books that incorporate different age groups, both males and females, a variety of cultural groups, and people with disabilities. For example, the class examined the problems of the elderly in *Grandpa and Me* (Tolan, 1978), a story about a family that has to decide what to do about their aging grandfather, who has always lived with them. The story highlights the special friendship between the grandfather and granddaughter. A particular favorite of the class was *Summer of the Swans* (Byars, 1974), a story told from the perspective of the sister of a boy with a mental disability. The story tells how the girl comes to know and understand herself better because of her brother.

Water Sky (George, 1987) is a story about a young man living with an Eskimo family in Alaska. There he learns the importance of whaling in the Eskimo culture. *The Black Snowman* (Mendez, 1989) describes a young African-American boy who discovers the beauty of his heritage and self-worth. For a list of books about a variety of cultural groups, see Table 4.2.

Materials Selection and the Stages of Learning

You may use a variety of instructional materials to meet the needs of your students at each of

Table 4.2 Multicultural Literature

African-Americans

Angelou, M. (1989). Writers' voices selected from *I know why the caged bird sings* and *The heart of a woman*. New York: Readers House.

Bryan, A. (1989). *Turtle knows your name*. New York: Antheneum.

Greenfield, E. (1989). *Nathaniel talking*. New York: Writers & Readers.

Lester, J. (1989). *How many spots does a leopard have? And other tales*. New York: Scholastic.

Mendez, P. (1989). *The black snowman*. New York: Scholastic.

Miller, D. (1988). *Frederick Douglass and the fight for freedom*. New York: Crowell.

Myers, W. D. (1990). *Scorpions*. New York: Harper Collins.

Patterson, L. (1989). *Martin Luther King, Jr., and the freedom movement*. New York: Facts on File.

San Souci, R. (1989). *The talking eggs: A folktale from the American South*. New York: Dial.

Sanfield, S. (1991). *The adventures of High John the Conqueror*. New York: Orchard.

Smith, K. (1991). *Skeeter*. New York: Houghton Mifflin.

Terry, W. (1987). *Bloods: An oral history of the Vietnam War by Black veterans*. New York: Random House.

Asian-Americans

Demi (1998). *The empty pot*. New York: Henry Holt & Company.

Goldman, P., & Fuller, T. (1983). *What happened to us in Vietnam?* New York: Morrow.

Huynh Quang Nhoung (1982). *The land I lost: Adventures of a boy in Vietnam*. New York: Harper.

Ike, J. H. (1982). *A Japanese fairy tale*. New York: Warne.

Kingston, M. H. (1990). Writers' voices selected from *China men and the woman warrior*. New York: Readers House.

Luenn, N. (1982). *The dragon kite*. San Diego, CA: Harcourt Brace Jovanovich.

Newton, P. C. (1982). *The five sparrows*. New York: Atheneum.

Nguyen Ngoc Bich (1975). *A thousand years of Vietnamese poetry*. Translated by B. Raffel & W. S. Merwin. New York: Knopf.

Pittman, H. C. (1986). *A grain of rice*. New York: Bantam.

Seros, K. (1982). *Sun and moon: Fairy tales from Korea*. Winslow, WA: Holly.

Vuyon, L. D. (1982). *The brocaded slipper and other Vietnamese tales*. Reading, MA: Addison-Wesley.

Hispanics

Aardema, V. (1979). *The riddle of the drum: A tale from Tizapan, Mexico*. New York: Four Winds.

Anaya, Rudolfo A. (1989). Writers' voices selected from *bless me, Ultima*. New York: Readers House.

Bethancourt, T. E. (1987). *The me inside of me*. Neward, DE: Lerner.

Bierhorst, J. (1987). *Doctor Coyote: A Native American Aesop's fables*. New York: Morrow.

Bierhorst, J. (1986). *The monkey's haircut and other stories told by the Maya*. New York: Morrow.

Griego y Maetras, J., & Anaya, R. A. (1980). *Cuentos: Tales from the Hispanic Southwest*. Santa Fe, NM: Museum of New Mexico.

Jagendorf, M. A., & Boggs, R. W. (1960). *The king of the mountains: A treasure of Latin American folk stories*. New York: Vanguard.

Lattimore, D. (1987). *The flame of peace: A tale of the Aztecs*. New York: Harper & Row.

Marrin, A. (1986). *The Aztecs and Spaniards: Cortez and the conquest of Mexico*. New York: Atheneum.

White, C. (1976). *César Chávez, man of courage*. Champaign, IL: Gerrard.

Native Americans

Carter, F. (1990). *The education of Little Tree*. Albuquerque, NM: University of New Mexico Press.

Erdrich, L. (1989). Writers' voices selected from *Love medicine*. New York: Readers House.

Esbensen, B. (1988). *The star maiden*. Boston: Little, Brown.

Freedman, R. (1988). *Buffalo hunt*. New York: Holiday.

George, J. (1987). *Water sky*. New York: Harper & Row.

Highwater, J. (1998). *I wear the morning star*. New York: Harper & Row.

Hortze, S. (1990). *A circle unbroken*. New York: Clarion.

Hudson, J. (1992). *Dawn rider*. New York: Philomel.

Hudson, J. (1989). *Sweetgrass*. New York: Philomel.

Paulsen, G. (1992). *Canyons*. New York: Delacorte.

the stages of learning. At the acquisition level, materials should provide opportunities for extensive teacher participation. For example, to teach writing skills to your students, you may use materials that explain how to write a variety of sentence types and then require you to model what to do when writing sentences.

After your students have acquired skills, they need to practice them to gain fluency. Students should practice first in a controlled or guided situation under close supervision, then in independent situations. Therefore, you should select and develop a wide variety of materials and provide opportunities for extensive student involvement. Practice materials should foster participation on the part of students. You may use workbooks, magazines, practice exercises, audiotapes, software programs, and games to develop fluency in writing. In addition, you may use charts and graphs to monitor each student's progress.

After students have demonstrated fluency, you should provide instructional materials that allow them to maintain their skills. At this stage, you should provide materials that will encourage frequent use of the skills. Students with special needs can practice writing a variety of things to maintain their writing skills (such as a letter to the editor). In addition, maintenance is frequently enhanced by learning centers, where students work independently on such skills as writing different sentence types and writing reports.

The final stage of learning involves the generalization of skills across situations and settings. For example, you should help students identify the opportunities for using writing in real-life materials. Thus, you should select materials that require students to apply their writing skills to the types of writing they do in content area classes (e.g., English), on the job (e.g., taking orders), and personally (e.g., writing letters). One high school student confided to her teacher that her letters to her boyfriend were easier to write after she improved her writing skills.

 ACTIVITY 4.1

Examine a commercially produced instructional material for reading or literature and answer the following questions:

1. How does the material meet the needs of the students?
2. Is the material motivating and related to real life?
3. Does it provide opportunity for social interaction?
4. Does it share information about diversity?
5. Which stage of learning does it address?

(Answers for this activity and others are found in the Instructor's Manual.)

ANALYZING INSTRUCTIONAL MATERIALS

It is important to analyze instructional materials for their appropriateness for students to decide whether to incorporate them into the instructional program. Many commercial products are not appropriate because they possess characteristics that make their use extremely difficult for students with special needs. There are many reasons for the ineffectiveness of commercial materials, curricula, programs, and textbooks:

1. *The readability of text may be too difficult.* Many materials are written on a reading level that may be challenging for students with special needs. Sentences may be too long and complex, and vocabulary may be unnecessarily difficult, as in "The man, addressing the audience before him, told them that he had repented for all of his past offenses" instead of "The man told the people he was sorry for what he did."
2. *The vocabulary is often highly sophisticated.* Complex words may be used when easier synonyms would be just as effective (see preceding example). Unfortunately, when technical terms are introduced in some content

materials, definitions are omitted or not clearly stated. Wiig and Semel (1984) suggest the use of only five unfamiliar vocabulary words per lesson for students who have language or learning disabilities.

3. ***Too many concepts may be presented at one time.*** Students with special needs benefit when concepts are introduced one at a time. Unfortunately, math materials sometimes present more than one type of problem on a page. For example, in one text we examined, the division problems ($24/8 =$ ____ ; $38/5 =$ ____ ; and $215/3 =$ ____) required three different skills and levels of competence but were presented on the same page. Notice that the first problem can be divided evenly, the second has a remainder, and the third involves a two-digit quotient with a remainder. Each type should be mastered before the next is introduced.

4. ***The sequencing of skills may be inappropriate.*** Students with special needs may experience problems when skills are taught out of sequence. For instance, students should be taught initial consonant sounds before they are introduced to the concept of consonant blends (Spache & Spache, 1977).

5. ***Directions are not always clear.*** Some materials use different words for the same directions, as in the case of "Circle the best answer" and "Put a line around the best answer." It is less confusing for students if directions are worded consistently on assignments and tests.

6. ***There are insufficient opportunities for practice and review.*** Many workbooks, textbooks, and other printed products move too quickly, failing to provide sufficient practice. For example, students should spend sufficient time learning how to subtract two-digit numbers *without* regrouping before attempting similar problems *with* regrouping. Many commercial materials do not incorporate a review of previously learned skills in practical, relevant situations. For example, once students in an employability skills class have learned the steps for job interviewing, they need to apply those skills through role-playing scenarios, and videotaping. Students with special needs require practice to become fluent and to maintain a skill.

7. ***Key points and terms may not be given adequate emphasis.*** Printed products do not always highlight, print in bold type, print in italics, or define the most important terms and ideas. This may cause difficulty for students who do not easily identify key points and terms.

8. ***Organization, format, and layout are sometimes confusing.*** Printed materials do not always begin with an advance organizer or introduction of what is to come (e.g., list of objectives, key vocabulary list, outline), nor do they conclude with a postorganizer (e.g., summary, list of important points, questions). In addition, when tables, graphs, and illustrations are placed far away from the text that describes them, they may confuse students or be ignored, as the students do not see the connection between the text and the graphic aid. Imagine trying to follow an explanation of how to record checks in a check register, when the instructions are on one page and a diagram of the check register is on another. In addition, pages may be cluttered with too much information. Crowded formats may confuse students and discourage them from even beginning a task. Students may be unable to pinpoint relevant information and screen out nonessential information when a page is overcrowded. Pages with lots of white space are more student friendly.

9. ***Materials may be unmotivating and uninteresting.*** Some commercially produced materials simply are not appealing or interesting because of format, level of difficulty, lack of color and illustrations, subject matter, age level targeted, typeface, or lack of relevance and functionality. Thus, they may not hold the learner's attention.

10. *Materials and text are sometimes too abstract.* Some written materials contain long passages of text with no clues to the definitions of abstract vocabulary and concepts. For example, a social studies chapter on justice, democracy, and freedom may not make these concepts concrete. Another example is math material that contains the term *congruent* with no examples, definitions, or illustrations of the term.

11. *Students may be limited in their response modes.* Unfortunately, some materials require only one type of response from students. For example, a science text that provides only end-of-chapter questions limits response. In contrast, a science text that provides suggestions for experiments, topics for discussion, suggestions for group activities, ideas for field trips, and chapter questions provides a variety of ways for students to respond.

12. *A variety of ethnic, cultural, and gender groups may not be represented or they may be inaccurately represented.* Some instructional materials do not include exposure to a variety of ethnic and cultural groups and genders, thereby limiting their appeal. This omission may communicate to students that some ethnic and cultural groups are less important than others (Gollnick & Chinn, 1990). Some materials include descriptions of people and activities that stereotype individuals in terms of culture, ethnic group, religion, gender, or age. Biases may exist within both the printed and graphic sections of materials (Baca & Cervantes, 1989). Although some progress has been made, Asian-Americans, Latinos, Native Americans, and women continue to be underrepresented in instructional materials (Hernandez, 1989).

The U.S. Department of Education, Office of Special Education Projects, which focused on instructional materials for students with mild disabilities, identified features that are typically examined in a textbook analysis: vocabulary, reading level, and concept development (Burnette, 1987). Knowing the reading levels of your students and of a textbook helps you judge the suitability of the text. Analyzing a textbook as part of your selection process helps you determine the amount of repetition, review, and material that is included. You should be sure that your students can handle the concept load and that the text provides ample opportunities for your students to check their understanding. Supplementary materials may include study aids, activity sheets, and overviews. You should also make sure that the format (layout, print, graphics) is compatible with the needs of your students. By analyzing elementary and secondary textbooks for content, organization, supplementary materials, and format, you can identify elements that cause problems for students and then adapt the textbooks accordingly.

You may also want to check the readability level of your textbooks and other reading materials. Typically, readability formulas are used to evaluate the complexity of the sentences in a passage (e.g., sentence length) and the level of difficulty of the vocabulary (word length or frequency). Figure 4.1 contains the Fry Readability Graph for Estimating Readability. You can use these steps to obtain a general idea of the difficulty level of a passage. Although readability formulas are typically used to determine readability level, they should be used with caution and as only one means of evaluating the appropriateness of a text or reading passage. Standal (1978) recommends using a readability formula as a "general indicator of a possible range of materials" (p. 646) and a good starting point for estimating the readability of a passage.

Most readability formulas are based on sentence complexity and vocabulary and do not take into consideration other aspects of a textbook, such as the way it is organized and formatted (headings, graphic aids, important points, definitions in margins, etc.). Beals

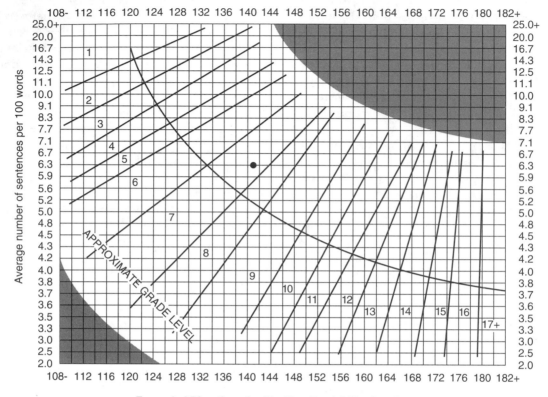

GRAPH FOR ESTIMATING READABILITY—EXTENDED
by Edward Fry, Rutgers University Reading Center, New Brunswick, NJ 08904

Average number of syllables per 100 words

Expanded Directions for Working Readability Graph

1. Randomly select three (3) sample passages and count out exactly 100 words each, beginning with the beginning of a sentence. Do count proper nouns, initializations, and numerals.
2. Count the number of sentences in the hundred words, estimating length of the fraction of the last sentence to the nearest one-tenth.
3. Count the total number of syllables in the 100-word passage. If you don't have a hand counter available, an easy way is to simply put a mark above every syllable over one in each word, then when you get to the end of the passage, count the number of marks and add 100. Small calculators can also be used as counters by pushing numeral 1, then push the + sign for each word or syllable when counting.
4. Enter graph with *average* sentence length and *average* number of syllables; plot dot where the two lines intersect. Area where dot is plotted will give you the approximate grade level.
5. If a great deal of variability is found in syllable count or sentence count, putting more samples into the average is desirable.
6. A word is defined as a group of symbols with a space on either side; thus, *Joe, IRA, 1945,* and *&* are each one word.
7. A syllable is defined as a phonetic syllable. Generally, there are as many syllables as vowel sounds. For example, *stopped* is one syllable and *wanted* is two syllables. When counting syllables for numerals and initializations, count one syllable for each symbol. For example, *1945* is four syllables, *IRA* is three syllables, and *&* is one syllable.

Figure 4.1 Fry Readability Formula

Note. This "extended graph" does not outmode or render earlier (1968) version inoperative or inaccurate; it is an extension of the earlier version. (REPRODUCTION PERMITTED—NO COPYRIGHT)

(1989) suggests that teachers should also evaluate vocabulary load, syntax, and style and recommends the following steps:

1. Determine the reading level of the student who will be using the text/material.
2. Select an easy-to-use readability formula, such as the Fry Readability Formula (Fry, 1968), to get a general estimate of readability (see Figure 4.1).
3. Examine the passages that you used to determine readability, and mark any words that the student might not understand (those that require direct instruction or use of context).
4. Analyze the syntax in the passage by identifying the basic sentence types.
5. Compare the sentence types typically used by the student (e.g., simple, compound, complex) with those found in the passage.
6. Analyze the style of the writing by looking for anything that might cause problems for the student.

By analyzing material using a readability formula to obtain a general indication of a range of materials (Standal, 1978) and assessing vocabulary load, syntax, and style (Beals, 1989), you should be able to judge the suitability of reading materials for your students. Remember also to take into consideration the characteristics of the reader as you make your selection of materials that are reader friendly.

There are numerous forms and checklists available, both commercial or teacher-made (like the one following), for teachers to use when analyzing instructional materials for students. You should use some type of evaluation procedure to help you decide whether to use a given material as it is, use it with modifications, or not use it at all. In addition to evaluating materials themselves, some teachers borrow or obtain sample sets of commercial materials from publishers and ask their students to try them out and provide feedback about them.

Complete the following:

Title: _____

Author: _____

Publisher: _____

Copyright: _____

Cost: _____

Purpose: _____

Rate the following:

	Acceptable	Unacceptable
Directions	_____	_____
Readability	_____	_____
Sequencing	_____	_____
Interest level	_____	_____
Pace	_____	_____
Examples	_____	_____
Opportunities for practice	_____	_____
Opportunities for self-monitoring	_____	_____
Multicultural emphasis	_____	_____

Respond to the following:

1. How would you use this material (e.g., supplementary, required, to help with generalization)? _____
2. In what type(s) of instructional arrangement(s) would you use this material (e.g., individual, group)? _____
3. Give your overall impression of the material.

_____

◆ **ACTIVITY 4.2**

Select a classroom material (kit, program, game, workbook) and analyze it using the teacher-made materials analysis form previously discussed. Present the material and your findings to the class. Now, select a passage from this text or from an elementary or secondary textbook and apply the Fry Readability Formula. Discuss your results with the class.

ADAPTING MATERIALS

Once you have analyzed materials and identified any shortcomings, you may need to adapt the materials for use with students who have special needs. Materials should be usable under different instructional conditions with students who have varying abilities. If students experience difficulty with assignments or activities, teachers may make changes to help meet their needs. The number of students with disabilities being educated in general education classrooms is continuing to grow (Fuchs & Fuchs, 1994), thus increasing the need for general education teachers to be knowledgeable about adapting materials and instruction. Unfortunately, observational studies of actual instruction provided by general education teachers to mainstream students show that few, if any, adaptations in instruction are being made (Baker & Zigmond, 1990; McIntosh, Vaughn, Schumm, Haager, & Lee, 1993). Therefore, one of the most important roles of the special education teacher is to assist general education teachers in the adaptation of materials and instruction to ensure the successful participation of students with special needs in the general classroom community.

Printed Products

Printed products include textbooks, workbooks, worksheets, transparencies, kits with cards or written information, tests and quizzes, and flash cards—in short, anything that contains written text. Following are areas to modify and techniques that you may utilize for students with special needs.

Readability

To modify the readability level:

1. Reword content by shortening sentences and simplifying vocabulary. Table 4.3 provides an example of how to reword test items, while maintaining the original intent of the questions.

2. Provide outlines or study guides to accompany the text.
3. Highlight essential information.
4. Limit the amount of information on a page.
5. Make the topic sentence of a paragraph the initial sentence (Wood & Wooley, 1986).

Vocabulary

To modify vocabulary:

1. Use the marginal gloss technique. Write terms and their definitions in the margins of a textbook page (Figure 4.2).
2. Underline or highlight key terms.
3. Locate all boldface, italicized, or new concept words from the text and list them with the corresponding page number (Wood & Wooley, 1986).
4. Record essential words, definitions, and sentences on language master cards or on audiotapes.
5. Provide vocabulary lists or glossaries with simplified definitions and use the words in sentences.

Presentation of Concepts

To modify the presentation of concepts:

1. Supplement print material with concept-teaching procedures.
2. Present concepts one at a time.
3. Provide visual supplements, such as transparencies, illustrations, and diagrams.
4. Use modeling and demonstration to clarify concepts.
5. Use games, manipulatives, and hands-on activities to reinforce concepts.
6. Draw upon the different cultural backgrounds and experiences of your students to make concepts meaningful.

General Comprehension

To increase understanding of materials:

1. Include prereading organizers and end-of-text summaries.
2. Provide study guides or outlines.

Table 4.3 Test Questions with Lowered Readability

These are examples of how you can rewrite test questions in order to lower the readability level. Notice that the original intent of each question is maintained.

Original	Earthquakes are produced by what forces within the earth?
Revised	What causes earthquakes?
Original	Compare and contrast the personal attributes and characteristics of Ulysses S. Grant and Robert E. Lee.
Revised	How were Ulysses S. Grant and Robert E. Lee alike? How were they different?
Original	What is the sensation of seeing two objects when only one is viewed?
Revised	What is double vision?
Original	Discuss the rationale of the secessionists in regard to their threat to secede from the union in 1860.
Revised	Why did the southern states decide to leave the union in 1860?
Original	According to the Gadsden Purchase, the United States procured thousands of square miles of unsettled land located in New Mexico and Arizona along the southern borders of both states.
Revised	The Gadsden Purchase gave the United States unsettled land along the southern border of New Mexico and Arizona.
Original	List the four primary taste sensations that are each sensitive to a particular kind of chemical stimulus.
Revised	List the four primary taste sensations.
Original	Describe the three environmental conditions required for the prolific growth of mold and mildew.
Revised	List three things mold and mildew need in order to grow.
Original	Crystal Thompson needs insurance for her personal belongings, but not for her residence, since she lives in an apartment. If her annual insurance premium is $63.00, what amount will she have paid in three years?
Revised	Crystal Thompson lives in an apartment and needs to insure her belongings. The insurance premium costs $63.00 a year (annually). How much will she pay in three years?

Adapted from D. A. Murphy, C. C. Meyers, S. Olesen, K. McKean, and S. H. Custer, *Exceptions: A Handbook of Inclusion Activities for Teachers of Students at Grades 6–12 with Mild Disabilities* (Longmont, CO: Sopris Press, 1996).

Figure 4.2 Marginal Gloss Technique

3. Insert stop points in text and have students summarize what they have read.
4. Include periodic reviews in the form of statements or questions.
5. Have students generate their own questions about printed materials.
6. Highlight main ideas in one color and supporting details in another. Post a key to the coding system in the classroom.
7. Give short, frequent quizzes instead of one long test.
8. Provide summaries on tapes.
9. Use graphic organizers (Figure 4.3).
10. Conduct brainstorming sessions.

Directions

To clarify written directions:

1. Simplify the directions.
2. Shorten the directions.

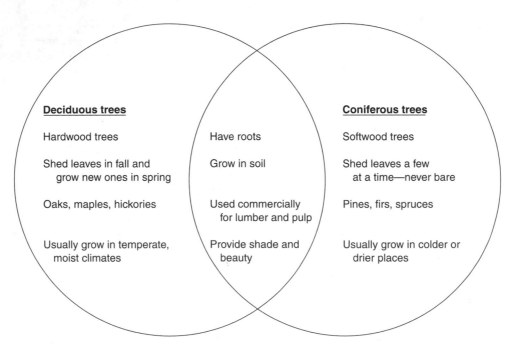

Figure 4.3   Graphic Organizer

3. Use concise, boldface directions.
4. Put the words typically used in directions on language master cards.
5. Highlight the key words in a set of directions (e.g., "**Write** a *t* in the blank if the answer is **true** and an *f* if the answer is **false.**").
6. Have the students underline what they are supposed to do (e.g., "<u>Write</u> your answer <u>in the blank</u> provided for you.").
7. In a set of multiple directions, use colored dots or numbers to differentiate the separate directions (Lambie, 1980).
8. Record directions on audiocassette.

Practice
To provide sufficient practice:

1. Have students move laterally before they move vertically to a new skill (e.g., have students practice multiplying one-digit numbers by one-digit numbers to mastery level before you teach them to multiply one-digit numbers by two-digit numbers).

2. Supplement practice in printed products with games, audiotapes, and manipulatives.
3. Provide repetition, review, and application of skills.
4. Provide opportunities to practice previously taught skills within learning centers.

Manageability of Materials
To increase the manageability of printed materials:

1. Shorten assignments by cutting worksheets in half or circling even-numbered questions for students to complete.
2. Clip a piece of paper to a page so that it covers half of the page, and have the student complete the other half.
3. Draw a box around the questions that the student should answer (Figure 4.4).
4. Use bookmarks to help students locate words and keep their place.
5. Underline or highlight specific information that is being introduced or emphasized.

Figure 4.4 Shortening an
Assignment

Name _____ Date _____

Directions: Write your answers to the subtraction problems in the space provided.

Do the problems that are inside the box.

1. $5.10
    −2.51
	2. $6.28
	    −2.99
		3. $4.43
		    −1.76
			4. $8.11
			    −5.86

5. $7.56
    −6.78
	6. $4.41
	    −3.85
		7. $9.05
		    −2.79
			8. $6.43
			    −4.78

9. $3.10
    −2.98
	10. $8.83
	    −5.99
		11. $6.76
		    −3.97
			12. $5.20
			    −4.91

13. $5.84
    −1.96
	14. $4.12
	    −3.87
		15. $8.03
		    −5.75
			16. $7.07
			    −2.49

(Problems 2, 3, 6, 7, 10, 11, 14, and 15 are enclosed inside a box.)

6. Mask out certain areas of print material to emphasize specific concepts, eliminate unnecessary visual stimuli, and encourage task performance.
7. Color-code newly introduced material, major concepts, or material to be memorized.
8. During presentations with transparencies, put a star by the important points and underline the details (Lambie, 1980).
9. Cover each transparency with a piece of paper and move the paper downward one line at a time (Lambie, 1980).
10. For students who have difficulty reading lengthy chapters, tape-record every other page. Have the student read one page and listen to the next (Lambie, 1980).

Organization

To organize printed materials in a clear, consistent manner:

1. Use advance and post organizers for each activity (e.g., give students an outline or a set of questions at the beginning of a lesson and print a summary or list important points on a transparency to use for review at the end of a lesson).

2. Reorganize poorly designed worksheets to create simple, easy-to-follow layouts and formats.
3. Provide graphics that are clear and understandable. Be sure graphics clarify and support the printed text (e.g., give students a photocopy of a check that has been filled out so that, as they read the text, they can see where the date, amount, signature, etc., belong).

Response Modes

To increase the options for student responses:

1. Allow students to tape their responses on audiocassette.
2. Provide opportunities for students to work in groups with games, flash cards, and hands-on activities in response to printed assignments.
3. Allow students to take tests orally.
4. Let students dictate stories, themes, and book reports.
5. Allow students to use the computer instead of writing spelling words, themes, and reports.
6. Provide role play and discussions.
7. Make materials self-correcting.

Motivation

To increase motivation and interest in printed materials:

1. Use concrete examples and demonstrations to supplement printed materials.
2. Draw upon prior knowledge to make material more interesting to students.
3. Supplement text materials with nontraditional printed materials, such as newspapers, magazines, and comic books (e.g., use stories dictated by students about popular athletes and other celebrities to develop reading lessons for students).
4. Allow students to use self-correcting materials and manipulatives.
5. Use materials that interest students while simplifying vocabulary.
6. Use audiovisual aids, such as filmstrips, videotapes, language master cards, computer software, and audiotapes to increase interest in printed materials.
7. Use Think/Pair/Share—after asking a question, ask students to find a partner, share their response to the question, remember their partner's response, and share with the class.
8. Incorporate multicultural materials into your classroom.

Content Delivery

Use audiotapes to present printed materials (Deshler & Graham, 1979). When you prepare tapes:

1. Highlight important points.
2. Include questions to facilitate recall and critical analysis.
3. Repeat key concepts.
4. Provide feedback.
5. Differentiate between main ideas and supporting details.
6. Explain how to use graphics.
7. Explain how to use chapter titles, boldface subheadings, section summaries, and questions to gain information.

8. Show students how to use a marking system (Figure 4.5) in connection with an audiotape (Deshler & Graham, 1979). Use a solid line to indicate that the material will be read verbatim on the audiotape. Use a dotted line to indicate that the material will be omitted from the audiotape. Use a wavy line to mean that the material will be paraphrased. Use a star to mean that students must stop the audiotape to complete an activity. Such a marking system helps students coordinate audiotaped material with printed material.

Abstract Concepts and Materials

To make materials more concrete:

1. Provide demonstrations.
2. Use concrete examples.
3. Present or construct models.
4. Use role play.
5. Associate concepts with music or art.
6. Relate materials to students' cultural backgrounds and experiences.

Chapter Questions

To modify end-of-chapter questions:

1. Ask fewer questions.
2. Reword the questions in simpler terms.
3. Increase response time.
4. Write the number of the page on which the response can be found next to each question at the end of the chapter (see Figure 4.6). Or next to the response in the chapter, write the number of the question, then highlight the response (Wood & Wooley, 1986).

Software Programs

Commercially produced software programs may not accommodate students with special needs. Furthermore, many commercial software programs are protected by programming codes that make them impossible to modify. Chiang (1986) suggests a number of modifications:

The Civil War was fought between the North and the South. Differences and major disagreements had developed between these two regions of our country. People on both sides tried to figure out ways to solve problems and work out differences. Although some of the suggestions were promising, nothing seemed to last. The two sides seemed doomed to disagree.

One of the reasons the North and the South differed to such a degree was that the two regions were developing so differently. The North was developing into a major manufacturing center with its textile mills and its emphasis on trade with other countries. Factories were plentiful and were run by thousands of immigrants arriving daily from across the sea.

On the other hand, the South was developing into a major agricultural area with cotton as its major crop. The Southern plantation thrived on its cotton crop and exported it to other countries.

These differences between an agrarian society (the South) and one that focused on manufacturing and trade (the North) further divided the two regions. The North wanted to pass laws that would help its interests such as a tax on imported goods. This tax would make goods produced in the North look very attractive.

A tax on imported goods would not help the South. The Southerners wanted to pay the lowest price they could for manufactured goods. They opposed the idea of a tax on imported goods.

The Growth of Slavery in the South

Southerners used slaves to work their plantations and produce a bountiful cotton crop. Therefore, the increased emphasis on cotton as the South's major crop led to the growth of slavery.

Figure 4.5 Marking System

Directions: Read each question carefully. Next to each question is the page on which the answer may be found. Find the page in the chapter and look for the answer. Write your answers at the bottom of this paper.

1. What are bacteria? (Page 16)
2. What shape are bacteria? (Page 16)
3. Where do bacteria live? (Page 17)
4. How are bacteria harmful to us? (Page 19)
5. How are bacteria helpful to us? (Page 21)

Figure 4.6 Chapter Questions

1. *Add a word file editor.* A word file editor allows you to make a Dolch word list accessible to activities like *Hangman* and *Spell-n-Time.*
2. *Provide a performance summary upon quitting a program.* Performance summaries give students their scores in terms of number correct and rate before they abandon a program.
3. *Include clear, concise directions.* Be sure students can review the directions at any time, in case they have forgotten them or are confused about them.

4. *Provide opportunities for self-correction.* Self-correction encourages self-monitoring of performance and allows for error analysis.
5. *Provide prompts about where to enter the response.* Use a flashing cursor or question mark to show students where to enter the next response.
6. *Control the duration of the screen display.* Lengthening the duration of the display may prove advantageous to students.

For an extensive discussion of technology-related materials and software programs, see Chapter 11.

SELECTING, ANALYZING, AND ADAPTING MATERIALS FOR STUDENTS FROM CULTURALLY AND LINGUISTICALLY DIVERSE POPULATIONS

Baca and Cervantes (1989) suggest 10 guidelines to follow in making decisions about materials. Some of their recommendations overlap suggestions in the previous discussion and therefore are not repeated; however, others have not been mentioned and are important to consider. Baca and Cervantes (1989) recommend that teachers include appropriate cultural experiences in the materials they develop or adapt. For example, Ms. Higgins developed a unit called "Holidays Around the World" for her primary students. She teaches the students to sing a song in five different languages. For her discussion of customs, she presents a different holiday custom from each country and encourages the students to share a holiday custom that their families practice.

Baca and Cervantes (1989) suggest that teachers continue to try out different materials and adaptations until they achieve an appropriate education plan for all students who are culturally and linguistically diverse. For example, in her history class, Mrs. O'Mara has to adapt and supplement the history textbook significantly to include the perspective of Native Americans in the study of Western expansion. The textbook presents only the U.S. government's perspective. She feels that the Native American students in her class and students of other cultures should read more than one perspective.

Teachers should be knowledgeable about particular cultures and heritages and the compatibility of the cultures and heritages with selected materials. For example, a text that is limited to the contributions of the European settlers in the United States does not present a balanced perspective (Gollnick & Chinn, 1990). Many students would fail to learn about the contributions of their own cultural groups in the development of their country. Such a text would have to be significantly modified or supplemented.

Ortiz (1989) recommends that teachers consider specific factors when adapting materials for students who have limited English proficiency (LEP). He suggests that teachers analyze vocabulary and syntax for verbal load and regional forms and rewrite the text if necessary. He feels that teachers should support texts with pictures, media, and action to make the content understandable. For example, Mr. Bonavidez uses videotapes and CD-ROM technology to supplement his discussion of famous inventors. His students are able to see different parts of the United States and the world as each videotape and CD-ROM traces the origin and background of one inventor. Mr. Bonavidez provides glossaries that contain terms, definitions, and pictures to help students who are not proficient in English.

Winzer and Mazurek (1998) state that the materials teachers use have a major impact on students' cognitive and affective domains and can help develop understandings. They recommend that you include the following in your classroom:

1. Fiction, nonfiction, dual-language texts, poetry, magazines, and newspapers.
2. Books that have predictable features, invite conversation, have meaningful illustrations, support the curriculum, and are linked to the student's culture.

3. Materials that are culturally appropriate, meaningful, accurate, and in the student's language.
4. Manipulatives, technology, and bulletin boards.

 ACTIVITY 4.3

Locate the instructional material you analyzed in Activity 4.2 and think about the limitations you identified. Now, use some of the strategies we've presented to modify the material to make it more appropriate for students with special needs. Remember to include multicultural and gender considerations.

◇ **IMPORTANT POINTS**

1. When selecting instructional materials, teachers should be aware of individual learner needs, interest and motivation levels of materials, opportunities that materials provide for social interaction, and the level of attention to diversity within the materials.
2. Materials should be developmentally, culturally, linguistically, age, and interest appropriate for students.
3. Instructional materials may be used to address the needs of students at each of the stages of learning (acquisition, fluency, maintenance, and generalization).
4. It is important to analyze instructional materials for their appropriateness with students to decide whether to incorporate them into the instructional program.
5. Materials and texts that are not appropriate for students with special needs in special or inclusive education settings may be adapted.
6. Strategies for adapting printed products include highlighting, color coding, and simplifying, among others.

7. To facilitate the effective and appropriate use of instructional materials with students who are culturally and linguistically diverse, strategies include modification of vocabulary; use of media, pictures, and glossaries; and incorporation of supplementary materials that emphasize different languages and cultures.

DEVELOPING MATERIALS

Some instructional materials cannot be adapted or modified to a level that is acceptable for use with students who have special needs. For example, we have worked with some math and spelling materials that required an almost complete reconstruction because of inappropriate sequencing of skills, problems with format, and print quality. Other materials have been inappropriate because of cultural or gender bias. Still other materials have introduced too much new vocabulary.

Because of such problems and others, you may choose to develop your own materials. When developing instructional materials, avoid the problems that are characteristic of ineffective commercial products. For example, design materials that provide sufficient practice, repetition, and review and consider factors that will affect the performance of your students. Consider how the learner is going to interact with the material. The input may be auditory, with directions given on an audiotape, and the output may be written, with the student required to write something. Vary the input (auditory, visual) and output (written, verbal), depending upon the activity and the characteristics of your students.

You should also attend to the complexity of the material and match it to the level of your students. Some teachers develop manipulative materials to help their students better grasp abstract concepts. The complexity of the material can also be related to the stages of learning.

For example, when Ms. Roberts teaches place value to her students, she gives them popsicle sticks to help them understand the concept (acquisition stage).

As you develop materials, consider how your students will receive feedback. Some of your materials should be self-correcting, so that your students can monitor their own performance. Computers can provide automatic feedback. With other materials, you should provide positive and corrective feedback to your students.

In materials development, you should give careful consideration to the concept load of the material. This includes the number of new concepts you present at one time, the amount of practice you provide, and the rate of presentation. For example, Mr. Saunders spends a class period with his high school students going over a diagram that he developed after examining several textbooks. He consolidated into one diagram nearly everything he could find on the topic of prejudice. Concentrating on the one concept, the class defines prejudice, identifies characteristics of it, and gives examples.

In materials development, you should also consider your level of involvement with the materials and whether it is extensive (teacher-directed) or minimal (student-directed, individual, or group). Rewriting materials and then presenting them to your students (teacher-directed) will require quite an investment of your time. Giving the students self-correcting materials requires less teacher interaction and time. Finally, you should consider the affective aspects of materials, such as cultural emphasis, age bias, and gender bias.

Development of Specific Materials

Teacher-made materials may include worksheets, folder activities, educational games, and self-correcting materials. These materials may increase the effectiveness of the overall instructional program because they ensure individualization and because they are designed to reinforce, motivate, and enhance pupil participation. For example, Marco, a third grader, had trouble learning vocabulary in its written form in his reading workbook. Ms. Micelli, his special education teacher, made him a word bank that contained the reading vocabulary on language master cards. Marco practiced his words on the language master, which presented the words to him both visually and aurally. Marco said each word aloud as he practiced and again, later, as Ms. Micelli checked him. Ms. Micelli noted Marco's progress on a chart that listed each of the words. Marco learned the words quickly because he received positive and corrective feedback and found the material interesting and motivating.

Laurie, a seventh-grade student, had just been taught a technique to improve her comprehension of reading material. Because she works successfully in groups and learns well from others, her teacher, Mr. Nohmura, grouped her with two other students to practice, repeat, and review the steps of the comprehension monitoring technique. Mr. Nohmura developed worksheets for the students to use for written practice, let them verbally rehearse the steps with one another, and then, using a teacher-made checklist, evaluated each student for mastery of the steps. Use of the teacher-made materials and attention to affective concerns, in combination with learner interactions with the materials and feedback and evaluation, increased Laurie's opportunities for success.

Worksheets

In developing worksheets for students, you should make directions clear and concise and be careful not to overload the page with items. Worksheets should focus on one concept at a time and provide adequate practice. Worksheets should be manageable in appearance, not overwhelming, with a clear, easy-to-follow, inviting format. In addition to developing your own worksheets, you may also adapt or rewrite worksheets. Figure 4.7 contains a sample of a poorly designed worksheet. Figure 4.8 shows how that worksheet has been adapted.

Notice how the poorly designed worksheet is crowded and lacks clear, specific directions. For example, there are no directions for Part A (the true/false items), there are incomplete directions for Part B (the vocabulary section), and the directions lack specificity in Part C (the written response section). The list of 20

words looks overwhelming, and the worksheet looks crowded. The adapted worksheet is easier on the eye because of the way it is organized (e.g., boxes around sections and better spacing). Introductory directions are provided and directions for Parts I, II, and III are clear and specific. Part I contains boxes in which students may write their responses, and the directions specify that students are to write *true or false*. The directions for Part II state where to write the words and definitions. The long list of 20 words has been divided into

---

Name _____ Date_____

Read Chapter 5 about the rainforest and answer the following questions.

A. TRUE/FALSE
   1. Rainforests are characterized by vast, dry, sunny regions.
   2. Destruction of the world's rainforests may affect plants, animals, and climate.
   3. It is humid and rains almost every day in a rainforest.
   4. Rainforests are dense forests that are found in tropical regions around the equator.
   5. Rainforests are very heavily populated areas with many people.
   6. The trees of a rainforest grow so close together that sunlight rarely reaches the forest floor.

B. Look up the following words in the Glossary of your social studies book.
   1. uninhabited
   2. vegetation
   3. tropical
   4. frontier
   5. agriculture
   6. lumbering
   7. ecologists
   8. economy
   9. climate
  10. temperature
  11. Amazon
  12. equator
  13. continents
  14. minerals
  15. extinction
  16. humidity
  17. minerals
  18. petroleum
  19. resources
  20. carbon dioxide

C. Read another story or article about rainforests. Compare the information in Chapter 5 with your new article. Or write a story about a rainforest including how it would look, sound, smell, and feel.

Figure 4.7 Example of a Poorly Designed Worksheet

Name _____ Date _____

The Rainforest

Directions: Read pages 43–52 in Chapter 5 of your social studies book. Then complete Parts I, II, and III about the rainforest.

Part I—True/False

Directions: Read each of the following statements. Write "True" in the box if the statement is true, and "False" if it is false.

1. Rainforests are characterized by vast, dry, sunny regions.
2. Destruction of the world's rainforests may affect plants, animals, and climate.
3. It is humid and rains almost every day in a rainforest.
4. Rainforests are dense forests that are found in tropical regions around the equator.
5. Rainforests are very heavily populated areas with many people.
6. The trees of a rainforest grow so close together that sunlight rarely reaches the forest floor.

Part II—Vocabulary

Directions: Look up the following words in the Glossary in the back of your social studies book. Write the word and its definition in your notebook.

List 1	List 2
1. uninhabited	1. lumbering
2. vegetation	2. ecologists
3. tropical	3. climate
4. agriculture	4. temperature
5. frontier	5. economy

List 3	List 4
1. carbon dioxide	1. extinction
2. Amazon	2. humidity
3. equator	3. petroleum
4. populated	4. resources
5. continents	5. minerals

Part III—Take Your Choice

Directions: Complete *either* Choice #1 or Choice #2.

Choice #1

1st — Read another story or article about rainforests.

2nd — Write two things that are the same as the information in Chapter 5 of your book.

3rd — Write two new things that you learned.

Choice #2

Write a story about a rainforest including how it would look, sound, smell, and feel.

Figure 4.8 Example of an Adapted Worksheet

four smaller, more manageable lists. The directions for Part III clearly state that students have a choice of *two* activities for the written response question.

You can make worksheets self-correcting by printing the answers on the back, on the bottom (upside down), or along the right margin (which can be folded over to conceal them). You may also provide oral and written feedback. Whenever you utilize worksheets, be sure they serve a valid purpose and are not used merely to fill time.

Folder Activities

File folders meet the needs of students by providing opportunities for practice and reinforcement of a wide range of skills. File folders are convenient to use and store, and teachers who float from classroom to classroom can easily transport them. Because folder activities are usually student directed, they should contain clear, concise directions. Many folder activities include some means of self-monitoring, such as access to an answer key.

Folders may be constructed to include activities that are multilevel. For example, in her preparation of a math unit, Mrs. Barkwell set up folder activities that used a restaurant menu. In one folder activity, students were asked to locate the cost of various items, such as hamburgers, soft drinks, french fries, and milkshakes. In another folder activity, students were required to order several items and compute the total cost. In still another activity, students had to figure the total cost plus tax. In a more advanced folder activity, students determined the total cost and tax, then figured out how much change they would receive from $10 and from $20. Notice how the difficulty level of the activities varied, making them appropriate for students functioning at several different levels. The activities were set up to be self-correcting, with the answers written on the reverse side (e.g., a card with a picture of a hamburger on one side and the price on the back).

Educational Games

Educational games do not take the place of instruction, but they do provide motivating ways to help reinforce skills (Heit, 1980). By creating games, you help students attain skills and solve problems that are important to their success both in and out of school. A teacher-made game must provide (a) a clearly stated purpose, or rationale, and outcome; (b) complete yet uncomplicated directions and rules; (c) reinforcement and practice of skills already acquired; and (d) a method of monitoring and evaluating progress.

You may construct your own board game or use a commercial board. Little Kenny Publications has wipe-off game boards, cards, spinners, and game pieces available for purchase. You can use this generic equipment to create your own instructional games to support the sequential development of the academic skills your students need. The game boards can be adapted to any academic skill and content that you want to reinforce, including simplifying fractions, reviewing science vocabulary, and practicing long vowel sounds. You may also construct a spinner for a game by attaching a paper fastener to the center of a transparency. By drawing a circle on the transparency, dividing it into eighths, and writing numbers 1 through 8 in consecutive sections, you can make a generic spinner that is appropriate for use with any game and is usable with the entire class or a small group.

Cosgrove (1992) recommends creating board games from computer programs, or adapting boards from old, unused games (e.g., recycle a Candyland board by adding math fact questions to the color-coded game cards). Matrix boards (e.g., checkers) or a deck of cards may also be adapted (Cosgrove, 1992) to make Concentration and Jeopardy games for vocabulary and math.

Self-Correcting Materials

Many teachers include a self-correcting component in the materials they develop because of the importance of immediate feedback to learning.

Mercer, Mercer, and Bott (1984) point out some advantages of self-correcting materials:

◆ Students avoid practicing mistakes.
◆ Students learn better with immediate rather than delayed feedback.
◆ Students can function independently.
◆ Students tend to remain on task with self-correcting materials.

You can develop self-correcting materials in a variety of formats (e.g., answer on the back, audiocassette, matching, etc.). The following ideas are based on suggestions by Mercer, Mercer, and Bott (1984).

Answer on the Back. You can write a problem on one side of a card and put the answer on the back. You may use such cards for math facts and their answers or for vocabulary terms and their definitions. Alternatively, you can write terms or math facts and their answers on the same side of the card. Then cut each card in half in a different zigzag pattern, so the question is on one half of the card and the answer is on the other half. That way, the two parts fit together each time your students respond correctly. You may also use this technique for the states and their capitals.

Audiocassette. You can use an audiocassette to record a problem, question, or direction, then pause before dictating the answer. This self-correcting technique is also effective with spelling words, science vocabulary, and word problems.

Matching. For practicing a word and its abbreviation, a math problem and its answer, or a date in history and the event that took place on that date, prepare sets of cards with a problem or question on one card and the answer on another card. Be sure the back of each pair of cards contains some type of picture completion. After students respond to the problems, they should turn the cards over. If the answer is correct, the pictures should either match or fit together to complete an object or design.

 ACTIVITY 4.4

Part 1. Develop a math worksheet on telling time for a third-grade student. Make sure the directions are clear and the worksheet is self-correcting.

Part 2. Develop a self-correcting activity appropriate for an elementary student (such as states and their capitals) and one for a secondary student (such as subject-verb agreement).

◇ **IMPORTANT POINTS**

1. In developing instructional materials, it is important to provide sufficient practice, repetition, and review.
2. Key variables during materials development include the learner's interactions with the materials, the concept load, the extent of teacher involvement, and affective aspects of materials.
3. Teacher-made materials may include worksheets, folder activities, educational games, and self-correcting materials.

Development of Multilevel Learning Centers

A learning center is an area within the classroom that contains a collection of activities and materials to reinforce initial teaching, clarify concepts, provide drill and practice, enrich, and motivate (Cooper, 1981; Kaplan, Kaplan, Madsen, & Taylor, 1973). Learning centers do not replace the teacher, nor are they responsible for initial teaching. Instead, they provide opportunities for students to work independently with materials on their own level and with activities that are interesting, motivating, meaningful, and relevant. Learning centers may help your students become more self-directed, independent, and task oriented. Multilevel learning centers are frequently found in general education settings at all grade levels and are an effective way to meet the needs of academically diverse students in inclusive classrooms. When developing learning centers, consider (a) goals and functions, (b) key components, (c) organization, (d) development, (e) scheduling, (f) teacher and student roles, (g) record keeping, and (h) evaluation.

Goals and Functions

Teachers may use learning centers to meet a variety of goals. Kaplan et al. (1973) suggest using learning centers as vehicles for independent study, as follow-ups for teacher-taught lessons, as enrichment or extension activities, and as substitutes for regular assignments. You may use learning centers for either individual or group activities. Learning centers perform varied functions, including assessing, monitoring, and evaluating; reviewing, drilling, and practicing; reteaching; reinforcing; contracting; and increasing interest and motivation.

Cosgrove (1992) suggests that learning center activities may be organized by skills (punctuation, creative writing, fractions, listening), interests (sports, computers, archaeology), or integrated themes (using all content areas to teach specific objectives). For example, when teaching fraction skills, you could include a variety of activities for working with fractions:

◆ Following a recipe by measuring amounts of solids and liquids (¾ of a cup)
◆ Computing distances (5½ miles from your house to school)
◆ Completing worksheets with adding, subtracting, multiplying, and dividing fractions
◆ Providing activities that involve solving problems with fractions (dividing a pizza, sharing equally the proceeds from a garage sale)

Learning centers may be developed around student interests (topics not in the curriculum but interesting to students and related to content). Ms. Monroe developed a Sports Center in her classroom and motivated her students to extend their knowledge and thinking about topics such as:

◆ Ethical behavior in sports
◆ Athletes as role models

Integrated themes may complement a unit that you are teaching. For example, a teacher at the elementary level developed a "What's Bugging You?" center to enhance his unit on insects. He had the students:

◆ Write stories about each insect being studied (language arts)
◆ Solve math problems using insect manipulatives (math)
◆ Identify the insects that live in each region of the United States (science and social studies)
◆ Make models of insects utilizing various media (science and art)
◆ Describe jobs that involve insects (career education)

Notice how various content areas were incorporated to achieve the learning center goal of review, reinforcement, and enrichment of instruction about insects.

Figure 4.9 illustrates a learning center in which students are required to read and write about Alaska. Materials and activities revolve around the topic of the center. Student-developed materials, such as the scrapbook and summaries of articles or news broadcasts, could also be included as part of the center display.

Key Components

A learning center should possess multilevel capabilities; that is, it should include activities at a variety of levels, so that each of your students can work at his or her level. The materials and activities must not only cover a range of abilities, from simple to complex, but also include tasks that are concrete and tasks that are abstract. A learning center should be geared to the interests, abilities, and needs of

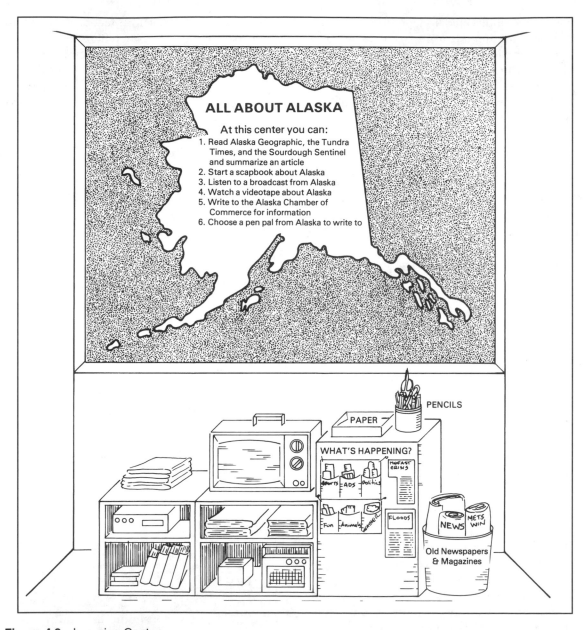

ALL ABOUT ALASKA

At this center you can:
1. Read Alaska Geographic, the Tundra Times, and the Sourdough Sentinel and summarize an article
2. Start a scrapbook about Alaska
3. Listen to a broadcast from Alaska
4. Watch a videotape about Alaska
5. Write to the Alaska Chamber of Commerce for information
6. Choose a pen pal from Alaska to write to

Figure 4.9   Learning Center

the students in that classroom (Kaplan et al., 1973). The basic components of a learning center are:

1. *A name or topic.* Examples: Alphabetizing, tall tales, mollusks, or recognizing individual differences.

2. *A wide variety of materials to support the theme, concept, or skill.* Examples: Games, audio and videotapes, worksheets, charts, books, manipulatives, puzzles, folder activities.

3. *Clear, complete directions about who can work at the center, how to complete the activities, how to*

correct work and record performance, when students are scheduled at the center, how many students can work at the center at one time, and which materials each student should use. Example: "Please consult the learning center schedule to find out what center to report to. Centers will be open from 9:00 to 10:30 Friday morning for all groups. Check the folder in your center for directions."

Organization

As you develop learning centers in inclusive classrooms, consider how to organize the centers within the physical environment. Special education teachers in pull-out models are frequently given small classrooms. They must make optimal use of the space they have, while providing a variety of resources for their students. Other special education teachers must be able to set up learning centers in general education classrooms, work with existing centers in those classrooms, or transport their learning centers from classroom to classroom.

Development

Construction of a learning center should be systematic and careful. You may use the following steps as a guide:

1. *Identify an area of need.* Example: Reading comprehension.
2. *Determine the objectives.* Examples: Identifying main idea, identifying supporting details, answering questions and retrieving information from text, paraphrasing, summarizing, sequencing, or selecting a title.
3. *Develop learning center activities.* These could take the form of file folder activities, games, word searches, manipulative activities, listening to audiotapes, reading, or writing. Examples:
   - Students complete a folder activity in which they match main idea and detail statements.
   - Students read a short story and then select the best name or title for the story.
   - Students create their own questions about a reading passage, give them to another

student, and provide feedback about the responses.

4. *Prepare clear, concise directions for the learning center overall and for each activity in the center.* Overall center directions are important so that students will know exactly which activities they are supposed to do. Clear directions for each activity increase the likelihood that the student will be able to work independently.
5. *Select, develop, and collect the materials and equipment to be used in the learning center.*
6. *Construct the learning center.* Drawing a sketch or floor plan may be helpful.
7. *Develop a schedule for learning center use.* Example: The center may be open for 2 hours in the morning and 1 hour in the afternoon, with specific students assigned to use it at different times.
8. *Develop a record-keeping system and a method of providing feedback and monitoring student progress.* Example: After students complete an activity, such as sequencing the events in a story, they check the answer key for the accuracy of their responses. They enter the name of the activity and their scores before and after corrections on the learning center log or checklist.

Scheduling

The way you schedule time for learning centers depends upon how they are used in your classroom. You must decide whether you want your students to have a voice in the scheduling or whether the scheduling will be teacher-directed. Time spent at the learning centers may be incorporated into students' daily assignments or be indicated on a separate schedule for learning centers. Once you have determined your needs and those of your students, select the scheduling technique that best suits your situation. You may utilize a variety of techniques to schedule students into learning centers, including (a) rotational scheduling, (b) use of contracts, and (c) assignment to centers based on diagnosed needs, interests, and daily work. Rotational scheduling involves having students rotate from one center to another at times that you specify. With contracts (Blackburn & Powell, 1976), teachers and students develop a contract, set goals, and decide what the student will accomplish in each learning center (see Figure 4.10). With assignment to centers, you assess each student's skills and interests, then assign students to centers or let them choose from specified centers. For example, after instructing students in small groups, Ms. Peterson assigns them learning center activities for practice.

Teacher and Student Roles

Teachers and students have different roles and expectations in relation to the development, use, maintenance, and evaluation of learning centers. You should develop learning centers in relation to the needs and interests of your students. Then you should identify the objectives that will meet these needs and incorporate them into the learning centers. You are responsible for setting up meaningful activities, clear directions, and effective methods of evaluation.

You should introduce one learning center at a time. Remember to change learning centers frequently to maintain student interest, motivation, and participation. Finally, prepare your students by providing a thorough orientation to the use and maintenance of centers as well as student behavior standards. Modeling and role playing are useful orientation strategies. During the orientation, thoroughly explain the roles of students in relation to learning centers. You should expect your students to follow directions, keep accurate and thorough records, exercise care when using materials and equipment, adhere to the prearranged schedule, and clean up and put away activities when finished. Also, you may ask students to evaluate the effectiveness of learning centers.

Record Keeping

Record keeping is extremely important in planning for and evaluating student learning. It makes your students more aware of their progress and increases their responsibility for their learning. It assists you in making data-based decisions about your students' performance. It yields records you can show to parents to report participation in specific activities or to demonstrate overall progress. For special education teachers using learning centers in pull-out programs, these records can be shared with mainstream teachers and used to make decisions about participation in general education classroom activities. For special education teachers who are providing consultative or itinerant services in the general education classroom, or who are co-teaching with the general education teacher, the records are valuable in discussing student progress and setting new goals. Because record keeping is so valuable, it is important to include it in learning center activities.

Both you and your students may evaluate progress in learning center activities. You may perform spot checks; evaluate folders, products, and completed work on a daily basis; review contracts; and schedule individual conferences with students. Your students may set goals and evaluate their progress toward those goals, utilize self-checking procedures, monitor their progress toward meeting the terms of their contracts, chart and graph their performance, and request conferences with you. Figure 4.11 shows an example of record keeping used to monitor a student's progress. Notice how the teacher, Mrs. Tinsdal, has provided feedback and how Mandy has set her own goals to work on. Records should be simple and uncomplicated and should communicate at a glance what the student has accomplished and how well he or she has done.

Evaluation

Of equal importance to the development of a learning center is the evaluation of the learning

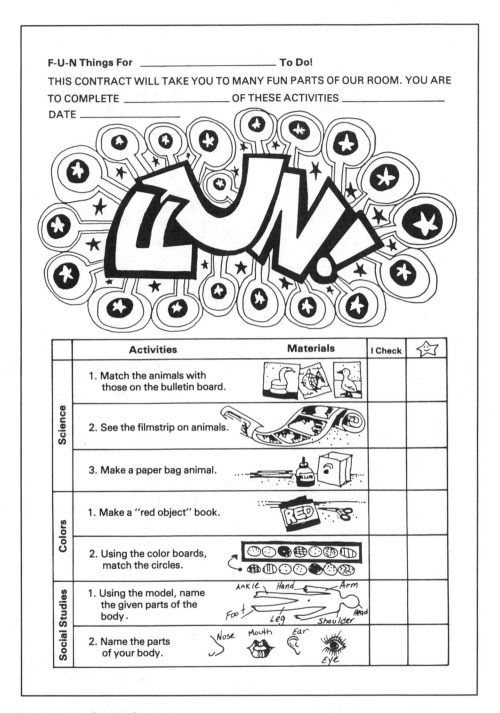

F-U-N Things For _____ **To Do!**

THIS CONTRACT WILL TAKE YOU TO MANY FUN PARTS OF OUR ROOM. YOU ARE

TO COMPLETE _____ OF THESE ACTIVITIES _____

DATE _____

	Activities	Materials	I Check	⭐
Science	1. Match the animals with those on the bulletin board.			
	2. See the filmstrip on animals.			
	3. Make a paper bag animal.			
Colors	1. Make a "red object" book.			
	2. Using the color boards, match the circles.			
Social Studies	1. Using the model, name the given parts of the body.			
	2. Name the parts of your body.			

Figure 4.10 Learning Center Contract

Note. From *One at a Time All at Once: The Creative Teacher's Guide to Individualized Instruction Without Anarchy* (p. 130) by J. E. Blackburn and W. C. Powell. A GoodYear book. Copyright © 1976 by Scott, Foresman and Company. Reprinted by permission.

Learning Center Check Sheet

Name <u>Mandy Markowicz</u>

Directions: Put a check mark next to the center you worked in each day. For example, if you worked on Creative Writing on Monday, put a check mark next to Creative Writing and under Monday.

Centers	Days				
	Mon.	Tues.	Wed.	Thur.	Fri.
Measurement	✓		✓		
Creative Writing		✓		✓	
Social Studies		✓		✓	
Reading	✓		✓		✓

Feedback from teacher:

Measurement <u>Excellent progress. All work correct.</u>

Creative Writing <u>Content and organization of "Trip Around the World" are outstanding.</u>

Social Studies <u>You need to add two more landforms to your map. Please check my note.</u>

Reading <u>Your quiz score shows you are using the paraphrasing strategy. Now, write a summary of "North Pole Adventure."</u>

Goals for next check sheet:

<u>I need to add two landforms to my map in social studies and write a summary of "North Pole Adventure"</u>

Teacher <u>Ms. Tinsdal</u>   Date <u>11/19</u>
Student <u>Mandy Markowicz</u> Date <u>11/19</u>

Figure 4.11   Learning Center Check Sheet

center. Before presenting a learning center to your students, you should ask yourself the following questions:

1. Does it have multiage, multilevel capabilities?
2. Is it interesting and age appropriate?
3. Does it have clear, concise directions?

4. Are a wide variety of activities and materials included?
5. Will students have opportunities to use different response modes?
6. Does the center have a clear purpose, along with objectives that relate to student needs?
7. Does the center have eye appeal?

8. Is the schedule workable?
9. Are record-keeping procedures included?
10. Is there a plan to orient students to the center?

If you responded positively to these questions, then you are ready to introduce learning centers into your instructional program.

 ## ACTIVITY 4.5

With four or five of your fellow students, assume the role of a teacher of students with special needs. Several of your students are included in multiage general education classrooms at the intermediate grade level. Identify the needs of your students, develop objectives, and select a theme for a learning center. Simulate the steps and procedures you would follow in developing the learning center, dividing the responsibilities for this task among group members. Be sure to include a list of materials, a sketch, directions, a time schedule, and methods for record keeping and monitoring progress. Present your learning center to the class. Ask another group to consider the 10 evaluation points provided in the chapter and evaluate your center.

 ## IMPORTANT POINTS

1. Learning centers should possess multiage and multilevel capabilities and be geared to the interests, abilities, and needs of students.
2. Teachers may use learning centers as vehicles for independent study, follow-ups to lessons, enrichment activities, and substitutes for regular assignments.
3. The basic components of a learning center include a name or theme, a variety of materials, and clear directions.
4. The steps involved in developing a learning center include (a) identify an area of need; (b) determine the objectives; (c) develop the skill or concept into learning, application, and extending activities; (d) prepare directions for the activities; (e) collect the materials; (f) construct the center; (g) develop a time schedule; and (h) develop a record-keeping system.
5. Teachers and students have different roles in the development, use, maintenance, and evaluation of learning centers.
6. Teachers should evaluate each learning center before they present it to students.

◆ DISCUSSION QUESTIONS

1. Provide examples to support the statement, "One of the most important roles of the special education teacher is to assist general education teachers in the adaptation of materials and instruction."
2. Discuss how you are going to provide materials in your classroom that are appropriate for culturally and linguistically diverse groups of students.
3. Justify the use of multilevel learning centers with elementary, middle, and high school students in special and general education settings.

5

COLLABORATIVE
CONSULTATION
AND
COMMUNICATION

The field of special education is u[ndergoing] many changes. Two major reform effor[ts] Chapter 1), the Regular Education Initia[tive] (Will, 1986) and inclusion (NASBE, 1992), have focused on redefining or restructuring the relationship between general and special education. Among the recommendations for implementing these reform efforts were that general and special educators increase their collaborative efforts in planning and providing instruction to students with disabilities in inclusive settings (Kamens, 1997; Stainback & Stainback, 1984; Wang & Reynolds, 1985). Increasing numbers of students with special needs are receiving services in general education classrooms. In order to provide successful experiences for these students, teachers need to become more involved in collaborative planning and problem solving (Voltz, Elliot, & Cobb, 1994). According to Bondy and Brownell (1997, p. 112), "teachers and other members of school communities are increasingly recognizing the need for collaboration." Collaborative interactions are occurring in inclusionary schools, where students previously excluded from their neighborhood schools are now included in general education classrooms (Friend & Bursuck, 1996; Stainback, Stainback, & Stefanich, 1996). It has become more the norm than the exception that teachers of children and adolescents with special needs are working less in isolation and more as members of an educational team. Thus, the ability to communicate and collaborate with other members of a team (general classroom teachers, administrators, paraprofessionals, other direct- and related-service providers, and families) may have a significant impact on the quality of services that special educators provide for their students.

ing the ra-
n, describ-
ollaborative
some of the
ative interac-
overcoming or

preventing them. Then we provide recommendations for planning and implementing paraprofessional programs, strategies for communicating and collaborating with parents/families, and a final comment about collaborating with other partners in the school and community.

TATION

In a dynamic ... stantly undergoing reform, school professi... s continue to search for alternative methods for serving students with special needs. An alternative that has received increased attention and support is that of collaborative consultation. Collaborative consultation originates from a triadic model (Tharp, 1975; Tharp & Wetzel, 1969). The triadic model consists of three components: (a) the target (T), or student with a problem; (b) the mediator (M), or someone who has the ability to influence the student; and (c) the consultant (C), or someone with the knowledge and skills to work with the mediator. Idol, Paolucci-Whitcomb, and Nevin (1994) indicate that consultants and mediators may be general education teachers, special education teachers, speech pathologists, principals, paraprofessionals, parents, or other members of the educational community. Correct use of the model results in participatory decision making, collaborative solutions to carefully specified problems, and shared responsibility for outcomes. Special education professionals refer to this as collaborative consultation. According to Idol, Paolucci-Whitcomb, and Nevin (1994):

> Collaborative consultation is an interactive process that enables people with diverse expertise to generate creative solutions to mutually defined problems. The outcome is enhanced, altered, and produces solutions that are different from those that the individual team members would produce independently. The major outcome of collaborative consultation is to provide comprehensive and

effective programs for students with special needs within the most appropriate context, thereby enabling them to achieve maximum constructive interaction with their nonhandicapped peers. (p. 1)

In collaborative consultation, participants such as general education teachers, special education teachers, parents, administrators, paraprofessionals, school counselors, employers, and speech pathologists serve as consultants in their respective areas of expertise, so that all participants have the opportunity to exchange their knowledge and skills (Blalock, 1997). Through this collaborative effort, it is possible to share information about a student's strengths and weaknesses and to identify potential teaching strategies and curricular adaptations that could prove beneficial (Knackendoffel, 1996). Successful resolution of problems is dependent upon the skills of the collaborators. Since most educators may not possess a strong background in collaborative strategies, it is recommended that they receive training in order to serve in collaborative roles (Berdine & Cegelka, 1995; Erchul & Conoley, 1991; Gersten, Darch, David, & George, 1991).

Rationale and Need for Collaborative Consultation

Collaboration between special and general educators is being viewed as an essential component in the success of students with disabilities who are being served in general education classes (Dettmer, Thurston, & Dyck, 1993; Pugach & Johnson, 1995; Voltz & Elliot, 1997). The field of education is moving toward increased integration and inclusion of students who are educationally heterogeneous and diverse (Bauwens, Hourcade, & Friend, 1989), necessitating greater collaboration among school professionals. The purpose of collaborative consultation in special education is to facilitate the cooperative efforts of general and special educators in developing specific interventions for students with learning and behavior problems (Pugach & Johnson, 1988). General education teachers sometimes have difficulty adapting instruction or integrating specific strategies into instruction for the students with disabilities whom they serve (Scanlon, Deshler, & Schumaker, 1996) and may be unprepared to meet the needs of heterogeneous student populations (Margolis & McGettigan, 1988) and increasingly diverse groups of children and adolescents (Reynolds, Wang, & Walberg, 1987). Collaborative consultation may provide a way to help teachers integrate students with varying academic abilities, including those who qualify for special education (Bauwens, Hourcade, & Friend, 1989).

Collaborative consultation focuses on the prevention of learning and behavior problems by meeting the needs of students prior to referral and possible placement. Studies have demonstrated that the use of consultation may contribute significantly to reducing the number of students referred for special education and may facilitate the mutual problem solving and sharing of expertise among general and special educators (Gable, Young, & Hendrickson, 1987).

Consultation-based programming has received support as an alternative service delivery option (Phillips & McCullough, 1990) and as a problem-solving process (West & Idol, 1990). Support for consultation among general educators was shown in a survey by Myles and Kasselman (1990) in which half of the teachers surveyed reported using collaborative consultation, even though a formal consultation program was not available in their schools. Similarly, in a survey of 100 general educators, Myles and Simpson (1989) reported that tation as a method to assist streaming exceptional students.

Kamens (1997) found that collab tivity increases job satisfaction and self-e promotes better working relationships, a contributes to professional development. When teachers collaborate, they tend to become more knowledgeable about their fields, become more involved in school decision making (Sindelar, Griffin, Smith, & Watanabe, 1992), and improve their skills and those of their students (Elliott & Sheridan, 1992). According to Dynak, Whitten, and Dynak (1997), teaching should not be an isolated act; elementary education, special education, and content-area teachers should collaborate as part of their regular school day. Educators should be interdependent and make use of each other's knowledge and expertise (Lieberman, 1995).

IMPORTANT POINTS

1. The ability to communicate and collaborate with other members of a team (general classroom teachers, administrators, paraprofessionals, other direct- and related-service providers, and families) may have a significant impact on the quality of services that special educators provide for their students.
2. Collaborative consultation is an interactive process that enables people with diverse expertise to generate creative solutions to mutually defined problems.
3. The purpose of collaborative consultation in special education is to facilitate the cooperative efforts of general and special educators in developing specific interventions for students with learning and behavior problems (Pugach & Johnson, 1988).
4. Collaborative consultation focuses on the prevention of learning and behavior problems by meeting the needs of students prior to referral and possible placement.

ing. Members of these teams range from general education teachers to special education teachers, counselors, social workers, or other members of the school community. In all three approaches, the intent is to work collaboratively through formal, structured stages to solve problems and make decisions about students. These approaches tend to reduce the number of inappropriate or unsuitable referrals for special education placement (Blalock, 1997), provide support to students (Bos & Vaughn, 1994), and expand the instructional alternatives that teachers have at their disposal (Olson & Platt, 1996). The coaching, consulting teaching, and cooperative teaching options for implementing collaborative consultation usually involve close collaboration between general and special education teachers in actual classroom settings.

Teacher Assistance Teams

Teacher assistance teams (TATs) are support systems for teachers (Chalfant & Pysh, 1989; Chalfant, Pysh, & Moultrie, 1979). Such teams provide opportunities to brainstorm solutions to problems and exchange ideas, methods, and techniques for developing instructional alternatives to help students referred to the team (Hayek, 1987). The philosophy behind teacher assistance teams is that classroom teachers have the skills to teach students with learning and behavior problems by working together in a problem-solving, collaborative manner. Teacher assistance teams are composed of general classroom teachers and function to help the referring teachers resolve problems. The use of teacher assistance teams has resulted in benefits to students, their families, and professionals (Chalfant & Pysh, 1989; Chalfant, Pysh, & Moultrie, 1979).

Teacher Referrals. A teacher who is having difficulty with a student submits a referral to the team. The referring teacher describes the student's performance, strengths, and weaknesses;

---

ob satisfac-
etter work-
professional
mproves skills

5% selected consul-
them in main-

133

ic of discussion in education to the aspect of collaboration as your topic, locate an article in a professional journal, a paper that was presented at a national meeting, or an education or special education Web site and report your findings to a peer or in a small group at your next class meeting.

(Answers for this and other activities are found in the Instructor's Manual.)

Options for Implementing Collaborative Consultation

Several options or models have been found to be effective in the implementation of collaborative interactions (i.e., mutual problem solving and shared decision making) among professionals. They include teacher assistance teams (Chalfant & Pysh, 1989; Chalfant, Pysh, & Moultrie, 1979), mainstream assistance teams (Fuchs, Fuchs, & Bahr, 1990), prereferral intervention (Blackhurst & Berdine, 1993; Graden, Casey, & Christianson, 1985; Winzer & Mazurek, 1998), coaching (Costa & Garmston, 1994; Knackendoffel, 1996; Showers, 1990), consulting teacher (Idol, 1986, 1988; West & Cannon, 1988), and cooperative teaching (Bauwens, Hourcade, & Friend, 1989; Bauwens & Hourcade, 1997).

The teacher assistance team, mainstream assistance team, and prereferral intervention are examples of a team approach to problem solvthe interventions already attempted; and other pertinent information, such as health history or assessment results.

Reviews of Referrals. The team coordinator reviews the referral and asks the team members to read it prior to a team meeting so that the team members may devote the meeting time to actual problem solving (Chalfant & Pysh, 1981).

Requests for Specific Information. The team coordinator responsible for the case may need to contact the referring teacher for clarification of information submitted or for additional information, may observe in the classroom if necessary, and develops a problem-interaction diagram that summarizes the concerns (Chalfant & Pysh, 1992).

Classroom Visits. It may be helpful if one of the team members observes the student in the classroom. This team member may be able to collect additional pertinent information through observation of the student and the environment.

Problem-Solving Meetings. The teacher assistance team meeting lasts for 30 minutes and includes the following steps recommended by Chalfant and Pysh (1981):

1. Reach a consensus about the nature of the problem.
2. Negotiate one or two objectives with the referring teacher. Be sure that the objectives specifically state the behaviors the student should achieve.
3. Brainstorm alternatives.
4. Select the methods the referring teacher would like to try and define the methods.
5. Assign responsibility for carrying out the recommendations (who, what, when, where, how).
6. Establish a follow-up plan for continued support and evaluation.

Recommendations. The meeting should result in recommendations for the referring teacher to implement, recommendations for informal assessment for the teacher or a team member to complete, or a referral for special help.

Mainstream Assistance Teams

The mainstream assistance team (Fuchs, Fuchs, & Bahr, 1990) is a multidisciplinary, preventative intervention process to serve students with mild disabilities and students without disabilities who are difficult to teach. Fuchs, Fuchs, and Bahr (1990) developed a prescriptive approach in which the specialist (e.g., special education teacher) serves as a consultant and collaborates with the consultee, the general education teacher. Both general and special education teachers have expressed satisfaction with the process and outcomes of the program (Bos & Vaughn, 1998). The school-based mainstream assistance team follows a series of four stages that were found to be critical to improved student behavior (Fuchs, Fuchs, & Hamlett, 1989; Fuchs, Fuchs, Bahr, Fernstrom, & Stecker, 1990):

- Problem identification
- Problem analysis
- Plan implementation
- Problem evaluation

Prereferral Intervention

Prereferral intervention refers to "a systematic set of activities in which students believed to be at risk for school failure are evaluated with regard to their learning and educational needs as well as their abilities" (Blackhurst & Berdine, 1993, p. 51). Prereferral intervention is designed to prevent inappropriate placements in special education and to help general classroom teachers interact effectively with students who have special needs. Prereferral consultation is done in a highly collaborative manner (Welch, Judge, Anderson, Bray, Child, & Franke, 1990) and focuses on instructional and behavioral interventions as opposed to testing and place-

Table 5.1 Modifications for Prereferral

Materials modifications	Make materials self-correcting. Highlight critical features. Block out extraneous elements.
Instructional modifications	Use mnemonic devices. Shorten directions. Provide mediators. Use advance organizers. Preface all remarks with a title or the main idea of the lesson. Use cognitive learning strategies.
Cues, feedback	Provide more prompts. Use corrective feedback. Provide visual cues.
Management	Use contingency contracts. Change seating. Use cooperative strategies. Use peer tutoring.
Content	Slow pace; use wait time.
Grouping	Use learning centers.
Test taking	Teach test-taking skills.
Study	Teach study skills. Note all assignments on a special bulletin board.

Psychosocial	Use the following:
	    Counseling
	    Support groups
	    Social services
	    Crosscultural counseling

NOTE. From Winzer, M. A., and Mazurek, K. M., *Special Education in Multicultural Contexts.* 1994. Prentice Hall, Upper Saddle River, NJ. Reproduced by permission of the publisher.

ment. Some professionals dislike the use of the term *prereferral,* as it implies that referral to special education is imminent (Graden, 1989; Pugach & Johnson, 1989). Graden (1989) prefers the term *intervention assistance,* as it more clearly describes the purpose and procedures associated with prereferral intervention. Through prereferral interventions, teachers can gather data on a student's learning and behavior, design a support system to assist the student in general classrooms, and adapt curriculum and modify the classroom environment (Winzer & Mazurek, 1998). Thus, prereferral intervention has two areas of emphasis: *problem solving* and *adaptations/modifications. Problem solving* involves collaborative consultation among members of a school-based problem-solving team to which referrals are sent and whose members suggest instructional interventions. *Adaptations and modifications* are recommended when students' needs are not being met in the existing classroom setting. Table 5.1 contains examples of modifications for prereferral recommended by Winzer and Mazurek (1998). Look back at Chapter 4 for additional suggestions of how to adapt materials for students with special needs in inclusive settings.

Graden, Casey, and Christianson's (1985) model includes both problem solving and adaptations. They suggest that intervention begin at the point of initial referral and recommend a prereferral system comprised of six stages: four in the prereferral process and two in the referral/assessment of eligibility process if needed.

Stage 1: Referral for Consultation. The classroom teacher requests assistance from a consultant (such as a school psychologist, a social worker, a special education teacher, or a counselor) or seeks assistance from a school-based problem-solving and screening team (school psychologist, other classroom teachers, special education teacher, principal, social worker, counselor).

Stage 2: Consultation. The consultant or team collaborates with the classroom teacher to define the problem, explore intervention strategies, try them, and evaluate the outcomes. If the intervention attempts are successful, the process ends. If they are not, the process moves to a third stage.

Stage 3: Observation. During the observation stage, additional information is collected through observation of the student and the environment. Then alternate intervention plans are implemented and evaluated. At Stages 2 and 3, the participants must specify the roles and responsibilities of those implementing the plan. For example, the school psychologist may be responsible for observing the student, the classroom teacher may be responsible for collecting work samples and performing an error analysis, and the special education teacher may be responsible for adapting instructional materials.

Stage 4: Conference. At this stage, a conference is held with a child review team to communicate the results of interventions and make decisions. This team comprises some of the school resource people mentioned in Stage 1 (school psychologist, general classroom teachers, special education teachers, etc.). All information is reviewed and the team makes recommendations to continue the interventions, try alternative interventions, or refer the student for consideration for special education placement.

Stage 5: Formal Referral. At this stage, the student may be referred for a psychoeducational assessment. Information previously gathered and interventions tried during the previous stages can be vitally important. The team members may want to ask themselves what additional data are necessary to make a decision. They may want to reexamine student work samples, records of assignment completion, observations of classroom behavior and participation, screenings of academic skills, and modifications made in the classroom. Further assessment could include curriculum-based assessment, criterion-referenced testing, and additional observation measures.

Stage 6: Formal Program Meeting. A formal meeting of the child study team is held to review information from the first five stages. The team discusses alternative placements and services and writes IEP goals if appropriate.

Cultural and Linguistic Diversity as Factors in the Prereferral Process. Students with limited English proficiency and students from culturally diverse backgrounds tend to be overrepresented in special education and remedial classes (Winzer & Mazurek, 1998). One reason may be that language and cultural characteristics may be interpreted as disabilities instead of differences. The prereferral process should include considerations related to the education of multicultural populations.

Ortiz and Garcia (1989) developed an eight-step prereferral process for preventing inappropriate referrals of Hispanic students to special education. Their prereferral system addresses very specific questions that include but are not limited to the following:

1. Is the student experiencing academic difficulty?
2. Is the curriculum known to be effective for language minority students?
3. Has the student's problem been validated?

4. Is there evidence of systematic efforts to identify the source of difficulty and take corrective action?

5. Do difficulties continue in spite of the programming alternatives?

Although Ortiz and Garcia (1989) provide this prereferral process to use with Hispanic students, it may be used effectively with members of other language minority and multicultural populations as well.

Coaching

Another model found to be effective in implementing collaborative interactions among teachers is that of coaching. Although different terms have been used for coaching, such as cognitive coaching, peer coaching, and others, it typically refers to individuals engaged in helping one another to improve their skills or practices or to learn something new. Cummings (1985) defines coaching as the process of giving teachers structured feedback about the practices they used in a lesson. In the school community, coaches may be teachers, administrators, or other school professionals. In an examination of studies on coaching, Showers (1990) reports that approximately 80% of teachers who were in coaching programs implemented new teaching strategies compared with approximately 10% of uncoached teachers.

Collaborative interactions between general and special education teachers and the learning outcomes of their students may be enhanced through coaching. Coaching typically involves observations of instructional practice, followed by discussions and reflections on that practice by the coaching partners. The coaching partners usually identify and focus on a specific instructional practice with which the teacher is experimenting (Showers, 1985). The coaching partners, or teachers, may also use the coaching relationship to share with each other methods for adapting instruction and materials, suggestions for checking student understanding during lesson presentations, specific teaching techniques, ideas for classroom management, methods for teaching various content areas, and strategies for monitoring student progress. Successful coaching relationships depend upon trust, openness, mutual learning, and a willingness to change. "Cognitive coaching is a nonjudgmental process—built around a planning conference, observation, and a reflecting conference" (Costa & Garmston, 1994, p. 2). During the *planning conference,* the partners identify what the teacher is going to work on, establish what one teacher will observe the other teacher do, and prepare or rehearse the lesson. For example, Ms. Johnson (general education teacher) selected her instructional language, and specifically, her questioning strategies, as an area that she wanted to improve. She asked her coaching partner, Ms. Washington (special education teacher), to give her some suggestions for phrasing her questions so that her students would raise their hands instead of calling out the answers and so that more students would respond to questions instead of the same few students each time. She also asked Ms. Washington to listen carefully to the questions she asked during the lesson and to check how long she waited for students to respond (wait time). The teachers developed sample questions at various levels of difficulty that could be used during the lesson. They practiced how to allow sufficient wait time after asking a question.

During the *observation,* Ms. Johnson taught the lesson and Ms. Washington observed by jotting down the questions that Ms. Johnson used and recording the amount of time that she gave for students to respond. During the observation stage of coaching, "the intent is to cast the teacher in the role of experimenter and researcher and the coach in the role of data collector" (Costa & Garmston, 1994, p. 21). Notice that the process is nonjudgmental and highly collaborative, with both teachers committed to solving the problem.

The *reflecting conference* is held after the observation. The coach may want to organize or revise the notes and data taken during the observation before sharing them with the teacher. During the reflecting conference, coaches usually ask teachers to share their impressions of the lesson, thereby encouraging them to judge their own performance. It is important for teachers to reflect on the relationship between their own actions and student outcomes. It is very difficult for teachers to change their actions or behaviors when they are not aware of them.

In our example, after examining the data that Ms. Washington collected, Ms. Johnson may decide that the way she phrased her questions had a direct impact on how her students responded during the lesson and that providing sufficient wait time after asking questions definitely resulted in more students responding. The reflecting conference may be used by the teacher to reflect about the lesson that was just observed and to plan for future lessons based upon new learnings resulting from the coaching experience. During this conference, the partners should also evaluate the coaching experience and devise ways to strengthen it.

Consulting Teacher

Consulting teaching is "a process for providing special education services to students with special needs in which special education teachers, general education teachers, other school professionals, or parents collaborate to plan, implement, and evaluate instruction conducted in general classrooms for the purpose of preventing or ameliorating students' academic or social behavior problems" (Idol, 1986, p. 2). As a service delivery system, the pure consulting teacher model is one of indirect service to students (Idol, 1986; Lilly & Givens-Ogle, 1981). As a problem-solving process, it is meant to be highly collaborative, with general and special education teachers working as partners in planning instruction.

The intent of the consulting teacher model is to provide general classroom teachers with the skills necessary to instruct students who have special needs. In other words, the goal is

not to relieve general classroom teachers of the responsibility for instructing students with mild disabilities and other low-achieving students (Huefner, 1988). Idol (1988) feels that consultation should support, not supplant, general education programs.

West and Cannon (1988) surveyed individuals in 47 states to identify the competencies essential for consultation and found that the highest ratings were given to interpersonal skills, personal and professional attitudes and beliefs, and personal qualities needed. Reeve and Hallahan (1994) report that the technical skills associated with effective teaching of students with disabilities were not included in West and Cannon's (1988) survey, and they question whether communication and compatibility are sufficient for successful collaboration when the ultimate target is student outcomes. We suggest that consulting teachers should possess excellent listening, interpersonal, communication (verbal and nonverbal), problem-solving, and teaming skills, as well as effective technical skills (e.g., task analysis, content enhancement, direct instruction, questioning, etc.).

The role of the consulting teacher requires knowledge of large- and small-group instruction, familiarity with the general education curriculum, ability to adapt and modify materials and instruction, flexibility, and expertise in working with others. For example, a high school teacher was concerned that the readability level of her history textbook was too high for many of her students, that the text failed to represent the contributions of different cultural groups to the development of the United States, and that it did not present a balanced perspective. She worked with the consulting teacher in the development of materials to supplement the text. They used videotapes, books that represented different ethnic groups, and reference materials from the media center. Consulting teachers may also design curriculum units, participate in prereferral systems, and co-teach with general classroom teachers.

For consulting teachers engaged primarily in problem solving/decision making, there are several methods and models available. Bergan (1977) suggests following four steps in consultation: problem identification, problem analysis, plan implementation, and plan evaluation. Following this sequence of steps allows special and general education teachers to utilize systematic procedures in working collaboratively, thus providing an excellent vehicle for consultation.

As part of their *Teaming Techniques* series, Knackendoffel, Robinson, Schumaker, and Deshler (1992) focus on basic communication skills, the problem-solving process, partnership-building skills, and the instructional principles needed in decision-making situations. They *use a problem-solving worksheet* that provides general and special education teachers with a systematic method of collaborating to solve student problems. Thurston (1987) uses the POCS method of problem solving in which general and special education teachers cooperatively complete a worksheet with the POCS steps for problem solving (problems, options, consequences, and solutions). This method promotes collective thinking in generating viable alternatives for students with special needs.

Figure 5.1 contains an example of a cooperative planning guide, which employs the four steps in consultation. Notice that the form was completed cooperatively by the special education teacher, Judy Hernandez, and the classroom teacher, Don Whitley. They began by *defining the problem*. Through an exchange of information including listening, questioning, and clarifying, they were able to target Marcus's problem—he does not pay attention in science class and this affects his performance on tests and projects.

Second, they *analyzed the problem*. They did this by listing (a) the factors in the classroom that might be contributing (e.g., the class is primarily lecture), (b) the behaviors of the student that might be contributing (e.g., he doesn't write anything down), and (c) the strengths of the student (e.g., he learns well from visuals). As you can see by examining Figure 5.1, they learned a great deal about Marcus by using environmental variables and student strengths and weaknesses to analyze his problem.

Third, they *implemented a plan*. They did this by first generating and then prioritizing several recommendations. They also decided who would be responsible for carrying out each recommendation. For example, their first priority was to award points to Marcus for coming to class prepared, with the science teacher assuming the responsibility for implementing this. The next priority was to teach Marcus to take notes. The special education teacher assumed responsibility for this.

Finally, they determined how they would *evaluate the plan*. They did this by deciding how they would fulfill their roles and responsibilities. For example, the science teacher kept a daily record of the points Marcus earned by coming to class prepared. The special education teacher agreed to evaluate Marcus's notes for technique, and the science teacher assumed responsibility for checking the notes for content.

The consulting teacher may use any of the previously mentioned methods for collaborative problem solving. The key is to use teamwork and shared decision making to create, implement, and evaluate realistic alternatives for students.

Cooperative Teaching

Given the increased diversity in today's public school classrooms, it is essential to develop alternative forms of service delivery within the general education setting. Cooperative teaching has emerged as an effective way to facilitate the inclusion of students with diverse needs (Bauwens & Hourcade, 1997). According to Bauwens, Hourcade, and Friend (1989), "Cooperative teaching (or co-teaching) refers to an educational approach in which general and special educators work in a co-active and coordinated fashion to jointly teach academically and behaviorally heterogeneous groups of students in educationally integrated settings (i.e.,

Cooperative Planning Guide

Student's Name: Marcus Wyler
Date: 11/10

1. Define the problem:

Marcus doesn't pay attention in science class and this affects his performance on tests and projects.

2. Analyze the problem:
   a. List the factors in the environment that may be contributing to the problem

   - The pace is fast.
   - The class is large.
   - The class is primarily lecture.

   b. List the behaviors of the student that may be contributing to the problem

   - He doesn't come to class prepared with pencil and paper.
   - Ho doesn't watch when information is put on the board.
   - He doesn't write anything down, so he probably doesn't study.

   c. Discuss the student's strengths

   - He likes working with peers
   - He has excellent attendance.
   - He learns well from visuals.

3. Implement a plan:
   a. List and prioritize five recommendations

   - Award points for coming prepared. (1) DW
   - Present material on transparencies when possible. (4) D.W.
   - Cue him when to write something down.(3) D.W. & J.H.
   - Teach him to take notes. (2) J.H.
   - At the end of class, review the key points of the presentation and let him compare his notes to a peer's. (5) D.W.

   b. Go back and write the initials of the person responsible for implementing each recommendation next to that recommendation

4. Evaluate the plan:
   For each recommendation listed in 3(a), specify how it will be monitored and evaluated

   - Science teacher will keep a record of points earned.
   - Special education teacher will check notes for technique and science teacher for content.
   - Science teacher will keep track of the effectiveness of cueing.
   - Science teacher and special education teacher will check notes for evidence of material presented on transparencies.
   - Science teacher and special education teacher will check notes for key points.

Special education teacher: Judy Hernandez
Science teacher: Don Whitley
Comments: Let's meet next Thursday after school to review Marcus's progress.

Figure 5.1   An Example of a Cooperative Planning Guide

general classrooms)" (p. 18). In co-teaching, cooperative planning and instructing are emphasized. Both the general and special education teachers are present in the classroom and assume responsibility for instruction. Roles and responsibilities are determined on the basis of the strengths and skills of the teachers.

By combining the planning and teaching skills of general and special education professionals in a cooperative arrangement, it may be

Regular Education	Collaborative Teaching	Special Education
Content knowledge Curriculum objectives Curriculum materials Content resources support Content development Curriculum sequence Learning environment	Shared teaching Evaluation Classroom management Student supervision Team problem solving Communication skills Response to change Professional growth Social and emotional needs addressed	Knowledge of each disability Individual learning styles Adaptation of curriculum Learning strategies Modifications to learning environment Legal issues Motivational techniques

Figure 5.2   Interaction Curriculum Content

NOTE. From "A Collaborative Model for Students with Mild Disabilities in Middle Schools" by A. E. White and L. L. White, 1992. *Focus on Exceptional Children,* 24(9), p. 7. Copyright 1992 by PRO-ED. Reprinted by permission.

possible to achieve successful reintegration of students with special needs into general classrooms. Most general education teachers are skilled in content and curriculum and in providing instruction to large groups, while most special education teachers are adept at analyzing and adapting materials and are knowledgeable in special teaching methodologies. In planning instruction, general educators typically identify a theme or topic related to district or state competencies and then develop activities, while special educators, who are accountable for student mastery of IEP objectives, focus on student learning first and then generate activities to help students meet the objectives (Dyck, Sundbye, & Pemberton, 1997). Figure 5.2 illustrates the interaction of curriculum content (the specialty of general education) and specialized methodology (the specialty of special education) to produce a more effective instructional situation through cooperative teaching (White & White, 1992).

In our world of specialists, we need to be careful that the contributions of general education teachers are not overlooked. Pugach and Johnson (1989) describe a presentation that they observed by a collaborative team of two general educators and one special education teacher. After

the team had shared their collaborative efforts, members of the audience commented on how much the general education teachers must have learned from working with the special education teacher. The special education teacher asked the audience why they didn't ask her about all the things she had learned from the general education teachers. We hope you will think about this as you work collaboratively with classroom teachers—for the learning is reciprocal.

Figure 5.3 lists some of the tasks that special education teachers may perform as co-teachers to help students with special needs succeed in regular classrooms. Of course, both teachers should provide input into the appropriateness of these tasks for a given situation.

Bauwens, Hourcade, and Friend (1989) recommend three approaches to co-teaching—team teaching, supportive learning activities, and complementary teaching—and suggest that, at times, two or more of these approaches may occur simultaneously in the classroom.

Team Teaching. In the team teaching approach, general and special educators jointly plan and present content to all of the students. At times, one teacher may take the lead for some aspect of instruction, such as teaching

Figure 5.3 Possible Tasks of the Special Education Teacher in Cooperative Teaching

Lectures and Presentations
1. Provide visuals.
2. Prepare study guides and chapter outlines.
3. Use modeling and demonstration.
4. Prepare glossaries.
5. Teach note taking.

Textbooks and Other Printed Materials
1. Physically alter printed material.
   a. Insert stop points in text.
   b. Use marginal gloss.
   c. Highlight.
   d. Underline.
2. Tape-record printed material.
3. Have the students develop their own end-of-chapter questions.
4. Teach the use of mnemonic devices.
5. Show the students how to preview a textbook and chapter.

Interest and Motivation
1. Use story starters.
2. Alternate listening and doing activities.
3. Allow students to demonstrate knowledge in a variety of ways (e.g., writing, telling, making, working with a partner or group).
4. Provide written feedback.
5. Use calculators, games, word searches, puzzles, audiovisuals (videotapes, language master cards, slides, and filmstrips).
6. Develop learning centers.
7. Develop self-correcting materials.

Teacher Assistance
1. Cooperatively plan lessons and activities.
2. Help teachers locate and adapt materials.
3. Monitor student progress (academic and social).
4. Help grade assignments.

the steps for a bill to become a law. At other times, the other teacher takes the responsibility for part of a lesson, such as instructing students in how to interpret the graphics in their social studies texts. Knackendoffel (1996) refers to team teaching as teaching in concert with each other.

For example, Mr. Milaki (special education teacher) and Mr. Webster (sixth-grade teacher) jointly planned a social studies lesson for the sixth grade. Mr. Milaki began the lesson by using direct instruction to introduce new vocabulary to students. Mr. Webster presented the lesson content using the overhead projector to emphasize key points and show examples. Both teachers monitored student attention to, and acquisition of, the social studies content. In addition to this example, Bauwens and Hourcade (1997) suggest other ways of team teaching such as (a) dividing students into two heterogeneous groups to receive similar instruction, but in smaller groups, (b) having one teacher present the content while the other moves around the classroom to monitor student progress, (c) having one teacher present content while the other poses questions, and (d) having one teacher present content while the other conducts a review for those who need it.

Supportive Learning Activities. In this approach to cooperative teaching, both general and special education teachers plan and present content (Bauwens & Hourcade, 1997). General education teachers present the essential content, while special education teachers are responsible for designing and implementing supplementary and supportive learning activities (Bauwens, Hourcade, & Friend, 1989). Both teachers are present during instruction to monitor student performance.

For example, Ms. Parrish (classroom teacher at the high school level) presented a lesson on the different forms of government. She described the forms of government, provided examples, and discussed characteristics. She asked the students several questions to check their understanding of the material. After she finished her presentation, Ms. Ramirez (special education teacher) organized the students into cooperative learning groups and asked them to describe how their history class would be run under a democracy, dictatorship, or parliamentary government. Ms. Ramirez also planned a trip to the media center later in the week to examine some supplementary materials on the topic. Through cooperative teaching, these teachers provided their students with the essential content as well as supplementary and supportive activities to reinforce, enrich, and supplement the content.

Additional ways of using supportive learning activities include (a) dividing students into two groups with each teacher presenting content to that group, then dividing students into peer tutoring teams to tutor each other; (b) having one teacher provide small-group instruction while the other monitors the rest of the class; and (c) breaking the class into four groups while the two teachers rotate around the class to provide support or supplementary information (Bauwens & Hourcade, 1997). A final way to use supportive learning activities is by having one teacher work with the majority of the class while other students work at learning centers with the second teacher monitoring and supporting their efforts.

Complementary Instruction. Students in intermediate grades, middle school, and high school may have difficulty with some of the skills necessary for school success, such as organization, studying, test taking, report writing, use of reference materials, and note taking. In the complementary instruction approach to cooperative teaching, general education teachers assume the responsibility for presenting specific content (e.g., science), while special education teachers instruct students in how to access that content by teaching strategies (note taking and test taking) (Bauwens & Hourcade, 1997). Complementary instructional activities are typically worked into a classroom schedule as mini-lessons (Bauwens & Hourcade, 1997).

For example, Ms. Ruiz (special education teacher) spent the first 12 minutes of science class instructing students in note taking. She had the students divide their papers into two columns. Next, she showed them how to write the science teacher's key words and points on the right side of the page during the teacher's presentation. Then she showed them how to summarize the teacher's notes and jot down questions on the left side of the page after the presentation. While Mr. Peterson (science teacher) presented some information on ecosystems, Ms. Ruiz took notes so that she would have a model to show the students later. Mr. Peterson stopped about 20 minutes before the end of class so that he and Ms. Ruiz could circulate and give feedback to the students about their note-taking content and technique. Then Ms. Ruiz showed her notes to the class on the overhead projector. With this type of cooperative teaching, students are presented with strategies to access content directly and, therefore, generalization is facilitated.

Other models of cooperative teaching are available, and you are referred to the work of Friend and of Bos and Vaughn.

◆ **ACTIVITY 5.2**

Read the following scenario. Work with a partner to complete the scenario using the cooperative planning guide in Figure 5.1.

TENTH-GRADE TEACHER: Beth, thanks for stopping in. I have a problem I need help with.

SPECIAL EDUCATION TEACHER: What seems to be the problem?

TENTH-GRADE TEACHER: Some of the students with learning problems who are included in my third-period class can't seem to write a theme. Every time I assign one, they fail.

SPECIAL EDUCATION TEACHER: What is it about the assignment that's giving them trouble?

TENTH-GRADE TEACHER: Well, they can't seem to write enough. Actually, they can't even write a variety of sentences. In fact, they don't always write complete sentences.

SPECIAL EDUCATION TEACHER: I can see this is a real problem for you. Let me see if I understand the situation. They are having trouble writing themes because they don't know how to write a variety of sentences and sometimes their sentences aren't correct.

TENTH-GRADE TEACHER: Right. I thought maybe you could help me.

Barriers to and Ingredients of Effective Collaborative Consultation

Although collaboration has many benefits as a service option, a number of barriers may interfere with its effectiveness (Bondy & Brownell, 1997; Haight, 1984; Idol, 1988; Mitchell, 1997; Tindal, Shinn, & Rodden-Nord, 1990). In this section, we discuss some of the barriers to collaboration and provide suggestions for overcoming them.

1. PROBLEM: *Insufficient time and overwhelming caseloads*

Lack of time is frequently cited as a barrier to developing interactive relationships (Tindal, Shinn, & Rodden-Nord, 1990) and may be one of the greatest obstacles to collaborative consultative efforts (Idol, 1986). Because of the demands of multiple roles and responsibilities, some teachers state that consultation is just one more thing to do (Evans, 1980; Idol-Maestas & Ritter, 1985; Nowacek, 1992).

SOLUTIONS:

In situations in which cooperative teaching has been implemented, time has not been found to be a problem, perhaps because with more efficient communication, duplication of instruction to students with mild disabilities is minimized (Bauwens, Hourcade, & Friend, 1989). Furthermore, as teachers gain more experience with the roles of consulting teacher and co-teacher, responsibilities may become more evenly distributed. Teachers who participate as members of collaborative consultation teams, such as prereferral, teacher assistance teams, and mainstream assistance teams, may initially find the procedures time consuming; however, with increased use, these structured procedures may expedite decisions about students. Finally, school administrators can play an important part in easing the time and scheduling problems of teachers. Administrators may help alleviate the time problem by providing adequate planning and scheduling time for teachers and by assigning concurrent preparation periods to those who need them. West and Idol (1990) report several strategies for increasing consulting time that have been successfully used in elementary and secondary settings. We present an adapted version of their work in Table 5.2.

2. PROBLEM: *Lack of administrative support*

Lack of administrative support was found to be the major barrier to developing and implementing consultation efforts between general

Table 5.2 Strategies for Increasing Consulting Time

1. Have the principal or other support staff member teach a period each day on a regular basis.
2. Cluster students for independent assignments and study activities in large rooms with fewer staff supervising.
3. Ask a business or community organization that has adopted your school to supply a permanent floating (no cost) substitute.
4. Use teaching assistants or volunteers to supervise at lunch and as classes change.
5. Ask the principal to assign a specific time each week for professionals to collaborate.
6. Use part of regularly scheduled in-service days for collaborative teams to meet, or designate a half day each month without students (third Monday afternoon of each month) to use for collaboration.

NOTE. "Collaborative Consultation in the Education of Mildly Handicapped and At-Risk Students" by J. F. West and L. Idol, 1990, *Remedial and Special Education, 11*(1), p. 30. Copyright 1990 by PRO-ED, Inc. Adapted and reprinted by permission.

classroom and special education teachers (Nelson & Stevens, 1981). Administrative support is necessary for effective consultation programs (Idol-Maestas & Ritter, 1985) and for designing and implementing consultation efforts (Phillips & McCullough, 1990).

SOLUTIONS:

School administrators can create a climate in which collaborative consultation is valued. Their involvement in promoting consultation, controlling caseloads, providing adequate time for consultation, financing programs, facilitating teachers' efforts, breaking down barriers, and addressing implementation issues is crucial to the success of consultation-based programming. Teachers should share their ideas and suggestions for how to schedule cooperative planning time with their principals, provide incentives and support for teachers engaged in consultation, and solve implementation issues. Active involvement of teachers in planning and decision making helps increase collaboration

(Rozenholtz, Bassler, & Hoover-Dempsey, 1985) and ensures ownership (Duke, Showers, & Imber, 1980) and implementation (Fullan & Pomfret, 1977). When administrators include teachers from the initial planning stage through implementation and evaluation, they significantly increase support for new programs. Platt and Olson (1997, p. 174) provide the following suggestions for school administrators:

◆ Promote a climate that is conducive to collaboration.
◆ Take a leadership role in promoting collaborative consultation, and model collaboration for faculty and staff.
◆ Have a clear understanding of the basic principles of collaborative consultation and facilitate similar understanding by others (by providing speakers, written information, visits to other sites, and ample opportunities for dialogue).
◆ Develop an awareness of probable roadblocks to consultative efforts and of effective solutions for managing them.
◆ From the beginning, include faculty and staff in participatory planning and decision making. Secure their ownership.
◆ Provide necessary staff development training for all participants.
◆ Know how to plan, finance, implement, and evaluate collaborative consultation.
◆ Provide incentives and support for professionals engaging in collaborative consultation.

3. PROBLEM: *Differences in background and areas of expertise*

Historically, the roles and responsibilities of special and general educators have been different. Phillips and McCullough (1990) cited a lack of understanding between general and special educators in regard to each other's roles. In fact, general and special education teachers may have very different priorities. According to Glatthorn (1990), "the special education teacher is more often concerned with one student and how learning might be individualized; the classroom teacher worries about the entire class and how

Table 5.3   The Top 10 Technical Skills and Personal Qualities of Effective Collaborators

Technical Skills	Personal Qualities
Effective collaborators typically know how to	*Effective collaborators typically are*
1. Manage resistance	1. Respected by others
2. Facilitate change	2. Socially competent
3. Resolve conflict	3. Warm, sensitive, understanding
4. Adapt curriculum and instruction	4. Flexible
5. Use principles of effective instruction	5. Risk-takers
6. Manage the learning environment	6. Knowledgeable and experienced
7. Use effective communication skills	7. Good listeners
8. Monitor student progress	8. Confident
9. Work as a member of a team	9. Able to think on their feet
10. Engage in problem solving	10. Energetic

NOTE. From Platt, J., and Olson, J., *Teaching Adolescents with Mild Disabilities,* 1997, Brooks/Cole Publishing Company, Pacific Grove, CA. Reproduced by permission of Wadsworth Publishing Company.

overall achievement might be advanced. The special education teacher tends to be concerned with developing a wide range of learning and coping skills; the classroom teacher focuses on academic skills and content" (p. 307). The beliefs general and special educators have about each other may pose barriers to collaboration (Bondy, Ross, Sindelar, & Griffin, 1995) and may cause each to question the credibility of the other.

SOLUTIONS:

The options for implementing collaborative consultation, such as consulting teacher or co-teacher, may reverse negative attitudes, misunderstandings, and resistance. Combining a professional who possesses knowledge in curriculum, content, and large-group instruction with a professional who is skilled in adapting instructional materials and implementing effective teaching strategies may enhance the progress of *all* students. Once teachers experience the power of collaboration, they will not view their differences as weaknesses, but as strengths.

The competencies presented in Table 5.3 are derived from the work of Friend and Cook (1992), Idol, Paolucci-Whitcomb, and Nevin (1994), Little (1982), and Platt and Olson (1997). They represent the types of technical

skills and personal qualities that are likely to facilitate effective collaboration for all professionals regardless of field, background, and training.

4. PROBLEM: *Lack of knowledge about collaborative consultation and the change process*

Training is necessary in order to deal effectively with change in the educational setting. Preservice and in-service teachers should be given opportunities to develop these skills, as most individuals do not develop them automatically.

SOLUTIONS:

As we mentioned at the beginning of the chapter, training in collaboration is a must if we expect teachers to serve in collaborative roles (Berdine & Cegelka, 1997; Erchul & Conoley, 1991; Gersten, Darch, David, & George, 1991). Comprehensive training programs should be available at preservice and in-service levels for general and special education teachers and school administrators. For teachers, the training should include, but not be limited to, clarification of roles, consultation skills, techniques for adapting to change (Idol, 1988), and peer coaching skills. For administrators, training should include, but not be limited to, role and responsibility clarification, techniques for implementing change, awareness of barriers to implementation, strategies for promoting and implementing school consultation (Idol, 1988), and coaching skills.

Studies indicate that people move through specific stages when adapting to change. Hall and Hord (1984) report seven stages: (1) awareness ("I'm really not involved that much."), (2) informational ("Tell me more."), (3) personal ("What is my role going to be?"), (4) management ("How will I implement this?"), (5) consequence ("Let's see how this is going to impact . . ."), (6) collaboration ("By cooperating on this we can . . ."), and (7) refocusing ("This has worked well, but I have a suggestion for making it even better."). Teachers and administrators need training in consultation-based programming and in adapting to change. Once consultation-based programming has been established, ongoing training and support are essential to maintain it. Effective support strategies include observation, practice, experimentation, feedback, formation of support teams, and peer coaching (Joyce & Showers, 1983).

5. PROBLEM: *Differences and difficulties in communication*

Special education teachers may use a communication code not easily understood by general classroom teachers. Teachers of students with special needs may use abbreviations such as LRE, IEP, FAPE, WRAT, ITP, CRT, and CBM, unaware that classroom teachers may not understand them. This may pose a major barrier to effective communication (Stamm, 1980).

SOLUTION:

Use a shared language to communicate about students and school-related activities. This may help strengthen the bond that should exist among professionals who share responsibility for the same students. Suggestions for enhancing communication include:

◆ Using a common language that is easily understood by all participants (avoiding jargon, abbreviations, and vocabulary specific to one person's experiential background, but not to others') (Platt & Olson, 1997).

◆ Using effective communication techniques, which we describe later in the chapter, like active listening, reflective statements, nonverbal techniques, questions, and providing adequate verbal space.

◆ Showing respect for others' knowledge, valuing their expertise, and pooling the talents of all team members (Platt & Olson, 1997).

◆ Developing an attitude of shared ownership for ideas and activities, and assuming joint responsibility, accountability, and recognition for problem resolution (Phillips & McCullough, 1990).

◆ ACTIVITY 5.3

Examine the following statements made by general education teachers about collaborative consultation. In a group, brainstorm ways of responding to these concerns:
1. "I don't have time for all those meetings. I have too much to do."
2. "When will I plan with the special education teacher? She has planning during sixth period and I have it during fourth."
3. "I don't understand all those terms they use in special education."
4. "There's too much paperwork. How will I keep up?"
5. "How will these collaborative consultation procedures help my students?"

◇ IMPORTANT POINTS

1. Options for implementing collaborative consultation include teacher assistance teams, mainstream assistance teams, prereferral intervention, coaching, consulting teacher, and cooperative teaching.

2. The teacher assistance team is a support system for teachers that provides opportunities for brainstorming solutions to problems in order to develop alternatives for students referred to the team.

3. The mainstream assistance team is a multidisciplinary, preventative intervention process to serve students with mild disabilities and students without disabilities who are difficult to teach.

4. In prereferral intervention, a consultant or team collaborates with a teacher to define a problem, explore intervention strategies, try them out, and evaluate the outcomes.

5. Coaching involves individuals helping each other improve their skills or practices through self-reflection.

6. Cognitive coaching is a nonjudgmental process that includes a planning conference, an observation, and a reflecting conference.

7. Consulting teaching is conducted in general education classrooms and involves providing support services to teachers and students in order to prevent or ameliorate students' academic or social behavior problems.

8. Co-teaching is an approach in which general and special educators work together and jointly teach academically and behaviorally heterogeneous groups of students in educationally integrated settings.

9. Barriers to effective collaborative consultation include insufficient time and overwhelming caseloads, lack of administrative support, differences in background and areas of expertise, preparation in collaborative consultation and the change process, and differences and difficulties in communication.

10. Ingredients of effective collaborative consultation include administrative support, teacher involvement in decision making, training in collaborative consultation, support teams, peer coaching, and use of a shared language with general educators.

COLLABORATION WITH PARAPROFESSIONALS

Over the last few years, a substantial growth in the use of paraprofessionals in special education has had a positive impact on the delivery of services to students with disabilities (Harrington & Mitchelson, 1987; Pickett, 1988). Pickett (1986) defines a paraprofessional as:

> a person whose position is either instructional in nature or who delivers direct services to students and/or their parents; and who serves in a position for which a teacher or another professional has ultimate responsibility for the design and implementation of individual education programs and other services (p. 2).

The term *teaching* or *educational assistant* is frequently used to describe paraprofessionals as is *paraeducators,* which Blalock (1997) describes as more reflective of the expanded roles that paraprofessionals fill (e.g., job coach, human service technician). The phenomenal growth rate of paraprofessionals has been attributed to (a) the high marks that paraprofessionals have received in serving exceptional students (Frith, Lindsey, & Edwards, 1981; Guess, Smith, & Ensminger, 1977; Palmer, 1975); (b) the ability of paraprofessionals to work with a variety of exceptionalities in a variety of settings (Bayes & Neill, 1978; Frith & Lindsey, 1980); (c) the cost-effectiveness of utilizing paraprofessionals (Frith & Lindsey, 1982); (d) a change from the emphasis on performing clerical tasks to that of providing instructional support (Boomer, 1982, Evans & Evans, 1986); and (e) the beliefs of administrators, teachers, and paraprofessionals that utilization of paraprofessionals is an effective method of service delivery (Jones & Bender, 1993). Case (1986) found that 98% of paraprofessionals interviewed believed that their presence in the classroom enabled teachers to attend better to the individual needs of students. This was supported in another study that illustrated that paraprofessionals feel they make a positive difference in special education class-rooms and that teachers are satisfied with their performance (Frank, Keith, & Steil, 1988).

Unfortunately, although paraprofessionals have a great deal to offer, their skills are not al-ways accurately identified or utilized to enable them to contribute in a meaningful way (McKenzie & Houk, 1986). Training and super-vision have been informal, haphazard, or non-existent (Frith & Lindsey, 1982), and place-ment decisions have not always been made systematically. Blalock (1991) reports that many schools are not providing training at all for paraprofessionals, which is contrary to what is recommended in the literature. Therefore, it is necessary to examine ways to improve current practices and maximize the positive effects that these important members of the educational team can have on students.

Planning Paraprofessional Programs

There are several aspects to consider in order to utilize best the skills and talents of paraprofes-sionals in meeting the needs of teachers and students. They include matching skills with needs, utilizing paraprofessionals with cultur-ally and linguistically diverse populations, and defining role expectations/responsibilities.

Matching Skills with Needs

From time to time, you may overhear special ed-ucation teachers discussing their needs, such as "I could really use some help making flash cards, self-correcting materials, and games for my stu-dents" or "I am trying to get my class checked out on their job application and job interview competencies, but it's impossible to do by my-self." A paraprofessional should be placed with a teacher whose needs and expectations match the skills of the paraprofessional (McKenzie & Houk, 1986). Frank, Keith, and Steil (1988) found that paraprofessionals need to possess dif-ferent competencies based upon the educa-tional setting in which they are working.

McKenzie and Houk (1986) suggest the use of an inventory (see Figure 5.4) to be filled out by both the special education teacher and the paraprofessional. Teachers can use the inven-tory to identify the types of support they need, while paraprofessionals can use it to indicate their skills and interests. In this way, a parapro-fessional who is skilled at materials develop-ment may be assigned to a teacher who needs self-correcting materials and games, while someone with effective instructional skills and good rapport with students may be assigned to a teacher who needs someone to go over vo-cabulary with the students, monitor progress during practice activities in an inclusive setting, or help students review for tests. Others, with skills in monitoring, data collection, and pro-viding feedback, may assist with the reintegra-tion of students to general education class-rooms or by helping students to make the transition into work settings. Special education teachers who are co-teaching with general edu-cation teachers may want to enlist the assistance of a paraprofessional in preparing study guides, making transparencies, tape-recording por-tions of textbooks, and making supplementary activities, such as games, folder activities, and learning centers.

Utilizing Paraprofessionals with Culturally and Linguistically Diverse Populations

Teachers are expected to possess the knowl-edge, skills, and experience to be effective with students from increasingly diverse cultural, lin-guistic, and socioeconomic backgrounds (Ortiz & Garcia, 1989). It may be helpful to have a teaching assistant who can work effectively with culturally and linguistically diverse groups and can speak languages other than English.

Paraprofessionals can and have assisted non-English-speaking students and students from culturally diverse backgrounds. One of the au-thors of this text set up a program that utilized volunteers to work individually and in small groups with students to teach them to speak

Name _____ Date _____

Directions: Listed below are a number of tasks which a paraprofessional may perform. If you are a paraprofessional, mark with a "P" those activities/duties which you feel you could conduct. If you are a teacher, mark with a "T" those areas in which you intend to use a paraprofessional.

Instructional Support

1. _____ Reinforce concepts already presented by the teacher, by assisting students in reading, math, spelling, articulation, vocabulary development, signing, mobility, and/or self-care.
2. _____ Listen to students read.
3. _____ Read to students.
4. _____ Supervise independent or small group work.
5. _____ Modify written materials, e.g., tape record stories, rewrite to lower level.
6. _____ Help students work on projects or assignments.
7. _____ Help students select library books.
8. _____ Assist physically disabled students, e.g., feeding, positioning.
9. _____ Help students explore careers and special interests.
10. _____ Practice vocabulary with non–English speaking students.
_____ Other. Please describe.

Behavior Management Support

11. _____ Provide and/or supervise earned reinforcement.
12. _____ Supervise time out.
13. _____ Be a resource for students who are experiencing stress.
14. _____ Monitor progress on contracts.
15. _____ Enhance students' self-concept by providing positive feedback.
_____ Other. Please describe.

Diagnostic Support

16. _____ Correct and grade assigned activities.
17. _____ Observe and record academic behavior and progress, e.g., math facts learned, vocabulary growth, reading rate.
18. _____ Observe and record social behavior(s).
19. _____ Administer informal assessments, e.g., unit tests and criterion-referenced measures.
_____ Other. Please describe.

Classroom Organization

20. _____ Make instructional games.
21. _____ Develop and manage learning centers.
22. _____ Prepare displays.
23. _____ Locate instructional materials.
24. _____ Assist in daily planning.
25. _____ Make bulletin boards.
_____ Other. Please describe.

Clerical Support

26. _____ Type.
27. _____ Duplicate materials.
28. _____ Take attendance.
29. _____ Record grades.
_____ Other. Please describe.

Figure 5.4 Inventory of Paraprofessional Skills and Teacher Needs

NOTE. From "Paraprofessionals in Special Education" (p. 249) by R. G. McKenzie and C. S. Houk, 1986, *Teaching Exceptional Children,* 19 (4). Reprinted by permission.

English. Through the volunteers, the students were able to share some of their culture, language, and customs with their peers. It is an asset to the classroom to have an assistant who could explain in two languages something about the diversity within cultures and who could create learning activities compatible with student characteristics!

Another way to involve assistants in ensuring that students from culturally and linguistically diverse backgrounds succeed is to have them develop multisensory teaching aids, such as language master cards, games, audiovisual aids, computer programs, multimedia, and learning centers in which material can be learned in a variety of ways. Assistants may also help you monitor diversified grouping patterns, such as cooperative learning and peer tutoring. These instructional arrangements allow more students to participate, regardless of their cultural and linguistic backgrounds.

Defining Role Expectations and Responsibilities

The lack of a clear job description appears to be one of the problems most commonly experienced by paraprofessionals. According to Frith and Mims (1985), "Paraprofessionals who possess a realistic perception of what is expected of them are more likely to perform admirably and to be more satisfied with their work" (p. 226). Teachers should clearly specify what the teaching assistant is expected to do within the areas of instructional support, behavior management support, diagnostic support, classroom organization, and clerical support. As you can see from Figure 5.5, a paraprofessional can accomplish many tasks in the special education setting and in the general education classroom. The key is careful communication of tasks, roles, expectations, and responsibilities.

Carefully specifying role expectations and responsibilities may also help prevent the awkward situation of a teaching assistant who tries to assume a supervisory role. Regularly scheduled conferences in which you and your assistant talk about student progress, clerical activities, development or modification of materials, and scheduling are ideal for reviewing and clarifying the assistant's assignments and responsibilities. Some teachers prepare a written schedule each day for their assistants, in order to clarify roles and responsibilities. Praising and reinforcing your assistant for performing agreed-upon assignments is an effective way to ensure that these, and not other, assignments are carried out.

Implementing Paraprofessional Programs

Planning is the first step in organizing a paraprofessional program. In order to implement the program effectively, you should include orientation and training, scheduling, communication, feedback, and evaluation.

Orientation and Training

Lindsey (1983) suggests that paraprofessionals attend an initial meeting with other members of the school faculty and staff. Such a meeting should include the following activities: (a) introductions, (b) definition of the paraprofessional's role, (c) distribution of information about assessment and instructional techniques, (d) audiovisual presentations, (e) simulations, and (f) a question-and-answer session. An initial session may include discussions about confidentiality, rules, and school procedures. Then a general orientation from a building-level administrator may occur, followed by specific training by the teacher. The training session provides an excellent opportunity for the teacher to clarify roles and responsibilities. Training may involve anything from how to conduct multimedia presentations, to how to develop study guides, to how to monitor the progress of students in inclusive settings.

Training is necessary at the outset and on an ongoing basis (Frith & Lindsey, 1982; Frith & Mims, 1985). Training may be provided in the

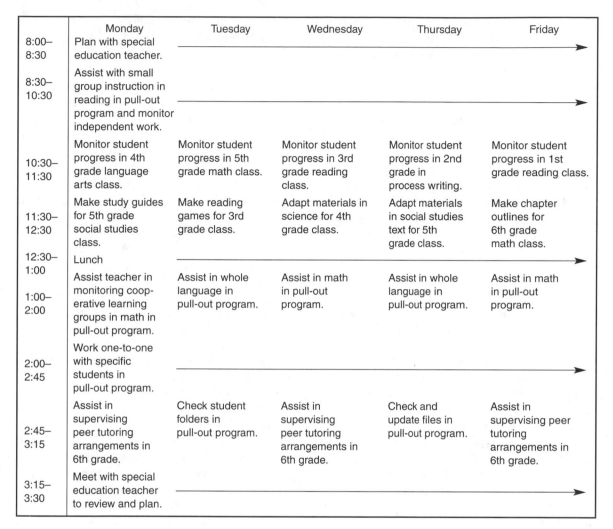

	Monday	Tuesday	Wednesday	Thursday	Friday
8:00–8:30	Plan with special education teacher.	→			
8:30–10:30	Assist with small group instruction in reading in pull-out program and monitor independent work.	→			
10:30–11:30	Monitor student progress in 4th grade language arts class.	Monitor student progress in 5th grade math class.	Monitor student progress in 3rd grade reading class.	Monitor student progress in 2nd grade in process writing.	Monitor student progress in 1st grade reading class.
11:30–12:30	Make study guides for 5th grade social studies class.	Make reading games for 3rd grade class.	Adapt materials in science for 4th grade class.	Adapt materials in social studies text for 5th grade class.	Make chapter outlines for 6th grade math class.
12:30–1:00	Lunch	→			
1:00–2:00	Assist teacher in monitoring cooperative learning groups in math in pull-out program.	Assist in whole language in pull-out program.	Assist in math in pull-out program.	Assist in whole language in pull-out program.	Assist in math in pull-out program.
2:00–2:45	Work one-to-one with specific students in pull-out program.	→			
2:45–3:15	Assist in supervising peer tutoring arrangements in 6th grade.	Check student folders in pull-out program.	Assist in supervising peer tutoring arrangements in 6th grade.	Check and update files in pull-out program.	Assist in supervising peer tutoring arrangements in 6th grade.
3:15–3:30	Meet with special education teacher to review and plan.	→			

Figure 5.5   Example of a Paraprofessional's Schedule

classroom by the teacher and in separate training workshops as needed. Separate training sessions may focus on topics such as how to work with culturally diverse populations; how to work in co-teaching situations; how to teach learning strategies and study skills; how to implement cooperative learning activities; how to use effective questioning; or how to work effectively in inclusive settings. Lindsey (1983) suggests providing ongoing inservice activities to maintain the diagnostic, instructional, and interpersonal relationship competencies of the paraprofessional and recommends monthly staff meetings to provide support.

Once a teacher and paraprofessional clarify role expectations, they should decide on (a) the specific tasks the paraprofessional will complete (e.g., collecting data on students' knowledge of multiplication facts), (b) the skills necessary to accomplish the tasks (e.g., charting and graphing), and (c) any training or modeling of strategies that would help the paraprofessional complete the tasks (e.g., strategies for monitoring students' performance). For example, if a paraprofessional were going to help a teacher make data-based decisions about a student's learning by using precision teaching to monitor progress, he or she would need specific training or instruction in how to use it. McKenzie and Houk (1986) suggest developing a plan that specifies the skills a paraprofessional must have in order to accomplish the tasks assigned. The plan should indicate exactly how the paraprofessional will acquire the skills, such as through on-the-job training, through in-service workshops, or by reading information on the topic.

Scheduling

Once identified, the tasks or job descriptions may be written on a task sheet (Salvia & Hughes, 1990) or schedule (see Figure 5.5). Daily and weekly schedules are helpful in clarifying assignments and structuring the activities of an assistant. This is an important point: What is written down is more likely to be accomplished than what is just mentioned. You may have encountered this when you made a to-do list in the morning compared with when you had ideas in your mind of things you wanted to do that day. On which day did you accomplish more?

The responsibilities of a teaching assistant should change as the classroom needs change. For example, during the month of September, Ms. Hernando's students were preparing for a young author's conference to be held in October. Ms. Hernando's teaching assistant, Ms. Talbot, helped students write stories, complete illustrations, type them in final form, and bind them in covers. During late October, Ms. Talbot helped students prepare for their end-of-the-quarter exams. She made sets of review cards with questions on the front and answers on the back. Her responsibilities changed because the needs of the students and classroom changed.

Communication and Feedback

Kahn (1981) suggests including time each day to meet with your teaching assistant. You may use this time to review the day, plan the next day, make modifications and adjustments, or revise job responsibilities, but most importantly, to keep communicating. You should make a point of providing both positive and corrective feedback to your teaching assistant.

For example, Ms. Brizo provided positive feedback to her teaching assistant, Ms. Grant, by reinforcing her work on the many multicultural activities she had developed to go with their learning center on famous American poets. On another occasion, when they were having a weekly planning session, Ms. Brizo noticed that Ms. Grant had left out some information on a chapter outline that she had been developing for some of the mainstreamed sixth graders. Ms. Brizo showed Ms. Grant a new technique to use in pulling the essential information out of a chapter. Ms. Grant used the technique to rework the outline, and Ms. Brizo gave her feedback and reinforcement for her work.

Evaluation

Some teachers plan a brief conference in the morning before school begins and another brief meeting at the end of the day. Others plan a conference once each day, in the morning, to plan the day. The next morning, they review the previous day and make adjustments, if necessary, as they devise a schedule for that day. Still others prefer to meet at the end of the day for planning and scheduling.

Evaluation is greatly facilitated when teachers and assistants schedule daily conferences. During the conference, the teacher and assistant can examine the responsibilities of the paraprofessional to make sure that they are still an important use of the assistant's time. The teacher may use this time to provide positive or corrective feedback to the assistant. The assistant may use the conference as an opportunity to clarify assignments and share information about students' progress. The greater the specificity of the assistant's duties and the greater the structure in identifying the tasks in writing, the easier it is to evaluate performance. If paraprofessionals are to provide services to students with special needs, then special education teachers must provide adequate training, schedule their time effectively, and give them ample feedback and recognition.

 ACTIVITY 5.4

1. You are a teacher of students with special needs at the elementary level. Several of your students are integrated into general education classrooms for math and reading. Make a list of the ways you would utilize the skills of a paraprofessional to help these students in the general education classroom.
2. You are a teacher of secondary students with special needs. You work with your students in school in the morning and in the community by supervising them on the job in the afternoon. In what ways could you utilize a paraprofessional in these situations?

◇ **IMPORTANT POINTS**

1. There has been substantial growth in the use of paraprofessionals in special education, and this growth has positively affected the delivery of services to students with special needs.
2. A paraprofessional, sometimes called a teaching/educational assistant or paraeducator, is a person whose position is either instructional or who delivers direct services to students and/or their parents, and who serves in a position for which a teacher or other professional has ultimate responsibility for the design and implementation of IEPs and other services.

3. In planning paraprofessional programs, it is important to (a) match the skills of the paraprofessional with the needs of the teacher, (b) examine ways to utilize the skills of paraprofessionals in working with culturally and linguistically diverse populations, and (c) clearly define role expectations and responsibilities.
4. Implementation of paraprofessional programs should include (a) orientation and training, (b) scheduling, (c) communication and feedback, and (d) evaluation.

COLLABORATION WITH PARENTS/FAMILIES

Historically, parents did not play a significant role in the education of their children with disabilities. School districts frequently assessed and placed children in special education settings without parental input or notification (Turnbull & Turnbull, 1986). However, with the passage of Public Law 94–142 (1975), now known as Public Law 105–17 (1997), the Individuals with Disabilities Act, many parents began to assume a more active role in decision making and program implementation for their children with disabilities.

Not only are parent roles changing in the school community, but they are also changing in society at large. Ever-increasing numbers of women are entering the workforce. The number of single-parent families is on the rise due to such factors as escalating divorce rates, desertion, and the growing acceptance of single parents (Ascher, 1987; Peterson, 1987; Turnbull & Turnbull, 1986). Approximately 47% of all African-American families, 26% of all Hispanic, and 14% of all Anglo households are headed by women (Bureau of the Census, 1997). Parents are relying more and more on day-care centers, extended family members, or persons other than a biological parent as caregivers. It is not unusual for Native American tribes to assign child-rearing responsibilities to grandparents (Devore & Schlesinger, 1987). Throughout this chapter, and the entire text, the terms *families* and *parents* will be used interchangeably, and may refer to mothers, fathers, stepparents, foster parents, aunts, uncles, grandparents, guardians, older siblings, and others.

With all of these factors affecting families, it is a challenge for special educators to form collaborative relationships with families to meet students' needs. Encouraging parents to visit the school, increasing the frequency of communication by making phone calls, sending positive notes home, and using telephone answering machines for recorded messages are just a few techniques that encourage a collaborative relationship between the school and families (Haring, Lovett, & Saren, 1991; Minner, Beane, & Prater, 1986). The foundation for any collaborative effort between families and school personnel is based on clear, open communication. Therefore, in this section on parents/families, we focus on effective communication techniques.

Communicating with Parents/Families

To encourage professional–family (school–home) collaboration, you must be aware of some of the barriers to effective communication, the content of both nonverbal and verbal messages, and ways to communicate during a crisis confrontation. Although we specifically address parents/families in this section, the verbal and nonverbal communication techniques we present are equally effective with administrators, faculty, and staff in the schools.

Communication Barriers
Sonnenschein (1981) identified attitudes of professionals that interfere with communication. These include the beliefs that parents are helpless, that parents are responsible for the child's conditions, that parents' opinions are not worth-

while, that parents are pushy or adversarial, and that parents and professionals should not become overly friendly. A belief particularly attributed to family members from minority cultures is that they lack interest in their child's development (Rounds, Weil, & Bishop, 1994). As Harry (1992) explains, this belief is exacerbated by the fact that some cultures stress respect for and deference to authority, which interferes with active participation at IEP and other meetings.

A first step in communicating with parents is viewing parents as partners, showing trust and respect, and having empathy for their problems. An attitude of respect and trust is particularly important when working with parents from various cultural groups (S. Chan, 1987; Johnson, 1987; Olion, 1989). Lack of respect from teachers and other school personnel is often mentioned as one of the reasons for infrequent involvement with their child's educational program (Marion, 1981).

Imagine what it would be like to have a child with you all day who is in constant motion or has frequent temper tantrums and to worry constantly about how that child will function as a productive adult. The Native American saying, "Oh, Great Spirit, grant that I may not criticize my neighbor until I have walked a mile in his moccasins," reminds us to consider the perspectives and experiences that parents bring to the communication process. Remember, the parent is the child's first teacher.

Nonverbal Skills
Eighty-five percent of communication is primal, nonverbal communication (Crisis Prevention Institute, 1983). Nonverbal communication is essentially all communication other than the spoken or written word. It is an important component of communication: When there is a discrepancy between a person's verbal and nonverbal message, people more often attend to the nonverbal message (Argyle, 1975; Mehrabian, 1969). If a friend of yours says everything

is fine, but has a scowl on his face, do you really want to ask if you can borrow his car? Nonverbal communication consists of proxemics, kinesics, and paraverbal components.

Proxemics. *Proxemics* refers to personal space, or the amount of distance you need in order to feel comfortable in your interactions with others. It is an imaginary circle that surrounds your body and is your comfort zone. When others cross it, you become uncomfortable. If you have ever worked with students who have behavior problems, you know that many problems develop because these students frequently do not respect the personal space of others. In fact, some teachers even take masking tape and tape personal spaces around each student's desk with the stipulation that other students can cross only with permission.

Culture influences a person's comfort zone. Many Asian-Americans require more personal space and are uncomfortable with the physical closeness of a teacher, whereas people from the Hispanic culture frequently need less personal space (Briganti, 1989). Most Arabs and southern Europeans stand closer when they talk than do Indians, Pakistanis, northern Europeans, and African-Americans (Baxter, 1970; Watson, 1970).

The personal space you are comfortable with is also often influenced by the sex, age, race, and size of the other person. Do you stand closer to an unfamiliar female or male? Anxiety also plays a part in personal space. A person who is anxious usually requires more personal space. When communicating with parents during a conference, you may want to place the chairs so that there is room for the parents to move and adjust their comfort zone.

Kinesics. Body language, such as postures and gestures, also conveys a message. Again, cultural effects are evident in this nonverbal communication. For some cultures, looking down, not at the teacher, is a sign of respect. Many Native Americans avoid eye contact (Simpson, 1982), as do many Asian-Americans, who are taught that avoiding direct eye contact conveys respect (S. Chan, 1987). Many individuals from Hispanic (Briganti, 1989) and African-American cultures (Grossman, 1994) teach children to lower their heads and not maintain eye contact when they are being reprimanded. In fact, eye contact with authority figures is frequently a sign of disrespect in the African-American culture (Gilliam & Van Den Berg, 1980; Grossman, 1994).

It is a good idea when communicating with parents to maintain a supportive stance. A supportive stance requires physical positioning so you are not sitting or standing directly in front of a parent. Many people connect a straightforward position with an authoritarian figure, which may decrease verbal communication (Crisis Prevention Institute, 1983). Instead of sitting or standing in front of parents, try sitting or standing to the side.

◆ ACTIVITY 5.5

You will need the help of a friend for this activity. With about seven feet between you, stand directly across from your friend. Looking at your friend, have him or her walk toward you. Hold your hand out and say stop when you begin to feel uncomfortable. Now reverse roles. Was your friend's personal space different from your own? Try the same experiment without the stop cue when you are with people you do not know as well. Did your comfort boundary change? Did it differ from theirs?

Paraverbal Communication. The tone, volume, and cadence of your voice are involved in paraverbal communication. Paraverbal communication is what your dog understands, causing it to hop around when you say, "Let's, go for a

Table 5.4 Nonverbal Communication Skills

Desirable	Undesirable
Facial Expressions	
• Direct eye contact (except when culturally proscribed) • Warmth and concern reflected in facial expression • Eyes at same level as client's • Appropriately varied and animated facial expressions • Mouth relaxed; occasional smiles	• Avoidance of eye contact • Eye level higher or lower than client's • Staring or fixating on person or object • Lifting eyebrow critically • Nodding head excessively • Yawning • Frozen or rigid facial expressions • Inappropriate slight smile • Pursing or biting lips
Posture	
• Arms and hands moderately expressive; appropriate gestures • Body leaning slightly forward; attentive but relaxed	• Rigid body position; arms tightly folded • Body turned at an angle to client • Fidgeting with hands (including clipping nails, cleaning pipe) • Squirming or rocking in chair • Slouching or placing feet on desk • Hand or fingers over mouth • Pointing finger for emphasis
Voice	
• Clearly audible but not loud • Warmth in tone of voice • Voice modulated to reflect nuances of feeling and emotional tone of client messages • Moderate speech tempo	• Mumbling or speaking inaudibly • Monotonic voice • Halting speech • Frequent grammatical errors • Prolonged silences • Excessively animated speech • Slow, rapid, or staccato speech • Nervous laughter • Consistent clearing of throat • Speaking loudly
Physical Proximity	
• Three to five feet between chairs	• Excessive closeness or distance • Talking across desk or other barrier

NOTE. From *Direct Social Work Practice: Theory and Skills,* Third Edition, by Dean H. Hepworth and Jo Ann Larsen. © 1990 by Wadsworth, Inc. Reprinted by permission of the publisher.

walk," or hide when you say, "It's bath time." It's the type of communication that interfered with the first speech you ever had to give in front of a large, unfamiliar audience. Remember the sweaty palms and the quaking voice? Suggestions for desirable nonverbal language communications with parents are found in Table 5.4.

Verbal Skills

The verbal skills of active listening, rephrasing, open-ended questioning, and summarizing are powerful during communication (FDLRS East, 1982; Roberds-Baxter, 1984; Turnbull & Turnbull, 1986). Coupled with nonverbal skills, they can lead to productive communication sessions.

Active Listening. Many teachers use active listening. In active listening, you communicate to parents that you are interested in what they have to say, will work to understand what they mean, and are comfortable with the feelings underlying their message. You echo what parents say, including their emotions, and they can either confirm or correct the accuracy of your understanding. For example, if a parent says, "I just can't understand why Janet is the way she is!" an active listening response is, "You sound very sad about Janet's disability." Active listening allows parents the freedom to express their feelings, to feel accepted, and to accept themselves (FDLRS East, 1982).

Rephrasing. When you rephrase, or reframe, what a parent is saying, you are attempting to use your own words to restate the parent's message (FDLRS East, 1982). Unlike active listening, in which you concentrate on both the affective and cognitive parts of the message, in rephrasing you concentrate on the meaning, or cognitive part. For example, look again at the parent's message, "I just can't understand why Janet is the way she is!" A possible rephrasing response is, "You are having difficulty understanding Janet's disability." With this response, you are not attempting to describe the feeling (e.g., sadness), but the cognitive part of the message. Rephrasing changes the words to help parents hear what they are saying and perhaps approach their problems from a different perspective.

Open-ended Questioning. Open-ended questions encourage parents to share information and participate more. The questions may be unstructured (e.g., "What do you think about Hector's program?") or structured, which limits the responses (e.g., "What have you found that works with Susan when she begins to cry?") (Turnbull & Turnbull, 1986). According to Hepworth and Larsen (1990), open-ended questions may take the form of a polite command (e.g., "Would you please tell me how the

notes are working with Jock?") or an embedded question (e.g., "I'd like to know how the notes are working with Jock."). This doesn't mean that you should never ask a closed-ended question, such as "Do you feel Lashonda is making progress?" or "Does Lashonda frequently appear tired?" Such questions are useful for finding factual information, but a preponderance of these questions limits discussion.

Summarizing. To summarize, simply restate what the parents said, highlighting the major points. Summarization helps to acknowledge that a topic has been exhausted and that the major points are understood.

 ACTIVITY 5.6

A parent has said that she is upset that you are allowing the other children to pick on her daughter. Write down two active listening statements and an open-ended question in response to this comment.

Crisis Confrontation

Handling a parent who is upset is never easy, even for veteran teachers. If you know that communication with a particular parent has the potential to become quarrelsome, you may wish to practice first what you plan to say with other people and ask them for feedback (Roberds-Baxter, 1984). But how do you handle communication when you are surprised by an irate parent? The Crisis Intervention Institute (1983) recommends the following procedures for handling verbal, aggressive behavior.

1. *Stay calm.* Trying to remain calm when a parent is shouting at you is easier said than done. Wanting to shout back or to escape is normal. Breathe deeply or think a pleasant thought before you engage in conversation.

2. *Isolate the parent.* Remove the parent from the public area. There is no need for others to be involved, and it is often difficult to change an attitude when others are observing. For example, you might say, "Ms. Herman, I'm sorry you're upset about Joe's quiz score. Let's go to my classroom, so I can get his quiz and we can sit down and talk about the problem." Don't forget the nonverbal behaviors of a calm, steady, low voice and a supportive stance.

3. *Listen and be aware of nonverbal cues.* Remember the nonverbal postures specified in Table 5.4. Try to pick up on any nonverbal cues, such as relaxation of the shoulders, to show that the parent is moving from an anxious stage and is ready to listen and discuss the problem rationally.

4. *After listening to the complaint, attempt to restate the parent's comment.* Restating what the parent said gives you time to think and possibly break the parent's pattern of irate communication. For example, "I can see that you are upset with Joe's grade because you feel the quiz was unfair and I'm picking on him." You may even agree with part of the criticism (e.g., "I know this was a difficult quiz").

5. *Question for specifics.* When you question for specifics, try to promote a rational reaction to the problem and show that you are willing to look at the problem from the parent's viewpoint. Open-ended, structured questions are often the best (e.g., "I have the quiz. Let's see what questions you feel were unfair."). Avoid making judgmental comments like, "Oh, Ms. Herman, you are so wrong."

6. *Keep communication simple.* Refrain from long explanations until the parent has calmed down. An anxious person is usually not ready or willing to listen to others. Spend more time listening than talking.

7. *Try not to take the action personally.* Do not automatically assume that the parent dislikes you. People lose control for many reasons be-sides personal animosity, including displaced anger, loss of personal power, confusion, fear of the unknown, attention getting, or psychological or physical disorders (Crisis Prevention Institute, 1983). Think of the reasons people lose control and try not to take the comments personally.

8. *Be assertive.* This is a step we have added in training our students to deal with verbal aggression. If Ms. Herman continues to scream, attempt to reschedule the conference with an assertive comment, "Ms. Herman, I appreciate your concern and I would like to resolve the problem with you, but it is difficult to do right now. Let's reschedule for tomorrow morning." Or "Ms. Herman, we don't seem to be able to resolve this. Sometimes, it helps to talk to another person. Why don't you come in tomorrow and we'll talk with the principal, Ms. Martinez, and maybe she can help us with our discussion."

◇ **IMPORTANT POINTS**

1. Treating parents/families with respect and having empathy for their problems may remove communication barriers.

2. Eighty-five percent of communication is nonverbal.

3. Nonverbal communication includes proxemics (personal space), kinesics (posture and gestures), and paraverbal components (tone, volume, and cadence).

4. Nonverbal behaviors such as proxemics are influenced by a person's culture (e.g., Hispanics often require less personal space than Asian-Americans and African-Americans).

5. Effective verbal communication skills include active listening, rephrasing, open-ended questioning, and summarizing.

6. Active listening involves echoing the cognitive and affective components of a verbal message.

7. Rephrasing involves restating the cognitive component of a verbal message.
8. Open-ended questioning such as "How is sending the note home working with Vivian?" tends to foster active interchanges.
9. Summarizing requires highlighting the major points of an interaction.
10. During a crisis confrontation, teachers should stay calm, isolate, listen, restate, question, keep the communication simple, view it as not personal, and be assertive.

Parent-Teacher Conferences

Effective communication skills should be practiced during parent conferences. In a longitudinal survey conducted by Harry, Allen, and McLaughlin (1995), parents of preschool special education students from the African-American culture identified four deterrents to participation: inflexible scheduling, limited conference time, emphasis on documentation rather than parent participation, and role structure of professionals as authoritarians. Hopefully, we will avoid these deterrents with the following suggestions for successful parent-teacher conferences. Parent-teacher conferences generally involve three steps: (a) planning the conference, (b) conducting the conference, and (c) following through on the conference. We present a checklist identifying procedures for these three steps in Figure 5.6.

Planning the Conference

Since many parents feel that a parent-teacher conference signifies some sort of problem (Flake-Hobson & Swick, 1984), be specific about the purpose of the meeting in addition to specifying the date and time. You may notify parents of the parent-teacher meeting by a note or by phone. A phone call provides an opportunity for the parents to ask questions and for you to check their understanding of the purpose of the meeting. If you are working with families from diverse cultures, Hyun and Fowler (1995) suggest that you encourage the parents to invite other people who are important to them to the conference.

Before the conference, review the student's folders, gather examples of work, and prepare materials, including a skeleton script of what you are planning to say. Scripting the content allows you to check your communication to determine whether or not it is free of educational jargon, to organize your thoughts, and in many cases, to listen carefully to the parents (because you have planned the important points you want to mention). A script also allows you to check with other teachers to obtain their input. In a co-teaching situation, it is essential that you meet with the general education teacher ahead of time for his or her input. In fact, you may want to sit down together and complete the script.

Educational jargon often interferes with communication. If you must use educational jargon, define or give examples of the terms. For instance, if you use the term *short-term objective,* add a definition, "the small steps students must master to reach a goal," or an example, "Jason must master the short-term objective of changing percentages, such as 70%, to decimal numbers, such as 0.70, before he can figure out sales tax."

When scripting the content, include student strengths, your concerns, and possible solutions. Remember the cultural implications of solutions. For example, in many cultures, such as Asian-American (Chinn & Plata, 1987), Latino (Briganti, 1989), and Native American (Walker, 1988), child rearing is shared by grandparents or others who live in the home. Therefore, consistency in helping children and adolescents with disabilities can be achieved only if whole families agree to participate in the intervention.

Another consideration in offering solutions is to recognize that some resources may

Planning the Conference

_____ 1. Notify
   - Purpose, place, time, length of time allotted
_____ 2. Prepare
   - Review student's folder
   - Gather examples of work
   - Prepare materials
_____ 3. Secure co-teacher's input, if appropriate
_____ 4. Script important points you wish to make
_____ 5. Arrange environment
   - Select site
   - Choose comfortable seating
   - Eliminate distractions

Conducting the Conference

_____ 1. Build rapport
   - Welcome
   - Introduce yourself and others
   - Describe roles of all individuals at conference
_____ 2. Preview meeting
   - Purpose
   - Time limitations
   - Note taking
   - Emphasize importance of parents' input
_____ 3. Share information
   - Use open-ended questions
   - Use active listening/rephrasing
   - Discuss strengths, concerns, and solutions
   - Pause once in a while
   - Look for nonverbal cues
_____ 4. Complete parent-conference form
_____ 5. Summarize information
   - Review high points
   - Schedule other meetings or follow-ups
   - Thank them for taking the time to come and for their contributions

Following Up on the Conference

_____ 1. Review conference with student, if appropriate
_____ 2. Share information with other school personnel, if needed
_____ 3. Mark calendar for planned follow-up
_____ 4. File parent-teacher form

Figure 5.6   Conference Checklist

NOTE. Adapted from the University of New Mexico/Albuquerque Public Schools Center for Parent Involvement, Albuquerque, 1979.

not be available to the parents. For example, Johnson (1987) cautions that it is not appropriate to suggest that a child play with water at

Student's Name _Bill_

Grade _Ninth_

1. _Strengths_ (Check vocabulary.)
   - Participates in discussions.
   - Makes insightful comments that often describe the point the author is trying to make.
   - Is a leader during cooperative learning groups. (Cooperative learning groups involve students of different ability working together on a project.) For example, Bill helps organize the other students by suggesting how they might all work together, asking such questions as, Who wants to draw the graph? and Who wants to look up the information in the encyclopedia?

2. _Concerns_ (Check jargon and specific examples.)
   - Bill is constantly late for his first-period history class, which is resulting in a failing grade.
   - His ninth-grade class teacher and I kept a record of the number of times late the past 3 weeks—late 11 of 15 days an average of 20 minutes each day. On time about 1 day a week.
   - Bill says he oversleeps or he rides with a friend who oversleeps.
     (Ask parents if they have any idea why he is late.)

3. _Possible Solutions_ (Initiate by asking parents if they have any solutions. If none, ask them about each of the following and see if they think any one would work.)
   - Bill rides the bus instead of riding with a friend.
   - Set up a home reinforcer system. At the end of the week the teacher will call the parent. If Bill is on time 3 out of 5 days, he can go to the football game or dance or out on Friday night. If not, he stays home.
   - Bill and both teachers write out a contract. If Bill is on time 3 out of 5 days, he earns the negotiated reinforcer at school, such as leading a small-group discussion with materials provided by the teacher.

Figure 5.7   Sample Script

home, if water must be hauled to the home. For these reasons, it is important to secure parent input concerning solutions; the ones you write during the planning should never be etched in stone. A sample script appears in Figure 5.7.

A final part of planning is selection of the environment for the conference. Try to use the classroom. There, you have immediate access to the files, plus the setting serves as a reminder of things the student said or did and that the pur-

---

Parent-Teacher Conference Form

Student's Name: Bill Jacobs   Grade: 9th

Date: 10/12

Place: Milton High School

Purpose: To discuss Bill's lateness to his first-period history class, which is resulting in a failing grade. Tardy 11 out of 15 days the past 3 weeks. On time 4 out of 15 days, about once a week.

Possible Solutions:

Solutions	Evaluation
1. Parents will talk with Bill.	Question effectiveness.
2. If late for more than two days during the week, he must ride the bus the entire week.	Negative, too long of a punishment.
3. If on time for three days during the week, Bill's father will take him out to drive the car on Saturday.	Positive, must do every week.
4. If on time for three days a week for five or six weeks, Bill's father will take him to a professional football game.	Positive, six weeks' time.

Solution Selected: #4
Bill's parents feel he will work for football and they want him to take driving lessons at school. His teachers will make up a chart for Bill, so he can see his progress.

Follow-Up Procedures:
Ms. Gonzalez will call Bill's parents weekly to report Bill's progress.

Signatures: *Jim & Diane Jacobs*   (parent/s)
                      Linda Gonzalez   (teacher)

Figure 5.8 Conference Form

pose of the meeting is to discuss educational goals (Stephens, Blackhurst, & Magliocca, 1988). Be certain to provide all participants with adult-sized chairs.

Spend time before the meeting relaxing. Roberds-Baxter (1984) recommends that you visualize yourself before the conference as being nondefensive, assertive, listening, and showing confidence.

Conducting the Conference

Establishing rapport, previewing the conference, sharing information, and summarizing the information are ingredients for successful completion of a conference. We also recommend the completion of a conference form during the conference to serve as a written verification of the content. A completed form dealing with the problem of Bill's being late for class is found in Figure 5.8. Beginning with *Possible Solutions,* the information was completed with parent input.

Establishing Rapport. Greeting parents at the door is a way to add to the comfort of parents from diverse cultures (Kuykendall, 1992). Begin the conference by introducing yourself and any other individuals, indicating their responsibilities. Be certain to address the parents respectfully. Hyun and Fowler (1995) suggest using greeting words in the family's language. Perl (1995) suggests you begin the conference with small talk and something nonalcoholic to drink to help relax parents. If you are part of a co-teaching situation and the general education teacher and you are both present, the person who contacted the parents should take charge. If you are in charge, remember to ask opinions of your co-teacher as well as the parents as you conduct the conference. Arrange adult seating for the parents and place your chair next to the parents and not directly across from them.

Previewing the Conference. At this time, state the purpose of the meeting, identify time limitations, and emphasize to the parents their importance in providing input and solutions. If you plan to take notes, inform the parents and ask them if they would like a copy. Take notes openly, so that they can see what you are writing (Turnbull & Turnbull, 1986). If you are going to complete a conference form similar to that in Figure 5.8, show and explain the form.

Sharing Information. In sharing information, remember to use open-ended questions, active listening, and rephrasing. Make every attempt to involve the parents actively. In many cultures, parents are passive receivers of information in school matters. For example, in the Asian culture, schooling is viewed as the responsibility of the school (Chinn & Plata, 1987). In the Hispanic culture, parental involvement in school matters is not expected or encouraged (Echevarria-Ratleff & Graf, 1988). The inclination to be a passive receiver of information is also often found in the Native American parent, whose culture promotes a re-

luctance to share information with authorities (Johnson, 1987).

Always start on a positive note, mentioning the strengths of the student. Next, move to the concerns, using specific examples or work samples. You may want to ask parents if they see similar behavior at home. Once your concerns are thoroughly discussed, move to possible solutions, asking for parent input. Throughout the conference, remember to listen to the parents, refrain from interruptions, and give the parents many opportunities for input. If you do not understand what a parent is saying, ask the parent for clarification (Hyun & Fowler, 1995). Wait for the parents to respond before adding another point: In some cultures, it is impolite to interrupt others. For example, in some Native American tribes, it is an unwritten rule that an individual waits for the speaker to finish talking before saying anything (Johnson, 1987).

Summarizing the Information. Before concluding the conference, review the major points, including the concerns and the solution agreed upon. Schedule any future meetings, phone calls, or follow-through plans. Be certain to thank the parents for their ideas and contributions, and offer to send them a copy of your notes or the conference form.

Following Through After the Conference

If you are planning to review the conference with the student, you should mention this at the end of the parent conference and ask the parents for their permission, or summarize what you plan to say. If you need to share the information with other professionals, remember that any written information that is shared with other school personnel must be revealed to parents upon request (Morgan & Jensen, 1988). Finally, be certain to file the conference form.

ACTIVITY 5.7

Examine the description below and script the information using the script in Figure 5.7 as an example. Include strengths, concerns, and possible solutions.

Rosa is having problems turning in homework. She keeps telling her fifth-grade teacher and you that her younger brother rips it or that she forgets it, but it is finished. At this time, her grade is a D due to her incomplete homework assignments. She is able to score Bs and Cs on the weekly quizzes.

Table 5.5 Desired Qualities of an Exemplary Collaboration

1. Unconditional support based on shared goals, mutual decision making with the agreement to disagree.
2. Positive attitudes and interactions combined with mutual respect among partners/collaborators.
3. Shared responsibility and no-fault teaming.
4. A total commitment by the partners to resolve problems/conflict.
5. Team spirit that is enhanced by building on existing strengths and skills of partners.
6. Professional development and support of partners to learn and grow.
7. Ongoing, positive interactions with the community.

COLLABORATION WITH OTHER PARTNERS

Throughout this chapter, we have focused on collaboration with general educators, paraprofessionals, and parents/families. However, a variety of other partners are critical for the success of school and community programs (Blalock, 1997). These partners include administrators (e.g., principals, assistant principals), other teachers or specialists (e.g., Chapter 1, bilingual, transition specialists), related service providers (e.g., speech/language pathologists, counselors, school psychologists), community and state agency personnel, or job coaches. The key to success in working effectively with these and other partners is through communication and collaboration. Many of the techniques and procedures we have suggested that you use with teachers, paraprofessionals, and parents/families will work effectively with these partners as well. Please see, in particular, our suggestions for administrators in the section of this chapter on barriers to and ingredients of effective collaboration. In addition, we have included an ex-

ample of the desired qualities of an exemplary collaboration inspired by the work of Hunt (1995). We believe that these seven suggestions (Table 5.5) can be used in collaborative interactions with all partners.

 IMPORTANT POINTS

1. Parent-teacher conferences involve (a) planning the conference, (b) conducting the conference, and (c) following through on the conference.
2. Before the conference, review the student's folders, gather examples of work, and prepare materials, including a skeleton script of what you want to say.
3. During a parent-teacher conference, a teacher should establish rapport; preview the meeting; share strengths, concerns, and possible solutions; and summarize the conference content.
4. Prior to concluding the conference, review the key points, including the concerns agreed upon.
5. Schedule a follow-up to the conference.

6. A variety of other partners are critical for the success of school and community programs, including administrators, other teachers or specialists, related service providers, community and state agency personnel, or job coaches.

◆ DISCUSSION QUESTIONS

1. Discuss the impact of coaching on collaborative interactions among teachers, administrators, and other school professionals.

2. Give examples of the verbal and nonverbal communication skills that you, as a teacher, feel would be most effective in the following situations:

   a. The planning conference, the observation, and the reflecting conference involved in cognitive coaching.

   b. A feedback session with a paraprofessional.

   c. A meeting with parents who are concerned about their child's progress.

PART

2

INSTRUCTIONAL TECHNIQUES

6

THE
INSTRUCTIONAL
CYCLE

In Chapter 1, we referred to a general instructional framework for making decisions about teaching students with special needs. This framework includes planning the lesson, presenting the lesson with guided practice and feedback, providing for independent practice, and evaluating the effectiveness of the lesson. We discussed beginning-of-the-year planning in Chapter 2, and in this chapter, we examine some of the decisions teachers must make in the daily teaching process. In the daily planning phase, teachers make decisions about instructional language, instructional time, motivation, and subject content. In presenting the lesson, they make decisions about strategies for presenting new subject content, activities for practice, positive and corrective feedback, and summarization of the content. During independent practice activities, teachers decide on activities that reinforce the content presented and ways to generalize the information. After the lesson, they make evaluative decisions concerning student performances and the necessity of reteaching the content. They also reflect and self-evaluate. Teacher effectiveness research supports this instructional cycle (Berliner, 1984; Brophy, 1979; Christenson, Ysseldyke, & Thurlow, 1989; Englert, 1984; Rosenshine, 1980; Rosenshine & Stevens, 1986).

We feel this instructional cycle provides a useful framework whether a teacher follows the reductionist or constructivist paradigm. For example, during the lesson presentation, a teacher may present the subject matter (reductionist paradigm) or encourage a classroom dialogue (constructivist paradigm).

169

PLANNING

The IEP is crucial in planning instruction, as students' needs and characteristics are considered. A student's annual goals and short-term objectives form the foundation for planning. We discussed creating IEPs in Chapter 2 and developing annual goals and short-term objectives from assessment data in Chapter 3. Consequently, we do not discuss them again in this chapter. Moreover, instructional arrangements (e.g., large group, small group, peer tutoring, and individual instruction), which are also considered in the planning stage, are not discussed in this section, as they are discussed in other chapters. This section focuses instead on the teacher decisions involved with instructional language, instructional time, motivation, and content.

Instructional Language

Providing clear, explicit instructions is a strategy related to positive academic achievement (Coker, Medley, & Soar, 1980; Fisher et al., 1980; Rosenshine, 1983). Yet many teachers have problems communicating instructions to students who have special needs, especially students from diverse language backgrounds (Wohlge, 1983). To give directions, you must gain the attention of the students, examine the syntax and semantic content of the message, give visual cues, rephrase instructions, use comprehension checks, and select appropriate vocabulary.

A first step in giving directions or beginning instruction is to make certain that everyone is listening. This is easier said than done. Sometimes, teachers are in such a hurry to teach a concept that they forget that John isn't going to learn it if he is asleep or is talking to Susie. A verbal cue such as "Listen" or "Look at me," followed by silence and then praise for the students who are attending can ensure that all are listening. "May I please have everyone's attention?" followed by "Thank you" is appropriate

for secondary students. This cue is particularly effective when stated while standing close to a nonattending student. Other effective cues are silently standing in front of the room until all are quiet at the secondary level and gesturing with one finger in front of the lips for silence at the elementary level.

Syntax and semantics are also considerations for instructional language. An active sentence, such as "The boy hit the ball," is easier to understand than a passive sentence, such as "The ball was hit by the boy" (Wiig & Semel, 1984). Watson, Northcutt, and Rydele (1989) suggest avoiding idiomatic expressions, such as "busy as a bee," when instructing bilingual students. Simple sentences are recommended for students whose ability to understand instructional language lags behind their understanding of social language (Wohlge, 1983). Wiig and Semel (1984) suggest a sentence length of not more than 8 to 10 words.

Visual cues also help students understand instructional language. Simply writing the number 74 on the board clarifies the direction "Turn to page 74 in your math book." Writing the major points of a lecture on a transparency makes the lecture easier for secondary students to follow. Likewise, repeating a direction in a different way often helps students comprehend instructional language. For example, "Locate all the adjectives and underline them in the 10 sentences," can be rephrased as, "Find the descriptive word, or adjective, in each of the sentences and then underline it." These two suggestions are particularly effective for giving instructions to bilingual students with disabilities (Gersten & Woodward, 1994).

Comprehension checks are a necessity when working with students who have special needs. Specific questions are more effective than are general questions (Rosenshine & Stevens, 1986). "Are there any questions?" often results in silence, even though the students do not understand the task, whereas the question, "Robert, what are you to do first?" clarifies whether Robert understands the task and lets you know whether or not you should repeat it. Additionally, specific questions give students opportunities to listen to information again. Frequent comprehension checks are particularly recommended for bilingual students with disabilities (Gersten & Woodward, 1994). We discuss more about comprehension checks later in the chapter.

Vocabulary selection is another important consideration for instructional language. Wiig and Semel (1984) suggest the use of only five unfamiliar vocabulary words per lesson for students with language and learning disabilities. Marker words (such as "remember" or "the first step is" or "this is important") and voice emphasis assist poor listeners (Alley & Deshler, 1979; Burns, 1980). Brigham, Scruggs, and Mastropieri (1992) report that animated facial expressions, frequent eye contact, expressive and varied voice tones, dramatic body movement, and overall energy had positive effects on attention, behavior, achievement, and attitudes

◆ ACTIVITY 6.2

Work with your partner again and notice the improvement in your instructional language and your friend's performance as you describe these four figures:

of students with mild disabilities in junior high school classes.

Instructional Time

Instructional time is usually divided into time allocated to various instructional activities (allocated time) and time that students are engaged in academic tasks (Greenwood, 1991). In Chapter 2, we discussed allocated time, so here we concentrate on engaged time. Academic learning time (ALT) is the amount of time that students spend engaged in successful completion of relevant learning activities (R. Wilson, 1987). It is closely linked to achievement in elementary students (Fredrick & Walberg, 1980) and students with disabilities (Rieth & Frick, 1982; Sindelar, Smith, Harriman, Hale, & Wilson, 1986), including those from culturally diverse backgrounds (Gettinger & Fayne, 1982).

Time on task varies, depending on the special education setting and the instructional techniques. Rich and Ross (1989) report that elementary students in resource room settings have higher levels of on-task behavior than do those in special classes and special schools. They also observed that students spent about 90% of the time on task during teacher instruction and only 60% during seatwork activities. Greenwood (1991) reports that high socioeconomic status (SES) students in suburban schools spent more instructional time in academic-oriented instruction than did low SES students in urban schools.

Presenting shorter and more frequent lessons per hour, using appropriate positioning and eye scanning to monitor the class, and reinforcing appropriate behavior facilitate student task involvement (Englert & Thomas, 1982).

Sometimes students are off task because they are waiting for teacher assistance or for other students to finish assignments. Listing alternatives, such as "go on to the next problem" or "ask for help from your assigned partner," may keep students on task (Olson, 1989). Designing help signs for younger students to place on their desks or having older students take a number for help may decrease the tendency of students to discontinue work because they have their hands raised as they wait for assistance (Olson, 1989). Other times students may be off task as they finish assignments before the period ends. Instead of giving them more of the same work, you may provide (a) a free area or learning center with games or listening activities; (b) magazines such as *National Geographic, People, Seventeen,* and *Hot Rod* for students to read at their desks; (c) social areas in the room for quiet talk (especially appropriate for secondary students who enjoy peer interaction); (d) self-selected worksheets to complete for extra credit; and (e) 3-by-5-inch index cards with creative, enjoyable tasks, such as reading to the rabbit or calculating the area of the teacher's desk, for students to complete (Olson, 1989). You may also wish to preselect specific software programs or CD-ROMs for students (see Chapter 11).

Off-task talk prevents on-task behavior. For example, in answer to a question, students sometimes talk about a personal experience that is totally unrelated to the task. To redirect the student to the task at hand and to maintain the momentum or pace of the lesson, you may state that what the student has said does not have anything to do with the topic ("This doesn't relate to our topic. Remember, we are talking about electricity.") or suggest that the topic should be talked about at a later time ("I know that's im-

portant, but let's talk about it later."). Of course, you must remember to discuss the topic later if you've promised to do so.

For academic progress to occur, students must not only be on task, but must also achieve at a high accuracy level. When answering questions or participating in practice connected with presentation of new material, students should achieve an accuracy level of approximately 80% (Christenson, Thurlow, & Ysseldyke, 1987; Englert, 1984; Wilson, 1987). Christenson, Thurlow, and Ysseldyke (1987) recommend a success rate between 90% and 100% during independent practice and review.

Kounin and his colleagues (Kounin, 1970; Kounin & Gump, 1974; Kounin & Obradovic, 1968) identified several teacher behaviors that decrease noninstructional time and increase appropriate behaviors and time on task. These behaviors, with examples, are explained in Table 6.1.

 ACTIVITY 6.3

Meet with three peers and develop three ideas for dealing with students who finish work early at the secondary level and three ideas for the elementary level.

Motivation

As a teacher, you will be faced with the challenge of motivating your students. Offering structured choices relative to curriculum content and procedures can be motivational (Adelman & Taylor, 1983). Even simple choices of whether to do the odd- or even-numbered problems or when to do various worksheets may motivate reluctant adolescents. You may schedule a variety of activities for student selection during independent practice. You may also of-

Table 6.1 Ways to Increase Instruction Time and Decrease Off-Task Student Behaviors

Behaviors	Definition	Example
Withitness	Constant awareness of what is going on in classroom. Selecting the correct inappropriate behavior, stopping it before it escalates, and offering alternative behaviors.	The teacher sees Mike is about to throw a spit ball at Jane and comments, "Mike, please continue—we're on the third paragraph."
Overlapping	Attending to more than one situation at a time.	The teacher is teaching a reading mastery lesson when Sally approaches with a question. As part of the class routine Sally knows to sit in the help chair next to the teacher. A few minutes later, the teacher tells the reading group students to practice reading to each other. She then helps Sally quickly and returns to the reading group, praising them for reading so well together.
Movement: Smoothness	Staying on track (not reacting to or interjecting irrelevancies).	During the science demonstration, the teacher, instead of listening to Jim's story about what he did last night, quickly states, "We need to talk about science now," and refocuses the attention of the students onto the science demonstration.
Movement: Smoothness	Absence of flip-flop or dangle; i.e., starting an activity, stopping it, and then returning to original or dropping it altogether.	Instead of starting the science lesson and then assigning the spelling homework she had forgotten during spelling class, the teacher makes a note in her science text. After science is completed, she reviews homework for the day and includes the spelling words.
Movement: Slow Down	Keeping lessons moving briskly, avoiding staying on a topic too long or fragmenting.	When the teacher sees that Tim has his feet in the aisle, she quickly moves toward Tim and taps his leg as she continues with the lecture, as opposed to the teacher who says, "I see some children with their feet in the aisle. Keeping feet in the aisle is dangerous as other students may trip over them. . . ."
Group Attention	Taking action to ensure students are attending to task.	The teacher varies individual and group responses or avoids a predictable pattern for calling on students.
Group Attention	Encouraging students to participate at all times, even during individual responses.	While Hector works a division problem on the overhead, the rest of the students complete the problem at their desks.
Accountability	Letting students know their participation will be monitored.	The teacher circulates as students read to each other.

fer a variety of ways for students to demonstrate their knowledge. One of the most common responses in education is a paper-and-pencil response, which requires students to answer questions on dittos, workbook pages, or at the end of a chapter (Rieth, Polsgrove, Okolo, Bahr, & Eckert, 1987). But students can present their knowledge in other ways as well. In Figure 6.1, we present a sample choice sheet designed for secondary students. The sheet lists different ways to exhibit content knowledge. You may instruct students in how many activities to com-

Name _____

Date _____

I will do _____ of these to show I understand the

material found in Chapter _____ of

_____ .

_____ 1. Take a test.

_____ 2. Design a technology presentation of the
           major points.

_____ 3. Write a summary and answer the questions
           at the end of the chapter.

_____ 4. Tape a summary and the answers to the
           questions at the end of the chapter.

_____ 5. Complete _____ worksheets.

_____ 6. Discuss the major points with two peers over
           a tape recorder.

_____ 7. Complete a notebook of major facts.

_____ 8. Your option as approved by the teacher

           _____ .

(The following numbers are required by all

_____ .)

Figure 6.1 Sample Choice Sheet for Secondary
Students

plete and let them choose the activities. The variety of choices considers the learning styles, interests, and diversity of students. There is also a
self-choice option.

Motivation is further enhanced when learning is personally relevant (Good & Brophy,
1984). Explaining why it is necessary to learn the
material and applying the objectives to real life
are adaptations that teachers can easily make to
motivate students (Adelman & Taylor, 1983).
"We are studying about business letters because
next week we will be writing to the embassies of
various countries to ask for information" is an
example of giving relevance to the study of

business letters. Adding personal relevance is
also achieved by linking a student's prior knowledge to the new knowledge. For example, "Jim
visited Mesa Verde over the summer so he saw
one of the land forms, mesas, that we are studying today. What did you notice about the mesas,
Jim?" The consideration of students' personal
interests in the selection of materials motivates
secondary students (Zigmond, Sansone, Miller,
Donahoe, & Kohnke, 1986). Driver's training
manuals, newspapers, sports stories, or student-
selected materials are often more reinforcing
than a standard secondary text.

Making a commitment to learning and setting
goals gives students a sense of participation in the
learning process. One of the techniques used in
the learning strategies curriculum model from
the University of Kansas Center for Research on
Learning is to ask adolescents to make a commitment to learning a new strategy before you introduce it. The self-advocacy strategy of the learning
strategies curriculum increased adolescents' participation in setting their own goals during IEP
conferences (VanReusen & Bos, 1994).

Some teachers even write individual student
contracts. In these contracts, students often set
their own goals. We have found that students
frequently set unrealistic goals, such as "completing 100 problems in a minute" or "scoring
100% on all spelling tests." Therefore, it is helpful to share common performance standards
with the students (see Chapter 3) in order to in-
still realistic expectations of success. In Figure
6.2, we present a sample contract for a secondary student. The student typed his responses using a word processing program.

In a discussion of the literature concerning
motivation for adolescent low achievers, Mercer and Mercer (1998) note the benefit of student involvement. While teaching a secondary
basic science class, Ms. Moore motivated students with special needs by asking for student
volunteers to lead the class in a discussion of science questions. Before the science discussion,
she had written the questions on transparencies

Math Contract

Objective I Will Be Working On:

I will learn to add, subtract, multiply, and divide like fractions and reduce the answers to the lowest terms.

Materials and Techniques:

Participation in teacher-directed lessons during the weeks of November 1–29. Completion of all worksheets and assigned activities.

Goal:

90% on at least 1/2 of the worksheets and activities.
80%–90% on the unit exam.

I have selected the goal and feel it is one I can achieve.

Signed _____ Jose H. _____
(Student)

Figure 6.2 Academic Contract

and the answers on a piece of notebook paper. Each volunteer took turns sitting on the teacher's high stool at the front of the class and acting as the teacher. The acting teacher read a question and called on a student to read the section of the textbook that contained the answer. The acting teacher then showed the transparency with the question printed on it, called on a different student for the answer, and wrote the answer on the transparency using the teacher's model. Some of the students led lively discussions and wrote their own answers; others just followed the procedures.

Task-attraction and task-challenge behaviors motivate students to become involved in lesson presentations (Florida Performance Measurement System, 1984). Task attraction is teacher behavior that "expresses or shows genuine zest for a task" (p. 157). Task challenges are statements that indicate "to the students that an exercise or activity will be hard to do" (p. 157). Enthusiastic statements, like "This next activity is going to be fun" (task attraction), or challenging statements, like "This is a very difficult concept" or "You'll need your thinking cap on for this one. Hope I don't fool you" (task challenge), are easy to incorporate into a lesson.

The fooler game is a task-attraction activity designed to motivate elementary students to pay attention during lesson presentations. Demonstrated by Engelmann during a Distar reading program workshop (personal observation, Chicago, 1978), it involves a game with the teacher playing against the class. First, write sounds, facts, words, or other items on the board. Then explain to the class that they will play a fooler game to practice a particular skill. Continue with, "In this game, I'm going to try to fool you. If I fool you, I get a point, but if I don't, the class gets a point. I'm going to write some letters on the board and tell you the sound. You have to tell me whether I'm right or wrong. Remember, I'm going to try to fool you, so I won't always say the correct sound. Let's see if I can fool you." Then, point to the letter *i* and say, "This is *aa*. Right?" If children say no, reply, "What sound? Yes, a point for you." If the children answer incorrectly, reply, "No, it's *ii*. What sound?" and then, following student repetition of the correct sound, say, "A point for me." Engelmann adapted components of this game into his Direct Instruction reading program.

Ms. Gaines plays a similar game during guided practice of writing skills with her primary class of students with special needs. After teaching the correct printing of a letter, she writes the letter on the board, sometimes correctly and other times incorrectly, and asks each student to tell her whether the letter is correctly printed. If the student is correct, the class gets a point; if not, the teacher does.

A classroom reinforcement system may motivate students to reduce disruptive behaviors and increase academic efforts (Sprick, 1985). A system that many of our student teachers and beginning teachers find effective is a lottery reinforcement system adapted from the Assertive Discipline program (Canter & Associates, 1986). To set up the lottery system, identify the behaviors that you wish to reinforce, then give the students slips of paper when they display these appropriate behaviors. Have the students write their names on the slips of paper and place them in a container. At the end of the week, draw two names. Have the two winners then draw cards to determine what they have won. Each card should have a number from 1 to 7, representing the number of the reinforcers, except for one card, which says that the student wins all seven prizes. In Table 6.2, we show a lottery system designed to increase the academic performance of a class of secondary students.

Table 6.2 Lottery Motivation Example

You will earn chances for the room lottery held every Friday by:

• Returning homework on time.
• Bringing in paper and pencil.
• Participating in class.
• Scoring 80% or above on assignments.
• Turning in assignments.

The homework and paper-and-pencil tickets will be given out at the beginning of class. All other tickets will be given out at the end of class. Write your name on the tickets and drop them into the lottery container.

On Friday, two winners will be drawn. Being a winner entitles you to draw a card to determine which prize you have won. Each card has a number from 1 to 7, representing the numbers of the prizes. However, one card allows you to win all seven prizes.

 IMPORTANT POINTS

1. Teachers enhance instruction when they gain the attention of the students, examine the syntax and semantic content of the message, give visual cues, rephrase instructions, use comprehension checks, and select appropriate vocabulary.

2. Short, active sentences that do not contain idiomatic expressions are easier for students to understand.

3. Comprehension checks involve asking specific questions instead of general ones and require students to repeat the information.

4. Marker words and voice emphasis to stress important points help students comprehend instruction.

5. Academic learning time is the amount of time students spend engaged in successful completion of relevant learning activities.

6. Time on task is influenced by setting (e.g., students in resource rooms spend more time on task than do those in special classes or schools) and instructional strategies (e.g., students spend more time on task during teacher-directed presentations and less time during seatwork activities).

7. Providing students with alternatives for what to do when waiting for assistance from the teacher or waiting for others to finish their work decreases the amount of time students spend not engaged in academic activities.

8. For profitable academic learning time, students should maintain an accuracy level of 80% during lesson presentation and between 90% and 100% during independent practice.

9. Offering choices, making learning personally relevant, asking students to make commitments and set goals, actively involving students, making task-challenge and task-attraction comments, and implementing a reinforcement system motivate students to achieve academically and to display appropriate behaviors.

Subject Matter

According to Meier (1992), state and local education agencies usually determine the broad content of required courses and subjects, local school district administrators and teachers determine the specific subject area content, and individual teachers usually determine the content for a particular day or lesson. As a special education teacher, you may teach all subject areas, so you need to be certain you are knowledgeable of the subject matter.

Selection of Subject Matter

Teachers' manuals often assist in the daily selection and sequencing of subject matter. For example, the following teacher information is presented in the *Guide to Basic English Grammar* (B. Walker, 1988), the manual accompanying a text used to teach English to middle school students with special needs: "Remind students that the subject of a sentence is the person, place, or thing that is being talked about" (p. 37). This statement furnishes the definition of subject as used in the text. There is also a suggested sequence for instruction: "Discuss the meaning, pronunciation, and spelling of each vocabulary word. Then discuss the information and examples on pages 101 and 102. Have students complete the three warm-up exercises" (p. 20). In some popular commercial curriculum programs used in the teaching of students with special needs, such as *Reading Mastery* (Engelmann & Bruner, 1988), *Skills for School Success* (Archer & Gleason, 1989), and the *Learning Strategies* curriculum (Deshler & Schumaker, 1986), the subject matter is clearly specified and the lessons are scripted.

In addition to teachers' manuals, students' ideas and background information may provide a resource for the selection and sequencing of content. In an example from the Foxfire approach used with students with disabilities, the teacher presents the objectives mandated by state or local guidelines and the IEP, but students develop their learning experiences and negotiate how the objectives are to be achieved (Ensminger & Dangel, 1992).

Whether you use a manual or students' ideas and background information, you must analyze the subject matter to determine if students have the necessary prerequisite skills to master the new material. In the planning stage, you should ask yourself if the students might have difficulty with the new information because it builds on information that they are lacking. For example, Miller and Milam (1987) found that students with learning disabilities had difficulty mastering the new content of division because they had difficulty with subtraction or multiplication. A systematic way to identify prerequisite skills is to complete a task analysis.

Task Analysis

Task analysis involves breaking down a task or objective being taught into simpler components. To perform a task analysis, you must identify "the terminal behavior, list the necessary prerequisite skills and list the component skills in sequence" (Alberto & Troutman, 1999, p. 277). Prerequisite skills are skills that students must master *before* they can be taught a terminal behavior. In the previous division example, students were unsuccessful at mastering division problems (the terminal behavior) because they could not subtract or multiply accurately (prerequisite skills). They may also be unsuccessful because you have not identified the component skills that must be mastered *on the way* to reaching the terminal behavior. The component skills may be either parallel or sequential (Desberg & Taylor, 1986). Parallel component skills have no sequential order; that is, it doesn't matter which component skill you teach first. Skills are sequential if their order is invariant; that is, each component skill cannot be mastered unless the previous one has been mastered. For example, if the terminal behavior is to discriminate between mass and weight, it doesn't matter whether you teach students to define *mass* or *weight* first (parallel component skills). However, you must teach students the definition of *mass* and *weight* before you can teach them to discriminate between the concepts (sequential component skills).

Thus, when you are planning a lesson, you need to consider prerequisite and component skills. For example, let's say that your objective involves teaching Heather to multiply accurately problems with percents, such as 25% × 33. In your plan, you need to make certain Heather knows the prerequisite skills of multiplying two-digit times two-digit problems with and without regrouping. Thus, you should begin the lesson by having her multiply two-digit times two-digit problems, such as 15 × 24. By including such problems, you automatically check whether she knows the multiplication process, addition process, multiplication facts, and addition facts, the prerequisite skills required for success. The next step in your planning is to think about the component skills: "What steps should I teach first?" Performing the task yourself shows that Heather must convert the percents to decimals (25% = .25), multiply (.25 × 33), and then place the decimal point in the proper place in the answer (8.25).

If you are planning to assign a commercial worksheet or lesson from a commercial text for the students to work on independently, a task analysis may identify the content to emphasize during instruction. For example, from the commercially prepared worksheet in Table 6.3, Ms. Monti decided that she had better emphasize

Table 6.3 Capitalization Worksheet

Directions: Circle the capitalization errors below in the nine sentences.

1. Look at the old Car with the shiny hubcaps.
2. they did a fun activity in class.
3. Yesterday i went to see dr. jones.
4. did you like the movie *gremlins*?
5. Chicago is a City in Illinois.
6. monkeys are funny to watch at the zoo.
7. We went to see mother.
8. Do you know dr. smith, the dentist?
9. I really enjoyed reading *a wrinkle in time.*

---

the following capitalization rules during her lesson presentation:

1. Capitalize the beginning of a sentence (Sentences 2 and 6).
2. Capitalize the pronoun *I* (Sentence 3).
3. Capitalize the names and titles of persons and things (Sentences 3, 4, 8, and 9).
4. Capitalize the word *mother* when it is used as a substitute for a name (Sentence 7).
5. Do not capitalize common nouns (Sentences 1 and 5).

 ACTIVITY 6.4

Using task analysis, identify the capitalization rules that students must know to complete these two sentences successfully.

1. we have left our airline Tickets at home.
2. Sunfa did not like the movie *roger rabbit.*

Types of Subject Matter

The academic subject matter found in classrooms typically falls into the categories of basic concepts or skills, concepts, rules, laws, lawlike principles, and value judgments (Engelmann & Carnine, 1982; Florida Performance Measurement System, 1984). As you are planning, correct identification of the types of subject matter leads to the correct selection of the content that you should directly teach or elicit from the students. For example, when you are teaching concepts, you need to be certain you include the definition, examples, and nonexamples when you present the lesson (Engelmann & Carnine, 1982; Florida Performance Measurement System, 1984). Conversely, if you are teaching basic concepts or skills, you would not include a definition. Concepts and basic concepts/skills may be found in all subject areas. Rules are often found in reading, spelling, grammar, and math content; laws in the natural sciences; and lawlike principles in social studies. Value judg-

Table 6.4 Types of Subject Matter

What Content to Include if You Are Teaching

Concepts—Abstract or generic idea
Verb (example)
Definition—*A verb is a word that indicates action or state of being*
Examples—*run, jump, is,* and *are*
Nonexamples—*girl, man,* and *to.*
Characteristics (optional)—*Verbs often follow subjects.*
Comparisons (optional)—*"A verb doesn't name a person, place, or thing like a noun does."*

Basic Concepts—Skills, abstract or generic idea
The color red (example)
Examples—*red apple, red block, red truck*
Nonexamples—*blue truck, blue block, green square*

Rule—A prescribed guide for action
A capitalization rule (example)
Rule identification—*Begin a sentence with a capital letter.*
Application items—*the boy is my friend* and *off the chair*

Laws or Principles—Explanation of physical behavior
Movement of electricity (example)
Law identification—*Electricity can pass through a closed circuit only.*
Cause and effect—*If the circuit is closed, then electricity can pass through.*
Application items—*Experiment with wires and a battery cell to turn on a light bulb.*

Lawlike Principles—Explanation of human or animal behaviors
Camouflage (example)
Principle identification—*Animals use camouflage to hide from their enemies.*
Cause and Effect—*If a chameleon thinks an enemy is near, it will turn the color of its surroundings.*
Application items—*Discover other animals and ways they camouflage themselves.*

Value Judgment—Evaluation of the value of things
Pam's behavior was appropriate (example)
Development of criteria—*Calm voice, polite*
Identification of facts—*Pam asked, "May I please borrow a pencil?"*
Comparison—*Calm voice—yes*
                       Polite—yes

ments are often found in social skills and self-help content. See Table 6.4 for specific guidelines concerning subject matter types.

Amount and Complexity of Subject Matter

From a review of the effective teaching research, Berliner (1982) reports that presenting concepts in small steps is particularly successful when teaching young students, remedial students, and students of all ages and abilities during the acquisition stage of learning. For exam-ple, in teaching the skills of long division, effective teachers of low-achieving students in math first taught the students the estimation step and had the students practice that step (Englert, 1984). Then the teachers described the next step and followed it with practice.

Proponents of the constructivist model feel that teachers should refrain from breaking tasks down into small steps, because that results in a lack of meaning (Poplin, 1988; Heshusius, 1989). Instead, they believe effective teachers use scaffolding strategies. The rationale for scaffolding originates from Vygotsky's zone of proximal development, which is the distance between what an individual can do independently and what an individual can do with assistance from more competent individuals. With scaffolding, a teacher supports and guides young learners in taking the risk to achieve a task just beyond the learner's capabilities. Procedural facilitators and anticipation of students' errors to decrease content complexity are examples of some scaffolding strategies (Rosenshine, 1990).

Procedural facilitators may include hints, cue cards, and half-done examples. Listing the steps of rounding hundreds, beginning with the first step of "1. Look at the number in the ten's position" provides hints to students. Montague and Leavell (1994) used grammar cue cards to improve the quality and length of stories by junior high students with learning disabilities. The cue cards contained key words like *where, when, characters, problem and plan,* and *story ending.* These key words reminded students to include this information in their stories. Half-done examples provide questions or statement starters, such as "That doesn't sound right because *cold* means _____ ," for students to complete.

In anticipating student errors, effective teachers point out the material that is easily misunderstood. For example, Mr. Anderson, in discussing the spelling of *all right,* mentioned that most students forget that it is two words and spell it as *alright.* Palincsar and Brown (1989) suggest that teachers discuss the vocabulary that they feel may give their students problems before they teach reading comprehension. It may be difficult to anticipate mistakes at first, but with experience you will begin to recognize content that may prove particularly troublesome for students.

Instructional Alignment

Instructional alignment is the amount of congruence among the objectives, instructional procedures, and evaluation procedures of a lesson (Cohen, 1987). What you intend to teach should match what you teach and what you assess (West, Idol, & Cannon, 1989). An example of nonalignment is found in the following lesson. The teacher, Ms. Harper, planned to teach students to identify adjectives. During the lesson, she asked students to circle the adjectives in each sentence, and then during evaluation, she required them to write sentences with adjectives. Ms. Harper has matched the objective to the instructional procedures, but not to the evaluation procedures. Requiring students to write a sentence with *beautiful* in it (the evaluation task) is more difficult than her objective of requiring students to circle the adjective in a sentence, as in, "The beautiful girl is crying." To correct this nonalignment, Ms. Harper should require students to identify adjectives in sentences during evaluation. Cohen (1987) finds that students with academic difficulty have problems with lack of instructional alignment.

◆ **ACTIVITY 6.5**

Part 1. Label each of the following statements as a concept, rule, law, lawlike principle, or value judgment. Next, select one of the four items and identify the subject matter you plan to teach. For example, if the item you selected is a concept, you need to identify the definition, examples, and nonexamples you would include.

1. A triangle is a figure with three sides and three angles.
2. Flossing your teeth is a good health habit.
3. When you round off a number, you should compare it to 5.
4. If water reaches 212 degrees Fahrenheit, then it will boil.

Part 2. Create a procedural facilitator to help a student who is having problems remembering the rounding rule (Item 3).

◇ IMPORTANT POINTS

1. Task analysis requires the identification of prerequisite skills, component skills, and terminal behaviors or objectives.
2. Prerequisite skills are skills that students must master *before* they can master the terminal objective. Component skills are skills that must be mastered *on the way* to mastering a terminal objective.
3. Definitions, examples, and nonexamples are usually presented when teaching concepts; examples and nonexamples are used when teaching basic concepts or skills.
4. The use of examples, nonexamples, and the defense of whether or not a rule applies are necessary in teaching rules.
5. When teaching laws and lawlike principles, effective teachers state and discuss cause and effect and lead students in applications.
6. Development of criteria is necessary in the teaching of value judgments.
7. When students are first learning a new skill, effective teachers present a number of small, sequenced steps or decrease the complexity of the materials by using procedural facilitators and anticipating possible student errors.
8. With scaffolding, a teacher supports and guides young learners in taking the risk to achieve a task just beyond the learner's capabilities.
9. Procedural facilitators are prompts that help students when they begin to learn a skill.
10. Instructional alignment is the amount of congruence among the objectives, instructional procedures, and evaluation procedures of a lesson (Cohen, 1987).

PRESENTATION

Archer and Isaacson (1990) divide lessons into three parts: opening, body, and closing. We bor-row this terminology for our discussion of the next step of the instructional framework: presentation. Within lesson presentation, we also discuss guided practice and feedback.

Opening

To teach students, you must *gain their attention.* Sometimes, this is done by verbally cueing the students with "Look at me" for young students or "I need everyone's attention" for older ones. Sometimes, nonverbal cues, like silently waiting in front of the room or flicking the light switch, are used. Hunter (1981) recommends an anticipatory set as a way to cue attention and open a lesson. An anticipatory set is a statement or an activity that introduces the content and motivates students to learn. For example, one of our student teachers dressed up like a pilgrim to lead a discussion of the first Thanksgiving.

Once you have everyone's attention, Rosenshine and Stevens (1986), in their summary of the teacher effectiveness research, suggest beginning a lesson with a *short review of prerequisite skills.* We previously discussed the use of task analysis to identify prerequisite skills. *Relating the current lesson to previous lessons* is also recommended when introducing a new skill to students with special needs (Cohen, 1986; Englert, 1984; Goodman, 1985). For example, a review of the definition of a paragraph from the previous lesson should precede a new lesson dealing with various kinds of paragraphs.

An *overview* or preview of the instructional activities quickly informs the students of the day's events. For example, Ms. Maddalozzo begins her lesson, "Today we are going to spend time discussing some major holidays in November. First, we will discuss the information, then we'll do a few of the items together on the worksheet, and then you will do a few items alone. After we finish with the worksheets, we will do an activity involving a holiday in November."

An introduction that is especially effective for students with problem behaviors is *sharing*

What Do You . . .

Know?	Think You'll Learn?	Know You Learned?
She was a teacher.	How she trained for the flight?	
She died in an explosion of the shuttle.	Why she wanted to be an astronaut?	
She had to compete to be selected to join the crew.	How many children she had?	
She was married.	What classes she taught?	

Figure 6.3   Prediction Form

expectations concerning the behavior rules of the lesson (Borg & Ascione, 1982; Englert, 1984; Evertson & Emmer, 1982; Rosenberg, 1986). Sharing behavioral expectations is particularly important at the beginning of the year and when new students enter a program. Schumaker (1989) recommends that teachers share their expectations regarding student involvement in a learning strategies lesson, for example, "(a) watch the demonstration, (b) pay particular attention to what the teacher says and does, and (c) imitate what has been demonstrated" (p. 1).

Other opening strategies include *sharing rationales* (Archer & Isaacson, 1990; Palincsar & Brown, 1989; Schumaker & Sheldon, 1985) and discussing situations where the skill may be used (Palincsar & Brown, 1989; Schumaker & Sheldon, 1985). Duffy, Roehler, and Rackliff (1986) found that sharing the objective of a lesson and relating its importance to real life motivated readers who were reading one or more years below grade level. Rationales, such as "This lesson should help you read the back of a cereal box," influenced the amount of information that the low achievers remembered from the lesson. Describing the benefits of using different learning strategies in school, for employment, and in general also motivate secondary students with mild disabilities (Lenz, Alley, & Schumaker, 1987).

Since students come to school with prior information, *activating background knowledge* is an effective way to open a lesson (Palincsar &

Brown, 1989; Rosenshine & Stevens, 1986). One of the techniques to use to activate this prior knowledge is prediction (Langer, 1984; Ogle, 1986). In Figure 6.3, we present a form for using prediction in preparation for reading an article about Christa McAuliffe, the first teacher scheduled to make a shuttle flight. The first two columns are completed with the students before reading and the last after the students have read the article. Notice that in the first column, guided by the teacher, the students discuss what they already know from their background experiences and create a group knowledge base. In the "Think You'll Learn" column, students examine titles, pictures, and captions to make predictions about the content. The last column, "Know You Learned," requires students to compare their predictions to the events described. For students from different cultural backgrounds, Ruiz (1989) suggests a variation of the prediction routine. In her variation, the teacher identifies the major idea of the selection, asks the students to relate any similar experiences, and then asks the students to predict what will happen in the story.

For students who may not have the necessary prior knowledge to understand text information, Hasselbring (1998) recommends the use of *anchoring activities* to help build backgrounds. Anchoring is using real-world situations to develop meaningful knowledge (Bransford, Sherwood, Hasselbring, Kinzer, & Williams, 1990). For example, in the *Young Explorers* multimedia reading program, teachers show a videotape of the story before they expect students to read the text (Hasselbring, Goin, Taylor, Bottge, & Daley, 1997). Brown (1991) recommends bringing in concrete objects, showing a film, or role-playing to help build background information for the Native American student.

◆ **ACTIVITY 6.6**

Part 1. For a group of elementary students with special needs, decide how you would open a lesson with the following objective: When presented with two-digit numbers and asked to round them off to the nearest 10, students will round off the numbers at a rate of at least 20 digits correct and no more than 2 digits incorrect per minute for three sessions.

Part 2. For a group of secondary students with special needs, decide how you would open a lesson with the following objective: When presented with a paragraph from the reading text, students will paraphrase the content with 100% accuracy.

Body

Modeling, lecturing, questioning, and guided practice occur during the body of a lesson when new information is presented (Archer & Isaacson, 1990; Christenson, Ysseldyke, & Thurlow, 1989; Deshler & Schumaker, 1986; Palincsar & Brown, 1989). We also include a discussion of feedback here, even though feedback permeates a lesson.

Modeling

Modeling is defined as a "teacher's active performance of a skill" (Haring & Eaton, 1978, p. 25). Teacher modeling is recommended when students are just acquiring a skill (the ac-

quisition stage). Teachers may model the steps to a problem or use think-alouds. In think-alouds, teachers model their thought processes (Rosenshine, 1990). Think-alouds are frequently used in the teaching of learning strategies and in the use of reciprocal teaching practices (see Chapter 8). Modeling is effective for all levels and ethnic groups of exceptional students (Cohen, 1986; Englert, 1984; Graham, 1985; Rivera & Smith, 1988).

An example of modeling the steps of a problem is found in Mr. Clarke's oral introduction to long division: "The first step to work the problem 365 divided by 5 is to ask if 3 can be divided by 5. It cannot, so 36 will have to be divided by 5. Thirty-six divided by 5 is about 7, because 7 times 5 is 35. The next step is to subtract 35 from 36, which yields a remainder of 1. One cannot be divided by 5, so bring down the 5, which makes the number 15. Fifteen divided by 5 is 3. The answer is 73." Of course, Mr. Clarke is drawing a visual model of each step of the problem on the board as he completes each step verbally.

Duffy, Roehler, and Rackliff (1986) described a think-aloud for low-achieving readers. In this think-aloud, teachers talk about their thought processes and the steps to the strategy. We have modeled the following think-aloud after theirs.

Mr. Clarke begins: "Today, I'd like to share with you a strategy I use when I come to a word that I don't know when I'm reading. I'll think out loud so you can hear my thoughts.

First, I read the unknown word in the sentence. The weather forecaster said there will be snow flurries. I know I've heard the word *flurries* before, but I don't know what it means.

My **second** step is to see if there are any other words in that sentence that can help me figure out the word. The word before *flurries* is *snow,* so it has something to do with snow. Hm. It may mean it's going to snow a lot or it may mean it isn't going to snow much.

The **third** step is to read more of the sentences. OK, I'll read on. The next sentence says, "When the little boy heard the weather report, he became angry, because he wanted to build a snowman."

The **fourth** step is to use any background information. I think that sentence can help me figure the word out, because I know that you have to have a lot of snow to build a snowman. My brother and I used to make snowmen all the time.

The **fifth** step is to guess at the meaning. Now I bet I know what *flurries* means. I think it means light snow.

The **last** step is to substitute the meaning and reread the sentences. Let me go back and check. "The weather forecaster said there will be snow flurries or light snow. When the little boy heard the weather report, he became angry, because he wanted to build a snowman." Yep, I'm right.

 ACTIVITY 6.7

Take the example of Mr. Clarke's long division and change it to a think-aloud modeling procedure.

Lecturing

Often, at the secondary level, especially in an inclusive classroom, teachers present information through the lecturing technique. Research shows that active student involvement is essential during lesson presentation (Christenson, Ysseldyke, & Thurlow, 1989; Schumaker, Nolan, & Deshler, 1985). The three-statement rule—the teacher will make no more than three statements without having a student make a response—typifies the importance of student participation (Schumaker, Nolan, & Deshler, 1985).

Some effective adaptations to ensure that students with disabilities are engaged during a lecture is to use the instructional-pause procedure and guided notes. In the instructional-pause procedure, the teacher lectures and then allows time for student discussion. During the brief discussion, the students may identify the main idea and important points and predict the next section of the lecture, or they may share notes and review information. In a secondary social studies class, the following co-teaching instructional-pause routine was established. The general educator, Mr. Green, lectured for 10 minutes, then had the students repeat the important points in small peer groups for about 3 minutes while he and the special education teacher monitored the comments of the various groups. Both teachers then listed the major points on an overhead projector, asked questions of the groups to summarize the relevant features of the lecture, and clarified any misunderstandings that they heard while monitoring the group discussions.

With guided note taking, students are actively involved during a lecture as they complete a teacher-prepared handout to assist them in taking notes from the lecture. The guided note handout consists of cues and spaces for students to write key facts, concepts, and important relationships while the teacher is lecturing. For example, guided notes concerning the taxes levied by the British on the colonists may include a statement that says:

1. To increase revenue, the British decided to levy _____ on the colonists. Some of the products taxed were
   a. _____
   b. _____
   c. _____

Guided notes resulted in the taking of more accurate notes and in improved quiz scores for middle and secondary students with disabilities (Heward, 1994). Heward (1994) recommends that guided notes include the use of consistent cues (lines, bullets, etc.), more than a simple fill-in-the-blank format, daily quizzes as a follow-up activity, and minimal student writing, along with the inclusion of all facts, concepts, and relationships that students must learn. In Chapter 9, we discuss guided notes in detail with more examples.

Questioning

Teachers use questioning during lesson presentation to elicit student involvement (Engelmann & Carnine, 1982), to foster cognitive learning (Florida Performance Measurement System, 1984), to reinforce concepts, to scaffold (Pressley, Hogan, Wharton-McDonald, Mistretta, & Ettenberger, 1996), and to monitor and adjust instruction during the checking of comprehension (Christenson, Ysseldyke, & Thurlow, 1989). In reciprocal teaching, Palincsar and Brown (1984) teach students to generate their own questions and to ask questions of others as they compose a dialogue to learn new information (see Chapter 8).

Involving Students. Questioning students is a way to increase their academic responding time. Academic responding time is the time that students spend making active, overt responses. It is positively related to achievement (Greenwood, Delquadri, & Hall, 1984). Even though teacher questioning can effectively involve all students, minority and low-achieving students are not given as many opportunities to respond in class as other students (Reid, 1986; Stanley & Greenwood, 1983). Teachers advance the following reasons for not calling on low achievers: to protect the student from embarrassment, to prevent a slowdown of the lesson, and to ensure that everyone will hear a good answer (Christenson, Thurlow, & Ysseldyke, 1987). To ensure that every student is given an opportunity to respond to questions, you may call on students in a fixed order or put each student's name on an index card, which you flip once the student is called on. Another strategy

to involve all students is to call on students with disabilities first whenever you ask a question with many parts. For example, a question such as "What were the three causes of the uprising?" is easier for a student to answer when first asked than after other students have responded with two causes.

Fostering Cognitive Learning. A number of studies (Englert, 1984; Goodman, 1985) demonstrate that it is best to use low-level, fast-paced questions that produce many correct responses and elicit the involvement of special students when teaching basic concepts or skills. These low-level questions generally fall into the knowledge domain of Bloom's taxonomy of cognitive development (1956). Use of only low-level questions (recall questions) hinders the development of higher-level thinking skills (Meier, 1992). Higher-level thinking skills include comprehension, application, analysis, synthesis, and evaluation (Bloom, 1956). Asking students to list the effects of the Civil War is an example of a low-level recall question; asking students to compare and contrast the effects of the Civil War on the northern states as opposed to the southern states is an example of a high-level question. See Table 6.5 for some key words to assist in asking different levels of questions based on Bloom's taxonomy.

◆ ACTIVITY 6.8

Using the sample question stems found in Table 6.5, write questions for each of the levels about the movie *Titanic* or about one of your favorite books.

Reinforcing and Repeating Information. Teachers also use questioning to reinforce and repeat information (Engelmann & Carnine, 1982). For example, Mr. Pratt asked these two questions to

Table 6.5 Sample Question Stems Based on Bloom's Taxonomy

1. Knowledge

    Who, what, when, and where

2. Comprehension

    What is the main idea . . . ? What is meant by . . . ?

3. Application

    How would you . . . ? What would happen if . . . ?

4. Analysis

    Why? What was the author's purpose in . . . ?

5. Synthesis

    Do you suppose that . . . ? What if . . . ?

6. Evaluation

    Which is better . . . ? What do you think . . . ? Would you tend to agree that . . . ?

NOTE. Adapted from Morgan, N., & Saxton, J. (1994). *Asking Better Questions.* Markham, Ontario: Pembroke Publishers.

reinforce the fact that three-fourths of the earth is covered with water: (a) "How much of the earth is covered with water?" and (b) "Three-fourths of the earth is covered with what?" With these questions, the fact that three-fourths of the earth is covered with water is repeated. Repetition is frequently recommended for bilingual students with disabilities (Gersten & Woodward, 1994).

Scaffolding. Questions also serve as prompts or scaffolds to help students arrive at the correct answer. In prompting, teachers sometimes increase assistance until the student is able to respond correctly (Alberto & Troutman, 1999). For example, if you receive no response or an incorrect response after asking the question, "How do we change *lady* to *ladies?*" you should proceed with a more intrusive verbal prompt: "What is the rule?" to remind the student that there is a rule. If necessary, continue with "What do we do when a word ends in *y* to make it plural?" to give the student a part of the rule. You should always remain positive when prompting.

Monitoring and Adjusting Instruction During Comprehension Checks. Specific questions, like "What is the next step in the operation, Bob?" or "What kind of punctuation marks do you use at the end of a sentence?" serve as checks of comprehension and enable you to monitor and adjust instruction. The answers to specific questions will inform you if you should reteach concepts or skills or change the content of the lesson. If the students cannot answer the questions, you should reteach the concept instead of continuing with a new one. Rosenshine and Stevens (1986) identify three errors teachers frequently make in monitoring for understanding: (1) asking a general question (e.g., "Do you understand?") and then assuming, if there are no questions, that everyone understands; (2) calling only on volunteers, who usually know the answers, and assuming that other students know the answers, too; and (3) asking only a few questions. An effective routine is to ask specific questions after giving instructions or directions.

Nonacademic Questioning. Nonacademic questions frequently disrupt the flow of a lesson (Florida Performance Measurement System, 1984) and may lead to noncompliant behavior. Remember, an academic focus increases academic learning time, which results in higher achievement for students with special needs. For example, during her experience in a primary setting with students with special needs, a student teacher asked a 7-year-old student, "Joey, will you read the next two paragraphs?" to which he replied, "No, let Jamey do it." Now the student teacher was faced with another problem. This type of response to a nonacademic question is not unusual for noncompliant students. A nicely stated command, "Please read the next two paragraphs, Joey," is a better way to proceed.

Wait Time. There are two types of wait time connected with questioning. One involves the amount of time a teacher waits for a student's response after asking a question. The other concerns the amount of time a teacher waits after a student's response to ask another question. Rowe (1974) investigated both types of wait time in elementary science classes and found that teachers waited an average of 1 second for a student's response after asking a question and 0.9 seconds after a student's response before asking another question. When teachers increased the amount of wait time, students responded with longer answers, volunteered answers more frequently, and even initiated more questions. Teachers who use appropriate wait time are more flexible, ask a greater variety of questions, listen more carefully to answers, expect more of students, and demonstrate more genuine interest (Rowe, 1987).

In a review of wait time research, Tobin (1987) stated that a 3- to 5-second wait time enhanced achievement in all content areas with all levels of students, kindergarten through twelfth grade. Wait time is also important for bilingual students who have language-processing difficulties (Watson, Northcutt, & Rydele, 1989).

The suggestion to increase wait time may seem to contradict the instructional procedure of asking many questions that require quick, short student responses when teaching basic skills. It certainly is not appropriate for a teacher to wait 5 seconds when asking a child what sound a short *a* makes. Tobin (1987) suggests that the amount of wait time is a function of the type of question. He contends that low-level cognitive questions require less wait time and high-level questions require more. This is a logical explanation of the difference between the results of the wait-time research, which shows achievement enhanced by a 3- to 5-second pause after questioning, and the teacher effectiveness research, which shows that a brisk pace of teacher questioning and a high frequency of accurate student responses are effective for teaching basic skills.

 ACTIVITY 6.9

Change the following ineffective questioning techniques to effective ones:

1. A secondary teacher asks, "Sarah, why is this an example of a narrative paragraph? What is the relevant cue? How can you tell?"
2. A primary teacher asks, "Why do we hear a long sound in that word?" (No response.) The teacher continues, "Because it has a silent *e* at the end."

Guided Practice

Guided practice is active participation directed by the teacher. After presenting subject matter, the teacher leads the students in practice of the information. Often, guided practice is alternated with teacher modeling and demonstration, so that presentation and practice appear as one (Rosenshine & Stevens, 1986). A common practice routine in general education classrooms is to call on one student to demonstrate the answer to a problem on the board while other students watch. To increase the active participation of and extra practice for all students, simply have the other students complete the problem at their desks. One of our interns supplied her students with Etch A Sketch pads, while another created small chalkboards made with special paint for each student. You may also use peer tutoring or cooperative learning instructional formats during guided practice (see Chapter 10).

Guided practice activities should always align with the objective of the lesson and actively involve the students. For example, if the objective of the lesson is to write a descriptive sentence, then guided practice activities should involve students in writing descriptive sentences, not identifying which of two sentences is a descriptive one. During guided practice, effective teachers provide prompts, check for understanding, repeat and rephrase lesson content, provide examples and nonexamples, and give feedback (Gettinger & Fayne, 1982; Good & Grouws, 1979; Rosenshine & Stevens, 1986). Often, a teacher continues with guided practice until students reach a mastery level, usually 80% (Brophy, 1980).

Guided practice activities may include repeated readings, repetitive routines, and choral responding practices. In repeated readings, the teacher first reads the selection. Then the students read it in unison. Next, the teacher and students reread together, and finally, the students read it alone. In a comparison with worksheets, repeated readings resulted in improved reading rate and comprehension for students with special needs (Henk, Helfeldt, & Platt, 1986; O'Shea & O'Shea, 1988; O'Shea, Sindelar, & O'Shea, 1985). Suggestions for repetitive routines for both elementary and middle school students with special needs include telling students to "Repeat the rule with your eyes closed," "Whisper the rule to a neighbor," and "Say it with your right hand raised."

Choral responding is an effective strategy for providing practice for students with disabilities (Heward, 1994; Sainato, Strain, & Lyon, 1987). Choral responding was more effective than turn taking in teaching sight words to elementary students with learning disabilities or mild mental disabilities (Sindelar, Bursuck, & Halle, 1986). The normal choral responding routine is to ask a question or model a response, pause, cue students to respond together, and give feedback (see "Reading Mastery" in Chapter 7). For example, after telling students that an adjective tells which, what kind of, or how many, the teacher signals, pauses, and asks, "Everyone, what does an adjective tell?" Then all the students respond and the teacher acknowledges with feedback, "Absolutely correct, a perfect answer." Notice in the preceding example that a cue word, *everyone,* was used to elicit the group response. If a cue word is not used, the fastest and brightest students often blurt out the answers, defeating the purpose of the choral response. Interspersing choral responses with individual responses tends to keep students actively involved. Heward, Courson, and Narayan (1989) recommend the use of choral responding when a short and specific answer is required and when presenting information at a fast pace.

Response cards may be used instead of oral choral responding. Studies found that elementary and middle school students with or without disabilities participated more, scored higher on quizzes, and preferred response cards as compared to hand raising and one-student-at-a-time recitation in answering teachers' questions during math, social studies, and science classes (Gardner, Heward, & Grossi, 1994; see Heward, 1994, for master and doctoral studies results; Narayan, Heward, Gardner, Courson, & Omness, 1990). Ms. Otto used 3-by-5-inch cards in a nonverbal guided practice activity involving adjectives and adverbs for middle school students. She passed out two cards to each student and had them write *adjective* on one card and *adverb* on the other. She also made two cards for herself. She read a sentence written on the transparency (e.g., "The dilapidated window shutter was flapping wildly in the breeze."), asked a question (e.g., "What part of speech is *dilapidated*?"), followed with a pause, then cued the students to respond in unison (e.g., "Now"). Upon hearing the cue word, the students held up one of the cards. At the same time, she held up her adjective card so students could compare their answers with hers.

With this immediate feedback, it is not so embarrassing for students to have an incorrect answer, because they usually correct it before their peers notice. With a quick glance, the teacher can identify students who looked at others' cards for the answer or who were holding up the incorrect card. Such a format for eliciting active participation is particularly effective when teaching bilingual students (Watson, Northcutt, & Rydele, 1989).

Heward (1994) recommends "pinch" cards with multiple answers instead of a single set of cards. Students respond by holding up the card and then pinching the correct response with either the thumb and forefinger or with a colored clothespin. In the previous example, Ms. Otto may have had students write *adverb* and *adjective* on one card and then pinch with a clothespin the correct response.

You may also wish to preprint some general cards such as Yes/No or True/False that students can use for any curriculum. Whatever type of response cards you may choose to use, model several question-and-answer trials first, elicit many responses during a short time period of about 5 or 10 minutes, provide cue words such as, "everyone," give specific feedback based on the majority response, repeat items missed, and allow students to look at their peers' response cards (Heward, Grander, Cavanaugh, Courson, Grossi, & Barbetta, 1996).

 ACTIVITY 6.10

Correct the following mistakes made by two student teachers.

1. A student teacher was teaching a reading lesson to primary students with special needs by calling on one student to sound out 10 words, then calling on another student to sound out 10 words.
2. A student teacher was teaching a math lesson to a group of five middle school students. He spent the first 20 minutes lecturing to the students.

 IMPORTANT POINTS

1. Effective ways to open a lesson include the use of an anticipatory set, a short review of either prerequisite skills or previous lessons, an overview, sharing expectations and rationales, activating background knowledge, and anchoring activities.
2. Modeling may involve orally presenting the steps to a problem.
3. In think-alouds, teachers share their thought processes.
4. Instructional-pause routines and guided notes are suggested to insure more active student participation during lecturing.
5. Questioning is used to elicit active student involvement, to foster cognitive learning, to reinforce concepts, to prompt, to monitor, and to adjust instruction.
6. Low-level, fast-paced questions produce many correct responses and elicit much student involvement when teaching basic skills, whereas high-level, slow-paced questions are generally required in the teaching of higher-level cognitive thinking.
7. Specific questions, such as "What is the next step in the operation, Bob?" serve as checks of comprehension and enable teachers to monitor and adjust instruction.

8. Nonacademic questions frequently disrupt the flow of a lesson and may lead to non-compliant student behavior.

9. Wait time refers either to the amount of time a teacher waits for a student's response after asking a question or the amount of time a teacher waits after a student's response to ask another question.

10. Guided practice is teacher-led practice that must be aligned with the objective and independent practice. Examples of guided practice activities are repeated reading, repetitive routines, and choral responding.

Feedback

Feedback often follows an Initiate (teacher questions or elicits student response), Respond (a student or students chorally respond), and Evaluate (teacher evaluates answer) cycle (Pressley et al., 1996). Rieth and Frick (1983) report that only 8% to 9% of academic learning time is given to feedback, even though research shows that 12% to 14% increases the likelihood of student engagement and achievement gains. Teachers can give feedback by acknowledging, amplifying, rephrasing, and correcting (Anderson, Evertson, & Brophy, 1979; Florida Performance Measurement System, 1984).

Acknowledgment

Acknowledgment involves telling a student that an answer is correct or wrong, such as "Yes, that is correct" or "No, that is not correct." Acknowledgment also involves the use of specific praise. Specific praise requires specification of the appropriate behavior. It is not merely "Good," but "Good reading" or "Good remembering." Stating a specific behavior (reading, remembering) helps students recognize why they are receiving positive statements from you. They know the exact behavior that earned your approval. In response to a general statement like "Good boy," a student may think, "Oh, yes,

I read well," or "Oh, the teacher must be in a good mood today." Many students with special needs have problems connecting a behavior with the praise when the behavior is not specified. Soldier (1989) recommends praising a Native American's efforts rather than the product.

Positive comments may also be made in the feedback of written products. Marking the correct items in color or writing positive comments on the paper ("Excellent printing," "Great idea") take a little more time, but they help students view school more positively.

Amplification and Rephrasing

Amplification is expansion of a student's response by either the teacher or another student, such as "Yes, Jim, you are correct. We do multiply to solve that problem and the reason we do that is . . ." or "Yes, Sue, that is a good start. Now, Pat, would you explain it further?" Amplification is used during the teaching of learning strategies to help students discriminate between good and poor student modeling of the teacher's think-alouds (Schumaker, 1989). Rephrasing is often used to emphasize the steps or methods used to arrive at a correct answer (e.g., "Yes, Jimmy, you first divide and then you multiply.") or to repeat the relevant points of a lesson (e.g., "Yes, that's correct, the rule is *i* before *e* except after *c*.") (Anderson, Evertson, & Brophy, 1979).

Correction

Correcting a wrong response usually follows a supply or scaffolding format, or adaptations of them. A teacher who employs the supply format simply supplies or has another student supply the correct answer. For example, after a student's incorrect response, you or another student model the correct one ("No, the word is *heat*." or "Susie, please read the word."), lead the student ("Let's say it together."), and test the student ("Now, you read the word."). Alternatively, you may just model and test, as in "No, the word is *heat*. What word?" (Engelmann & Carnine, 1982; Meyer, 1986).

With the scaffolding format, the teacher follows up the question with more questions, prompts, and hints "to probe students' understandings and as a guide for individualized instruction, rather than for evaluation only" (Pressley et al., 1996, p. 142). For example, now you may suggest a strategy ("Is this a word that can be sounded out?") or provide information that the student can use to deduce the correct answer ("Is there any vowel rule we may be able to use here?"). With both formats, the process should end with the student responding with the correct answer (Collins, Carnine, & Gersten, 1987).

◆ **ACTIVITY 6.11**

- Student Teacher 1 asked a third-grade student to make up a sentence with the word *me.* The student said, "*Me* am happy," to which the teacher replied, "me and my shadow," and then asked the student to write the word *fan.* How could the student teacher have given the student more appropriate feedback?
- Student Teacher 2 responded, "That's correct," when a student answered the question of why the astronauts are weightless in space by saying that there is no gravity. Provide a rephrasing type of feedback to emphasize the effect of gravity. Provide a specific praise acknowledgment.

Closing

Frequently, the lesson ends with (a) a review of the information presented (Archer & Isaacson, 1990; Schumaker, 1989), (b) a preview of the future use for the information (Archer & Isaacson, 1990; Schumaker, 1989), (c) a statement of expectations (Archer & Isaacson, 1990; Schumaker, 1989), (d) a cue to chart progress or self-evaluate (Palincsar, 1986b; Schumaker, 1989),

and (e) an introduction of the independent work (Archer & Isaacson, 1990). Following is an example of each feature.

Review. Students or teachers may review the major points of the lessons with summaries or by asking questions, for example, "Today we discussed the three types of sentences. What was the first type of sentence, Shari?" or "Shari, please summarize what you learned today." One of our interns led students in a listing of major points under the column, "What Did We Learn Today?" Another intern had students enter major points in their learning journal at the end of each math lesson.

Preview. Teachers frequently use previews to tie together information. "Today we prepared our published books. Tomorrow we will visit the retirement home and read them to our grandparent partners."

Expectations. You may either summarize how students met your behavior expectations or what they may expect as a result of their new knowledge. For example, one of our student teachers, in commenting on behavior expectations of the tenth graders, noted: "You all really listened today. You remembered to write down the major points and you listened to others' comments without interruptions. Thank you."

Self-Evaluation. You may have students monitor their own progress using any of the procedures discussed in Chapter 3. In the self-advocacy strategy, VanReusen, Bos, Schumaker, and Deshler (1994) have students keep track of their mastery of the strategy using goal dates and completion dates.

Introduce Independent Work. Give a specific assignment that relates to the content taught by discussing the directions and checking for comprehension.

INDEPENDENT PRACTICE

It is recommended that students move to independent practice activities when they are making few errors during guided practice (Rosenshine & Stevens, 1986). Independent practice activities are completed by students with minimal teacher assistance. Independent practice should result in fluency, maintenance, and generalization of skills. Teachers must design generalization activities, as students with disabilities often have a difficult time relating content they are learning to other settings and situations. For example, if you are teaching the job-related social skill of giving compliments appropriately, you may assign an activity that requires students to record each time they give compliments at home for 1 week.

Independent practice is not to be confused with a student's interacting with a worksheet. Ineffective teachers often expect students to learn too much from worksheets (Medley, 1979; Rieth, Polsgrove, Okolo, Bahr, & Eckert, 1987; Rosenshine & Stevens, 1986; Squires, Huitt, & Segars, 1983). It is appropriate to use worksheets or dittos during independent practice, but only to reinforce a concept that has already been taught. Remember, independent practice should relate to objectives and guided practice activities, even though new examples are provided. For example, if the objective of the lesson is to identify possessive nouns, then students should practice the identification of possessive nouns during both guided and independent practice activities.

A success rate of 90% to 100% is suggested for independent practice of basic skills for effective learning (Christenson, Thurlow, & Ysseldyke, 1987). To ensure a 90% success rate, give instructions telling what you expect during the independent activity and, if necessary, adapt the activities. Wong, Wong, and LaMare (1982) caution against the use of general instructions like "Read the assignment carefully." Instead, to promote optimal learning and on-task behavior, they suggest that teachers inform students of the specific objectives of the assignment. In working with students from the African-American culture, Kuykendall (1992) recommends that teachers set aside a few minutes for the stage-setting behaviors often practiced by these students before they begin an assignment. These stage-setting behaviors, which are applicable for all students, include "pencil sharpening, rearranging posture, checking paper and writing space, asking for repeat directions, and even checking perceptions with their neighbors" (Kuykendall, 1992, p. 63).

Teachers may adapt the directions or content of worksheets for independent practice. (Refer to Chapter 4 for an extensive discussion of ways to adapt materials.) They may also complete the first problem on the worksheet with the students.

Instead of sitting at their desks, effective teachers circulate and give extra help and individual feedback during independent practice (Brophy & Evertson, 1977). But if you need to spend more than a few minutes explaining a problem to a student, you should probably reteach that lesson. Beginning teachers often run into management problems during independent practice because they spend too much time with one student or they position themselves with their backs to the other students, making it impossible to monitor behaviors.

EVALUATION

The last step in the instructional framework is to evaluate whether students have learned the skills, strategies, and content of the lesson. Evaluation procedures should be aligned with the lesson objectives, guided practice, and independent practice. For example, if the objective of the lesson is to teach students to write descriptive sentences, then students should practice writing descriptive sentences during guided and independent practice activities and be evaluated on how well they write descriptive sentences.

In Chapter 3, we discussed different ways to monitor student progress. The procedures of precision teaching, curriculum-based measurements, and alternative assessments are just as effective for individual lesson evaluations. For example, Mr. LaRue has students chart the number of words they read correctly during the reading story. Ms. Smythe observes the strategies students use in solving math problems as she moves from one student to another during independent practice. Ms. Gonzalez uses oral questions to check comprehension. Some general evaluation guidelines are to specify the criteria, vary evaluation methods, and teach students to self-evaluate and reflect on the teaching episode.

Specify the Criteria

Students need to know how you plan to evaluate them. One way to share evaluation expectations is to use expert products (Rosenshine, 1990). With expert products, you present the students with a project that you feel demonstrates the quality of work you expect. M. J. Johnson (1991) noted that a completed expert project assists Native Americans, who frequently do not exhibit risk-taking behaviors and are hesitant to complete unstructured assignments. Asking a student to make a copy of a well-done project for later use in other classes is easy to do.

Another way to specify criteria is to prepare a holistic or analytic scoring rubric (see Chapter 3). Archbald (1992) adds the feature of assigning percentages to each of the standards in a rubric dealing with the scoring of written essays. For example, the organization standard of the essay accounts for 30% of the total score, the sentence structure standard for 25%, usage accounts for 20%, mechanics for 20%, and format for 5%. Now, students know that a high-level score of 5 on the sentence structure standard not only meets the indicator of "sentences are complete and varied in length and struc-

ture" but also is worth 25% of the final essay grade.

One of our student teachers presented students with an evaluation sheet as they began an assignment. Before he divided students into cooperative groups to write a report about Ohio, he presented them with a checklist of items such as (a) Did you describe three of the major occupations of the state? (12 points) and (b) Did you write complete sentences in the two-page report? (10 points). Thus, he shared with his students the information he expected to see on the report and the importance of including it. He also listed the point value for each question on an exam or quiz and taught students to spend more time answering the questions worth more points.

Vary Ways to Evaluate

Teachers frequently use ditto sheets or pencil-and-paper tests to evaluate performance. There are many other ways for students to show that they know the information. You may allow students to give an oral report, complete a homework project, or prepare a portfolio. In the section on motivation, we presented a sample choice sheet for secondary students to select ways to demonstrate their knowledge. When you give students choices as to ways to share information, you are providing for the different learning styles of students, which makes the experience more meaningful. Evaluation should be linked to meaningful and relevant tasks.

Teach Students to Self-Evaluate

In Chapter 3, we discussed strategies to teach students to self-evaluate as they monitor their progress in the general education classroom setting and as they complete their portfolios. Self-evaluation is an important aspect of authentic evaluation, as evidenced in its use in portfolio assessment, learning logs, and journals. One of our interns required her secondary students in a pull-out setting to complete a daily journal entry. During the last 15 minutes of class, the students independently or in a small group answered the questions: (a) What did you learn today? and (b) Do you have any concerns? She then responded to the entries and used their concerns to reteach any confusing information during the next day's lesson.

Complete Self-Evaluation

Before ending our discussion of evaluation, effective teachers frequently reflect on the teaching episode (Costa & Garmston, 1994). The use of videotapes, cognitive coaching, student evaluations, and self-questioning are multiple ways of gathering data for reflection. Some questions that you may wish to ask for reflection are: (a) What did I want to have happen? (b) Is what happened different? (c) What strategy was particularly effective today? (d) What strategy didn't work as well as I thought? (e) How should I change what happened? and (f) What did I learn that I may use in the future?

 IMPORTANT POINTS

1. Feedback involves responding to students' answers and correcting students' errors.
2. Acknowledgment involves telling a student that an answer is correct or wrong.
3. Specific praise requires specification of an appropriate behavior and an evaluative word, such as *good,* etc.
4. Rephrasing is often used to emphasize facts that make an answer correct or the steps or methods used to arrive at a correct answer.
5. Amplification is an expansion of a student's response by either the teacher or another student.
6. Correction procedures often consist of either a supply format or a scaffolding format.
7. Frequently, lessons close with a review of the information presented, a preview of the future use for the information, a statement of expectations, a self-evaluation measure, and an introduction of the independent work.
8. Independent practice activities should relate to objectives and guided practice activities and reinforce previously taught information, even though new examples are provided.
9. Instead of sitting at their desks, effective teachers move around the classroom to give extra help and individual feedback during independent practice.
10. Evaluation procedures should be aligned with the lesson objectives, guided practice, and independent practice.
11. Some general guidelines to follow in evaluation are to specify the criteria, vary evaluation methods, teach students to self-evaluate, and reflect on the teaching episode.

LESSON PLAN

As a way of summarizing the parts of the instructional cycle, Figure 6.4 contains a sample lesson plan. Notice that a short explanation is given in parentheses after each section of the plan.

◆ DISCUSSION QUESTIONS

1. Discuss how you plan to involve **all** your students actively during lesson presentation.
2. Research shows that motivation is further enhanced when learning is personally relevant for students. Describe how you plan to make learning personally relevant for your students.
3. Discuss why it is necessary to identify subject matter as laws, rules, etc.
4. Discuss two results of the teacher effectiveness research and the implications for teaching students with special needs.

Objective: When presented with an independent practice sheet of 10 fractions, students will write equivalent fractions with 90% accuracy. (Fractions were identified on each of the students' IEPs.)

Subject Matter Content:
For presentation: Concept
        Definition—Equivalent fractions are fractions that name the same number (from text, *Applying Mathematics*, 1986, Laidlaw Brothers, p. 538.)
        Attribute—Equivalent fractions are equal.
        Examples—$\frac{1}{2} = \frac{2}{4} = \frac{4}{8} = \frac{8}{16}$, $\frac{1}{4} = \frac{2}{8} = \frac{4}{16}$, $\frac{1}{8} = \frac{2}{16}$, $\frac{2}{4} = \frac{4}{8} = \frac{8}{16}$, etc.
        Nonexamples—$\frac{1}{2} = \frac{3}{4}$, $\frac{1}{4} = \frac{3}{8}$, $\frac{1}{8} = \frac{4}{16}$, $\frac{2}{4} = \frac{7}{8}$, etc.

For review: Basic concept/skill—write fractions from pictures. Examples—see Transparency A.
        Basic concept/skill—identification of fraction kits

(Since this is a concept, a definition, examples, and nonexamples must be identified. Teacher reviewed prerequisite basic concepts/skills. See Step 4 of plan and Transparency A.)

Questions:
    How many eighths are in one-half? How many fourths are in one-sixteenth?
    Why aren't $\frac{3}{4}$ and $\frac{7}{8}$ equivalent fractions?
    What does *equivalent* mean?
    Are $\frac{1}{2}$ and $\frac{2}{4}$ equivalent fractions?
    Why are these fractions equal?
    How can you prove that the fractions are equal?

(Notice, the teacher identified both low- and high-level questions.)

Feedback:
    Correct—You certainly know how to find equivalent fractions, well done, (name). You are absolutely correct, $\frac{1}{2}$ does equal $\frac{2}{4}$.
    Incorrect—What was the first step? What fraction pieces do you think you need?

(Notice, the teacher plans to use specific praise and amplification for correct answers and a scaffolding strategy for incorrect.)

Materials:
    Math Journal
    Teacher Fraction Kit (same as students' kits, but made from transparencies, produced by a graphics software program and color printer)
    Students' Fraction Kits made from construction paper:
        One sheet of yellow construction paper represents 1 whole.
        One sheet of green construction paper cut into 2 equal pieces represents halves.
        One sheet of blue construction paper cut into 4 equal pieces represents fourths.
        One sheet of orange construction paper cut into 8 equal pieces represents eighths.
        One sheet of purple construction paper cut into 16 equal pieces represents sixteenths.

Figure 6.4 Sample Lesson Plan

Transparency A with pictures for review (Students must write the fraction from the picture.)

Transparency A

Number 1

Number 2

Number 3

Number 4

Transparency B, which has the definition of equivalent fractions written on it.

Transparency B

Definition—Equivalent fractions are fractions that name the same number.

Independent Practice Sheet—(Of course, all of the materials would be in larger print for the actual presentation.)

Independent Practice Sheet

Directions: Convert the fractions into equivalent fractions:

1. ½ = /4   2. ¾ = /8   3. $^6/_{16}$ = /8   4. ¾ = /8   5. ⅘ = /16

6. ¼ = /16   7. $^2/_{16}$ = /8   8. ⅘ = /4   9. $^4/_{16}$ = /8   10. $^{10}/_{16}$ = /8

Figure 6.4 *continued*

196

Lesson Presentation

Opening:

1. Overview: "Today we will talk about equivalent fractions and use our fraction kits to explore equivalent fractions. We'll start off working problems together, then you will work with a partner, and then alone on identifying equivalent fractions."
2. Rationale: "Why do you think we need to know about making equal fractions?"
3. Expectations: "During today's lesson I expect all of you to remain seated, to be good listeners, and to raise your hand to answer questions. I know you will enjoy class today."
4. Review: "But, first, let's quickly review writing fractions and our fraction kit values."
    a. Show Transparency A and have students write down fractions on a sheet of paper. Then check with unison response, "Everyone, what is this fraction?" Give feedback.
    b. Hold up yellow construction paper and ask, "What do we call the yellow pieces of our fraction kit, everyone? Blue? Purple? Orange? Green?"

(Notice, the teacher selected overview, rationale, expectations, and review as components to use to introduce this lesson. She cued with "Everyone" in eliciting a student response and then gave feedback.)

Body:

5. After review, state and show the definition of equivalent fraction (Transparency B). Ask students questions about the definition. (Emphasize that they are equal parts of the whole.) Have students copy the definition into their math journals.
6. Model doing an equivalent fraction using Transparency A, Example 2, and fraction kit. "Let's see, I've identified that fraction as ½ so I need to find all the fractions equivalent to ½. Let me start by pulling out my green ½ pieces from my fraction kit. Now, I'll pull out my fourth pieces, the blue ones from the kit. How many fourth pieces do I think equal the ½ piece? Hm, let's try 3. Nope. That doesn't work. They do not fit on top of each other. So ½ doesn't equal 3 pieces of the fourths or ¾. Let's try 2 pieces. They fit fine. So ½ equals ²⁄₄. So ½ and ²⁄₄ are equivalent fractions; they cover an equal portion of the whole. They are equal." (Write ½ = ²⁄₄ on the board.).
7. Do another example (Write ½ = /₈ on the board.), asking students questions as they watch you, beginning with, "Now, I wonder if I can find an equal number of eighths to equal ½. What should I do first, Jack?"

Guided Practice:

8. Have students take out their fraction kits. "Let's see if you can find an equal number of sixteenths. (Write ½ = /₁₆ on the board.) What should you do first? Yes, start with your green or half sheet."
9. Do two more examples (⁸⁄₁₆ = /₂, and ¾ = /₈), asking the students questions.
10. Divide the students into pairs, having one student show one fraction with the kit and another student the equivalent fraction. Model with two students first, "Jim and Jason are partners. They are working the problem of ⁶⁄₁₆ = /₈. Jason, show us ⁶⁄₁₆ with your fraction kit. Now, Jim, take out your eighths. What do you do now?" (Remember, to have students write both fractions.)
11. Circulate while students are working five more examples (taken from the examples listed in subject matter).
12. Call on each group to write one of the problems, explaining and showing how they got their answers. Then have all students copy the five examples into their Math Journal underneath the definition.

Closing:

13. "Let's do a quick review. What is the definition of an equivalent fraction? How do you use your fraction kit to find an equivalent fraction?"
14. Have students write what they learned from today's Math Lesson in their Math Journal.

Independent Practice:

15. Have the student helper pass out the worksheets. Go over the directions and do the first problem with the students. (See Independent Practice sheet in Materials section.)
16. Have students interview parents to see how they use equivalent fractions. (This is a first step in a generalization activity.)

Evaluation:

17. Circulate as the students are completing the worksheets. Plan to reteach the lesson to any student who misses more than one problem (90% accuracy).

Figure 6.4 *continued*

7

CONTENT
INSTRUCTION

In special education, the Direct Instruction model is often used to teach academic content. This model is the basis for various popular commercial reading, math, and spelling curriculum programs such as *Distar Arithmetic, Corrective Spelling Through Morphographs,* and *Reading Mastery,* all created by Engelmann and his colleagues. *Direct Instruction Mathematics,* by Silbert, Carnine, and Stein (1990) and *Direct Instruction Reading* by Carnine, Silbert, and Kameenui (1990) are also examples of the Direct Instruction model.

As we described in Chapter 1, the Direct Instruction model has its basis in the reductionist paradigm. The teacher is directly in charge of instruction: The teacher's role is to present well-structured sequences of subject matter, supervise practice, provide feedback, maintain a brisk pace, and ensure a high success rate. We follow the Direct Instruction discussion with a discussion of a combination, or balanced, approach that combines the Direct Instruction strategies and other techniques. From an examination of about 28 studies dealing with whole language or phonics reading instruction, Stahl, McKenna, and Pagnucco (1994) recommend a balanced approach. The balanced approach includes open-ended tasks and self-selection (more aligned with the constructivist paradigm), plus teacher-directed explicit phonics and comprehension instruction (more aligned with the reductionist paradigm). Gersten and Woodward (1994) also recommend a combination approach for the instruction of bilingual students with disabilities.

Next, we examine the Unit Approach, which has been used in classes to teach content to students with mild disabilities (Englert, Raphael, & Mariage, 1994) and in classes for students with learning disabilities (Swicegood & Parsons, 1991). You may also encounter the Unit Approach in an inclusive setting. With the Unit Approach, students usually participate in various activities and are exposed to a variety of instructional techniques and arrangements. Depending on the structure of the unit, the Unit Approach may fall under either the reductionist or constructivist paradigm. Generally, the Unit Approach promotes meaningful contexts and establishes classroom communities. The teacher's role may vary from the direct purveyor of knowledge to that of a facilitator as students assume responsibility for their own learning.

We conclude the chapter with a discussion of teaching content using a single text. Fre-quently, instruction in the areas of science, social studies, health, math, and other content areas are based on the use of a single text. In her description of textbooks, Kovalik (1994) laments the importance given to them: "Parents demand that they be brought home, teachers won't start class without them, and academic departments spend months examining new texts for adoption" (xiii). Even though we agree with Kovalik's belief that textbooks do not equal curriculum and instruction but are the tools of schooling, we do realize that many of our students with disabilities will be expected to learn from textbooks. Therefore, we discuss some adaptations that will make textbook learning more meaningful and effective.

DIRECT INSTRUCTION

Direct Instruction (DI) is used in this chapter to refer to the structured, teacher-directed curriculum program first designed by Becker and Engelmann as a model for Project Head Start, a federally funded preschool intervention program for disadvantaged children from low-income homes. In 1967, when Head Start was extended to Project Follow-Through (an intervention program with a focus on the primary grades), Direct Instruction (with the Distar language, math, and reading programs) was retained as one of the 22 experimental models selected for evaluation (Peterson, 1987). There is a wealth of empirical evidence that supports the use of the Direct Instruction model with these children.

The Direct Instruction model began to be used with special education elementary students in the late 1960s with similar success, especially in the teaching of basic skills (Gersten, 1985; Gersten, Woodward, & Darch, 1986; Lloyd, Cullinan, Heins, & Epstein, 1980; Stein & Goldman, 1980). Direct Instruction has also been shown to increase the academic performance of adolescents with mild disabilities (Pol-loway, Epstein, Polloway, Patton, & Ball, 1986), senior high school readers with reading problems (Gregory, Hackney, & Gregory, 1982), and preadolescents and adolescents with mild mental disabilities (Gersten & Maggs, 1982). Remember, as reported in Chapter 1, Direct Instruction is one of the effective interventions identified by Forness, Kavale, Blum, and Lloyd (1997) from a meta-analysis examination of special education research.

Rationale

The Direct Instruction model is based on behavioral principles. Its fundamental premise is that students must master basic academic skills before they can master higher-level cognitive skills. According to Tarver (1986), "Instruction begins with specific decoding skills and strategies and progresses in a highly structured, spiraling fashion to higher-level comprehension skills and strategies" (p. 370).

Another premise of Direct Instruction is that the best way to teach both basic and higher-level skills is to present carefully sequenced content using task analysis and mastery learning principles.

In discussing the basis of *Distar Arithmetic* (Engelmann & Carnine, 1972, 1975, 1976), Gersten and Carnine (1984) posit that "all children can learn mathematics if the lesson is designed so students can understand what is being presented, if they are given adequate practice with corrective feedback and their progress through the curriculum is assessed regularly" (p. 396).

Description

The Direct Instruction model features a well-designed curriculum and detailed instructional procedures. As described by Tarver (1986), "The curriculum design components constitute the cognitive elements of DI and the presentation components constitute the behavioral elements" (p. 369). The curriculum features include sequential order, examples, well-constructed formats, prompts, independent practice activities, and mastery learning.

Curriculum Features

In Direct Instruction, skills and concepts are presented in sequential order and in logical steps within well-constructed, repetitive formats. All skills are taught directly, with minimal reliance on incidental learning. Each lesson includes teacher-scripted presentations, individual tests, and independent practice activities. Mastery tests are interspersed throughout the curriculum.

Sequential Order.
In all of the content areas, skills and concepts are analyzed thoroughly to make certain that preskills necessary for success are taught, easy skills are taught before more difficult ones, similar skills are taught nonconsecutively, and high-utility skills are taught before less-used ones.

◆ *Preskills are skills that must be taught before a task is introduced* (Silbert, Carnine, & Stein, 1990). Before teachers teach students to add the fast way in *Direct Instruction Mathematics* (Silbert, Carnine, & Stein, 1990), they teach the preskills of (a) drawing lines to correspond to a numeral (making 3 lines to represent 3), (b) rote counting from a number other than 1 (beginning with 5), (c) rational counting (touching lines as they count), and (d) reading equations ($5 + 3 = $ _____). Then the students are ready for this lesson: Write on board: $5 + 3 = $

1. "I'll touch and you read."
2. "We're going to work this problem a fast way. We draw lines under the number after the plus." (Point to $+3$.) "What does this say? So, how many lines are we going to draw? I'll make the lines." Draw three lines under the 3.
3. "Watch me count the fast way." Touch 5 and then each line. "Fiiiivvve, six, seven, eight" (p. 147).

◆ *Skills are sequenced according to difficulty levels.* In symbol identification, the teen numerals of 14, 16, 17, 18, and 19 are taught before 11, 12, 13, and 15 due to the way the numeral names are pronounced (Silbert, Carnine, & Stein, 1990). The names of the first set of numerals are pronounced beginning with the numeral in the ones column, such as 14 ("four-teen") and 16 ("six-teen"), while the names of the last set are not; that is, 11 is not read "one-teen," nor is 12 read "two-teen." Sounding out words that begin with continuous sounds is taught before sounding out words that begin with stop sounds (Carnine, Silbert, & Kameenui, 1990) because it is much easier to sound out words beginning with sounds that can be held, such as *a* in *an* and *m* in *mat,* than it is to sound out words beginning with sounds that cannot be held, such as *p* in *pan* and *t* in *tot.*

◆ *Similar information, or strategies that are likely to be confused, are not introduced together.* For example, the sound of *d* is introduced in Presentation Book A, Lesson 27, and the sound of *b* is introduced in Presentation Book C, Lesson 121. The sounds are not introduced close together because students frequently have difficulty discriminating the letters visually.

◆ *High-utility skills are taught before less-used ones.* Irregular words, such as *was, said,* and *have,* are taught before less-used irregular words, like *tomb, heir,* and *neon* (Carnine, Silbert, & Kameenui, 1990).

Examples. According to Engelmann and Carnine (1982), the inclusion of a wide range of positive examples, negative examples, and test examples is important for unambiguous communication and in teaching generalizations. The range of positive examples must demonstrate "only one identifiable sameness in quality" (Engelmann & Carnine, 1982, p. 5). For example, when teaching the concept red, the example of red should not always be accompanied with round objects, because students might incorrectly conclude that red is round. The only sameness of the objects should be red. Thus, red apples, red wagons, red squares, and other objects that are red are used.

In turn, a negative example must be minimally different from a positive one to prevent students from overgeneralizing and to help the students make discriminations. For example, negative examples of red should differ only in the color attribute. A red ball should be compared with a yellow ball (difference only in color attribute) instead of a red square with a yellow ball (difference in color plus shape attributes). In the latter example, students may focus on the shape and interpret red as something that has corners, instead of using the color as the discriminating factor.

In the test examples, you should present new positive and negative examples that require students to apply their knowledge. For instance, in a test example of red, present a red scarf if it was not one of the objects used as an example during the lesson.

One last guideline in example selection is to include examples that are consistent with the strategy before exceptions (Carnine, Silbert, &

Kameenui, 1990). If the rule states that the letters *ea* in the middle of a word often have the long *e* sound, examples such as *thread* and *breath,* which are exceptions to the rule, should not be selected until students become proficient with the rule.

◆ **ACTIVITY 7.1**

1. In teaching elementary students, identify some positive, negative, and test examples you might use to teach the following concept: "A sum is the answer you get when you add." A positive example may be 3 + 8 = _____ .
2. In teaching middle school students, identify some positive, negative, and test examples you might use to teach the following rule: "We change a decimal to a percent by adding a percent sign after the number and moving the decimal point two places toward the percent sign" (Silbert, Carnine, & Stein, 1990, p. 414).

(Answers for this and other activities are found in the Instructor's Manual.)

Well-Constructed Formats. Well-constructed, fast-paced, repetitive formats with teacher scripts are designed to teach skills, basic concepts, related concepts, rules, and cognitive operations (Tarver, 1986). In each format, the wording of the teacher script is consistent and clear to make the information easier for the students to acquire and for the teacher to present (Engelmann, Osborn, & Hanner, 1978). The use of scripts permits teachers to focus on monitoring student performance, instead of concentrating on the use of clear instructional language and appropriate examples (Stein, Carnine, & Dixon, 1998).

A typical format for teaching new sounds appears in Figure 7.1. In this format, the teacher: (a) models and repeats twice (Items 1–3),

S

The teacher models the sound and repeats twice.

1. Touch the first ball of the arrow. **Here's a new sound. My turn to say it. Get ready.** Move quickly to the second ball. Hold. **sss.**
2. Touch the first ball of the arrow. **My turn again. Get ready.** Move quickly to the second ball. Hold. **sss.**
3. Touch the first ball of the arrow. **My turn again. Get ready.** Move quickly to the second ball. Hold. **sss.**
   The teacher prompts the students to practice the sounds in unison.
4. Touch the first ball of the arrow. **Your turn. Get ready.** Move quickly to the second ball. Hold. sss. **Yes, sss.**
5. Touch the first ball of the arrow. **Again. Get ready.** Move quickly to the second ball. Hold. sss. **Yes, sss.**
   The teacher directs students to repeat sound until firm.
6. Repeat **5** until firm.
   The teacher tests individuals.
7. Call on different children to do **4.**
   The teacher gives feedback.
8. **Good saying sss.**

Figure 7.1 Sample DI Format for Teaching Sounds

NOTE. From *Reading Mastery: Distar Reading I* (p. 102) by S. Engelmann and E. C. Bruner, 1988. Chicago: Science Research Associates. Copyright 1988 by McGraw-Hill, Inc. Reprinted by permission.

(b) prompts the students to practice the sound in unison (Items 4 and 5), (c) directs students to repeat the sound until firm (Item 6), (d) tests individual children (Item 7), and (e) gives feedback (Item 8). This same format with similar wording continues from lesson to lesson whenever a new sound is introduced.

There are also specific feedback formats. A frequently used format consists of model, lead, test, and retest when an error is made (Engelmann & Carnine, 1982). For example, when a student does not say the short *a* sound correctly, the teacher models the correct answer ("the sound is *aaa*"), leads the student ("Say it with me. Get ready."), tests the student ("Your turn. Get ready."), and retests ("Again. Get ready.") (Engelmann & Bruner, 1988, Presentation Book A, Lesson 2, p. 9). Sometimes, the teacher asks other students to model the correct answer during the modeling step. Scripted feedback for correct answers often directs the teacher to either acknowledge the correct response (e.g., "Yes, the sound is *sss*.") or to use specific praise statements (e.g., "Good, saying it fast, Ted.")

Prompts. A prompt is a visual detail that is added to an example to highlight a relevant feature (Engelmann & Carnine, 1982). Eventually, the prompts are faded. Some of the frequently used visual cues in the beginning reading program are exemplified in the following word:

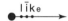

A macron (—) marks the long *i* vowel sound, the silent letter *e* is reduced to smaller print to prompt students that "when a word has a little sound, you don't say that sound" (Engelmann & Bruner, 1988, Presentation Book A, p. 221), and an arrow underlines the word to prompt students to proceed from left to right when reading. Dots, or balls, under a word tell students that they must make that sound. A larger dot prompts students where to begin. In beginning math, one 10 is written as 1°, so 16 is 1°6 and 106 is 1°°6.

Independent Practice. With independent practice activities, students complete exercises in their workbooks. The activities include a mixture of examples in which the new skill or rule is applied and some in which previously taught skills are applied (Silbert, Carnine, & Stein, 1990). For example, after Mr. Phillips introduces addition with regrouping, he gives the students independent assignments containing problems that require regrouping (application of the new skill), such as 35 + 27, and problems that do not require regrouping (application of a previously taught skill), such as $35 + 12$.

Mastery Learning.   Mastery learning, which requires students to reach a certain criterion, is built into the Direct Instruction model. During the lesson presentations, students do not practice material alone until the group response is firm. Notice Number 6 in Figure 7.1, which directs the teacher to continue to repeat Number 5 until the sound is firm. In the choral reading of a story, the students must read to a certain point with a limited number of errors. If they make more errors, they must reread the section as a group until the error goal is reached.

Mastery tests appear throughout the curriculum. For example, the first mastery test in *Reading Mastery 1* (Engelmann & Bruner, 1988) appears after Lesson 8. Placement tests are also available for the initial placement of students in the program.

Instructional Procedures

As we noted at the beginning of this chapter, Direct Instruction incorporates teaching strategies from the teacher effectiveness literature and the reductionist paradigm. The effective instructional procedures include cueing attention and providing overviews to open the lesson; modeling, eliciting overt student responding, providing immediate feedback, and guiding practice activities during the body of the lesson; and introducing independent practice activities to close the lesson. The teacher usually presents the lesson to small groups of children.

Opening.   Often, lessons begin with cues for students to attend. For example, some lessons begin with attention getters such as, "Everyone, look at me." Each section of the lesson usually begins with an overview, such as, "First, you're going to say the word slowly without stopping between the sounds. Then you're going to say the word fast" (Engelmann & Bruner, 1988, Presentation Book A, p. 190).

Body and Guided Practice.   The body of the lesson often consists of the teacher modeling or presenting scripted information and then cueing students to practice the content in unison. After leading the group in practice, the teacher asks individual students to respond. Throughout the lesson presentation, the teacher gives structured, immediate feedback for both incorrect and correct answers.

Closing.   Most lessons conclude with the teacher introducing and discussing the practice activities in the workbook following a script. Often, the teacher will complete the first few problems with the students.

Use

Many school districts have adopted the previously discussed commercial programs for Direct Instruction in the areas of reading, spelling, math, and language. Thus, you may find a kit with a teacher's manual, student workbooks, and other materials in the classroom. Although you should try to follow the scripted teacher presentation, Gersten, Carnine, and Woodward (1987) discovered that immediate correction of student errors and the number of correct student responses were linked to student success more often than was following the script word for word.

Even if Direct Instruction commercial programs are not available, it is possible to incorporate the curriculum design features and instructional procedures into a lesson. For example, Darch and Gersten (1986) incorporated Direct Instruction procedures as they used an advance organizer with high school students with learning disabilities. They used a well-constructed format, carefully worded definitions, and carefully selected examples to open the science lesson. The format consisted of (a) the teacher reading the item, (b) the students reading the item in unison, and (c) the teacher asking fast-paced questions of the students after several items were read. The scripted lesson began:

TEACHER: Today we are going to learn about ocean currents and how these currents can affect the weather on land. Everybody look at 1. A current moves like a river. Say that.

STUDENTS: A current moves like a river.

TEACHER: Everybody look at 1A. Water moves in parts of the ocean. These are called currents. Say that.

STUDENTS: Water moves in parts of the ocean.

TEACHER: Touch 1B. These currents can be very wide—sometimes as wide as 100 miles. Say that. . . . Let's review what we have covered so far. Everybody, can an ocean have currents?

STUDENTS: Yes.

TEACHER: Do these currents move?

STUDENTS: Yes.

TEACHER: Everybody, how wide can these currents be? (p. 238)

Lesson Plan

In the following sections, we use Direct Instruction to design a lesson for the rule, "When a word has a short vowel sound followed by one consonant, double the consonant before adding *ing*," adapted from a fourth-grade spelling book (Silver Burdett, 1986). We first adapt the curriculum features and then present a scripted lesson presentation. In order to teach the rule, we identify it, give examples for student application, and have students defend its application (Florida Performance Measurement System, 1984).

Adapting Curriculum Features

As we plan the lesson, we consider the curriculum features of sequential order, examples, well-constructed formats, feedback, prompts, independent practice activities, and mastery. We have already taught short vowel sounds, and students know consonants, so students should be ready to learn the rule **(sequential order).** We select the positive **examples** *bat* and *slip,* because they represent different vowel sounds (short *a* and *i*) and different beginning consonants (a single consonant, *b,* and a blend, *sl*). We use the negative **examples** *jump* and *rain. Jump* differs in the number of consonants and *rain* in the vowel sound. Other examples include positive ones, like *skip, hem,* and *hop,* and negative ones, like *batch, bow,* and *meet.*

We plan to present the lesson using the following **format** (the teacher script appears in Figure 7.2):

Step A. Teacher tells students the rule.

Step B. Students repeat the rule.

Step C. Teacher asks questions about the rule and gives feedback.

Step D. Teacher models the use of the rule with a positive example.

Step E. Students repeat the application.

Step F. Teacher gives feedback.

Step G. Teacher tests individuals (Steps E and F).

Step H. Teacher drops model and asks questions to prompt rule application.

Step I. Teacher tests individuals, repeating Step H with other positive examples and feedback.

Step J. Teacher repeats the rule.

Step K. Teacher models the use of the rule with a negative example.

Step L. Students repeat the application.

Step M. Teacher gives feedback.

Step N. Teacher tests individuals (Steps L and M).

Step O. Teacher tests individuals, repeating Step L with other negative examples and feedback.

Depending on the needs of the individual student, the teacher may model more positive examples before Step H or the teacher may present negative examples during the next day's lesson.

The **feedback** format includes acknowledgment with rule repetition or specific praise for correct answers and a model, lead, and test procedure for incorrect answers.

In selecting **prompts,** we want the students to be aware of the vowel sound and the one consonant in this rule, so we darken the vowels and circle the consonants following the vowels at the beginning of the lesson. These visual prompts should cue the students to the relevant features of the word. For **independent practice,** we present the students with 10 words, some that apply the rule, like *fan,* and some that do not, like *sing.* They are instructed to add *ing* to the words that fit the rule and write "No" by the words that do not fit the rule. Throughout the lesson, we include mastery checks (Step G) to make certain every student is able to apply the rule before we assign the independent practice problems.

Adapting the Instructional Procedures

We present a script to demonstrate the instructional procedures of modeling, asking fast-paced questions, involving students with choral responding, giving immediate feedback, and checking comprehension. We have attempted to use uniform, unambiguous wording in the script. A hand drop is the signal for choral responding. Please see Figure 7.2 for the sample plan.

◆ ACTIVITY 7.2

Use Direct Instruction procedures to teach that *y* at the end of a two-syllable word often has the *e* sound (e.g., *baby, pretty, slowly*). First, adapt the curriculum features: What preskills should the students know? What examples do you plan to use? What prompts? What independent activities? How do you plan to ensure mastery? Now adapt the instructional procedures and write the script.

 IMPORTANT POINTS

1. The Direct Instruction model as demonstrated commercially in such programs as *Distar Math, Spelling Through Morphographs,* and *Reading Mastery* created by Engelmann and his colleagues and *Direct Instruction Mathematics* by Silbert, Carnine, and Stein is effective in teaching basic skills to students from ethnically diverse cultural backgrounds and students with special needs.

2. Curriculum features of Direct Instruction include the components of sequential order, examples, well-constructed formats, prompts, independent practice activities, and mastery learning.

3. The guidelines for sequential order are (a) teach preskills, (b) teach easy skills before more difficult skills, (c) teach similar skills nonconsecutively, and (d) teach high-utility skills before less-used ones.

4. Positive, negative, and test examples should be selected; examples should consistently follow the rule, with exceptions introduced later.

5. Well-constructed formats with teacher scripts are usually used to teach different types of skills (e.g., to teach new sounds, the teacher models, repeats, elicits student responses, tests individuals, and gives feedback).

6. Prompts are visual details that are added to an example to highlight the relevant features.

7. Independent activities in the workbook are presented after the lesson, while mastery learning activities are presented during the lessons and mastery tests are interspersed throughout.

8. Cueing attention and providing overviews to begin the lesson; modeling, eliciting student participation, providing immediate feedback, and guiding practice activities during the body of the lesson; and introducing independent practice activities to close the lesson are instructional procedures often used.

Teacher: Listen. Today we are going to be learning a new spelling rule. First I'll teach you the rule, we'll practice together, and then you'll use the rule alone.

Body and Guided Practice

Our lesson proceeds using the format described in Adapting Curriculum Features:

(Step A—Teacher tells students the rule.)

Teacher: Listen. I'm going to present a new spelling rule. Here's the new spelling rule: When a word has a short vowel sound followed by one consonant, double the consonant before adding *ing.*

(Step B—Students repeat the rule.)

Teacher: Say the rule. (Signal)
Students: When . . . .

(Step C—Teacher asks questions about the rule and gives feedback.)

Teacher: When a word has a short vowel sound followed by one consonant, double the consonant before adding *ing.*
What do you do when a word has a short vowel sound followed by one consonant? (Signal)
Students: Double the consonant.
Teacher: Yes, we double the consonant. You are absolutely correct.

or

No, listen. The rule is when a word has a short vowel sound followed by one consonant, double the consonant before adding *ing.* So what do you do when a word has a short vowel sound followed by one consonant? Double the consonant. Say it with me. Say it alone.

(Step C—Teacher asks questions about the rule and gives feedback.)

Teacher: When do you double the consonant? (Signal)
Students: When the word has a short vowel sound followed by one consonant.
Teacher: Yes, we double the consonant when the word has a short vowel sound followed by one consonant.

or

No, listen. The rule is when a word has a short vowel sound followed by one consonant, double the consonant before adding *ing.* So when do you double the consonant? When the word has a short vowel sound followed by one consonant. Say it with me. Say it alone.

(Step D—Teacher models use of the rule with a positive example.)

Teacher: (Write *bat* on the board with colored chalk and circle the *t.*) Look at this word. My turn. Does *bat* have a short vowel sound? Yes. Does one consonant follow the vowel? Yes. Do I double the consonant before adding *ing?* Yes. How do I know? Because the word has a short vowel sound followed by one consonant. Add *ing* to bat: b-a-t-t-i-n-g.

(Step E—Students repeat application of the rule.)

Teacher: Your turn. Does *bat* have a short vowel sound? (Signal) Does one consonant follow the vowel? (Signal) Do you double the consonant before adding *ing?* (Signal) How do you know? (Signal) Add *ing* to bat. (Signal)

(Step F—Teacher gives feedback.)

Teacher: Good spelling *batting.* (If they are incorrect, say, No, listen and repeat Steps D and E.)

(Step G—Teacher tests individuals [Steps E and F].)

Teacher: Your turn, Larry. Does *bat* have a short vowel sound? (Continue with Steps E and F.)

Figure 7.2 Sample Lesson Plan

(Step H—Teacher drops the model and asks questions to prompt rule application.)

Teacher: Look at this word *slip.* (Write *slip* on the board with colored chalk and circle the *p.*) Your turn. Does *slip* have a short vowel sound? (Signal) Does one consonant follow the vowel? (Signal) Do you double the consonant before adding *ing*? (Signal) How do you know? (Signal) Add *ing* to *slip.* (Signal) Good using the rule.

(Step I—Teacher tests individuals, repeating Step H with positive examples of skip, hem, *and* hop *and gives feedback.)*

Teacher: Your turn, Sarah. . . . Good using the rule, Sarah.

(Step J—Teacher repeats the rule.)

Teacher: Remember, the rule is when a word has a short vowel sound followed by one consonant, double the consonant before adding *ing.*

(Step K—Teacher models the use of the rule with a negative example.)

Teacher: (Write *jump* on the board with colored chalk and circle the *m* and *p.*) Look at this word. My turn. Does *jump* have a short vowel sound? Yes. Does one consonant follow the vowel? No. Can I use the *ing* rule? Oh, no, I can't use this *ing* rule. Why? Because it doesn't have only one consonant following the vowel.

(Step L—Students repeat the application.)

Teacher: Your turn. Does *jump* have a short vowel sound? (Signal) Does one consonant follow the vowel? (Signal) Can I use the *ing* rule? (Signal) Why? (Signal)

(Step M—Teacher gives feedback.)

Teacher: You are correct. We can't use our rule.

(Step N—Teacher tests individuals [Steps L and M].)

Teacher: Your turn, Hector. Does *jump* have a short vowel sound? . . . Good using the rule, Hector.

(Step O—Teacher tests individuals, repeating Step L with negative examples of batch, bow, *and* meet, *and gives feedback.)*

Teacher: Your turn, Annie. . . . Good using the rule, Annie.

Closing

Teacher: Let's review our new rule we learned today. What do you do to add *ing* to a word that has a short vowel sound followed by one consonant? (Signal) (Give feedback.) Let's say the rule together. The rule is, when a word has a short vowel sound followed by one consonant, double the consonant before adding *ing.* Say it alone. Let's look at the directions and the first problem on our worksheet. Please read the directions, Sharon.

Evaluation

The teacher checks worksheets and expects students to master items at 100% accuracy.

Figure 7.2   (continued)

BALANCED INSTRUCTION (COMBINATION APPROACH)

Hefferan and O'Rear (1991) developed a program that integrates Direct Instruction commercial reading programs with the whole language or literature-based model. Called BALANCE (*B*lending *A*ll *L*earning *A*ctivities *N*urtures *C*lassroom *E*xcellence), the program promotes the use of Direct Instruction, precision teaching, quality literature, the writing process, and integrated subjects to enhance the teaching of skills. A sample BALANCE lesson on the unit theme "Accepting Myself and Others" proceeds in the following manner:

Day 1, 50-minute period

10 minutes:	Read *Leo the Late Bloomer* (a trade book)—use Preview and Predict.
5 minutes:	Do character chart of Leo.
20 minutes:	Teach Reading Mastery Lesson 11—use Preview and Predict, model reading, and modify questions from teacher's guide.
5 minutes:	Do character chart of Arf.
5 minutes:	Do precision teaching timing with partners.
5 minutes:	Introduce writing assignment, which students complete on their own. Draw a picture of yourself in a place where you like to spend time.
Homework:	Reading Mastery Lesson 11 Take-Home (Hefferan & O'Rear, 1991, p. 1).

Prediction, a character chart, and writing assignments add the balance to the Direct Instruction components of the Reading Mastery lesson and precision teaching. Science Research Associates, the publisher of many Direct Instruction commercial materials, provides teachers with a free handbook of literature selections correlated with each story theme in Reading Mastery.

Some of our student teachers have adapted the reading of stories from the Direct Instruction curriculum programs of Reading Mastery and Corrective Reading. These adaptations include:

1. Have students practice reading with a partner before taking turns to read the story.
2. Read a poor reader's part first and then have him or her read it.
3. Rephrase, or have the students rephrase, the story at stopping points.
4. Review the previous day's section of the story before starting today's.
5. Remind students that some words, like *mopper*, are not used that frequently and have students substitute other, more commonly used words or phrases, such as *janitor*.
6. Expand on a story theme with creative activities.

We want to spend a little more time discussing Suggestion 6, "expand on a story theme with creative activities," as expansion activities lead to inclusion of the two effective strategies of student choice and open-ended tasks. Art and drama activities are easy to add to the Direct Instruction Curriculum of Reading Mastery and Corrective Reading. One of our interns had students participate in their own treasure hunt after reading about a treasure hunt in their Corrective Reading text. The teacher divided the students into cooperative groups to plan the hunt. One group drew the map, one wrote the clues and hid the treasure, and one group formulated a search plan and then searched for the treasure. They then dictated their experiences to the teacher, who published their accounts in a class book. Throughout the week, they selected one of the accounts to read during the reading class. Another student teacher had students make puppets of their favorite characters from the stories they read that month. They made a puppet stage from a refrigerator box and then presented the plays to other classes.

Writing activities are also easy to correlate to the Direct Instruction curriculum. Experience stories may be completed after each class period. For example, Ms. Phillips has her students retell the story they read each day. As they are retelling it, she transcribes the story on chart paper. The children then read the story and several are selected to draw a picture to go with the story. The next day, Ms. Phillips begins class by having the students read their own story as a review before reading the new part of the story. Depending on the students, you may want them to write their own story or even think of their own endings.

Ms. Anderson had her children create big books from literature selections that were correlated to a particular theme from the Reading Mastery curriculum. A Big Book is usually made after children are quite familiar with a story. The children retell the story, and the teacher prints one or two sentences at the top of each 12-by-18-inch piece of light cardboard until the children's version of the story is complete. Then the children, either individually or in small groups, draw illustrations that correspond to the text on each page. A cover page with the title and author and a preface page that explains why the children selected the story to retell are also included (Herald-Taylor, 1987). The pages are sequenced by the children and then bound with a heavy-duty stapler or book-binding tape.

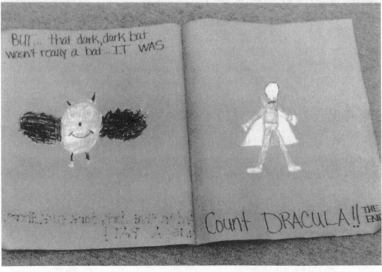

This big book was designed by primary-age students with special needs.

THE UNIT APPROACH

The Unit Approach integrates subject matter with a topic, theme, or interest area. For example, instead of teaching students about electricity by having them read page by page in the science text, you may teach about electricity through interrelated activities. Students may calculate the average cost of the school's electric bill for the past 6 months, set up an experiment demonstrating the idea of a circuit, or read about Thomas Edison and his experiments with electricity.

Mastropieri and Roser (1994) posit that students with disabilities are less likely to encounter difficulties with language and literacy demands with a hands-on science approach that includes manipulative activities and thematic units instead of a text-oriented one. Roser, Hoffman, and Farest (1990) found that literature units contributed to improved language arts and reading test scores on the California Test of Basic Skills for second graders at risk, many of them from the Hispanic culture. Thematic units were part of a school-based literacy learning project that improved the reading and writing performance of students with mild disabilities over that of a control group (Englert, Raphael, & Mariage, 1994).

The Unit Approach is also recommended for integrating multicultural content into the curriculum (Baker, 1983; Banks, 1987; Grant & Sleeter, 1989; Tiedt & Tiedt, 1986). For example, if you are teaching a unit dealing with different shelters, it is easy to include such diverse cultural elements as shelter on a reservation and shelter in a ghetto. A unit on folktales may include a selection of tales of African origin, such as *Mufaro's Beautiful Daughters* by John Steptoe (1987); tales of Native American origin, such as dePaola's (1983) *The Legend of the Bluebonnet;* and tales of Hispanic origin, such as Belpre's (1973) *Once in Puerto Rico.*

Rationale

The Unit Approach is based on the premise that students learn and assimilate information by actively participating in a variety of activities. Current brain research shows us that the brain does not process information in a step-by-step, one-item-at-a-time process, but by continuously multiprocessing information and emotions through all of our senses at the same time (Stanciak, 1997). Integration of information promotes real purposes and audiences for language, factors important in learning (Rhodes & Dudley-Marling, 1988). Furthermore, units are motivational because they can take advantage of a student's special interests, natural curiosity, experiences, and cultural background and incorporate student choice.

Description

Units may differ in the amount of student input they require (Baker, 1983). In a teacher-prepared unit, the teacher decides the topics and information to be presented. In a teacher-student-prepared unit, the teacher generally selects the topic but guides the students in their selection of the content and ways to learn the information. In a student-prepared unit, the students decide the topic, ways to learn the information, and how much time to spend on a topic. Units may contain activities centered around different content areas, learning styles, or multiple intelligences.

Units Related to Content and Themes

Lewis (1993) suggests the organization of units around the areas of cognition, self-help, expressive language, receptive language, gross motor, fine motor, socialization, and preacademics for preschool; writing, speaking/listening, science/health, reading comprehension, word recognition, arithmetic/mathematics, and humanities for elementary; and social studies, English, math, geography, humanities, science, and foreign language/cultures for secondary. Englert, Raphael, and Mariage (1994) arrange their units around the four levels of literacy: "(a) performative literacy (e.g., decoding and printing facility); (b) functional literacy (the use of literacy for interpersonal exchange); (c) informational literacy (literacy used to communicate and acquire knowledge); and (d) epistemic literacy (literacy in pursuit of creative, exploratory, and evaluative purposes)" (p. 3).

Swicegood and Parsons (1991) created a unit that integrated speaking, listening, reading, and writing around the theme of offshore petroleum exploration for adolescents with learning disabilities. In *The Unit Organizer Routine* (Lenz, Bulgren, Schumaker, Deshler, & Boudah, 1994), the teacher and students create a graphic worksheet to identify the important content and relationships of a unit. For example, the Unit Organizer contains key words to identify the theme, lines, and labels to help students see connections, schedules of assignments, topics, tasks, activities, and a list of questions (see our example shown in Figure 7.3).

An additional part that some teachers like to use is the Expanded Unit Map. The Expanded Unit Map is completed as the unit is taught and expands upon the major topics and subtopics. We present our example of a partially completed Expanded Unit Map dealing with cold deserts in Figure 7.4.

Thematic units are organized around themes, which state a point of view or perspective, not topics (Shanahan, Robinson, & Schneider, 1995). For example, a theme may be, "we need to respect individual differences," whereas a topic is a subject, such as "transportation." Often, teachers then integrate that theme into math, reading, and other academic content.

Units Related to Learning Styles and Multiple Intelligences

Even though research concerning learning styles and brain hemisphere preferences is con-

troversial (Dunn, Griggs, Olson, Beasley, & Gorman, 1995; Kavale, Hirshoren, & Forness, 1998; Snider, 1992), this approach provides teachers with a model for individualizing instruction and honoring diversity. Thinking about learning styles and multiple intelligences reminds us to present information in a variety of ways and to provide students with choices of ways to demonstrate their knowledge.

The 4MAT System. In the 4MAT system for preparing a unit, McCarthy (1987) recommends correlating subject matter to the learning styles and brain hemispheric preferences of students. The four learning styles are imaginative (Type 1), analytic (Type 2), common sense (Type 3), and dynamic (Type 4). According to McCarthy, the imaginative learner needs personal involvement in the learning experience and learns through social interaction; the analytic learner wants to know what experts think and learns by thinking through ideas; the commonsense learner wants to know how things work and learns through hands-on activities; and the dynamic learner enjoys being involved with a variety of activities and learns through self-discovery. In an examination of brain hemispheric preferences research, McCarthy finds that some individuals process information in a nonverbal global manner (right hemisphere); some in a linear, sequential, logical manner (left hemisphere); and some show no preference. Thus, the teacher organizes information with a specific type of learner in mind, using either a logical, step-by-step format (left hemisphere) or an overview presentation (right hemisphere).

Unit activities and the teacher's role vary depending on learning styles and hemispheric preferences. The teacher's role also changes during the unit from direct teaching to becoming more of a facilitator. See Figure 7.5 for a sample of the activities one of our interns planned for a solar system unit based on this model.

NAME _____
DATE _____

LAST UNIT/Experience	CURRENT UNIT	NEXT UNIT/Experience
Grasslands	Deserts	Forests

UNIT MAP

is about...

Chapter 10

A dry, barren region where plants, animals, and people find that water is scarce.

inhabited by → Desert Animals
- Mammals
- Reptiles
- Insects

covered with → Vegetation
- Creosote Bush
- Mesquite
- Cactus

divided into → Certain types of deserts
- Tropical
- Temperate
- Cold
- Semi-Arid

4/17	Introduce unit organizer ✓
4/18	Describe types of deserts ✓
4/19	Read pp. 1–6 in Chapter 10 ✓
4/20	Make desert collages
4/21	Show video on desert vegetation
4/24	Discuss pp. 7–12
4/25	Complete a cloze activity on desert vegetation
4/26	Read pp. 12–18
4/27	Discuss desert animals
4/28	Construct a bulletin board of desert animals
5/1	Write a journal entry called: "One Day in the Desert"
5/2	Review
5/3	Test

UNIT RELATIONSHIPS
- compare/contrast
- cause/effect
- descriptive

UNIT SELF-TEST QUESTIONS

1. In what ways do tropical, temperate, cold, and semi-arid deserts differ?
2. How do desert plants get water?
3. How do desert animals withstand the extreme heat of the desert?
4. What are three examples of desert vegetation?

Figure 7.3 Unit Organizer

NOTE. The unit organizer is an instructional tool developed and researched at the University of Kansas Center for Research on Learning (Bulgren, Schumaker, & Deshler, 1988). Reprinted by permission.

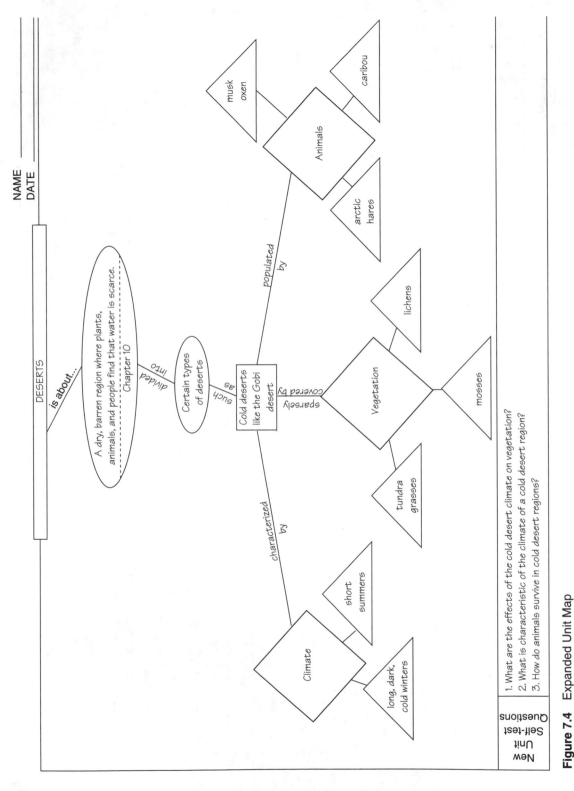

Figure 7.4 Expanded Unit Map

NOTE. The Expanded Unit Map is an instructional tool developed and researched at the University of Kansas Center for Research on Learning (Bulgren, Schumaker, & Desher, 1988). Reprinted by permission.

214

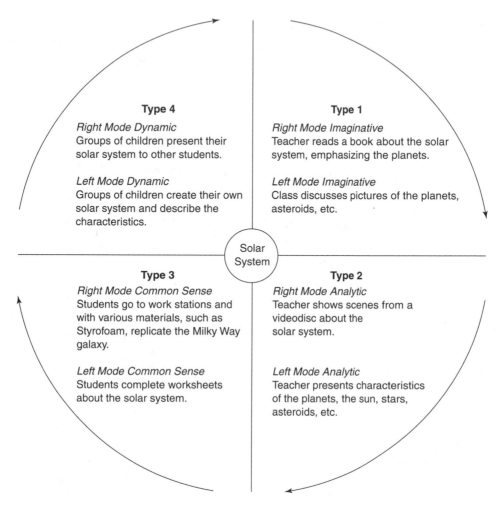

Figure 7.5 Sample 4MAT Unit

Multiple Intelligences. Gardner (1983) posits the existence of multiple intelligences that enable people to solve problems. These intelligences are verbal/linguistic, logical/mathematical, visual/spatial, musical/rhythmic, body/kinesthetic, interpersonal, and intrapersonal. Verbal/linguistic is related to words and language; logical/mathematical is related to numbers and the recognition of abstract patterns; visual/spatial includes the ability to create mental images; musical/rhythmic is related to recognition and sensitivity to rhythms and beats; body/kinesthetic includes physical movement and body awareness; interpersonal relies on relationships and communications; and intrapersonal centers on metacognition and inner awareness (Lazear, 1991).

Building on this theory, Maker, Nielson, and Rogers (1994) devised a thematic curriculum that considers multiple intelligences, problem types, and cultural diversity. With a unit theme of "Connections" and the topic of

Native Americans in North Carolina, they devised different activities that, they feel, are appropriate for each intelligence:

A. *Verbal/linguistic:* Read a road map of North Carolina. List the Native American place names on the map.
B. *Logical/mathematical:* Compute the number of miles Cherokees walked per day during the Trail of Tears.
C. *Visual/spatial:* Trace the route of the Trail of Tears on a modern-day map.
D. *Musical/rhythmic:* Find a recording of Native American music and share it with your classmates.
E. *Body/kinesthetic:* Demonstrate a Native American game that teaches the skills of hunting.
F. *Interpersonal:* Identify the problems specific Native American groups have had with settlers in North Carolina. Which was the most severe? Why?
G. *Intrapersonal:* Choose your favorite event(s) from *Knots on a Counting Rope.* Show in some way the role you would play in the event(s) (p. 15).

Gardner (1995) believes that multiple intelligence theory may enhance education by: (a) presenting concepts in a variety of ways, although he cautions that not all topics may be approached via the seven intelligences; (b) cultivating more than verbal/linguistic or logical/mathematical intelligences, which comprise the focus of most school curricula; and (c) personalizing education with the emphasis on children's strengths. He also believes that most people possess all intelligences at various competence levels.

 ACTIVITY 7.3

With a colleague, discuss the various ways to organize a unit. Then select one of the ways and design some activities.

Planning

The suggestions for planning a unit are a compilation of ideas from Baker (1983); Englert, Raphael, and Mariage (1994); Pappas, Kiefer, and Levstik (1990); Rhodes and Dudley-Marling (1988); Swicegood and Parsons (1991); Weaver, Chaston, and Peterson (1993); and our own experiences. Although there is not a single correct way to create a unit, we suggest the following steps: (1) select the unit theme or topic, (2) brainstorm ideas, (3) group ideas into categories, (4) identify general goals, (5) identify specific objectives, (6) develop activities to meet the objectives, (7) evaluate the objectives, and (8) compile a list of resources. The steps are not always sequential, as sometimes it is easier to identify the activities before the objectives.

Select the Unit Theme or Topic

The selection of the unit theme or topic is often dictated by district curriculum guides, which list required topics and objectives in social studies, language arts, science, history, health, and other subject areas for various grade levels. Swicegood and Parsons (1991) suggest that teachers first give an overview of the possible topics that address the curricular objectives and then let students participate in the selection of the topic.

Roser, Hoffman, and Farest (1990) used children's literature to select unit themes or topics. They selected and grouped 10 children's books that focused on character traits and the ways these traits made characters special into the unit topic, "Being Different Is Being Special" (p. 556). Rhodes and Dudley-Marling (1988) suggest, "The topic can be selected because the teacher knows that it will inspire students' interests and meet some of their needs, or because the students themselves have suggested the topic or revealed a great interest in it during another instructional experience" (p. 93).

Brainstorm Ideas

After selection of the general theme or topic, the students and teachers list everything that

Figure 7.6 Sample Semantic Map

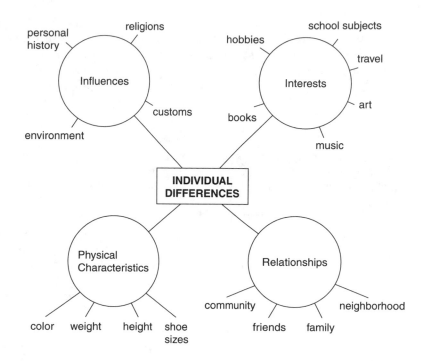

comes to mind. This brainstorming creates a collective group knowledge with equal access to information and a common vocabulary for all (Englert, Raphael, & Mariage, 1994). With young children, you may wish to show pictures or a book to elicit brainstorming.

During this process, you may want to think of your students' IEP objectives, current resources, and literature books. For example, the topic of *time* may elicit a list of hours, minutes, clocks, days, night, calendar, movement, and the book, *A Wrinkle in Time*. Hours and minutes may be related to your students' IEP objectives of telling time.

Group Ideas into Categories

Next, take these ideas and develop them into semantic maps or webs with categories that show relationships (see Figure 7.6). For example, students in the Early Literacy Program talked about snapping, poison, and box turtles, which were categorized under different kinds of tur-

tles (Englert, Raphael, & Mariage, 1994). Another example shows simple clocks, manual clocks, and mechanical clocks mapped under "measuring time" (Pappas, Kiefer, & Levstik, 1990). The software program of Inspiration may assist in the creation of semantic maps (Inspiration Software, Inc., 7412 SW Beaverton, Hillsdale Hwy., Suite 102, Portland, OR 97225; 1-800-877-4292). Students and teachers continue to update the map or web as students secure more information and check the accuracy of their brainstormed ideas. This, then, leads to the identification of goals and objectives.

Identify General Goals

General goals may include such words and phrases as, "to have a greater appreciation, to better understand, to be able to enjoy, to develop respect for" (Baker, 1983, p. 108). A general goal found in a multicultural unit is, "to help students understand the role and contributions of different ethnic groups in the development of the District of Columbia" (Baker, 1983, p. 109). A general goal for the unit on time may be, "to help students understand the role of time in history."

 ACTIVITY 7.4

> Brainstorm with another student ideas concerning global warming. Then draw a semantic map with the ideas grouped into categories.

Identify Objectives

Behavioral objectives specify the learner, condition, criterion, and target behavior (see Chapter 2). They describe outcomes that can be measured and correlated with the categories and the major goals of the unit. For example, an objective for the general goal just discussed may be, "Following a discussion of ways time was measured over the centuries, the students will build a water clock and use it to tell time at 100% accuracy." Students may wish to develop their own objectives based on the questions that they would like answered.

Develop Activities and Learning Experiences

Ideas for activities may come from suggested experiments, enrichment activities found in teachers' manuals, your own creativity and experiences, or again, from the questions students are asking. Activities may be tied to subject areas, literacy stages, themes, learning styles, and multiple intelligences, as discussed in the description section. Englert and Mariage (1996) suggest that students now transform their ideas into written or oral reports after they use the semantic map to make decisions about the relevant ideas and the relationships of the ideas. Swicegood and Parsons (1991) include speaking and listening activities (such as debates and role-plays), reading activities (such as constructing tree webs), and written expression

activities (such as keeping journals and diaries) for their secondary unit on offshore petroleum exploration.

Weaver, Chaston, and Peterson (1993) recommend dividing the students into cooperative groups, based on their interests. Students then research the topic and decide on the activities. One of our student teachers used this procedure in a co-taught health class on substance abuse. After weeks of researching information, one group wrote a play about the dangers of smoking. Another group presented posters dealing with statistics on teenage substance abuse and a comparison with their own school from interviews and surveys that they had conducted. A third group videotaped a day in the life of a teenage substance abuser, emphasizing the effects on work, school, and relationships. After researching the causes of substance abuse, a fourth group wrote 10 two-minute television spots dealing with handling peer pressure and how to help a friend who may be having difficulties.

Students' presentation of information may be enhanced through the use of software programs, such as Amazing Animations (Claris), Hyperstudio (Roger Wagner), Kid's Studio (Cyber Puppy), Microsoft Creative Writer 2 (Microsoft), The Print Shop Deluxe or New Print Shop (Broderbund), and Visual Planner (Steck Vaughn). Kid's Studio, Amazing Animations, and Hyperstudio allow students to create multimedia productions that may incorporate text, graphics, animation, movie clips, and sounds.

Many times, teachers plan a culminating activity to tie together the information and understandings the students have developed in a unit. For example, after studying about Mexico, students in a co-taught inclusion class invited parents and members from other classes to visit the various booths designed by each cooperative group. Visitors were treated to sample foods in the food booth, dramatizations in the arts booth, oral reports in the government booth, and visual displays in the lifestyles booth.

The culminating activity was so motivating to one student who was essentially a nonreader that he volunteered to read one of the group-prepared reports. He had memorized the report, but pretended to read from the typed project.

Evaluating the Objectives

Swicegood and Parsons (1991) recommend both quantitative (product) and qualitative (process) evaluation procedures. Some of their examples of quantitative procedures include evaluating the amount of work, scoring writing mechanics, and comparing work samples over time. Some of their examples of qualitative procedures include audiotaping class participation, judging debates, and scoring writing holistically. Barnes (1993) recommends that both teachers and students reflect on the product and process.

Compiling a List of Resources

Since no single text is used in the Unit Approach and since you want to include many activities when presenting the information, you must compile a list of resources. Englert, Raphael, and Mariage (1994) had their students list additional sources of information with the following results: "Ask brothers and sisters, look in books, look on the book cover, library, dictionary, encyclopedia, ask parents, and look in books at home" (p. 11). To this resource list, we add films and CD-ROMs, such as First Connections: Eyewitness Children's Encyclopedia (Dorling Kindersley), First Connections: The Golden Book Encyclopedia (Hartley/Josten), Mammals: A Multimedia Encyclopedia (National Geographic Society), and Microsoft Encarta (Microsoft). In Table 7.1 we provide ideas for other resources and free materials.

Sometimes, students may secure supplemental materials. One teacher, who organized the social studies curriculum into units with various countries as topics, had the students write to the embassies located in Washington, DC, for in-

Table 7.1 Sources of Free Materials

Educator's Guide to Free Materials
Educator's Progress Service, Inc.
214 Center St.
Randolph, WI 53956
(*Phone:* 920-326-3126)

Free Stuff for Kids
Meadowbrook Publishers
Distributed by Simon & Schuster
1230 Avenue of the Americas
New York, NY 10020

Free Publications from U.S. Government Agencies
Library Unlimited
P.O. Box 3988
Englewood, CO 80155-3988
(*Phone:* 800-237-6124)

Educator's Guide to Free Health, Physical Education, and Recreation Materials and Educator's Guide to Free Social Studies Materials
Educator's Progress Service, Inc.
214 Center Street
Randolph, WI 53956
(*Phone:* 920-326-3126)

The Kid's Address Book
by Michael Levine
A Perigree Book (Putnam Publishers Group)
405 Murray Hill Pkwy.
Rutherford, NJ 07073
(*Phone:* 800-631-8571)

formation about each country. Frequently, embassies send addresses of other places to write to for free materials as well as free pamphlets about their countries. At the beginning of the school year, this same teacher had parents identify any special skills or topics they or their friends might share from a list of planned unit topics for the coming school year. Crocker (1983) recommends having students file the information and materials they collect in large vertical files for use by other students in the future. Other sources for published units may be found in Table 7.2. We adapt examples from

Table 7.2 Sources for
Published Units

Multicultural Teaching: A Handbook of Activities, Information, and Resources by
Tiedt & Tiedt (1986)
The authors suggest ideas for various multicultural units.

The 4MAT System by McCarthy (1987)
Sample elementary unit topics—living and nonliving things
Sample middle school–level topics—probability and energy
Sample secondary-level topics—due process and respiration/breathing

ITI: THE MODEL: Integrated Thematic Instruction by Kovalik (1994)
The author identifies research, basic information to be learned, activities, and
resources for weekly and monthly units, based on brain-compatible learning and
brain research.

*An Integrated Language Perspective in the Elementary School: Theory into
Action* by Pappas, Kiefer, and Levstik (1990)
Sample primary grade themes—spaces, wash and wear, changes, explorations,
let's eat, and giants
Sample fourth- through sixth-grade themes—explorations and digging up the
past

◆ **ACTIVITY 7.5**

Develop a unit based on 4MAT, multiple intelligences, literacy stages, or subject areas. Be sure
to identify the major goal, categories, objectives,
activities, and evaluation.

Pappas, Kiefer, and Levstik's theme of wash and
wear to summarize the steps to unit preparation
(see Figure 7.7).

THE SINGLE-TEXT APPROACH

In some inclusive settings, teachers rely on the
textbook for instructing students. Frequently,
the instruction proceeds with students taking
turns reading paragraphs orally or reading the
text silently and answering questions. For students with disabilities who often have reading,
organization, memory, and attention problems,
these instructional strategies are ineffective.
Adaptations should be made before, during,

and after lesson presentation. We present adaptations dealing with a health lesson on skin,
hair, and nail care, taken from *Decisions for
Health Book One* (Bernstein, 1997), a textbook
written for students with special needs. We feel
these adaptations require minimal teacher time
and are easy to implement.

Before Instruction
Content area texts frequently include chapters
with independent practice items. As a first step,
you need to examine the practice items and ask
yourself the following questions: (a) How are
the items presented? (b) Are there enough
items? (c) Are the independent practice items
aligned with the objectives and content of the
lesson and with students' needs and objectives?
(d) What do I need to emphasize in the lesson
so that my students will successfully complete
the items? (e) Does the student text cover the
information that my students need to complete
successfully the independent practice items?

EXAMPLE: Ms. Robinson read the four-page
Chapter 6 of the health text and examined the
independent practice items. She found that

Figure 7.7 A Sample Unit

Step 1. Select a topic or theme.
  Example: wash and wear
Step 2. Brainstorm ideas.
  Example: drip dry, washing machines, rocks, ringers, cotton, pioneer, cave dwellers, keeping clean, safety clothes, dress-up clothes, working clothes, playing clothes, nylon, wool, sewing, hand, etc.
Step 3. Group ideas into categories
  Example: Types of clothes people wear—safety, dress-up, working, playing
          What clothes are made of—nylon, wool, cotton
          Ways to wash—rocks, washing machines, hand, ringers
          How clothes are made—sewing machine, by hand
Step 4. Identify the general goals.
  Example: Students will develop an understanding that fibers go through many changes to make clothes.
Step 5. *Identify the specific objectives.
  Example: (A) After listening to the book, *Charlie Needs a Cloak* (dePaola, 1974), the children will make a picture chart showing the various steps with 100% accuracy.
  Example: (B) After watching a demonstration on how raw wool becomes a woven coat, children will place samples of wool that demonstrate the various stages in order with 100% accuracy.
  (*Note: Sequencing is listed in the IEP objectives for four students in the inclusive class.)
Step 6. Develop activities and learning experiences
  Example: To go with (A) teacher reads the book, and children discuss the steps of making Charlie's cloak. The teacher then presents them with four pictures, and they practice putting them in order. The children then tell the teacher in their own words how to make Charlie's cloak as the teacher transcribes their steps on chart paper. Some students are given a blank sheet, and they draw their pictures in order for making Charlie's cloak, while some select the teacher-made worksheet with the four pictures. If they selected the teacher worksheet, they then cut and paste them in order to make their own picture chart.
Step 7. Evaluate objectives.
  Example: Teacher observes as the students work in groups and then she checks students' picture charts. She also has some of the students individually tell her about the pictures.
Step 8. Compile a list of materials and resources.
  Example: Books such as *Mrs. Wishy-Washy* (Cowley & Melser, 1981), *The Five Hundred Hats of Bartholemew Cubbins* (Geisel, 1938). Visitors such as a seamstress. Centers with looms to make potholders; with paper bag vests that can be decorated with various materials; with pictures of articles of clothing that they must sort into working, playing, safety, and dress-up clothes. Pictures or three-dimensional objects that show different ways to wash items. Field trips to department stores, clothes museums, etc.

there were **four vocabulary** items, **six comprehension** questions, and **six analogy** questions. The **vocabulary** items were fill-in-the-blank that required students to select the correct word from three choices (e.g., Pimples form when blocked _____ become infected (moles, pores, glands).) The **comprehension** questions gave the students the answers and required them to write the questions (e.g., You shouldn't squeeze blackheads or pimples because this can spread acne. Why _____). In the **analogy** questions, students selected a word from a group of words to finish each sentence (e.g., Shampoo is to hair as _____ is to skin (skin, oil, acne, sun, soap).)

After rereading the chapter, she decided to include **more vocabulary** items (10 important vocabulary terms). To emphasize the problems and care of the skin, hair, and nails, she replaced the comprehension activity with **comprehension** questions, such as, "Why shouldn't you squeeze a pimple or blackhead?" that the students had to answer. She eliminated the **analogies,** as she felt they were not important to her objectives and were not aligned with the information found in the text.

During Instruction

To introduce the lesson, you may wish to ask students questions to bring in their background information, to list important key points or vocabulary, to complete a **K** (Know Already) **-W** (Want to Learn) **-L** (Learned) (Ogle, 1986) activity, to bring in concrete objects, or to act out simulations. For example, one of our student teachers brought in Native American artifacts to introduce a chapter on the Plains Indians. Another student teacher had all the students measure their heart rate, run in place for 2 minutes, and then measure their heart rate again to introduce a chapter on physical fitness.

Frequent adaptations in the body of the lesson include the use of guided notes, instructional pausing, vocabulary simplification, concrete objects, paraphrasing, questioning, and graphic organizers. We discussed guided notes and instructional pausing procedures in other sections of the text, so we do not discuss them again here. Paraphrasing and questioning involve turn-reading, but stopping after a few paragraphs are read and then either the teacher or student paraphrases what was read (paraphrasing) or either the teacher or student asks questions after the

previously read material (questioning). Some examples of graphic organizers are presented in Figure 7.8. More examples of graphic organizers are presented in Chapter 9.

EXAMPLE: To open the lesson, Ms. Robinson used the K column of the K-W-L procedure and asked students what they already knew about skin, hair, and nail problems and cures. Students looked at the pictures and titles in the text to add ideas. She then directed student attention to the vocabulary words that they needed to know for successful completion of the independent practice items.

Ms. Robinson next used the instructional pause procedure: one student read two paragraphs and then the students discussed the main idea and two details. Ms. Robinson wrote the main idea on a transparency and students wrote it in their health journal. In her discussion of the details, she referred to the word on the board and listed a short definition or a key word (e.g., bacteria—tiny living things/can lead to sickness; glands—oil and sweat). She also decided to use a chart for each of the topics, for example:

Hair	
Problems	Cures

After reading about a problem and cure, the students then told her what to write in the chart. To close the lesson, she used the L column of the K-W-L procedures and had students tell what they had learned about hair, skin, and nail problems and cures as she wrote the information on an overhead. She then asked them to compare this information to what they listed in the K column at the beginning of the lesson.

1. Sequence

The Titanic hit an iceberg.

↓

Some people climbed into the lifeboats.

↓

The ship sank.

2. List 3 or more details   Identify the Main Idea

The skin holds your internal organs in place. The skin keeps you from getting too hot or too cold. The skin keeps bacteria out of your body.	→	The skin protects you.

3.   CAUSE   EFFECT

Oil glands produce too much oil.	→	Blocks the pores and produces acne.

Figure 7.8 Sample Graphic Organizers

After the Lesson

Teachers now select activities that reinforce, enrich, generalize, or apply the information. Brown (1991) recommends that these activities build on students' interests, skills, and talents and that they include written, oral, and visual experiences. We like to emphasize generalization activities, as generalization of new information or skills is such a problem for students with disabilities.

EXAMPLE: Ms. Robinson puts the students in cooperative groups and assigns two vocabulary words to each group with the directions to draw or find a picture in a magazine and write a short definition of each word on a poster. These posters are then displayed around the room.

◆ ACTIVITY 7.6

Select a chapter from a content area text and design two graphic organizers.

Ms. Robinson then gives a homework assignment that requires students to interview peers or parents to see how they care for certain skin, hair, and nail problems.

Each group writes a list of five questions and then presents the list to the entire class. Students may select any five questions for their interviews.

◇ IMPORTANT POINTS

1. The Unit Approach relates instruction in a variety of academic areas to a topic, a problem, a theme, or an area of interest.
2. The Unit Approach extols student involvement, individualization, motivation, and multicultural concerns.
3. A unit may incorporate activities to correspond with various subject areas, themes, learning styles, or multiple intelligences.
4. In planning a unit, (1) select the unit theme or topic, (2) brainstorm ideas, (3) group ideas into categories, (4) identify general goals, (5) identify specific objectives, (6) develop activities to meet the objectives, (7) evaluate the objectives, and (8) compile a list of resources.
5. Unit topics may be selected from curriculum guides, classroom texts, children's literature, and students' interests.
6. Objectives identify specific behaviors and correlate with the categories and major goals of the unit and relate to students' IEP objectives.
7. Activities and learning experiences should relate to the unit objectives, require student participation, and provide for various instructional arrangements.
8. Teaching content with a single text requires various adaptations, such as changing or adding more practice items; using guided notes or instructional pausing; simplifying vocabulary; adding concrete objects, paraphrasing, questioning, and using graphic organizers.

◆ DISCUSSION QUESTIONS

1. Opponents of the Direct Instruction model frequently assert that the lessons are boring and not motivating to the students due to the constant repetition and controlled vocabulary. How might you respond to such criticism?
2. Discuss the pros and cons of designing a unit that considers learning styles.
3. What are some effective adaptations that you may make if you are using a single text for content instruction?

STRATEGY
INSTRUCTION

The adage, "Give me a fish and I eat for a day. Teach me to fish and I eat for a lifetime," typifies the current emphasis in special education on teaching students how to learn. If you teach students *how* to learn, then you do not have to help them prepare for every test, assist them with each report, or help them answer the questions at the end of every chapter they are assigned. In other words, you provide them with the strategies that will empower them to act independently and master skills across a variety of situations and settings. These skills may include finding the main idea in a paragraph, summarizing a passage, accessing information on their own, or writing a research paper (Rosenshine, 1990).

In this chapter, we discuss the use of cognitive strategies to teach students with special needs to become strategic information processors and problem solvers. First, we provide a discussion of cognitive strategies in general. Then we describe how cognitive strategies are taught through the use of metacognition, cognitive behavior modification, reciprocal teaching, the Strategic Instruction Model (SIM), and the Self-Regulated Strategy Development (SRSD) Model, all of which include aspects of both the reductionist (scientific) and constructivist (holistic) paradigms described in Chapter 1. These approaches rely on systematic instruction, modeling, verbal rehearsal, checking for understanding, practice, feedback, and active student involvement—characteristics of the reductionist paradigm. They also place an emphasis on how students think, embed instruction in meaningful contexts, and provide opportunities for students to assume responsibility for their own learning by setting their own objectives and learning from one another—characteristics of the constructivist paradigm. Metacognition, cognitive behavior modification, reciprocal teaching, the Strategic Instruction Model (SIM), and the Self-Regulated Strategy Development (SRSD) Model begin with the teacher assuming the major responsibility for teaching, then gradually shifting the responsibility to the students.

COGNITIVE STRATEGIES

Cognitive strategies are the "behaviors of a learner that are intended to influence how the learner processes information" (Mayer, 1988, p. 21). For example, Joshua may use the cognitive strategy of writing a long-distance phone number five times to help him memorize it, while B. J. may use the cognitive strategy of clustering, so the phone number is processed as 305 452 38 10. Thus, cognitive strategy instruction empowers students by giving them techniques or methods for acquiring, remembering, and demonstrating information in order to solve problems.

Rationale

Students with learning problems may lack certain cognitive strategies, fail to use them, or choose them inappropriately (Swanson, 1989). Students with learning disabilities, mild mental disabilities, or behavior problems often fail to take an active role in their own learning, and they frequently fail to develop strategies that could be used to complete tasks (Torgesen, 1982). Others may actually use strategies but may not choose them wisely (as in repeating a long list of words over and over in order to memorize it instead of using mnemonics or visual imagery). Jones, Palincsar, Ogle, and Carr (1987) indicate that if students do not already possess a strategy for completing certain tasks, then teaching an appropriate strategy is likely to improve achievement, especially for less proficient students. Since low-achieving students are not likely to develop cognitive strategies spontaneously, it is important to provide specific strategy instruction (Jones et al., 1987). Cognitive strategies provide students with a set of self-instructional steps that assist them in addressing a specific need (e.g., writing an essay) and in learning, organizing, retaining, and expressing information. Cognitive strategies offer promise for students with mild disabilities to set goals, devise strategies, and monitor their own progress (Meese, 1994).

In addition to knowing how to use a cognitive strategy, it is important for students to know why the strategy is useful or how to evaluate its effectiveness (Billingsley & Wildman, 1990). Students need to know (1) what the strategy is for; (2) how, when, and where to use the strategy; (3) why the strategy is important and useful; and (4) how to evaluate its effectiveness (Winograd & Hare, 1988). This knowledge is critical to generalization efforts. Studies have shown that cognitive strategy training has a significant impact on academic performance when generalization of the training to natural environments occurs (Ellis, 1983; Schmidt, 1983).

Strategic Teaching and Learning

In classroom settings where strategic teaching and learning are taking place, teachers and students think and make decisions about strategy selection, application, and evaluation. If you walked into a classroom in which the teacher was using cognitive strategy instruction, you might notice the teacher (1) tailoring instruction to meet students' needs and difficulties, (2) modeling the use of strategies by "thinking aloud," (3) making sure that students understand the task and the significance of the strategy to the task, (4) actively involving students, (5) helping students create their own strategies, (6) assisting students to personalize the strategies they use, (7) providing feedback regarding students' use of strategies, and (8) gradually transferring the responsibility for teaching and learning to the students. In that same classroom you would see students (1) applying strategies to various academic content, (2) actively participating, (3) monitoring their own progress, (4) interacting with teachers and with each other, and (5) taking responsibility for their own learning through self-instruction, self-evaluation, and self-regulation.

In describing strategic teaching and learning, we borrow from the ideas of Jones and associates (1987), along with the principles of effective teaching (Englert et al., 1992). Strategic teachers:

◆ Spend time thinking/reflecting about instructional planning and teaching
◆ Focus on students' prior learning experiences
◆ Possess a wide variety of strategies and explain to students the purpose and significance of each strategy
◆ Are rich in content knowledge
◆ Know how to achieve a balance between strategies and content
◆ Understand characteristics of learners
◆ Are knowledgeable about the organization of instructional materials and curriculum
◆ Actively collaborate with their students in selecting, applying, and monitoring the use of strategies to meet specific goals

As you read the next sections on metacognition, cognitive behavior modification, reciprocal teaching, the Strategic Instruction Model (SIM), and the Self-Regulated Strategy Development (SRSD) Model, notice that the strategic teaching and learning behaviors previously described are included in each of them. Note

also that each of these approaches begins with the teacher assuming the major responsibility for teaching, then gradually shifting the responsibility to the students. Metacognition is the knowledge (awareness) and control (monitoring) that individuals have over their learning. Cognitive behavior modification teaches self-regulation and problem solving. Reciprocal teaching involves gaining meaning from text through the use of teacher-student dialogues. Both SIM and SRSD include how to plan and complete a task, monitor progress, and make adjustments and modifications. Although there are some differences among these five approaches, the many similarities qualify each of them in the category of cognitive strategies. Each approach (1) has a set of steps or procedures, (2) uses cognitive modeling, (3) involves explicit instruction, (4) includes practice and feedback, (5) incorporates a gradual transfer of responsibility and ownership, and (6) promotes generalization. Table 8.1 provides a comparison of metacognition, cognitive behavior modification, reciprocal teaching, the Strategic Instruction Model, and the Self-Directed Strategy Development Model in terms of definition, components, instructional procedures, instructional approach, and content taught. Figure 8.1 illustrates an example of a cognitive/metacognitive strategy for mathematical problem solving (Montague, 1997).

METACOGNITION

The general knowledge (awareness) and control (monitoring) that an individual has over his or her thinking and learning is known as metacognition (Flavell, 1976; Paris, Lipson, Jacobs, Oka, Debritto, & Cross, 1982). Awareness, the first component of metacognition, involves a person's knowledge about his or her cognitive resources and the relationship between those capabilities and the demands of the task. For example, if you notice that you can study better with the radio off, you are demonstrating an understanding of how you best function in a specific situation or with a certain task. If you are aware of what you need to do to perform effectively, you may be able to regulate and control activities to solve a problem or complete a task. For example, when Rebekah observes that she is more successful in afternoon classes than in morning classes because she performs better in the afternoon, she is demonstrating metacognitive awareness.

The second component of metacognition involves self-regulatory mechanisms that enable a person to monitor, adjust, correct, and control his or her cognitive activities and task performance. For example, when you estimate the length of time it will take to complete an activity and adjust your pace to allow yourself sufficient time to finish, you are exercising control and regulating your actions. You are actively participating in, and assuming control over, the learning situation. Active monitoring of cognitive activities is necessary for efficient learning (Baker & Brown, 1980). For example, Brady has learned self-regulation by adjusting his rate when he reads different materials. He reads *The Sporting News* magazine and the daily comics quickly, but reads his science textbook more slowly and methodically, looking back frequently to check his comprehension. Notice how he first demonstrates an awareness of the need to read materials at different rates (metacognitive awareness) and then exercises control over the situation by actually adjusting his reading rate with different materials (metacognitive monitoring).

Rationale

The reason we teach metacognitive strategies to students is to influence how students interact with a learning task (Palincsar, 1986a). Metacognitive instruction is designed to empower students to assume control over their own learning and problem solving. It allows students to be more independent, to understand

 ACTIVITY 8.1

Part 1. Read the following passage. As you read it, try to observe what you do by asking yourself these questions, which are based on H. A. Robinson's (1975) work:

1. Do I look back at the words I have just read?
2. Do I look at each word?
3. Do I think of other things when I read?
4. Do I read and think about the meaning of every word, or do I put words together into groups?
5. Do I really know what I am reading? When you finish reading, write down all the things you did while you were reading (activity adapted from Platt, 1987; Platt & Williams, 1988).

Beneath their feet the diesel engine thudded slowly, sending a thrust of power trembling through the deck. Across Tauranga Harbor, against the wharf at Mount Maunganui, a Japanese timber ship lifted her long black hull fretfully on the tide, dragging at the hawser with a dark, clumsy impatience. Farrer looked away, out to the harbor mouth, mentally checking off Matakana Island, impatient to be past it, as though the approaching bird sanctuary barred their passage to the open sea and the thing he knew awaited him there. The sun, still rising, spread hot, multi-fingered hands across the water. (Burns & Roe, 1985)

Part 2. Now that you have completed a metacognitive awareness activity, try a metacognitive monitoring activity. If you were to read this passage again, what would you do to improve your reading of it? Write down any strategies you would use or adjustments you would make. For example, would you look back? Would you adjust your pace?

(Answers for these and other activities are found in the Instructor's Manual.)

Table 8.1 Comparison of Cognitive Approaches

	Metacognition	Cognitive Behavior Modification	Reciprocal Teaching	Strategic Instruction Model	Self-Regulated Strategy Development Model
Definition	The knowledge (awareness) and control (monitoring) that individuals have over their own thinking and learning	A technique in which the teacher models his or her thinking processes while performing a task; then the student practices overtly and covertly by him- or herself	An interactive teaching strategy that takes the form of a dialogue between teachers and students to construct the meaning of text jointly	Learning *how* to learn and perform Focus on tasks and curriculum demands	An integrated approach that assists students in developing composition skills and self-regulation strategies
Components	Active involvement of students Systematic steps or procedures Cognitive modeling Self-awareness Self-monitoring Gradual transfer of ownership and regulation Generalization	Active involvement of students Systematic steps or procedures Cognitive modeling Guided practice Verbalizations Overt and covert processing Gradual transfer of ownership and regulation Generalization	Active involvement of students Systematic steps or procedures Instruction in useful strategies Guided interactive instruction Well-informed learners Readable, meaningful practice materials Scaffolding Cognitive modeling Gradual transfer of ownership and regulation Generalization	Active involvement of students Systematic steps or procedures Cognitive modeling Overt and covert processing Guided and independent practice Gradual transfer of ownership and regulation Generalization	Active involvement of students Systematic steps or procedures Cognitive modeling Overt and covert processing Instruction in useful strategies Gradual transfer of ownership and regulation Individualization of instruction Criterion-based instruction Generalization

	Metacognition	Cognitive Behavior Modification	Reciprocal Teaching	Strategic Instruction Model	Self-Regulated Strategy Development Model
Instructional procedures	Identify task Determine student's performance Select a strategy Teach the strategy Provide practice Provide feedback Teach generalization	Explain strategy Share rationale Perform task while thinking aloud Have student perform task overtly and covertly Provide feedback	Teach summarizing, question generating, clarifying, and predicting Read title, ask for predictions Read a segment of text Ask a question about content Summarize/ask for elaborations Discuss clarifications Discuss predictions regarding next segment Provide feedback	Pretest Describe/obtain commitment Model Verbal practice Controlled practice and feedback Advanced practice and feedback Confirm acquisition and obtain generalization commitment Generalization	Develop background knowledge Discuss it Model it Memorize it Support it Independent performance
Instructional approach	Integration of reductionist and constructivism	Integration of reductionist and constructivism	Integration of reductionist and constructivism	Integration of reductionist and constructivism	Integration of reductionist and constructivism
Content	Academic subjects Social behaviors	Academic subjects Social behaviors	Academic subjects	Academic subjects Social behaviors	Academic subjects Social behaviors

NOTE. Adapted from Platt, J., & Olson, J., *Teaching Adolescents with Mild Disabilities*. 1997. Brooks/Cole Publishing Company, Pacific Grove, CA. Reproduced by permission of the publisher.

Figure 8.1 A Cognitive/ Metacognitive Strategy for Mathematical Problem Solving

Read (for understanding)
Say: Read the problem. If I don't understand, read it again.
Ask: Have I read and understood the problem?
Check: For understanding as I solve the problem.

Paraphrase (your own words)
Say: Underline the important information. Put the problem in my own words.
Ask: Have I underlined the important information? What is the question? What am I looking for?
Check: That the information goes with the question.

Visualize (a picture of a diagram)
Say: Make a drawing or a diagram.
Ask: Does the picture fit the problem?
Check: The picture against the problem information.

Hypothesize (a plan to solve the problem)
Say: Decide how many steps and operations are needed. Write the operation symbols ($+ - \times \div$).
Ask: If I do—, what will I get? If I do—, then what do I need to do next? How many steps are needed?
Check: That the plan makes sense.

Estimate (predict the answer)
Say: Round the numbers, do the problem in my head, and write the estimate.
Ask: Did I round up and down? Did I write the estimate?
Check: That I used the important information.

Compute (do the arithmetic)
Say: Do the operations in the right order.
Ask: How does my answer compare with my estimate? Does my answer make sense? Are the decimals or money signs in the right places?
Check: That all the operations were done in the right order.

Check (make sure everything is right)
Say: Check the computation.
Ask: Have I checked every step? Have I checked the computation? Is my answer right?
Check: That everything is right. If not, go back. Then ask for help if I need it.

NOTE. From "Cognitive Strategy Instruction in Mathematics for Students with Learning Disabilities" by M. Montague, 1997, *Journal of Learning Disabilities, 30(2)*, p. 171. Copyright (1997) by PRO-ED, Inc. Reprinted by permission.

the purpose behind their academic assignments, and to realize the results of their actions. Metacognitive instruction is designed to promote generalization and transfer of skills across content areas and settings and is effective in teaching higher-level skills like summarizing, paragraph writing, and self-questioning. Wong (1986) found that students who think they are in control of their environment appear to be the most successful learners, and that therefore remedial programs for students with learning disabilities should include a metacognitive component to help them become independent learners.

Description

Cognitive psychology is an important source of information for teachers working with students who have special needs. Using the contributions of cognitive psychology, special educators can design interventions that emphasize the maintenance and generalization of metacognitive skills and strategies (Wong, 1986). For example, a self-questioning procedure taught to students with learning disabilities resulted in systematic self-monitoring and enhanced reading comprehension (Wong & Jones, 1982). Other investigations have studied the effects of metacognitive instruction on the memory (Paris, Newman, & McVey, 1982) and written expression skills (Harris & Graham, 1985) of students with academic problems. Researchers in the fields of cognitive developmental psychology and instructional psychology have developed systematic procedures for teaching metacognitive strategies (Collins & Smith, 1980; Garner & Kraus, 1982; Palincsar, 1982; B. M. Taylor & Beach, 1984; Wong & Jones, 1982), and teachers may use these procedures with students who have special needs.

There are a variety of metacognitive strategies for you to use as you work with students with special needs. We could compare a student's having a variety of metacognitive strategies to a good rock group that has a repertoire of hits that it can perform at a concert. Students with special needs require a number of strategies at their disposal to respond to the academic demands of the classroom. Besides knowing a variety of strategies, students need to know which strategies to use and when to use them. The members of the rock group will consider their audience and the acoustics of the facility in which they are playing (setting demands); the lighting, equipment, their voices, instruments (strengths and weaknesses); and what they are trying to accomplish at each concert they hold, such as fundraising or plugging a new release (personal goal or objective). Students need to consider the de-

mands and problems they encounter in the classroom, what strengths they bring to a learning activity, what typically gives them problems, and what they are trying to do, such as understand a reading passage, remember a list of words, or write a theme. Successful musicians monitor throughout the concert how they are received by the crowd. They may decide to rearrange the sequence of hits they are performing based upon the reaction of the audience, or they may resurrect some of their old classics if they get lots of requests for them or if the new ones are not getting a good reaction. You may have been to a concert that started out in a sequenced and organized manner and then noticed signals being passed among the group members to change the original plan and try something else.

Just as the rock group members monitored and made adjustments in their performance at the concert, students who are metacognitively aware and know how to regulate their learning make adjustments as they proceed through a task. Karim could not remember what he had read when he got to the bottom of the page in his history book (awareness), so he reread the page, this time pausing after each paragraph to paraphrase what he had just read (monitoring). Angel was having difficulty studying for tests at the end of a unit because she could not understand her own notes or remember what the teacher had said (awareness). She began to rewrite her notes after each class, thereby engaging in a cumulative review (monitoring). These two students were demonstrating metacognitive knowledge. When students possess good metacognitive skills, they are able to interact effectively with learning situations and perform independently.

 ACTIVITY 8.2

Give an example of a metacognitive awareness activity and a metacognitive monitoring activity.

Implementation

Teachers initially assume the responsibility for helping students identify tasks for which they need metacognitive training. They begin metacognitive training by modeling self-regulation activities. Then, gradually, through scaffolding, they shift the responsibility to the students, who participate in applying metacognitive skills. Metacognitive strategies become student-directed when students show independent application of them, or generalization.

A review of the literature in metacognition suggests the existence of specific elements to include in metacognitive instruction. We present the following critical steps adapted from the work of Palincsar and Brown (1987) and Pressley, Borkowski, and O'Sullivan (1984), in combination with our own thoughts.

1. Identify the task.
   Example: Remembering what was read
2. Choose a strategy to facilitate completion of the task.
   Example: Inserting stop points in a text and then telling students to paraphrase what was read.
3. Explicitly teach the strategy.
   Example: Modeling for students what they should do when they come to a stop point
4. Explain the benefits to be expected.
   Example: Describing that grades will improve, frustration will decrease, and reading will be easier and more fun
5. Provide guided practice.
   Example: Working through an activity with students; having them apply the strategy
6. Provide feedback.
   Example: Giving positive and corrective comments, oral and/or written, regarding consistent and appropriate use of the strategy
7. Teach students how to generalize the use of the strategy.
   Example: Showing students how to use this technique with reading materials in school (content-area subjects) and out of school (magazines, mail, written directions)

Let's take a look at a metacognitive intervention for increasing class participation (Ellis, 1989). It consists of four parts (PREP, SLANT, RELATE, and WISE) that teach students to think ahead, think during class discussions, and think after class discussions. PREP (prepare materials, review what you know, establish a positive mindset, and pinpoint goals) activates students to prepare themselves for class discussions. During actual class discussions, SLANT (sit up, lean forward, act like you're interested, nod, and track the teacher) cues students to demonstrate appropriate nonverbal behaviors. RELATE (reveal reasons, echo examples, lasso comparisons, ask questions, tell the main idea, and examine importance) directs students to the verbal behaviors essential for class participation. WISE (were goals met, itemize important information, see how information can be remembered, and explain what was learned) requires students to think back and evaluate their participation after class is over. Figure 8.2 shows the WISE strategy for thinking after a lesson, and Figure 8.3 shows the PREP/WISE score sheet.

Ellis's (1989) class participation intervention (CPI) for students with special needs addresses metacognitive awareness ("Am I prepared for class?") and monitoring ("Does that make sense? No, I had better ask a question."). Ellis recommends teaching PREP and WISE together and, after they are mastered, he recommends teaching SLANT and RELATE together. Ellis specifies that the CPI strategies should be taught by (a) motivating students to learn them, (b) describing and modeling the strategies, (c) requiring verbal elaboration and then rote memorization of the strategies, (d) providing group and individual practice, and (e) periodically checking for maintenance of the strategies. He reports that students who master the CPI strategies come to class better prepared and increase academic responding during class.

Think Back with WISE

Were goals met?

- Did you learn what you wanted to learn?
- Did you meet your participation goals?

Itemize important information

- Review study guide, notes, or textbook
- Mark key information

See how information can be remembered

- Draw graphic displays
- Create mnemonic devices
- Create study cards

Explain what was learned to somebody

- Use your notes to teach somebody about the topic

Figure 8.2   The Metacognitive Strategy for Thinking After a Lesson

NOTE. From "A Metacognitive Intervention for Increasing Participation" by E. S. Ellis, 1989, *Learning Disabilities Focus,* 5(1), p. 37. Reprinted by permission.

 IMPORTANT POINTS

1. Cognitive strategies are the "behaviors of a learner that are intended to influence how the learner processes information" (Mayer, 1988, p. 21).
2. Students need to know the purpose for a cognitive strategy; how, when, and where to use it; why it is useful; and how to evaluate its effectiveness.
3. In classrooms where strategic teaching and learning are taking place, both teachers and students are constantly thinking and making decisions related to strategy selection, application, and evaluation.
4. Metacognition is the general knowledge (awareness) and control (monitoring) that an individual has over his or her thinking and learning.

5. Metacognitive awareness involves a person's knowledge about his or her own cognitive resources and the relationship between those capabilities and the demands of the task.
6. Metacognitive monitoring involves self-regulatory mechanisms that enable a person to monitor, adjust, correct, and control his or her cognitive activities.
7. Metacognitive instruction is designed to improve student problem solving, increase student independence, promote generalization and transfer of skills, and teach higher-level skills like summarizing and self-questioning.
8. Metacognitive teaching procedures include the following: (a) identify the task, (b) choose a strategy, (c) teach the strategy, (d) explain the benefits, (e) provide guided practice, (f) provide feedback, and (g) teach generalization.

COGNITIVE BEHAVIOR MODIFICATION

Cognitive behavior modification involves "specific techniques that teach self-control through increased awareness of cognitive processes and knowledge of how behavior affects academic outcomes" (Swaggert, 1998, p. 235). The teacher models his or her thinking processes in performance of a task and then the student practices the teacher model, overtly with assistance, and then covertly alone. It requires the teacher to analyze the task and the thinking processes involved in performing the task. In turn, the students are active participants as they attempt to change their cognitive behaviors. Students are taught to monitor continuously their progress toward preset goals (Swaggert, 1998). Thus, students are able to regulate their own actions (Fraser, Belzner, & Conte, 1992).

Cognitive behavior modification training was first introduced by Meichenbaum and Goodman (1971) to improve the self-control of hyperactive children. Since then, various components of CBM

PREP/WISE score sheet

PREP   WISE

Student name: _____

Prepare materials for class

yes no N/A

☐ ☐ ☐ Textbook
☐ ☐ ☐ Notebook
☐ ☐ ☐ Pen/pencil
☐ ☐ ☐ Homework
☐ ☐ ☐ Study guide
☐ ☐ ☐ Other _____

yes no N/A
☐ ☐ ☐ Difficult areas marked on notes/book

PREP/WISE Process

of "yes" boxes   Score
☐
_____
☐   Process Score
categories evaluated

Were goals met?

yes no N/A
☐ ☐ ☐ Noted whether topic question had been answered during the lesson/what answer was

Itemize important information

yes no N/A
☐ ☐ ☐ Marked on notes/book perceptions of most important information from lesson

See how information can be remembered

yes no N/A
☐ ☐ ☐ Remembering devices created

Review what you know

(at least 3 items known about topic listed)

What I already know:

1. _____
2. _____

yes no N/A
☐ ☐ ☐

3. _____

Explain what was learned to somebody

yes no N/A
☐ ☐ ☐ Explained what was learned to someone else

Establish positive mindset

yes no
☐ ☐

Positive statement about myself: _____

Pinpoint goals

Question about the topic has been noted

yes no N/A
☐ ☐ ☐

I want to find out _____

_____

I found out   I still don't know
☐   ☐

yes no N/A
☐ ☐ ☐

My participation goal is to _____

_____

☐   ☐

Participation goals noted

I met my goal   I didn't meet my goal

Figure 8.3 PREP/WISE Evaluation Sheet

NOTE. From "A Metacognitive Intervention for Increasing Participation" by E. S. Ellis, 1989, *Learning Disabilities Focus*, 5(1), p. 39. Reprinted by permission.

have been found to be effective in developing cognitive, behavior, and academic skills in students with learning and behavior problems (Armstrong & Frith, 1984; Burgio, Whitman, & Johnson, 1980; Davis & Hajicek, 1985; Hughes, Ruhl, & Misra, 1989; Rooney, Polloway, & Hallahan, 1985).

Rationale

One of the premises of cognitive behavior modification is that language is thought to affect the socialization and learning processes (Vygotsky, 1962). According to Vygotsky, children first use language to mediate their actions overtly (e.g., "If I touch the stove, I will get burned."). These overt processes (thinking aloud) eventually change to covert processes (thinking to yourself), and the child no longer uses external language-mediation to avoid the hot stove. Overt behavior can be changed by modifying a person's pattern of thoughts; that is, changing the way a person thinks about a task can change how he or she approaches it. For example, labeling a task as interesting or boring will often determine whether the person attacks the task vigorously or approaches it reluctantly (Mahoney, 1974). As a teacher, you can share your thought processes with students as you attempt to solve problems and complete tasks, providing a model for students to imitate.

The procedures used in CBM training can be adapted to fit a variety of tasks (Meese, 1994), situations, and settings. Cognitive behavior modification is effective in assisting students to remember the steps needed to solve an academic or social problem, such as computing a long division problem or responding to peer pressure (Swaggart, 1998; Williams & Rooney, 1986). It is also a way for students to improve their self-control (Fraser, Belzner, & Conte, 1992).

Description

Cognitive behavior modification is an approach that teaches students self-regulation and problem solving. Its essential components are cognitive modeling, guided practice, and verbal mediation.

Cognitive Modeling

Cognitive modeling is used as the primary means of instruction (Bos & Vaughn, 1998). In cognitive modeling, you model your thoughts by thinking aloud for students as you attempt to solve an academic or social problem. As a first step, Albion (1980) suggests that you identify the specific steps if the task deals with a skill such as dividing numbers or the generic steps if the task deals with such behaviors as being prepared for class. Once the steps are identified, you should reconceptualize them into the conversational styles of the students. For example, Ms. Williams used think-aloud procedures as she completed long division problems ("I know I can solve this problem. Let's see . . . first I divide. Yes, that's right. Now, what do I do next? I

remember . . . I multiply. Let's see, did I multiply correctly? Yes. Next, I need to subtract. Okay—that looks good. Now, the last thing I do is bring down the next number. This looks right—I knew I could do it!").

Guided Practice

An adaptation of a training sequence developed by Meichenbaum and Goodman (1971) is usually used to teach students to imitate the teacher's verbalizations (Alberto & Troutman, 1999). The sequence proceeds from overt verbalization (in which students perform out loud the same task that was modeled by the teacher) to covert verbalization (in which students perform the task via private speech). It also moves from external guidance provided by the teacher as he or she assists the students in performing the task to internal guidance in which the students complete the steps alone.

Verbal Mediation

Self-instruction, self-reinforcement, self-regulation, and self-evaluation are generally included, individually or in combination, as part of the verbal mediation procedure. *Self-instruction* is the use of language to mediate the completion of a task. *Self-reinforcement* includes selecting and administering a reinforcer, contingent upon meeting some performance standard (Hughes, Ruhl, & Misra, 1989). *Self-evaluation* refers to monitoring the quality or acceptability of the behavior, whereas *self-regulation* refers to monitoring whether the strategies are working and changing them if they are not (Paris & Oka, 1986). Examples of these various components follow in our description of two different verbal mediation procedures, one recommended by Meichenbaum (1977) and Meichenbaum and Goodman (1971) and one that we and our students have found effective.

Adaptations of the verbal mediation strategy created by Meichenbaum (1977) are frequently found in studies that measure the effectiveness of cognitive behavior modification (Alberto &

Troutman, 1999). The verbal mediation strategy includes the following steps:

1. *Problem definition:* "What is it I have to do?"
2. *Focusing attention and response guidance:* "Oh, proofread the paragraph I've just written."
3. *Self-reinforcement:* "Good, I'm remembering to check to see if I've capitalized everything I'm supposed to."
4. *Self-evaluative coping skills and error-correction options:* "That's okay; even if I make an error, I can go slowly." (p. 23)

You may have noticed that the last step also includes self-regulation, as students are taught how to monitor their errors and how to decrease them (in this case, "go slowly").

We have adapted a problem-solving type of verbal mediation strategy appropriate for teaching elementary and middle school students with problem behaviors (MARC, 1983).

1. *Define the problem:* "I talk out during independent practice time."
2. *Study the problem and its consequences:* "I am breaking one of the class rules. It gets me into trouble with the teacher. I don't finish my work, I don't do well on my math quizzes, and I miss important points."
3. *Make a value judgment:* "I really don't like the teacher to be angry with me. I don't like it when my friends get mad because I disturb them. I'd like to get better grades on my math quizzes. I really need to be quiet and concentrate on my work."
4. *Identify alternative solutions:* "I can count to five when I feel the urge to talk out. I can draw a picture of an open mouth with a slash through it and tape it on my desk and mark on it each time I feel the urge to talk out."
5. *Evaluate the solutions:* "If I count to five, I may just end up shouting the number out loud. If I try marking on the picture of the mouth, I won't bother anyone and I won't be saying anything at all."
6. *Make a decision and be happy about it:* "I think I'll try the picture of the open mouth with

the slash through it. I think it will work well. Yeah, that sounds good."
7. *Implement the decision and evaluate it:* "I just made the picture and taped it to my desk. Now I'll check 2 days from now to see how I did. Maybe I'll buy myself a candy bar if I have only a few marks. I really think this will help me."

A teacher who taught his students this problem-solving procedure prepared the poster shown in Figure 8.4 to cue the students to use the strategy. He hoped these reminders would assist the students in using the technique independently.

Implementation

Like most cognitive strategies, this one should be introduced with an explanation, purpose, and rationale to implement cognitive behavior modification. Then model your strategy and elicit student participation to model the strategy overtly and then covertly. The steps, adapted from Meichenbaum and Goodman (1971) and Meichenbaum (1977), usually proceed in the following manner:

1. *Explain the technique:* "You seem to be having problems with talk-outs, Lupa. I have a neat strategy that I use whenever I am having problems. Let me show it to you."
2. *Share the purpose:* "The strategy should help you stop your talk-outs."
3. *State its value:* "Last year it helped one of my students make new friends because she listened to them when they spoke. It should help you get your work done because you won't talk out as much."
4. *Select a verbal mediation procedure:* The teacher selects the steps of the problem-solving techniques found in Figure 8.4.
5. *Model your thoughts out loud, using appropriate vocabulary:* "Let's see . . . my first step is to define my problem. Uh, I seem to have difficulty with talk-outs." (The teacher continues

Figure 8.4 Problem-Solving Poster

modeling each of the steps of the problem-solving procedure.)

6. *Prompt and guide the student in imitating your model:* "What do you plan to do first? What are your options?"

7. *Have the student practice overtly without guidance, but with feedback:* "Lupa, you try it alone." "Well done, Lupa, you remembered each of the steps." Or, "Not quite, Lupa, you forgot to look at all the solutions."

8. *Fade overt practice:* "Whisper the problem-solving steps now, Lupa."

9. *Have the student practice the model silently:* "Practice the problem-solving steps just by thinking about them now, Lupa."

Anita Gearhart, a teacher of middle school students with behavior problems, adapted the technique into a Think Sheet (see Figure 8.5). She has the student identify the problem (My behavior), study the problem (Reasons), and suggest alternative ways to behave (Acceptable alternatives). We added the requirement of selecting a strategy to try the next time a similar incident occurs (Next time I will try). She has the student take the sheet home for parent signatures.

◆ **ACTIVITY 8.3**

Design a verbal recitation procedure using self-reinforcement and self-evaluation, then give examples to implement a student's use of cognitive behavior modification procedures.

◇ **IMPORTANT POINTS**

1. Cognitive behavior modification is a technique in which the teacher models his or her thinking processes in performance of a task. The student practices overtly with assistance and eventually covertly (internalizing the procedure).

2. Cognitive behavior modification includes the components of cognitive modeling, guided practice, and verbal mediation.

3. Cognitive modeling involves modeling your thoughts by thinking aloud while students watch you solve an academic or social problem.

Figure 8.5 Think Sheet

My behavior: _____
_____
_____

Rule: I will be held responsible for my own behavior (copy).
_____
_____
_____

Reasons for my behavior: _____
_____
_____

Acceptable alternatives (acceptable behavior I could have decided on):
_____
_____
_____
_____

Next time, I will try (which of the above): _____
_____

☐ I am ready to return to task.

Student _____
Teacher _____
Parent (s) _____

4. Guided practice involves having students perform a task that was modeled by the teacher, first overtly (out loud) with external teacher guidance, then covertly (using private or internal speech) with internal guidance (completing the steps alone).

5. Verbal mediation involves the use of overt verbalization (thinking aloud) through self-instruction, self-reinforcement, self-regulation, and self-evaluation, which is gradually faded to covert verbalization (private or internal speech).

6. Cognitive behavior modification may be implemented by completing the following steps: (a) explain the technique, (b) share its purpose, (c) state its value, (d) select a verbal mediation procedure, (e) model your thoughts using appropriate vocabulary,

(f) prompt and guide the student in imitating your model, (g) have the students practice overtly without guidance but with feedback, (h) fade overt practice, and (i) have the student practice the model silently.

RECIPROCAL TEACHING

Reciprocal teaching is a research-based instructional procedure designed to encourage students' active participation in lessons (Speece, MacDonald, Kilsheimer, & Krist, 1997). Like the other approaches in this chapter, reciprocal teaching concentrates on teaching students how to learn, specifically, how to gain meaning from reading text. Essentially, "reciprocal teaching is a dialogue between teachers and students for the purpose of jointly constructing the meaning of the text" (Palincsar, 1986a, p. 119). The approach helps students understand how to study and learn from a text and promotes metacognitive monitoring of comprehension (Palincsar & Brown, 1986, 1987). The instruction is teacher directed at first, but then a student assumes the teacher's role as other students comment upon the student's questions, elaborate upon the student's summary, and assist in constructing meaning and predicting new information. Students take turns assuming the role of the teacher as they lead discussions using the four reading strategies of summarizing, questioning, clarifying, and predicting text information (Bos & Anders, 1990). The context in which these four strategies are learned is social, interactive, and holistic in nature (Englert & Palincsar, 1991). To move from teacher-directed to student-directed instruction, the teacher uses a scaffolding procedure, decreasing the intensity and frequency of the prompts and supports (Palincsar & Brown, 1984).

The technique is usually taught to students individually or in groups of four to seven, and the lessons last approximately 30 minutes for 20 days (Palincsar & Brown, 1986, 1988). Many of the techniques identified in the teacher effectiveness literature (see Chapter 6) are the same as those utilized in reciprocal teaching, and we point out the similarities in our discussion.

Much of the research on the effectiveness of reciprocal teaching was conducted by the creators of the model with junior high students in remedial reading classes as the subjects, and expository or informational text as the reading material. The students were identified as "adequate decoders but poor comprehenders" (Palincsar & Brown, 1986, p. 775). In the studies (Brown & Palincsar, 1982; Palincsar & Brown, 1984), students improved in comprehension, measured by daily curriculum-based tests of 450-word passages and 10 comprehension questions. They also improved in comprehension of material presented in their general education classes, demonstrating that reciprocal teaching produced generalization.

Additionally, Palincsar and Brown (1989) found that reciprocal teaching was effective with first and second graders judged to be at risk for academic failure. In these studies, the teachers, instead of the students, read the text. It was found that 75% of the first-grade children achieved criterion performance on comprehension. In addition, the first-grade children attempted to apply the procedure to spontaneous discussions and were able to maintain the procedures in a follow-up study conducted when the students entered second grade.

Rationale

The idea behind reciprocal teaching is that the teacher is teaching the students strategies that will enable them to learn how to gain information from the printed page. Once the students learn the strategies, they can apply them to different situations without the presence of the teacher. The strategies improve self-concept, because students learn to attribute their success to their ability to use the strategies and not to luck (Palincsar, 1986a). The emphasis on en-suring that the students are well informed about the procedures, purposes, and applica-tions finds its basis in metacognition and in the premise that students with learning problems acquire information more readily when they are well informed (Duffy, Roehler, Meloth, Put-nam, & Wesselman, 1986). The interactive na-ture of the approach, which requires a joint construction of meaning, is based on the belief that students can learn from each other (Pal-incsar & Brown, 1988).

Description

The essential components of reciprocal teach-ing are strategies that teach students how to gain information from text, guided interactive instruction, and informed learners. The teacher instructs the students in the strategies of summarizing, questioning, clarifying, and predicting. In guided interactive instruction, control of the lesson moves from the teacher to the students. Students are informed about the procedures, purposes, and applications.

Strategies

The teacher teaches the four strategies: sum-marizing, questioning, clarifying, and predict-ing. For the first 4 days of the procedures, the teacher teaches the students the strategies. On the fifth day, the teacher begins modeling the strategies in constructing a dialogue. For exam-ple, Palincsar and Brown (1986) suggest that you teach students to generate information—seeking questions by first asking them to gener-ate questions concerning everyday events, such as, "If you are interested in knowing what time the afternoon movie begins, you call the theater and ask" (p. 773). The teacher spends only about a day introducing each strategy, because the emphasis is on teaching the strategies through the interaction between teacher and students in a dialogue (Palincsar & Brown, 1986).

Summarizing.
Summarizing involves identify-ing and paraphrasing the main ideas. Students are taught first to summarize the content in a paragraph or section and then to integrate the content across paragraphs.

Questioning.
Questioning requires students to question themselves about the content. Stu-dents become more involved when they must generate questions than when they merely re-spond to teacher questions (Palincsar & Brown, 1986). At the beginning, students often gener-ate questions that cannot be answered using the information presented in the text, which is a clue that they are not focusing on the text in-formation (Palincsar & Brown, 1988).

Clarifying.
Clarifying is discerning when there is a breakdown in comprehension and identify-ing appropriate strategies to restore meaning. To do this, students must know that they are not comprehending the information (metacogni-tive awareness). Readers who have comprehen-sion problems often cannot discriminate when they do not understand materials, as they are more interested in decoding words than in making sense of the words (Palincsar & Brown, 1986). At first, students attribute lack of vocab-ulary knowledge as the cause for not under-standing the meaning of a passage, so they fo-cus on the unknown words in a selection for clarification. Eventually, however, they realize that unfamiliar ideas or difficult content may block understanding of the text, so they at-tempt to clarify these concepts (Palincsar & Brown, 1988).

Predicting.
Predicting is hypothesizing the next event in the text. Students often use pic-tures and text structures, such as headings and italicized words, to aid them in making predic-tions. Predicting requires students to activate background information concerning the pas-sage and to link that information to the au-thor's intent. Often, however, students who

come from different cultural backgrounds find that their background information does not relate to the classroom materials that they are using, and they have difficulty comprehending the author's message (Ruiz, 1989). For example, if you are reading a selection about plants of the desert, you probably will predict that sometime in the text the author will mention cactus. Think of the advantage for the student who has read about or visited a desert compared with one who has never encountered the desert environment before.

Predictions can also let teachers and students know when there is a breakdown in comprehension and a student's background knowledge is incorrect. Palincsar and Brown (1988) relate the example of students not using the facts of a selection to check an incorrect prediction. In reading the title and looking at the picture in the selection "Ships of the Desert," some students predicted that the author would talk about camels storing water in their humps. When asked to summarize, these same students said the author told how camels stored water in their humps, when in fact the author had stated that camels store fat in their humps. The students did not correct their prediction and, thus, didn't glean the correct meaning from the selection. They failed to use metacognitive monitoring to check their incorrect prediction.

Guided Interactive Instruction

During guided interactive instruction, you model the use of the four preceding strategies. Remember, you have already spent four days teaching the strategies. During the initial modeling, you attempt to involve the students by having them answer questions, elaborate upon your summary, and add predictions and clarifications (Herrmann, 1988). You gradually transfer responsibility for these activities to the students until, eventually, you just provide feedback and coach the students through the dialogue as they interact with each other. For example, if the student discussion leader can-

not generate a question, you may prompt by suggesting that the student begin the question with *when*. If that doesn't work, then you may modify the task by asking the student to identify a fact instead of a question. If that doesn't work, you may model the task: "I might ask the question . . ." You may also give corrective feedback using the prompt format (e.g., "I think you forgot an important point in your summary. Remember . . .") and praise for correct answers (e.g., "Good summary, James").

High-risk students frequently have difficulty constructing summarizing statements and generating appropriate questions, so during the beginning stages, you should construct paraphrases and questions for the students to mimic (Brown & Palincsar, 1982). Eventually, however, high-risk students are able to use the strategies on their own. In a comparison of student performance on the beginning dialogue sessions (when the teacher assumed most of the responsibility) and the end sessions (when the students assumed most of the responsibility), Brown and Palincsar (1982) report that nonquestions were reduced from 19% to 0%, and student responses needing clarification were reduced from 36% to 4%. Only 11% of the students' summary statements described main ideas in the beginning sessions, whereas 60% of the statements did at the end of the study.

Informed Learners

At the beginning of every reciprocal teaching session, inform learners about the strategies they will be using, the importance of using the strategies, and ways to generalize them. In addition, inform learners of the consequences of learning the strategies. Specifying what happens when a strategy is employed leads to a better understanding of the relationship between the strategic learning and successful performance (Paris & Oka, 1986). Students must feel that the effort of learning the strategies produces success with a task (Paris & Oka, 1986). Direct and frequent measurements are suggested as a means to convince students of the worth of reciprocal teaching (Palincsar, 1986b). Frequent graphing of the results of comprehension testing and taping of the reciprocal sessions help prove to students that the use of reciprocal teaching leads to positive consequences (Palincsar & Brown, 1984).

Implementation

Implementation of reciprocal teaching requires careful planning and incorporation of the activities of summarizing, questioning, clarifying, and predicting into the lesson presentation. The steps for planning and presentation are adapted from the work of Palincsar and Brown (1986, 1988, 1989) and Herrmann (1988). These steps are not rigid, nor is the exact wording given for the modeling, the prompting, or the feedback. Unlike Direct Instruction, with its emphasis on teacher control and scripted lessons, much of the learning interaction in reciprocal teaching is controlled by the students, so teacher responses cannot be specifically worded.

Planning

To prepare for a reciprocal teaching session, first select text segments. Criteria for text selection are that the students can decode the material with at least 80 words-per-minute (wpm) accuracy with no more than 2 errors and that the text is representative of the materials that students read and study in the general education class (Palincsar, 1986b). Remember, most reciprocal teaching research was completed with expository or informational materials.

Other planning activities include (a) generate possible predictions, (b) identify questions, (c) summarize each section, (d) circle difficult vocabulary or concepts, and (e) identify supports that students will need to help them learn the information (Hermann, 1988). We present each of these activities with an example in Table 8.2.

Presentation

We suggest the following steps for presentation in a reciprocal teaching lesson during the initial stages of teacher modeling and after the students have been taught the four strategy skills. We follow each step with an example of its implementation in teaching a group of middle school students with special needs. Since this is an initial lesson, the teacher is more in charge, and the students are participating mostly by answering questions generated by the teacher, elaborating on the summary, and adding predictions and clarifications. The teacher explains, instructs, models, guides the students, and praises (Palincsar & Brown, 1986). We use the plan in Table 8.2 to assist in generating the dialogue.

1. Begin with a review of the four strategies, their importance, and the context in which the strategies are useful.
2. Read the title and ask the students to predict what they will learn. For example:

TEACHER: The title of the passage is *Langston Hughes: He Believed Humor Would Help Defeat Bigotry and Fear.* In your own words, by looking at the pictures, what do you think this story will be about?
STUDENT 1: A man.
TEACHER: Correct. Any other predictions?
STUDENT 2: A black man.
STUDENT 3: He thinks humor is powerful and can beat fear.
STUDENT 4: I bet he's a comedian.
STUDENT 5: No, look at the picture. He's signing autographs. I bet he's a writer.
TEACHER: Those are excellent predictions. Let's begin.

3. Read a small portion of the text orally or have the students read it silently, depending on the group.
4. Ask a question about the content. In the beginning ask students to answer your question. Then ask if students have any additional

Table 8.2 Planning Steps with Examples for Reciprocal Teaching

---

1. *Select the text segment for the first modeling.*
Langston Hughes: He Believed Humor Would Help Defeat Bigotry and Fear by L. Morgan (Ed.). (Seattle, Washington: Turman Publishing Company, 1988)

   "I've known rivers," wrote Langston Hughes in *The Negro Speaks of Rivers,* one of his best-known poems. "I've known rivers ancient as the world and older than the flow of human blood in human veins. My soul has grown deep like the rivers."

   Langston, one of America's greatest writers, was a powerful artist. He was able to capture in his writing both the humor and sadness of life.

   Langston had a very difficult childhood. Not long after he was born in Missouri on February 1, 1901, Langston's father James left home. James had studied law for years and learned he could not become a lawyer because he was black. Angry and bitter, James moved to Mexico to become a lawyer there. (p. 9)

2. *Generate possible predictions.*
He was an author.

3. *Identify questions.*
   • How do you think Langston's father's leaving affected his writing?
   • Why did Langston's father leave home?
   • Why did his father have to leave for Mexico?
   • Did Langston think life was only funny?
   • What did he compare his soul to?
   • Who is Langston Hughes?

4. *Summarize each section.*
Include who he was and why he had a difficult childhood.

5. *Circle difficult vocabulary or concepts.*
Bigotry. "My soul has grown deep like the rivers." Effect that a difficult childhood may have on writing.

6. *Identify supports.*
   • Kendra will need help on questions.
   • Ali will need a prompt for prediction.

7. *Generate possible predictions for the next section.*
It will tell more about Langston's childhood.

---

questions of their own to ask about the text material. For example:

TEACHER: After reading the first three paragraphs my question is, Why did Langston's father leave home?
STUDENT 1: To go to Mexico.
TEACHER: To do what?
STUDENT 1: To become a lawyer.
TEACHER: Why did he go to Mexico?
STUDENT 1: Because he was black.
TEACHER: And . . .

STUDENT 1: Oh, yeah, he couldn't practice law in this country.
TEACHER: That's correct. Does anyone else have a question to ask?

5. Summarize the section and invite elaboration from the group members. Herrmann (1988) recommends that you also explain how you arrived at the summary. For example:

TEACHER: My summary begins with the statement that Langston Hughes was a famous black writer who wrote about the humor and sadness in life. He had a difficult childhood. His father left to become a lawyer in Mexico, because he wasn't allowed to practice law in this country. This is a summary because I have included only information that we have already read.

6. Discuss any clarification that needs to be made concerning ideas or words.

TEACHER: Let me ask you something. Do you know what *bigotry* in the title means?
STUDENT 1: No.
TEACHER: Let's see if we can find the meaning somewhere in the text. I see an example in the story. Langston's father had to move to Mexico to practice law because he was black. This is an example of bigotry. Does anyone know what it means now?
STUDENT 4: Oh, it's when people do not like you because your skin is black.
TEACHER: Any other ideas?
STUDENT 2: Yes, bigotry means having bad feelings about someone
TEACHER: I guess you could say that it is having bad feelings without a good reason.

7. Predict the next section of the text.

TEACHER: I think the next part of the story may be about some more unhappy childhood experiences. Anyone have another prediction?

IMPORTANT POINTS

1. The essential components of the reciprocal teaching model are strategies to teach students how to gain information from text, guided interactive instruction, and informed learners.
2. The comprehension and monitoring strategies of summarizing, questioning, clarifying, and predicting are taught to structure the dialogue of reciprocal teaching.
3. Teachers employ a scaffolding procedure, decreasing and adjusting support as they

◆ ACTIVITY 8.4

Prepare a reciprocal teaching lesson identifying possible predictions, questions, a summary, and difficult words or concepts from the following selection from *Langston Hughes*. Check the plans in Table 8.2.

> Carrie Hughes, Langston's mother, moved to Topeka, Kansas. She worked in a law office. Carrie wanted Langston to go to a public school that did not allow black children. She went to the school board and won her fight to place Langston in the school. Even though his mother won that fight, Langston had to struggle every day to fit in at the school. Many of the children, and one teacher especially, were mean to Langston and made fun of him. Langston later wrote about his school years in *The Big Sea,* a book about his life. [Morgan, *Langston Hughes* (Seattle: Turman Publishing Company 1988), p. 9]

model the techniques, assist the students in the transfer of the technique, and move into a coaching and feedback role.
4. Careful planning includes identification of the text segment, possible predictions, questions, a summary, difficult words or concepts, and supports that students may need.
5. Presentation includes (a) sharing a brief review of the strategies, (b) reading the title for student predictions, (c) reading a small portion of the text, (d) asking questions, (e) summarizing and encouraging the students to elaborate on the summary, and (f) adding clarifications.

STRATEGIC INSTRUCTION MODEL (SIM)

The purpose of the Strategic Instruction Model (SIM) is to teach students how to learn and perform academic, social, and job-related tasks so that they can cope with immediate setting demands and generalize these skills across situations and settings throughout their lives (Deshler & Schumaker, 1988). The model employs techniques that encourage students to think and act strategically in their problem solving (e.g., know what information to memorize for a test and know when an outline will be helpful).

Rationale

As students with special needs progress through the grades, the gap widens between what they can do (their levels of functioning) and what they are expected to do (curriculum demands). By the time such students reach secondary school, the demands have increased more than their skills. Research conducted at the University of Kansas Center for Research on Learning indicates that low-achieving students, just after tenth grade, appear to plateau at about a fourth- to fifth-grade level in reading and writing and at a sixth-grade level in math (Deshler, Schumaker, Alley, Warner, & Clark, 1982). It seems appropriate to change the curricular approach to one that teaches students how to learn, solve problems, monitor performance, and take control of their cognitive processing.

Research conducted at the University of Kansas Center for Research on Learning indicates that low-achieving students do not use effective or efficient study techniques, have difficulty completing assignments, do not organize information well, and have problems distinguishing important information from unimportant information (Alley, Deshler, Clark, Schumaker, & Warner, 1983). These problems can be addressed by assisting students to select appropriate strategies, to monitor their own execution of the strategies, and to generalize the strategies across situations (content) and settings (school, home, work, and community). Students with special needs may not be actively involved in, nor assume responsibility for, learning and applying specific strategies to help themselves acquire the skills needed to meet the demands of the curriculum (Torgesen, 1982). Research has shown that students with learning disabilities do not typically apply techniques to facilitate their comprehension of reading materials (Wong & Jones, 1982). However, students have shown significant improvement in performance when taught appropriate strategies (Torgesen, 1977). Through strategic instruction, a teacher actively involves students in learning and gives them opportunities to set their own goals. Many low-achieving students fail to generalize the skills they have learned to new situations and settings (Ryan, Weed, & Short, 1986; Schneider, 1985). The Strategic Instruction Model emphasizes mastery and includes specific procedures to promote generalization.

Description

The Strategic Instruction Model consists of three components. They include a strategic curriculum (what strategies are taught), strategic instruction (how strategies are taught), and a strategic environment (how the environment is arranged to promote and enhance learning) (see Table 8.3).

Strategic Curriculum

The strategic curriculum component consists of four types of strategies: (1) learning strategies (memorizing information, paraphrasing, test taking), (2) social skill strategies (getting along, conversational skills, problem solving), (3) motivation strategies (goal setting), and (4) executive strategies (selecting and designing appropriate strategies). Learning strategies are critical for understanding, retaining, and expressing content. Social skill strategies are needed for students to be successful in school, at home, and on the job. Motivation strategies assist students in problem solving and decision making. Executive strategies enable students to create their own strategies, monitor their effectiveness, and make the adaptations necessary to improve the strategy's effectiveness.

Table 8.3   Components of the Strategic Instruction Model

Strategic Curriculum Component

The Strategic Curriculum Component of the Strategic Instruction Model specifies *what* will be taught to low-achieving or at-risk students. This component consists of four types of strategies.

Learning Strategies: designed to teach students how to cope with the academic demands encountered across a variety of school, home, community, and employment settings. These learning strategies teach students how to respond to critical reading, writing, listening, remembering, and test-taking demands.

Social Skill Strategies: designed to teach the student how to interact appropriately across a variety of situations and settings. Strategies such as resisting peer pressure, accepting criticism, negotiating, following directions, and asking for help are included.

Motivation Strategies: consist of strategies that enable students to become active in planning the direction of their lives. Strategies that teach students how to set, monitor, and attain goals related to important areas of their lives and then communicate these goals to others are included.

Executive Strategies: designed to teach students how to solve problems independently and generalize learning. These strategies are taught to students after instruction in three to five learning strategies.

Strategic Instruction Component

The Strategic Instruction Component includes procedures for *how* strategies should be taught to students. In addition, it includes procedures for the effective delivery of content to low-achieving and at-risk students.

Acquisition Procedures: provide teachers with a sequenced set of steps for teaching the strategies to mastery.

Generalization Procedures: provide teachers with a sequenced set of steps for teaching and ensuring generalization and maintenance of newly acquired strategies to other settings and situations.

Strategic Teaching Behaviors: provide teachers with the critical teaching behaviors that should be infused throughout all steps and phases of strategy and content instruction to promote maximum learning by low-achieving and at-risk students.

Content Enhancement Procedures: provide teachers with routines and devices for delivering subject-matter information in a manner that can be understood and remembered by students.

Strategic Environment Component

The Strategic Environment Component deals with how to manage and organize educational settings and programs to promote and prompt strategic learning and performance.

Teaming Techniques: consist of methods related to teaching teachers, students, parents, and other professionals how to work as a team to bring about maximum student learning.

Management Techniques: consist of methods related to how to manage materials, time, instructional arrangements, and student behavior to promote student independence and success.

Evaluation Techniques: consist of systems related to evaluating student performance, program performance, and teacher performance and providing feedback to those involved in a manner that will promote student learning and success.

Development Techniques: consist of methods related to systematically implementing program components and developing strategies responsive to student needs.

NOTE. From *Students with Learning Disabilities,* 4th ed. (p. 371), by C. D. Mercer, 1992, Upper Saddle River, NJ: Merrill/Prentice Hall. Copyright 1992 Merrill/Prentice Hall. Reprinted by permission.

All four types of strategies are essential for success. In this section, we focus on strategies that deal specifically with academic content. The learning strategies curriculum is divided into three strands: (1) the acquisition strand helps students acquire information from printed materials, (2) the storage strand helps students store important information, and (3) the expression and demonstration of competence strand helps students with writing, proofreading, and organization (see Table 8.4). The learning strategies curriculum is

Table 8.4 Learning Strategies Curriculum

Acquisition Strand

Word Identification Strategy: teaches students a problem-solving procedure for quickly attacking and decoding unknown words in reading materials, allowing them to move on quickly for the purpose of comprehending the passage.

Paraphrasing Strategy: directs students to read a limited section of material, ask themselves the main idea and the details of the section, and put that information in their own words. This strategy is designed to improve comprehension by focusing attention on the important information of a passage and by stimulating active involvement with the passage.

Self-questioning Strategy: aids reading comprehension by having students actively ask questions about key pieces of information in a passage and then read to find the answers for these questions.

Visual Imagery Strategy: designed to improve students' acquisition, storage, and recall of prose material. Students improve reading comprehension by reading short passages and visualizing the scene which is described, incorporating actors, action, and details.

Interpreting Visuals Strategy: designed to aid students in the use and interpretation of visuals such as maps, graphs, pictures, and tables to increase their ability to extract needed information from written materials.

Multipass Strategy: involves making three passes through a passage for the purpose of focusing attention on key details and main ideas. Students survey a chapter or passage to get an overview, size up sections of the chapter by systematically scanning to locate relevant information which they note, and sort out important information in the chapter by locating answers to specific questions.

Storage Strand

First-Letter Mnemonic Strategy: designed to aid students in memorizing lists of information by teaching them to design mnemonics or memorization aids, and in finding and making lists of crucial information.

Paired Associates Strategy: designed to aid students in memorizing parts or small groups of information by using visual imagery, matching pertinent information with familiar objects, coding important dates, and a first-syllable technique.

Listening and Notetaking Strategy: designed to teach students to develop skills which will enhance their ability to learn from listening experiences by identifying the speaker's verbal cues or mannerisms which signal that important information is about to be given, noting key words, and organizing their notes into an outline for future reference or study.

Expression and Demonstration of Competence Strand

Sentence Writing Strategy: This strategy is designed to teach students how to recognize and generate four types of sentences: simple, compound, complex, and compound-complex.

Paragraph Writing Strategy: designed to teach students how to write well-organized, complete paragraphs by outlining ideas, selecting a point of view and tense for the paragraph, sequencing ideas, and checking their work.

Error Monitoring Strategy: designed to teach students a process for detecting and correcting errors in their writing and for producing a neater written product. Students are taught to locate errors in paragraph organization, sentence structure, capitalization, overall editing and appearance, punctuation, and spelling by asking themselves a series of questions. Students correct their errors and rewrite the passage before submitting it to their teacher.

Theme Writing Strategy: teaches students to write a five-paragraph theme. They learn how to generate ideas for themes and how to organize these ideas into a logical sequence. Then the student learns how to write the paragraphs, monitor errors, and rewrite the theme.

Assignment Completion Strategy: teaches students to monitor their assignments from the time an assignment is given until it is completed and submitted to the teacher. Students write down assignments; analyze the assignments; schedule various subtasks; complete the subtasks and, ultimately, the entire task; and submit the completed assignment.

Test Taking Strategy: designed to be used by the student during a test. The student is taught to allocate time and read instructions and questions carefully. A question is either answered or abandoned for later consideration. The obviously wrong answers are eliminated from the abandoned questions and a reasonable guess is made. The last step is to survey the entire test for unanswered questions.

NOTE. From the University of Kansas Center for Research on Learning. Reprinted by permission.

organized in the form of a series of instructor's manuals with accompanying student activities, detailed lesson plans for teachers, and teaching materials.

Strategic Instruction

The strategic instruction component consists of four stages that are critical to the success of the model: (1) stages of acquisition, (2) stages of generalization, (3) strategic teaching behaviors, and (4) content enhancement procedures. Table 8.5 provides a description of the stages of acquisition and generalization that are used to teach strategies and content to students. It is important to adhere to these stages during instruction if maximum results are to be achieved.

The strategic teaching behaviors are the critical teaching procedures that must be utilized throughout strategy and content instruction in order to meet the needs of low-achieving students. Strategy instruction is more effective when teachers actively involve their students and make instruction motivating and interesting. The strategic teaching behaviors include:

◆ Using advance and post organizers
◆ Communicating rationales
◆ Communicating expectations
◆ Reviewing and checking for understanding
◆ Facilitating independence
◆ Ensuring intensity of instruction
◆ Providing instructional monitoring
◆ Providing feedback
◆ Requiring mastery of learning

Please note the similarities between the instructional procedures that are part of the Strategic Instruction Model and those described in Chapter 6 in our presentation of teacher effectiveness research (e.g., prompting, active student involvement, self-charting of progress, promoting generalization).

Content enhancement procedures are used to help make decisions about what content to teach and how to present it in a meaningful way. Content enhancement procedures provide teachers with planning and teaching routines and devices for presenting content in a way that can be organized, comprehended, and remembered by students. The use of content enhancement planning and teaching routines is based on the premise that students learn more effectively when:

◆ they are actively involved,
◆ abstract concepts are presented in concrete forms,
◆ information is organized for them,
◆ relationships among pieces of information are made explicit, and
◆ important information is distinguished from unimportant information.

Look back at Chapter 7 and examine the content enhancement planning and teaching device called the Unit Organizer. As we mentioned, the unit organizer is a visual or graphic worksheet used by the teacher to plan, chart, monitor, and evaluate the teaching of a unit. It can be used to teach any subject, with or without a textbook. It may be prepared by the teacher alone, or by the teacher in combination with the students for maximum ownership of the subject matter and topic. It may be used by the teacher as an advance organizer to introduce a unit; by students as a monitoring device to help keep up with assignments, meet deadlines, and review for a test; and by anyone who wants to see where a current topic fits in relation to other topics.

Strategic Environment

The Strategic Instruction Model consists of four types of techniques designed to promote a learning environment that is strategic: (1) teaming techniques, (2) management techniques, (3) evaluation techniques, and (4) development techniques. Teaming techniques relate to preparing the members of the educational community (teachers, parents, students, psychologists, vocational rehabilitation

Table 8.5 The Stages of Strategy Acquisition and Generalization Developed by the University of Kansas for Research on Learning

---

Stage 1: Pretest and Make Commitments
Purpose: To motivate students to learn a new strategy and establish a baseline for instruction

Phase 1: Orientation and pretest
  Give rationales and overview
  Administer pretest
  Discuss how decisions are made
  Assess student's current learning habits
  Determine whether strategy is appropriate

Phase 2: Awareness and commitment
  Review pretest results
  Describe:
    the alternative strategy
    what is required to learn the strategy
    results others have achieved
  Ask for a commitment to learn the new strategy
  Affirm and explain the teacher's commitment

Stage 2: Describe the Strategy
Purpose: To present a clear picture of the overt and covert processes and steps of the new strategy

Phase 1: Orientation and overview
  Give rationales for the strategy
  Describe situations where the strategy can be used
  Prompt comparisons with old learning habits

Phase 2: Present the strategy and the remembering system
  Describe the overall strategic processes
  Describe the overt and covert processes in each step
  Explain the remembering system and its relationship to self-instruction
  Compare/contrast the new strategy to old approaches
  Set goals for learning the strategy

Stage 3: Model the Strategy
Purpose: To demonstrate the cognitive behaviors and physical actions involved in using the strategy

Phase 1: Orientation
  Review previous learning
  Personalize the strategy
  Define lesson content
  State expectations

Phase 2: Presentation
  Think aloud
  Self-instruct
  Problem solve
  Self-monitor
  Perform task

Phase 3: Student enlistment
  Prompt involvement
  Check understanding
  Correct and expand responses
  Engineer success

Table 8.5 *(continued)*

Stage 4: Verbal Elaboration and Rehearsal

Purpose: To ensure comprehension of the strategy and facilitate student mediation

Phase 1: Verbal elaboration
   Have students describe the intent of the strategy and the process involved
   Have students describe what each step is designed to do and why it is important to the overall process

Phase 2: Verbal rehearsal
   Require students to name each of the steps at an automatic level

Stage 5: Controlled Practice and Feedback

Purpose: To provide practice in controlled materials, build confidence and fluency, and gradually shift the responsibility for strategy use to students

Phase 1: Orientation and overview
   Review the strategy steps
   Review previous practice attempts
   Discuss group progress and errors
   Prompt reports of strategy use and errors
   Prompt reports of strategy use or potential use

Phase 2: Guided practice
   Give directions for activities
   Model strategy applications
   Prompt student completion of activities as teacher models
   Prompt increasing student responsibility
   Give clear instructions for peer-mediated practice

Stage 6: Advanced Practice and Feedback

Purpose: To provide practice in advanced materials (e.g., regular class, work related) and situations and gradually shift the responsibility for strategy use and feedback to students

The instructional sequence for Advanced Practice and Feedback is the same as the instructional sequence used for Controlled Practice. However, this level of practice should:
   Use grade-appropriate or situation-appropriate materials
   Require application of the strategy to a variety of materials
   Provide practice in poorly designed materials
   Fade prompts and cues for use and evaluation

Stage 7: Confirm Acquisition and Make Generalization Commitments

Purpose: To document mastery and to build a rationale for self-regulated generalization

Phase 1: Confirm and celebrate
   Assign task to confirm mastery
   Congratulate student on meeting mastery (if mastery is not met, provide additional explanation, encouragement, and practice)
   Discuss achievement and attribution for success
   Identify ways to recognize accomplishment

Phase 2: Forecast and commit to generalization
   Explain goals of generalization
   Identify consequences of focusing and not focusing on generalization
   Explain the phases of generalization
   Prompt increasing student responsibility
   Prompt commitment to generalize
   Affirm and explain teacher's commitments

Table 8.5 *(continued)*

Stage 8: Generalization
Purpose: To ensure the use of the strategy in other settings

Phase 1: Orientation
    Prompt students to:
        discuss rationales for strategy use
        identify settings in which the strategy might be used
        discuss how to remember to use the strategy
        identify cues within settings that signal use
        identify materials in other settings
        discuss most and least helpful aspects of the strategy
        identify other strategies to combine
    Construct cue cards and affirmation statements
    Evaluate appropriateness of the strategy in various settings and materials

Phase 2: Activation
    Prompt and monitor student application across settings
    Enlist assistance of other teachers
    Request feedback from other teachers
    Reinforce progress and success
    Prompt students to:
        apply the strategy in a variety of settings, situations, materials, and assignments
        set goals for the use of the strategy
        develop a plan to increase application
        review affirmation cards
    Prompt regular classroom teachers to:
        understand the strategy
        identify cues that the students have been taught
        provide sufficient cues for students to identify when to use the strategy
        monitor whether the strategy is being used
        cue use of strategy
        model how to apply the strategy, if necessary
        provide feedback on strategy use

Phase 3: Adaptation
    Prompt students to:
        describe the strategy and its parts
        discuss the overt and covert processes
        identify cognitive strategies embedded in the strategy
        identify where these processes and strategies are required across settings
        identify how the strategy can be modified
        repeat application with the modified strategy

Phase 4: Maintenance
    Prompt students to:
        discuss rationales related to long-term use of the strategy
        identify barriers to continued use
        determine how they can monitor long-term use and how the teacher can help
        set goals related to monitoring long-term use
        determine how use of the strategy will be evaluated
        identify self-reinforcers and self-rewards

NOTE. From *Students with Learning Disabilities,* 4th ed. (pp. 384–387), by C. D. Mercer, 1992, Upper Saddle River, NJ: Merrill/Prentice Hall. Copyright 1992 by Merrill/Prentice Hall. Reprinted by permission.

counselors, and others) to work together cooperatively. Management techniques are related to managing time, materials, and the expertise and contributions of professionals in order to facilitate student learning and performance. Evaluation techniques emphasize the provision of feedback to teachers and students. Finally, development techniques refer to the systematic and continued design and development of strategies and other program components to meet student needs.

Implementation

In teaching learning strategies, you begin by pretesting students and gaining their commitment to learn the strategy. You then describe and model the strategy; conduct verbal elaboration and rehearsal, provide controlled and advanced practice; and then posttest and gain a commitment to generalize the strategy.

If you utilize the following stages of acquisition, you can teach students such strategies as error monitoring, paraphrasing, sentence writing, and word identification. The following systematic application of these stages is vital to the success of the model (See Table 8.5).

Pretest and Make Commitments
Establish the student's current level of performance and secure his or her agreement to learn a strategy. For example, after Rudy takes his pretest, he and his teacher, Ms. Olan, review the results and determine that his written work is messy and contains quite a few capitalization and punctuation errors. Ms. Olan makes a commitment to help him improve and motivates Rudy to make a commitment to proofread his work by learning and applying the error monitoring strategy (Schumaker, Nolan, & Deshler, 1985).

Describe the Strategy
Discuss the rationales and benefits for learning the strategy, then carefully describe the steps of the strategy. You may notice that this step was also included in reciprocal teaching and metacognitive instruction. Ms. Olan shows Rudy how the error monitoring strategy will help him improve his grades in school, his chances for employment, and his ability to write error-free letters to his girlfriend. Then she describes and gives examples of each step of the error monitoring strategy.

Model the Strategy
The modeling stage is based on the premise that students learn a skill better if they see it performed, rather than just hear it described. Therefore, Ms. Olan models the steps of the strategy by thinking aloud and using self-instruction, self-regulation, and self-monitoring. For example, she says, "Let's see. I will look at this sentence to see if there are any capitalization errors. Hm, I have capitalized all of the proper nouns. Oh, I forgot to capitalize the first word in the sentence. Good, now I don't have any capitalization errors." After Ms. Olan models the cognitive processes by thinking aloud as she examines a written passage for errors, she enlists Rudy's participation in finding errors in the passage.

Conduct Verbal Elaboration and Rehearsal
The next stage consists of two parts—verbal elaboration and rehearsal. With verbal elaboration, you ask questions about the strategy. Ms. Olan asks, "Why is it important to prepare papers that are error-free and neat in appearance?" "What are the most common mistakes students make in their written work?" "In which of your classes do your teachers penalize you for spelling, punctuation, and grammatical errors?" With verbal rehearsal, you review the steps of the strategy until the student knows them on an automatic level. For example, Rudy and Ms. Olan practice the steps to error monitoring until he has committed them to memory.

Provide Controlled Practice and Feedback
Provide ample guided practice in easy materials (controlled) until mastery is reached. Give in-

dividual feedback to reinforce efforts and avoid practice of incorrect responses. For example, Ms. Olan gives Rudy practice exercises and then provides verbal and written feedback regarding his performance of detecting and correcting errors in passages. This type of practice usually begins by having the teacher and students work together, and then with partners or in groups.

Provide Advanced Practice and Feedback

Provide advanced practice in grade-level materials found in the mainstream setting while providing positive and corrective feedback. For example, Ms. Olan checks some of Rudy's work from selected mainstream classes and gives him feedback regarding his ability to detect and correct errors in these more difficult materials.

Posttest and Elicit Commitments to Generalize

Give a posttest to determine progress and to provide feedback. Ask students to agree to generalize use of the strategy to other settings.

Promote Generalization

After ensuring that students have acquired a strategy, teachers should focus on the stages of generalization. Although teachers should be promoting generalization throughout the teaching of a strategy, they should focus on a systematic set of generalization procedures after they have completed the stages of acquisition. For strategy instruction to be effective, students must generalize the use of strategies. The following stages of generalization provide

◆ **ACTIVITY 8.5**

Use the describe stage of acquisition to teach someone to parallel park a car. Remember to include the rationale and benefits of the strategy and to describe the steps carefully.

students with the steps necessary to ensure successful transfer of skills across situations and settings.

Orientation: Make the student aware of the need to apply the strategy. For example, Ms. Olan and Rudy discuss where Rudy could use the error monitoring strategy, how he will remember to use it, and why it is important to use it in a variety of classes.

Activation: Prompt the student to use the strategy and monitor use of it. For example, Ms. Olan checks with mainstream teachers to see if Rudy is using the error monitoring strategy and helps Rudy set goals.

Adaptation: Prompt the student to examine the strategy for the cognitive behaviors he or she is using (e.g., self-questioning) and to modify the strategy to the demands of new situations. For example, Rudy and Ms. Olan work together to figure out how Rudy can use the error monitoring strategy as he takes tests.

Maintenance: Promote long-term use of the strategy across situations and settings. For example, Ms. Olan conducts periodic checks to see that Rudy is still using the error monitoring strategy effectively in a variety of situations (home, school, and on the job).

The Strategic Instruction Model stresses collaboration among support agents: general education teachers, special education teachers, students, parents, and administrators. Ongoing, systematic, collaborative efforts among support agents will assist in ensuring generalization. Special education teachers could be responsible for teaching strategies or co-teaching them with general education teachers in inclusive classrooms, general education teachers and parents could be responsible for cueing strategy use and reinforcing students when they apply strategies at school and home, and administrators could promote and reinforce the use of strategies on a schoolwide basis.

◆ ACTIVITY 8.6

Choose a partner to work with. Use the stages of acquisition and generalization to teach your partner to add three one-digit numbers (e.g., 5 + 2 + 3 =). Now switch roles and have your partner use the acquisition and generalization stages to teach you the steps in long division (e.g., 46 divided by 8 =).

SELF-REGULATED STRATEGY DEVELOPMENT (SRSD) MODEL

Harris and Graham developed the Self-Regulated Strategy Development (SRSD) instructional approach (Harris, Schmidt, & Graham, 1997), which has been used in a variety of content areas (e.g., reading, writing, spelling, and math) (Case, Mamlin, Harris, & Graham, 1995) over the last 15 years. SRSD is an integrated approach that assists students in developing composition skills and self-regulation abilities (Harris & Graham, 1996).

Rationale

Many students, particularly those who exhibit significant difficulties with writing, lack self-regulation and composition strategies and skills (Harris, Schmidt, & Graham, 1997). Their compositions do not typically show evidence of planning, effort, and monitoring (Graham & Harris, 1993). Students with problems in reading and writing need structured and explicit instruction in strategies crucial to literacy (Graham & Harris, 1994). Self-regulated strategy training focuses on strategies for planning, writing, editing, and managing the writing process (Harris, Schmidt, & Graham, 1997) as well as on self-regulation strategies such as self-instruction, self-assessment, self-monitoring, and self-reinforcement. The use of Self-Regulated Strategy Development has resulted in improved writing skills of both normally achieving students and students with learning disabilities (Graham, Harris, MacArthur, & Schwartz, 1991). SRSD has had a significant impact on students' goal setting (Graham, MacArthur, & Schwartz, 1995), self-monitoring (Harris, Graham, Reid, McElroy, & Hamby, 1994), organization of writing content (Sawyer, Graham, & Harris, 1992), and revising of written products (Graham, MacArthur, & Schwartz, 1995), among others.

Description

Self-Regulated Strategy Development is an instructional approach that directly addresses students' affective, behavioral, and cognitive characteristics, needs, and strengths (Harris & Graham, 1996). SRSD complements existing effective practices in writing; involves teachers as collaborators in the learning process through dialogues, sharing, and scaffolding; and actively engages students in writing instruction, in the development of their own strategies, and in the transfer and generalization of strategies. It is important to note that SRSD is only as explicit and supportive as is required by individual students, due to the fact that students vary in their needs for writing and self-regulation strategies. Although Harris and Graham have worked primarily with students in elementary and middle school, SRSD has also been used with high school students (Harris, Schmidt, & Graham, 1997). In the area of writing, the three major goals of SRSD include:

◆ "Assist students in developing knowledge about writing and powerful skills and strategies involved in the writing process, including planning, writing, revising, and editing.

◆ Support students in the ongoing development of the abilities needed to monitor and manage their own writing.

◆ Promote children's development of positive attitudes about writing and themselves as writers" (Harris, Schmidt, & Graham, 1997, p. 1).

Characteristics of Self-Regulated Strategy Development

Harris and Graham (1996) list six characteristics that are essential for the effective implementation of SRSD. We list them here with our own descriptions.

1. Collaborative learning: As with other types of cognitive strategy instruction discussed in this chapter, the teacher takes the initial responsibility for teaching and learning and then gradually shifts the responsibility to the students. For example, students work with one another in goal setting, monitoring, executing, and modifying writing strategies and self-regulation procedures.
2. Individualization of instruction: Instructional decisions are based upon the needs of students. For example, students will vary in terms of goals, strategies, pace of instruction, amount of repetition and practice, ability to select and modify strategies, as well as many other considerations.
3. Criterion-based instruction: Students progress through the stages at their own pace and focus on their own individual goals. As previously stated, not all students will need to work at each stage.
4. Anticipate and plan for areas of instruction that may be difficult: Collaborate with students to plan ahead for potential problems (e.g., difficulty setting realistic goals for initial acquisition and later generalization of strategies). Once you have identified possible pitfalls, you can plan ways to address them, such as providing extra practice sessions or using more examples.
5. Enthusiastic teachers and a supportive network: The level of enthusiasm and ownership a teacher has for the SRSD model, or any teaching practice, will affect its success. This, along with support from other professionals and parents within the school, can have a major impact on instruction.
6. Developmental enhancement: Each student's developmental level as a writer and as a strategic learner must be considered. As mentioned earlier in the chapter, it is important to help students understand the meaning and significance of strategy use and assist them in making decisions about how and when to apply strategies. Teachers must be knowledgeable about each student's stage of development and how strategies can best assist them at that level.

Implementation

In teaching SRSD, you generally follow six stages of instruction and choose from a variety of strategies. These strategies may be presented by the teacher or may be developed and/or modified by the students.

Stages of Instruction

Although six stages are provided for the implementation of self-regulated strategy development, these stages serve only as a general guideline. In other words, some stages will not be needed by some students; stages may be combined, modified, reordered, or revisited. For example, some students may be able to skip Stage 1, as they already possess sufficient background knowledge. Others may need to revisit Stage 3 for additional instruction or Stage 5 for additional support. The model is flexible and focuses on addressing individual needs of students. Note, for example, in Table 8.6 that some students who are learning an essay writing strategy may need to revisit Stage 5 for additional support. Perhaps they need more help writing supporting reasons for their premise, or maybe they need additional assistance with self-regulation procedures (e.g., "Slow down and take my time. Then my work will be better."). Students set their own goals and work at their own pace. As with the Strategic Instruction Model, procedures for maintenance and generalization are integrated throughout the six stages of the SRSD model (see Table 8.6).

Table 8.6 Self-Regulated Strategy Development Instructional Stages: Using the TREE Strategy to Teach Essay Writing

---

Stage 1—Develop Background Knowledge

Find out what students already know about essays and build on it.

Look at samples of well-written essays.

Identify the effective features of these well-written essays.

Look for these features in essays they are reading in class and in essays of classmates.

Using a variety of topics, brainstorm ideas for essay parts.

Stage 2—Discuss It

Have an individual conference with each student to discuss their essays and identify any strategies or self-statements currently being used.

Introduce the idea of a strategy for writing essays along with the self-monitoring components of self-assessment and self-recording.

Discuss the benefits of using the strategy.

Determine each student's current performance.

Set goals.

Describe the TREE strategy (note **T**opic sentence, note **R**easons, **E**xamine reasons, note **E**nding) in an interactive session with students.

Provide strategy charts and lists of self-statements.

Stage 3—Model It

Model the TREE strategy while thinking out loud.

Elicit student help during modeling.

Use self-statements throughout the modeling (e.g., "What do I need to do next?" "Yes, that is a good reason. I'll write that.").

Stage 4—Memorize It

Have students memorize the strategy and practice using self-statements.

Stage 5—Support It

Collaborate with the students in supporting their use of the strategy and the self-regulation procedures.

Revisit the rationale for using the strategy and the self-statements, as needed.

Model the correction of errors in the use of the strategy and include a self-statement (e.g., "I'm going to change this supporting reason. I need to remember to follow all of the steps of the strategy so that I will write a good essay.").

Adjust the level of support as students become more proficient, gradually fading prompts or reminders.

Use goal setting and self-assessment (e.g., Have students assess their work to see if they have met their goals. Have them provide feedback to one another.)

Stage 6—Independent Performance

Have students plan and write essays independently.

Provide positive and constructive feedback.

Encourage students to work without their strategy charts and self-statement lists.

Promote generalization of the strategy and self-regulatory procedures.

NOTE. Information taken from *Every Child Can Write: Strategies for Composition and Self-Regulation in the Writing Process* by K. Harris, T. Schmidt, & S. Graham (1997). In *Teaching Every Child Every Day: Learning in Diverse Schools and Classrooms* by S. Graham & K. Harris (Eds.). Cambridge, MA: Brookline Books.

Strategies

Harris and Graham (1996) have developed writing strategies in a variety of areas that include but are not limited to planning, brainstorming, story writing, essay writing, and report writing. We provide examples of some of their strategies for assisting students with planning and writing. Notice how the same six stages of instruction are used in teaching each of these strategies.

Three-Step Planning Strategy for Story Writing.

The teacher introduces a planning and writing strategy to students by explaining that these three steps will help them write better stories and essays. Students are asked to think about who will read the story or essay and why they are writing it. Then the students are instructed to use the SPACE mnemonic, which will help them plan what to say in their story or essay. As they write, they may think of more things to say and should be encouraged to do so.

1. Think.
   Who will read this? Why am I writing this?
2. Plan what to say.
   Use SPACE (Setting, Purpose, Action, Conclusion, Emotions)
3. Write and say more.

Three-Step Writing Strategy.

This strategy is similar to the planning and writing strategy. However, this time the mnemonic, TREE, is used to help students make note of their **T**opic sentence (e.g., "My topic sentence is that it is better to be the oldest child in the family instead of the youngest."); note **R**easons (e.g., "One of my reasons is that you get privileges that your younger brothers and sisters do not get. Now, I need to think of others."); **E**xamine reasons (e.g., "Hm, I think I'll cross out the one about getting to boss the others around—that's a little weak."); and note **E**nding (e.g., "Now I need to write a good ending.").

1. Think, who will read this, and why am I writing it?
2. Plan what to say using TREE (note Topic sentence, note Reasons, Examine reasons, note Ending).
3. Write and say more.

W-W-W or Story Grammar Strategy.

This strategy teaches students how to write stories by focusing on seven questions that prompt the story parts. Significant improvements were noted in the quality and length of students' stories after they learned and practiced this strategy.

1. Think of a story you would like to share.
2. Let your mind be free.
3. Write down the story part reminder (W-W-W)

   Who is the main character?

   When does the story take place?

   Where does the story take place?

   What = 2

   What does the main character do or want to do, and what do the other characters do?

   What happens when the main character does or tries to do it, and what happens with other characters?

   How = 2

   How does the story end?

   How does the main character feel, and how do other characters feel?

4. Make notes of your ideas for each part.
5. Write your story—use good parts, add, elaborate, revise as you write or afterwards, and make sense.

STOP and LIST Writing Strategy.

The strategy of STOP (Stop Think of Purpose) and LIST (List Ideas and Sequence Them) assists students to set goals, brainstorm, and sequence when writing or performing other tasks. It can be used for completing writing assignments, planning a report, or preparing for other activities (e.g., deciding what supplies or resources will be needed for a project and in what order you will proceed, completing homework assignments).

Evaluation Procedures

Harris, Schmidt, and Graham (1997) suggest several basic principles for assessing SRSD methods and procedures:

♦ *Involve students as co-evaluators.* Co-evaluation increases the sense of ownership and enriches the evaluation process. Students may use self-assessment, peer evaluation, and other reflective techniques.
♦ *Consider the level of evaluation needed.* Harris, Schmidt, and Graham (1997) recommend that teachers find out if students are using the strategy, whether it is having a positive effect on performance, and if students think the strategy is valuable and manageable.
♦ *Assess changes in performance, attitudes, and cognition.* It is important to determine changes in the quality and quantity of students' writing and any changes in attitude (e.g., enthusiasm for writing, confidence in writing abilities) and cognitive processes (e.g., spontaneous statements about writing).
♦ *Assess how students actually use the strategy.* It is helpful to observe students directly as they write and also to look for evidence of strategy use by examining students' written work.
♦ *Assess students' use of the strategy over time and in new situations.* In order to be sure that students are continuing to use a strategy and use it appropriately, it is beneficial to find out how students are using and/or modifying strategies. In other words, conduct spot checks by asking the student to share information about using the strategy, asking a general education teacher if the student is using the strategy in that class, or looking at samples of the student's written work.
♦ *Collaborate with colleagues during the evaluation process.* It is important to collaborate with other teachers in promoting generalization and in monitoring strategy use in other classroom settings. This teamwork should result in more effective use of strategies by students and more consistent application and generalization of strategies.
♦ *Use portfolio assessment procedures.* We discussed portfolio assessment in Chapter 3. As it relates to SRSD, portfolio assessment is an excellent way to encourage students to engage in reflection and self-assessment of their writing and self-regulation strategies and to ensure that they are taking more responsibility for their own learning.

 ACTIVITY 8.7

You are an elementary level special education teacher working in a fifth-grade classroom. You have asked the students to write a theme about someone they would consider their hero. They will be reading their themes to the fourth graders. The students are having difficulty developing a quality product, one that has the essential elements of a well-structured theme and that is of sufficient length. How can you help them?

 IMPORTANT POINTS

1. The Strategic Instruction Model is a model that includes a strategic curriculum component, a strategic instruction component, and a strategic environment component.
2. The strategic curriculum component addresses what to teach, the strategic instruction component includes how to teach, and the strategic environment component incorporates how the environment is arranged to enhance performance.

3. The Strategic Instruction Model focuses on teaching strategies directly to students and having the students apply the strategies to general classroom materials and generalize their use.

4. The Self-Regulated Strategy Development Model is an integrated, instructional approach that assists students in developing composition skills and self-regulation abilities (e.g., goal setting, self-instruction, self-monitoring, self-assessment, and self-reinforcement).

5. The Self-Regulated Strategy Development Model directly addresses students' affective, behavioral, and cognitive characteristics, needs, and strengths.

6. The characteristics of SRSD emphasize collaborative learning, individualization, criterion-based instruction, anticipating and planning for problem areas, enthusiastic, supportive teachers, and attention to developmental levels of students.

◆ DISCUSSION QUESTIONS

1. Differentiate between the reductionist and constructivist elements of cognitive strategy instruction.

2. One of the three components of the Strategic Instruction Model is a strategic environment. Describe how you will create a strategic environment in your classroom.

3. Explain the benefits for students when you "think aloud" during instruction.

9

STUDY SKILLS
INSTRUCTION

School settings present many challenges for students with special needs, particularly in view of the increased inclusion of students with mild disabilities in general education settings. Students are expected to arrive at school on time with their materials, prepared to listen, participate, and respond. During a typical school day, students in K–12 settings may be asked to acquire new content; demonstrate understanding and mastery of the content through completion of tests, projects, or other assignments; demonstrate good work habits; and perhaps work with several school professionals who may have different expectations and requirements and whose teaching styles may vary. Students with special needs may have problems meeting these expectations because of poor organizational and information-processing skills as well as other difficulties. It has been suggested that integrated study skills programs be provided throughout students' schooling and as lifelong skills (Hoover & Patton, 1995) to help students meet these expectations. The purpose of this chapter is to present study skills and strategies that will assist students with special needs to acquire information, organize it, and express it.

RATIONALE FOR STUDY SKILLS INSTRUCTION

Study skills are those competencies associated with acquiring, recording, organizing, synthesizing, remembering, and using information and ideas (Devine, 1993). They typically include listening, note taking, outlining, textbook usage, test taking, reference skills, and others that are needed for success in academic (e.g., science class) and nonacademic (e.g., the workplace) settings (Platt & Olson, 1997). Utilization of study skills may lead students with special needs to exhibit more active learning styles and to demonstrate proactive approaches to academic tasks. Incorporation of study skills instruction into the curriculum may help students attribute their learning successes to the systematic selection and application of strategies instead of to luck or the assistance of others. Study skills represent the key to independent learning by helping students acquire and use information effectively (Bos & Vaughn, 1997).

Since evidence suggests the need for study skills in elementary and secondary settings for students with special needs (Hoover, 1997), we recommend the introduction of study skills instruction at the elementary level followed by continuous instruction throughout middle and high school. Systematic instruction in study skills can show students the relationship between their approach to a learning task and the result of that approach (e.g., using a mnemonic device to memorize a list of words may facilitate memorization of that list better than simply repeating the words in the list). The application of study skills and strategies may, therefore, increase the independent functioning of learners.

COMPONENTS OF STUDY SKILLS INSTRUCTION

In order for study skills training to be effective, teachers must be aware of the components that contribute to its success. The following five criteria derived from Paris (1988) should be included in study skills training. These are similar to the critical features of strategy instruction that we presented in Chapter 8.

1. *Study skills should be functional and meaningful.* Identify your students' needs and determine the study skills that would be most effective in meeting those needs. For example, if Jesse is required to memorize lists of terms for his fourth-grade health class, you may want to teach him a mnemonic strategy to help him memorize material and prepare for tests. Suppose Jesse has to memorize the parts of the digestive system. He may make a list with all the parts and then look at the first letter of each of the words. Perhaps they spell a word, or maybe he can make a sentence out of them.

2. *Students should believe that study skills are useful and necessary.* Your students must be convinced that study skills are important, necessary for success, worth using, and effective in solving problems; therefore, it is helpful to demonstrate to your students that their current methods are not effective and to explain the rationale for each specific strategy (Alley & Deshler, 1979). For example, Mr. Waldo asked his students to take notes on one of his math lessons. When he evaluated their notes with them, he pointed out the shortcomings and ineffective practices. He elicited from the students the rationale for taking effective notes and had them suggest situations in which they might need to use this skill. One student mentioned she could use it in her social studies class, while another said that it would help him as a reporter for the school newspaper. Then Mr. Waldo presented some effective note-taking techniques to the class. By first demonstrating how note-taking techniques are useful and necessary, he was able to motivate and interest the students in note taking.

3. *Instruction should be direct, informed, and explanatory.* According to Rosenshine (1983), instruction should include (a) presenting material in small steps, (b) focusing on one aspect at a time, (c) organizing the material sequentially for mastery, (d) modeling the

skill, (e) presenting many examples, (f) providing detailed explanations for difficult points, and (g) monitoring student progress. For example, in their instruction of report writing, Ms. Tartaglia and Ms. Dearden took their co-taught fifth-grade class to the media center and modeled the steps that they wanted the students to follow as they used reference materials. They provided several different topics and modeled the steps sequentially for each one. They spent time teaching the students how to use the automated card catalog or similar computer system before they assigned them topics to look up. Then, as the students worked through the steps they had modeled, the two teachers carefully monitored their progress.

4. *Instruction should demonstrate what study skills can be used, how they can be applied, and when and why they are helpful.* For example, Mr. Johansen, working with his high school students on test taking, taught the students study skills to apply when taking tests. Next, he elicited from the students when and why the study skills would be helpful (content classes, job seeking, and taking the driver's test or the test for the military). Finally, he showed the students how to apply the study skills to each of the situations they had identified.

5. *Instructional materials must be lucid and enjoyable.* The materials you use as part of study skills instruction must be motivating, meaningful, relevant, and easy to understand. For example, working with a group of fifth graders in a general education classroom, Ms. Barnhart incorporated information about the students into a lesson that showed them how to use the graphic aids in textbooks. She taught her fifth-grade students to read graphs by graphing the students' birthdays, favorite movies and television shows, and their interests and hobbies. These activities were instrumental in holding student interest and attention.

Because we believe the preceding components of effective study skills instruction should be included in the teaching of all of the study skills presented in this chapter, we do not mention them each time a new study skill is introduced. However, we urge you to incorporate them into your instruction.

ACQUISITION OF INFORMATION

As mentioned in Chapter 1, students with special needs often have difficulty with reading, mathematics, oral and written language, attending, and organizing. Therefore, they must be taught techniques to help them acquire the skills and content expected of them. In this section, we present strategies for listening, taking notes, and comprehending.

Listening

Students spend more than half of their time in school listening (Mandlebaum & Wilson, 1989). In fact, listening skills are needed to complete most academic tasks or requirements (Hoover & Patton, 1995). Students with special needs should be made aware of the fact that listening is more than hearing words, and it may require practice and training (Carlisle & Felbinger, 1991; Masters & Mori, 1993). Devine (1987) suggests that listening can be improved through systematic teaching and practice. The following strategies are provided for students who have difficulty listening effectively, have developed poor listening habits, do not attend to relevant stimuli, or are inattentive.

Prelistening Strategies
In adaptations of the work of Alley and Deshler (1979), Barker (1971), Nichols and Stevens (1957), and Taylor (1964), Suritsky and Hughes (1996) present the following prelistening strategies. They include mental preparation, physical preparation, and vocabulary preparation.

Mental Preparation. Before your students attend a class lecture or presentation, they should prepare for listening by practicing the three R's of listening preparation—review, read, and relate—using procedural facilitators or cues. They can do this by reviewing previous notes, reading about the topic that is going to be covered, and relating the topic to what they already know and to what they have learned in class. You may model this for them by thinking aloud what you want your students to say and do. For example, you may say, "Let's see, I need to look back at Monday's notes. Oh, I remember. We were talking about clouds, and today we are going to talk about two types: cumulus and cirrus. I know how clouds are formed, because I put hot water in a jar and held ice over the jar. I watched a cloud form in the jar. O.K., I'm ready to learn more about clouds. I'm ready for today's class."

Physical Preparation. Your students should select seats that will increase their opportunities for attending to and concentrating on what is presented. They should come to class with the necessary materials, such as textbook, notebook, pens, pencils, tape recorder, and/or highlighter.

Vocabulary Preparation. If the class topic is known in advance, students may be able to ask for a list of the vocabulary that will be included, or teachers may have the words written on the board. Teachers of students with special needs sometimes tape-record words and their definitions or prepare glossaries for students to use in the mainstream. Students may be taught to prepare their own note cards with the word, a brief definition, and a picture that relates to the word.

Listening Strategies

Alley and Deshler (1979) suggest the following strategies to improve listening skills. They include organizing cues, verbal and nonverbal cues, main and supporting details, and questioning.

Organizing Cues. Students may attend to cues that indicate how the teacher is organizing con-

tent or information. Some teachers use verbal cues to emphasize the most important points of a presentation. Teach your students to listen for statements like, "The main reasons Cuban Americans immigrated to the United States are . . ." or "The most important thing to remember about crop rotation is . . ." Also, teach students to look for written cues to spoken content. Some teachers identify the main points of their presentation by writing them on the chalkboard or an overhead projector. Students may take this as a cue to copy the information.

Verbal and Nonverbal Cues. Show students how to identify important points by attending to speaking pace, volume, pauses, and stress on words and phrases. Also, alert students to the nonverbal behaviors that teachers use to make important points while speaking. These include eye contact, hand signals, facial expressions, and posture. You may model these verbal and nonverbal cues by videotaping class lectures and then pointing out cues as they occur. For example, Ms. Jackson videotaped herself teaching a history class. She played the videotape for her students and pointed out the fact that each time she mentioned a new term, she wrote it on the board and underlined it. She also alerted her students to other cues, such as holding her hand up, increasing her volume, and slowing her speaking rate each time she emphasized an important point.

Main and Supporting Ideas. Specific activities may help students distinguish main ideas from supporting material during a lecture or presentation. For example, Mr. Wong presented the following three statements and asked the students to identify which was the main idea and which were supporting statements:

- The air is becoming polluted.
- The environment is undergoing significant changes.
- Our water supply is insufficient in some areas.

Then Mr. Wong showed his students how the first and last sentences were actually examples, or supporting details, of the second sentence.

Another activity involves having the students listen to a class presentation and then identify the main ideas. At first, give your students a worksheet from which to choose the main ideas. After they select the main ideas, the students should explain why the other choices are not main ideas. Such activities prepare students to separate essential information from extraneous, irrelevant materials—a skill that is essential to listening comprehension.

Questioning.   One way to determine whether your students have listened effectively is to have them ask questions about what they have heard. For example, after a presentation about dolphins to a third-grade class, the teacher was convinced that her students had listened when they asked these questions: Where did the word dolphin come from? What is the difference between a dolphin and a porpoise? Is the dolphin a fish or a mammal? What do dolphins eat? How do dolphins breathe?

Additional listening activities for students with special needs at both the elementary and secondary level are:

1. Alert your students before they listen to a class presentation that there will be at least one factual error in the presentation. Ask the students to write down the error(s) after the information has been presented (Wallace & Kauffman, 1986). For example, during a presentation on the size, population, major cities, and important industries of New Jersey, Mr. Feldman erroneously identified the capital as Newark. We recommend telling the students what the error is if they cannot identify it themselves.
2. Prior to a lecture or presentation, list the five most important points of the talk on the chalkboard, an overhead projector, or a handout. Then ask your students to listen for those five points and arrange them in the correct sequence before the conclusion of the presentation (Devine, 1981).
3. Show a videotape containing subject matter that is interesting and age appropriate. Ask the students to listen for specific information, such as the speaker's intent, definitions of certain words and how context affects them, factual information, or the general theme. You may stop the videotape at any time to ask questions about the content or ask for predictions of what will happen next. For example, Mr. Johnson showed a series of videotapes to his students about the lives of four African-Americans who made great contributions to our country: (a) Paul Lawrence Dunbar, (b) Booker T. Washington, (c) Dr. Martin Luther King, Jr., and (d) Dr. George Washington Carver. He periodically stopped the videotape to ask questions and to give his students a specific fact to listen for.
4. Ask your students to listen to television or radio advertisements and explain how the advertisers are trying to influence listeners to buy their products. For example, some advertisers ask celebrities to advertise and endorse their products, others use catchy tunes, and some tell about the money you will save. This listening activity may be done in the classroom or as a homework assignment (Lerner, 1985).

Students need to learn how to listen effectively and practice the skill of listening just as they practice other skills. It is never too late to learn how to listen.

 ACTIVITY 9.1

During your next class lecture, note all of the verbal and nonverbal cues that the instructor utilizes. Compare these to what other class members identify.

(Answers for this and other activities are found in the Instructor's Manual.)

Note Taking

The move toward inclusion of students with learning problems in general education classrooms where they must meet the demands of that environment, combined with the fact that college is a viable option for many students with learning disabilities, has increased the need for learning how to take notes during class presentations (Czarnecki, Rosko, & Fine, 1998; Deshler, Ellis, & Lenz, 1996). In general education high school settings, teachers spend at least half of their class time presenting information through lectures (Putnam, Deshler, & Schumaker, 1993). Although many students without disabilities develop note-taking skills on their own (Beirne-Smith, 1989), many students with learning disabilities may not develop note-taking skills (Suritsky & Hughes, 1993) or may evidence deficient note-taking skills (Carlson & Alley, 1981; Suritsky & Hughes, 1993; Saski, Swicegood, & Carter, 1983). Note taking is difficult and tedious for many students with learning and behavior problems. Therefore, many of them do not take notes in class. You may need to convince your students of the importance of taking notes. One effective way is to make them aware of what they currently do during a lecture or class presentation. For example, Ms. Malone presented information on the recycling of products as a way to protect the environment. She asked her students to take notes during her presentation, using the activity as a pretest to show the students that improvement might be needed. After instruction in note-taking techniques, she used the activity as a posttest to show the students their improvement in note taking.

Pauk (1989) found that non–note takers forget 80% of a lecture within 2 weeks. Therefore, it is important for you to teach note taking directly and to reinforce its use. Many strategies are available to improve note taking, although "no evidence indicates that any one technique is consistently superior to another" (Devine, 1981, p. 173). You may want to show your students a variety of ways to take notes so that they can find the ways that are effective for them.

Guided Notes

In Chapter 6, we introduced the topic of guided notes as an effective adaptation to ensure that students with disabilities are engaged throughout a lecture. For students who have difficulty taking notes, it is helpful to begin with guided notes, since students do not have to generate all of the notes themselves. Guided notes are the skeleton outlines that contain the main ideas and related concepts of a lecture, including designated spaces for students to complete as the lecture/presentation occurs (Lazarus, 1991, 1998). Guided notes assist students who have mild disabilities to participate actively in note taking, to follow along with the sequence of the lecture/presentation, and to write useful notes for later review (Lazarus, 1991). First, the teacher provides the students with a structured outline of a class presentation (Shields & Heron, 1989). As the teacher presents the information, the students follow the outline and fill in missing words, underline key words, and mark the important points. The advantages of guided notes include their applicability across subject areas and settings, their emphasis on the major points of a topic, their assistance with retention of information, and the opportunities for student involvement (Kline, 1986).

Shields and Heron (1989) recommend including three components in a set of guided notes, as illustrated by this example of a presentation on ecosystems:

1. *Key terms:* ecology, ecosystem, atmosphere, hydrosphere, geosphere, biosphere, ecosphere, energy, matter, and organisms.
2. *Two brief paragraphs that provide definitions of the terms and explain the key concepts.* For example, the goal of *ecology* is to discover how air, water, soil, and organisms work and how they sustain themselves.

3. *Several questions that the student must answer after reading the notes.* What is an ecosystem and what are its most important living and nonliving components? What roles do different organisms play in an ecosystem, and how do they interact?

Figure 9.1 contains an example of another approach to using guided notes. This example illustrates what a teacher might give to students at the beginning of a lecture/presentation. Notice that the student's copy of the guided notes contains main ideas and key concepts and fol-

lows a specific sequence. It contains a minimal amount of information, giving students maximal opportunities and flexibility to respond (Lazarus, 1996). Note how Lazarus (1996) includes cues (e.g., blanks, labels, etc.) along with a review tally so that students can self-record how many times they review their own notes. Figure 9.2 contains an example of the teacher's completed notes on transparencies, which may be shown to students before the lecture/presentation to introduce and provide an overview of a lesson/unit and communicate the expectation that students will complete their own

Figure 9.1 Student's Copy of Guided Notes with Cues and Review Tally

Review Tally

Chapter 20

Cell Reproduction

I. All life starts out as a _____ ____.

  A.   ----------------------

  B.

II. _____ _____ are formed by _____ _____.

III. Types of cell division.

  A. Mitosis—DEFINITION:

    1. Mitosis is used for replacement of:

      a.

      b.

      c.

      d.

      e.

    2.

    3.

NOTE. From "Flexible Skeletons, Guided Notes for Adolescents with Mild Disabilities" by B. D. Lazarus, *Teaching Exceptional Children,* 28(3), 1996, 38. Copyright (1996) by The Council for Exceptional Children. Reprinted with permission.

Figure 9.2 Teacher's
Transparencies with Completed
Guided Notes that Correspond
with the Students' Copies

Chapter 20

Cell Reproduction

I. All life starts out as a <u>single</u> <u>cell.</u>

   A. single cells ------------------------- millions of cells

   B. Humans have millions of cells.

II. <u>New</u> <u>cells</u> are formed by <u>cell</u> <u>division.</u>

III. Types of cell division.

   A. Mitosis—DEFINITION: process of cell division in which two cells are
                  formed from one cell.

      1. Mitosis is used for replacement of:

         a. red blood cells

         b. skin cells

         c. muscle cells

         d. root tips

         e. leaf cells

      2. Before cells divide, the cell parts are copied so the result is two
         identical cells.

      3. Mitosis is a series of steps.

NOTE. From "Flexible Skeletons, Guided Notes for Adolescents With Mild Disabilities" by B. D. Lazarus, *Teaching Exceptional Children,* 28(3), 1996, 38. Copyright (1996) by The Council for Exceptional Children. Reprinted with permission.

notes. The completed notes may be shown to students during and after a lecture/presentation so that students may monitor the accuracy of their own work and so that teachers can provide immediate feedback regarding students' notes. After the lecture/presentation, the completed notes may be used to review the material together as a class or in small groups.

The Five-Step Method for Taking Lecture Notes

The five-step method for taking lecture notes (Bragstad & Stumpf, 1987) includes the following:

1. *Surveying.* Many teachers give an advance organizer or preview of what they are going to cover. Students can take notes on these points, thereby alerting themselves to what to expect during the lecture.

2. *Questioning.* Encourage your students to have a questioning attitude to help them focus on what is happening in the presentation. They may ask themselves, What is the main idea of this presentation? What am I supposed to know when the speaker is finished? What is being said about the topic? Effective ways to teach students to have a questioning attitude during a lecture presentation include (a) modeling question asking for them and (b) setting up role plays so that they can practice with each other.

3. *Listening.* Encourage students to employ listening strategies to help them listen carefully

for content, cues, organization, main points, and supporting statements.

4. *Organizing.* Have your students determine how you are organizing the information being presented. Perhaps you use the chalkboard, an overhead projector, or handouts to organize content. If you do not provide these clues, your students may listen for verbal cues to organization, such as, "The most important point to remember is . . . " or "Note this . . ." You may also repeat important points or say them slowly with emphasis and then a pause.

5. *Reviewing and revising.* As soon after the lecture or presentation as possible, your students should review their notes. In this way, they can add, change, or delete material while the information is still fresh in their minds. Encourage your students to conduct frequent cumulative reviews of their notes. By going back over that day's notes along with all previous notes after each class session, your students will be committing the material to memory.

Two- and Three-Column Methods of Note Taking

Two- and three-column methods of note taking provide opportunities for students to interact with content. The two-column method (Aaronson, 1975; Bragstad & Stumpf, 1987) may be varied and modified for individual purposes. With this system, students divide their papers into two sections by drawing a line from top to bottom, thus forming two columns. The wider column is used to record the teacher's ideas as presented in class. The narrower column is used after the lecture to write questions or to summarize the major points and ideas. For example, Ms. Tuttle asked one of her students to read the following information about bats while she took notes using the two-column method.

Today we are going to talk about bats. Bats are classified as mammals—a group of vertebrates that include people, dogs, and mice. Like all mammals, bats nurse their young on milk. Like

most mammals, they bear living young and have hair on their bodies. However, in one way, bats are different from all other mammals, because bats can fly! Bats fly through the air with wings. . . .

Ms. Tuttle shared with the class what she wrote in each column. First, she filled out the "Teacher's comments" column by writing down information from the presentation in the form of key words. Next, she filled out the "Student's summary statements and questions" column with words, phrases, and sentences that clarified what she had written under "Teacher's comments." It is helpful if teachers give students class time to fill in their summary statements and questions (see Figure 9.3), so that students can remember how the information in the two columns is related. They can also use this time to connect the information in their textbook to the notes in class by jotting down additional material from the text.

Some students prefer to have a third, narrow column to define key terms or to paraphrase material from the class presentation. Students in Ms. Tuttle's class preferred a third column to write the definition of terms (e.g., mammals— any of the group of vertebrate animals, including humans, that nourish their young with milk) and to paraphrase information (e.g., Bats are like other mammals except that bats can fly).

Additional Note-Taking Tips

In teaching note taking to students, you should model effective note taking. Bragstad and Stumpf (1987) suggest playing a tape of a lecture and, while the class is watching, taking notes on an overhead projector so that the students see what you write. At the conclusion of the demonstration, you and your students can discuss the note-taking techniques that you utilized.

You should provide your students with ample practice in note taking before asking them to take notes in general education classes. Devine (1981) recommends using how-to-do-it presentations, such as how to change a tire,

Student's Summary Statements and Questions	Teacher's Comments
	Bats
–All of these animals are classified as mammals	–Mammals
	• Bats
	• People
	• Dogs
	• Mice
–How are bats like all other mammals?	–Nurse young
	–Bear living young
	–Have hair on bodies
–How are bats different than other mammals?	–Fly

Figure 9.3   Two-Column Method of Note Taking

how to look up a word in the dictionary, or how to make a peanut butter sandwich. Have your students take notes as you present one of these topics.

Bragstad and Stumpf (1987) suggest giving students a set of notes that contain errors. Then have the students work in groups to correct the errors and to improve the notes. Remember to provide positive and corrective feedback to students, so that they will know what they did well and will be aware of exactly where the errors were.

To reinforce the importance of taking notes, Devine (1981) recommends having a note-taking contest in which main ideas and supporting details are each worth a specified number of points. Then have the students calculate the scores of the different sets of notes. You may also specify other aspects to look for in a set of notes, such as underlining of key points or defining of technical vocabulary in the margins, and then ask the students to judge which notes contain all of the important elements.

Czarnecki, Rosko, and Fine (1998) developed two note-taking strategies for middle and high school students with special needs. The first, CALL UP, was designed for students to use while they are taking notes in class. The second, "A" NOTES, was created for students to use when reviewing notes after a lecture/presentation. They developed these strategies so that students with special needs participating in inclusive settings would be able to take notes in their general education classes. After instruction, both teachers and students reported greater competency in taking notes (Czarnecki et al., 1998).

CALL UP

Copy from board or transparency.

Add details.

Listen and write the question.

Listen and write the answer.

Utilize the text.

Put it in your own words.

A NOTES

Ask yourself if you have a date and a topic.

Name the main ideas and details.

Observe ideas also in text.

Try margin notes and use SAND strategy.

Star important ideas.

Arrange arrows to connect ideas.

Number key points in order.

Devise abbreviations.

Examine for omissions or unclear ideas.

Summarize key points.

Platt and Olson (1997) recommend that whatever methods are used for note taking, the following general tips may help your students organize, understand, and retain information for later recall.

1. Before going to class, review notes from the previous class, review vocabulary, read assigned pages, and think about the topic that will be covered.
2. Use a looseleaf notebook so that you can keep notes, handouts, and tests in order and together. You can take out materials, add materials, and move them around as needed.
3. Divide your notebook into different sections for each class, or use a different notebook for each class.
4. Bring materials to class each day (pens, pencils, highlighters, calculator, etc.).
5. Sit in front where you can see and hear, away from distractions, and pay close attention.
6. Write the name of your class and the date at the top of the paper and number each page.
7. Write on only one side of the paper.
8. Write quickly but clearly and legibly. Do not write everything the teacher says—just key words and phrases.
9. Write a main idea. Then indent details under the main idea in outline form. Add an example of your own or one of the teacher's. Skip a line or two before moving to another idea.
10. Leave a blank column on your paper to record your own questions and ideas. Take advantage of pauses in the presentation to make your own notes.
11. Put a question mark by items that you do not understand or that you need more information about, and ask the teacher for clarification.
12. Put a blank where you missed a word and check on it later.
13. Use a marking system to distinguish main ideas from details and examples, perhaps by drawing a box around main ideas and underlining, highlighting, or color coding certain items.
14. Use abbreviations:

    e.g. = example
    def = definition
    info = information
    # = number
    etc. = and so forth
    impt. = important
    ref. = reference
    p = page
    vs = versus
    > = greater than
    < = less than
    i.e. = that is
    s = summary
    & = and

15. Listen and look for verbal and nonverbal cues.
    - Points that are repeated
    - Key points ("The most important point to remember is . . .")
    - Words and definitions
    - A change in the speaker's volume, rate, and posture
    - Gestures used to emphasize points
    - Information that is written on the board or overhead
    - Lists ("The five types of . . .")

- ◆ Use of absolute words (all, always, never, none, best)
- ◆ Words and phrases that signal or alert you to something:
  - ◆ "In conclusion"
  - ◆ "In summary"
  - ◆ "Finally," "For example"
  - ◆ "In comparison"
  - ◆ "Prior to"
  - ◆ "The opposite of"
  - ◆ "Remember"

16. After class, fill in any missed information, and ask the teacher to clarify anything you did not understand.

17. Make sure your notes are organized chronologically along with supporting handouts.

18. As soon as possible after class, examine your notes and check to see how they support, supplement, and/or explain the information in your textbook.

19. Review your notes before the next class. Cumulative review assists with understanding, retention, and test preparation.

20. Compare your notes to those of a peer and check for accuracy and consistency, consulting your textbook if necessary.

◇ IMPORTANT POINTS

1. Study skills are those competencies associated with acquiring, recording, organizing, synthesizing, remembering, and using information and ideas (Devine, 1987).

2. The components of effective study skills instruction include: (a) study skills should be functional and meaningful; (b) students should believe that study skills are useful and necessary; (c) instruction should be direct, informed, and explanatory; (d) instruction should demonstrate what study skills can be used, how they can be applied, and when and why they are helpful; and (e) instructional materials must be lucid and enjoyable.

3. To listen effectively, students should physically and mentally prepare to listen; identify organizational, verbal, and nonverbal cues; learn how to identify main and supporting details; and practice self-questioning.

4. Strategies for giving students purposes for listening are (a) alerting them to listen for factual errors in a presentation, (b) listing the five most important points of a lesson and directing the students to listen for those points, (c) asking students to listen for certain information as they view a videotape, (d) having students listen to advertisements to determine how listeners are being influenced to buy products, and (e) using a pause procedure to assist students with recall of information.

5. Guided notes are the skeleton outlines that contain the main ideas and related concepts of a lecture, including designated spaces for students to complete as the lecture/presentation occurs (Lazarus, 1991, 1998).

6. Guided notes consist of a teacher-prepared, structured, sequenced outline of a class presentation. Students follow along, fill in missing words, underline or write key words, and mark important points.

7. A five-step method of taking notes includes (1) surveying, (2) questioning, (3) listening, (4) organizing, and (5) reviewing and revising.

8. The two- and three-column methods of note taking provide students with opportunities to interact with content.

9. Additional note-taking tips include following an outline, using abbreviations, listening and looking for verbal and nonverbal cues, using a marking system, organizing notes chronologically, and leaving blanks where you missed something.

Comprehension

In order to succeed in content classes, students with special needs are expected to acquire information from textbooks and from material presented orally in lectures, class discussions, demonstrations, and student presentations (Herr, 1988). Because your students may lack a systematic approach to comprehending content material, you must provide specific strategies to help them structure their efforts. In this section we present study skills and strategies that will improve comprehension; they include the use of advance organizers, mapping, concept teaching, and textbook usage.

Advance Organizers

An advance organizer is material that is presented "in advance of, and at a higher level of generality, inclusiveness, and abstraction than, the learning task itself" (Ausubel & Robinson, 1969, p. 606). Advance organizers may be verbal or written (Gleason, 1988) and set the stage for and contribute to comprehension. They are activities that the teacher uses before teaching a task or skill that give organizational structure to that task/skill (Lenz, 1983).

An advance organizer may consist of an activity for obtaining student attention, a statement of the lesson objectives, a confirmation of the teacher's expectations, or a presentation of a graphic organizer (Putnam & Wesson, 1990). Mr. Row used a written advance organizer in the form of a handout to introduce a lesson on the parts of a story. The first part of the handout contained the lesson objectives, and the second part listed the parts of a story and then identified them in an actual story. While co-teaching with a general education teacher, Mr. Dunn used a verbal advance organizer to introduce a lesson on rocks. He began by showing the students a display of different kinds of rock formations and then said, "Today we are going to learn about the three types of rocks: igneous, sedimentary, and metamorphic." In both of these classrooms, the teachers used advance organizers to provide clues to important information that they wanted their students to acquire.

Mapping

Mapping is making a word picture of ideas. It involves structuring information on a topic into categories using a graphic or web (Bulgren & Lenz, 1996). Maps may have boxes, arrows, lines, or other figures; they are visual representations that show relationships among conceptual ideas. Mapping is an excellent method for acquiring information from printed materials. It enhances comprehension, allows students to think about the relationships among concepts and ideas, and facilitates the condensing of material to be studied.

A type of mapping technique that promotes comprehension of reading content involves the use of a character web. A character web is a type of map that allows students to study characters, their traits, and examples of those traits. Figure 9.4 contains a character web that the teacher and class co-constructed about Big Anthony, a character in *Strega Nona* by Tomie dePaola. This is a delightful folktale about an elderly woman with special, magical powers and the young man who takes care of her and helps her with her house. When Strega Nona leaves him alone with her magic pasta pot, Big Anthony is determined to show the townspeople how it works. The story goes on to describe what happens when Big Anthony tries to show off for the town instead of doing what Strega Nona asked him to do. Note how the use of this web with second graders enhances their understanding of the story and opens up opportunities for lessons in character and career education. After initial instruction in how to develop a character web, students can construct them independently, with a peer, or in a cooperative group.

Concept Teaching

Concept teaching possesses many of the same characteristics as mapping. The Concept Mastery Routine, which utilizes concept diagrams (Bulgren, Schumaker, & Deshler, 1988), is effective for helping students acquire information.

Figure 9.4   Character Web

CHARACTER	TRAITS	EXAMPLES
Big Anthony	Likeable	He means well and tries hard to do the right thing.
	Lazy	He wanted the magic pasta pot to do his work for him.
	Show-off	He bragged that he could make the magic pasta pot work.
	Poor Listener	He did not listen to Strega Nona about how to make the magic pasta pot work.

This teaching routine is particularly useful in facilitating the comprehension of content material (e.g., science, social studies, history). It requires the teacher to select and become familiar with textbook or unit content before initiating instruction with students.

The Concept Mastery Routine, developed at the University of Kansas Center for Research on Learning, consists of (a) a visual device called a Concept Diagram (see Figure 9.5), (b) a set of linking steps used to develop the Concept Diagram (see the seven steps listed below and represented by the acronym CONCEPT), and (c) instructional procedures that help the teacher cue the students to use the Concept Mastery Routine, interact with the students in completing the Concept Diagram, and review understanding of the concept. For a detailed description of this teaching routine, please contact the University of Kansas Center for Research on Learning in Lawrence, Kansas 66045. Bulgren, Schumaker, and Deshler (1988) successfully assisted general education teachers in using concept diagrams with students with learning disabilities and with other students by using the following procedures (CONCEPT):

1. *Convey the targeted concept.* Name a word or phrase that represents a category or idea. *Example:* cooperation.

2. *Offer the overall concept.* Explain the category into which the targeted concept can be grouped. *Example:* a way to do tasks.

3. *Note key words.* List words or phrases that are related to the concept. *Examples:* sports team, lab partners in science, rewards, two or more people, competition.

4. *Classify characteristics as always, sometimes, or never present.* For each word or phrase that is classified as a characteristic, decide whether it is always, sometimes, or never present. *Example:* two or more people—always-present characteristic of cooperation; study—sometimes-present characteristic of cooperation; only individual—never-present characteristic of cooperation.

5. *Explore examples and nonexamples.* Decide which words or phrases represent examples or nonexamples. *Examples:* lab partners in a science class—example of cooperation; a person playing golf—nonexample of cooperation.

6. *Practice with a new example.* Generate your own examples and nonexamples of the concept. These are words or phrases that were not on the original key word list. *Example:* construction team—example of cooperation; movie theater audience—nonexample of cooperation.

7. *Tie down a definition.* Use the always-present characteristics to form a definition. *Example:*

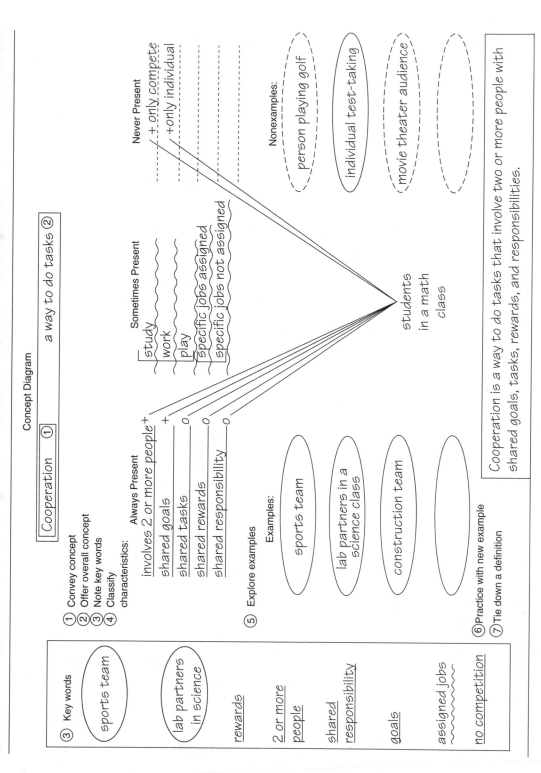

Figure 9.5 Concept Diagram

NOTE. The Concept Diagram is an instructional tool developed and researched at the University of Kansas Center for Research on Learning (Bulgren, Schumaker, & Deshler, 1988). It is a teaching device designed for teachers to use as they teach content information to classes containing diverse student populations. It is a data-based teaching instrument found effective when used with a planning routine, as well as a teaching routine that combines cues about the instruction, specialized delivery of the content, involvement of the students in the cognitive processes, and a review of the learning process and content material (Bulgren, Deshler, & Shumaker, 1993). Reprinted by permission.

Cooperation is a way to do tasks that involves two or more people with shared goals, tasks, rewards, and responsibilities.

The preceding information is plotted in Figure 9.5. The sixth step, practice with a new example, gives you and your students the opportunity to generate additional examples and nonexamples. For example, in Figure 9.5 you will note that + (yes) or 0 (no) is used to decide whether *students in a math class* is an example or a nonexample of *cooperation*. An example has all the always-present characteristics, none of the never-present characteristics, and possibly some of the sometimes-present characteristics. A nonexample lacks at least one of the always-present characteristics or has at least one of the never-present characteristics. *Students in a math class* is a nonexample, because it meets these criteria. Remember, the Concept Mastery Routine is intended to be dynamic, with a great deal of teacher and student interaction with the concept being studied. The Concept Diagram has not been shown to be an effective tool if it is simply distributed to students. Like mapping, concept teaching routines help students comprehend content material. Concept diagrams condense material into manageable chunks and facilitate the acquisition of information.

 ACTIVITY 9.2

Select one of the following concepts and develop a concept diagram: conservation, democracy, pollution.

Textbook Usage

Almost 44% of the information that students are responsible for learning is contained in textbooks but is not discussed in class (Zigmond, Levin, & Laurie, 1985). Students with special needs frequently encounter problems when try-

ing to read, use information, or locate it in textbooks. Many secondary students with disabilities experience difficulty reading (Schloss, Smith, & Schloss, 1995) and comprehending content area textbooks (Meese, 1994). Thus, strategies in textbook usage provide valuable assistance, particularly to students who are expected to use textbooks independently in general education classes. We present suggestions for previewing textbooks, surveying textbooks and textbook chapters, and using graphic aids.

Textbook Previewing. Davis and Clark (1981) indicate that by focusing on 10 specific aspects of a textbook, students concentrate on the fewest number of words that contain the greatest amount of information. After previewing these 10 components, your students will know a great deal about the textbook. Following are the 10 keys to textbook previewing (Davis & Clark, 1981):

1. Title
2. Introduction
3. Summary
4. Pictures and maps
5. Chapter questions
6. Subtopic titles
7. First paragraphs following subtopics
8. First sentences of paragraphs
9. Special print (italics)
10. Bold print

Textbook and Chapter Surveying. Prior to using a new textbook, a valuable activity for your students to perform is surveying that textbook. This allows the students to become familiar with the parts of a textbook: table of contents, preface, glossary, appendix, bibliography, and index. This activity may be performed in small groups or individually.

After a textbook is surveyed and students become familiar with its contents, an additional activity may be performed: surveying a chapter. This allows students to predict from the title what the chapter is about, to turn headings into questions, to identify study aids (e.g., bold print, italics, graphs, and charts), and to divide the chapter into manageable sections. Class discussions, co-operative learning activities, and class presentations may facilitate the sharing of information about the chapter before the students read and study it. Another way to survey a chapter is to use the chapter survey routine called TRIMS (Schumaker, Deshler, & McKnight, 1989):

Title

Relationship

Introduction

Main parts

Summary

An important part of TRIMS involves identifying the common relationship structures and signal words associated with these relationship structures (Bulgren & Lenz, 1996). These include listing, compare/contrast, cause/effect, and general/specific. These structures are organized on a worksheet that the teacher and students can use to complete a TRIMS of the chapter. For a thorough description of the procedures involved in using TRIMS, consult the work of Schumaker, Deshler, and McKnight (1989).

Table 9.1 illustrates textbook and chapter surveying. If students know how to use a textbook and are aware of how to read and study individual chapters, they are more apt to interact with the content presented. This interaction may promote more independent functioning in both special and inclusive settings.

 ACTIVITY 9.3

Utilize the form in Table 9.1 to survey this textbook and one of its chapters.

Graphic Aids. Many students with learning problems do not automatically activate and utilize strategies to help them acquire information from text (Torgesen, 1982). This problem is intensified in the content areas because of the prevalence of inconsiderate text (e.g., a text that lacks structure, unity, coherence, and audience appropriateness) (Armbruster & Anderson, 1981). Graphic aids may alleviate the problems inherent in content area textbooks. Graphic aids may take the form of a table of contents, chapter headings, tables, a glossary, an appendix, a bibliography, or an index, as well as maps, graphs, and illustrations. These graphic aids help students gather clues about the content of the text and organize facts so that they are easy to understand.

We recommend that you specifically teach the use of each of the graphic aids rather than assume that your students know how and when to use them to acquire information. For example, Mr. Alonzo taught beginning map skills to his primary students by drawing a map of the neighborhood around the school. He showed the students how to use the compass rose (the symbol that has lines or arrows that point in the four main directions on the map). He gave them many opportunities to practice by asking them questions such as, "If you wanted to walk from Spruce Street in front of the school to Twin Oaks Drive behind the school, in which direction would you walk?" Next, he showed them how to use the distance scale on the map to determine the distance between streets and between stores. On his map, the scale stated that 1 inch is equal to 3 miles. After modeling how to figure distance with the distance scale and a ruler, he asked them questions such as, "If I live on Bellvedere Street and I want to walk to school, how far will I have to walk?"

Another effective graphic aid is the graphic organizer, a visual means for organizing material to be learned. We presented some examples of graphic organizers in Chapter 7. A different type of graphic organizer is the tree diagram (see Figure 9.6), which contains vocabulary related to a specific concept (Barron, 1969). Alvermann (1983) suggests using a modified graphic organizer: a tree diagram that contains empty spaces to represent missing information for students to fill in while reading their textbooks. It focuses attention on what is important in the textbook and secures the students' involvement by requiring them to search for the missing information.

Table 9.1   Surveying a Textbook and Chapter

Surveying Your Textbook

1. Name of textbook _____

2. Author(s) _____

3. List two things you can tell about the book by its title. _____

   _____

4. List three points that the author makes in the introduction. _____

   _____

5. Look at the table of contents. List three things you know about the textbook by reading the chapter titles.

   _____

   _____

6. Does the textbook contain an index, glossary, and appendix? If so, how will you use each of them?

   _____

   _____

Surveying a Textbook Chapter

1. Title of chapter _____

2. List two things that the chapter title suggests. _____

   _____

3. Read the first and last paragraphs and the boldface headings in the chapter. What do you think the author wants you to

   learn? _____

   _____

4. What graphic aids does the chapter contain?

   _____ maps   _____ italics

   _____ graphs   _____ questions

   _____ charts   _____ definitions

   _____ illustrations   _____ bold print

   _____ diagrams   _____ other

5. What other clues does the chapter have that might help you understand it? _____

   _____

   _____

Initially, the teacher may assume responsibility for constructing the graphic organizer in order to assist students with the understanding of concepts, the meaning of vocabulary, the relationship among terms and ideas, and the organization of textbook material. Eventually, students will be able to construct these diagrams in collaboration with the teacher and, finally, on their own. To construct a graphic organizer, you should follow these steps adapted from Alvermann (1983):

1. *Choose the portion of a textbook chapter* (e.g., a few pages) *that you are ready to teach next.* In

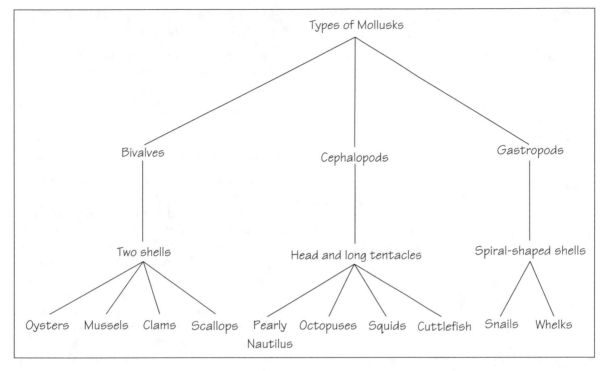

Figure 9.6   Tree Diagram

our example, we have selected a section that describes types of mollusks (see Figure 9.6).

2. *Write down the words that represent your topic* (e.g., types of mollusks).

mantle	clams	cuttlefish
bivalves	scallops	tentacles
oysters	cephalopods	gastropods
pearly nautilus	octopuses	mussels
whelks	snails	squids

3. *Arrange the words in a tree diagram to show their relationship to the concept* (e.g., types of mollusks). You may need to add or delete words to connect terms and ideas and to clarify relationships. We added *two shells* to describe *bivalves, head and long tentacles* to describe *cephalopods,* and *spiral-shaped shells* to describe *gastropods.* We deleted *mantle.*

4. *Draw your tree diagram on the board or overhead transparency to discuss with the students.* We rec-

ommend giving each student a copy. If you use a modified graphic organizer (a tree diagram with some empty spaces), students must have a copy so that they can supply the missing information.

5. *Demonstrate for the students how the information on the diagram simplifies, clarifies, and relates to the information in the textbook.*

Once you have taught the use of graphic aids, provide opportunities to practice. For example, for practice in using maps with intermediate and middle school students, Ekwall (1985) recommends setting up a travel bureau in the classroom. Students (customers) may visit the travel bureau to plan family vacations, identify the best mode and route of travel, and locate landmarks and historic sites. After students have practiced using graphic organizers, they may try constructing graphic organizers individually or in groups.

◇ IMPORTANT POINTS

1. An advance organizer is material that is presented "in advance of, and at a higher level of generality, inclusiveness, and abstraction than, the learning task itself" (Ausubel & Robinson, 1969, p. 606).
2. An advance organizer may be verbal or written and may consist of an activity for obtaining student attention, a statement of the lesson objectives, a confirmation of the teacher's expectations, or a presentation of a graphic organizer.
3. Mapping is a word picture of ideas and involves structuring information into categories using a graphic or web.
4. Maps are visual representations that show relationships among concepts.
5. A character web is a type of map that allows students to study characters, their traits, and examples of those traits.
6. The Concept Mastery Routine consists of selecting the targeted and overall concept; selecting key words or phrases; identifying characteristics as always, sometimes, or never present; identifying examples, nonexamples, and new examples; defining the concept; and plotting this information on a concept diagram.
7. A textbook may be previewed by attending to the title, introduction, summary, pictures and maps, chapter questions, subtopic titles, first paragraphs following subtopics, first sentences of paragraphs, italics, and bold print.
8. Graphic aids, the parts of a textbook that provide clues to content and assist in organizing facts, include the table of contents; chapter headings; maps, graphs, and other illustrations; tables; glossaries; appendices; bibliographies; and indexes.
9. Graphic organizers, such as tree diagrams, provide a visual means of organizing material.

ORGANIZATION AND MEMORIZATION OF INFORMATION

In this section, we present strategies that relate to how students organize and memorize information. We describe mnemonic and general memory strategies, underlining and highlighting, and study guides.

Memory Strategies

Memory plays an important part in the academic success of students. Memory skills affect the organization and storage of information for later retrieval. Memory skills are among the most commonly reported areas of weakness among students in special education and remedial classes (Scruggs & Mastropieri, 1984). Students with disabilities may have difficulty memorizing information for tests, presentations, and written work (Ashbaker & Swanson, 1996). Consequently, it is important to teach specifically strategies that will enhance memory skills.

Specific Mnemonic Strategies

Mnemonic strategies are systematic strategies to facilitate the organization, storage, and retrieval of information (Bellezza, 1983; Levin, 1985; Masters & Mori, 1993). *Mnemonics* comes from a Greek term and refers to the art of improving memory by using formulae or other aids (Bragstad & Stumpf, 1987). The following mnemonic strategies may be helpful to students who have difficulty with remembering.

Keyword Method. The keyword mnemonic method has been used successfully for learning and recalling information (Mastropieri, Scruggs, & Levin, 1986b; Mastropieri, Scruggs, Levin, Gaffney, & McLoone, 1985). Atkinson (1975) used the keyword method in foreign language vocabulary tasks. Additionally the keyword method has been used in the teaching of subjects such as history and science to students with learning disabilities (Scruggs, Mastropieri, Levin, & Gaffney, 1985; Veit, Scruggs, & Mastropieri, 1986).

The keyword method is a mnemonic strategy that assists in the retention of facts by using auditory and visual cues as well as visual imagery (Mastropieri, 1988). It employs the steps of recoding, relating, and retrieving. In recoding, an unfamiliar word is associated with a familiar, acoustically similar keyword. The relating element allows the learner to link the keyword to the actual word through a picture or image. Finally, the retrieving component enables the learner to call to mind systematically the original word (Mastropieri, Scruggs, & Levin, 1986a). For example, Mastropieri (1988) suggests that to learn the word *apex,* you recode it to a word that sounds similar, like *ape.* This is a good keyword for students who are familiar with the concept of ape. Next, relate the keyword, *ape,* by creating an image of the keyword and the definition of the word *apex.* Since *apex* means highest point, you would picture an ape at a highest point. A good interactive image may be an ape (possibly King Kong) sitting on the highest point of something, for example, the Empire State Building. To retrieve the word *apex* and its definition, you would tell the student to think of the keyword, think back to the picture, and state the definition. It is important to consider students' experiential and cultural backgrounds when choosing keywords. You want to be sure to include concepts with which they are familiar.

Pegword Method. A method for learning and remembering a list of items is the number rhyme, or pegword, method. A pegword is a rhyming word for the numbers from 1 to 10:

1. Bun	6. Sticks
2. Shoe	7. Heaven
3. Tree	8. Gate
4. Door	9. Vine
5. Hive	10. Hen

To learn a list of words, you create an image that associates the number 1, the word *bun,* and the first word on the list of items to be learned. For example, if you wanted to remember the five senses (sight, hearing, smell, taste, and touch), you would picture (1) a large bun wearing glasses, (2) a shoe with big ears, (3) a tree with an oversized nose sniffing its blossoms, (4) a door with an open mouth licking its lips, and (5) a beehive with long arms extending from its sides that were getting stung by bees because they kept touching the hive. This technique utilizes the visualizing and associative potential of the learner to help aid memory.

Other Mnemonic Aids. Although mnemonic aids are not to be used as a substitute for studying and understanding, they may provide useful cues for students who are required to memorize lists, items, causes, laws, or equations. Some commonly used mnemonics are suggested:

1. Directions (north, east, south, west)— *Never eat soggy waffles*
2. Parts of the atom (proton, electron, neutron, shell)— *PENS*
3. Simple machines (lever, pulley, wheel, axle, inclined plane, screw, wedge)—*Lisa pushed Wendy Adams in pretty Susan's way*
4. Spelling *dessert*—Two s's because *so sweet*
5. Colors of the spectrum (red, orange, yellow, green, blue, indigo, violet)— *Roy G. Biv*
6. Time changes—Spring forward, fall back
7. Coordinating conjunctions (for, and, nor, but, or, yet, so)— *fan boys*
8. Operations (multiplication, division, addition, subtraction)— *My Dear Aunt Sally*
9. *b* and *d* reversals—two thumbs-up to represent the headboard and foot of a bed
10. Spatial relations in handwriting
   Grass letters—grow only to middle line (*a, s, c*) Sky letters—reach to the top line (*b, f, l*) Root letters—grow as high as grass letters and then dig down (*g, j, p*)

◆ **ACTIVITY 9.4**

Develop a mnemonic strategy for each of the following situations:

1. Teach a fifth grader to memorize the following parts of speech: noun, verb, adverb, adjective, preposition, conjunction.
2. Show a ninth grader an effective way to memorize the following types of trees: spruce, oak, willow, sycamore, elm, palm, maple.

Underlining and Highlighting

Some study strategies help students organize information by physically altering the text or material. Underlining is one of the most popular and frequently used study strategies (Anderson & Armbruster, 1984; Annis & Davis, 1978; Glynn, 1978). It is accomplished by drawing a line under the important text. Highlighting is accomplished by going over the text with a transparent marker. Underlining and highlighting are particularly useful with consumable materials. Underlining and highlighting may facilitate studying by isolating the information to be recalled (Blanchard, 1985). You should underline only after you have read the material by going back and picking out a few words (not whole sentences) that summarize the author's main point (Murphy, Meyers, Olesen, McKean, & Custer, 1996). Effective underlining identifies the main ideas and supporting statements in a passage and conveys the same meaning as the entire passage (Raygor, 1970). For example, consider the following passage that Ms. Rodriguez used with her students:

Every now and then, a <u>moving light</u> may appear in the <u>night sky.</u> That light may be a <u>comet.</u> A comet has a <u>head</u> and a <u>tail.</u> The <u>head</u> of the comet is <u>made up of</u> a large cloud of <u>gases called</u> the <u>coma.</u> The <u>tail</u> actually <u>forms when</u> the cloud of <u>gases</u> is <u>blown back</u> by the wind.

Notice that the same meaning is conveyed when you read the entire passage and when you read only the underlined portions.

The results of many of the studies conducted in the area of underlining (Anderson & Armbruster, 1980; Cashen & Leicht, 1970; Fowler & Barker, 1974; Idstein & Jenkins, 1972; Johnson & Wen, 1976; Rickards & August, 1975) suggest that teachers should do the following:

1. Give preunderlined material whenever possible.
2. Provide training in effective underlining.
3. Encourage students to underline important general ideas.
4. Remind students that with underlining, less is more.
5. Encourage students to use the time saved by underlining to study the material.

For example, Ms. Rodriguez frequently gives handouts to her students to accompany their fifth-grade science textbook chapters. Her handouts contain sections that she has underlined prior to assigning the chapter. This has helped her students focus on important concepts, key terms and their definitions, study questions, and other elements that she wants them to study in preparation for a quiz or test. Sometimes, she passes out handouts that have not been underlined and models for her students what they should underline. She uses cognitive modeling techniques to demonstrate by saying, "I am going to underline *moving light* and *night sky* because it is important to know that comets move and that we can see them against the dark sky at night. I will underline *comet, head,* and *tail* because I need to remember that a comet has a head and tail. I am going to underline *head made up of gases called coma* so that I will remember what the head is composed of. That sounds as if it might be a test question."

After modeling for her students, she gives them another handout and asks them to practice underlining the way she has shown them. When Ms. Rodriguez began this procedure, her students tended to underline almost everything on a page, but after repeated practice, the amount of underlining decreased and was limited to the most essential information. Her students had learned to focus on the underlined information to prepare for tests.

Study Guides

Study strategies that help students organize information, both visual (e.g., reading assignment, overhead transparency, chalkboard, laboratory work) and auditory (e.g., lecture, audiotape, and videotape) may take the form of study guides. Because many students with special needs have difficulty organizing information, they may benefit from a guide presenting information in a well-sequenced, structured format. A study guide may function as a map to guide the student through an assignment (Devine, 1981). Study guides may help students with poor reading skills gain information from texts that have heavy concept loads and high readability levels (Olson, 1980). By directing attention to specific points, study guides provide organized ways to view a videotape or listen to an audiotape. They may also prove valuable to students as a means of reviewing for tests.

Study guides may be used with elementary and secondary students before, during, and after instruction. A child in the elementary grades would benefit from a guide illustrating the four steps in long division or an outline with the names of the five parts of a friendly letter and an example of each. Mario, a second-grade student, was given a study guide with the five short vowels (*a, e, i, o, u*) on it. Next to each vowel was a picture that represented the sound that the vowel made (apple, elephant, igloo, octopus, umbrella). Bonita, a fifth-grade student, received the following guide prepared by her teacher:

Topic	Writing four types of sentences
Terms	Declarative, interrogative, exclamatory, and imperative
Definitions	Declarative: a sentence that states or declares something. Interrogative: a sentence that asks a question. Exclamatory: a sentence that expresses emotion or surprise. Imperative: a sentence that gives a command or order.
Examples	Don ran all the way home from Bob's house. (declarative) Do you think I could have left my notebook in school? (interrogative) I'll never do that again as long as I live! (exclamatory) Close the door. (imperative)

Riegel, Mayle, and McCarthy-Henkel (1988) recommended different levels of study guides depending on a student's reading level. Table 9.2 illustrates three different types of study guides. The *independent* study guide includes critical information and is appropriate for students who have good reading and study skills, know how to use an index, can skim and scan for information, and can make inferences (Riegel et al., 1988). The *prompted* study guide includes critical information and prompts (e.g., page numbers) to help students locate the information. The *directed* study guide identifies, provides prompts for, and defines critical information.

Students at the secondary level may profit from a listing of (1) title or subject, (2) purpose, (3) key vocabulary and definitions, (4) a brief outline of subject matter, (5) questions, and (6) text references with pages. For example, Leroy needed to prepare for a test on Japan. Utilizing the six elements just listed, his teacher, Ms. Delgado, developed a study guide to help structure his studying and organize the information.

1. *Title/Subject* The island of Japan
2. *Purpose* To describe the environment of Japan and the way of life of its people
3. *Key vocabulary and definitions*

bonsai:	potted plants and trees kept small through specific cultivation techniques
monsoon:	a periodic wind that reverses direction seasonally

Table 9.2 Independent, Prompted, and Directed Study Guides

Sample Independent Study Guide

Define the following terms:
1. Axis
2. blitzkrieg
3. neutral
4. isolation

Answer the following questions:
1. What happened on December 7, 1941?
2. Describe two factors that contributed to war in Europe.

Sample Prompted Study Guide

Define the following terms:
1. Axis (page 123)
2. blitzkrieg (page 130)
3. neutral (page 129)
4. isolation (page 125)

Answer the following questions:
1. What happened on December 7, 1941? (page 132)
2. Describe two factors that contributed to war in Europe. (pages 121 & 122)

Sample Directed Study Guide

Define the following terms:
1. Axis (page 123)—Germany and its allies
2. blitzkrieg (page 130)—lightning warfare
3. neutral (page 129)—to take no side between nations at war
4. isolation (page 125)—a belief that a nation should not become involved in foreign (other countries') problems

Answer the following questions:
1. What happened on December 7, 1941? (page 132) The Japanese bombed Pearl Harbor, Hawaii.
2. Describe two factors that contributed to war in Europe. (pages 121 & 122) Economic factors and political conditions contributed to war in Europe.

NOTE. From *Beyond Maladies and Remedies: Suggestions and Guidelines for Adapting Materials for Students with Special Needs in the Regular Class* by R. H. Riegel, J. A. Mayle, & J. McCarthy-Henkel, 1988. Novi, MI: RHR Consultation Services. Reprinted by permission.

archipelago: a body of salt water interspersed with numerous islands
typhoon: a tropical cyclone that occurs in the western Pacific
tsunami: a huge wave caused by an underwater disturbance

4. *A brief outline*
  I. Climate
  II. Population distribution
  III. Landforms
    A. Mountains
    B. Plateaus
    C. Plains
  IV. Natural resources
  V. Life in Japan
    A. Urban
    B. Rural

5. *Questions*
What are the advantages and disadvantages of Japan's location?
What are Japan's greatest natural resources?
Describe urban and rural life in Japan.

6. *Text references*
World Cultures, pages 56–67
Japan Today, page 34 and pages 117–129

Next month, after Leroy has become used to the format of the study guide, Ms. Delgado may

Table 9.3 Study Guide to Assist with Reading Assignments

Questions to Guide Your Reading about Wild Plants and Animals
Directions: Read this study guide before you begin reading the material or responding to the questions.

1. The main idea can be found in the first paragraph. Write it in your own words. (p. 68)

2. Read pp. 68–73 and then stop and write in your own owrds two major points the author is making. Now read pp. 74–79 and do the same.

3. Terms you should know are: (pp. 68–79)

extinct	wildlife management
species	wildlife refuges
depleted	ethics
resources	predator
endangered	poaching
threatened	migration

   Be prepared to use them meaningfully in a class discussion.

4. What wild plants and animals are in danger of becoming extinct? Six are listed on pages 70–75.

5. The author gives three reasons why we should not let these endangered species die. Write them and give one of your own. (Hint: Think about our speaker from the Audubon Society as well as the debate we had in class.)

6. Make sure you read the captions under the pictures. They give excellent descriptions of the California condor, snow leopard, whooping crane, black-footed ferret, Florida manatee, and black lace cactus.

7. Write down any words that you are unsure of and bring them to class. Remember first to use context clues and the glossary in the back of the book to help figure them out.

8. Think about what you have read and how this material relates to the previous unit on land and water resources. List at least two things in the previous unit that helped you with this unit.

leave some blanks in his study guide and require him to fill in these sections, increasing his involvement with the material. Perhaps he will have to supply some of the definitions, generate some questions about the topic, or fill in parts of the outline.

Students at both elementary and secondary levels can benefit from study guides to assist them with school or home reading assignments. For example, Ms. Donahue gave her students a reading assignment on wild plants and animals and prepared a study guide to accompany their reading (see Table 9.3). Notice how Ms. Donahue made this reading assignment meaningful by developing a study guide to accompany it.

Study guides may take many different forms, depending on the age of the student, the purpose of the guide, the subject matter, and the needs of the students. They provide an excellent way to facilitate the organization of information for students with special needs.

 ACTIVITY 9.5

Select a chapter from this textbook and develop a study guide for it. Switch with someone else. How would his or her guide assist you in reading the chapter? In preparing for a test on the chapter? Critique the guide, using some or all of the suggestions given in the chapter. Now have the other person do the same for yours.

 IMPORTANT POINTS

1. To organize and remember information effectively, students may use memory strategies, underlining or highlighting techniques, and study guides.

2. Mnemonic strategies are strategies that facilitate the organization, storage, and retrieval of information.

3. The keyword method uses auditory and visual cues as well as visual imagery to enhance memorization.

4. The pegword method utilizes a number rhyme technique to assist in memorizing a list of items.

5. Underlining and highlighting help students organize information to be studied by physically altering the material.

6. Effective underlining identifies the main ideas and supporting statements and conveys the same meaning as the entire passage.

7. Study guides help students organize information presented visually (in reading assignments, on the board or overhead, in laboratory work) and auditorily (through lectures and audiotapes or videotapes).

8. Study guides may include topic, terms, definitions, and examples.

9. Independent study guides include critical information and are appropriate for students who have good reading and study skills, know how to use an index, can skim and scan for information, and can make inferences. Prompted study guides include critical information and prompts; directed study guides identify, provide prompts for, and define critical information.

EXPRESSION OF INFORMATION

In this section, we present study skills and strategies that relate to how students express information. Students are expected to possess skills that will enable them to demonstrate their knowledge and mastery of content in school. Therefore, in this section, we provide techniques to improve two skill areas important for success in school and later at work and in life: (1) test preparation and test taking and (2) report writing and presentation.

Test Preparation and Test Taking

Most students are required to take tests before they enter elementary school, during the elementary and secondary years in school, and be-

fore they leave high school. Even though students spend their school years taking quizzes, unit tests, and minimum competency tests, they are not necessarily proficient at doing so. Students with special needs encounter problems preparing for and taking tests because of difficulties with organization, comprehension, memory, task completion within time limits, studying, self-confidence, and test-wiseness.

Just as you prepare your students in computation, handwriting, and theme writing, you may also prepare them to take tests. After all, your students are tested in every aspect of the curriculum, from reading to vocational skills. We present several suggestions to help your students improve their skills in test taking. Studying the content, using the study skills previously mentioned in this chapter (e.g., listening, note taking, memory techniques, study guides), and utilizing these test-taking tips should help your students improve their performance on tests.

The following suggestions, adapted from the work of Bos & Vaughn (1998), Bragstad & Stumpf (1987), and Mercer & Mercer (1998), may assist your students before they take a test, during the completion of a test, and after a test is returned.

Before the Test

Following are some of the specific procedures you can suggest to your students as they prepare for a test.

1. *Keep reviewing.* Students should review after each class, week, or section. A spaced or cumulative review is more effective than a massed review of the information just before a test. You may suggest that your students keep a study log to help keep up with information. The study log may contain things to do, such as review prior work, rewrite notes, or highlight important information.

2. *Determine the specifics about the test.* Suggest that your students find out the following from the teacher: date of test, sources to be studied (text, notes, presentations), types of questions (objective, essay), and time allowed.

3. *Guesstimate about the test.* Prompt your students to use past tests and quizzes, clues from their teachers, and brainstorming with other students to predict questions on the test. This will help them allocate study time more efficiently.

4. *Think positive thoughts.* Encourage your students to tell themselves that they will do well because they have studied the right sources of information, prepared for specific types of questions, and thought about how to allot their time.

During the Test

Following are some specific techniques you can suggest your students use as they actually take a test:

1. *Situate yourself where you can concentrate.* If seats are not assigned, remind the students to choose one that will allow them to concentrate. For some it will be in the back and for others in the front—away from friends, noise, or other distractions.

2. *Survey the test.* Suggest that the students take a few deep breaths before starting. They should then put their names on their tests and look over the entire test before beginning. This will help them decide how much time to spend on each section and how the points are allocated. If this is not clear to them, they should ask the teacher.

3. *Complete the test.* Alert the students to read the directions carefully and to respond as directed, since failure to do so may result in a loss of points. They should answer the easy questions first (to earn points quickly and gain confidence) and place a mark by each question that they are unsure of. Then they can later go back to the questions they left unanswered. Unless there is a penalty for guessing, they should answer all of the questions, even if they must guess.

4. *Review the test.* Remind the students that after they have completed the test, they should look it over again. They should make sure they have followed the directions, answered all of the questions, and put their name on the test.

They should check to see if their writing is legible and all words are spelled correctly. Caution the students to change an answer only if they are absolutely certain it is incorrect.

After the Test

Following are some of the suggestions you can give to your students after they turn in their tests. Have the students systematically analyze their test-taking strengths and weaknesses.

Directions: This is an analysis of your test-taking performance. Please mark *Yes* or *No* for each of the following statements.

	Yes	**No**
1. Studied for test		
2. Put name on paper		
3. Surveyed test		
4. Decided order to do test		
5. Read and followed directions		
6. Answered easy questions first		
7. Marked/left difficult questions		
8. Went back to unanswered questions		
9. Answered all questions		
10. Proofread test		

Students typically need to spend a significant amount of time trying to comprehend and retain information in order to take tests (Hughes, 1996). Therefore, it is extremely important for them to have good test preparation skills that they can use across content areas and in a variety of situations and settings. We suggest that, in addition to following specific suggestions *before taking a test,* which we listed previously, students also understand the language of tests, use flash cards, and employ strategies like EASY and RCRC described on page 291.

Managing Instructional Language and Terms

Tests and quizzes are accompanied by directions that contain key words requiring students to respond in a specific way. It is vital for students to have a clear understanding of these words in order to complete short-answer and

Table 9.4 Instructional Language of Tests

Apply	Using examples, explain how an idea or concept would work.
Compare	Show similarities and differences of two or more things.
Contrast	Highlight just the differences of two or more concepts.
Define	Provide a general description of the concept.
Discuss	Provide a more detailed description, including pros and cons.
Evaluate	Discuss the concept, including your opinion and the facts to support the opinion.
Explain	Tell why something occurred.
Illustrate	Use examples, including diagrams and pictures, to explain your idea further.
Justify	Offer reasons and provide facts to support your statements.
Outline	Condense material into major topics with their subpoints underneath.
Relate	Show the connection between several thoughts and ideas.
Solve	Arrive at a desired outcome using facts and knowledge.
State	Offer main point without providing details.
Summarize	Bring knowledge together with emphasis on main points only.

essay questions accurately. Several authors have identified commonly used terms (Bos & Vaughn, 1994; Pauk, 1989; Riegel, Mayle, & McCarthy-Henkel, 1988), which we have listed in Table 9.4. To check for understanding of these terms, Bos and Vaughn (1994) recommend asking students to respond to test items that use different instructional language. This enables students to see how varying the instructional language varies their responses. Consider the different responses you would get to the following two instructions:

Define autocratic. *Discuss* autocratic.

Flash Cards

McCarney and Tucci (1991) suggest putting information to be learned for tests on flash cards using a who, what, where, when, how, why format. The questions are written on one side, and the answers are written on the back and may be prepared by the teacher, a teaching assistant, or the students themselves. Students can study independently or with a partner. This technique can be adapted for younger children by using pictures instead of words. Our example shows a sample of the flash cards a fifth-grade teacher had his students use to study for a test on a unit about heroes and heroines.

Who: was Molly Pitcher?
What: did she do to help the soldiers during the Revolutionary War?
Where: was she born?
When: did she live?
How: did she earn her nickname, Molly Pitcher?
Why: was she proclaimed a heroine at the Battle of Monmouth?

Who: Molly Hays McCauley (called Molly Pitcher) was a heroine of the Revolutionary War.
What: She cooked for and fed the soldiers and the wounded during the Revolutionary War.
Where: She was born in New Jersey.
When: She lived from 1754 to 1832.
How: She got her nickname by carrying pitchers of water to the wounded during the Battle of Monmouth. They called, "Molly, Pitcher!"
Why: She fought with the soldiers by loading and firing cannons during the Battle of Monmouth.

EASY

Ellis and Lenz (1987, p. 99) developed a strategy for students to use independently to prepare for tests by organizing and prioritizing information.

E = **Elicit** "Wh" questions (who, what, when, where, why) to identify important information.

A = **Ask** yourself which information is the least troublesome.

S = **Study** the easy parts first and the hardest parts last.

Y = Say **"Yes"** to self-reinforcement.

RCRC

Archer and Gleason (1994) have developed a strategy that students can use independently to prepare for tests by verbally rehearsing information from class presentations, notes, handouts, and textbooks.

R = **Read.** Read a section of material from the textbook, notes, or handouts and read it again.

C = **Cover.** Cover the material so you cannot see it.

R = **Recite.** Tell yourself what you have read.

C = **Check.** Uncover the material and check to see if you are right.

Most tests require students to read directions and questions and to work independently (Ritter & Idol-Maestas, 1986). Two options that give students a systematic procedure for taking tests are SCORER and SPLASH. Both involve having students preview the test before starting, skipping questions and returning to them later, and checking over the test before turning it in.

SCORER

Carman and Adams (1972) designed a technique called SCORER for students to use when they take tests:

1. **S**chedule time
2. **C**lue words
3. **O**mit difficult questions
4. **R**ead carefully
5. **E**stimate answers
6. **R**eview the work

Schedule Time. Students should begin their test by looking it over and planning how much time they will spend on each section. They can determine this by identifying the items that are easy and difficult for them, the point values of items, and how many items are on the test.

Clue Words. Students should look for clue words in multiple-choice and true-false items. Words like *never, none, every, always, all,* and *only* are "100 percent words," which imply that the response is true 100 percent of the time (Pauk, 1989). In most cases, students should avoid choosing responses that contain these words in multiple-choice items, and should answer *false* to true-false items containing these words.

Omit Difficult Questions. A good rule of thumb in taking tests is to answer the questions you know first and mark the ones you do not know. Come back later to the marked questions. Sometimes a question that a student has already answered on the test contains information that will help with an abandoned item.

Read Carefully. It is important that students read directions and test items carefully so they will not miss points because they did not follow the directions, answer the actual question, or answer all parts of a question.

Estimate Answers. Carman and Adams (1972) suggest that students performing mathematical calculations should estimate the answer before performing the calculation in order to avoid careless errors. Mercer and Mercer (1998) suggest that if guessing is not penalized, students should eliminate obvious choices and make their best guess.

Review Your Work. Students should go back over the entire test to make sure they have followed directions accurately, answered all abandoned items, and responded to all questions. Lee and Alley (1981) found that junior high students with learning disabilities demonstrated significantly improved unit test scores using the

SCORER approach. Ritter and Idol-Maestas (1983) used SCORER with high school students with mental disabilities and found the students who received instruction in SCORER performed better than the control group on content tests.

SPLASH

Simmonds, Luchow, Kaminsky, and Cottone (1989, p. 101) developed a method for taking tests that can be used for all content areas and types of tests.

S = **S**kim the entire test.
Note the easy and hard parts, directions, and point values so that you can best allocate the available time.

P = **P**lan your strategy once you have a general idea of the test.

L = **L**eave out difficult questions in a planned manner.

A = **A**ttack immediately those questions you know.

S = **S**ystematically guess after exhausting other strategies. (Here teachers must first instruct students to look for clues and answers on the test to help answer unknown questions. If there is no penalty for guessing, students should be told to guess the best choice after eliminating incorrect choices.)

H = **H**ouse cleaning.
Leave 5–10% of your allotted time to make sure all answers are filled in, clean up erasures, and check answers.

Report Writing and Presentation

Students are frequently required to express information through the writing and presentation of reports. This begins in elementary school, with children in the primary grades using show-and-tell activities, language experience stories, and process writing, and with students in the intermediate grades creating paragraphs, short stories, book reports, and themes. Students in middle and high school express themselves in writing (through paragraph and theme writing, preparation of written reports, and research papers requiring extensive use of references) and orally (through presentations of themes and reports).

It is helpful for students to have a time line to follow in the development of a paper or report. Some teachers ask for a topic, outline, and first draft by specific dates. These deadlines may be planned cooperatively with students, thus involving them in setting their own goals. You may want to instruct your students in how to do the following:

1. *Choose a topic.* When possible, topic choices should reflect student interests. For example, Mr. Bruno wanted his elementary students to write a report in his science class. He gave his students several choices of topics (e.g., the greenhouse effect, environmental pollution, depletion of resources, waste disposal) to motivate them to do the research and prepare the report. With choices, students had more involvement in the assignment from the start.

2. *Use reference materials in the media center* (e.g., Reader's Guide, encyclopedia, fiction and nonfiction, and technology resources—World Wide Web, CD-ROMs, videodiscs, software, etc.). It may be necessary to demonstrate for students how to locate reference materials and use them effectively. Some teachers take their classes to the media center during class time to review how to use the automated card catalog and conduct a search on the Internet, and to introduce the students to current Web sites that may be helpful to their research. Ms. Taylor took her tenth-grade students to the media center to give them guided practice in using reference materials and technology resources. She showed them how to make a card or create a file for each reference they used.

This helped them later as they put together their bibliographies.

3. *Prepare an outline (for organization and prioritization) and submit it for approval.* Many teachers require their students to submit outlines of their reports prior to the preparation of the actual report. This is an excellent way to monitor the progress of your students and to guide them in organizing and expressing themselves. For example, Mr. Tseng helped two of his students sequence the events of the Civil War by changing the order of the items on their outlines.

4. *Write and submit a thesis statement.* Your students should begin with a thesis statement and make sure that all of their information contributes to and supports that thesis. Show your students how to write a sample thesis statement such as, "Insects have an effect upon people and the environment." Then list several facts about insects, and ask your students to decide which statements contribute to the thesis.

   ◆ Insects have three body regions: the head, thorax, and abdomen.
   ◆ Insects are the largest class of organisms, including three-fourths to five-sixths of all known types of animals.
   ◆ Some insects transmit diseases to humans, plants, or animals.
   ◆ Some insects feed on crops and stored products.
   ◆ The expense in combating insects and the cost in loss or damages is at least $4 billion per year.
   ◆ Insects play an important role in soil improvement.

   This step helps your students organize their writing so that what they write relates to and supports the thesis statement.

5. *Prepare a rough draft of the report.* Many teachers require a rough draft of a report as a monitoring device. They assign points or credit to emphasize its importance in the preparation of a report. Suggestions, adjustments, and corrections can result in an improved final product. For example, out of a possible 300 points, Jeremy received 30 points for his outline, 90 points for his rough draft, 15 points for his bibliography, and 110 points for his final report.

6. *Prepare a bibliography.* Your students should include a list of the references and resources they used in completing their reports. This task is made easier when they make a card for each of their references as they find them.

7. *Develop a final copy of the report.* By incorporating any changes suggested during the rough draft stage of the report preparation, students have the opportunity to earn the maximum points possible. If students voice reluctance with "doing the report twice," remind them that their work will be more complete and polished and more likely to earn them a better grade when they complete the final copy.

8. *Proofread all work.* Some teachers award extra points when students turn in perfect papers because this indicates that they have proofread their work.

9. *Submit the paper or give the report orally.* You may require a written paper or an oral report as a final product. Either way, it is helpful for students to follow a well-sequenced, systematic set of procedures. Smith, Boone, and Higgins (1998) suggest that students may want to share their reports with students in other schools, states, or countries by posting it to a school or classroom Web site. This is an excellent way for students to receive feedback about their work from a variety of sources and to disseminate their research and writing to others.

Whether your students are presenting the information orally or in writing, they should follow the preceding steps. You may want to give your students the nine points listed above in the form of a checklist. Let this form serve as a monitoring tool for your students as they complete each stage of the presentation or the report.

ACTIVITY 9.6

Part 1. Evaluate your test-taking skills. Think of the last test you took. How many of the suggestions for what to do before, during, and after taking a test did you follow? What are your favorite types of test items to answer? What are your least favorite? Which, if any, part(s) of SCORER did you use? What aspects of your test-taking performance do you think you should change? Be specific.

Part 2. Practice writing a thesis statement. List several facts about the topic, including both extraneous and relevant issues. Justify which ones relate to the thesis statement and which ones do not.

◇ IMPORTANT POINTS

1. Techniques to use before taking a test are to review using a study log, determine specifics about the test, guesstimate about the test, and think positive thoughts.
2. Techniques to use during a test are to sit where it is possible to concentrate, survey the test, complete the test, and review the test.
3. A suggestion to use after taking a test is to analyze test-taking performance, including strengths and weaknesses.

4. Short-answer and essay questions contain instructional language that is important to understand in order to respond accurately to questions.
5. Specific test preparation strategies include EASY, RCRC, and the use of flash cards that follow a who, what, where, when, how, why format.
6. Specific test-taking strategies are SCORER and SPLASH.
7. The steps for developing an oral or written report are to choose a topic, use reference materials, prepare an outline, write a thesis statement, prepare a rough draft, prepare a bibliography, develop a final copy, proofread all work, and submit or give the report.

◆ DISCUSSION QUESTIONS

1. Justify the inclusion of study skills instruction in an already overcrowded curriculum.
2. Describe what you would include in a study skills program in elementary, middle, and high school.
3. Why do you think some students leave high school without a repertoire of study skills to enhance their success in postsecondary education? What can be done about it?

10

Social Skills and Peer-Mediated Instructional Strategies

In the early days of American education, when one-room schoolhouses were prevalent, older students instructing younger students was often a necessity, as the teacher usually taught four to eight grades (Allen, 1976). Today, teachers are again turning to the idea of students working with and instructing each other to meet the needs of the diverse population in inclusive classes. Cooperative goal structures are emphasized as students work together to accomplish goals and to create collaborative learning communities.

In this chapter, we examine some peer-mediated strategies that focus on students helping others learn. In particular, we concentrate on peer tutoring and cooperative learning, as both are recommended as effective strategies for inclusive settings (Johnson & Johnson, 1996; King-Sears & Bradley, 1995; Mathes, Fuchs, Fuchs, Henley, & Sanders, 1994; Slavin, 1988a). Peer tutoring involves students working together whereas cooperative learning usually occurs in groups of three or more. Peer tutoring and cooperative learning draw from both the reductionist and constructivist paradigms. Once the procedures are directly taught, the teacher's role changes to that of a facilitator, and the students participate in classroom communities. However, before we discuss these peer-mediated strategies, we spend time discussing social skills. Teachers must teach social skills before and during peer-mediated instruction for effective learning to occur (Allsopp, 1997; Cohen, 1994).

SOCIAL SKILLS

As discussed in Chapter 1, many students with special needs display inappropriate social skills. The lack of social skills tends to isolate these students from their peers, prevent positive interactions with teachers, and limit successful transitions to the world of work. Meta-analysis of social skills training finds only a modest effect for both students with learning disabilities and students with emotional disabilities (Kavale & Forness, 1995; Kavale, Mathur, Forness, Rutherford, & Quinn, 1997). Some possible explanations for the modest effect of social skills training may be intervention vagueness, imprecision in assessment procedures, lack of generalization of social skills, absence of a conceptual framework, and questionable social validity of social skills (Mather & Rutherford, 1996). As with all intervention strategies, the individual teacher should rely on data collection procedures to monitor the effectiveness of social skills training (see Chapter 3), as one cannot argue with the necessity of teaching social skills to students with special needs.

Identification of Social Skills

An examination of the literature finds varied definitions of social skills. McFall (1982) conceptualized a two-tiered model of social competence and social skills. According to his model, social competence involves the overall effectiveness of social behavior. A person who is socially competent perceives and interprets social situations and knows how to modify behavior when the situation changes (Chadsey-Rusch, 1986). Social skills are the specific strategies (accepting criticism, initiating conversation) and tactics that students use to negotiate daily social tasks.

Kavale and Forness (1995) discuss three types of social deficits: skill, performance, and self-control:

1. A skill deficit exists when a student has not learned the skill.

2. A performance deficit occurs when the student knows the skill but doesn't perform it due to a problem with motivation or discrimination (Smith, 1995). Students who are unmotivated do not perform the skill unless they are provided external motivation, while students with discrimination deficits are skilled and motivated, but don't know when to exhibit the skill.

3. Self-control deficits result when a student displays behaviors that interfere with the acquisition and performance of appropriate social skills. These behaviors include impulsivity, distractibility, hyperactivity, etc. (Smith, 1995).

With these various ways of conceptualizing social skills, how does a teacher decide which social skills will promote the behaviors necessary for effective peer tutoring and cooperative learning practices? You may check two sources: the empirical literature and consumer preferences (Walker, Schwarz, Nippold, Irvin, & Noell, 1994). In a review of the literature, offering encouragement and assistance, accepting compliments and criticism, taking turns, listening to what others are saying, avoiding sarcasm and criticism, and presenting a positive and friendly manner are frequently mentioned as skills that promote the behaviors necessary for effective peer tutoring and cooperative learning (Nelson, 1988; Mathes, Fuchs, Fuchs, Henley, & Sanders, 1994).

A survey of consumer preferences involves social validation or whether a skill is valued by the individuals in a particular setting. Students who display socially valued behaviors are more likely to be reinforced and accepted by peers. Walker et al. (1994) identify compromising, assisting, cooperating, and contributing to achievement of a valued outcome as behaviors that are highly preferred by peers and lead to peer acceptance and popularity. Nelson (1988) lists smiling, making eye contact, asking for help, sharing, and saying "thank you" as behaviors that have a high probability of being reinforced by peers. Thus, you may wish to interview your students to identify the social skills that they feel are necessary for peer tutoring or cooperative learning to work.

Knapczyk and Rodes (1996) suggest that teachers look at the setting demands and the social behavior of students who display appropriate skills. Greenwood (1996) followed this suggestion as he examined the behaviors of effective students during peer-tutoring sessions and found that they provided more encouragement and praise to their peers. It is also extremely important to make certain that students understand the meaning of the social skill. For example, Ms. Christensen (1992) prepared the poster in Figure 10.1 to make certain students understood what was meant by encouragement.

Social Skills Interventions

Social skills interventions generally fall into two areas or combinations of the two areas of skill-based approaches and problem-solving approaches (Walker et al., 1994). Smith (1995) recommends a skill-based approach for students who demonstrate skill deficits and a problem-solving approach for students who demonstrate performance deficits or self-control deficits. The skill-based approach adheres to the effective teaching strategies mentioned in Chapter 6: (a) teaching definition, steps, and rationale; (b) modeling; (c) presenting examples and nonexamples; (d) scheduling opportunities for students to practice the skill; (e) prompting; (f) giving feedback; (g) providing contingent reinforcement; and (h) teaching generalization of the skill. The problem-solving approach frequently teaches students to identify their feelings, tell what is happening, decide on a goal, identify alternative responses, envision possible outcomes for each response, select the best solution, decide on one solution, emit the behavior, and self-evaluate for future problem solving (Elias & Tobias, 1996). Whether you plan to use the skill-based approach or the problem-solving approach or elements of both, teachers should directly teach social skills, provide practice opportunities, integrate social skills with other curriculum, and emphasize generalization of the skills to other settings.

Figure 10.1   Sample Social Skills Poster for Peer-Mediated Strategies

NOTE. Adapted from Marge Christensen (1992). *Motivational English for At-risk Students: A Language Arts Course That Works,* Copyright 1992 by the National Education Service, 1252 Loesch Road, Bloomington, IN 47404, Telephone: 800-733-6786. Reprinted by permission.

◆ ACTIVITY 10.1

Select a social skill other than encouragement and design a poster to help students remember the definition.
(Answers for this and other activities are found in the Instructor's Manual.)

Directly Teach

As with academic skills, students with disabilities have difficulty learning social skills incidentally. Teachers should directly teach the skills and then use scaffolding (prompting) to facilitate social skills performance. Elias and Tobias (1996) recommend teaching students problem-solving strategies by using questioning techniques. They suggest that open-ended questions such as, "What happened? What were you trying to do? How are you feeling? What was the other person doing? What happened before this?" (p. 24) assist students to become competent and independent thinkers. For the resistant or younger child, they suggest teaching students to make choices, such as, "Were you trying to keep the toy for yourself?" or "Did you just want to play with it a little longer?" A two-question rule is used to encourage children to think. For example, before putting children into cooperative groups, you may ask them to think about these questions: "How do you plan to show you do not agree with your partner's idea? What are some words you could start with?" The idea is to lead students to reflect on their own behaviors. Rosenthal-Malek (1997) used six 10-minute daily instruction periods to teach her preschool children self-interrogation questions such as, "What will happen if _____ ?" to develop social skills. She asked each child to repeat the questions, she then wrote the questions on the board, and she developed games for application of the questions.

Modeling social skills is another effective way to directly teach social skills. Teachers or other students may model the skill. Often the skill is modeled in an appropriate manner and then in an inappropriate manner, and students must discriminate between them. For example, Ms. Trailer modeled the appropriate way to disagree with a peer and then the inappropriate way. The children designed their own evaluation to help discriminate the appropriate example from the inappropriate.

Elias and Taylor (1995) suggest the use of videos to teach social skills. They first show a segment of a television program or a movie. Then they ask students to discuss the main characters, the problems they have, their expressed feelings, the character's goals, their solutions, the roadblocks, the plan, and evaluation of the plan. Instead of using a movie, Ms. Fearis videotaped each cooperative group for five minutes and then presented the tape to the students and asked them to pinpoint any problems they saw that the group was having, brainstorm some solutions, vote on one solution, and agree to try the solution the next time the group met.

Practice

Practice for social skills frequently occurs during role playing. Role playing allows students to identify and learn skills and to solve problems in a group context with impersonal materials. During role playing, an effective teacher provides prompts and feedback. Many commercial social skills curriculum kits provide role-playing suggestions (see chapter 12). However, you or your students may generate the role-playing situations. At the end of one of the peer-tutoring sessions, Ms. Bright had students role-play how to give corrective feedback, as she noticed many tutors were having problems correcting their peers in an effective manner.

Another effective strategy is to provide students with mnemonics to cue students to remember and practice a skill. The SLAM (McIntosh, Vaughn, & Bennerson, 1995) strategy does just that. After skills instruction, teachers may use SLAM to remind students how to handle negative feedback: "**S**top whatever you're doing. **L**ook the person in the eye. **A**sk the person a question to clarify what he or she means. **M**ake an appropriate response to the person."

Integrate

If you use peer tutoring and cooperative learning groups frequently in your class, it is easy to integrate social skills, as both arrangements incorporate academic and social skills. The writing process also promotes the use of social skills, especially if you have students evaluate each other's work. During student feedback and evaluation of other students' writings, Zaragoza (1987) teaches her students to react positively to each other's work through the simple steps of TAG: "(a) *T*ell what you like, (b) *A*sk questions, and (c) *G*ive ideas" (p. 293).

Elias and Tobias (1996) suggest that social problem-solving frameworks may be applied to language arts, social studies, and health. For example, a "Book Talk" format brings problem-solving ideas into language arts for young readers:

My character's problem is . . . .

How did your character get into this problem . . . ?

How does the character feel?

What does the character want to happen?

What questions would you like to be able to ask the character you picked, one of the other characters, or the author? (p. 109)

Generalize

Students with disabilities have great difficulty in generalizing new information to other situations and settings (Rivera & Smith, 1997). Therefore, you must incorporate generalization strategies into your teaching of social skills. Skills that possess social validity are often easier to transfer, as they are maintained by naturally occurring behaviors, such as peer approval and attention. Prompting social skill use throughout the day and giving homework assignments are two strategies that often assist students to generalize behaviors. In her primary, inclusive, lit-

eracy-based classroom, Burke (1993) provides an example of the former by immediately attending to a social problem through the use of "Blue Chairs." Students who are involved in the conflict move to a separate part of the room and follow these procedures:

(1) Only people who are part of the problem sit in the Blue Chairs.
(2) No touching, yelling, or name calling.
(3) One person tells his/her feelings at a time. "I feel _____, because _____." The other person must wait his/her turn. There are no interruptions.
(4) The people who are part of the problem must solve the problem. Each person must be satisfied with the solution (p. 84).

The teacher acts as a mediator, prompting students to remember the steps and making suggestions if the students are having difficulty resolving the problems. The teacher then leaves and allows the students to continue the process independently.

Salend, Jantzen, and Giek (1992) found that a peer confrontation system was effective in modifying inappropriate verbalizations and low levels of on-task behavior for students with mild disabilities. Whenever the 8- through 10-year-olds displayed either behavior during the language arts classes, the teacher initiated the procedure by asking the group to respond to these questions: "_____ seems to be having a problem. Who can tell _____ what the problem is? Can you tell _____ why that is a problem? Who can tell _____ what he/she needs to do to solve the problem?" (p. 214). The teacher verbally praised appropriate responses to the questions and verbally praised the student who had been confronted for accepting and displaying the alternative suggested by the group. Twelve of the 13 students reported that they felt the teacher should continue the intervention, even though some felt it was embarrassing to be singled out. An adaptation is to direct the confrontation to the group and not a single subject; for example, "Our group seems to be having a problem . . . ."

Date: January 1. 1999   Name: Jason C.

Practice Skill: Encouragement

Where I did it: At home

What I did: I told my brother that he really was a good drawer and I
knew he'd draw a good map.

How I felt: Good. Happy.

How it worked: Good. He smiled at me. And Mom told me that I was
being thoughtful.

Figure 10.2 Homework Entry for Social Skills Journal

◆ **ACTIVITY 10.2**

Describe a social skills generalization activity
that you plan to use in your classroom.

Teachers may give homework assignments
for students to generalize social skills in addition to academic skills. Ms. Holt noticed that
students were not demonstrating encouraging
behavior to each other during group work. Using peer confrontation procedures, the group
defined the problem and discussed how to
show more encouragement to others. Ms. Holt
then gave the students a homework assignment
to complete for their social skills journals (see
Figure 10.2). Chances are with the peer-mediated strategies of peer tutoring and cooperative learning, social skills instruction will become an integral part of your curriculum.

◇ **IMPORTANT POINTS**

1. Meta-analysis of social skills training finds only
   a modest effect for both students with learning
   disabilities and students with emotional disabilities (Kavale & Forness, 1995; Kavale,
   Mathur, Forness, Rutherford, & Quinn, 1997).

2. Social competence is the overall demonstration of social behaviors as judged by
   others.
3. Social skills are specific skills or strategies
   that individuals use to negotiate daily social
   tasks.
4. Surveying the literature and interviewing significant peers and adults are two ways to
   identify social skills for instruction.
5. The skill-based approach for teaching social
   skills involves teaching the definition, steps,
   and rationale; modeling; presenting examples and nonexamples; scheduling opportunities for students to practice the skill;
   prompting; giving feedback; providing contingent reinforcement; and teaching generalization of the skill.
6. The problem-solving approach teaches students to identify their feelings, tell what is
   happening, decide on a goal, identify alternative responses, envision possible outcomes
   for each response, select the best solution,
   decide on one solution, emit the behavior,
   and use their self-evaluation for future problem solving (Elias & Tobias, 1996).
7. Whichever approach is used, teachers must
   directly teach social skills, provide practice
   opportunities, integrate social skills with
   other curriculum, and emphasize generalization of the skills to other settings.

Peer Tutoring

Peer tutoring consists of one student acting as a tutor, or the person who transmits the information, and one student acting as the tutee, or the person who receives the information. A tutor may be the same age as the tutee (same-age tutoring) or a different age (cross-age tutoring). Students may also assume reciprocal roles: sometimes as a tutor and sometimes as a tutee.

Peer tutoring enjoys much empirical support in the field of special education for students with mild disabilities in both elementary and secondary grades in all subject areas (Durrer & McLaughlin, 1995; Utley et al., 1997). Peer tutoring was identified as one of the promising interventions from a meta-analysis of special education research (Forness, Kavale, Blum, & Lloyd, 1997). Greenwood (1996) reports the successful implementation of a type of peer tutoring known as ClassWide Peer Tutoring (CWPT) as an inclusion strategy in 20 school districts and 11 special education cooperatives. Results of a 12-year follow-up study of a group of at-risk, urban first graders found that students who participated in CWPT procedures in math, reading, and spelling for four years were less likely to drop out of school (Greenwood & Delquadri, 1995). Fewer of these students were referred to special education services than a control group, and those who did receive special services were in less-restrictive settings. Moreover, teachers reported the procedures as very "teacher-friendly."

Rationale

The rationale behind the use of peer tutoring is that the procedures promote more active student responding, a direct link to higher achievement. Students have more opportunities to correct errors, are given immediate feedback, and are exposed to more social and academic support than in teacher-mediated instruction (King-Sears & Bradley, 1995; Utley, Mortsweet, & Greenwood, 1997). Furthermore,

peer tutoring is another way to accomplish individualized instruction, because instructional material may be matched to the learner's interest and ability. Peer tutoring is also an effective way to reinforce concepts previously taught by the teacher. A peer who has similar experiences and is closer to the developmental age of the tutee can often interpret the teacher's ideas or content in the child's language.

Description

Within peer tutoring, we examine instructional procedures that involve two peers working together, such as Reciprocal Peer Tutoring (Fantuzzo, King, & Heller, 1992) and the Reciprocal Peer Revision Strategy (MacArthur, Schwartz, & Graham, 1991). Additionally, we present models that involve peers working together as part of a team, such as ClassWide Peer Tutoring (CWPT; Delquadri, Greenwood, Stretton, & Hall, 1983), and Peer-Assisted Learning Strategies (PALS; Mathes, Fuchs, Fuchs, Henley, & Sanders, 1994). We select these particular models to describe, as they are supported in the literature for their effectiveness for students with mild disabilities and students at risk (Utley, Mortsweet, & Greenwood, 1997).

Reciprocal Peer Tutoring

The routine for Reciprocal Peer Tutoring (RPT) includes 20 minutes of peer tutoring, followed by 7 minutes of testing to teach math and spelling skills. We describe the math tutoring procedures (Fantuzzo et al., 1992; Fantuzzo, Davis, & Ginsburg, 1995). Students are paired randomly in same-age dyads and work with flash cards selected for them individually, based on their score on a math pretest. They also select their rewards and performance goals from teacher-prepared options. Sometimes students begin the procedures by completing a 5-minute multiplication drill, while other times they begin by reminding themselves of their individual and group goals. The format proceeds in the following manner:

a. Peer teacher presents flash card with answer and strategy on back to student.

b. Student completes problem on a worksheet that is divided into sections (Try 1, Try 2, Help, and Try 3).

c. If student is correct, peer teacher praises and presents next problem.

d. If student is wrong, peer teacher provides structured help (strategy on back of card) and personal suggestions.

e. Student attempts problem again in Try 2 section.

f. If still incorrect, the peer teacher completes the problem, explaining the procedures in the Help section on the worksheet.

g. Student attempts to solve problem again in Try 3 section.

h. At the end of 10 minutes, students change roles.

i. Both students take a 16-problem quiz.

j. Students grade each other's quizzes using an answer sheet.

k. Students compare their team score with team goal.

l. If the score exceeds the team goal, the students score a "win."

m. After a certain set of "wins," the team earns the predetermined reward.

Reciprocal Peer Revision Strategy

The Reciprocal Peer Revision Strategy combines strategy instruction and peer interaction. MacArthur, Schwartz, and Graham (1991) designed the highly structured approach to teaching revision skills, which are usually taught more informally in the process approach to writing instruction. The teacher introduced the peer editing strategy, shared its importance, taught the steps and rationale for each step, modeled the steps, and provided practice opportunities. At the conclusion of the teacher instruction, pairs of students worked together in a structured routine to improve composition writing. The routine required the peer editor to (a) listen and read along as the peer author reads; (b) tell the peer author the main idea of the paper and the part liked best; (c) reread the paper, take notes, and address whether the material is clear and is written with enough details; and (d) discuss suggestions with the peer author. Both students completed Steps (a) and (b) as a peer editor and as a peer author. At Step (c), each student worked independently on each other's composition. Students asked two questions during this step: "(1) Is there anything that is not CLEAR? and (2) Where could more DETAILS and information be added?" (MacArthur et al., 1991, p. 203). They then discussed the suggestions (Step d), and each student revised his/her composition. At the second meeting, the pair discussed revisions that they had made and completed a checklist that concentrated on four types of errors: complete sentences, capitalization (beginning of sentences), punctuation (end-mark), and spelling. The students with learning disabilities in the strategy group made more revisions and produced papers of higher quality with peer support than those who did not participate in the Reciprocal Peer Revision Strategy.

ClassWide Peer Tutoring

Initially developed by researchers to work with poor, culturally diverse children, the second phase of the Juniper Garden Children's Project extended the program to special education settings (Greenwood & Delquadri, 1995). Although many different versions of ClassWide Peer Tutoring (CWPT) are evident in the literature, certain core components are usually incorporated into the various adaptations. These core components include direct teacher presentation of new material to be learned, teacher monitoring of the tutoring process, whole-class instructional activity, explicit presentation formats for peers to follow, active student responding, reciprocal roles in each session, teams competing for the highest team point total, contingent point earning, systematic error correction strategies, public posting of student performance, and social awards for the winning team (Greenwood & Delquadri, 1995; Greenwood, 1996). We describe the use of CWPT in a secondary social studies inclusive classroom (Maheady, Sacca, & Harper, 1988). However, CWPT has been just as successful with elementary-age students and in math, reading, and spelling.

Maheady, Sacca, and Harper (1988) instituted the following CWPT approach in an inclusive secondary social studies class using study guides developed by the general and special education teachers. On Monday and Tuesday, the general education teacher presented the material; on Wednesday and Thursday, the peer tutoring occurred; on Friday, the students took a quiz during class time. Students with disabilities were paired with general education students. The pair was assigned to one of two teams by randomly drawing colored squares. The students then contributed points to each team as the teams competed with each other. The team membership stayed the same for two weeks.

During the 30-minute peer tutoring sessions, the tutor dictated the study guide questions to the tutee, who wrote and said the correct answer. The tutors gave feedback: either "that's right" or "wrong" and the correct answer. Tutees earned three points for each correct answer. When tutees gave an incorrect answer, the tutors instructed them to write the correct answer three times and awarded two points instead of three. After 15 minutes elapsed, the students reversed roles and continued with the same procedures.

The teachers' roles were also structured. Each teacher moved around the classroom and awarded up to 10 bonus points to tutors for following the presentation format. The individual scores of tutor and tutee were totaled for the daily team scores and posted on a chart in front of the class. On Friday, an individual quiz was given, and each student earned five team points for each correct answer. The winning team was announced following the weekly quiz.

Another variation of the ClassWide Peer Tutoring procedure is ClassWide Student Tutoring Teams (CSTT) (Harper, Mallette, Maheady, & Brennan, 1993). Now, students play a game during the peer-tutoring session as different team members are assigned to tables (Utley et al., 1997). For example, in a math class, the teacher assigned one student with high math ability, one student with low math ability, and two students with average math ability to each table (Harper et al., 1993). At each table is a folder with the task (e.g., study guide, math problems, etc.), answer sheet, paper and pencils, and deck of cards. The cards contain numbers on them that correspond to the items. Students take turns at being the teacher. The first peer teacher draws a card and reads the corresponding question from the study guide. Each student then writes an answer. The peer teacher checks each answer against the answer sheet and awards five points. If an answer is not correct, the peer teacher gives the correct answer and awards two or three points to the students after they successfully write the answer three times. The teacher's responsibility is then moved to the next student and the procedures are repeated. At the game's end, the teacher collects team points and posts the results on the board. The teacher may also give bonus points to teams who follow the steps and who demonstrate appropriate interactions. The most improved team is recognized, the teams that reached the preset criterion are recognized, and the most outstanding team members are recognized (Utley et al., 1997).

A common complaint of teachers in using CWPT is the amount of time that it takes for the score-reporting process and the planning. Currently, a computerized system is available that provides support to teachers in both these processes (Greenwood, Finney, Arreaga-Mayer, Carta, Delquadri, Walker, Innocenti, Lignugaris-Kraft, Harper, & Clinton,

1993). Other concerns are increased noise levels, complaints about partners, and cheating on point counts (Maheady, Harper, & Mallette, 1991).

 ACTIVITY 10.3

> Share ideas with another student for correcting some of the common complaints of teachers in using CWPT procedures.

Peabody Peer-Assisted Learning Strategies

In the Peabody Peer-Assisted Learning Strategies (PALS), also referred to as the Peabody ClassWide Peer Tutoring procedure, the reading strategies of summarization, main idea identification, and prediction are combined with peer interactions (Mathes, Fuchs, Fuchs, Henley, & Sanders, 1994). Teachers directly instruct the students in the key procedures of the tutoring process and in the strategies. Mathes et al. (1994) recommend that teachers teach each of the strategies separately for a week at a time. The teachers model the procedures and give students practice in them.

Once the students are trained in the strategies and the tutoring procedures, PALS typically occurs for three 35-minute periods each week for 15 weeks (Mathes et al., 1994; Fuchs, Fuchs, Mathes, & Simmons, 1996). Each strategy takes about 10 minutes, and the rest of the time is spent on taking out and putting materials away and for transition time between strategies. Readers of various levels work together and assume reciprocal roles. Teachers rank order their students and then split the class into high and low performers. The top-ranked student in the high performing group is then matched to the top-ranked student in the low performing group until all students from each group are paired (Mathes et al., 1994). Pairs may read from different texts.

Each pair is then assigned to one of two teams. Individuals earn points for their teams and then at the end of the week, the teacher's and each student's points are totaled, and the winning team is announced. Teachers may give points to students for following the procedures correctly and for exhibiting cooperative behaviors. The team receives applause from the other team. After four weeks, new peers and teams are assigned. In Table 10.1, we outline the specific format for peer teaching of the reading strategies.

There are also PALS procedures for math and group story mapping and writing. Table 10.2 presents a list of manuals for peer-tutoring procedures.

Implementation

Teachers must carefully plan peer-tutoring activities. The steps necessary for a successful peer-tutoring program follow whether you plan to use one-to-one tutoring or a classwide peer-tutoring format.

Selecting Objectives

Your first step in deciding to institute peer tutoring is to formulate the objectives of the peer-tutoring program. Usually, basic academic skills are taught directly, and positive social interaction is achieved indirectly. IEPs are a good source of objectives for peer tutoring.

Eiserman (1988) organized a peer-tutoring activity where elementary students with learning disabilities tutored general education students in sign language for the primary purpose of promoting improved attitudes among the students. Delquadri, Greenwood, Whorton, Carta, and Hall (1986) designated the following target behaviors as appropriate for peer-tutoring selection: "answering comprehension questions; practicing in reading workbooks; practicing spelling word lists; practicing math facts; and practicing vocabulary words, their meanings, and definitions" (p. 536). Allsop

Table 10.1   Peer Teaching of Reading Strategies

Partner Reading (Mathes et al., 1994)

   The instructional format for partner reading is:
      5 minutes—Best reader reads orally while worse reader tutors.
      5 minutes—Worse reader reads the same passage.
      1 or 2 minutes—Worse reader retells in sequence what is read.
      After the retell sequence, partners reward themselves 10 points if they feel they have worked hard and tried their
         best.

   The routine for correction of word recognition errors for each student is:
      Peer teacher says, "You missed this word. Can you figure it out?" Pauses 4 seconds (p. 45)
      If correct, student rereads sentence.
      If incorrect, peer teacher says, "That word is _____." (p. 46).
      Student rereads the word and then the sentence.
      Peer teacher rewards a point for each sentence read correctly, no matter the trials.

   The routine for the retell sequence is:
      Peer teacher says, "What did you learn first?" "What did you learn next?" (p. 46)

   If incorrect or the student can't remember, the peer teacher provides the information.

Paragraph Shrinking (Fuchs et al., 1996)

   The instructional format for paragraph shrinking is:
      5 minutes—Best reader orally reads one paragraph.
      Worse reader prompts tutee to recall main idea by reading cue cards:
         "Who or what was the paragraph mainly about? Tell the most important thing learned in the paragraph" (p. 10).
      Best reader identifies main idea with not more than 10 words.
      Worse reader awards 1 point for correct who or what, 1 point for main idea, and 1 point for shrinking the
         statement to 10 words.
      5 minutes—Worse reader reads next paragraph.
      Best reader prompts worse to recall main idea with the same questions.
      Best reader assigns points.

   The routine for correction for each student is:
      Incorrect answer, peer teacher says, "Try again."
      Still incorrect answer, peer teacher says, "Read the paragraph silently and try again."
      Still incorrect answer, peer teacher provides the answer.

Prediction Relay (Mathes et al., 1994)

   Prediction Relay is introduced after the students become better at summarizing and identifying the main idea.

   The instructional format for prediction relay is:
      5 minutes—Best reader makes a prediction about content, reads half page, confirms or disconfirms prediction,
         summarizes content in 10 words or less, makes a new prediction about next half page, and continues with
         routine until 5 minutes are up.
      Worse reader decides if answers are correct and assigns 1 point for each step, totaling 4 points.
      5 minutes—Roles reverse and same procedures are followed.

(1997) explored the possibility of the use of CWPT procedures with higher-order skills.

Selecting and Matching Students

If you are planning to assign reciprocal roles to students, you may use any of the selection and matching procedures that we have already discussed. If you are not planning for students to act as both tutors and tutees, choose tutors who have (a) demonstrated the initial acquisition of a skill but need more practice for mastery and application, and (b) are eager to participate and

Table 10.2 Sample Peer-Mediation Teacher's Manuals

ClassWide Peer Tutoring Manual
Educational Achievement Systems
319 Nickerson, Suite 112
Seattle, WA 98109

ClassWide Student Tutoring Teams Video and Manual
ClassWide Student Tutoring Teams
Department of Education
State University of New York
College of Fredonia
Fredonia, NY 14063

L. S. Fuchs, D. Fuchs, N. Phillips, & K. Karnes (1994)
Peer-Mediated Mathematics Instruction: A Manual
George Peabody College of Vanderbilt University
Nashville, TN 37203

D. Fuchs, P. G. Mathes, & L. S. Fuchs (1993)
Peabody ClassWide Peer Tutoring Reading Methods
Unpublished teacher's manual
(Available from Douglas Fuchs, Box 328,
George Peabody College, Vanderbilt University,
Nashville, TN 37203)

capable of learning appropriate procedures (Chiang, Thorpe, & Darch, 1980; Olson, 1982; Scruggs, Mastropieri, & Richter, 1985). Tutees should be selected from students who need to be taught the skill or information. Students with mild disabilities have benefited from peer tutoring, both as tutors and tutees. Gartner and Riessman (1993) suggest that students become tutors only after they have been tutored (the tutees).

Research provides no clear guidelines for the best matching procedures. Students with special needs have been matched to both same-age and younger general education students and students with disabilities with similar results (Eiserman, 1988). However, if you select different-age peers, you must make certain that the tutor is more competent than the tutee in the subject being taught: Nothing is as embarrassing to an older student as being corrected by a younger one. On the first day of class, Mr. Herman had his students list their strengths and interests to

 ACTIVITY 10.4

Choose one of the peer-mediated models and describe how you plan to use it.

assist him in the selection and matching of peer tutors (see Table 10.3).

Preparing Materials

Either the student or you may prepare the materials depending on the objective. If you target spelling words as the objective for peer tutoring, the tutor may just use the class text. If you select memorizing math facts, the tutor may write each fact on a 3-by-5-inch card. If the objective is studying for a test, you should prepare a study guide. For a shared reading objective, you may guide tutors in selecting a book for the session. Administration of a pretest and the selection of 10 missed items comprised the content for math tutoring sessions designed by

Table 10.3 Peer Tutor Application

Name _____ Grade Level _____
Date _____

I am good at:
_____ Listening to younger children read.
_____ Holding up flash cards for younger students.
_____ Reading to younger children.
_____ Correcting math errors.
_____ Drawing with younger children.
_____ Watching and talking about a filmstrip with younger children.
Other — _____
_____

I like:
_____ Talking about sports.
_____ Talking about movies.
_____ Talking about stories I have read.
_____ Working with numbers.
_____ Talking to students who have had different experiences than I have had.
Other — _____
_____
_____

Miller, Barbetta, and Heron (1994). Monitoring sheets may also be prepared by the tutors or by you. This step requires substantial time initially, but materials may be reused.

Determining Schedules and Selecting Sites

The popular length of a tutoring session is 30 minutes two or three times a week for five to seven weeks, with about 15 to 20 minutes for the actual student contact time (the rest of the time is spent organizing materials). Remember, in their ClassWide Peer Tutoring approach, Maheady, Sacca, and Harper (1987) schedule teacher-directed instruction for two days, peer tutoring of practice activities for two days, and a quiz on the fifth day.

The site should be a place where the tutors and tutees can work together undisturbed. If you use any of the reciprocal peer procedures, tutoring is scheduled as part of the class routine, so there is no problem with site selection; students may just be instructed to move their desks together. Two unsatisfactory areas for peer tutoring are outside the school building and in the hallways, where distractions tend to be excessive.

Planning the Presentation Format

You may decide on the presentation format or you may ask for student input. You may wish to select or adapt any of the models that we discussed previously (e.g., CWPT, PALS), where students assume reciprocal roles or you may adapt those models with only one student acting as the tutor. Remember, you should identify how the tutor retrieves and returns materials, presents the information, gives feedback, and monitors the progress of the tutee. You may even wish to script the procedures.

Yasutake, Bryan, and Dohrn (1996) report that attribution statements such as "You're getting smart because of your hard work" for correct responses and strategy statements such as "Try to sound out the word" for incorrect responses were of benefit to students with mild disabilities and those at risk for special education referral. Both tutors and tutees in third through eighth grade perceived themselves more positively in academic and affective performance than those students who did not receive the same type of feedback.

Training Tutors

Once you have decided on the presentation format, you must train your tutors to follow the format and to display appropriate teaching behaviors (Warger, 1990). These behaviors include waiting for the response instead of immediately telling the answer, avoiding sarcasm and criticism, and proceeding in a positive, friendly manner.

You should plan an orientation session in which you share the purpose, responsibilities, general guidelines, expected outcome, and information about the tutees with the tutors (Lazerson, Foster, Brow, & Hummel, 1988). For example, in the Reciprocal Peer Revision Strategy (MacArthur, Schwartz, & Graham, 1991), the teachers gave a general introduction to the purpose and importance of the strategy and related the strategy to the students' previous work on revisions. This is also a good time to teach the tutors how to set up and put away the tutoring materials (Schuler, Ogulthorpe, & Eiserman, 1987).

Following the orientation session, you should model the presentation format, guide the tutors in their imitation of the model, and point out the important behaviors. In a co-teaching situation, modeling is frequently presented with one teacher acting as the tutor and the other as the tutee.

In the Reciprocal Peer Revision Strategy (MacArthur, Schwartz, & Graham, 1991), students view and discuss a videotape of two students following the presentation format. In the Peabody ClassWide Peer Tutoring program (Mathes, Fuchs, Fuchs, Henley, & Sanders, 1994), teachers provide the tutors with prompt cards to assist them through the procedures. Checklists are also effective reminders of essential behaviors. Ms. James prepared the following list for her students: (a) I have all the materials, (b) I have examined the materials, (c) I plan to _____ when my student says something wrong, (d) I know when to say, "Good answer," and other nice things, (e) I will remember to smile, and (f) I will count to five to give my tutee a chance to answer after I ask a question. To prevent tutor burnout, you may wish to hold special luncheons or parties or give academic grades or credit for tutoring (Montague, Mecham, & McLaughlin, 1991).

Monitoring Progress

You should collect academic and social data to document the progress of both tutors and tutees. This data may be particularly helpful to answer any parent concerns about the tutoring process (Durrer & McLaughlin, 1995). If you are using a classwide peer-tutoring procedure, you have the individual quiz scores and the team points for accountability. If it is one-to-one tutoring, you may

wish to have the tutors chart the progress of the tutee. For example, the tutor may count and chart the number of words the student reads correctly each day or the number of addition facts the tutee answers correctly. Be sure to monitor and praise tutors for following the procedures.

Evaluating the Tutoring Session

Both tutors and tutees should evaluate the tutoring session. After each session, you should give tutees forms to mark whether they learned anything and how the session went. See Figure 10.3 for a sample elementary evaluation form.

Maher (1984) suggests support conferences for tutors to discuss group concerns and meetings with the teacher individually if necessary. Gartner and Riessman (1993) suggest an assigned time for both tutors and tutees to meet and reflect on their

Figure 10.3 Elementary Evaluation Form

Figure 10.4 Tutor Feedback Form

Tutor Form

Date: _____

Name: _____

My tutee learned: _____

_____

_____

He/She made _____ many _____ some _____ few mistakes

	Yes	No
He/She seemed to like the sessions.	____	____
I enjoyed the sessions.	____	____
I used praise.	____	____
I paused after I asked a question.	____	____

Next week I plan to: _____

_____

_____

tutoring experiences. In Figure 10.4, we present feedback forms for tutors to complete.

Informing Significant Others

You should be certain to notify parents of peer tutoring programs. Parents need to understand when their children come home and talk about working with other students. Tell them why, when, and how tutoring will be used. It is important to indicate that teacher-directed instruction is still occurring and to document that their children are continuing to learn.

 ACTIVITY 10.5

With a partner, design a peer-tutoring system for elementary, middle school, or secondary students with mild disabilities. Identify the objective, plan the presentation format, and describe how you are going to notify and inform parents.

 IMPORTANT POINTS

1. Peer tutoring may consist of one student acting as a tutor, or the person who transmits the information, and one student acting as the tutee, or the person who receives the information or students may assume reciprocal roles.
2. Reciprocal Peer Tutoring (Fantuzzo, King, & Heller, 1992), Reciprocal Peer Revision Strategy (MacArthur, Schwartz, & Graham, 1991), ClassWide Peer Tutoring (CWPT; Delquadri, Greenwood, Stretton, & Hall, 1983), and Peer-Assisted Learning Strategies (PALS; Mathes, Fuchs, Fuchs, Henley, & Sanders, 1994) are peer-tutoring models supported in the literature for their effectiveness for students with mild disabilities and students at risk (Utley, Mortsweet, & Greenwood, 1997).
3. Reciprocal Peer Tutoring involves students paired randomly in same-age dyads and self-selection of rewards and performance goals.

4. In the Reciprocal Peer Editing Strategy, instruction and peer interaction are combined to teach written revision skills.

5. The core components of CWPT include direct teacher presentation of new material to be learned, teacher monitoring of the tutoring process, whole-class instructional activity, explicit presentation formats for peers to follow, active student responding, reciprocal roles in each session, teams competing for the highest team point total, contingent point earning, systematic error correction strategies, public posting of student performance, and social awards for the winning team (Greenwood & Delquadri, 1995; Greenwood, 1996).

6. In PALS, students are taught strategies in reading, math, and story mapping combined with peer interactions.

7. The steps for implementing peer-tutoring procedures consist of (a) selecting objectives, (b) selecting and matching students, (c) preparing materials, (d) determining schedules and selecting sites, (e) planning the presentation format, (f) training tutors, (g) monitoring progress, (h) evaluating the tutoring session, and (i) informing significant others.

8. Tutors must be taught to follow a lesson presentation format, wait for a response, and avoid sarcasm and criticism.

COOPERATIVE LEARNING

Like peer tutoring, cooperative learning relies on peers working together to solve problems or share information. But cooperative learning groups consist of teams of three or four students working together to master academic tasks or content, rather than just two students as in peer tutoring. The students are usually of varying ability levels, races, and ethnic groups. Slavin and his colleagues at the Center for Research on Elementary and Middle Schools at Johns Hopkins University and Johnson and Johnson at the University of Minnesota have studied cooperative learning extensively.

The effectiveness of cooperative learning with students with disabilities is equivocal in the research literature (Tateyama-Sniezek, 1990). Brandt and Ellsworth (1996) found cooperative learning effective in increasing academic performance and attendance and in decreasing discipline problems of adolescents with learning disabilities from diverse cultures. However, O'Connor and Jenkins (1996) judged that cooperative practices were only effective for 40 to 44% of third- through sixth-grade students with learning disabilities. They found that students with learning disabilities required more help and contributed less to the group activities than those students without disabilities.

The reasons for the discrepant findings may lie in the differences in student populations and the institution of the cooperative procedures. It appears that students with behavior disorders, those with visual disabilities, and those with mental disabilities participate less in the group process (Cohen, 1994; Pomplun, 1996). The instructional processes of individual accountability and group rewards are required for positive effects (Stevens & Slavin, 1991). Teacher behaviors that promote effective cooperative learning procedures include (Johnson & Johnson, 1996; O'Connor & Jenkins, 1996; Slavin, 1984, 1985, 1988a, 1988b):

1. Public identification of students who demonstrate cooperative behaviors
2. Validation of low-status students' contributions to the group process
3. Insistence that all students participate
4. Direct instruction of cooperative behaviors
5. Repeated review and reinforcement of group cooperation
6. Monitoring of cooperative behaviors
7. Explicit explanation of expectations for group process and individual products

Two common special education practices that seem to defeat the effectiveness of cooperative learning are differential assignments and teacher assistance. O'Connor and Jenkins (1996) found that students with disabilities participated more in cooperative learning groups when their assignments matched those of their peers and that teachers who provided more assistance to students with disabilities or joined the cooperative learning group interfered with peers working together. Thus, the difference in the research findings may be due to the nature of the student population and to the instructional practices.

Rationale

Cooperative learning is proposed as a way to ensure successful inclusion of students with special needs (Johnson & Johnson, 1996; Slavin, 1988a) based on the premise that students who work together tend to come to like each other (Johnson & Johnson, 1980). A long tradition of research in social psychology "has shown that people working for a cooperative goal come to encourage one another to do their best, to help one another do well, and to like and respect one another" (Slavin, 1988b, p. 8). Cooperative learning also provides more opportunities for students of all abilities to participate and engage in class activities.

Cooperative learning also relies on peer pressure, a powerful reinforcer for adolescents in particular (Alberto & Troutman, 1999). Urging other students to complete a task for the good of the group frequently motivates reluctant adolescents.

Description

There are essentially four models of cooperative learning: (1) the jigsaw approach, (2) the group project, (3) the competitive team approach, and (4) Team-Accelerated Instruction, formerly titled Team-Assisted Individualization. Each has a different purpose and format.

The Jigsaw Approach

In the jigsaw format (Aronson, 1978), each member of the jigsaw group becomes an expert in some aspect of the task or material and teaches the others what he or she knows. For example, in preparing a report or answering a worksheet about the life of Martin Luther King, Jr., each student in the group may select to study one aspect of Reverend King's life. Once each student has mastered the specific content, he or she shares the information with the rest of the group. Then the group as a whole combines the individual information for the final project, whether it is a report or a worksheet about King's life.

The idiom of jigsaw is appropriate for this technique, for each student has a puzzle piece (e.g., Hector has information concerning Reverend King's childhood and Lashonda has information concerning King's educational background) that must be joined together with the puzzle pieces of the other students before it is possible to complete the entire puzzle (a report on the life of Martin Luther King, Jr.). But student absenteeism can be a problem in the jigsaw approach. If Hector is absent, he cannot contribute the information concerning Reverend King's childhood. Slavin (1988b) suggests assigning two students from each group to the same subtopic (Hector and Kendra would both be assigned to gather information concerning Reverend King's childhood) or selecting an activity that may be completed during one class period if absenteeism is a problem.

A variation of the jigsaw technique is a "counterpart" group (Aronson, 1978). In this adaptation, all students working on a particular subtopic meet together. After sharing information on this subtopic, they rejoin their original group members and complete the report.

Group Projects

In this format, students pool their knowledge and skills to create a project or complete an assignment. These groups are informally structured and usually are organized for a specific task. Cohen (1994) suggests that open-ended tasks with nonroutine solutions may increase effectiveness of students with mild disabilities. In using the cooperative learning model to teach the concept of area, Wells (1981) suggests that complex tasks, such as measuring areas of the floor and other objects in the classroom, produce more cooperation than simple ones, such as completing a worksheet of problems dealing with the calculation of area.

Competitive Teams

In the competitive teams approach, competition among different groups is emphasized. Slavin and his colleagues at Johns Hopkins University have created two different cooperative learning techniques that emphasize team competition. These two structured formats include Student Teams-Achievement Divisions (STAD) and Teams-Games-Tournaments (TGT).

Student Teams-Achievement Divisions (STAD). In Student Teams-Achievement Divisions, the students are divided into learning teams of three to five members. The teacher introduces new material in a lecture or discussion, usually on Mondays and Tuesdays. The team members study worksheets concerning the material on Wednesdays and Thursdays. Answer sheets are provided to the team, because the idea is to learn the concepts, not to simply complete the worksheets. Students may study in pairs, quiz each other, or choose whatever techniques they want to ensure that everyone on the team knows and understands the material.

On Fridays, the students, individually, take 30-item quizzes to demonstrate the knowledge that they gained from the class presentations and team practice. Then the individual scores are added for a total team score. Slavin (1988b) suggests giving points based on the "amount the student's quiz score exceeds his or her past quiz average" (p. 26). The past average quiz score is called the base score. For example, if Keisha's base score was 20, then she has the possibility of contributing 10 points if she scores 100% on the 30-item quiz. Since there is the

possibility of a ceiling effect on improvement scores (i.e., a student who scores a base score of 30 can never show an improvement), Slavin (1988b) suggests setting base scores 5 points below the student's average past quiz scores. You may also want to administer a pretest on Monday before teaching the concept and then administer the same quiz as a posttest on Friday to arrive at improvement scores. You may adjust the base scores at any time.

Teams-Games-Tournaments (TGT). An adaptation of the STAD is TGT (Teams-Games-Tournaments) (Devries & Slavin, 1978). The procedures are the same as in STAD, except the students participate in a tournament at the end of the week instead of taking a quiz. The teacher still presents the concepts and students still study in teams to master the information. However, students earn points for their teams by participating in the weekly tournament. A student from each team is assigned to a separate table to compete against other students of similar skill levels. To play the game, the students draw cards; the person who draws the card with the highest number begins the game. Play proceeds in a clockwise direction. The rules appear in Figure 10.5.

Team-Accelerated Instruction (TAI). Team-Accelerated Instruction combines individualized instruction and cooperative learning (Slavin, Leavey, & Madden, 1984; Slavin, 1988a, 1988b; Slavin, Stevens, & Madden, 1988). Unlike other cooperative learning techniques, in which all group members are working on the same objective, project, or set of materials, students in TAI are first tested to determine their skill levels and then assigned to materials that pertain to these levels only. For example, in math, there may be one student working on addition, one working on fractions, one on decimals, and one on word problems in the same group (Slavin, 1984). The students bring individual math units to the group. The group

Figure 10.5 Teams-Games-Tournaments Rules

NOTE. From *Student Team Learning: An Overview and Practical Guide* (2n d ed.) (p. 34) by R. E. Slavin, 1988, Washington, DC: National Education Association. Reprinted by permission.

Game Rules (TGT)

Reader

1. Picks a numbered card and finds the corresponding question on the game sheet.
2. Reads the question out loud.
3. Tries to answer.

1st Challenger

Challenges if he or she wants to (and gives a different answer), or passes.

2nd Challenger

Challenges if 1st challenger passes, if he or she wants to. When all have challenged or passed, 2nd challenger checks the answer sheet. Whoever was right keeps the card. If the *reader* was wrong, there is no penalty, but if either challenger was wrong, he or she must put a previously won card, if any, back in the deck.

members help each other and check each other's work. Team members earn points for their teams by completing the math unit and for making no more than one error. Since special materials are required, we recommend that you contact the Project Director at The Johns Hopkins University Team Learning Project, Center for Social Organization of Schools, Johns Hopkins University, 3505 North Charles Street, Baltimore, MD 21218 for more information concerning the materials and procedures.

Building on the guidelines of TAI, O'Melia and Rosenberg (1994) designed a Cooperative Homework Teams (CHT) model for secondary students with learning disabilities. The model uses peer teams to grade and make corrections on individual homework assignments. At the end of each math period, the teacher gives the students eight computation and two story problems. The next day, after opening activities, the CHT groups meet for 10 minutes. Each day, a different student assumes the role of the checker. The checker in each group checks the other students' homework assignments using teacher-made answer sheets, then reports the grades to the teacher and returns the papers to the team members for review and corrections. Students help each other correct the errors before they return the papers to the teacher.

The teacher awards daily points based on the completion of the assignment and the percentage of correct answers. The teacher then converts the mean individual scores to mean team scores and presents certificates to those teams who exceed a certain criterion. With this model in effect, seventh- and eighth-grade students with mild disabilities completed more homework assignments and increased their accuracy scores. We present a summary of the co-operative models and their components in Table 10.4.

 ACTIVITY 10.6

Part 1

Describe an appropriate activity for use with the jigsaw approach to cooperative learning for elementary students with special needs. Describe one for secondary students.

Part 2

With a peer, discuss the role you might play in the STAD procedure in a co-teaching situation.

Implementation

You should follow certain steps when implementing cooperative learning procedures. These steps apply no matter what the model is.

Specifying Objectives

Specify both academic and collaborative objectives. You may emphasize collaborative objectives (such as all students need to know how to do the work and students need to help each other learn). Slavin (1988a) insists that the group objective must be important to the group members and suggests that awarding certificates, free time, or bonus points for appropriate group participation may motivate each group member to cooperate.

Table 10.4 Comparison of Cooperative Models

Model	Teacher's Role	Student's Role	Outcome	Grade Level/ Subject Area
Jigsaw	Facilitator	Serves as expert.	Product or assignment completed.	Grades 3–12 in social studies, literature, science. Any material with no one right answer.
Group Project	Facilitator	Member of group.	Product or assignment completed.	Grades 1–12 in any subject.
Teams				
• STAD	Instructs 2 days.	Members of team study information together.	Quiz passed. Earn points for team.	Grades 2–12 in mathematics, language arts, science, graph reading, geography. Any material with one right answer.
• TGT	Instructs 2 days.	Members of team study information together.	Weekly game. Earn points for team.	Grades 2–12 in mathematics, language arts, science, graph reading, geography. Any material with one right answer.
• TAI	Varies—direct teaching, monitoring.	Complete individual worksheets and help others complete work.	Complete individual tasks. Earn points for team.	Grades 2–12 in mathematics, homework.

NOTE. Data in last column from *Student Team Learning: An Overview and Practical Guide* (2nd ed.) (p. 19) by R. E. Slavin, 1988, Washington, D.C.: National Education Association. Reprinted by permission.

Selecting the Model

Decide which of the previously discussed models to select. In addition to the following considerations, Table 10.4 should help in your decision. Remember, TAI follows explicit procedures and requires the purchase of special materials, unless you use the math homework procedures of O'Melia and Rosenberg (1994). Because TGT is very competitive, it may not be appropriate for students who cannot handle losing in a game format or have problems relating to others. Both STAD and TGT are teacher-directed. Students work with each other completing worksheets or on independent practice activities from information already presented by the teacher.

The jigsaw technique and the group project models may not be as motivating, because team points are not earned. Safeguards must be designed to ensure participation by all students, so that the project is not completed by only one or two students instead of the group.

Assigning Students to Groups

It is recommended that you assign students of various ethnic backgrounds and ability levels to each group (Johnson & Johnson, 1986; Slavin, 1988a). In a co-teaching situation, make certain that students with special needs are evenly distributed among the different groups. O'Connor and Jenkins (1996) emphasize that this step is extremely important, as students with disabilities need peers who are both willing and compassionate. Much of the research that shows positive effects for students with special needs has combined two students who are performing the skill or task at a low level and two who are performing the skill at a higher level in each group (Slavin, 1984; Slavin, Stevens, & Madden, 1988). The recommended size of a group is three to five members (Johnson & Johnson, 1986). To ensure the cohesiveness of the team, Slavin (1988b) stresses that you should make clear to the students that "putdowns, making fun of teammates, or refusing to help them are ineffective ways for teams to be successful and not acceptable kinds of behavior" (p. 52).

Deciding Team Schedules

As with anything new, you should first try the cooperative learning approach with one class or in one area. Students may stay on one team from 4 to 10 weeks. However, if teams do not work out, reassign the students after 3 or 4 weeks (Slavin, 1988b). The idea is to give every student an opportunity to work with all students in the classroom.

Arranging the Room and Materials. Group members should be close together and groups should be far apart (Schniedewind & Salend, 1987). Johnson and Johnson (1986) recommend a circle arrangement to accommodate student communication. Such an arrangement allows students to share and discuss materials and to maintain eye contact. The physical arrangement must allow clear access for the teacher. Each group also needs an area to store materials or the group project. One teacher bought square laundry baskets that each group decorated and used for the storage of their materials. The decorations were removable to accommodate the frequent changes in group membership.

Guaranteeing Individual Accountability and Participation

It is important to make certain each member is participating in the group and that the project or activity is not being completed by only one or two students. This is not a problem with STAD or TGT, because individual accountability is ensured by the weekly quiz or tournament, nor is it a problem with TAI, because students are assigned different materials to complete. However, assign student roles to ensure participation of all members when using the jigsaw and group project techniques.

Johnson and Johnson (1986) recommend assigning the roles of checker, accuracy coach, summarizer, elaboration seeker, and reporter, so that each group member has a specific responsibility. The checker makes certain that all students can understand the information. The accuracy coach corrects any mistakes in another member's explanation or summary. The summarizer restates major conclusions or answers of the group. The elaboration seeker asks members to relate material they previously learned. The reporter writes down the information or completes the worksheet. Assigning a specific role to students is particularly important for cooperative learning activities in an inclusive setting as, often, students with disabilities are left out if no particular role is assigned to them.

Another way to ensure individual accountability and participation is to select only one student's product to represent the group effort (Johnson & Johnson, 1986). Of course, this selection is kept secret until the end of the project. Salend and Allen (1985) ensure participation of all students by limiting the number of times each student may talk. Before the group activity, each member is given a certain number of tokens. Each time a student addresses the group, he or she must surrender a token. Once all of the tokens are used, the student may no longer address the group. A final technique for ensuring group participation is to limit the amount of material given to the group (Slavin, 1988a). If only one worksheet is given to the group, then four members cannot complete the worksheet individually. A "think, pair, share" routine also ensures individual participation. In this routine, two students think for a minute, discuss the topic, and then share with the whole group.

Teaching and Role-Playing Cooperative Behaviors

For students with mild disabilities, role-playing such cooperative behaviors as "Use a quiet voice," "Stay with your group," and "Say one nice thing to everyone in your group" (Putnam, Rynders, Johnson, & Johnson, 1989) is necessary, because many of these students have an inability to relate to others in socially appropriate ways. You should model cooperative behavior first. Then have students role-play appropriate and inappropriate ways to show cooperation and evaluate whether the demonstrated behavior is an example of cooperative or uncooperative behavior. Continue to review appropriate cooperative behaviors whenever you plan to form cooperative groups.

You may also use games to teach cooperative behaviors. Cooperative games require players to cooperate in order to overcome some obstacle. For example, Cartledge and Cochran (1993) created a circular game board with the goal that everyone must complete the entire circle before time ran out. Thus, students helped each other complete the game as they raced against time. Students were reinforced for their cooperative interactions instead of win-lose behaviors. Sapon-Shevin (1986) described a nonelimination musical chairs game. The object was to keep everyone in the game as the chairs were eliminated. The children had to find ways to make room for more and more children. The verbal behavior during the game was of a cooperative nature: "Come sit on/with me," or "Make room for Johnny" (p. 284).

For older students, a checklist of cooperative behaviors for students to self-monitor is often useful. Examples may include (a) I listened to others' opinions, (b) I complimented a person's idea in the group, (c) I spoke in a pleasant voice, (d) I didn't get angry if my ideas weren't used, and (e) I made constructive comments when I thought another student's idea was outrageous or not appropriate.

Monitoring Cooperative Behaviors

Once you have taught the concept or given directions for the required activity or project and modeled cooperative behavior, your role becomes that of a monitor. You monitor each member's cooperative behavior, keep the group on task, and intervene when necessary to provide task assistance. For young students, praise the sharing or helping behaviors publicly (Putnam, Rynders, Johnson, & Johnson, 1989) with such comments as "Sunny shared her article with Juan. She was being very cooperative." Your comments should also include validation statements, such as "Matt has the correct idea. He is on target," directed to students with disabilities who are often perceived as incompetent by peers.

One teacher instituted a system for students to self-monitor everyone's participation in the cooperative learning group. On a grid of names of team members and question numbers, one student placed yellow Post-its next to a student's name when he or she participated. Strategy cards with a list of questions can remind students to monitor participation and understanding: Am I listening to group members? Do I understand the directions and goal? If not, ask others in the group; if not, ask teacher? Am I helping group members? (Goor, Schwenn, Elridge, Mallein, & Stauffer, 1996). Students using the cards made more on-task comments and were better able to explain the main idea of the group discussion.

Evaluating Both the Product and Process
You should evaluate both the product and process of the group. If you are using STAD, TAI, or TGT procedures, you already have evaluated the product from quiz grades, individual tasks, or points earned during a tournament. In the jigsaw or group project approaches, you may elect to grade the group project or the individual student's project selected to represent the group work. Some teachers, when they know what individual members have contributed, grade the students' individual contributions in addition to assigning a group grade. Another strategy is to average the group grade with the individual student's grade. For example, if Joe scored 10 points on his individual project and his group scored 20 points, his final score would be 15.

According to Slavin (1988a), the group grade should be based on an average of the performances of all of the students. Johnson and Johnson (1986) suggest using different criteria to evaluate the project of a student with special needs, giving bonus points to the groups that have members with special needs. Some teachers also give grades for the group process. Remember, Slavin (1988b) recommends giving points to the students for appropriate participation. Even if you don't grade the process, you and the students should evaluate how the group functioned. See Table 10.5 for a sample evaluation form. In fact, you may want to have students role-play problem areas and possible solutions for evaluation of the process.

Recognizing the Group Effort
In STAD and TGT, Slavin (1988b) recommends the use of newsletters or bulletin boards to recognize team accomplishments. If you select the group project model, invite your principal, secretary, or colleagues to judge the projects. Then display the projects with pictures of the group members. In Table 10.6, we present a checklist of decisions you need to make before you use cooperative learning techniques. Remember, teachers make instructional decisions and monitor their effectiveness.

 ACTIVITY 10.7

With a group of three other students, solve the problems Mr. Hernandez encountered when working with cooperative groups. First identify the problem, then describe a solution.
1. Sam is frequently absent during the jigsaw procedure.
2. Manu contributes no points to the team, as he always scores 20 out of 20 on his papers.
3. Rupert monopolizes the group discussion.
4. Only two of the four members of the Tiger Team are completing the projects.

Table 10.5 Student Evaluation of Cooperative Session

What was learned in the group today? _____
_____
_____

Describe an example of cooperative behavior (a helpful action).
• You did _____
_____

• Others did _____
_____

Describe an example of uncooperative behavior (not a helpful action).
• You did _____
_____

• Others did _____
_____

Examine the example of uncooperative behaviors and change them to cooperative behaviors.
_____
_____

The completion of this sheet is worth 10 points toward your grade.

Table 10.6 Teacher Checklist

1. Specify group objective.
   Academic:
   _____
   _____
   _____

   Motivated to attain by:
   ___ a. Points
   ___ b. Certificates
   ___ c. Free time
   ___ d. Praise
   ___ e. Homework pass
   ___ f. Other
2. Specify other group objective.
   Collaborative:
   _____
   _____

   Motivated to attain by:
   ___ a. Points
   ___ b. Certificates
   ___ c. Free time
   ___ d. Praise
   ___ e. Homework pass
   ___ f. Other
3. Select model.
   ___ a. Jigsaw
   ___ b. Group project
   ___ c. STAD
   ___ d. TGT
   ___ e. TAI
4. Assign students.
   ___ a. Even number of girls/boys
   ___ b. Two high-level/two low-level

   ___ c. Special students divided
   ___ d. Students of various cultures/interests divided
   ___ e. Random
5. Decide team schedule.
   Time Frame:
   ___ a. No. of weeks
   ___ b. No. of days
6. Arrange room materials.
   ___ a. Clear access for teacher
   ___ b. Storage for materials
7. Guarantee individual accountability.
   ___ a. Grade individual quizzes or projects
   ___ b. Assign roles
   ___ c. Select one student's project
   ___ d. Tokens
   ___ e. Other
8. Have students evaluate their own cooperative
   behaviors.
   ___ a. Complete student evaluation form
   ___ b. Answer questions
9. Evaluate the students' work.
   The product: The process:
   ___ a. Points   ___ a. Points
   ___ b. Grades   ___ b. Grades
   ___ c. Other   ___ c. Other
10. Recognize the group effort.
    ___ a. Bulletin board
    ___ b. Newsletter
    ___ c. Other

◇ IMPORTANT POINTS

1. Cooperative learning groups consist of teams of three or four students who work together to master academic tasks or content.
2. The effectiveness of cooperative learning with students with disabilities is equivocal in the research literature (Tateyama-Sniczek, 1990).
3. There are four models of cooperative learning: (1) the jigsaw approach, (2) the group project, (3) the competitive team approach, and (4) Team-Accelerated Instruction.
4. In the jigsaw approach, each student has a piece of the puzzle, which must be combined with all the other students' pieces to produce a group report or project.
5. In the group project, students pool their knowledge and skills to create a project or complete an assignment, such as a chart on objects that sink or float.
6. In Student Teams-Achievement Divisions (STAD), students are divided into learning teams of three to five members who work together to master content presented by the teacher and earn points for the team based on weekly quiz scores.
7. In the Teams-Games-Tournaments (TGT) approach, students work together to learn the information and earn points for their team by answering questions correctly during a weekly tournament.
8. In the TAI approach, students help each other work on individual objectives and sets of materials, earning points for the team by completing materials that pertain to their objectives only.
9. To implement cooperative learning, the following steps are recommended: (a) specify objectives, (b) select the model, (c) assign students to groups, (d) decide team schedules, (e) plan room and material arrangements, (f) guarantee individual accountability and participation, (g) role-play cooperative behaviors, (h) monitor cooperative behaviors, (i) evaluate both the product and the process, and (j) recognize the group effort.

◆ DISCUSSION QUESTIONS

1. With the increased emphasis on academic standards, defend the incorporation of social skills objectives in your curriculum.
2. When Lashona went home and told her mother that she was teaching Susanna how to add during math class, her mother immediately called you to complain. She commented that you are the teacher and her child is not. How would you respond to this criticism of peer tutoring?
3. Compare and contrast the peer-tutoring models of Reciprocal Peer Tutoring, Reciprocal Peer Revision Strategy, ClassWide Peer Tutoring, and Peer-Assisted Learning Strategies.

PART

3

FACTORS
AFFECTING
INSTRUCTION

11

TECHNOLOGY FOR TEACHING AND LEARNING

By Dianne Mathews, Eileen Pracek, and Judy Olson

◆ KEY TOPICS

Technology as a Support for the Curriculum
Traditional Applications
Exploratory Applications
Tool Applications
Communication Applications

Technology as a Tool for Students
Organization
The Writing Process
Productivity Tools
Reference Material Tools
Cognitive Assistance Tools

Software Selection

Internet
General Information
Lesson Presentations
Professional Development
Safeguards

Technology as a Tool for Teachers
Planning
IEP Generation
Record Keeping and Classroom Management
Presentation Tools
Preparation of Classroom Materials
Authoring

Assistive Technology
Assistive Technology Devices
Assistive Technology Services
Modifications

Augmentative and Alternative Communication

Emerging Technologies
Artificial Intelligence
Virtual Reality

The use of technology is widespread in classrooms at all levels—as a tool for teachers to develop, monitor, and provide instruction and as a tool for students to access and engage in learning. Today technologies play a critical role in the education of all students, including students with disabilities. Benefits of technology use for students with disabilities include improvement of both academic and behavioral performance, sustained task performance, and empowerment (Lewis, 1993). Unmotivated students suddenly become interested in the task of writing a friendly letter when given the option of using a word processing program and adding graphics. Students whose spelling problems interfered with their writing skills are suddenly accomplishing an assignment that they have never done before: turning in papers free of spelling errors.

Legislation such as PL 99–457 and PL 100–407 were instrumental in promoting the use of technology tools for children and adolescents with disabilities. PL 99–457, Part G of the Education for All Handicapped Children Act of 1986, authorized the Technology, Educational Media, and Materials Program for Individuals with Disabilities to research and develop technology tools for students with disabilities (Hauser & Malouf, 1996). PL 100–407, The Technology-Related Assistance for Individuals with Disabilities Act of 1988 (Tech Act) was designed to enhance the availability and quality of assistive technology (AT) devices and services to all individuals and their families throughout the United States (Behrmann, 1995).

The purpose of this chapter is to focus on technology as a tool for students and teachers. We first look at technology tools as powerful enablers that help students access curriculum, engage in learning, meet required outcomes, and transition to the workplace. We next discuss technology tools as an integral part of the curriculum to support effective instructional interventions. Finally, we describe assistive technology tools that make a positive impact on the lives of children and adolescents.

We include computers, videodiscs, videocassettes, and the Internet plus assistive technology devices in our discussion of technology applications. Roblyer (1989) suggests that teachers use technology in the curriculum when the content or skills: (a) are difficult for students to understand, (b) present hurdles such as too much calculation or handwriting that interfere with or are irrelevant to the main objective of the lesson, (c) require extensive homework, and (d) need more interesting ma-

terials when the present materials are tedious or uninteresting.

A caveat in writing any chapter on technology is the impossibility of presenting current information, as technology is always changing. Two months later, that powerful computer is no longer so powerful, as another computer is on the market with more RAM (random access memory) and faster processor speeds (megahertz). The Web site that last month provided you with valuable lesson plans and information has disappeared. Please remember this caveat as you read the chapter and continue to stay current by reading professional journals, participating in professional organizations, visiting new Web sites, and taking technology classes.

TECHNOLOGY AS A SUPPORT FOR THE CURRICULUM

In the past we generally categorized programs into computer-assisted instruction and computer-managed instruction. Computer-assisted instruction provided computer-based lessons for students, and computer-managed instruction used computer systems to manage information about the learning process.

In an adaptation of Means' (1997) classification scheme for technologies, we suggest the broad categories of traditional, exploratory, tool, and communication applications. Although these categories are not mutually exclusive, they highlight the differences in instructional applications.

Traditional Applications

Tutorial, drill and practice, simulation, and problem solving are examples of traditional applications of software. This use of software represents the traditional view of learning where information is transmitted to the student. In our experience, it has been the one that con-

tinues to be most frequently used with students with disabilities.

Tutorial Programs

Tutorials are designed to teach new concepts and skills. They may be simple to very complex in design. They may be linear, with all students completing the same program, although the pace may be different for each student. More complex programs may offer multiple branching opportunities, with different responses taking students to different parts of the program for review, remediation, or advanced information. Good interactive tutorials can provide students with disabilities the kind of individual instruction that matches learner needs to a specific concept or skill.

Drill and Practice Programs

Drill and practice programs give students opportunities to practice skills and concepts. Good drill and practice programs offer corrections, hints for improvement, and even simple reteaching. They provide immediate feedback and do not allow students to make the same mistakes over and over again. When well designed and used as an integral part of the curriculum, drill and practice programs can help students with disabilities gain fluency in required skills. When poorly designed and used without instructional planning, drill and practice programs can be an inappropriate use of a powerful computer and a student's academic time.

Simulation Programs

Simulation programs offer students opportunities to see the consequence of their choices. These programs model reality and allow students to use their skills to make decisions and solve problems in a safe learning environment. Well-designed simulation programs provide some of the authentic experiences students need to succeed outside school (e.g., vocational, education, and transition). They may provide opportunities for instruction in settings that may not generally be available in schools.

Problem-Solving Programs

Problem-solving programs generally give students practice in identifying a problem, finding alternative solutions, selecting appropriate strategies, and evaluating results of the decisions made. Students may need to collect information, take notes, discover patterns, make generalizations, chart data, apply strategies, use inductive or deductive reasoning, or create a product. Some of these programs encourage students to work together in pairs or teams. Problem-solving software can offer students with disabilities the opportunity to develop and apply the higher-order thinking skills that are required for success in school and in the world of work. Although it is critical that students have the prerequisite skills for using the program, teachers need to remember that students with disabilities may be capable of solving more complex problems than their mastery of basic skills indicates.

Exploratory Applications

This category represents software that allows the student to navigate through a program and select information for learning. Examples are electronic encyclopedias, atlases, and multimedia databases of animals, plants, people, places, and things. Today, the ability to access and manage information is a required skill for success in school and in the world of work.

Tool Applications

These programs include the familiar applications like the word processor, database, and spreadsheet. Here, the technology facilitates the performance of tasks like writing, organizing, and presenting information. All students and teachers need tools. Students with disabilities may need special tools or need to use common tools in a special way. Technology tools provide access to the curriculum, offer alternative experiences for learning, allow students to demonstrate performance, and provide alternative options for assessment.

Communication Applications

This category refers to the technologies that provide opportunities for students to send and receive information from anywhere in the world. It includes interactive distance learning and electronic field trips. As more schools are connected to the Internet, more students with disabilities are getting the opportunity to participate in the technologies that can minimize differences.

 ACTIVITY 11.1

Describe when you might use a tutorial program with students and when you might use an exploratory application with students. Share your ideas with a partner.
(Answers for this and other activities are found in the Instructor's Manual.)

TECHNOLOGY AS A TOOL FOR STUDENTS

We need to give students experiences in selecting appropriate technology tools and in applying those tools to support the performance of complex, authentic tasks that will prepare them for a technology-laden world. Authentic uses of technology provide students with experiences that include features such as (a) supporting the use of technology for tasks that are similar to tasks performed by workers in nonschool settings, (b) integrating technology into activities that are a core part of the classroom curriculum, and (c) treating technology as a tool to accomplish a complex task.

You may use technology to assist students with mild disabilities in organization, the writing process, productivity, accessibility to reference materials, and cognitive assistance (Lahm & Morrisette, 1994). In each of these areas there is a wide range of technology available, from low-tech tools to more sophisticated tools that may require the use of a computer.

Organization

Your students may benefit from low-tech electronic organizers that are commonly available in office supply and major discount stores. These small, portable planners, sometimes referred to as personal digital assistants (PDAs), can help compensate for poor organizational skills, illegible handwriting, and memory deficits. Students can use a variety of inexpensive PDAs to keep track of homework assignments or due dates for projects, write to-do lists, store short notes or spelling words, consult a calendar, or set an alarm as a cue to perform some task such as stopping to check for understanding.

High-tech technology tools enable your students to organize and communicate their thoughts with story webs, character charts, tree diagrams, time lines, and other graphic organizers (see Chapters 2, 7, and 9 for other examples). Two examples of high-tech organization tools are the software programs of Inspiration (Inspiration) and TimeLiner (Tom Snyder Productions). Inspiration allows students to create a picture of ideas or concepts in a diagram (see Figure 11.1). Using TimeLiner, students can print out a visual display of critical dates on a time line. One of our student teachers assigned students to organize their personal histories or life maps using TimeLiner and then to relate their own time lines to events in American history.

The Writing Process

Videocassettes, computers, videodiscs, and the Internet are invaluable tools to assist students with disabilities in the steps of the writing process: prewriting, writing, editing and revising, and publishing. In the **prewriting** stage, instead of reading resource books or magazines, students may collect information by clicking on to a Web site, pausing a videodisc, viewing a video, or inserting a CD-ROM. Salend (1995) suggests the use of videotaping on field trips or community-referenced instruction trips to allow students to discuss and relate their field trip experiences to class content. We suggest that videotaping may also be used to assist students in finding topics during the prewriting stage.

In the **writing** stage, instead of paper and pencil, students may use word processing, word predictions, and abbreviation expansion programs. Even young children can begin to use word processors such as ClarisWorks for Kids (Claris Corporation) and Kid Works 2 (Davidson & Associates). Word prediction and abbreviation expansion help students with disabilities compose text and overcome problems with word recall, spelling, and keyboarding.

For example, in word prediction, students enter the beginning letters of a desired word. The program produces a list of predicted words that begin with that letter. For example, if the student enters "th," a predicted list might look like:

1. them	4. think
2. then	5. thing
3. their	6. this

Figure 11.1 Sample Graphic Organizers from Inspiration Software

NOTE. From Inspiration Software, 7412 SW Beaverton, Hillsdale Hwy., Suite 102, Portland, OR 97225. Reprinted by permission.

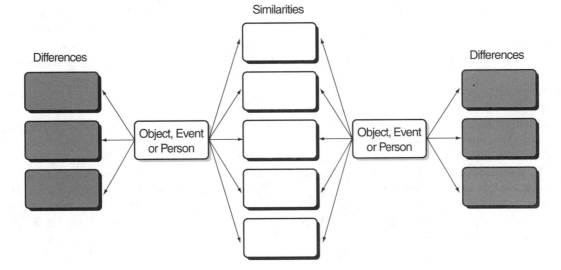

When students see or hear the word that they want from the list, they enter the corresponding number, and the word is added to their text. If the word is not on the list, students keep typing the next letter until the word appears.

In programs with abbreviation expansion, a long word or phrase can be coded using a few consonants. When the word or phrase is needed, students type the code, and the full word or phrase is entered into the text. For example, if Jim is writing a story about Tyran-nosaurus Rex and doesn't want to type out the word each time, he can type in a code such as TYR, and the full name (Tyrannosaurus Rex) will appear in the body of the text. Co:Writer (Don Johnston, Inc.), TypeIt4Me by Riccardo Ettore (Shareware), E Z Keys (Words +, Inc.), and Telepathic II (Madenta Communication, Inc.) are word predictors that allow for abbreviation expansion. These word prediction programs can be used in conjunction with any word processors. Many word processors include macros that can be used for abbreviation expansion. For example, in Microsoft Word, Autotext allows for coding and expansion of words.

Students who are struggling with reading or writing may use "talking" word processors during the writing stage. Such programs as Write: Out Loud (Don Johnston, Inc.) and Intellitalk (IntelliTools) help students make critical connections among saying, writing, and reading words. Students of all ages can enter their own words into the program, hear the computer speak them, and print them out to be read.

A technology solution that may help some students overcome difficulties related to the physical process of writing is the portable keyboard. It is a low-cost and lightweight alternative to a computer. Several models are available, including the AlphaSmart, DreamWriter, Laser PC5, and the QuickPad. The student turns the keyboard on, does some writing, and turns it off. The system saves several files, which allows for students to share the keyboard. The files will load into any computer word processing file by attaching a cable from the portable word processor to the computer. The student can then use spell check and other features of the word processing software.

Smith, Boone, and Higgins (1998) suggest that during the **revision and editing** stages, students paste their word processed story into a Web publishing program called Home Page (Claris Corporation). Next, they select graphics and create a hypertext link to other Web sites. They also e-mail their draft to other students or to experts for help in the revising process. In their example, Smith, Boone, and Higgins relate how Billy, at this stage, selects the word *skull* from his story and links the word to a Web site that has a picture of a dinosaur's head. When the teacher and his peers read Billy's story, they may click on to the underlined word *skull* and see the close-up picture of the head of the dinosaur from another Web site. Spelling and grammar check programs are also invaluable at this step.

The **publishing** stage provides for an exciting use of technology. Smith, Boone, and Higgins (1998) suggest that students now establish a Web site address, or URL, and register the story for international access.

A publishing alternative is to use software programs that create a multimedia presentation such as HyperStudio (Roger Wagner) and LinkWay (IBM). Students may use these programs to build interactive presentations that combine text, graphics, sound, animation, and movie clips to present ideas and information. Students create a stack of screens or cards that are interrelated and cross-referenced by hot spots or buttons on each card (Ray & Warden, 1995). Students may easily program buttons to perform functions such as move to another card, play a sound, play a QuickTime movie, play a videodisc or CD-ROM, start an animation, keep a running test score, or direct an Internet browser to open a specific home page or site on the Internet. For example, Sherry published her story about dinosaurs using HyperStudio. On her first card, she located a button on her dinosaur picture. A click on the button took the reader to a QuickTime movie of a dinosaur eating.

There are many other software programs available that make the writing process motivational. EasyBook Deluxe (Sunburst) allows students to make double-sided books by writing and illustrating each page. Hollywood High (Theatrix) lets adolescent students write a script with 10 characters and 20 places designed to reflect typical high school hangouts, including a mall, the arcade, or the beach.

 ACTIVITY 11.2

Jorge has trouble writing and spelling, so he dislikes both. He seldom finishes his written work, and although he thinks clearly, his thoughts seldom find their way to paper. Jorge has become discouraged and frustrated with school. He frequently shows his frustration by misbehaving. His attention span is short. Discuss the technology tools that you would use to help Jorge in writing and that would motivate him to succeed.

Productivity Tools

Students with disabilities need to use productivity tools to become independent and lifelong learners. There is an ever-increasing number of productivity tools available to enable your students to work effectively in all subject areas. They may be handheld devices like the Bookman Speaking Merriam Webster Dictionary and Thesaurus from Franklin Learning Resources. Students type in a word, such as *enuf*, and see the word, *enough*, on the screen and hear the word pronounced. Students can also store the word in a customized list to practice for a spelling test. Optional headphones eliminate classroom noise and provide privacy.

There are also handheld devices like calculators or spreadsheet programs. Simple calculators perform rote tasks while students use higher-order thinking skills to solve real math problems. Graphing calculators may help students who are visual learners "see" abstract algebraic concepts. Talking calculators may assist students who transpose digits to verify the sequence of their numbers.

For students with special needs, "an electronic spreadsheet helps students organize their math problems and print them out so they can be read. Since computers do most of the calculations, students can only get the correct answer by understanding how to set up the problem, a key thinking and problem-solving skill" (Male, 1988, p. 68). The Cruncher (Davidson & Associates) is a full-featured, easy-to-use spreadsheet for young children through adults. It includes tutorials to introduce students to spreadsheet functions and will read text and numbers out loud.

There are many opportunities to learn to work with spreadsheets in any classroom. Using a spreadsheet, a student can keep track of expenses for a field trip or project. The student can estimate expenses item by item, calculate the actual total, and compare the differences. A unit on weather yields many statistics that can be stored, sorted, calculated, and analyzed. Hypotheses can be tested. Which month has the hottest average temperature in Florida? Is it the same month as it is in Alaska? Are warm months more windy than cool months?

Many students who have poor math skills have excellent abilities to recall and interpret sports statistics. Spreadsheets may be used to record statistics from the daily paper, make comparisons, and predict outcomes. Who will have the best batting average? Which team had the most touchdowns at the end of the season? Students can also use spreadsheets to manage their allowances and prepare personal budgets or keep statistics during simulations.

Reference Material Tools

As we discussed in the prewriting stage of the writing process, technology has given students other ways to gain information in addition to the library book. The explosion of CD-ROM technologies has made electronic access to encyclopedias, atlases, dictionaries, and other reference materials a common occurrence in school media centers and classrooms. Most of the electronic encyclopedias provide basic information on a wide range of topics. They may contain a speech output option where the program will read selected passages to students. Most offer Internet links to Web sites for additional information.

To choose reference materials for your students, you need to check such features as the reading comprehension level of the material; the ease of searching for information; the ability to cut and paste pictures and text into a word processor; and the use of video, sound, animation, charts, and illustrations to bring content alive. If your students cannot access the reference material because they cannot read the passages (and the program will not read it to them), you can use a tool such as the Ultimate Reader (Universal Learning Technologies). This program allows students to import the text from CD-ROMs or other files and have the text read to them.

Another great source of reference materials is the Internet. As of January 1998, there were an estimated 5 million Web sites (Network Wizards, 1998). We discuss the Internet in more detail later in this chapter.

Cognitive Assistance Tools

Many technology tools are available to help students develop and improve cognitive and problem-solving skills. Well-designed, multimedia systems support students in learning both basic and more complex literacy skills. Videotape technology was effective in teaching students with disabilities problem-solving skills (Elias & Taylor, 1995), and videodisc technology increased the math skills of secondary students with mild disabilities (Woodward & Gersten, 1993).

Through multimedia presentations students see the text and hear it read aloud. Simultaneous presentation of written words and sounds assists students in building decoding skills. An example of this technology is the interactive book. With an interactive book, students can follow the highlighted text as the passage is read. Then they can click on individual words to hear them pronounced. They can also explore the engaging hot spots on each page. For example, in *Just Grandma and Me* by Mercer Mayer (Broderbund), the student can click on the cow to see and hear it moo.

The Peabody Learning Lab, a multimedia software program developed for middle school students from disadvantaged backgrounds who have reading and spelling problems, enlists a virtual tutor (Melvin) to take students through a series of skill-development activities in reading, spelling, and writing. First, the students watch a segment of a video, which gives them some background for their upcoming reading. After students view the video, they may either read a related text passage, with Melvin helping them with individual words, or they may ask Melvin to read the passage slowly (word by word) or fluently (sentence by sentence) to them (Hasselbring, Goin, Taylor, Bottge, & Daley, 1997). In a two-year pilot study of the Peabody Learning Lab Program, the average vocabulary and reading comprehension scores of 376 students improved significantly (Hasselbring et al., 1997).

One of the suggestions Broome and White (1995) make for the use of videotapes in classrooms serving youth with behavioral disorders is to give students practice to self-monitor their behaviors. Students view the tape, tally appropriate and inappropriate behaviors, use a scale to evaluate their behaviors from 1 to 5, and reinforce themselves for successful performance. Salend (1995) suggests the use of videotapes to prepare students with disabilities for inclusive settings. Students may view segments of an inclusive class and discuss the general education teacher's expectations, rules, and routines.

In a videodisc lesson of Mastery Fractions (System Impact), students first view a 3-minute presentation of the concept of reducing fractions with computer graphics and narration. The videodisc program then presents a set of two to four guided-practice problems. Each set is a still frame, and students in cooperative groups can use the remote to advance the frame (Woodward & Gersten, 1993). Secondary students with mild disabilities improved math performances with this program (Woodward & Gersten, 1993).

◇ **IMPORTANT POINTS**

1. Legislation such as PL 99–457 and PL 100–407 were instrumental in promoting the use of technology tools for children and adolescents with disabilities.
2. Roblyer (1989) suggests that teachers use technology in the curriculum when the content or skills: (a) are difficult for students to

understand, (b) present hurdles such as too much calculation or handwriting that interfere with or are irrelevant to the main objective of the lesson, (c) require extensive homework, and (d) need more interesting materials when the present materials are tedious or uninteresting.

3. An adaptation of Means' classification scheme includes the broad categories of traditional, exploratory, tool, and communication technology applications.

4. Authentic uses of technology provide students with experiences that include features such as (a) supporting the use of technology for tasks that are similar to tasks performed by workers in nonschool settings, (b) integrating technology into activities that are a core part of the classroom curriculum, and (c) treating technology as a tool to accomplish a complex task.

5. You may use low- and high-level technology to assist students with mild disabilities in organization, the writing process, productivity, accessibility to reference materials, and cognitive assistance (Lahm & Morrisette, 1994).

6. Technology greatly enhances the prewriting, writing, revising and editing, and publishing stages of the writing process.

7. Word prediction and abbreviation expansion programs help students with disabilities compose text and overcome problems with word recall, spelling, and keyboarding.

8. Students who have difficulty with mathematics may manipulate numbers and perform complex calculations using productivity tools such as spreadsheets.

9. Videotapes, videodiscs, and multimedia systems support students in learning both basic and more complex literacy skills.

SOFTWARE SELECTION

Thousands of software programs are available for teachers and students to use. Many schools or districts purchase site licenses for software packages for everyone to use. The daunting task is to match the appropriate software to the curriculum and students' needs. Komoski (1995) recommends seven steps to responsible software selection:

Step 1—Analyze Needs: The major question to ask here is whether the computer is the most appropriate medium to meet the instructional goals and objectives or if the strategies of direct instruction, worksheets, or videotapes are more efficient.

Step 2—Specify Requirements: Questions here involve analyzing learners' characteristics and needs and matching the software to these characteristics and needs. Komoski (1995) also recommends thinking about compatibility of software to current hardware, user friendliness, and access to technical support. For new multimedia programs in which students are developing their own presentations, questions may include: How easy is the program for students to use? Can students incorporate the elements they need to produce an effective presentation? What is the learning time required? Does the program work consistently well so that the students don't have downtime when the program crashes?

Step 3—Identify Promising Software: Sources such as *Closing the Gap* and *Technology and Learning* frequently provide listings of software appropriate to a particular subject area or unit of instruction. The Technology and Media Division of the Council for Exceptional Children also includes information about computer software in its journal. These sources and others frequently present ideas for integrating computers into the curriculum and for using application programs in the classroom.

Another source for finding software is software advertisements. You should carefully examine the advertising claims about the effectiveness or the content of software, as believing all of the claims may lead to disappointment. Remember, software producers are not likely to identify the poor qualities or limitations of the program in an advertisement.

Komoski (1995) recommends that teachers join a listserv on the Internet and post questions to other teachers about software. For example, "I am a teacher of students with behavior disorders and I want to find an interactive software program that teaches a fourth-grade student to handle temper tantrums " may lead to many suggestions.

Step 4—Read Relevant Reviews: Software reviews are reports of evaluations by experts. However, even a piece of software that has received a good review may not be appropriate for a particular situation or student. It is important to consider the needs, strengths, and weaknesses of students as well as the expert's viewpoint of the software.

Step 5—Preview Software: Many companies now let you download a demonstration version of their software from their Web site that you can preview before you decide to purchase it. The most effective way to preview software is to watch students as they interact with the program.

Step 6—Make Recommendations: At this step, Komoski (1995) suggests teachers complete an evaluation form (see Table 11.1 for a sample one) and also keep a record of the optimal uses for the piece of software.

Step 7—Get Post-Use Feedback: Accountability requires a check that the software program is meeting the instructional goals and objectives identified in Step 1 and the needs of the students.

The following are additional criteria to consider when selecting software for students with special needs (Lewis, 1993; Powers, 1986):

1. *Flexibility:* Can the software be used by many students? Can it be used by a single student many times? Does the software offer a large number and variety of presentations to facilitate the acquisition of new skills? Can you use an authoring mode to insert vocabulary and other content appropriate to the objectives? Can you select parts of the program for a specific student or group?

2. *Student or teacher control of the presentation of the materials:* Can students work at their own pace? Is the rate of movement through the program response controlled rather than time controlled? Can you control the response time in timed drill and practice programs? Can the response time be set at a very slow rate? Is the slowest rate slow enough for students with special needs? Can the rate be increased in small increments? Is the material presented and practiced in a variety of formats, contexts, and arrangements to facilitate transfer of skills? Are a variety of presentation techniques employed throughout the program to maintain the learners' attention?

3. *Number of problems or length of lesson:* Does the program maintain the students' attention? Can you control the number of problems presented so that students are challenged but attention is maintained? Are students able to stop a program and continue it later from the same point?

4. *Type of feedback:* Does feedback include an indication of correct responses, incorrect responses, and reasons why a response is incorrect? Does the feedback compare an incorrect response with the correct response in order to help the student judge his or her performance? Is feedback intermittent and varied? Does the program refrain from negative feedback? Are prompts and hints provided?

5. *Program content:* Is the software built upon clearly specified learning objectives? Is the mode of instruction direct? Is the instruction focused on predetermined objectives? Does the program offer content flexibility and personalization? Are record-keeping mechanisms present and adequate? Is the reading level of information presented in the program carefully controlled and specified in

Table 11.1 Software Evaluation Form

Title _____ Date _____
Publisher _____
Address _____
Subject Area _____ Grade Level _____ Price _____
Directions: Place a check mark under Y if yes, N if no, or NA if not applicable.

	Y	N	NA
Appropriateness:			
• Age	____	____	____
• Interest	____	____	____
• Level	____	____	____
Hardware Considerations:			
• Compatible with computer	____	____	____
• Sufficient memory	____	____	____
• Color monitor required	____	____	____
• Peripherals required (printer, mouse, etc.)	____	____	____
Documentation:			
• Manual provided	____	____	____
• Additional materials included (worksheets)	____	____	____
• Adaptations suggested	____	____	____
Program:			
• Content interesting	____	____	____
• Content accurate	____	____	____
• Information up to date	____	____	____
• Information free from stereotypes	____	____	____
• Content well organized	____	____	____
Interaction:			
• Active participation required of learner	____	____	____
• Varying levels of difficulty available	____	____	____
• Learner control of presentation rate	____	____	____
• Learner control of exit function	____	____	____
• Feedback provided	____	____	____
• Concepts and skills reinforced	____	____	____
Technical Considerations:			
• User friendly	____	____	____
• Sound optional	____	____	____
• High-quality graphics	____	____	____
Record Keeping:			
• Reporting of scores option	____	____	____
• Capable of printing out scores	____	____	____

the program manual? Do supplementary materials that provide extensive and varied practice accompany the software? Do the content and the presentation meet the needs of the students? Do they fit the curriculum?

6. *Screen design:* Is the screen display simple and uncluttered? Is color used to add interest and motivation? Does the use of color com-plement the content? Is the visual display free of unnecessary distractions? Are relevant stimuli clearly identified and emphasized through flashing, underlining, color, or contrast? Are graphics utilized to provide realistic and concrete illustrations of abstract concepts? For students with visual problems, is the lettering large and clear?

◆ **ACTIVITY 11.3**

Using an educational software catalog, find some programs designed specifically to help you. Locate at least one title that will help you:

1. Write a lesson plan.
2. Generate an IEP.
3. Generate a puzzle, game, or worksheet.
4. Generate a test.
5. Generate a certificate, bookmark, or reward.
6. Store and calculate your grades.
7. Make materials for the bulletin board.
8. Generate an overhead transparency.
9. Author a program.
10. Contact an electronic bulletin board.

If possible, preview at least one of these programs. How do you think the program would be useful to you? How would it help to make you more productive? More professional?

INTERNET

The Internet is a network of computers throughout the world that are connected to each other to share information. In the last five years the use of the Internet has grown tremendously. In this section, we discuss general information, instructional use, and safeguards of the Internet.

General Information

To connect to the Internet, your computer must have available a minimum of 8—preferably 16—megabytes of RAM (random access memory) and a very fast processor (Heflich, 1998). Many schools have access to the Internet either through local area networks (LANs) or through modems and telephone lines. An Internet service provider (ISP) connects you to the World Wide Web (WWW). Many school districts have a dedicated computer that has been assigned as a gateway (ISP) to connect to the

WWW for their teachers, staff, and students. Information on the WWW is basically organized by a Web site of individual Web pages that pertain to a similar subject. Browsers (software programs such as Netscape Navigator and Microsoft Internet Explorer) allow you to move from page to page and site to site. Netscape Navigator is available on the WWW and is free to educators, whereas Microsoft Internet Explorer is bundled with the Windows operating system (Heflich, 1998).

On the Web page, you may see some text that is highlighted in different colors or highlighted and underlined. By clicking your mouse on this highlighted text, you are automatically connected to different pages or sites. All Web pages at a site have addresses or URLs (uniform resource locators). For example, if you wish to go to the Council for Exceptional Children (CEC) Web site, you would type the URL of http://www.cec.sped.org/ in the location box at the top of Netscape Navigator and find information concerning CEC divisions and other special education information.

Let's say that you do not have a specific site in mind, but you want to explore a general topic. You can access directories such as Yahoo or Yahooligans (a directory for children ages 8–12) or such search engines as AltaVista to find sites that contain information concerning your topic (Wissick & Gardner, 1998).

Through these WWW connections, students and teachers are able to tap into resources previously unavailable. There are on-line dictionaries, encyclopedias, databases, picture databases, movie clips, sound clips, chat rooms with subject area experts, and virtual tours. For a more detailed discussion of the Internet, please see Volume 30, Issue 5 of *TEACHING Exceptional Children* (1998).

Lesson Presentations

We already briefly discussed the use of the Internet in the writing process. Teachers may use

Table 11.2 Sample Internet Sites

Site Name	WWW (URL) Address	Description
AskEric	http://ericir.syr.edu	Lesson plans for all levels and content, education information, search engine for educational professional literature
ATEN	http://www.aten.ocps.k12.fl.us	Resources and links for assistive technology
BCK2SKOL Lessons	http://web.csd.sc.edu/bck2skol/fall/	Lessons on using the Web and search engines
Busy Teacher Website	http://www.ceismc.gatech.edu/busyt/	Materials, lesson plans, class activities, interactive Web projects for students
Classroom Connect	http://www.classroom.net/	Site for K–12 educators and students
EXCEL (4Mat)	http://www.excelcorp.com/	Information on teaching/ learning, lesson exchange
Internet island—Miami Science Center	http://www.miamisci.org/ii/	Teaches students to use the Internet via a story
Multicultural Sites on the Internet	http://www.ithaca.edu/library/htmls/multi.html	Links to Asian American, Hispanic, Native, Gay, and Women's Studies
On-Line Books	http://www.cs.cmu.edu/books.html	Source of on-line books and out of copyright ones

NOTE. Site addresses may change without notice. If you are unable to find the site, use Web search engines and search by subject area(s).

the Internet to enrich and to support their lesson presentations and to develop professionally (Goldstein, 1998; Lewis, 1998; Mosca & Perkins, 1997; Wissick & Gardner, 1998). In Table 11.2 we present some popular sites and descriptions.

Many WWW sites provide lesson plans to enrich your lesson presentations. One of our student teachers used a lesson plan downloaded from the WWW to build a cell from jello, jelly beans, and other common materials. You may incorporate structured interactive activities for students to follow using the WWW. Goldstein (1998) suggests the creation of specific tasks and structured lessons for students to perform as groups using the WWW for lesson presentations. For example, you may design a "treasure hunt" of items and questions for students to answer as they browse through the WWW. Using groups is particularly effective, as some students with disabilities who cannot read may have difficulty answering the questions when so much of the information on the WWW is in written format

(Peters-Walters, 1998). Wissick and Gardner (1998) also recommend the Web for designing thematic units. They give an example of how the topic of whales quickly leads to various sites, information, and integrated activities. Educators Toolkit (http://www.eagle.ca/~matink/) and Thematic Units (http://www.ed.sc.edu/caw/theme.html) are two sites that provide a hotlist of sites grouped thematically (Wissick & Garnder, 1998).

The virtual trips especially enrich a lesson for students who will never be able actually to visit a place. They can experience the site through virtual pictures or video. Some software allows the user to manipulate pictures of objects in a museum so that they can look at the object from all angles. Even if the students were to visit a museum, they wouldn't be allowed to pick up or touch a valuable artifact. The other way virtual tours are useful is in performing tasks such as dissecting a virtual frog or other scientific experiments that may be too costly or too dangerous to perform in a classroom setting.

Since many special educators are co-teaching in inclusive settings, the WWW is an invaluable tool to enhance background information. Lewis (1998) notes that there are many sites that focus on diverse populations, such as details about Native American tribes and brief biographies of African-American scientists. Materials can be downloaded from the net to enhance the lessons. For example, one of our special education student teachers in a co-teaching setting downloaded the production graph from the M & M corporation. The students then compared their class graph of the various M & M colors to the company's production.

Professional Development

In addition to the ability to assess current, up-to-date information from professional organizations, listservs and Usenet Newsgroups may provide support and encouragement to teachers. Listservs provide forums for discussing topics with people who have similar interests (Lewis, 1998). People subscribe to a listserv, read messages, and send messages to the listserv (Morgan, 1997). Usenet Newsgroups are an electronic bulletin board system that consists of discussion forums on thousands of topics (Morgan, 1997). Using e-mail, teachers can interact with other professionals in solving everyday problems. For example, Terry Perkins (Mosca & Perkins, 1997) relates how she requested help for 10 students with emotional disabilities and learned of curriculum guides, lesson plans, and behavior systems from colleagues via a Usenet Newsgroup.

Safeguards

Although many schools have enlisted the aid of software that helps create a safer environment for students, they can still get to sites that are not appropriate. It is important to teach students "Net safety" in the same manner that they are taught drug safety and stranger safety (Bakken & Aloia, 1998; Goldstein, 1998). Some general precautions to teach students are that they should (a) let teachers know if any e-mail message or Web site information is inappropriate or makes them feel uncomfortable, (b) not believe everything that is on the WWW, (c) not give out personal information, and (d) not agree to meet anyone face-to-face (Bakken & Aloia, 1998; Goldstein, 1998). We want to reiterate the idea of evaluating carefully what you find on the WWW. Anyone can put information on the Internet without having it checked for accuracy, validity, or appropriateness. In fact, Caruso (1997) relates the story of how one of her seventh graders built his own Web site on computer repair and network consultation.

 ACTIVITY 11.4

Part 1. Find two sites on the Web and tell how you might use the information in your class. Share your site with a peer.

Part 2. Using the Internet, download a demonstration version of a talking word processor such as Write: Out Loud from Don Johnston, Inc. Describe the features of the program and its advantages for students who have reading and writing problems.

TECHNOLOGY AS A TOOL FOR TEACHERS

As technology becomes more common in the classroom, teachers are looking beyond school boundaries for new and innovative ways to integrate and infuse that technology into the curriculum (Craig, 1997). As previously discussed, on-line access to the Internet is helping teachers bring boundless resources to the classroom. Technology applications that can be used as a tool or a communications vehicle (word processing, spreadsheet, drawing program, network) can support any curriculum and can be fully assimilated into a teacher's ongoing core practice (Means, Blando, Olson, Middleton, Moroacco, Remz, and Zorfaass, 1993).

When instruction incorporates concept-based, integrated curricula and focuses on relevant issues, problems, and ideas, learning acquires a new depth (Erickson, 1995). When such instruction is paired with telecommunications and technology, students make the connection between academics and the world outside the classroom. This relevancy has a lasting impact on student learning. In the previous section, we included a discussion of the Internet. Therefore, we do not repeat the information on the application of the Internet for instruction here.

Planning

Good planning is critical to successful instruction. Since any word processing program allows you to enter, edit, format, print, and save text, you can easily produce lesson plans that are professional-looking, easily revised, and available when you need to retrieve them. By using a template, which is like filling in a blank form, you can develop a format that meets your needs and simplifies entering new lessons. Or you may want to develop a simple database of lesson plans. A database will allow you to categorize your plans according to such areas as content, objectives, developmental level, themes, and instructional strategies. Integrated programs such as Claris-Works (Claris Corporation) and Microsoft Works will allow you to pursue either option.

You may prefer to use a graphic organizer, such as Inspiration (see Figure 11.1), which allows you to map or diagram your lesson plans. This is a powerful tool for planning and developing integrated thematic units. A demonstration copy of the program is available from Inspiration at their Web site.

IEP Generation

Another popular use of technology in classrooms with students who have special needs is for developing and producing Individualized Education Programs (IEPs) (Krivacska, 1986; Maddux, 1986; Male, 1988, 1997). You can use your own word processor or database to enter, store, retrieve, and modify your required form, or you can use an IEP generation program. However, more and more districts and states are developing their own computerized IEPs or customizing commercial products to meet federal, state, and local requirements, curriculum objectives, and standards. Computerized IEPs offer the ability to enter data and edit without retyping. Larger systems may provide access to databases of annual goals and objectives, resources that have been correlated to local curriculum, and assessment data. They also allow generation of a variety of reports (Male, 1988, 1997). It is important to remember that IEPs should be written by teams of people, and computerization should not reduce the individualization of the process (Krivacska, 1986; Maddux, 1986).

Record Keeping and Classroom Management

Technology can help you manage your classroom. You can improve your record keeping by using a simple spreadsheet program or a spreadsheet template that is available with some integrated programs for educators, like ClarisWorks or Microsoft Works. You may be interested in a comprehensive classroom management program that includes grading, seating charts, and lesson plans, such as the one from Excelsior Software.

A wide range of software programs is available that have a number of different capabilities related to standardized tests. These programs offer interpretation of test results, information management of test results and data, report writing, and generation of instructional strategies, goals, and objectives (Male, 1997).

Programs are also available for sampling language and testing readability. Many schools are using programs like the Accelerated Reader (Advantage) to track what books students are reading and to measure comprehension of the material they read. It is important to examine informal or formal assessment programs for appropriateness to current curriculum goals and instructional practices.

Since the thinking behind how we deliver and measure learning is changing, digital or electronic portfolios for students are becoming more common as tools for assessment in many schools. Programs such as the Grady Profile Portfolio Assessment (Aurbach & Associates, 1995) and the Electronic Portfolio (Scholastic, 1996) allow teachers to track students' work samples in scanned images, sounds, full-motion video, graphics, text data, and other information pertinent to the students' educational history (see Chapter 3 for more information about portfolio assessment). An example of an entry in an electronic portfolio is found in Figure 11.2.

You also may wish to use videotape recording to monitor student behaviors. We discussed previously how the recording can promote self-monitoring. However, it is just as easy for a teacher to turn on the video and record classroom activities for a few minutes every day for evaluation of both student and teacher behaviors.

Presentation Tools

You may use a combination of graphics, text, sound, and video to introduce new topics, deliver necessary information, explain examples, demonstrate problems, and review previously covered material. Your computer presentations can be viewed by individual students or small groups or you can project them for larger groups. In fact, Middleton, Flores, and Knaupp (1997) recommend the elimination of one-student, one-computer thinking and the use of a high-end machine with a projection device that can involve an entire classroom of students in problem-solving and other interactive software.

You may transfer your computer presentations to videotape by use of a single cable from the computer to a videocassette recorder for students to view at home. Popular programs for computer presentations are PowerPoint (Microsoft), HyperStudio (Roger Wagner), Digital Chisel (Pierian Springs), and ClarisWorks Slideshow.

A videodisc player connected to a television monitor can also present graphics and sounds. For example, one of our student teachers used a videodisc to supplement her lecture on sea animals to her high school students. Checking in the teacher's guide that accompanied the videodisc, she found lists of images and video clips to enhance her presentation. She then entered a sequence of the frame numbers into the computer's database using a software program (Bar'N'Coder, Pioneer) and printed out the list. While she was lecturing to her students about the various animals, she passed a pen-shaped scanner over one of the barcodes and showed related pictures such as a picture of crabs eating.

Preparation of Classroom Materials

Technology can enhance instruction by helping you prepare materials for your classroom environment and curriculum. Computers can help you generate worksheets that match student needs for practice of skills and concepts. Programs such as Worksheet Magic (Teacher Support Software) allow you to produce a variety of creative formats, including crossword puzzles, scrambled words, word searches, and secret codes. Math Worksheet and Fraction Worksheet Generator (EPC) will help you to develop pretests, posttests, and practice problems to meet individual student needs. Problems can be printed horizontally or vertically, with or

Einsein's Academy for the Advancement of Science and Violin Middle School Division

Demo-Student, Ann   **Work Sample—Graphic**

Assignment   Draft
The student was asked to explain some math problems.   X Final
The goal of the exercise was to assess the student's   Typical
ability to verbalize the operations performed.   Atypical
                                                         X Printing
                                                           Cursive

Legend
$-$ = performance does not meet expectation
$\sqrt{}$ = performance meets expectation
$+$ = performance exceeds expectation

Title: 3/02/94—math problems
Evaluator: Ms. A. Nelson
Skill-Set: Mathematics
Date: 9/25/98

Student	Parent	Teacher	
+		+	Explanation shows math understanding
+		+	Explanation is accurate
+		+	Explanation is thorough

Ann

2) $(5^3 + 25) + (50 + 50) = 250$

3) $7 \cdot 6^3 - (42 - 36) - 150 = 1,356$

4) $9 \cdot 3 - 9 \div 3 + 3 = 27$

5) $6 \cdot 3 \div 2 + 2^2 = 36$

Reflections
My teacher asked me to give an example of my best math work this quarter and write a complete explanation. I picked these problems because they show that I know how to write long problems. I know that you are supposed to do the work inside the parentheses before you follow the signs outside them. Then you do multiplication first before the adding to get the right answer. I know how to use an integer (that's the little number three up in the air by the 5 in problem #2). That means to multiply that number by itself three times. Another word for that is cubed. If that number is a 2, it's called squared. You do this cubing or squaring first before you multiply. So here's the order you should go in if you get a problem like this. First look at stuff in parentheses and get those answers done. If there's an integer do that the very first. Then follow the math directions outside the parentheses. Do times and dividing first, then add or subtract. You'll get the right answer every time!

Miscellaneous Remarks
This is the first semester report for all students at Einstein. We the faculty hope you like our new output format. It is part of our new student profile system.

Notes
3/6/94 Ann shows understanding of the process of grouping and order of operations. She also understands squaring and cubing. I'd like her to learn to use the word "operation." Alice Einstein.

Figure 11.2   Electronic Portfolio Entry
NOTE. Grady Profile Portfolio Assessment Software (1998). Aurbach & Associates, Inc.; St. Louis, MO. Reprinted by permission.

without answers, with the procedure being shown, or with an example problem.

You can create certificates, awards, banners, signs, bookmarks, and bulletin board signs to enhance your themes, and instructional activities on such programs as Print Shop Deluxe (Broderbund) and PrintMaster Gold (Mindscape). Colored paper or color printers will add to the appearance of your products.

With desktop publishing programs you can add a professional polish to instructional materials and reports. Templates for newsletters in many word processing programs will allow you to add columns, rules, boxes, and shading to your work. Programs like the Student Writing Center (Learning Company) and the more professional PageMaker (Adobe) will offer more publishing options.

With multimedia software, teachers can incorporate graphics, video, animation, sound, and text into customized curriculum that reflects what students are actually doing in the school environment. You can digitize photographs of students or capture live video of field trips and performances. For example, students in a kindergarten class photographed a cooking class, downloaded the pictures to the computer, and used software to crop and alter their pictures (Pastor & Kerns, 1997). Eventually, the students wrote captions for their photo book, creating their own reading material.

Authoring

Although there are an enormous number of software programs available, you may still have difficulty finding the exact program that will meet a specific objective for your student. You may also lack the resources to purchase such a program. Few teachers have the programming skills or the time to author software, but there are viable options that can meet most needs for customized software.

Some commercially available programs have capabilities that allow you to customize the program to address specific instructional needs. You can actually build the modifications into the program. Through teacher options, you can adjust the levels, choose the range of difficulty, and determine the content of the software program appropriate for a specific student.

Digital Chisel and HyperStudio (Roger Wagner) are hypermedia programs that can be used for authoring. You can create instructional materials that not only include text, graphics, sound, animation, music, and video but that also access CD-ROMs or laserdiscs or link to resources on the Web. You can add digitized, familiar photos and video, or include explanations in your own voice or the voices of your students.

 ACTIVITY 11.5

Go to a software preview lab (university learning resource center, special education resource centers, local school, etc.) and preview an interactive media program (i.e., HyperStudio). Preview sample files for examples of lessons. Describe how you would use this program to design a lesson for any subject area.

 IMPORTANT POINTS

1. Komoski (1995) identifies the following steps for analyzing software: (1) analyze needs, (2) specify requirements, (3) identify promising software, (4) read relevant reviews, (5) preview software, (6) make recommendations, and (7) get post-use feedback.

2. The Internet is a network of computers throughout the world that are connected to each other to share information.

3. Goldstein (1998) suggests the creation of specific tasks and structured lessons for students to perform in groups using the WWW for lesson presentations.

4. Teachers may use the World Wide Web (WWW) to find lesson plans, background information, thematic units, virtual activities, professional information, and support.

5. Some general precautions to teach students are to let their teachers know if any e-mail message or Web site information is inappropriate or makes them feel uncomfortable, to not believe everything that is on the WWW, to not give out personal information, and to not agree to meet anyone face-to-face. (Bakken & Aloia, 1998; Goldstein, 1998).

6. Technology assists teachers in planning, IEP generation, record keeping and classroom management, lesson presentation, material preparation, and authoring.

7. It is important to remember that IEPs should be written by teams of people, and computerization should not reduce the individualization of the process (Krivacska, 1986; Maddux, 1986).

8. The Accelerated Reader program and electronic portfolios are samples of technology application for record keeping and classroom management.

9. Middleton, Flores, and Knaupp (1997) recommend the elimination of one-student, one-computer thinking and the use of a high-end machine with a projection device that can involve an entire classroom of students in problem solving and other interactive software.

10. Software programs are available to assist teachers in preparing individualized worksheets, crossword puzzles, certificates, and other motivational materials.

11. Authoring programs include customized software that allows teachers to adjust the levels, select the range of difficulty, and determine the content of the software program appropriate for a specific student.

ASSISTIVE TECHNOLOGY

Assistive technology addresses the special tools that students with disabilities must have in order to access curriculum, engage in learning, meet required outcomes, and transition successfully to the workplace. Assistive technology augments student learning by providing the tools, devices, and services necessary for circumventing particular learning problems or physical disabilities.

According to Hasselbring (1998), "assistive technology provides powerful tools for students with disabilities to become an integral part of schools and the community. Access to the assistive technology services and devices can remove barriers, unmask abilities and create opportunities for increased independence and inclusion for children and adults, regardless of the severity of their disability. Assistive technology provides avenues for people to increase expectations and to stretch their imaginations toward a future filled with possibilities" (p. 2).

When most people think of assistive or adaptive technology, they think of high-tech devices such as Stephen Hawking's speaking keyboard. Most adaptations are more mundane and address issues such as relocating the on/off button of the computer or pressing two keys at once or picking up a disk to slide into the drive. A pencil grip would qualify as assistive technology if it assists a student with writing problems to write better! It is technology that allows the student to do something that he/she would not be able to accomplish otherwise.

Much of the history related to the use of assistive technology in the classroom is based on three critical pieces of legislation: The Education for All Handicapped Children Act (EHA, PL 94-142), the Technology-Related Assistance for Individuals with Disabilities Act (Tech Act, PL 100-407), and the Individuals with Disabilities Education Act (IDEA, PL 105-17). Originally passed in 1975, Public Law 94-142 started the process of providing appropriate instructional interventions for students. The Tech Act (PL 100-407) was designed to enhance the availability and quality of assistive technology (AT) devices and services to all individuals and their families throughout the United States. It was the first law to define assistive technology and implement a consumer-responsive program of technology-related assistance for individuals with disabilities of all ages.

The Individuals with Disabilities Education Act reauthorization bill (IDEA Improvement Act PL 105-17) specified the consideration of assistive technology as part of the IEP development for a student receiving special education services. IDEA makes it possible for states and localities to receive federal funds to assist in the education of schoolchildren with disabilities when the school districts follow the federal guidelines. The definition of assistive technology includes both devices and services.

Assistive Technology Devices

Section 300.5 of IDEA defines assistive technology devices as "any item, piece of equipment or product system, whether acquired commercially off the shelf, modified, or customized, that is used to increase, maintain, or improve functional capabilities of individuals with disabilities" [20 U.S.C. Chapter 33, Section 1401 (25)]. This definition is broad and includes many of the modifications, adaptations, and accommodations made for a student in order to participate in a Free, and Appropriate Public Education (FAPE). As discussed previously, the devices

may range from low technology to high technology. With this definition, assistive technology does not have to be electronic or mechanical.

Hourcade, Parette, and Huer (1997) recommend a useful source of information on assistive devices, ABLEDATA. The U. S. Department of Education–sponsored database is accessed through a low-cost CD-ROM, Cooperative Database Distribution Network for Assistive Technology (CO-NET) through the Trace Center at the University of Wisconsin. The CD-ROM contains detailed descriptions of approximately 21,000 products from more than 3,000 manufacturers (Hourcade et al., 1997).

Assistive Technology Services

IDEA defines assistive technology service as "any service that directly assists an individual with a disability in the selection, acquisition, and use of an assistive technology device" [20 U.S.C. Chapter 33, Section 1401(25)]. Specifically, this service must include (a) evaluating an individual's assistive technology needs; (b) purchasing, leasing, or providing for acquisition of devices; (c) selecting, designing, adapting, maintaining, repairing, or replacing devices; (d) coordinating therapies, interventions, or services; (e) training and technical assistance for the individual and/or family; and (f) training and technical assistance for professionals. School districts are responsible for helping individuals with disabilities select and acquire an appropriate assistive technology device and assist in training them to use it.

Students, parents, and professionals together decide on the assistive technology needs of an individual student. Professionals who may be included are the teacher, speech therapist, occupational therapist, physical therapist, and any other person who works with the student.

Modifications

As we discussed previously, assistive technology may also include simple, low-tech modifications. Simple modifications are sometimes all that is needed to allow a student to use the computer software program. Some students may benefit from the use of bright stickers to code keys that are frequently used with a program. You may use word processing or graphics software to produce some special help cards for use at the computer. These cards can list frequently used commands or summarize directions in large, clear print with illustrations. Using screen capturing features of the computer allows you to print or download the image that appears on the screen. You can use screen capturing features to produce flash cards, prepare transparencies and task cards for a computer program, display and file exemplary work, and incorporate actual software graphics into student produced presentations.

In recent years, the operating systems of computers have accessibility features either built in to the system software or available at no cost. These features provide simple modifications that make using the computer more accessible to students. The features were designed primarily for individuals with motion-related disabilities who may have difficulty using the computer keyboard or mouse, for individuals who prefer visual feedback in place of sounds, and for some low-vision students. However, many of these features make the computer more user friendly for other students as well. The terminology for these features may vary from one computer system to another, but the accessibility features are offered in most of the system software.

Both the Macintosh and Windows operating systems include built-in controls that make standard functions simpler for individuals with special needs. For example, Ms. Perez slows down the speed at which the mouse pointer moves for Kimberly, who has some eye-hand coordination difficulties. More examples of built-in controls appear in Table 11.3.

Many programs give you and your students the option of using various peripheral devices to enhance instruction or provide the student with special access to use the program. Adapted standard computer input devices include different sizes of a mouse or a trackball, and different size or different key layouts of keyboards. Other examples include keyguards, touch-sensitive screens, alternate or adapted keyboards, switches, and voice entry systems.

Students usually respond to instructional software programs by typing on the computer keyboard. **Keyguards** reduce the possibility of hitting the wrong keys as students attempt to enter information. Keyguards fit over the regular computer keyboard and have holes cut out for the individual to access the keys on the keyboard with a finger, stylus, or stick. Keyguards may also have a latching key on certain function keys, such as the shift or control. With **touch-sensitive screens** (e.g., Touch Window, Edmark), students use a finger or stylus for input. To make a selection, the student simply points

Table 11.3 Sample Operating Systems Built-In Controls

These built-in controls include:
- The capability of switching from mouse control to keyboard control using the numeric keypad
- Control of the speed at which the mouse pointer moves
- Allowance for control key combinations to be pressed consecutively rather than simultaneously
- Use of the keyboard keys to select menu functions
- Adjustment of icons for size, spacing, and title text
- Change of the background screen color
- Custom features for controlling your mouse, trackball, or operating system
- An audible cue to tell when either the Caps Lock, Num Lock, or Scroll Lock keys have been made active or inactive
- A visual alert for persons with hearing disabilities or for those who are too easily distracted by the alert sounds

at the computer screen with a finger or a special penlike device. This often allows students who have fine-motor problems, inaccurate keyboard skills, or problems with spelling to complete programs without frustration.

Alternative or adapted keyboards, such as IntelliKeys (Intellitools) and DiscoverBoard (Don Johnston, Inc.) offer input methods that can be customized to a student's needs. Many of the same features that are system accessibility features are also included in these alternate keyboards. Most of these alternate keyboards have software that allows you to make customized overlays for the keyboards that will correspond to the specific software that the student is using.

The use of on-screen keyboards is an alternative input method that is software and hardware controlled. A graphical representation of the keyboard is displayed on the computer screen to allow individuals who cannot type with a standard keyboard to enter text using a pointing device (i.e., mouse, switch, or trackball).

Software devices such as Adaptive Firmware Card (Apple IIE and IIGS), Discover KE:NX (Macintosh), and DADA (IBM and compatibles) allow **switch activation** and a communication device to act in place of the computer keyboard. With switch activation, the software that comes with the specific device displays the computer keyboard. A switch activation signals the computer to start scanning the on-screen keyboard by row, column, or individual character. The scan can be customized for rate of scanning and activation as well as for different placements of characters on the on-screen keyboard. The simplest communication device activates a switch for selecting an actual object, whereas more advanced devices use intricate symbol codes to produce words on a display or for voice output.

Voice entry systems allow students to enter information into the computer simply by speaking into a microphone attached to the computer. Voice entry software is available as an alternative input system. Some computer systems have built-in systems providing voice access to the functions of the computer, but do not necessarily allow voice input of data. An individual may give a voice command, such as "Computer, open hard drive," and other commands to control the computer functions. However, the individual cannot tell the computer to enter the data. Instead, specific voice input software, such as Dragon Dictate, ViaVoice, or PowerSecretary, can be installed to provide for data input. These programs are fairly sensitive to voice discrepancies of different students. Therefore, they must be programmed to be used by one student at a time and in a fairly quiet environment. For some students with written expression problems, voice input can expedite the entering of text. Individuals who use voice input must have a fairly high cognitive level as well as extreme patience in working with the software to be successful.

Not all communication devices interface with the computer. These devices fall into a category of augmentative and alternative communication.

 ACTIVITY 11.6

With a colleague, list five modifications that you may make for your students.

AUGMENTATIVE AND ALTERNATIVE COMMUNICATION

Augmentative and alternative communication provides a method of communication for students whose speech is not fluent or understandable enough to communicate effectively. Communication devices include such things as symbol systems, manual communication boards and wallets, electronic communication devices, speech synthesizers, and communication enhancement software.

Augmentative and alternative communication (AAC) is the supplementation or replacement of natural speech and/or writing. AAC is thought of as a process of assessing and providing a variety of symbols, strategies, and techniques to assist people who are unable to meet their communication needs through natural speech and/or writing. Frequently, professionals and parents think that assistive technology (AT) and AAC are synonymous. It is important to remember that AAC is a process, whereas assistive technology refers to the tools used to assist individuals with functions and activities. We do not discuss AAC in depth here, as the students with disabilities whom we address in this book very rarely use these methods for communication.

EMERGING TECHNOLOGIES

Technology changes so quickly that it is very difficult to keep up with the latest developments. Artificial intelligence and virtual reality are two of the latest developments. However, these developments are happening more in research and development within the business world. In education, we have not yet seen the impact from these two areas.

Artificial Intelligence

Artificial intelligence is an application of computer science where people try to make computers act and think like a human being. One application of artificial intelligence is expert systems in which a "knowledge engineer" interviews experts in a certain subject area and tries to incorporate all the knowledge into a computer program for carrying out some tasks. An example of this in education might be a computer program that allows a teacher to input diagnostic and assessment information and to receive prescriptive teaching strategies, lessons, and resources based on the student information provided. The disadvantage of expert systems is that the computer can only analyze and produce information based on the information that the computer program has received. If, for example, this program was developed based on information from an expert who lives in another state and the state in which you reside uses different labeling, diagnostic criteria, or curricula, the results you receive probably will not be appropriate for your school environment.

An example of the application of artificial intelligence is speech recognition. This is probably the most usable form of artificial intelligence for students with learning disabilities. Speech recognition is the ability of the computer to recognize speech input and translate that into a text format that is understood by the computer. The computer must be trained to recognize the user's voice. For students who have problems with writing or spelling, voice input provides a way to express thoughts without the roadblocks of writing and spelling.

Virtual Reality

Virtual environments (sometimes called virtual reality or VR) is the use of 3D graphics with 3D models, combined with direct manipulation and a display technology that provides for or creates the illusion of immersion in the model world. There are several types of possible displays: monitors, head mounted displays (HMD), booms, and projection systems. All can be used to provide wide-angle stereoscopic views of a virtual world. Monitors with stereo glasses are the most inexpensive and provide for the lowest level of immersion.

Virtual environments are computer-generated, three-dimensional models of the real world. A student can "walk" around these environments using a joystick and interact with these environments using a touchscreen or mouse. Furthermore, a whole range of virtual environments can be built to model a rich and varied set of experiences. In this way, students with special needs can build a range of basic life skills in virtual environments to supplement their real-world experiences. Imagine students being able to move around the inside of the space shuttle and the excitement they would feel as the countdown begins.

Although education has not had widespread use of virtual environments or virtual reality within the classroom, the Internet has provided many virtual environments for students to explore. With the accessibility of the World Wide Web, a student can actually dissect a frog online, visit the Louvre in Paris, or visit a remote environmental habitat.

 IMPORTANT POINTS

1. Assistive technology addresses the special tools that students with disabilities must have in order to access curriculum, engage in learning, meet required outcomes, and transition successfully to the workplace.
2. Examples of assistive technology range from a high-technology solution such as a speaking keyboard to a low-technology solution such as a pencil grip.
3. The Education for All Handicapped Children Act (EHA, PL 94-142), the Technology-Related Assistance for Individuals with Disabilities Act (Tech Act, PL 100-407), and the Individuals with Disabilities Education Act (IDEA, PL 105-17) were three critical pieces of legislation in the technology movement.

4. In recent years, the operating systems of the computers have accessibility features either built in to the system software or are available at no cost that provide simple modifications that make using the computer more accessible to students.
5. Some operating system modifications include keyguards, touch sensitive screens, alternative or adapted keyboards, switches, and voice entry systems.
6. Augmentative and alternative communication is a process, whereas assistive technology refers to the tools used to assist individuals with functions and activities.
7. Artificial intelligence, specifically an expert system, allows you to talk with an expert via the computer.
8. Virtual reality uses computers to simulate moving through space and time.

◆ DISCUSSION QUESTIONS

1. Given the budget constraints placed on schools, make a case for expenditures in the area of technology, perhaps at the expense of other types of instructional materials.
2. Predict how students with special needs and their teachers will be using technology five years from now.
3. Describe how you will use technology to enhance your roles in teaching and learning.

TRANSITION FROM SCHOOL TO COMMUNITY LIVING

by Sara C. Pankaskie

Children with disabilities grow up to be adolescents and young adults with disabilities. One of the critical turning points in the lives of young people is the transition from secondary school to the world of postsecondary education, employment, and life in the community as an adult. Developing independence, examining one's talents and interests, deciding upon a career path, and pursuing either employment or additional schooling are just some of the challenges that all youth in transition face. In addition to these challenges, students with special needs face all unique challenges (Kranstover, Thurlow, & Bruininks, 1989; Wagner & Blackorby, 1996). They are unemployed at a higher rate than peers without disabilities, tend to drop out of school before graduation, are involved with the criminal system to a higher degree, and often are living in a dependent situation for a longer period of time (Edgar, 1988; Wagner & Blackorby, 1996).

The purpose of this chapter is to provide you with information and strategies to help adolescents with special needs make a successful transition from school to adult life. We begin the chapter with a summary of some of the best practices in transition found in the literature. Then we suggest activities for students during early school years to prepare them for the more intense transition programming during the late middle and high school years. As part of this, we define and describe career education. We address the legal requirements for transition planning under the Individuals with Disabilities Education Act (IDEA), including other federal laws related to transition, and information about the transition IEP. Next, we provide guidance in the areas of developing and maintaining linkages with families, with other people and agencies within the school, and with other people and agencies in the larger community. In the last section of the chapter, we suggest some practical programming and teaching approaches so you may assist students with special needs to complete high school, become employable, and emerge as independent and productive young adults. There are two main values underlying this chapter. One is that student and family in-volvement are critical for successful transition. The other is that transition is not a postschool experience. Instead, transition is everything we do with and for students while they are in school to help them succeed in their postschool lives.

BEST PRACTICES IN TRANSITION

The transition literature suggests many "best practices" in the area of transition from school to community living. Unfortunately, many of these best practices have not been substantiated by empirical, student outcomes research (Greene & Albright, 1995; Johnson & Rusch, 1993). A meta-analysis of various studies (Kohler, 1993) found that of the many practices thought to be critical, only four had been substantiated through data-based studies of student outcomes. These four are vocational training, parent involvement, paid work, and social skills training. However, there were several more practices that were strongly implied to be critical. These were inter-agency collaboration, individualized plans/plan-ning, community-based instruction, community-referenced curriculum, follow-up employment services, integration, and vocational assessment. Other areas that are considered important for students who plan to continue their education at colleges, universities, or vocational-technical schools include self-awareness and advocacy (Adelma & Vogel, 1990; Aune, 1991; Blalock & Patton, 1996; McGuire, Hall, & Litt, 1991), social-interpersonal (Aune, 1991), independent living (Brinkerhoff, Shaw, & McGuire, 1992), and academic preparation (Aune, 1991; HEATH Resource Center, 1990; Hoffman, Sheldon, Minskoff, Sautter, Steidle, Baker, Bailey, & Echols, 1987; McGuire, Hall, & Litt, 1991).

PREPARING FOR TRANSITION

Preparing for the many roles we will have as adults is a gradual process. A desirable long-term goal for all children and adolescents is for them to become productive members of society. Because children and adolescents with special needs may require a longer time to attain this goal, there are activities parents and teachers may do at school and at home to set the stage for the more direct and intense transition experience that will occur later in high school. After we identify some of these activities, we next discuss career education as career education prepares students for more intensive transition programming.

Activities

Pre-Kindergarten

◆ Design activities that encourage children to become more independent.
◆ Involve children in activities that build self-esteem and self-direction.
◆ Take young children into the community so they may see and learn about many possible careers and lifestyles.
◆ Spend time talking to children about what they might like to do when they grow older.
◆ Model a good work ethic and a joy of productive engagement.

Elementary Years

◆ Assign jobs to students within the classroom (or at home). Encourage completion of work in a timely and correct manner.
◆ Notice and praise good grooming and hygiene.
◆ Encourage parents to participate in the "Take Your Child to Work Day."
◆ Show films, bring in guest speakers, or visit different work sites where people with and

without disabilities from different career fields are employed.

◆ Encourage students to talk about what jobs they might like.

Middle School

◆ Complete vocational aptitude and interest inventories for each student.

◆ Address transition service needs on the IEP.

◆ Identify adult agencies from whom students may need assistance in the future.

◆ Engage students in career exploration activities.

Career Education

Career education is a term that was introduced into American education in 1971 (Brolin, 1995). It has been defined in several ways, but the basic concepts remain the same: career education is an *ongoing* process that *infuses* an emphasis on careers in *all subjects, K–12.* It includes employment and job-specific training as well as training in areas that prepare the student for many adult roles. Career education develops within stages:

Grades K–5: Self- and Career Awareness

Self-, career, and technology awareness activities are infused into the curriculum.

Grade 6: Personal Assessment and Technology Literacy

At this age, most students continue the process of assessing their academic, physical, and social/emotional strengths and weaknesses. They should have intense technological literacy instruction.

Grades 7 and 8: Career Orientation and Exploration

During this period, students identify broad goals to work toward. Four-year plans for grades 9–12 are developed with input from the students, families, and school personnel.

Grades 9–12: Academic and Specialized Skills Development

During high school, students attain the competencies necessary to go on for further education, training, and employment. This is done through academic programs and vocational programs and through applied learning in the community.

Postsecondary: Skills Development and Career Advancement

Career education is not a process that ends with high school. Many students choose to go on for further education or training either immediately after high school or at some point as adults.

Many elements of career education are found in functional curriculum, supported employment, and other transition-related programs. One of the best known and most widely used curricula is the Life Centered Career Education (LCCE) curriculum (Brolin, 1993). LCCE is a K–12 curriculum model that focuses on what an individual needs to know to function in society. It incorporates the basic tenets of the career education concept and provides teachers with a scope and sequence around which to teach children and young adults of all ages. A useful addition to the original LCCE, which targets students with mild disabilities, has been an edition of the LCCE for students with moderate disabilities.

 ACTIVITY 12.1

Reexamine the description of career education. Write down the things you did in kindergarten, elementary, middle, and high school that you think helped prepare you for the transition from school to the "real world." Who provided or helped you with these experiences? What other experiences might have been helpful?

(Answers for this and other activities are found in the Instructor's Manual.)

PLANNING FOR TRANSITION

One of the goals of the original landmark federal legislation, PL 94–142 Education for All Handicapped Children's Act, was to increase the personal independence and productivity of persons with disabilities through the provision of educational programming (Kruelle v. New Castle County School District, 1981). Although studies show some improvement in the employment percentages for students with disabilities after they had been out of school 3–5 years, they still lag substantially behind their peers without disabilities in all areas. Thus, the trend of unsuccessful postschool outcomes continues in spite of increased efforts over the past several years (Blackorby & Wagner, 1996; Wehman, 1993).

The Individuals with Disabilities Education Act and Transition

In 1990, PL 94–142 was amended and became the Individuals with Disabilities Education Act or IDEA (PL 101–476). IDEA required schools to address the transition needs of students in the Individualized Education Program (IEP) to help them plan for life after high school. The law contained a specific definition of transition services and mandated that all IEPs address needed transition services no later than age 16 and annually thereafter. IDEA defined transition services as follows:

> Transition services are a *coordinated set of activities* for a student, designed within an *outcome-oriented process,* which promote movement from *school to postschool* activities, including postsecondary education, vocational training, integrated employment (including supported employment), continuing and adult education, adult services, independent living, or community participation. The coordinated set of activities shall be *based upon the individual student's needs, taking into account the student's preferences and interests,* and shall include *instruction, community experiences,* the development of *employment* and other *post-school adult living* objectives, and, when appropriate, ac-

quisition of *daily living skills* and *functional vocational evaluation* (IDEA, PL 101–476) (italics added for emphasis by the authors).

The 1997 amendments to IDEA (PL 105–17) made small but important changes to the part of the law addressing transition from school to community living. The new amendments added language requiring that "beginning at age 14 and updated annually, each student's IEP must include a statement of the transition service needs under applicable components of the child's IEP that focuses on the child's courses of study" (Sec. 300.347 (b)(i)). In a subtle way, this requirement differs from the requirement at age 16 to have "a statement of needed transition services including interagency linkages." The new requirement (along with the legislative intent language) emphasizes the importance of early planning on the part of parents, teachers, and students. As soon as feasible, the student's curriculum should reflect courses that support desired postschool outcomes. For example, a student who is interested in a career in computers may have a statement connected to technology course work and a student who plans to go on to college may have a statement regarding participation in advanced placement courses. For all students, a statement regarding increased skills of self-advocacy and self-determination should be included (Cashman, 1998).

Other Laws Related to Transition

IDEA mandates supports and services for eligible students with disabilities pre-K through twelfth grade. Once a young adult graduates, permanently drops out, or "ages out," that student is no longer eligible under IDEA. The student may, however, come under the auspices of other related laws that support persons with disabilities. Some of these laws provide legal protection through the transition process for students while they are enrolled in school and other laws provide legal protection for the

Table 12.1 Legislation Since 1990 Affecting Transition for Students with Special Needs

Name	*Year*	*Major Purpose (relating to transition)*
Americans with Disabilities Act (ADA), PL 101–336	1990	ADA protects people with disabilities from discrimination in employment, public accommodations (including schools), state and local government services (including transportation), and telecommunications relay services. It also requires employers to make "reasonable accommodations" for employees with a disability.
Rehabilitation Act Amendments, PL 102–69	1992	New language in the Rehabilitation Act emphasizes that a person with a disability, regardless of the severity of that disability, can attain employment and other life goals if appropriate supports and services are made available.
Carl D. Perkins Vocational Education and Applied Technology Education Amendments, PL 101–392	1990	The new amendments replace set-asides mandated by the previous legislation with strong assurances and guarantees for equal access to services and support supplementary services for "special populations" (including students with disabilities). Controversy exists as to the elimination of the set-asides for special populations.
School-to-Work Opportunities Act (STW), PL 103–239	1994	The purpose of STW is to establish a national framework to expand educational and career opportunities for all youth (including young people with special needs). States may be funded to plan and develop a system that helps ensure a seamless transition from secondary education to meaningful, high-quality employment and continuing education.
Goals 2000: Educate America Act, PL 103–227	1994	Goals 2000: Educate America Act presents voluntary national standards describing what all students should know and be able to do at certain grade levels and establishes a national Skills Standards Board to promote development of occupational skills standards.

individual's lifetime. Table 12.1 describes some of the major laws related to transition. Two of these laws, the Rehabilitation Act of 1973 and the Carl D. Perkins Vocational Education Act of 1984, were passed several years ago but were amended in the 1990s. The table reflects just the amendments of these older laws. Section 504 of the Rehabilitation Act of 1973 is not listed because its substance is covered under the Americans with Disabilities Act (ADA).

The Transition Individualized Education Program (TIEP)

There are many similarities and a few important differences between Transition IEPs and the IEPs completed for students before they need transition services. Table 12.2 summarizes the components of the IEP process that are different for students in need of transition services

under IDEA. The components that are required for all IEPs before transition planning remain in effect.

The Transition IEP is different from a student's previous IEP in that participants now include the student and agency representatives, as appropriate, and the content must address postschool desires and needs. The Transition IEP is similar to the previous IEP in that it must be reviewed annually and the present level of performance, the goals, and the objectives should drive the services and supports provided to students.

Many local school districts develop Individualized Transition Programs (ITPs) separate from the IEPs. Some choose to incorporate transition planning into the student's IEP, but with more emphasis on preparing students to attain their desired postschool outcomes. Regardless of the way your school district elects to

Table 12.2 Transition-Related Elements of the IEP Process

Content of IEP

◆ A statement of transition service needs that focus on student's existing program or courses (beginning at age 14).

◆ A statement of needed transition services (beginning at age 16 or younger if appropriate).

◆ A statement of each agency's responsibilities and/or linkages.

◆ Goals and objectives addressing instruction, related services, community experiences, employment, postschool adult living (and, if appropriate, daily living skills and functional vocational evaluation).

◆ Because of the outcome orientation of the process, some statement of the student's desired postschool outcomes is implied. It should address, as appropriate, postsecondary education, vocational training, integrated employment (including supported employment), continuing and adult education, linkage with adult services, independent living, community participation. If services are not needed in these areas, the IEP team must indicate this and state the basis for making this determination.

Participants of IEP meeting

◆ The student must be invited.

◆ Representatives from agencies responsible for providing or paying for transition services.

Notice of meetings

◆ An indication that a purpose of the meeting is to consider transition services for the student.

◆ Beginning at least 1 year before the student reaches the age of majority, the student is informed of his or her rights as an adult (including signing the IEP).

---

accomplish transition planning, you will be responsible for writing goals and objectives that address the postschool needs of your students. Depending on the individual student, these objectives may include skills to prepare them for postsecondary education, competitive employment, and/or community participation.

You are encouraged to contact your local school district for copies of local transition guidelines and secondary IEP/Transition Planning formats. A partially completed TIEP appears in Figure 12.1.

As a teacher of adolescents with special needs, you will be involved in helping your students plan for transition. Although you may not be responsible for the entire transition planning process, you will be a key player. The complete transition planning process includes the following procedures (State of Florida, 1993):

◆ Becoming familiar with local adult services and supports

◆ Obtaining appropriate releases of information for your student

◆ Preplanning the TIEP meeting, which, most important, includes your student's input

◆ Scheduling the TIEP meeting to include teachers, administrators, counselors, family members, adult agency representatives, and your student

◆ Sending notice of the TIEP meeting to all participating members

◆ Preparing for the actual TIEP meeting, which may include preparing a packet of information and a survey of your student's job interests and adult living goals

◆ Initiating the TIEP meeting, which includes setting the tone for planning your student's future centered around living, employment,

Student's Name _Bobbie G._   **Teacher** _S. Carter_

Grade _11_   **Exceptionality** _Specific Learning Disabilities_

Standard Diploma _____   **Alternate Diploma** _X_

Desired Postschool Outcome

The student desires to: *enroll in a postsecondary program to become a child care worker, continue to live at home, learn to drive a car, and participate in a bowling league.*

The *Desired Postschool Outcome* statement is an expression of the student's dreams/visions 1–3 years after high school in the areas of employment, postsecondary education, community participation, residential preferences, etc. (i.e., live, work, and play).

Present Level of Performance

Based on student and parent interviews, past IEP summaries and other school records, and observation, Bobbie is on track to meet the requirements for an alternate diploma. She has mastered the performance objectives in the areas of functional academics at the independent level. Bobbie has volunteered at the on-campus day-care center and is near successful completion of the special needs vocational program in this area. She needs to investigate postschool training options available to her and have some paid work experience. Bobbie is independent in all daily living and most postschool adult living skills, but still has problems with budgeting money. She has taken Driver's Education but has not applied for her restricted license. Bobbie goes bowling with her siblings but has not found a league of her own. Her priority transition needs are (1) to participate in a work experience program (preferably one that is paid), (2) to apply for her restricted driver's license, (3) to learn money management, and (4) to locate and sign up for a bowling league.

(The *Present Level of Performance* should describe how the student is currently functioning. It should be stated so that a relationship between where the student is now and where he or she will need to be in order to attain desired postschool outcomes is apparent. It should include what the student *can* do and what the student *needs.* Test scores are acceptable if they are accompanied by an explanation of why they are important.)

Sample Annual Goal

Bobbie will find paid work experience.

(*Annual goals* should address discrepancies between the desired postschool outcomes and the present level of performance. The activity areas of instruction, community experience, training and employment, postschool adult living, functional vocational evaluation, adult agency services, financial management, daily living skills, and any other related services must be addressed either with a goal or a statement of why the IEP team feels a goal is not needed.)

Sample Short-Term Objectives	**Time Line**	**Responsible Person(s)**
1. Using classified ads, Bobbie will find 5 employment opportunities.	*November*	*OJT instructor and student*
2. Given 5 possible employment opportunities, Bobbie will fill out and submit 5 applications.	*December*	*OJT instructor and student*
3. When invited to interviews, Bobbie will meet with the interviewers and secure a position.	*January*	*OJT instructor and student*
4. When requested, Bobbie will provide evidence of her ongoing employment on a monthly basis.	*Feb.–May*	*OJT instructor and student*

(*Short-Term Objectives* must relate directly to the annual goal and must be measurable.)

Figure 12.1   Sample Transition IEP

community access, and friendship goals in the adult world

◆ Developing an outcome statement that projects future goals for your student 1 to 5 years after your student graduates

◆ Reviewing your student's present level of performance, needs, preferences, and interests

◆ Developing annual goals and short-term objectives in the transition activity areas of instruction, community experiences, employment, postschool adult living, daily living skills, and functional vocational assessment

◆ Assigning follow-up responsibilities for tracking the progress of transition services for your student after he/she graduates from high school

 IMPORTANT POINTS

1. Transition is not just a postschool experience as it includes everything we do during school to prepare students for adult living.

2. Some critical practices for successful transition found in the literature are vocational training, parent involvement, paid work, and social skills training (Kohler, 1993).

3. Other practices for successful transition implied to be critical include interagency collaboration, individualized plans/planning, community-based instruction, community-referenced curriculum, follow-up employment services, integration, and vocational assessment (Kohler, 1993).

4. Planning and preparation for adult roles do not begin in high school. The stage is set much earlier through experiences in the home, school, and community.

5. Career education is based on the infusion of critical skills for living and working throughout the school day from the earliest years and throughout a student's school life.

6. The Life Centered Career Education (LCCE) curriculum model is a unique scope and sequence to teach career education.

7. Transition is "... an outcome-oriented process ... which includes a coordinated set of activities ... which promotes movement from school to postschool activities ... must take into account the student's preferences and interests ... and must include instruction, community experiences, the development of employment and other postschool adult living objectives, daily living skills, and functional vocational evaluation" (IDEA, PL 101–476).

8. The 1997 amendments to IDEA lower the mandatory age to start the transition planning process to 14.

9. The Transition IEP is different from a student's previous IEP in that participants now include the student and agency representatives, as appropriate, and the content must address postschool desires and needs.

10. The Transition IEP is similar to a student's previous IEP in that it must be reviewed annually and the present level of performance, the goals, and the objectives should drive the services and supports provided to the student.

LINKING FOR TRANSITION

Planning and implementing transition supports and services is not something that can or should be done only by schools and teachers. Schools must join with *families, intragency* personnel (people inside the school system such as general and vocational educators and guidance counselors), and *interagency* personnel (people from the wider community, such as representatives from adult service agencies and employers). In this section, we provide you with some ideas about how to connect or link with these key stakeholders.

Family Linkages

Many families are very involved with their children during the early years. Young children require care and attention, and youngsters with special needs may evoke more nurturing and protective impulses in families than typical children. By the time students reach high school, however, family involvement in the IEP process has usually declined (Halpern & Benz, 1987). The 1990 amendments to IDEA attempted to re-emphasize the importance of family involvement by including a requirement of special notification to families when the purpose of the IEP meeting was to discuss transition services. Salembrier and Furney (1997) list three reasons as to the importance of family involvement in the transition planning and implementation process:

1. Families know more about their adolescents' needs, interests, and preferences.
2. The transition process prepares family members to think about the new roles and responsibilities they will have when their adolescent leaves the protective atmosphere of high school and the entitlement of IDEA.
3. If done correctly, involvement can empower the family to advocate for the adolescent during and after high school.

Families can be involved in many ways during transition. They may be involved in creating a vision, in the transition planning process, and in facilitating self-determination (Morningstar, Turnbull, & Turnbull, 1996). Training parents to become active partners and advocates for their youth with disabilities resulted in improved services and opportunities, both during school and after graduation (Katz, 1983). Family members need to be taught the process of adult agency referral, the mechanics of developing a TIEP, strategies for supporting the efforts of a working student, strategies for accessing adult community services, and other information specific to their adolescent's transition from school to the adult community. Table 12.3 lists some potential barriers along with solutions to family involvement in transition. Chapter 5 provides additional suggestions for promoting active parent involvement.

Intraagency Linkages

It is important for you and your students to develop linkages with people in the school environment because transition is not just a postschool experience. These people are the ones who help students acquire the knowledge

Table 12.3 Some Barriers and Solutions for Family Involvement in Transition

Barrier	*Solution*
If the family lacks knowledge or awareness:	**Then schools and teachers should:**
of rights and responsibilities during transition	share information in family-friendly formats (brochures, tapes, etc.)
about the continuum of programs offered in high school	discuss array of services; provide written or taped information
about graduation requirements	provide written information; discuss early and often; re-address during each TIEP meeting
about eligibility requirements for and services provided by adult agencies	hold Agency Fair; provide written information; invite agency personnel to TIEP meetings
about postsecondary options	share information about people with similar disabilities who have been successful; provide job shadowing
about community resources	provide written or taped information

and skills that will allow them to be successful after school. These intraagency linkages include general education, vocational education, and guidance and counseling.

General Education

Students who wish to pursue postsecondary education must first obtain a standard high school diploma or its equivalent. This makes linking with general education teachers important. Ways to support students academically in inclusive settings are discussed elsewhere in this text.

Vocational Education

About 99% of high school students with disabilities who stayed in school for four grade levels enrolled in some type of vocational education during that time (Wagner & Blackorby, 1996). Students with learning or speech problems, who took a concentration of vocational education during high school, were employed after high school at near or above the levels of the general population (Wagner & Blackorby, 1996). Vocational education may include school-to-work programs or work experiences.

School-to-Work. One of the most exciting initiatives related to vocational education and transition is the School-to-Work Opportunities Act. The purpose of the School-to-Work Opportunities Act (STW) is to establish a national framework to broaden educational, career, and economic opportunities for all youth through partnerships among business, schools, community-based organizations, and state and local governments. "All youth" includes young people with special needs (e.g., students with disabilities, disadvantaged youth, and youth with limited English proficiency). STW was designed to help states develop an integrated system that would provide students with a seamless transition from secondary education to meaningful, high-quality employment and continuing education. Successful school-to-work programs have three core components:

1. School-based learning (e.g., programs in which students learn math, science, language arts, technology, and other skills and standards in the context of the work world)
2. Work-based learning (e.g., programs in which students gain practical experience and training)
3. Connecting activities (e.g., links between employers, schools, teachers, students, and others)

These three components should be incorporated in kindergarten through postsecondary educational programs. The best-known types of school-to-work programs are Tech Prep, Career Academies ("Schools Within Schools"), Youth Apprenticeships, Cooperative Education, Vocational Technical Schools, Vocational Student Organizations (VSOs), and School-based Enterprises.

Work Experiences. Despite the common perception that work experience is effective in promoting future employment success (Edgar, 1987; Falvey, 1986), the National Longitudinal Transition Study (Wagner & Blackorby, 1996) found only a slight difference in the percentage of students competitively employed after high school (10.4%) between students with mild disabilities who did and those who did not have work experience. However, paid job experiences while in high school make a difference in postschool outcomes (Wise & Matthews, 1987; Sitlington, Frank, & Carson, 1993). Students with disabilities who engage in paid employment before high school completion are more likely to stay in school, remain employed after school completion, seek postsecondary education opportunities, and become self-supporting adults (Edgar, 1987).

Paid work experiences should be closely integrated with school-based instruction in job search and job maintenance skills training. Ideally, each student enrolled in job search and job maintenance skills training is simultaneously placed in a part-time job in the community. Skills learned in the classroom can then be practiced and generalized in the real world for permanency. A system for ongoing support and monitoring is critical for successful paid work experiences. Additionally, all members of the transition team should fully understand and implement the monitoring and evaluation process.

Guidance and Counseling

School counselors often take an active role in career planning for students with disabilities and initiate early career planning with parents and students. Students need to become aware of the many programs that can help them beyond high school, including community college programs, counseling and testing, disabled student services, occupational preparation programs, vocational training programs, and adult agency services.

School counselors should become an integral part of the transition team so they are informed and knowledgeable about the multitude of postschool program options for this group of students. High school special education teachers, job coaches, and other special education support personnel can play a vital role in collaborating with school counselors and soliciting their support on behalf of students with special needs in their quest for successful employment and adult living.

 ACTIVITY 12.2

> Interview a school counselor to determine the counselor's responsibilities as far as providing transition services to adolescents with mild disabilities. Design the interview form with a peer.

Interagency Linkages

Under IDEA, schools must provide a description of "interagency responsibilities and/or linkages" needed before a student leaves school. This im-

plies that schools need to have a working knowledge of and relationship with the public or private agencies that might provide or pay for services needed during transition. Unfortunately, students with disabilities often have little contact with representatives from postsecondary education, social, or rehabilitation agencies during their high school years (Hasazi, Gordon, & Roe, 1985; Roessler, Brolin, & Johnson, 1990).

The referral process to adult agencies must begin early so school personnel can assist with the application process and ensure active service status with the appropriate adult agency before graduation. Once a student with special needs graduates, there are a multitude of adult agencies to access. However, most of the agencies are burdened with high caseloads, bureaucratic complexities, discrepant eligibility criteria, and voluminous paperwork. Most adult agencies (such as state vocational rehabilitation agencies) require a formal application, medical exam, psychological exam, permission to access existing assessment information, interviews with the agency representative, eligibility determination, vocational evaluation, and/or extended vocational evaluation. This process can take anywhere from 12 to 24 months. A planned and systematic process of adult agency referral should be included in the student's TIEP during the tenth grade. The ultimate goal must be active client status with the adult agency, including postsecondary institutions, before the student's graduation date.

Once students with disabilities have completed the period of eligibility under IDEA (usually through age 21 or high school graduation, whichever comes first), they are no longer guaranteed services. The young adult will have to undergo the eligibility determination process for whatever adult services are desired. If determined eligible, the person may receive services from that agency as long as adequate state or federal funding is available or until the eligibility is reversed. There are many challenges in finding and getting the services necessary for young adults to make a successful transition. IDEA makes it clear that meeting these challenges is the shared responsibility of schools, parents, students, and agency personnel.

There are two main reasons for you to get to know local representatives of the adult agencies. First, the linkage gives you access to information that will be important to your students and their families, and second, it will give you a point of contact if one of your students has problems with an agency.

The most often accessed adult service agencies are listed and described in Table 12.4. This is not intended to be an exhaustive list but instead a beginning place for teachers, transition specialists, parents, and students.

Welfare reform is rapidly changing the types of programs available to people with limited means, including those with disabilities. As the federal government gives more and more discretion to state and local governments, fewer and fewer general statements can be made about national programs. You will need to become familiar with state requirements, especially for the programs described in Table 12.4. Because regulations change, including eligibility

Table 12.4 Adult Agencies That Serve Students with Disabilities in Transition

Agency	Description
Vocational Rehabilitation (VR)	VR's primary purpose is to assist eligible recipients to attain vocational goals and thereby become more economically self-sufficient. In order to be eligible for VR, a person must (1) have a physical and/or mental impairment that constitutes or results in a substantial impediment to employment, and (2) be able to benefit from an employment outcome from VR services. VR is a federally funded program (80%) with state match.
Job/Employment Services Job Training Partnership Act (JTPA)	Job or Employment Services are often administered by the same state agency that administers VR. The Job Training Partnership Act (JTPA) may also be in this agency (JTPA may be referred to by different names in different localities). This act provides job-training services for economically disadvantaged adults and others who face significant employment barriers.
Developmental Disabilities (DD) Services	Developmental disabilities services may include services in the areas of employment, residential, advocacy, and day activity programs. The most common developmental disabilities are mental retardation, autism, cerebral palsy, and epilepsy.
Community Colleges and Vocational Technical Schools	Community Colleges and Vocational Technical Schools typically have open enrollment and serve high school graduates from a certain catchment area. They can provide information about financial aid, academic counseling and guidance, special supports for students with disabilities, and, of course, an array of programs that usually includes both terminal degrees with certifications or 2-year programs that will allow students to go on to upper-division colleges and universities.
Social Security Administration (SSA)	The SSA is responsible for administering many federal and state funds for eligible elderly persons and persons with disabilities. The ones that may affect students in transition are: *Income Programs* [e.g., Supplemental Security Income Benefits (SSI)], *Medical Programs* [e.g., Medicare and Medicaid], *Work Incentive Programs* [e.g., Plans for Achieving Self-Support (PASS), Impairment-Related Work Expenses (IRWE), Student Earned Income Exclusion, etc.].

requirements, you should stay in close contact with local representatives of these agencies. For the most current and detailed information related to Social Security programs, contact your local SSA office. You may locate the SSA office closest to you by calling 1-800-772-1212.

 ACTIVITY 12.3

Working with a small group, plan an agency fair, an event that provides an opportunity for many different adult service agencies to share information with family members and students in a school or nonschool setting (e.g., a mall). Determine the agencies to include, incentives for student and parent participation, prior preparations, and follow-up activities.

 IMPORTANT POINTS

1. For effective transition to occur, families, intraagency personnel such as people inside the school system, and interagency personnel such as representatives from adult service agencies must work together.
2. The 1990 amendments to IDEA attempted to re-emphasize the importance of family involvement by including a requirement of special notification to families when the purpose of the IEP meeting was to discuss transition services.
3. Family members need to be taught the process of adult agency referral, the mechanics of developing a TIEP, effective strategies for supporting the efforts of a working student, strategies for accessing adult community services, and other information specific to their adolescent's transition from school to the adult community.
4. Intraagency linkages include general education, vocational education, and guidance and counseling.

5. Successful school-to-work programs have the three core components of school-based learning, work-based learning, and connecting activities.
6. Students with disabilities who engage in paid employment before high school completion are more likely to stay in school, remain employed after school completion, seek postsecondary education opportunities, and become self-supporting adults (Edgar, 1987).
7. Under IDEA, schools must provide a description of "interagency responsibilities and/or linkages" needed before a student leaves school.
8. Once students with disabilities complete the period of eligibility under IDEA (usually through age 21 or high school graduation, whichever comes first), they are no longer guaranteed services.

TEACHING FOR TRANSITION

The specific skills needed by a student with special needs to prepare for life after school will, of course, depend on the desired postschool outcomes of that individual. In this section, we address these skills in the context of the following transition domains of IDEA: Instruction, Related Services, Community Experiences, Postschool Adult Living, Employment, and, as appropriate, Functional Vocational Assessment and Daily Living Skills. When required, we further divide the skills in these domains into those that are more likely to be priorities for students who will be going (a) into postsecondary education or (b) directly into the workforce. These two outcomes are not mutually exclusive. Many students work while they attend school. Moreover, many of the same types of skills are necessary for young adults regardless of whether they go on to postsecondary education or directly into employment. It is impossible to teach students *all* the skills needed for the remainder of their lives. Therefore, you and the rest of the TIEP team must set priorities. In this section we describe general skill areas for students in transition and list some specific skills for transition to postsecondary educational settings and employment. Additionally, we describe commercially available programs for teaching these and other important skills.

Instruction

The teaching of academic skills is necessary for transitioning to either postsecondary education or employment. We have discussed strategies for teaching academic content throughout previous chapters so we just highlight information here.

Academic and Study Skills for Postsecondary Education

The importance of having an integrated transition planning process is especially relevant for students who are going on to postsecondary education. If the academic component of the TIEP is not developed in the context of the student's desired postschool outcomes, the student may not be adequately prepared for postsecondary education. Although most high school curricula are set up to be "college prep," teachers and parents must make sure that students not only enroll in the appropriate courses, but also that they are provided with supports and services to pass those courses. Necessary accommodations and modifications should be documented on each student's Transition IEP. This helps assure that the student will have a sufficient grade point average for college admission and be prepared academically for college level work. Additionally, teachers, parents, and the students should make formal preparation to take college entrance exams, including investigating possible testing accommodations that are available to students with documented disabilities (Hicks-Cooley & Kurtz, 1997).

Part of academic preparation is preparing for the increased study and organizational demands of postsecondary education. Students need to be taught study and work habits that will allow them to balance the demands of school with the need for some personal freedom and relationship building as a young adult (Hicks-Cooley & Kurtz, 1997; Hildreth, Dixon, Frerichs, & Heflin, 1994). See Chapter 9 for a thorough discussion of study skills that will enhance student success in postsecondary education and in the workplace.

 ACTIVITY 12.4

> Call a nearby community college and inquire about any supports and services available for students with disabilities. List and report to class.

Academic Skills for Employment

The SCANS (Secretary's Commission on Achieving Necessary Skills) Report (1991) identifies academic skill areas critical to functioning in the world of work. They include reading and writing on the job, figuring computations, estimating, making change, and using time wisely. Yet many students with special needs are not being exposed to functional curricula that prepare them for employment (California Education Transition Center, 1990). Students with special needs often have difficulty generalizing traditional academics to the real world of employment and adult living (Polloway, Epstein, Polloway, Patton, & Ball, 1986; Polloway, Patton, Epstein, & Smith, 1989). Job-related functional academics such as counting change, operating cash registers, and calculating net and gross pay are easily infused into existing mathematics courses.

Related Services

The term related services is defined as "transportation and such developmental, corrective, and other supportive services as are required to assist a child with a disability to benefit from special education..." (Sec. 300.22). Related services have been a required part of every student's IEP since the original PL 94–142 legislation. The 1997 amendments to IDEA highlight related services as part of transition planning by adding it to the areas that must be addressed on IEPs for students in need of transition services. Examples of related services that may be especially important for students in transition include transportation to a community-based instruction site, accommodations to a workplace environment, and parent counseling regarding the impact of a student's job on the income of the family. Related services are usually listed on the IEP separate from goals and objectives. However, if the need for the services is expressed or implied in the present levels of performance, there may also be annual goals to support them.

Community Experiences

Community experiences are mentioned specifically in IDEA for two major reasons: (1) some students with special needs do not have opportunities for a wide range of community experiences, and (2) many students with special needs require assistance to generalize knowledge and skills acquired in the classroom to real-life settings. Issues surrounding community-based instruction (CBI) or community-referenced instruction (CRI) include: (a) who should receive the instruction, (b) how much is appropriate, (c) which skills to teach in the community, and (d) what is the impact on inclusion efforts.

The amount of time spent in CRI should vary inversely with the student's ability to generalize. The more a student generalizes academic and social skills from school to nonschool settings, the less community-referenced instruction is needed. Conversely, the less a student demonstrates skills in real-life application situations, the more the student needs CRI.

Many school systems, community colleges, and colleges are promoting community service for *all* students. Community service projects are a positive step toward giving all students opportunities to feel connected to their communities.

For example, one of the authors is involved with a community service project for high school students with special needs. The students visit a retirement home weekly and read to the clients.

Postschool Adult Living

Postschool adult living is a broad area that encompasses the skills and knowledge required to survive in the "real" world and is not exclusively related to work or school. As adults, we shop for groceries, balance our checkbooks, make dental appointments, and go to parties. Some students with disabilities will incidently learn the skills to perform these activities successfully. In this section, we discuss self-advocacy and self-determination and social and interpersonal skills, two of the broad overarching skill areas for postschool adult living.

Self-Advocacy and Self-Determination

In the past, transition planning was done primarily by parents, teachers, and agency personnel. There are many curricula available that use a variety of approaches to help students develop self-determination skills. Table 12.5 lists and describes several of these curricula.

Students should be encouraged to participate in the planning for transition. Many students do not see themselves as an integral part of the transition planning process, and some professionals do not see students as active participants in TIEP development. Suggestions for ensuring student involvement in TIEP development include (a) have students write a rough draft of their own TIEP as a written class assignment, (b) encourage students to make a list of their strengths and weaknesses, (c) ask students to prepare a tentative list of their own transition goals to bring to the TIEP meeting, (d) allow students to be the prime decision makers relative to the time and place scheduled for their TIEP meeting, and (e) ensure that no TIEP meeting is held unless the students can be in attendance. See Figure 12.2 for an example of a way of involving students in the TIEP process.

Table 12.5 Sample Self-Determination Curricula

Title/Date	Author	Target Population	Comments
Become Your Own Expert (1995)	Carpenter	High school students with learning disabilities	One-semester course designed to teach self-advocacy skills
The Education Planning Strategy (1987)	VanReusen, Bos, Schumaker, and Deshler	High school students with learning disabilities	This strategy from the Learning Strategies curriculum teaches students to advocate for themselves during IEP and other conferences.
Learning with PURPOSE (1995)	Serna & Lau-Smith	Youth 12–25 with mild to moderate disabilities	Comprehensive curriculum
It's My Life (1995)	Curtis	Middle and high school students	Materials are designed to be fun for students (i.e., a card deck)
Whose Future Is It Anyway? (1995)	Wehmeyer	Students with mental disabilities	A student-directed transition planning process that is age and developmentally appropriate
Choicemaker Self-Determination Transition Curriculum (1996)	Martin, Huber, Marshall, Maxson, & Jerman	One part targets high school students with disabilities. Other parts target all students.	Comprehensive (and field tested). Includes *Self-directed IEP, Choosing Employment Goals,* and *Take Action*

Figure 12.2 Goals for My Future

Directions: Read each question and fill in the blanks.

One to three years after high school, I want to be living
_____ in an apartment.
_____ with my family
_____ Other _____

In order to do this, I will need to do the following:

1. _____ by _____
  (action)   (date)

2. _____ by _____
  (action)   (date)

I want to be employed as a _____
                                        (job title)

In order to get this job, I will need to do the following:

1. _____ by _____
  (action)   (date)

2. _____ by _____
  (action)   (date)

I want to continue my education at a
_____ community college
_____ university
_____ vocational technical center

In order to do this, I will need to do the following:

1. _____ by _____
  (action)   (date)

2. _____ by _____
  (action)   (date)

◆ **ACTIVITY 12.5**

Interview a student in a secondary program. Ask the student about his or her job interests, strengths and weaknesses, living plans for the future, and postsecondary education interests, if any. Fill out the Goals for My Future form (see Figure 12.2).

Self-Advocacy and Self-Determination in Postsecondary Education. The biggest difference between high school and postsecondary education is that the burden of advocacy shifts away from teachers and parents and toward the student. Under IDEA, schools and parents form a partnership to provide a free and appropriate education for the student. As discussed previously, students in postsecondary educational institutions have rights under ADA and Section 504, but they must be able to advocate for themselves. Self-determination and participation in one's own IEP has been discussed previously. The first step in preparing for postsecondary education for young people with disabilities is to open them up to the possibility and desirability of continuing education. For many of these students, school has been a struggle. Going on to college may not seem like a very good idea to high school students who struggle daily with academic work. Teachers and parents can promote continuing education by (a) helping the young person set and work toward goals, (b) pointing out people with similar disabilities who have entered and completed college and done well, and (c) helping the student develop a more positive self concept. This does not mean that you should encourage unrealistic goals, but you can help students develop realistic self-images in order to capitalize on strengths and accommodate deficits (Adelma & Vogel, 1990; Aune, 1991; McGuire, Hall, & Litt, 1991). Students need to know how they learn best. They not only need to be taught compen-

satory learning strategies, they need to understand why the strategies are necessary for them and the importance of their continued use. Learning disabilities do not disappear when a student leaves high school.

Good self-esteem and a realistic self-image are not enough, however. Students must also be effective at advocating for themselves for success in postsecondary education (Brinkerhoff, 1996; Dowdy, 1996; Koller, 1994). Several authors (Aune, 1991; Brinkerhoff, Shaw, & McGuire, 1992; McGuire, Hall, & Litt, 1991; McWhirter, 1990; VanReusen, Bos, Schumaker, & Deshler, 1987) suggest that students need to:

◆ be aware of their strengths, weaknesses, and learning preferences,

◆ understand their legal rights (federal laws and regulations such as ADA and applicable state laws),

◆ understand the circumstances under which they can and should request accommodations,

◆ maintain records that document their disability (e.g., IEP, medical records, descriptions of accommodations provided in high school),

◆ identify the types of supports and services that will help them most in their chosen postsecondary setting (e.g., note-takers, readers, transportation, etc.),

◆ identify specific services and resources available in the postsecondary institution they wish to attend, and

◆ identify the specific people or offices they should contact before, during, and after admission to their school of choice.

Self-Advocacy and Self-Determination Skills in Employment. Self-advocacy and self-determination skills are important to the worker with a disability. Some of these skills are more critical during the job-seeking process and some are needed to help workers maintain employment and feel good about their jobs. In the area of employment, several professionals (Hanley-Maxwell &

Collet-Klingenburg, 1997; Michaels, 1989) suggest the following self-advocacy skills:

◆ listing strengths and accomplishments (in writing a job application or in person during an interview),

◆ discussing the disability and requesting appropriate accommodations,

◆ responding to criticism in an appropriate manner,

◆ self-evaluating performance, monitoring task completion, and providing self-feedback,

◆ goal setting, including developing short- and long-term goals, and monitoring progress,

◆ developing a vocational plan that includes goals for career advancement and job upgrading, and

◆ standing up for one's rights on the job (not being taken advantage of).

Social and Interpersonal Skills

Interacting with other people is something we do every day in almost every aspect of our lives. Some of us are more socially adept than others. We seldom think of our social skills consciously. Research and anecdotal reports have clearly shown that for many students with disabilities, socialization is not a naturally occurring process (Chandler & Pankaskie, 1997). Lack of appropriate social skills may result in social isolation in the community and worse, involvement with the criminal justice system. If we do not provide systematic instruction in social skills for students with disabilities, we may be preparing students to fail in school and in the broader world of work and community.

There are many commercially available curricula that address many aspects of social-interpersonal skills. Some of them are listed and described in Table 12.6.

Social and Interpersonal Skills for Postsecondary Education. In addition to self-advocacy and academic skills, students in postsecondary educational settings need appropriate interpersonal skills (Aune, 1991; Hildreth et al., 1994; Koller, 1994). Social skills essential for postsecondary educational settings may include the ability to

Table 12.6 Sample Social Skills Curricula for Transition

Title/Author/Date	Description
ASSET Hazel, Schumaker, Sherman, & Sheldon-Widgen (1981)	A social skills program for adolescents age 13–18. It has a Leader's Guide, group activities, videotapes, and audiotapes.
Social Skills in the School and Community Sargent (ed.) (1991)	A CEC publication for mainstreamed primary, intermediate, junior, and senior high school levels.
Teaching Social Skills Rutherford, Chipman, DiGangi, & Anderson (1992)	A CEC publication that teaches socialization skills using a practical instructional approach.
Skillstreaming the Adolescent: A Structured Learning Approach to Teaching Prosocial Skills (Goldstein, Sprafkin, Gershaw, & Klein, 1980)	One of the most widely used, this curriculum provides a five-phase sequence to teach students critical social skills: (1) introduce the steps of the skill, (2) teach the steps, (3) demonstrate the skill, (4) have student rehearse and practice the skills, and (5) teach maintenance and generalization of the skill.
Social Skills Strategies Books A & B Gajewski & Mayo (1989)	This is a two-year program with daily activities that target students with skill, performance, and self-control deficits.

(a) use strategies to manage frustration and anger, (b) speak in a way that conveys a positive yet realistic self-image, (c) show awareness and concerns for the feelings of others, and (d) interact positively with college instructors, administrators, staff, and peers.

 ACTIVITY 12.6

In a small group or individually, review some of the social skills curricula listed in Table 12.6 and discuss their importance for students who plan to attend a community college, college, or university.

Social and Interpersonal Skills for Employment. Lack of social and interpersonal skills is often cited as the primary reason for unemployment and underemployment of individuals with special needs (Bullis & Foss, 1986). The specific skills related to successful employment are (a) independently managing one's activities, (b) meeting minimal cleanliness and dress requirements, (c) getting along with supervisors, (d) getting along with coworkers, (e) following directions, (f) being punctual, (g) managing time effectively and efficiently, (h) keeping an orderly work environment, (i) being friendly on the job, and (j) maintaining a moral work ethic (Archer & Gleason, 1994; Minskoff & DeMoss, 1994; Montague, 1988; Warger, 1990). *Job-Related Social Skills: A Curriculum for Adolescents with Special Needs* (Montague, 1988) and *Working II* (Foss & Vilhauer, 1986) are two programs that promote prosocial skills and address special considerations for social skills in employment settings.

The purpose of *Job-Related Social Skills: A Curriculum for Adolescents with Special Needs* (Montague, 1988) is to teach adolescents 18 job-related social skills that will increase their opportunity for job success. The skill sequence is hierarchical, with the skills ordered from simple to complex and easy to difficult. The social skills curriculum is developed around a task analysis of social behaviors to be learned, systematic instruction with repeated practice, and feedback to the learner regarding the appropriateness of responses. Since social skills are generally learned through observing the actions of others, students are taught to refine their observation skills. They are also taught to improve their interaction and problem-solving skills, in other words, to think before acting. Job-related social skills include: (a) ordering job responsibilities, (b) understanding instructions, (c) making introductions, (d) asking questions, (e) asking permission, (f) asking for help, (g) accepting help, (h) offering help, (i) requesting information, (j) taking messages, (k) having a conversation, (l) giving directions, (m) receiving compliments, and (n) giving compliments. *Job-Related Social Skills* comprises six sections: (1) an instructional guide, (2) job skills training format, (3) self-management strategies, (4) job-related social skills evaluation, (5) monitoring students on the job, and (6) appendices.

Working II (Foss & Vilhauer, 1986) is a job-related social skills program designed to develop social competence in a range of employment settings for adolescents and adults with mild mental disabilities. The program includes an assessment component, the Test of Interpersonal Competence for Employment (TICE), and an instructional component, the Interpersonal Skills Training for Employment (ISTE). The ISTE incorporates a nine-step teaching procedure designed to develop knowledge based on behavioral mastery of key job-related social competencies. Homework assignments are included to facilitate both application of learned skills in naturalistic settings and the transfer of training effects. The content areas of *Working II* include most of the critical areas listed in the literature, such as interactions with supervisors, following instructions, requesting assistance, handling criticism and correction, conflicts with coworkers, verbal teasing and provocation, interactions with coworkers, cooperative work behavior, and making requests.

With the *Working II* program, you use videotaped vignettes of job-related social skill situations to begin the problem-solving process. As the instructional sequence progresses, you model appropriate social skills for your students, then guide your students into their own behavioral rehearsal of the appropriate skills. The final step is for the students to demonstrate the appropriate skill in an actual job situation. You can adapt the instructional sequence to fit work-related social behaviors unique to your own students.

Employment

Knowing how to seek, find, and acquire employment is a critical element in transition programs for high school students with special needs (Cobb & Brody-Hasazi, 1987; Gerber & Brown, 1991; Polloway, Patton, Epstein, & Smith, 1989). Research has shown most former special education students rely on the self/family/friend network to find jobs (Frank, Sitlington, & Carson, 1991; Hasazi, Gordon, & Roe, 1985; Hasazi, Gordon, Roe, Hall, Finck, & Salembier, 1985). Adolescents with disabilities need instruction in skills like conducting a personal job search, filling out job applications correctly, and preparing a resume, as well as alternatives such as school-based vocational development and placement (Hasazi, Gordon & Roe, 1985; Roessler, Brolin, & Johnson, 1990). Some guidelines for infusing these components into the high school curriculum are listed below.

1. Include at least two to three weeks of skill building in how to search for job opportunities. Examine the classified ads, network with family and friends, and create an awareness of where job openings are posted in the local area.
2. Include instruction in developing a resume. Although young people may not have prior work experience, they do have life experiences that are transferable to the workplace. Critical content such as the mechanics of resume development may be included in an English course. Teachers may require the completion of a neat and accurate resume that can be mailed or taken to a prospective employer.
3. Include instruction in filling out job applications neatly, accurately, and completely. An English course may include the steps for filling out a job application using effective teaching methods so that the learned skill generalizes to the real world over time. Teachers should require students to complete a minimum of at least six real job applications to apply for jobs with local businesses (e.g., supermarkets, fast-food chains).
4. Include instruction in how to interview for a job. Instruction includes the skills of demonstrating appropriate personal appearance, personal hygiene, and the critical communication skills required for a successful job interview. Direct instruction and role playing using video technology may effectively teach these skills. Minimum proficiency should be the competent demonstration of interviewing skills for at least six jobs using video role-play techniques.
5. Include instruction on what essential documents are needed for getting a job. Cover what documents are necessary (e.g., birth certificate, state ID card, work permit, Social Security card), and how to obtain these documents.

Job success depends more on effective job maintenance skills (such as communication and interpersonal skills and good work habits) than upon the actual job skills (Chamberlain, 1988; Montague, 1988). Employers consider worker behaviors and attitudes to be important or essential to job performance (Campbell, Hensel, Hudson, Schwartz, & Sealander 1987; Hazler & Latto, 1987). When employers were asked to rank factors judged critical to job success for workers with disabilities, the five highest-ranking factors were: getting along well with others, interest in the job, efficiency, dependability, and being able to adapt to new work situations (Chamberlain, 1988).

Students with disabilities require systematic instruction in order to learn and practice the critical skills of keeping a job. They also need on-the-job support to ensure that appropriate job maintenance skills have been generalized in the workplace over time. Some implications for the high school curriculum and transition programs are:

1. Include at least a semester-long course in job maintenance skills. Emphasize job-keeping behaviors (e.g., how to dress appropriately on the job, how to fill out time cards, how to practice punctuality on the job) and job-related social behaviors (e.g., how to get along with supervisors and coworkers, how to interact with the public, how to ask for assistance, how to give and accept praise).

2. Include opportunities for part-time jobs while enrolled in a job maintenance skills course. The practice of learned skills in the natural environment is critical for generalization and also provides the opportunity for immediate feedback.

3. Provide ongoing and frequent support to working students. Support strategies may include teaching skills on the job, maintaining close employer communication, and implementing spontaneous crisis intervention. This process may require that systems change to allow support personnel to have time for supervision in the workplace.

As a teacher, it is important for you to communicate with your administrator and solicit the support necessary for a successful transition program.

 ACTIVITY 12.7

Make a list of the top 10 jobs in your county or city by using the Internet or calling the local Chamber of Commerce. Find out the educational requirements for three of these jobs.

Functional Vocational Assessment

As stated in IDEA, functional vocational assessment is required only "as appropriate." However, for students who want to enroll in vocational courses in high school and enter the workforce directly, it would be hard to imagine when it would not be appropriate. Alternative assessments are, and have been for many years, an integral part of vocational education. In the following section, we describe Curriculum-Based Vocational Assessment and Situational Assessment, two specific types of vocational assessment. We also discuss Portfolio Assessment. Any of these assessments serve the purpose of meeting the original IDEA requirements for a "functional vocational assessment" and provide an alternative way of assessing student progress.

Curriculum-Based Vocational Assessment (CBVA)

CBVA is similar to Curriculum-Based Measurement discussed in Chapter 3, but it has some unique characteristics. The main purpose of CBVA is to determine the career development and vocational instruction needs of students based on their ongoing performance within existing course content and curriculum. CBVA provides an alternative to the more traditional vocational assessment process. It has been found especially useful with students for whom written and simulated manipulation assessments are not appropriate. Table 12.7 provides a comparison of CBVA and traditional vocational evaluation.

There are three general assessment areas in CBVA: work-related behaviors, generalized skill outcomes, and specific skill outcomes. *Work-related behaviors* are the attitudinal, problem-solving, and interpersonal behaviors that are critical for student success both in classroom and community job settings. *Generalized skill outcomes* are the prerequisite concepts and knowledge necessary for students to perform successfully skills required in many occupational areas.

Table 12.7 Comparison of Two Vocational Assessment Approaches

Traditional Vocational Work Evaluation	*Curriculum-Based Vocational Assessment*
Requires a trained work evaluator experienced with special populations	Uses existing personnel such as vocational and special education teachers
High start-up costs and ongoing maintenance expenses	Minimal start-up and maintenance costs
The report is a "snapshot" of a student's abilities at the time of the evaluation	Assessments are ongoing from middle school through high school
Reports tend to very technical and require interpretation by a work evaluator	Reports are easily understood by parents and teachers
Has little or no relevance to what goes on in the classroom	Focuses on performance of course objectives and work-related outcomes
Provides information at the time of the work evaluation report	Provides a current base of information useful for transition planning

These skills include oral and written communication, math computation, and social-personal and problem solving. *Specific skill outcomes* are those skills needed for a particular occupational area. For example, in the woodworking trade, students may be observed for mastery of their use of hand tools and varnishes.

For students with special needs, the results of CBVA can assist in developing transition outcome statements, meaningful Transition IEP goals and objectives, and determining mastery of exit competencies for each outcome area. The results of CBVA may assist teachers in implementing and evaluating instructional plans and in making more suitable job placements.

Situational Assessment

Situational assessment is a system for evaluating work-related behaviors by observing a student in a controlled or somewhat controlled work environment. It is different from CBVA in that the assessed variables may be controlled during the assessment process. Situational assessments may be done in contrived or simulated settings, such as a mock work station in a classroom, or in a real work setting. Wherever it occurs, the underlying purposes of situational assessment are to observe and assess the individual in the work situation and provide feedback to the person and other interested parties about demonstrated work-related behaviors. The steps in a well-done situational assessment are:

1. Planning (considerations such as a work site that is of interest to the student, appropriate supervision, and a means for gathering information that can be used in vocational planning and feedback)
2. Scheduling (consideration of the dates and times of the observations, number of observations, and total time period of the observation—not longer than one month)
3. Recording (describing behaviors in observable, measurable terms; providing information about the work environment; recording the frequency, rate, or duration of behaviors when they occur)
4. Reporting (summarizing the observations and making recommendations, including job placement, work adjustment training, or another situational assessment in the same or different environment)

Portfolio Assessment

Although portfolio assessment has been discussed already in Chapter 3, a few words are in order here about the use of portfolio assessment in the area of employment. Students in secondary programs may use portfolios in a number of ways, but a common use is to document the student's employability skills (Stemmer, Brown, & Smith, 1992). Many of the basic academic, personal management, and teamwork skills that are important to employers may be taught, assessed, and documented in classroom settings. Examples of this include the ability to read and understand written materials, to attend class on time, and to work with people from diverse cultural and ethnic backgrounds. Both general and special education classroom teachers may provide this kind of documentation as part of their ongoing assessment of students. Either they or a transition specialist can help young adults decide what should go in the portfolio. The portfolio may be used to demonstrate to employers that young adults have the work-ready skills even if they have no actual work experience. If the student does have job training or experience, this may certainly be documented in the portfolio.

 ACTIVITY 12.8

Divide into small groups and discuss how you might use vocational portfolio assessment.

Daily Living Skills

Daily living skills include the many things that we need to know to help us meet the demands and expectations of each day. Daily living skills help us maintain our bodies, our personal possessions, and our homes. To some, they also include managing resources (money, time, and people), but these are more often included under postschool adult living skills. Most students with mild disabilities do not need direct instruction in daily living skills. They learn them, as most children do, through observation and guidance from parents. However, some children, especially those with moderate to severe disabilities, may need direct instruction in the how, where, and when of daily living skills.

The most effective and efficient way to teach most daily living skills is to break the skills down into their component parts (task analyze) and teach them sequentially in natural time and location using adequate amounts of prompts and reinforcement.

There are several curricula that offer guidance in teaching daily living skills. One example, *The Life Centered Career Education Curriculum* (LCCE) (Brolin, 1993), includes nine competencies in the daily living skills area. They are:

1. Managing personal finances
2. Selecting and managing a household
3. Caring for personal needs
4. Raising children and meeting marriage responsibilities
5. Buying, preparing, and consuming food
6. Buying and caring for clothes
7. Exhibiting responsible citizenship
8. Utilizing recreational facilities and engaging in leisure
9. Getting around the community

There are several subcompetencies under each competency (a total of 41 subcompetencies) along with suggested assessment and teaching strategies.

 IMPORTANT POINTS

1. Transition domains under IDEA include Instruction, Related Services, Community Experience, Postschool Adult Living, Employment, and, as appropriate, Functional Vocational Assessment and Daily Living Skills.

2. Although most high school curricula are set up to be "college prep," teachers and parents must make sure that students with disabilities not only enroll in the appropriate courses, but also that they are provided with supports and services to pass those courses.

3. The SCANS (Secretary's Commission on Achieving Necessary Skills) Report (1991) identifies academic skills such as reading and writing on the job, figuring computations, estimating, making change, and using time wisely as critical to functioning in the world of work.

4. Examples of related services that may be especially important for students in transition include transportation to a community-based instruction site, accommodations to a workplace environment, recreation/leisure programs in the community, and parent counseling regarding the impact of a student's job on the income of the family.

5. Generally speaking, students with moderate to severe disabilities will need more actual instruction in the community, but all students should have some community experience for practice and validation of skills.

6. Self-determination and self-advocacy skills will be needed by all young adults, whether they are going on to postsecondary education or directly into employment. The specific skills, however, may be somewhat different.

7. Lack of adequate social and interpersonal skills is often cited as the primary reason for unemployment and underemployment of individuals with special needs (Bullis & Foss, 1986).

8. Guidelines for teaching students with disabilities to find employment include (a) searching for a job, (b) developing a resume, (c) filling out job applications, (d) interviewing for a job, and (e) completing and obtaining essential documents.

9. When employers were asked to rank factors judged critical to job success for workers with disabilities, the five highest-ranking factors were getting along well with others, interest in the job, efficiency, dependability, and being able to adapt to new work situations (Chamberlain, 1988).

10. Guidelines for teaching students with disabilities to maintain employment include (a) emphasizing job-keeping behaviors and job-related social behaviors, (b) enrolling students in part-time jobs, and (c) providing ongoing and frequent support to working students.

11. Alternative functional vocational assessments include Curriculum-Based Vocational Assessment, Situational Assessment, and Portfolio Assessment.

12. Many students with mild disabilities do not require specific instruction in basic daily living skills, but may require prompts, encouragement, and reinforcement to use them.

◆ DISCUSSION QUESTIONS

1. Compare and contrast three functional vocational assessments.

2. Why do you think that students with disabilities still lag substantially behind their peers without disabilities in all areas of employment? What do you suggest to overcome this trend?

3. Your principal has asked you to create linkages for successful transition. What resources would you include and how do you plan to use them?

REFERENCES

Aaronson, S. (1975). Notetaking improvement: A combined auditory, functional, and psychological approach. *Journal of Reading, 19*, 8–12.

Adelma, P. B., & Vogel, S. A. (1990). College graduates with learning disabilities: Employment attainment and career patterns. *Learning Disabilities Quarterly, 13*, 154–166.

Adelman, H. S., & Taylor, L. (1983). Enhancing motivation for overcoming learning and behavior problems. *Journal of Learning Disabilities, 16*, 384–392.

Alberto, P. A., & Troutman, A. C. (1999). *Applied behavior analysis for teachers* (5th ed.). Upper Saddle River, NJ: Merrill/Prentice Hall.

Albion, F. M. (1980, April). *Development and implementation of self-monitoring/self-instruction procedures in the classroom.* Paper presented at CEC's 58th Annual International Convention, Philadelphia, PA.

Allen, V. L. (1976). The helping relationship and socialization of children: Some perspectives on tutoring. In V. L. Allen (Ed.), *Children as teachers: Theory and research on tutoring* (pp. 9–25). New York: Academic Press.

Alley, G. R., & Deshler, D. D. (1979). *Teaching students with learning problems.* (3rd ed.). New York: Merrill/Macmillan.

Alley, G. R., Deshler, D. D., Clark, F. L., Schumaker, J. B., & Warner, M. M. (1983). Learning disabilities in adolescent and young adult populations: Research implications (part II). *Focus on Exceptional Children, 15*(9), 1–14.

Allinder, R. M. (1996). When some is not better than none: Effects of differential implementation of curriculum-based measurement. *Exceptional Children, 62*(6), 525–536.

Allsopp, D. H. (1997). Using classwide peer tutoring to teach beginning algebra problem-solving skills in heterogeneous classrooms. *Remedial and Special Education, 18*(6), 367–379.

Alvermann, D. E. (1983). Putting the textbook in its place—Your students' hands. *Academic Therapy, 18*(3), 345–351.

Anderson, J., & Reilly, M. (1995). Establishing performance standards. In T. Azwell & E. Schmar (Eds.), *Report card on report cards: Alternatives to consider* (pp. 49–58). Portsmouth, NH: Heinemann.

Anderson, L., Evertson, C., & Brophy, J. (1979). An experimental study of effective teaching in first grade reading groups. *Elementary School Journal, 79*, 193–223.

Anderson, T. H., & Armbruster, B. B. (1980). *Studying.* (Report No. CS 005 205). Arlington, VA. (ERIC Document Reproduction Service No. ED 181 427)

Anderson, T. H., & Armbruster, B. B. (1984). *Studying.* In P. D. Pearson (Ed.), *Handbook of reading research* (pp. 657–679). New York: Longman.

Anderson-Inman, L. (1986). Bridging the gap: Student-centered strategies for promoting the transfer of learning. *Exceptional Children, 52*(6), 562–572.

Annis, L., & Davis, J. K. (1978). Study techniques: Comparing their effectiveness. *The American Biology Teacher,* pp. 108–110.

Archbald, D. A., (1992). Authentic assessment: Principles, practices, and issues. *School Psychology Quarterly, 6*(4), 279–293.

Archer, A. L., & Gleason, M. (1989). *Skills for school success.* North Billerica, MA: Curriculum Associates.

Archer, A. L., & Gleason, M. M. (1994). *Skills for school success.* North Billerica, MA: Curriculum Associates.

Archer, A. L., & Isaacson, S. L. (1990). Teaching others how to teach strategies. *Teacher Education and Special Education, 13*(2), 63–72.

Argyle, M. (1975). The syntaxes of bodily communication. In J. Benthall & T. Polhemus (Eds.), *The body as a medium of expression* (pp. 143–161). New York: E. P. Dutton.

Argyle, S. B. (1989). Miscue analysis for classroom use. *Reading Horizons 29*(2), 93–102.

Armbruster, B. B., & Anderson, T. H. (1981). *Content area textbooks* (Reading Education Report No. 23). Urbana, IL: University of Illinois, Center for the Study of Reading.

Armstrong, S. W., & Frith, G. H. (1984). *Practical monitoring for classroom use: An introductory text.* Springfield, IL: Charles C. Thomas.

Aronson, E. (1978). *The jigsaw classroom.* Beverly Hills, CA: Sage.

Ascher, C. (1987). *Trends and issues in urban and minority education.* New York: ERIC Clearinghouse on Urban Education.

Ashbaker, M. H., & Swanson, H. L. (1996). Short term memory operations and their contribution to reading in adolescents with and without learning disabilities. *Learning Disabilities Research and Practice, 11,* 206–213.

Atkinson, R. C. (1975). Mnemotechnics in second-language learning. *American Psychologist, 30,* 821–828.

Aune, E. (1991). A transitional model for postsecondary-bound students with learning disabilities. *Learning Disabilities Research and Practice, 6,* 177–187.

Aurbach, E. (1993). *Grady Profile* (Computer Software). St. Louis, MO: Aurbach & Associates.

Ausubel, D. P., & Robinson, F. G. (1969). *School learning: An introduction to educational psychology.* New York: Holt, Rinehart, & Winston.

Baca, L. M., & Cervantes, H. T. (1998). *The bilingual special education interface* (3rd ed.). Upper Saddle River, NJ: Merrill/Prentice Hall.

Baker, G. C. (1983). *Planning and organizing for multicultural instruction.* Reading, MA: Addison-Wesley.

Baker, J., & Zigmond, N. (1990). Are regular education classes equipped to accommodate students with learning disabilities? *Exceptional Children, 56*(6), 515–526.

Baker, L., & Brown, A. L. (1980). *Metacognitive skills and reading* (Technical Report No. 188). Urbana, IL: University of Illinois, Center for the Study of Reading.

Bakken, J. P., & Aloia, G. F. (1998). Evaluating the World Wide Web. *TEACHING Exceptional Children, 30*(5), 48–53.

Banjera, M., & Daily, R. (1995). A study of the effects of an inclusion model on students with specific learning disabilities. *Journal of Learning Disabilities, 28,* 511–522.

Banks, J. A. (1987). *Teaching strategies for ethnic students* (4th ed.). Needham Heights, MA: Allyn & Bacon.

Barker, L. L. (1971). *Listening behavior.* Upper Saddle River, NJ: Prentice Hall.

Barnes, D. (1993). Supporting exploratory talk for learning. In K. M. Pierce & C. J. Giles (Eds.), *Cycles of meaning: Exploring the potential of talk in learning communities* (pp. 17–34). Portsmouth, NH: Heinemann.

Barron, R. F. (1969). The use of vocabulary as an advance organizer. In H. L. Herber & P. L. Sanders (Eds.), *Research on reading in the content area: First-year report.* Syracuse, NY: University Press.

Baskwill, J., & Whitman, P. (1988). *New direction-evaluation: Whole language, whole child.* NY: Scholastic.

Bauman, J. (1986). Effects of rewritten content textbook passages on middle grade students' comprehension of main ideas: Making the inconsiderate considerate. *Journal of Reading Behavior, 18*(1), 1–21.

Bauwens, J., & Hourcade, J. (1994). *Cooperative teaching.* Austin, TX: PRO-ED.

Bauwens, J., & Hourcade, J. J. (1997). Cooperative teaching: Pictures of possibilities. *Intervention in School and Clinic, 33*(2), 81–89.

Bauwens, J., Hourcade, J. J., & Friend, M. (1989). Cooperative teaching: A model for general and special education integration. *Remedial and Special Education, 10*(2), 17–22.

Baxter, J. (1970). Interpersonal spacing in natural settings. *Sociometry, 33,* 44.

Bayes, M., & Neill, T. K. (1978). Problems for paraprofessionals in mental health services. *Administration in Mental Health, 6,* 133–146.

Beals, D. E. (1989). A practical guide for estimating readability. *Teaching Exceptional Children, 21*(3), 24–27.

Behrmann, M. M. (1995). *Assistive Technology for Students with Mild Disabilities* (ERIC Digest No E529). Syracuse, NY: ERIC Clearinghouse on Information and Technology.

Beirne-Smith, M. (1989). A systematic approach for teaching notetaking skills to students with mild handicaps. *Academic Therapy, 24,* 425–437.

Bellezza, F. S. (1983). Mnemonic-device instruction with adults. In M. Pressley & J. R. Levin (Eds.), *Cognitive strategy research: Psychological foundations* (pp. 51–73). New York: Springer-Verlag.

Belpre, P. (1973). *Once in Puerto Rico.* New York: Wame.

Berdine, W. H., & Cegelka, P. T. (1995). Collaborative consultation: A key to effective educational delivery. In P. T. Cegelka & W. H. Berdine (Eds.), *Effective instruction for students with learning difficulties* (pp. 19–43). Needham Heights, MA: Allyn & Bacon.

Bergan, J. R. (1977). *Behavioral consultation.* New York: Merrill/Macmillan.

Berliner, D. C. (1982). '82 issue: Should teachers be expected to learn and use direct instruction? *Association of Curriculum and Development Update, 24,* 5.

Berliner, D. C. (1984). The half-full glass: A review of research on teaching. In P. L. Hosford (Ed.), *Using what we know about teaching* (pp. 51–77). Alexandria, VA: Association for Supervision and Curriculum Development.

Bernstein, V. (1997). *Decisions for Health, Book One.* Austin, TX: Steck-Vaughn Company.

Best, G. A. (1990). Survival hints for the new teacher. *TEACHING Exceptional Children, 23*(1), 54–55.

Bietau, L. (1995). Students, parent, teacher collaboration. In T. Azwell & E. Schmar (Eds.), *Report card on report cards: Alternatives to consider* (pp. 131–153). Portsmouth, NH: Heinemann.

Bigge, J. (1988). *Curriculum-based instruction for special education students.* Mountain View, CA: Mayfield.

Biklen, D., & Zollers, N. (1986). The focus of advocacy in the LD field. *Journal of Learning Disabilities, 19,* 579–586.

Billingsley, B. S., & Wildman, T. W. (1990). Facilitating reading comprehension in learning disabled students: Metacognitive goals and instructional strategies. *Remedial and Special Education, 11*(2), 18–31.

Binder, C., Haughton, E., & Eyk, D. V. (1990). Increasing endurance by building fluency: Precision teaching attention span. *TEACHING Exceptional Children, 22*(3), 24–27.

Birdseye, T. (1990). *A song of stars.* New York: Holiday House.

Blackburn, J. E., & Powell, W. C. (1976). *One at a time all at once: The creative teacher's guide to individualized instruction without anarchy.* Glenview, IL: Scott Foresman.

Blackhurst, A. E., & Berdine, W. H. (1993). *An introduction to special education* (3rd ed.). New York: HarperCollins.

Blackorby, J., and Wagner, M. (1996). Longitudinal postschool outcomes of youth with disabilities: Findings from the National Longitudinal Transition Study. *Exceptional Children, 62,* 399–413.

Blalock, G. (1991). Paraprofessionals: Critical team members in our special education programs. *Intervention in School and Clinic, 26*(4), 200–214.

Blalock, G. (1997). Strategies for school consultation and collaboration. In E. A. Polloway & J. R. Patton (Eds.), *Strategies for teaching learners with special needs* (pp. 520–550). Upper Saddle River, NJ: Merrill/Prentice Hall.

Blalock, G., & Patton, J. R. (1996). Transition and students with learning disabilities: Creating sound futures. *Journal of Learning Disabilities, 29,* 7–16.

Blanchard, J. S. (1985). What to tell students about underlining . . . and why. *Journal of Reading,* 199–203.

Bloom, B. M. (1956). *Taxonomy of educational objectives, handbook I: Cognitive domain.* NY: David McKay Co., Inc.

Bondy, E., & Brownell, M. T. (1997). Overcoming barriers to collaboration. *Intervention in School and Clinic, 33*(2), 112–115.

Bondy, E., Ross, D. D., Sindelar, P. T., & Griffin, C. (1995). Elementary and special educators learning to work together: Team building processes. *Teacher Education and Special Education, 18*(2), 91–102.

Boomer, L. W. (1982). The paraprofessional: A valued resource for special children and teachers. *TEACHING Exceptional Children, 14,* 194–197.

Borg, W., & Ascione, F. (1982). Classroom management in elementary mainstreaming classrooms. *Journal of Educational Psychology, 71*(6), 733–750.

Bos, C. S., & Anders, P. L. (1990). Interactive practices for teaching content and strategic knowledge. In T. E. Scruggs and B. Y. L. Wond (Eds.), *Intervention research in learning disabilities* (pp. 116–185). NY: Springer-Verlag.

Bos, C. S., & Vaughn, S. (1994). *Strategies for teaching students with learning and behavior problems* (3rd ed.). Needham Heights, MA: Allyn & Bacon.

Bos, C. S., & Vaughn, S. (1998). *Strategies for teaching students with learning and behavior problems* (4th ed.). Needham Heights, MA: Allyn & Bacon.

Bott, D. A. (1990). Managing CBA in the classroom. In J. Salvia & C. Hughes, *Curriculum-based assessment: Testing what is taught* (pp. 270–294). New York: Macmillan.

Bragstad, B. J., & Stumpf, S. M. (1987). *A guidebook for teaching study skills and motivation.* Needham Heights, MA: Allyn & Bacon.

Brandt, F. J., & Ellsworth, J. J. (1996). Effects of cooperative learning on the academic achievement and self-esteem of urban adolescents with learning disabilities. *Learning Disabilities, 7*(1), 9–13.

Bransford, J. D., Sherwood, R. S., Hasselbring, T. S., Kinzer, C. K., & Williams, S. M. (1990). Anchored instruction: Why we need it and how technology can help. In D. Nix & R. Spiro (Eds.), *Cognitive, education, and multimedia exploration in high technology* (pp. 115–142). Hillsdale, NJ: Lawrence Erlbaum Associates, Inc.

Brigance, A. (1981). *BRIGANCE Diagnostic Inventory of Essential Skills.* North Billerica, MA: Curriculum Associates.

Brigance, A. (1983). *BRIGANCE Diagnostic Comprehensive Inventory of Basic Skills Student.* North Billerica, MA: Curriculum Associates.

Brigance, A. (1999). *BRIGANCE Diagnostic Comprehensive Inventory of Basic Skills (CIBS)—Revised.* North Billerica, MA: Curriculum Associates.

Briganti, M. (1989). *An ESE teacher's guide for working with the limited English proficient student.* Orlando, FL: Orange County Public Schools.

Brigham, F. J., Scruggs, T. E., & Mastropieri, M. A. (1992). Teacher enthusiasm in learning disabilities classrooms: Effects on learning and behavior. *Learning Disabilities Research and Practice, 7,* 68–73.

Brinkerhoff, L. C. (1996). Making the transition to higher education: Opportunities for student empowerment. *Journal of Learning Disabilities, 29*(2), 118–136.

Brinkerhoff, L. C., Shaw, S. F., & McGuire, J. M. (1992). Promoting access, accommodations and independence for college students with learning disabilities. *Journal of Learning Disabilities, 25*(7), 417–429.

Brolin, D. E. (1993). *Life Centered Career Education: A competency-based approach* (4th ed.). Reston, VA: Council for Exceptional Children.

Brolin, D. E. (1995). *Career Education.* Upper Saddle River, NJ: Prentice Hall.

Broome, S. A., & White, R. B. (1995). The many uses of VIDEOTAPE in classrooms serving youth with behavioral disorders. *TEACHING Exceptional Children, 27*(3), 10–13.

Brophy, J. E. (1979). Teacher behavior and its effects. *Journal of Educational Psychology, 71*(6), 733–750.

Brophy, J. E. (1980). *Recent research on teaching.* East Lansing, MI: Institute for Research on Teaching, Michigan State University.

Brophy, J. E., & Evertson, C. (1977). Teacher behaviors and student learning in second and third grades. In G. D. Borich (Ed.), *The appraisal of teaching: Concepts and process* (pp. 117–139). Reading, MA: Addison-Wesley.

Brophy, J. E., & Good, T. L. (1986). Teacher behavior and student achievement. In M. L. Wittrock (Ed.), *Handbook of research on teaching* (3rd ed.) (pp. 328–375). New York: Macmillan.

Brown, A. L., & Palincsar, A. S. (1982). Inducing strategic learning from texts by means of informed, self-control training. *Topics in Learning and Learning Disabilities, 2*(1), 1–17.

Brown, G. L. (1991). *Reading and language arts curricula in elementary and secondary education for American Indians and Alaska Natives* (Report No. RC 018 625). Washington, DC: Department of Education, Indian Nations at Risk Task Force. (ERIC Document Reproduction Service No. ED 343 766)

Bryan, T., Donahue, M., & Pearl, R. (1981). Learning disabled children's peer interactions during a small-group problem-solving task. *Learning Disability Quarterly, 4*(1), 13–22.

Bulgren, J., & Lenz, B. K. (1996). Strategic instruction in the content areas. In D. D. Deshler, E. S. Ellis, & B. K. Lenz (Eds,). *Adolescents with learning disabilities: Strategies and methods* (2nd ed.). Denver: Love.

Bulgren, J., Schumaker, J. B., & Deshler, D. D. (1988). Effectiveness of a concept teaching routine in enhancing the performance of LD students in secondary-level mainstream classes. *Learning Disability Quarterly, 11,* 3–17.

Bullis, L. P., & Foss, G. (1986). Assessing the employment-related interpersonal competence of mildly retarded workers. *American Journal of Mental Retardation, 91,* 43–50.

Bureau of the Census (1997). *Statistical abstract of the United States: 1997* (117th ed.). Washington, DC: Treasury Dept.

Burgio, L. D., Whitman, T. L., & Johnson, M. R. (1980). A self-instructional package for increasing the attending behavior in educable mentally retarded children. *Journal of Applied Behavior Analysis, 13,* 443–459.

Burke, C. M. (1993). Talk within the kindergarten: Language supporting a learning community. In K. M. Pierce & C. J. Giles (Eds.), *Cycles of meaning: Exploring the potential of talk in learning communities* (pp. 79–98). Portsmouth, NH: Heinemann.

Burnette, J. (1987). *Adapting instructional materials for mainstreamed students*. Washington, DC: Office of Special Education Programs, United States Department of Education.

Burnette, J. (1996). Including students with disabilities in general education classrooms: From policy to practice. In Educational Resources Information Center, U.S. Department of Education (Ed.), *Inclusion, 4*(3), 2–11.

Burns, P. C. (1980). *Assessment and correction of language arts difficulties*. Upper Saddle River, NJ: Merrill/Prentice Hall.

Burns, P. C., & Roe, B. (1985). *Informal reading inventory* (2nd ed.). Boston: Houghton Mifflin.

Bursuck, W., Polloway, E. A., Plante, L., Epstein, M. H., Jayanthi, M., & McConeghy, J. (1996). Report card grading and adaptations: A national survey of classroom practices. *Exceptional Children, 62*(4), 301–318.

Butler, S., Magliocca, L., Torres, L., & Lee, W. (1984). Grading the mainstreamed student: A decision-making model for modification. *The Directive Teacher, 6*(2), 6–7.

Byars, B. (1974). *Summer of the swans*. New York: Avon.

California Education Transition Center. (1990). *Synthesis of Individual Transition Plans: Format and Process*. Sacramento, CA: Author.

Calkins, L. M. (1986). *The art of teaching writing*. Portsmouth, NH: Heinemann Educational Books.

Callahan, J. F., Clark, L. H., & Kellough, R. D. (1998). *Teaching in the middle and secondary schools* (6th ed.). Upper Saddle River, NJ: Merrill/Prentice Hall.

Campbell, P., Hensel, J. W., Hudson, P., Schwartz, S. E., & Sealander, K. (1987). The successfully employed worker with a handicap: Employee/employer perceptions of job performance. *Career Development for Exceptional Individuals, 10,* 85–93.

Canter, L. (1979). Competency-based to discipline— It's assertive. *Thrust for Educational Leadership, 8,* 11–13.

Canter, L., & Associates. (1986). *Assertive discipline videotape No. 2: Implementing assertive discipline in the classroom*. Santa Monica, CA: Canter & Associates.

Carlisle, J. F., & Felbinger, L. (1991). Profiles of listening and reading comprehension. *Journal of Educational Research, 84,* 345–354.

Carlson, S. A., & Alley, G. R. (1981). *Performance and competence of learning disabled and high achieving high school students on essential cognitive skills*. Lawrence, KS: University of Kansas Institute for Research in Learning Disabilities.

Carman, R. A., & Adams, W. R. (1972). *Study skills: A student's guide for survival*. New York: Wiley.

Carnine, D., Silbert, J., & Kameenui, E. J. (1990). *Direct instruction reading* (2nd ed.). Upper Saddle River, NJ: Merrill/Prentice Hall.

Carnine, D., Silbert, J., & Kameenui, E. J. (1997). *Direct instruction reading* (3rd ed.). Upper Saddle River, NJ: Merrill/Prentice Hall.

Carpenter, C. D., Ray, M. S., & Bloom, L. A. (1995). Portfolio assessment: Opportunities and challenges. *Intervention in School and Clinic, 31*(1), 34–41.

Carpenter, W. D. (1995). *Become Your Own Expert! Self-Advocacy Curriculum for Individuals with Learning Disabilities*. Minneapolis, MN: Minnesota Educational Services.

Cartledge, G. (1996) with contributions by J. F. Milburn. *Cultural diversity and social skills instruction: Understanding ethnic and gender differences*. Champaign, IL: Research Press.

Cartledge, G., & Cochran, L. L. (1993). Developing cooperative learning behaviors in students with behavior disorders. *Preventing School Failure, 37,* 5–10.

Caruso, C. (1997). Before you cite a site. *Educational Leadership, 55*(3), 24–25.

Case, E. J. (1986). *Evaluation report: C-level aide program*. Albuquerque, NM: Albuquerque Public Schools.

Case, L. P., Mamlin, N., Harris, K. R., & Graham, S. (1995). Self-regulated strategy development: A theoretical and practical perspective. In T. Scruggs & M. Mastropieri (Eds.), *Toward a scientific practice of science education* (pp. 112–139). Hillsdale, NJ: Erlbaum.

Cashen, V. M., & Leicht, K. L. (1970). Role of the isolation effect in a formal education setting. *Journal of Educational Psychology, 61*(6), 484–486.

Cashman, J. (1998, Winter). DCDT offers preliminary on IDEA regulations. *DCDT Network, 22* (2), 8.

Castaneda, A. (1976). Cultural democracy and the needs of Mexican-American children. In R. L.

Jones (Ed.), *Mainstreaming and the minority child* (pp. 181–194). Reston, VA: Council for Exceptional Children.

Cegelka, P. T. (1995). Structuring the classroom for effective instruction. In P. T. Cegelka & W. H. Berdine (Eds.), *Effective instruction for students with learning difficulties* (pp. 135–159). Needham Heights, MA: Allyn & Bacon.

Chadsey-Rusch, J. (1986). Identifying and teaching valued social behaviors. In F. R. Rusch (Ed.), *Competitive employment issues and strategies* (pp. 273–287). Baltimore: Paul H. Brookes.

Chalfant, J. C., & Pysh, M. V. (1981, November). Teacher assistance teams: A model for within-building problem solving. *Counterpoint,* pp. 1–4.

Chalfant, J. C., & Pysh, M. V. (1989). Teacher assistance teams: Five descriptive studies on 96 teams. *Remedial and special education, 10*(6), 49–58.

Chalfant, J. C., Pysh, M. V., & Moultrie, R. (1979). Teacher assistance teams: A model for within-building based problem solving. *Learning Disabilities Quarterly, 2,* 85–96.

Chamberlain, M. (1988). Employers' rankings of factors judged to be critical to job success for individuals with severe disabilities. *Career Development for Exceptional Individuals, 11*(3), 141–147.

Chan, D. M. (1987). Curriculum development for limited-English-proficient exceptional Chinese children. In M. K. Kitano & P. C. Chinn (Eds.), *Exceptional Asian children and youth* (pp. 61–69). Reston, VA: Council for Exceptional Children.

Chan, K. S., & Kitano, M. K. (1987). Demographic characteristics of exceptional Asian students. In M. K. Kitano & P. C. Chinn (Eds.), *Exceptional Asian children and youth* (pp. 1–11). Reston, VA: The Council for Exceptional Children.

Chan, S. (1987). Parents of exceptional Asian children. In M. K. Kitano & P. C. Chinn (Eds.), *Exceptional Asian children and youth* (pp. 36–53). Reston, VA: The Council for Exceptional Children.

Chandler, S. K., & Pankaskie, S. C. (1997). Socialization, peer relationships, and self-esteem. In P. Wehman and J. Kregel (Eds.), *Functional Curriculum for Elementary, Middle, and Secondary Age Students with Special Needs* (pp. 123–153). Austin: PRO-ED.

Chiang, B. (1986). Modifying public domain software for use by the learning disabled student. *Journal of Learning Disabilities, 19*(5), 315–317.

Chiang, B., Thorpe, H. W., & Darch, C. B. (1980). Effects of cross-age tutoring on word-recognition performance of learning disabled students. *Learning Disabilities Quarterly, 3*(4), 11–17.

Chinn, P. C., & Plata, M. (1987). Perspectives and educational implications of southeast Asian students. In M. K. Kitano & P. C. Chinn (Eds.), *Exceptional Asian children and youth* (pp. 12–28). Reston, VA: The Council for Exceptional Children.

Christensen, M. (1992). *Motivational English for at-risk students.* Bloomington, IA: National Educational Service.

Christenson, S. L., Thurlow, M. L., & Ysseldyke, J. E. (1987). *Instructional effectiveness: Implications for effective instruction of handicapped students* (Monograph No. 4). Minneapolis, MN: University of Minnesota, Instructional Alternatives Project.

Christenson, S. L., Ysseldyke, J. E., & Thurlow, M. L. (1989). Critical instructional factors for students with mild handicaps: An integrative review. *Remedial and Special Education, 10*(5), 21–29.

Clark, F. L., Deshler, D. D., Schumaker, J. B., Alley, G. R., & Warner, M. M. (1984). Visual imagery and self-questioning: Strategies to improve comprehension of written materials. *Journal of Learning Disabilities, 17,* 145–149.

Cobb, B., & Brody-Hasazi, S. (1987). School-aged transition services: Options for adolescents with mild handicaps. *Career Development for Exceptional Individuals, 10*(1), 15–23.

Cohen, E. G. (1994). Restructuring the classroom: Conditions for productive small groups. *Review of Educational Research, 64,* 1–35.

Cohen, L. G., & Spencimer, L. J. (1998). *Assessment of children and youth.* New York: Longman.

Cohen, S. A. (1987). Instructional alignment: Searching for the magic bullet. *Exceptional Researcher, 16*(8), 16–20.

Cohen, S. B. (1986). Teaching new material. *TEACHING Exceptional Children, 19*(1), 50–51.

Coker, H., Medley, D., & Soar, R. (1980). How valid are expert opinions about effective teaching? *Phi Delta Kappan, 62,* 131–134.

Collins, A., & Smith, E. E. (1980). *Teaching the process of reading comprehension* (Technical Report No. 182). Urbana, IL: Center for the Study of Reading, University of Illinois.

Collins, J. L. (1997). *Strategies for struggling writers.* New York: Guilford.

Collins, M., Carnine, D., & Gersten, R. (1987). Elaborated corrective feedback and the acquisition of reasoning skills: A study of computer-assisted instruction. *Exceptional Children, 54*(3), 254–262.

Colvin, G., Ainge, D., & Nelson, R. (1997). How to defuse confrontations. *TEACHING Exceptional Children, 29*(6), 47–51.

Cooper, A. (1981). Learning centers: What they are and aren't. *Academic Therapy, 16*(5), 527–531.

Cosgrove, M. S. (1992). *Inside learning centers.* (ERIC Document Reproduction Service No. ED 358 875).

Costa, A. L., & Garmston, R. J. (1994). *Cognitive coaching: A foundation for renaissance schools.* Norwood, MA: Christopher-Gordon Publishers, Inc.

Council for Exceptional Children. (1995). *Mission statement.* [Online] Available http://www.cec.sped.org.ab/purpose.htm, August 27, 1998.

Council for Exceptional Children (1997). Special Education in the Schools. *Policy Manual.* [Online] Available http://www.cec.sped.org/pp/policies/ch3.htm, March 3, 1999.

Council for Exceptional Children Delegate Assembly. (1983). Code of ethics and standards for professional practice. *Exceptional Children, 50,* 8–12.

Cowley, J., & Melser, J. (1981). *Mrs. Wishy Washy.* Bothell, WA: Wright Group.

Craig, D. V. (1997). Telecurricular teaching and learning: The impact of World Wide Web access on the instructional process. *Telecommunications in Education News, 8*(3), 1.

Crisis Prevention Institute. (1983). *CPI workshop materials.* Milwaukee, WI: Author.

Crocker, M. (1983). Creating a vertical file. In J. Newman (Ed.), *Whole language: Translating theory into practice* (pp. 150–161). Halifax, NS, Canada: Dalhousie Univ.

Cummings, C. (1985). *Peering in on peers: Coaching teachers.* Edmonds, WA: TEACHING, Inc.

Curtis, E. (1995). *It's My Life: Preference-Based Planning, Facilitators' Guide and Planners' Workbook.* Salt Lake City, UT: New Hats.

Czarnecki, E., Rosko, D., & Fine, E. (1998). How to call up notetaking skills. *TEACHING Exceptional Children, 30*(6), 14–19.

D'Alonzo, B. J., D'Alonzo, R. L., & Mauser, A. J. (1979). Developing resource rooms for the handicapped. *TEACHING Exceptional Children, 11,* 91–96.

Darch, C., & Gersten, R. (1986). Direction-setting activities in reading comprehension: A comparison of two approaches. *Learning Disabilities Quarterly, 9*(3), 235–243.

Davis, A., & Clark, E. (1981, October). *High-yield study skills instruction.* (Report No. CS 006 323). Paper presented at the annual meeting of the Plains Regional Conference of the International Reading Association, Des Moines. (ERIC Document Reproduction Service No. ED 208 372)

Davis, R. W., & Hajicek, J. O. (1985). Effects of self-instructional training and strategy training on a mathematics task with severely behaviorally disordered students. *Behavioral Disorders, 10*(4), 275–282.

Delquadri, J., Greenwood, C. R., Stretton, K., & Hall, R. V. (1983). The peer tutoring game: A classroom procedure for increasing opportunity to respond and spelling performance. *Education and Treatment of Children, 6,* 225–239.

Delquadri, J., Greenwood, C. R., Whorton, D., Carta, J. J., & Hall, R. V. (1986). Classwide peer tutoring. *Exceptional Children, 52*(6), 535–542.

Demi (1990). *The empty pot.* New York: Henry Holt.

Deno, S. L. (1985). Curriculum-based measurement: The emerging alternative. *Exceptional Children, 52*(3), 219–232.

Deno, S. L., & Fuchs, L. S. (1987). Developing curriculum-based measurement systems for data-based special education problem solving. *Focus on Exceptional Children, 19*(8), 1–16.

Deno, S. L., Marston, D., & Mirkin, P. (1982). Valid measurement procedures for continuous evaluation of written expression. *Exceptional Children, 48,* 368–371.

Deno, S. L., Marston, D., Mirkin, P., Lowry, L., Sindelar, P., & Jenkins, J. (1982). *The use of standard tasks to measure achievement in reading, spelling and written expression: A normative developmental study* (Research Report No. 87). Minneapolis, MN: University of Minnesota, Institute for Research on Learning Disabilities.

Deno, S. L., Mirkin, P., & Chiang, B. (1982). Identifying valid measures of reading. *Exceptional Children, 49,* 36–45.

Deno, S. L., Mirkin, P., & Wesson, C. (1984). How to write effective data based IEPs. *TEACHING Exceptional Children, 16*(2), 99–104.

dePaola, T. (1974). *Charlie needs a cloak.* New York: Simon & Schuster.

dePaola, T. (1983). *The legend of the bluebonnet: An old tale of Texas.* New York: G. P. Putnam's Sons.

Desberg, P., & Taylor, J. H. (1986). *Essentials of task analysis.* Lanham, MD: University Press of America.

Deshler, D. D., Ellis, E. S., & Lenz, B. K. (1996). *Adolescents with learning disabilities: Strategies and methods* (2nd ed.). Denver: Love Publishing Co.

Deshler, D. D., & Graham, S. (1979). *Tape recording educational materials for secondary handicapped students.* Reston, VA: The Council for Exceptional Children.

Deshler, D. D., & Schumaker, J. (1986). Learning strategies: An instructional alternative for low-achieving adolescents. *Exceptional Children, 52*(6), 483–490.

Deshler, D. D., & Schumaker, J. B. (1988). An instructional model for teaching students how to learn. In J. L. Graden, J. E. Zins, & M. L. Curtis (Eds.), *Alternative educational delivery systems: Enhancing instructional options for all students* (pp. 391–411). Washington, DC: National Association of School Psychologists.

Deshler, D. D., Schumaker, J. B., Alley, G. R., Warner, M. M., & Clark, F. L. (1982). Learning disabilities in adolescents and young adult populations: Research implications (part I). *Focus on Exceptional Children, 15*(1), 1–12.

Dettmer, P., Thurston, L. P., & Dyck, N. (1993). *Consultation, collaboration, and teamwork for students with special needs.* Needham Heights, MA: Allyn & Bacon.

Devine, T. G. (1981). *Teaching study skills* (2nd ed.). Needham Heights, MA: Allyn & Bacon.

Devore, W., & Schlesinger, E. G. (1987). *Ethnic-sensitive social work practice* (2nd ed.). Upper Saddle River, NJ: Merrill/Prentice Hall.

Devries, D. L., & Slavin, R. E. (1978). Teams-games-tournaments (TGT): Review of ten classroom experiments. *Journal of Research and Development in Education, 12,* 28–38.

Dieker, L. A., & Barnett, C. A. (1996). Effective co-teaching. *TEACHING Exceptional Children, 29*(1), 5–7.

Dillard, J. M. (1983). *Multicultural counseling: Toward ethnic and cultural relevance in human encounters.* Chicago, IL: Nelson-Hall.

Dowdy, C. A. (1996). Vocational rehabilitation and special education: Partners in transition for individuals with learning disabilities. *Journal of Learning Disabilities, 29*(2), 137–154.

Duffy, G. G., Roehler, L. R., Meloth, M. S., Putnam, J., & Wesselman, R. (1986). The relationship between explicit verbal explanations during reading-skill instruction and student awareness and achievement: A study of reading teacher effects. *Reading Research Quarterly, 21*(3), 237–252.

Duffy, G., Roehler, L., & Rackliff, G. (1986). How teachers' instructional talk influences students' understanding of lesson content. *Elementary School Journal, 87*(1), 3–16.

Duke, D., Showers, B., & Imber, M. (1980). Teachers and shared decision making: The costs and benefits of involvement. *Educational Administration Quarterly, 16,* 93–106.

Dunn, R., Griggs, S. A., Olson, J., Beasley, M., & Gorman, B. S. (1995). A meta-analytic validation of the Dunn and Dunn model of learning style preferences. *The Journal of Educational Research, 88,* 353–362.

Durrer, B., & McLaughlin, T. F. (1995). The use of peer tutoring interventions involving students with behaviour disorders. *B.C. Journal of Special Education, 19*(1), 20–27.

Dyck, N., Sundbye, N., & Pemberton, J. (1997). A recipe for efficient co-teaching. *TEACHING Exceptional Children, 30*(2), 42–45.

Dynak, J., Whitten, E., & Dynak, D. (1997). Refining the general education student teaching experience through the use of special education collaborative teaching models. *Action in Teacher Education, 19*(1), 64–74.

Eaton, M. D. (1978). Data decisions and evaluation. In N. G. Haring, T. C. Lovitt, M. D. Eaton, & C. L. Hansen (Eds.), *The fourth R: Research in the classroom* (pp. 167–190). Upper Saddle River, NJ: Merrill/Prentice Hall.

Echevarria-Ratleff, J., & Graf, V. R. (1988). California bilingual special education model sites (1984–1986): Programs and research. In A. A. Ortiz & B. A. Ramirez (Eds.), *Schools and the culturally diverse exceptional student: Promising practices and future directions* (pp. 104–112). Reston, VA: The Council for Exceptional Children.

Edgar, E. (1987). Secondary programs in special education: Are many of them justifiable? *Exceptional Children, 53*(5), 555–561.

Edgar, E. (1988). Employment as an outcome for mildly handicapped students: Current status and future directions. *Focus on Exceptional Children, 2*(1), 1–8.

Eiserman, W. D. (1988). Three types of peer tutoring: Effects on the attitudes of students with learning disabilities and their regular class peers. *Journal of Learning Disabilities, 21*(4), 223–229.

Ekwall, E. E. (1985). *Locating and correcting reading difficulties* (4th ed.). Upper Saddle River, NJ: Merrill/Prentice Hall.

Electronic Portfolio (Computer Software). (1996). New York: Scholastic.

Elias, M. J., & Taylor, M. E. (1995). Building social and academic skills via problem solving VIDEOS. *TEACHING Exceptional Children, 27*(3), 14–17.

Elias, M. J., & Tobias, S. E. (1996). *Social problem solving: Interventions in the schools.* New York: The Guilford Press.

Elliott, S. N., & Sheridan, S. M. (1992). Consultation and teaming: Problem solving among educators, parents, and support personnel. *The Elementary School Journal, 92*(3), 315–338.

Ellis, E. S. (1983). *The effects of teaching learning disabled adolescents an executive strategy to facilitate self-generation of task-specific strategies.* Unpublished doctoral dissertation, University of Kansas, Lawrence.

Ellis, E. S. (1986). The role of motivation and pedagogy on the generalization of cognitive strategy training, *Journal of Learning Disabilities, 19,* 66–70.

Ellis, E. S. (1989). A metacognitive intervention for increasing class participation. *Learning Disabilities Focus, 5*(1), 36–46.

Ellis, E. S. (1994). Integrating writing strategy instruction with content-area instruction: Part 1. Orienting students to use organizational devices. *Intervention in School and Clinic, 29,* 169–179.

Ellis, E. S., & Lenz, B. K. (1987). A component analysis of effective learning strategies for LD students. *Learning Disabilities Focus, 2,* 94–107.

Emmer, E. T., Evertson, C., & Anderson, L. (1980). Effective classroom management at the beginning of the school year. *The Elementary School Journal, 80,* 219–231.

Emmer, E. T., Evertson, C. M., Clement, B. S., & Worsham, M. E. (1994). *Classroom management for secondary teachers* (3rd ed). Needham Heights, MA: Allyn & Bacon.

Englemann, S., Becker, W. C., Hanner, S., & Johnson, G. (1980). *Corrective reading program.* Chicago: Science Research Associates.

Engelmann, S., & Bruner, E. C. (1988). *Reading mastery: Distar Reading I.* Chicago: Science Research Associates.

Engelmann, S., & Bruner, E. C. (1988). *Reading mastery: Distar Reading II.* Chicago, IL: Science Research Associates.

Engelmann, S., & Bruner, E. C. (1988). *Reading mastery: Fast cycle.* Chicago, IL: Science Research Associates.

Engelmann, S., & Carnine, D. W. (1972). *DISTAR arithmetic level III.* Chicago, IL: Science Research Associates.

Engelmann, S., & Carnine, D. W. (1975). *DISTAR arithmetic level I* (2nd ed.). Chicago, IL: Science Research Associates.

Engelmann, S., & Carnine, D. W. (1976). *DISTAR arithmetic level II* (2nd ed.). Chicago, IL: Science Research Associates.

Engelmann, S., & Carnine, D. (1982). *Theory of instruction: Principles and applications.* New York: Irvington Publishers.

Engelmann, S., Osborn, J., & Hanner, S. (1978). *Corrective reading.* Chicago, IL: Science Research Associates.

Englert, C. S. (1984). Effective direct instruction practices in special education settings. *Remedial and Special Education, 5*(2), 38–47.

Englert, C. S. (1993). Writing instruction from a sociocultural perspective: The holistic, dialogic, and social enterprise of writing. *Journal of Learning Disabilities, 25,* 153–172.

Englert, C. S., & Mariage, T. V. (1996). A sociocultural perspective: Teaching ways-of-thinking and ways-of-talking in a literacy community. *Learning Disabilities Research & Practice, 11*(3), 157–167.

Englert, C. S., & Palincsar, A. S. (1991). Reconsidering instructional research in literacy from a sociocultural perspective. *Learning Disabilities Research and Practice, 6,* 225–229.

Englert, C. S., Raphael, T. E., & Mariage, T. V. (1994). Developing a school-based discourse for literacy learning: A principled search for understanding. *Learning Disability Quarterly, 17,* 2–32.

Englert, C. S., Tarrant, K. L., & Mariage, T. V. (1992). Defining and redefining instructional practice in special education: Perspectives on good teaching. *Teacher Education and Special Education, 15*(2), 62–87.

Englert, C. S., & Thomas, C. C. (1982). Management of task involvement in special education classrooms: Implications for teacher preparation. *Teacher Education and Special Education, 5*(1), 3–10.

Enright, B. E. (1983). *Enright Diagnostic Inventory of Basic Arithmetic Skills.* North Billerica, MA: Curriculum Associates.

Ensminger, E. E., & Dangel, H. L. (1992). The Foxfire pedagogy: A confluence of best practices for special education. *Focus on Exceptional Children, 24*(7), 2–15.

Erchul, W. P., & Conoley, C. W. (1991). Helpful theories to guide counselors' practice of school-based consultation. *Elementary School Guidance and Counseling, 25*(3), 204–211.

Erikson, H. L. (1995). *Stirring the head, heart, and soul.* Thousand Oaks, CA: Corwin Press.

Evans, S. S. (1980). The consultant role of the resource teacher. *Exceptional Children, 46,* 402–404.

Evans, S. S., & Evans, W. H. (1986). Training needs of special education paraprofessionals: Results of a survey conducted by a community college. *New Directions, 1,* 4–6.

Evans, S. S., Evans, W. H., & Mercer, C. E. (1986). *Assessment for instruction.* Needham Heights, MA: Allyn & Bacon.

Evertson, C., & Emmer, E. (1982). Effective management at the beginning of the school year in junior high classes. *Journal of Educational Psychology, 75,* 485–498.

Evertson, C. M., Emmer, E. T., Clements, B. S., & Worsham, M. E. (1994). *Classroom management for elementary teachers.* Needham Heights, MA: Allyn & Bacon.

Falvey, M. A. (1986). *Community-based curriculum: Instructional strategies for students with severe handicaps.* Baltimore: Paul H. Brookes.

Fantuzzo, J. W., Davis, G. Y., & Ginsburg, M. D. (1995). Effects of parent involvement in isolation or in combination with peer tutoring on student self-concept and mathematics achievement. *Journal of Educational Psychology, 87*(2), 272–281.

Fantuzzo, J. W., King, J. A., & Heller, L. R. (1992). Effects of reciprocal peer tutoring on mathematics and school adjustment: A component analysis. *Journal of Educational Psychology, 84*(3), 331–339.

Farr, R. F. (1989). A response from Robert Farr. In K. S. Jongsma (Ed.). Questions & answers: Portfolio assessment. *The Reading Teacher, 43*(3), 264–265.

FDLRS (Florida Diagnostic and Learning Resource System). (1982). *Communication skills materials.* Daytona Beach, FL: Author.

Fisher, C., Berliner, D., Filby, N., Marliave, R., Cahen, L., & Dishaw, M. (1980). Teaching behaviors, academic learning time, and student achievement: An overview. In C. Denham & A. Lieberman (Eds.), *Time to learn* (pp. 7–32). Washington, DC: National Institute of Education.

Fister, S. L., & Kemp, K. A. (1995). *TGIF: But what will I do on Monday?* Longmont, CO: Sopris West.

Flake-Hobson, C., & Swick, K. J. (1984). Communication strategies for parents and teachers, or how to say what you mean. In M. L. & E. M. Nesselroad (Eds.), *Working with parents of handicapped children: A book of readings for school personnel* (pp. 141–149). Lanham, MD: University Press of America.

Flavell, J. (1976). Metacognitive aspects of problem solving. In L. B. Resnick (Ed.), *The nature of intelligence.* Hillsdale, NJ: Erlbaum.

Flood, J., & Lapp, D. (1989). Reporting reading progress: A comparison portfolio for parents. *The Reading Teacher, 42*(7), 508–514.

Flores, D., Schloss, P., & Alper, S. (1995). The use of a daily calendar to increase responsibilities fulfilled by secondary students with special needs. *Remedial and Special Education, 16*(1), 38–43.

Florida Department of Education. (1994). *Specialized curriculum for exceptional students: Instructor's manual.* Tallahassee, FL: Bureau of Education for Exceptional Students.

Florida Performance Measurement System (FPMS). (1984). *Domains: Knowledge base of the Florida Performance Measurement System.* Tallahassee, FL: Florida Coalition for the Development of a Performance Measurement System, Office of Teacher Education, Certification and Inservice Staff Development.

Forness, S. R., Kavale, K. A., Blum, I. M., & Lloyd, J. W. (1997). Mega-analysis of meta-analyses: What works in special education and related services. *TEACHING Exceptional Children, 29*(6), 4–9.

Foss G., & Vilhauer, D. (1986). *Working I & II: Interpersonal skills assessment and training for employment.* Santa Monica, CA: James Standfield.

Fowler, R. L., & Barker, A. S. (1974). Effectiveness of highlighting for retention of text material. *Journal of Applied Psychology, 59,* 358–364.

Fradd, S., & Hallman, C. L. (1983). Implications of psychological and educational research for assessment and instruction of culturally and linguistically different students. *Learning Disability Quarterly, 6*(4), 468–478.

Frank, A. R., Keith, T. Z., & Steil, D. A. (1988). Training needs of special education professionals. *Exceptional Children, 55*(3), 253–258.

Frank, A. R., Sitlington, P. L., & Carson, R. (1991). Transition of adolescents with behavioral disorders—is it successful? *Behavioral Disorders, 16*(3), 180–191.

Fraser, C., Belzner, R., & Conte, R. (1992). Attention deficit hyperactivity disorder and self-control. *School Psychology International, 13,* 339–345.

Frederick, W. C., & Walberg, H. J. (1980). Learning as a function of time. *The Journal of Educational Research, 73,* 183–194.

Friend, M., & Bursuck, W. (1996). *Including students with special needs: A practical guide for classroom teachers:* Needham Heights, MA: Allyn & Bacon.

Friend, M., & Cook, L. (1992). *Interactions: Collaboration skills for professionals.* New York: Longman.

Frisby, C. (1987). Alternative assessment committee report: Curriculum-based assessment. *CASP Today, 36,* 15–26.

Frith, G. H., & Armstrong, S. W. (1986). Self-monitoring for behavior-disordered students. *Behavioral Disorders, 18*(2), 144–148.

Frith, G. H., & Lindsey, J. D. (1980). Paraprofessional roles in mainstreaming multihandicapped students. *Education Unlimited, 2,* 17–21.

Frith, G. H., & Lindsey, J. D. (1982). Certification, training, and other programming variables affecting special education and the paraprofessional concept. *Journal of Special Education, 16,* 229–236.

Frith, G. H., Lindsey, J. D., & Edwards, R. (1981). A noncategorical approach for serving exceptional children of low-incidence exceptionalities in rural areas. *Education, 101,* 276–278.

Frith, G. H., & Mims, A. (1985, Spring). Burnout among special education paraprofessionals. *TEACHING Exceptional Children, 17*(3), 225–227.

Fry, E. (1968). A readability formula that saves time. *Journal of Reading, 11*(7), 513–516, 575–578.

Fuchs, D., & Fuchs, L. (1994). Inclusive schools movement and the radicalization of special education reform. *Exceptional Children, 60*(4), 294–309.

Fuchs, D., & Fuchs, L. S. (1989). Exploring effective and efficient prereferral interventions: A component analysis of behavioral consultation. *School Psychology Review, 18,* 260–283.

Fuchs, D., Fuchs, L. S., & Bahr, M. W. (1990). Mainstream assistance teams: A scientific basis for the art of consultation. *Exceptional Children, 57*(2), 128–139.

Fuchs, D., Fuchs, L. S., Bahr, M. W., Fernstrom, P., & Stecker, P. M. (1990). Prereferral intervention: A prescriptive approach. *Exceptional Children, 56*(6), 493–513.

Fuchs, D., Fuchs, L. S., Mathes, P. G., & Simmons, D. C. (1996). *Peer-assisted learning strategies: Making classrooms more responsive to diversity.* (Report No. NCRTL-EC-304-716). East Lansing, MI: National Center for Research on Teacher Learning. (ERIC Document Reproduction Service No. ED 393 269)

Fuchs, L. S., & Deno, S. L. (1991). Paradigmatic distinctions between instructionally relevant measurement models. *Exceptional Children, 57*(6), 488–500.

Fuchs, L. S., & Fuchs, D. (1996). Combining performance assessment and curriculum-based measurement to strengthen instructional planning. *Learning Disabilities Research & Practice, 11*(3), 183–192.

Fuchs, L. S., Fuchs, D., & Hamlett, C. L. (1989). Effects of alternative goal structures within curriculum-based measurement. *Exceptional Children, 55*(5), 429–438.

Fuchs, L. S., Fuchs, D., Hamlett, C. L., & Stecker, P. M. (1990). The role of skills analysis in curriculum-based measurement in math. *School Psychology Review, 19*(1), 6–22.

Fuchs, L. S., Fuchs, D., Hamlett, C. L., & Stecker, P. M. (1991). Effects of curriculum-based measurement and consultation on teacher planning and student achievement in mathematics operations. *American Educational Research Journal, 28*(3), 617–641.

Fuchs, L. S., Fuchs, D., Hamlett, C. L., & Whinnery, K. (1991). Effects of goal line feedback on level, slope, and stability of performance within curriculum-based measurement. *Learning Disabilities Research & Practice, 6*(2), 66–74.

Fuchs, L. S., Hamlett, C. L., & Fuchs, D. (1990). *Monitoring Basic Skills Growth.* Austin, TX: PRO-ED.

Fuchs, L. S., & Shinn, M. R. (1989). Writing CBM IEP objectives. In M. R. Shinn (Ed.), *Curriculum-based measurement: Assessing special children* (pp. 130–152). New York: The Guilford Press.

Fullan, M., & Pomfret, A. (1977). Research on curriculum and instruction implementation. *Review of Educational Research, 47,* 335–397.

Gable, R. A., Young, C. C., & Hendrickson, M. J. (1987). Content of special education teacher preparation: Are we headed in the right direction? *Teacher Education and Special Education, 10*(3), 135–139.

Gajewski, N., & Mayo, P. (1989). *Social skills strategies, Books A & B.* Verona, WI: Thinking Publications.

Gallagher, P. A. (1988). *Teaching students with behavior disorders: Techniques and activities for classroom instruction* (2nd ed.). Denver: Love Publishing.

Gardner, H. (1983). *Frames of mind: The theory of multiple intelligences.* New York: Basic Books.

Gardner, H. (1995). Reflections on multiple intelligences: Myths and messages. *Phi Delta Kappan, 77*(3), 200–209.

Gardner, R., Heward, W. L., & Grossi, T. A. (1994). Effects of response cards on student participation and academic achievement: A systematic replication with inner-city students during whole-class science instruction. *Journal of Applied Behavior Analysis, 27,* 63–71.

Garner, R., & Kraus, C. (1982). Good and poor comprehension differences in knowing and regulating reading behaviors. *Educational Research Quarterly, 6,* 5–12.

Gartner, A., & Riessman, F. (1993). *Peer-tutoring: Toward a new model* (Report No. NCTRL-SP-034-776). East Lansing, MI. National Center for Research on Teacher Learning. (ERIC Document Reproduction Service No. ED 362 506)

Geisel, T. (Dr. Seuss). (1938). *The five hundred hats of Bartholemew Cubbins.* New York: Vanguard.

Gelzheiser, L. M., Shepherd, M. J., & Wozniak, R. H. (1986). The development of instruction to induce skill transfer. *Exceptional Children, 53*(2), 125–129.

George, J. C. (1987). *Water Sky.* New York: Harper & Row.

Gerber, P. J., & Brown, D. (1991). Report of the pathways to employment consensus conference on employability of persons with learning disabilities. *Learning Disabilities Research and Practice, 6*(2), 99–103.

Gersten, R. (1985). Direct instruction with special education students: A review of evaluation research. *Journal of Special Education, 19*(1), 41–58.

Gersten, R., & Carnine, D. (1984). Direct instruction mathematics: A longitudinal evaluation of low-income elementary school students. *Elementary School Journal, 84*(4), 395–407.

Gersten, R., Carnine, D., & Woodward, J. (1987). Direct instruction research: The third decade. *Remedial and Special Education, 8*(6), 48–56.

Gersten, R., Darch, C., David, G., & George, N. (1991). Apprenticeship and intensive training of consulting teachers: A naturalistic study. *Exceptional Children, 57*(3), 226–236.

Gersten, R., & Maggs, A. (1982). Teaching the general case to moderately retarded children: Evaluation of a five-year project. *Analysis and Intervention in Developmental Disabilities, 2,* 329–343.

Gersten, R., Vaughn, S., & Brengelman, S. (1996.) Grading and academic feedback for special education students and students with learning disabilities. In T. R. Guskey (Ed.), *ASCD Yearbook 1996 Communicating student learning* (pp. 47–57). Alexandria, VA: ASCD.

Gersten, R., & Woodward, J. (1994). The language-minority student and special education: Issues, trends, and paradoxes. *Exceptional Children, 60*(4), 310–322.

Gersten, R., Woodward, J., & Darch, C. (1986). Direct instruction: A research-based approach to curriculum design and teaching. *Exceptional Children, 53*(1), 17–31.

Gettinger, M., & Fayne, H. (1982). Classroom behaviors during small group instruction and learning performance in learning-disabled and nondisabled children. *Journal of Educational Research, 75*(3), 182–187.

Gilliam, H. V., & Van Den Berg, S. (1980). Different levels of eye contact: Effects on black and white college students. *Urban Education, 15*(1), 83–92.

Glatthorn, A. A. (1990). Cooperative professional development: Facilitating the growth of the special education teacher and the classroom teacher. *Remedial and Special Education, 11*(3), 29–50.

Gleason, M. M. (1988). Study skills: Teaching study strategies. *TEACHING Exceptional Children, 20*(3), 52–53.

Glynn, S. M. (1978). Capturing readers' attention by means of typographical cueing strategies. *Educational Technology, 18,* 7–12.

Goldstein, C. (1998). Learning at CyberCamp. *TEACHING Exceptional Children, 30*(5), 16–21.

Goldstein, M. J. (1986). Curriculum: The keystone for special education planning. *TEACHING Exceptional Children, 18*(3), 220–225.

Gollnick, D. M., & Chinn, P. C. (1990). *Multicultural education in a pluralistic society* (3rd ed.). Upper Saddle River, NJ: Merrill/Prentice Hall.

Gollnick, D. M., Sadker, M. P., & Sadker, D. M. (1982). Beyond the Dick and Jane syndrome: Confronting sex bias in instructional materials. In M. P. Sadker & D. M. Sadker (Eds.), *Sex equity handbook for schools* (pp. 60–90). New York: Longman.

Good, T. L., & Brophy, J. (1984). *Looking in classrooms* (3rd ed.). New York: Harper & Row.

Good, T. L., & Brophy, J. E. (1987). *Looking in classrooms* (4th ed.). New York: Harper & Row.

Good, T. L., & Grouws, D. A. (1979). The Missouri mathematics effectiveness project. *Journal of Educational Psychology, 71*, 355–362.

Goodman, L. (1985). The effective schools movement and special education. *TEACHING Exceptional Children, 17*(2), 102–105.

Goodrich, H. (Dec, 1996–Jan, 1997). Understanding rubrics. *Educational Leadership, 54*(4), 14–17.

Goor, M., Schwenn, J., Elridge, A., Mallein, D., & Stauffer, J. (1996). Using strategy cards to enhance cooperative learning for students with disabilities. *TEACHING Exceptional Children, 29*(1), 66–70.

Graden, J. L. (1989). Redefining "prereferral" intervention as instructional assistance: Collaboration between general and special education. *Exceptional Children, 56*(3), 227–231.

Graden, J. L., Casey, A., & Christenson, S. L. (1985). Implementing a prereferral intervention system. Part I: The model. *Exceptional Children, 51*, 377–384.

The Grady Profile™ (Computer Software). (1995). St. Louis, MO: Aurbach and Associates.

Graham, S. (1985). Teaching basic academic skills to learning-disabled students: A model of the teaching-learning process. *Journal of Learning Disabilities, 18*(9), 528–534.

Graham, S., & Harris, K. R. (1993). Self-regulated strategy development: Helping students with learning problems develop as writers. *Elementary School Journal, 94*, 169–181.

Graham, S., & Harris, K. R. (1994). The effects of whole language on children's writing: A review of literature. *Educational Psychologist, 29*, 187–192.

Graham, S., Harris, K. R., MacArthur, C., & Schwartz, S. (1991). Writing and writing instruction with students with learning disabilities: A review of a program of research. *Learning Disability Quarterly, 14*, 89–114.

Graham, S., MacArthur, C., & Schwartz, S. (1995). The effects of goal setting and procedural facilitation on the revising behavior and writing performance of students with writing and learning problems. *Journal of Educational Psychology, 87*(2), 230–240.

Grant, C. A., & Sleeter, C. E. (1989). *Turning on learning: Five approaches for multicultural plans for race, class, gender, and disability.* Upper Saddle River, NJ: Merrill/Prentice Hall.

Graves, D. K., & Bradley, D. F. (1997). Establishing the classroom as a community. In D. F. Bradley, M. K. King-Sears, & D. M. Tessier-Switlick (Eds.), *Teaching students in inclusive settings: From theory to practice* (pp. 365–383). Needham Heights, MA: Allyn & Bacon.

Graves, D. K., & Stuart, V. (1985). *Write from the start.* New York: New American Library.

Great Falls Public Schools. (1981). *Great Falls precision teaching training manual* (5th ed). Great Falls, MT: Author.

Greene, G., & Albright, L. (1995). "Best practices" in transition services: Do they exist? *Career Development for Exceptional Individuals, 18*, 1–2.

Greenwood, C. R. (1991). Longitudinal analysis of time, engagement, and achievement in at-risk versus non-risk students. *Exceptional Children, 57*(6), 521–535.

Greenwood, C. R. (1996). Research on the practices and behavior of effective teachers at the Juniper Gardens Children's Project: Implications for the education of diverse learners. In D. Speece & B. Keogh (Eds.), *Research on classroom ecologies: Implications for inclusion of children with learning disabilities* (pp. 36–67). Hillsdale, NJ: Lawrence Erlbaum Associates, Publishers.

Greenwood, C. R., & Delquadri, J. (1995). ClassWide peer tutoring and the prevention of school failure. *Preventing School Failure, 39*(4), 21–25.

Greenwood, C. R., Delquadri, J., & Hall, R. V. (1984). Opportunity to respond and student academic performance. In W. L. Heward, T. E. Heron, J. Trap-Porter, & D. S. Hill (Eds.), *Focus on behavior analysis in education* (pp. 58–88). Upper Saddle River, NJ: Merrill/Prentice Hall.

Greenwood, C. R., Finney, R., Terry, B., Arreaga-Mayer, C., Carta, J. J., Delquadri, J., Walker, D., Innocenti, M., Lignugaris-Kraft, J., Harper, G. F., & Clifton, R. (1993). Monitoring, improving, and maintaining quality implementation of the class-wide peer tutoring program using behavioral and computer technology. *Education and Treatment of Children, 16,* 19–47.

Gregory, R. P., Hackney, C., & Gregory, N. M. (1982). Corrective reading programs: An evaluation. *British Journal of Educational Psychology, 52,* 33–50.

Grossman, H. (1990). *Trouble-free teaching: Solutions to behavior problems in the classroom.* Mountain View, CA: Mayfield.

Grossman, H. (1994). *Special education in a diverse society.* Needham Heights, MA: Allyn & Bacon.

Guess, D., Smith, J., & Ensminger, E. (1977). The role of nonprofessional persons in teaching language skills to mentally retarded children. *Exceptional Children, 37,* 447–453.

Haight, S. H. (1984). Special education teacher consultant: Idealism versus realism. *Exceptional Children, 50,* 507–515.

Hale, J. E. (1981). Black children: Their roots, culture, and learning styles. *Young Children, 36*(20), 37–50.

Hall, G. E., & Hord, S. M. (1984). *Change in schools: Facilitating the process.* Albany: State University of New York Press.

Halpern, A. S., & Benz, M. R. (1987). A statewide examination of secondary special education for students with mild disabilities: Implications for high school curriculum. *Exceptional Children, 54*(2), 122–129.

Hanley-Maxwell, C., & Collet-Klingenburg, L. (1997). Curricular choices related to work. In P. Wehman and J. Kregel (Eds.), *Functional Curriculum for Elementary, Middle, and Secondary Age Students with Special Needs* (155–183). Austin: PRO-ED.

Hannah, G. G. (1982). *Classroom spaces and places.* Belmont, CA: Pitman Learning.

Haring, K. A., Lovett, D. L., & Saren, D. (1991). Parent perceptions of their adult offspring with disabilities. *TEACHING Exceptional Children, 23*(2), 6–10.

Haring, N. G., & Eaton, M. (1978). Systematic instructional procedures: An instructional hierarchy. In N. Haring, T. Lovitt, M. Eaton, & C. Hansen (Eds.), *The fourth R: Research in the classroom* (pp. 23–40). Upper Saddle River, NJ: Merrill/Prentice Hall.

Haring, N. G., & Gentry, N. D. (1976). Direct and individualized instructional procedures. In N. G. Haring & R. L. Schiefelbusch (Eds.), *Teaching special children* (pp. 77–111). New York: McGraw-Hill.

Haring, N. G., Lovitt, T. C., Eaton, M. D., & Hansen, C. L. (1978). *The fourth R: Research in the classroom.* Upper Saddle River, NJ: Merrill/Prentice Hall.

Harper, G. F., Mallette, B., Maheady, L., & Brennan, G. (1993). Classwide student tutoring teams and direct instruction as a combined instructional program to teach generalizable strategies for mathematics word problems. *Education & Treatment of Children, 16,* 115–134.

Harrington, R. G., & Mitchelson, D. (1987). Special education paraprofessionals: How effective are they? *New Directions, 3*–4.

Harris, K. R., & Graham, S. (1985). Improving learning-disabled students' composition skills: A self-control strategy training approach. *Learning Disability Quarterly, 8,* 27–36.

Harris, K. R., & Graham, S. (1992). Self-regulated strategy development: A part of the writing process. In M. Pressley, K. R. Harris, & J. T. Guthrie (Eds.), *Promoting academic competence and literacy in school* (pp. 277–309). New York: Academic Press.

Harris, K. R., & Graham, S. (1996). Making the writing process work: Strategies for composition and self-regulation. Cambridge, MA: Brookline.

Harris, K. R., Graham, S., Reid, R., McElroy, K., & Hamby, R. (1994). Self-monitoring of attention versus self-monitoring of performance: Replication and cross-task comparison studies. *Learning Disability Quarterly, 17,* 121–139.

Harris, K. R., & Pressley, M. (1991). The nature of cognitive strategy instruction: Interactive strategy construction. *Exceptional Education, 57*(5), 392–404.

Harris, K. R., Schmidt, T., & Graham, S. (1997). Every child can write: Strategies for composition and self-regulation in the classroom. *Every Child Every Day: Learning in Diverse Schools and Classrooms.* Cambridge, MA: Brookline Books.

Harry, B. (1992). *Cultural diversity, families, and the special education system: Communication and empowerment.* New York: Teachers College Press.

Harry, B., Allen, N., & McLaughlin, M. (1995). Communication versus compliance: African American parents' involvement in special education. *Exceptional Children, 61*(4), 364–377.

Hasazi, S., Gordon, L., & Roe, C. (1985). Factors associated with the employment status of handicapped youth exiting high school from 1979 to 1983. *Exceptional Children, 51*(5), 455–469.

Hasazi, S., Gordon, L., Roe, C., Hall, M., Finck, K., & Salembier, G. (1985). A statewide follow-up on post high school employment and residential status of students labeled "mentally retarded." *Education and Training of the Mentally Retarded, 20,* 222–234.

Hasbrouck, J. E., & Tindal, G. (1992). Curriculum-based oral reading fluency norms for students in grades 2 through 5. *TEACHING Exceptional Children, 24*(3), 41–44.

Hasselbring, T. S. (1994). *TECH TALK: A multimedia teleconference.* Orlando, FL: Orange County School Board.

Hasselbring, T. S. (1998). *The Future of Special Education and the Role of Technology.* Peabody College of Vanderbilt University. Retrieved July 15, 1998, from the World Wide Web: http://peabody.vanderbilt.edu/ltc/hasselbringt/futute.html

Hasselbring, T. S., Goin, L., Taylor, R., Bottge, B., & Daley, P. (1997). The computer doesn't embarrass me. *Educational Leadership, 55*(3), 30–33.

Hauser, J., & Malouf, D. B. (1996). A federal perspective on special education technology. *Journal of Learning Disabilities, 29*(5), 504–511.

Hayek, R. A. (1987). The teacher assistance team: A prereferral support system. *Focus on Exceptional Children, 20*(1), 1–7.

Hayes, M. L. (1985). Materials for the resource room. *Academic Therapy, 20*(3), 289–297.

Hazel, J. S., Schumaker, J. B., Sherman, J. A., & Sheldon-Wigden, J. (1981). *ASSET.* Champaign, IL: Research Press.

Hazler, R. J., & Latto, L. D. (1987). Employers' opinions on the attitudes and skills of high school graduates. *Journal of Employment Counseling, 24,* 130–136.

HEATH Resource Center (1990). *Transitions for young adults with learning disabilities and other special needs.* Washington, DC: National Clearinghouse on Postsecondary Education for Individuals with Handicaps.

Hefferan, M., & Diviaio, L. (1989). *A resource manual for the development and evaluation of special programs for exceptional students, Volume V-D: Techniques of precision teaching, Part 1: Training manual.* Tallahassee, FL: Bureau of Education for Exceptional Students.

Hefferan, M., & O'Rear, S. (1991). *B.A.L.A.N.C.E. Training Manual.* Orlando, FL: FDLRS/Action.

Heflich, D. A. (1998). Getting ready to connect to the World Wide Web. *TEACHING Exceptional Children, 30*(5), 6.

Heit, S. B. (1980). *Gameboards for everyone.* Carthage, IL: Good Apple.

Henk, W. A., Helfeldt, J. P., & Platt, J. M. (1986). Alternative approaches to reading instruction for learning disabled students. *TEACHING Exceptional Children, 18*(3), 202–206. Washington, DC: National Academy Press.

Hepworth, D. H., & Larsen, J. A. (1990). *Direct social work practice: Theory and skills* (3rd ed.). Homewood, IL: The Dorsey Press.

Herald-Taylor, G. (1987). How to use predictable books for K–2 language arts instruction. *The Reading Teacher, 40*(7), 656–663.

Hernandez, H. (1989). *Multicultural education: A teacher's guide to content and process.* Upper Saddle River, NJ: Merrill/Prentice Hall.

Heron, T. E., & Harris, K. C. (1987). *The educational consultant* (2nd ed.). Austin, TX: PRO-ED.

Herr, C. M. (1988). Strategies for gaining information. *TEACHING Exceptional Children, 20*(3), 53–55.

Herrmann, B. A. (1988). Two approaches for helping poor readers. *Reading Teacher, 42*(1), 25–28.

Heshusius, L. (1989). The Newtonian mechanistic paradigm, special education, and contours of alternatives: An overview. *Journal of Learning Disabilities, 22*(7), 403–415.

Heward, W. L. (1994). Three "low-tech" strategies for increasing the frequency of active student response during group instruction. In R. Gardner III, D. M. Sainato, J. O. Cooper, T. E. Heron, W. L. Heward, J. Eshleman, & T. A. Grossi (Eds.), *Behavior analysis in education: Focus on measurably superior instruction* (pp. 283–320). Monterey, CA: Brooks/Cole.

Heward, W. L., Courson, F. H., & Narayan, J. S. (1989). Using choral responding to increase active student response during group instruction. *TEACHING Exceptional Children, 21*(3), 72–75.

Heward, W. L., Gardner, R., Cavanaugh, R. A., Courson, F. H., Grossi, T. A., & Barbetta, P. M. (1996). Everyone participates in this class. *TEACHING Exceptional Children, 28*(2), 4–10.

Hicks-Cooley, A. & Kurtz, P. D. (1997). Preparing students with learning disabilities for success in postsecondary education: Needs and services. *Social Work in Education, 19*(1), 13–45.

Hildreth, B. L., Dixon, M. E., Frerichs, D. K., & Heflin, L. J. (1994). College readiness for students with learning disabilities: The role of the school counselor. *The School Counselor, 41,* 343–346.

Hillard, A. G. (1980). Cultural diversity and special education. *Exceptional Children, 46,* 584–588.

Hoffer, K. H. (1983). Assessment and instruction of reading skills: Results with Mexican-American students. *Learning Disabilities Quarterly, 6*(4), 458–467.

Hoffmann, F. J., Sheldon, K. L., Minskoff, E. H., Sauter, S. W., Steidle, E. F., Baker, D. P., Bailey, M. B., & Echols, L. D. (1987). Needs of learning disabled adults. *Journal of Learning Disabilities, 20*(1), 43–52.

Hoover, J. J. (1997). Study skills. In E. A. Polloway & J. R. Patton (Eds.), *Strategies for teaching learners with special needs.* Upper Saddle River, NJ: Merrill/Prentice Hall.

Hoover, J. J., & Patton, J. R. (1995). *Teaching students with learning problems to use study skills.* Austin, TX: PRO-ED.

Hourcade, J. J., Parette, H. P., Jr., & Huer, M. B. (1997). Family and cultural alert: Considerations in assistive technology. *TEACHING Exceptional Children, 30*(1), 40–43.

Howell, K. W., Fox, S. L., & Morehead, M. K. (1993). *Curriculum-based evaluation: Teaching decision making* (2nd ed.) Pacific Grove, CA: Brooks/Cole.

Howell, K. W., & Morehead, M. K. (1987). *Curriculum-based evaluation for special and remedial education.* Upper Saddle River, NJ: Merrill/Prentice Hall.

Huefner, D. S. (1988). The consulting teacher model: Risks and opportunities. *Exceptional Children, 54*(5), 403–414.

Hughes, C. A. (1996). Memory and test-taking strategies. In D. D. Deshler, E. S. Ellis, & B. K. Lenz (Eds.), *Adolescents with learning disabilities: Strategies and methods* (2nd ed.). Denver: Love.

Hughes, C. A., Ruhl, K. L., & Misra, A. (1989). Self-management with behaviorally disordered students in school settings: A promise unfulfilled. *Behavioral Disorders, 14*(4), 250–262.

Hughes, C. A., Ruhl, K. L., & Peterson, S. K. (1988). Promising practices: Teaching self-management skills. *Teaching Exceptional Children, 20*(2), 70–72.

Hunt, P. (1995). Collaboration: What does it take? What's working: Transition in Minnesota, p. 1. Minneapolis: University of Minnesota Institute on Community Integration.

Hunter, M. (1981). *Increasing your teaching effectiveness.* Palo Alto, CA: Learning Institute.

Hyun, J. K., & Fowler, S. A. (1995). Respect, cultural sensitivity, and communication: Promoting participation by Asian families in the Individualized Family Service Plan. *TEACHING Exceptional Children, 28*(1), 25–28.

Iano, R. P. (1989). Comments related to Professor Heshusius' application of paradigm change to special education. *Journal of Learning Disabilities, 22*(7), 416–417.

Idol, L. (1986). *Collaborative School Consultation* (Report of the National Task Force on School Consultation). Reston, VA: Teacher Education Division, The Council for Exceptional Children.

Idol, L. (1988). A rationale and guidelines for establishing a special education consultation program. *Remedial and Special Education Program, 9*(6), 48–62.

Idol, L., Paolucci-Whitcomb, P., & Nevin, A. (1986). *Collaborative consultation.* Rockville, MD: Aspen.

Idol, L., Paolucci-Whitcomb, P., & Nevin, A. (1994). *Collaboration consultation* (2nd ed.). Austin, TX: PRO-ED.

Idol-Maestas, L., & Ritter, S. (1985). A follow-up study of resource/consulting teachers: Factors that facilitate and inhibit teacher consultation. *Teacher Education and Special Education, 8,* 121–131.

Idstein, P., & Jenkins, J. R. (1972). Underlining versus repetitive reading. *Journal of Educational Research, 65,* 321–323.

Irmsher, K. (1996). Inclusive education in practice. In Educational Resources Information Center, U.S. Department of Education (Ed.), *Inclusion, 4*(3), 18–19.

Jensen, W. R., Sloan, H. N., & Young, K. R. (1988). *Applied behavior analysis in education: A structured teaching approach* (2nd ed.). Upper Saddle River, NJ: Prentice Hall.

Johnson, D. W., & Johnson, R. T. (1980). Integrating handicapped children into the mainstream. *Exceptional Children, 47,* 90–98.

Johnson, D. W., & Johnson, R. T. (1986). Mainstreaming and cooperative learning strategies. *Exceptional Children, 52*(6), 553–561.

Johnson, D. W., & Johnson, R. T. (1996). The role of cooperative learning in assessing and communicating student learning. In T. R. Guskey (Ed.), *ASCD Yearbook 1996* (pp. 25–46). Alexandria, VA: ASCD.

Johnson, D. W., Johnson, R. T., & Maruyama, G. (1983). Interdependence and interpersonal attraction among heterogeneous individuals: A theoretical formulation and a meta-analysis of the research. *Review of Educational Research, 53,* 5–54.

Johnson, D. W., & Wen, S. (1976). Effects of correct and extraneous markings under time limits on reading comprehension. *Psychology in the Schools, 13,* 454–456.

Johnson, J. R., & Rusch, F. R. (1993). Secondary special education and transition services: Identifications and recommendations for future research and demonstration. *Career Development for Exceptional Individuals, 16,* 1–18.

Johnson, M. J. (1987). American Indian parents of handicapped children. In M. J. Johnson & B. A. Ramirez (Eds.), *American Indian exceptional children and youth* (pp. 6–7). Reston, VA: Council for Exceptional Children.

Johnson, M. J. (1991). *American Indians and Alaska Natives with disabilities* (Report No. RC 018 629). Washington, DC: Department of Education. (ERIC Document Reproduction Service No. ED 343 770)

Jones, B. F., Palincsar, A. S., Ogle, D. S., & Carr, E. G. (1987). *Strategic teaching and learning: Cognitive instruction in the content areas.* Alexandria, VA: Association for Supervision and Curriculum Development.

Jones, K. H., & Bender, W. N. (1993). Utilization of paraprofessionals in special education: A review of the literature. *Remedial and Special Education, 14*(1), 7–14.

Jongsma, K. S. (1989). Questions and answers: Portfolio assessment. *Reading Teacher, 43*(3), 264–265.

Joyce, B. R., & Showers, B. (1983). *Power in staff development through research on training.* Alexandria, VA: Association for Supervision and Curriculum Development.

Kagan, S. (1992). *Cooperative Learning.* San Juan Capistrano, CA: Kagan Cooperative Learning.

Kahn, E. H. (1981). Aides in special education—A boon for students and teachers. *TEACHING Exceptional Children, 55*(3), 101–105.

Kamens, M. W. (1997). A model for introducing student teachers to collaboration. *The Teacher Educator, 33*(2), 90–102.

Kaplan, S. N., Kaplan, J. B., Madsen, S. K., & Taylor, B. K. (1973). *Change for children: Ideas and activities for individualizing learning.* Pacific Palisades, CA: Goodyear.

Katz, W.(1983). *Summary of three task force planning activities to provide recommendations to achieve effective parent/educator partnerships.* Washington, DC: National Association of State Directors of Special Education.

Kauffman, J. M. (1993). How we might achieve the radical reform of special education. *Exceptional children, 60*(1), 6–16.

Kavale, K. A., & Forness, S. R. (1995). Social skills deficits and training: A meta-analysis of the research in learning disabilities. In T. Scruggs & M. Mastropieri (Eds.), *Advances in learning and behavioral disabilities* (Vol 9, pp. 119–160). Greenwich, CT: JAI Press.

Kavale, K. A., Hirshoren, A., & Forness, S. R. (1998). Meta-analytic validation of the Dunn and Dunn model of learning-style preferences: A critique of what was done. *Learning Disabilities Research & Practice, 13*(2), 75–80.

Kavale, K. A., Mathur, S. R., Forness, S. R., Rutherford, R. B., & Quinn, M. M. (1997). Effectiveness of social skills training for students with behavior disorders: A meta-analysis. In T. Scruggs & M. Mastropieri (Eds.), *Advances in learning and behavioral disabilities* (Vol. 11, pp. 293–312). Greenwich, CT: JAI Press.

Kellogg, S. (1984). *Paul Bunyan: A tall tale.* New York: William Morrow.

Kerka, S. (1995). *Techniques for authentic assessment practice application brief.* Columbus, OH: ERIC Clearinghouse on Adult, Career, and Vocational Education Center on Education and Training for Employment.

Kimball, W. H., & Heron, T. E. (1988). A behavioral commentary on Poplin's discussion of reductionistic fallacy and holistic/constructivist principles. *Journal of Learning Disabilities, 21*(7), 425–428.

King-Sears, M. E., & Bradley, D. F. (1995). ClassWide peer tutoring: Heterogeneous instruction in general education classrooms. *Preventing School Failure, 40*(1), 29–35.

Kitano, M. K. (1987). Gifted and talented Asian children. In M. K. Kitano & P. C. Chinn (Eds.), *Exceptional Asian children and youth* (pp. 1–11). Reston, VA: The Council for Exceptional Children.

Kline, C. S. (1986). *Effects of guided notes on academic achievement of learning disabled high school students.* Unpublished master's thesis: The Ohio State University, Columbus.

Knackendoffel, E. A. (1996). Collaborative teaming in the secondary school. In D. D. Deshler, E. S. Ellis, & B. K. Lenz (Eds.), *Adolescents with learning disabilities* (2nd ed., pp. 579–616). Denver, CO: Love.

Knackendoffel, E. A., Robinson, S. M., Schumaker, J. B., & Deshler, D. D. (1992). *Developing collaborative relationships: Teaming techniques for communication, problem-solving, and decision making.* Lawrence, KS: Edge Enterprises, Inc.

Knapczyk, D. R., & Rodes, P. G. (1996). *Teaching social competence: A practical approach for improving social skills in students at-risk.* Pacific Grove, CA: Brooks/Cole.

Kohler, P. (1993). Best practices in transition: Substantiated or implied? *Career Development for Exceptional Individuals, 16*, 107–121.

Koller, J. R. (1994). Improving transition outcomes for persons with specific learning disabilities. *American Rehabilitation, 20*(2), 37–42.

Komoski, K. (1995). *Seven steps to responsible software selection.* Syracuse, NY: ERIC Clearinghouse on Information and Technology. (ERIC Digest No EDO-IR-95-6).

Koorland, M. A., Keel, M. C., and Ueberhorst, P. (1990). Setting aims for precision learning. *TEACHING Exceptional Children, 22*(3), 64–68.

Kounin, J. S. (1970). *Discipline and group management in classrooms.* New York: Holt, Rinehart, & Winston.

Kounin, J. S., & Gump, P. (1974). Signal systems of lesson settings and the task related behavior of preschool children. *Journal of Education Psychology, 66*, 554–562.

Kounin, J. S., & Obradovic, S. (1968). Managing emotionally disturbed children in regular classrooms: A replication and extension. *Journal of Special Education, 2*, 129–135.

Kovalik, S. with K. Olsen. (1994). *ITI: THE MODEL: Integrated thematic instruction* (3rd ed). Kent, WA: Books for Educators.

Kranstover, L. L., Thurlow, M. L., & Bruininks, R. H. (1989). Special education graduates versus nongraduates: A longitudinal study of outcomes. *Career Development for Exceptional Individuals, 12*(2), 153–166.

Krivacska, J. J. (1986). *Selection of the IEP management systems. Computers in the Schools, 3*(3), 91–95.

Kruelle v. New Castle County School District, 642 F.2d 687 (3rd Cir. 1981).

Kuykendall, C. (1992). *From rage to hope: Strategies for reclaiming Black & Hispanic students.* Bloomington, IN: National Educational Service.

Lahm, E., & Morrisette, S. (1994, April). *Assistive technology.* Paper presented at the annual meeting of the Council for Exceptional Children.

Lambie, R. A. (1980). A systematic approach for changing materials, instruction, and assignments to meet individual needs. *Focus on Exceptional Children, 12*(1), 1–12.

Langer, J. (1984). Examining background knowledge and text comprehension. *Reading Research Quarterly, 19*, 468–481.

Lazarus, B. D. (1988). Using guided notes to aid learning disabled students in secondary mainstream settings. *The Pointer, 33*, 32–36.

Lazarus, B. D. (1991). Guided notes, review, and achievement of learning disabled adolescents in secondary mainstream settings. *Education and Treatment of Children, 14*, 112–127.

Lazarus, B. D. (1996). Flexible skeletons: Guided notes for adolescents with mild disabilities. *TEACHING Exceptional Children, 28*(3), 36–40.

Lazear, D. (1991). *Seven ways of knowing: Teaching from multiple intelligences.* Palatine, IL: Skylight Publishing.

Lazerson, D. B., Foster, H. L., Brow, S. I., & Hummel, J. W. (1988). The effectiveness of cross-age tutoring with truant, junior high students with learning disabilities. *Journal of Learning Disabilities, 21*(4), 253–255.

Lee, P., & Alley, G. R. (1981). *Training junior high LD students to use a test-taking strategy* (Research Report No. 38). Lawrence, KS: University of Kansas, Institute for Research in Learning Disabilities.

Leinhardt, G., Zigmond, N., & Cooley, W. (1981). Reading instruction and its effects. *American Education Research Journal, 18*(3), 343–361.

Lenz, B. K. (1983). Promoting active learning through effective instruction: Using advance organizers. *Pointer, 27*(2), 11–13.

Lenz, B. K., Alley, G., & Schumaker, J. (1987). Activating the inactive learner: Advance organizers in the secondary content classroom. *Learning Disabilities Quarterly, 10*(1), 53–67.

Lenz, B. K., with Bulgren, J. A., Schumaker, J. B., Deshler, D. D., & Boudah, D. A. (1994). *The unit organizer routine* (Instructor's Manual). Lawrence, KS: Edge Enterprises.

Lerner, J. (1985). *Learning disabilities: Theories, diagnosis, and teaching strategies.* Boston: Houghton Mifflin.

Leslie, L., & Caldwell, J. (1990). *Qualitative reading inventory.* Glenview, IL: Scott Foresman.

Leung, B. (1987). Psychoeducational assessment of Asian students. In M. K. Kitano & P. C. Chinn (Eds.), *Exceptional Asian children and youth* (pp. 29–35). Reston, VA: The Council for Exceptional Children.

Leung, E. K. (1989). Cultural and acculturational commonalities and diversities among Asian Americans: Identification and programming considerations. In A. A. Ortiz & B. A. Ramirez (Eds.), *Schools and the culturally diverse exceptional student: Promising practices and future directions* (pp. 86–95). Reston, VA: The Council for Exceptional Children.

Levin, J. R. (1985). Educational applications of mnemonic pictures: Possibilities beyond your wildest imagination. In A. A. Sheikh (Ed.), *Imagery in education: Imagery in the educational process* (pp. 63–87). Farmingdale, NY: Baywood.

Lewis, J. D. (1998). How the internet expands educational options. *TEACHING Exceptional Children, 30*(5), 34–41.

Lewis, M. B. (1993). *Thematic methods and strategies in learning disabilities: Textbook for practitioners.* San Diego, CA: Singular Publishing Group.

Lewis, R. B. (1993). *Special education technology: Classroom applications.* Pacific Grove, CA: Brooks/Cole.

Lewis, R. B., & Doorlag, D. H. (1991). *Teaching special students in the mainstream* (3rd ed.). New York: Merrill/Macmillan.

Lieberman, A. (1995). Practices that support teacher development: Transforming conceptions of professional learning. *Phi Delta Kappan, 76*(8), 591–596.

Lilly, M. S., & Givens-Ogle, L. B. (1981). Teacher consultation: Present, past, & future. *Behavioral Disorders, 6*(2), 73–77.

Lindsey, J. D. (1983). Paraprofessionals in learning disabilities. *Journal of Learning Disabilities, 16,* 467–472.

Lindsley, O. R. (1990). Precision teaching: By teachers for children. *Teaching Exceptional Children, 22*(3), 10–15.

Little, J. W. (1982). Norms of collegiality and experimentation: Workplace conditions of school success. *American Educational Research Journal, 19,* 325–340.

Lloyd, J., Cullinan, D., Heins, E. D., & Epstein, M. H. (1980). Direct instruction: Effects on oral and written language comprehension. *Learning Disabilities Quarterly, 3*(4), 70–76.

Lovitt, D. L., & Harris, M. B. (1987). Important skills for adults with mental retardation: The client's point of view. *Mental Retardation, 25,* 351–356.

MacArthur, C. A., Schwartz, S. S., & Graham, S. (1991). Effects of a reciprocal peer revision strategy in special education classrooms. *Learning Disabilities Research & Practice, 6*(4), 201–218.

Maddux, C. D. (1986). Issues and concerns in special education microcomputing. *Computers in the Schools, 3*(3), 1–19.

Maheady, L., Harper, G. F., & Mallette, B. (1991). Peer-mediated instruction: A review of potential applications for special education. *Reading, Writing, and Learning Disabilities, 7,* 75–103.

Maheady, L., Sacca, M. K., & Harper, G. F. (1987). Classwide student tutoring teams: The effects of peer-mediated instruction on the academic performance of secondary mainstreamed students. *Journal of Special Education, 21*(3), 107–121.

Maheady, L., Sacca, M. K., & Harper, G. F. (1988). Classwide peer tutoring with mildly handicapped high school students. *Exceptional Children, 55*(1), 52–59.

Maher, C. A. (1984). Handicapped adolescents as cross-age tutors: Program description and evaluation. *Exceptional Children, 51*(1), 56–63.

Mahoney, M. (1974). *Cognition and behavior modification.* Cambridge, MA: Bollinger Publishing Co.

Maker, C. J., Nielson, A. B., & Rogers, J. A. (1994). Multiple intelligences: Giftedness, diversity, and problem-solving. *Teaching Exceptional Children, 27*(1), 4–19.

Male, M. (1988). Special magic: Computers, classroom strategies, and exceptional students. Mountain View, CA: Mayfield.

Male, M. (1997). *Technology for inclusion: Meeting the special needs of all students* (3rd ed.). Needham Heights, MA: Allyn & Bacon.

Mandlebaum L. H., & Wilson, R. (1989). Teaching listening skills in the special education classroom. *Academic Therapy, 24,* 449–457.

MARC: A resource manual for the development and evaluation of special programs for the students, V-C: Affective curriculum for secondary emotionally handicapped students. (1983). Tallahassee, FL: Florida Department of Education.

Margolis, H., & McGettigan, J. (1988). Managing resistance to instructional modifications in mainstreamed environments. *Remedial and Special Education, 9*(4), 15–21.

Marion, R. L. (1981). *Educators, parents, and exceptional children.* Rockville, MD: Aspen.

Markwardt, F. C. (1989). *Peabody Individual Achievement Test—Revised.* Circle Pines, MN: American Guidance Service.

Marston, D. (1989). A curriculum-based measurement approach to assessing academic performance: What it is and why do it. In M. R. Shinn (Ed.), *Curriculum-based measurement: Assessing special children* (pp. 18–78). New York: The Guilford Press.

Marston, D., Dement, K., Allen, D., & Allen, L. (1992). Monitoring pupil progress in reading. *Preventing School Failure, 36*(2), 21–25.

Marston, D., Fuchs, L., & Deno, S. L. (1985). Measuring pupil progress: A comparison of standardized achievement tests and curriculum-based measures. *Diagnostique, 11,* 77–90.

Marston, D., & Magnusson, D. (1985). Implementing curriculum-based measurement in special and regular education settings. *Exceptional Children, 52*(3), 266–276.

Martin, J. E., Huber Marshall, L., Maxson, L. I., & Jerman, P. (1996). *Self-directed IEP.* Longmont, CO: Sopris West.

Marzano, R., Pickering, D., & McTighe, J. (1993). *Assessing outcomes: Performance assessment using dimensions of learning model.* Alexandria, VA: Association for Supervision and Curriculum Development.

Masters, L. F., & Mori, A. A. (1993). *Teaching secondary students with mild learning and behavior problems: Methods, materials, and strategies.* Rockville, MD: Aspen.

Mastropieri, M. A. (1988). Using the keyword method. *TEACHING Exceptional Children, 20*(2), 4–8.

Mastropieri, M. A., & Scruggs, T. E. (1994). Text versus hands-on science curriculum: Implications for students with disabilities. *Remedial and Special Education (RASE), 15*(2), 72–85.

Mastropieri, M. A., Scruggs, T. E., & Levin, J. R. (1986a). Direct vs. mnemonic instruction: Relative benefits for exceptional learners. *Journal of Special Education, 20*(3), 299–308.

Mastropieri, M. A., Scruggs, T. E., & Levin, J. R. (1986b). Maximizing what exceptional students can learn: A review of keyword and other mnemonic strategy research. *Remedial and Special Education, 6*(2), 39–45.

Mastropieri, M. A., Scruggs, T. E., Levin, J. R., Gaffney, J., & McLoone, B. (1985). Mnemonic vocabulary instruction for learning-disabled students. *Learning Disability Quarterly, 8,* 57–63.

Mather, S. R., & Rutherford, R. B., Jr., (1996). Is social skills training effective with students for emotional or behavioral disorders? Research issues and needs. *Behavioral Disorders, 22*(1), 21–28.

Mathes, P. G., Fuchs, D., Fuchs, L. S., Henley, A. M., & Sanders, A. (1994). Increasing strategic reading practice with Peabody Classwide Peer Tutoring. *Learning Disabilities Research and Practice, 9*(1), 44–48.

Mayer, R. E. (1988). Learning Strategies: An overview. In C. Weinstein, E. Goetz, & P. A. Alexander (Eds.), *Learning and study strategies* (p. 21). New York: Academic Press.

McCabe, P. A. (July 22, 1997). *1994 elementary and secondary school civil rights compliance report: Projected values for the nation.* Washington, DC: Department of Education, Office for Civil Rights.

McCarney, S. B., & Tucci, J. K., (1991). *Study skills for students in our schools: Study, skills and intervention strategies for elementary and secondary students.* Columbia, MO: Hawthorne.

McCarthy, B. (1987). *The 4MAT system.* Barrington, IL: Excel.

McDougall, D., & Brady, M. P. (1998). Initiating and fading self-management interventions to increase math fluency in general education classes. *Exceptional Children, 64*(2), 151–166.

McFall, R. M. (1982). A review and reformulation of the concept of social skills. *Behavioral Assessment, 4,* 1–33.

McGill, D., & Pearce, J. K. (1982). British families. In M. Giodrick, J. K. Pearce, & J. Giordano (Eds.),

Ethnicity in family therapy (pp. 457–482). New York: Guilford Press.

McGuire, J. M., Hall, D., & Litt, A. V. (1991). A field-based study of the direct service needs of college students with learning disabilities. *Journal of College Student Development, 32,* 101–108.

McIntosh, R., Vaughn, S., & Bennerson, D. (1995). FAST social skills with a SLAM and a RAP. *TEACHING Exceptional Children, 28*(1), 37–41.

McIntosh, R., Vaughn, S., Schumm, J., Haager, D., & Lee, O. (1993). Observations of students with learning disabilities in general education classrooms. *Exceptional Children, 60*(3), 249–261.

McIntyre, T. (1998). The culturally sensitive disciplinarian. In K. Freiberg (Ed.), *Educating exceptional children 98/99* (pp. 110–114). Guilford, CT: Dushkin/McGraw-Hill.

McKenzie, R. G., & Houk, C. S. (1986). Use of paraprofessionals in the resource room. *Exceptional Children, 53*(1), 41–45.

McRobbie, J. (1992). *Using portfolios to assess student performance, knowledge brief, #9.* San Francisco, CA: Far West Laboratory for Educational Research and Development.

McWhirter, A. M. (1990). Whole language in the middle school. *The Reading Teacher, 43*(8), 562–567.

Means, B. (1997). *Critical issue: Using technology to enhance engaged learning for at-risk students* (On-line). Retrieved July 15, 1998, from the World Wide Web: http://www.ncrel.org/sdrs/areas/issues/students/atrisk/at400.html

Means, B., Blando, J., Olson, K., Middleton, T., Moroacco, C., Remz, A. R., & Zorfass, J. (1993). *Using technology to support education reform.* Washington DC: U.S. Government Printing Office, 1993.

Medley, D. M. (1979). The effectiveness of teachers: In P. L. Peterson & H. J. Walberg (Eds.), *Research on teaching: Concepts, findings, and implications* (pp. 11–27). Berkeley, CA: McCutchan.

Meese, R. (1994). *Teaching learners with mild disabilities: Integrating research and practice.* Pacific Grove, CA: Brooks/Cole.

Mehrabian, A. (1969). Significance of posture and position in the communication of attitude and status relationships. *Psychological Bulletin, 71,* 359–372.

Mehring, T. (1995). Report card options for students with disabilities in general education. In T. Azwell & E. Schmar (Eds.), *Report card on report cards: Alternatives to consider* (pp. 11–21), Portsmouth, NH: Heinemann.

Meichenbaum, D. (1977). *Cognitive behavior modification: An integrative approach.* NY: Plenum Press.

Meichenbaum, D., & Goodman, J. (1971). Training impulsive children to talk to themselves: A means of developing self-control. *Journal of Abnormal Psychology, 77,* 115–126.

Meier, F. E. (1992). *Competency-based instruction for teachers of students with special learning needs.* Needham Heights, MA: Allyn & Bacon.

Mendez, P. (1989). *The black snowman.* New York: Scholastic.

Mercer, C. D. (1992). *Students with learning disabilities* (4th ed.). Upper Saddle River, NJ: Merrill/Prentice Hall.

Mercer, C. D., Jordan, L. , & Miller, S. P. (1996). Constructivistic math instruction in diverse learners. *Learning Disabilities Research & Practice, 11*(3), 147–156.

Mercer, C. D., & Mercer, A. R. (1993). *Teaching students with learning problems* (4th ed). Upper Saddle River, NJ: Merrill/Prentice Hall.

Mercer, C. D., & Mercer, A. R. (1998). *Teaching students with learning problems* (5th ed). Upper Saddle River, NJ: Merrill/Prentice Hall.

Mercer, C. D., Mercer, A. R., & Bott, D. A. (1984). *Self-correcting learning materials for the classroom.* Upper Saddle River, NJ: Merrill/Prentice Hall.

Meyer, L. A. (1986). Strategies for correcting students' wrong responses. *Elementary School Journal, 87*(2), 227–241.

Michaels, C. A. (1989). Employment: The final frontier: Issues and practices for persons with learning disabilities. *Rehabilitation Counseling Bulletin, 33*(1), 67–73.

Middleton, J. A., Flores, A., & Knaupp, J. (1997). Shopping for technology. *Educational Leadership, 55*(3), 20–23.

Miller, A. D., Barbetta, P. M., & Heron, T. E. (1994). START tutoring: Designing, training, implementing, adapting, and evaluating tutoring programs for school and home settings. In Gardner III, D. M., Sainato, J. O., Cooper, T. E., Heron, W. L., Heward, J. W., & Eshelman, T. A. (Eds.), *Behavior analysis in education: Focus on measurably superior instruction* (pp. 265–282). Pacific Grove, CA: Brooks/Cole.

Miller, J. H., & Milam, C. P. (1987). Multiplication and division errors committed by learning disabled students. *Learning Disabilities Research, 2*(2), 119–122.

Miller, W. H. (1995). *Alternative assessment techniques for reading and writing.* New York: The Center for Applied Research in Education.

Minke, K. M., Bear, G. G., Deemer, S. A., & Griffin, S. M. (1996). Teachers' experiences with inclusive classrooms: Implications for special education reform. *Journal of Special Education, 30*(2), 152–186.

Minner, S., Beane, A., & Prater, G. (1986). Try telephone answering machines. *TEACHING Exceptional Children, 19*(1), 62–63.

Minskoff, E. H., & DeMoss, S. (1994). Workplace social skills and individuals with learning disabilities. *Journal of Vocational Rehabilitation, 4*(2), 113–121.

Mitchell, A. (1997). Teacher identity: A key to increased collaboration. *Action in Teacher Education, 19*(3), 1–14.

Montague, M. (1988). Job-related social skills training for adolescents with handicaps. *Career Development for Exceptional Individuals, 11*(1), 26–41.

Montague, M. (1997). Cognitive strategy instruction in mathematics for students with learning disabilities. *Journal of Learning Disabilities, 30*(2), 164–177.

Montague, M., & Leavell, A. G. (1994). Improving the narrative writing of students with learning disabilities. *RASE, 15*(1), 21–33.

Montague, M., Marquard, K., & LeBlanc, W. (1993, April). The effects of cognitive strategy instruction on the mathematical problem-solving of students with learning disabilities. Paper presented at the annual meeting of the American Educational Research Association, Atlanta, GA.

Montague, P., Mecham, M., & McLaughlin, T. F. (1991). Peer tutoring in special education: Effects on the academic achievement of secondary students with mild handicaps. *B.C. Journal of Special Education, 15,* 47–63.

Morgan, D. P., & Jenson, W. R. (1988). *Teaching behaviorally disordered students: Preferred practices.* Upper Saddle River, NJ: Merrill/Prentice Hall.

Morgan, L. (Ed.) (1988). *Langston Hughes: He believed humor would help defeat bigotry and fear.* Seattle: Turman.

Morgan, N. A. (1997). *An introduction to Internet resources for K–12 educators: Part II: Question answering, listservs, discussion groups, update 1997.* Syracuse, NY: ERIC Clearinghouse on Information and Technology. (ERIC Digest No EDO-IR-97–04)

Morgan, N. A., & Saxton, J. (1994). *Asking better questions.* Markham, Ontario: Pembroke Publishers.

Morningstar, M. E., Turnbull, A. P., and Turnbull, N. R., III. (1996). What do students with disabilities tell us about the importance of family involvement in the transition from school to adult life? *Exceptional Children, 62*(3), 249–260.

Mosca, F. J., & Perkins, T. (1997). Help from hundreds of people you've never met: Cruising the Internet's world. *Beyond the Classroom, 8*(1), 16–17.

Moskowitz, G., & Hayman, J. L. (1976). Success strategies of inner-city teachers: A year-long study. *Journal of Educational Research, 69,* 283–289.

Munk, D. D., & Bursuck, W. D. (1997). Can grades be helpful and fair? *Educational Leadership, 55*(4), 44–47.

Murphy, D. A., Meyers, C. C., Olesen, S., McKean, K., & Custer, S. H. (1996). *Exceptions: A handbook of inclusion activities for teachers of students at grades 6–12 with mild disabilities.* Longmont, CO: Sopris Press.

Myles, B. S., & Kasselman, C. J. (1990). Collaborative consultation: The regular educator's view. Manuscript submitted for publication.

Myles, B. S., & Simpson, R. L. (1989). Regular educators' modification preferences for mainstreaming mildly handicapped children. *Journal of Special Education, 22*(4), 479–492.

Narayan, J. S., Heward, W. L., Gardner, R., III. Courson, F. H., & Omness, C. (1990). Using response cards to increase student participation in an elementary classroom. *Journal of Applied Behavior Analysis, 23,* 483–490.

National Association of School Boards of Education (1992, October). *Winners all: A call for inclusive schools.* Alexandria, VA: Author.

National Committee on Excellence in Education. (1983). *A nation at risk: The imperative for educational reform.* Washington, DC: U.S. Government Printing Office.

Nelson, C. M. (1988). Social skills training for handicapped students. *TEACHING Exceptional Children, 20*(4), 19–23.

Nelson, C. M., & Stevens, K. B. (1981). An accountable model for mainstreaming behaviorally disordered children, *Behavioral Disorders, 6*(2), 82–91.

Network Wizards. (1998). *Internet domain survey* (On-line). Available: http://www.nw.com./zone/WWW/report.html

Newcomer, P. (1986). *Standardized Reading Inventory.* Austin, TX: PRO-ED.

New Mexico/Albuquerque Public Schools Center for Parent Involvement. (1979). Albuquerque, NM: University of New Mexico/Albuquerque Public Schools Center for Parent Involvement.

Nichols, R. G., & Stevens, L. A. (1957). *Are you listening?* New York: McGraw-Hill.

Nowacek, J. E. (1992). Professional talk about teaching together: Interviews with five collaborating teachers. *Intervention in School & Clinic, 27,* 262–276.

O'Connor, R. E., & Jenkins, J. R. (1996). Cooperative learning as an inclusion strategy: A closer look. *Exceptionality, 6*(1), 29–51.

Ogle, D. M. (1986). K-W-L: A teaching model that develops active reading of expository text. *The Reading Teacher, 39,* 564–570.

Olion, L. (1989). Enhancing the involvement of Black parents of adolescents with handicaps. In A. A. Ortiz & B. A. Ramirez (Eds.), *Schools and the culturally diverse exceptional students: Promising practices and future directions* (pp. 96–103). Reston, VA: The Council for Exceptional Children.

Olson, J. (1982). Treatment perspectives: Peer tutoring, Unit 2. In B. Algozzine (Ed.), *Problem behavior management* (pp. 40–44). Rockville, MD: Aspen.

Olson, J. (1989). Managing life in the classroom: Dealing with the nitty gritty. *Academic Therapy, 24*(5), 545–554.

Olson, J., & Platt, J. (1996). *Teaching children and adolescents with special needs* (2nd ed.). Upper Saddle River, NJ: Merrill/Prentice Hall.

Olson, M. W. (1980, February). *Pattern guides: An alternative for content teachers.* Paper presented at the annual meeting of the southwest regional conference of the International Reading Association, Albuquerque, NM.

O'Melia, M. C., & Rosenberg, M. S. (1994). Effects of Cooperative Homework Teams on the acquisition of mathematics skills by secondary students with mild disabilities. *Exceptional Children, 60*(6), 538–548.

Ortiz, A. A. (1989). *Factors to consider when adapting materials for ESE/LEP students.* Handicapped Minority Research Institute, Department of Special Education, University of Texas, Austin, TX.

Ortiz, A. A., & Garcia, S. B. (1989). A preferral process for preventing inappropriate referrals of Hispanic students to special education. In A. A. Ortiz & B. A. Ramirez (Eds.), *Schools and the culturally diverse exceptional student: Promising practices and future directions* (pp. 6–18). Reston, VA: The Council for Exceptional Children.

Ortiz, A. A., & Polyzoi, E. (1989). Language assessment of Hispanic learning disabled and speech and language handicapped students: Research in progress. In A. A. Ortiz & B. A. Ramirez (Eds.), *Schools and the culturally diverse exceptional student: Promising practices and future directions* (pp. 32–44). Reston, VA: The Council for Exceptional Children.

Osborne, S. S., Kosiewicz, M. M., Crumley, E. B., & Lee, C. (1987). It worked in my classroom. *Teaching Exceptional Children, 19*(2), 66–69.

O'Shea, L. J., & O'Shea, D. (1988). Using repeated readings. *TEACHING Exceptional Children, 20*(2), 26–29.

O'Shea, L. J., Sindelar, P. T., & O'Shea, D. J. (1985). The effects of repeated readings and attentional cues on reading fluency and comprehension. *Journal of Reading Behavior, 17,* 129–141.

Palincsar, A. S. (1982). *Improving the reading comprehension of junior high students through reciprocal teaching of comprehension-monitoring strategies.* Unpublished doctoral dissertation, University of Illinois, Urbana.

Palincsar, A. S. (1986a). Metacognitive strategy instruction. *Exceptional Children, 53*(2), 118–124.

Palincsar, A. S. (1986b). The role of dialogue in scaffolded instruction. *Educational Psychologist, 21,* 73–98.

Palincsar, A. S., & Brown, A. L. (1984). The reciprocal teaching of comprehension fostering and comprehension monitoring activities. *Cognition and Instruction, 1,* 117–175.

Palincsar, A. S., & Brown, A. L. (1986). Interactive teaching to promote independent learning from text. *The Reading Teacher, 39*(8), 771–777.

Palincsar, A. S., & Brown, A. L. (1987). Enhancing instructional time through attention to metacognition. *Journal of Learning Disabilities, 20*(2), 66–75.

Palincsar, A. S., & Brown, A. L. (1988). Teaching and practicing thinking skills to promote comprehension in the context of group problem solving. *Remedial and Special Education, 9*(1), 53–59.

Palincsar, A. S., & Brown, A. L. (1989). Instruction for self-regulated reading. In L. B. Resnick & L. E. Klopfer (Eds.), *Toward the thinking curriculum: Current cognitive research: 1989 ASCD yearbook* (pp. 19–39). Alexandria, VA: Association for Supervision and Curriculum Development.

Palincsar, A., & Klenk, L. (1992). Fostering literacy learning in supportive contexts. *Journal of Learning Disabilities, 25*(4), 211–225, 229.

Palmer, U. (1975). The value and training of paraprofessionals. *Journal of Rehabilitation of the Deaf, 8,* 3–9.

Pappas, C., Kiefer, B., & Levstik, L. (1990). *An integrated language perspective in the elementary school: Theory into action.* New York: Longman.

Paris, S. G. (1988). Models and metaphors of learning strategies. In C. E. Weinstein, E. T. Goetz, & P. A. Alexander (Eds.), *Learning and study strategies: Issues in assessment, instruction, and evaluation* (pp. 299–321). San Diego: Academic Press.

Paris, S. G., & Byrnes, J. P. (1989). The constructivist approach to self-regulation and learning in the classroom. In B. Zimmerman & D. Schunk (Eds.), *Self-regulated learning and academic achievement: Theory, research, and practice* (pp. 169–200). New York: Springer-Verlag.

Paris, S. G., & Cross, D. R. (1983). Ordinary learning: Pragmatic connections among children's beliefs, motives, and actions. In J. Disanz, G. L. Disanz, & R. Kail (Eds.), *Learning in children* (pp. 137–169). New York: Springer-Verlag.

Paris, S. G., Lipson, M. Y., Jacobs, J., Oka, E., Debritto, A. M., & Cross, D. (1982, April). *Metacognition and reading comprehension.* Symposium conducted at the annual meeting of the International Reading Association, Chicago, IL.

Paris, S. G., Newman, R., & McVey, K. (1982). Learning the functional significance of mnemonic actions: A microgenetic study of strategy acquisition. *Journal of Experimental Child Psychology, 34,* 490–509.

Paris, S. G., & Oka, E. R. (1986). Self-regulated learning among exceptional children. *Exceptional Children, 53*(2), 103–108.

Pascal, F. (1983–1989). *Sweet valley high series.* New York: Bantam.

Pastor, E., & Kerns, E. (1997). A digital snapshot of an early childhood classroom. *Educational Leadership, 55*(3), 42–45.

Pauk, W. (1989). *How to study in college* (4th ed.). Boston: Houghton Mifflin.

Pearson, P. D., & Johnson, D. (1978). *Teaching reading comprehension.* New York: Holt, Rinehart, & Winston.

Pepper, I. C. (1986). Social and cultural effects on Indian learning style: Classroom implications. *Canadian Journal of Native Education, 13*(1), 54–61.

Perl, J. (1995). Improving relationship skills for parent conferences. *TEACHING Exceptional Children, 28*(1), 29–31.

Peterson, N. L. (1987). *Early intervention for handicapped and at-risk children: An introduction to early childhood–special education.* Denver, CO: Love Publishing.

Peters-Walters, S. (1998). Accessible Web site design. *TEACHING Exceptional Children, 30*(5), 42–47.

Phillips, V., & McCullough, L. (1990). Consultation-based programming: Instituting the collaborative ethic in schools. *Exceptional Children, 56*(4), 291–304.

Pickett, A. L. (1986). *Paraprofessionals in special education: The state of the art.* New York: City University of New York, New Careers Training Laboratory.

Pickett, A. L. (1988). *A training program for paraprofessionals working in special education and related services.* New York: National Resource Center for Paraprofessionals in Special Education, New Careers Training Laboratory, City University of New York.

Platt, J. M. (1987). Increasing the independence of learning-disabled adolescents through self-detection of errors. *Ideas in Education, 4*(1), 17–23.

Platt, J. M., & Olson, J. (1997). *Teaching adolescents with mild disabilities.* Pacific Grove, CA: Brooks/Cole.

Platt, J. M., & Williams, K. (1988). Preservice and inservice teachers' reading comprehension skills and their metacognitive awareness of processing of text. *Eighth Yearbook of the American Reading Forum.* Sarasota, FL: American Reading Forum.

Polloway, E. A., Epstein, M. H., Bursuck, W. D., Roderique, T. W., McConeghy, J., & Jayanthi, M. (1994). Classroom grading: A national survey of policies. *Remedial and Special Education, 15,* 162–170.

Polloway, E. A., Epstein, M. H., Polloway, C. H., Patton, I. R., & Ball, D. W. (1986). Corrective reading program: An analysis of effectiveness with learning disabled and mentally retarded students. *Remedial and Special Education, 7*(4), 41–47.

Polloway, E. A., & Patton, J. R. (1997). *Strategies for teaching learners with special needs* (5th ed.). Upper Saddle River, NJ: Merrill/Prentice Hall.

Polloway, E. A., Patton, J. R., Epstein, M. H., & Smith, T. E. (1989). Comprehensive curriculum for students with mild disabilities. *Focus on Exceptional Children, 21,* 1–12.

Polloway, E. A., Patton, J. R., Payne, J. S., & Payne, R. A. (1989). *Strategies for teaching learners with special needs* (4th ed.). Upper Saddle River, NJ: Merrill/Prentice Hall.

Pomplun, M. (1996). Cooperative groups: Alternative assessment for students with disabilities? *The Journal of Special Education, 30*(1), 1–17.

Popham, W. J. (1997). What's wrong—and What's right—with rubrics. *Educational Leadership, 55*(2), 72–75.

Poplin, M. S. (1988). Holistic/constructivist principles of the teaching/learning process: Implications for the field of learning disabilities. *Journal of Learning Disabilities, 21*(7), 389–400.

The Portfolio Assessment Kit (Computer Software). (1996). New York: Super School.

Powers, D. A. (1986). Evaluating software for use by mentally handicapped learners. *Computers in the Schools, 3*(3–4), 41–49.

Pressley, M., Borkowski, J. G., & O'Sullivan, J. T. (1984). Memory strategy instruction is made of this: Metamemory and durable strategy use. *Educational Psychologist, 1,* 94–107.

Pressley, M., Hogan, K., Wharton-McDonald, R., Mistretta, J., & Ettenberger, S. (1996). The challenges of instructional scaffolding: The challenges of instruction that supports student thinking. *Learning Disabilities Research & Practice, 11*(3), 138–146.

Pressley, M., Symons, S., Snyder, B. L., & Cariglia-Bull, T. (1989). Strategy instruction research comes of age. *Learning Disability Quarterly, 12*(1), 16–31.

Pressley, M., Woloshyn, V., & Associates. (1995). *Cognitive strategy instruction that really improves children's academic performance.* Cambridge, MA: Brookline Books.

Public Law 94–142. (1975). *The Equal Education for All Handicapped Children Act.* Washington, DC: The U.S. Congress.

Public Law 98–199. (1983). *Amendments to PL 94–142: The School to Work Transition Initiative.* Washington, DC: The U.S. Congress.

Public Law 101–476. (1990). *Amendments to PL 94–142: The Individuals with Disabilities Education Act.* Washington, DC: The U.S. Congress.

Pugach, M. C., & Johnson, L. J. (1988). Rethinking the relationship between consultation and collaborative problem solving. *Focus on Exceptional Children, 21*(4), 1–14.

Pugach, M. C., & Johnson, L. J. (1989). The challenge of implementing collaboration between general and special education. *Exceptional Children, 56*(3), 232–235.

Pugach, M. C., & Johnson, L. J. (1995). *Collaborative practitioners, collaborative schools.* Denver, CO: Love.

Putnam, J. W., Rynders, J. E., Johnson, R. T., & Johnson, D. W. (1989). Collaborative skill instruction for promoting positive interactions between mentally handicapped and nonhandicapped children. *Exceptional Children, 55*(6), 550–558.

Putnam, M. L., Deshler, D. D., & Schumaker, J. B. (1993). The investigation of setting demands: A missing link in learning strategy instruction. In L. S. Meltzer (Ed.), *Strategy assessment and instruction for students with learning disabilities* (pp. 325–354). Austin, TX: PRO-ED.

Putnam, M. L., & Wesson, C. L. (1990). The teacher's role in teaching content-area information. *LD Forum, 16*(1), 55–60.

Ray, J., & Warden, M. K. (1995). *Technology, computers, and the special needs learner.* Albany, NY: Delmar.

Raygor, A. L. (1970). *Study skills test: Form A.* New York: McGraw-Hill.

Reeve, P. T., & Hallahan, D. P. (1994). Practical questions about collaboration between general and special educators. *Focus on Exceptional Children, 26*(7), 1–12.

Reid, D. K., Kurkjian, C., & Carruthers, S. S. (1994). Special education teachers interpret constructivist teaching. *Remedial and Special Education, 15*(5), 267–280.

Reid, E. (1986). Practicing effective instruction: The exemplary center for reading instruction approach. *Exceptional Children, 52*(6), 510–517.

Reynolds, M. C. (1991). Classification and labeling. In J. W. Lloyd, A. C. Repp, & N. N. Singh (Eds.), *The Regular Education Initiative: Alternative perspec-*

tives on concepts, issues, and models (pp. 29–41). Sycamore, IL: Sycamore.

Reynolds, M. C., Wang, M. C., & Walberg, H. J. (1987). The necessary restructuring of special and regular education. *Exceptional Children, 53*(5), 391–398.

Rhodes, L. K. (1981). I can read: Predictable books as resources for reading and writing instruction. *The Reading Teacher, 34*(5), 511–518.

Rhodes, L. K., & Dudley-Marling, C. (1988). *Readers and writers make a difference: A holistic approach to teaching learning disabled and remedial students.* Portsmouth, NH: Heinemann Educational Books.

Rich, H. L., & Ross, S. M. (1989). Student's time on learning tasks in special education. *Exceptional Child, 55*(6), 508–515.

Rickards, J. P., & August, G. J. (1975). Generative underlining strategies in prose recall. *Journal of Educational Psychology, 67,* 860–865.

Riegel, R. H., Mayle, J. A., & McCarthy-Henkel, J. (1988). *Beyond maladies and remedies.* Novi, MI: RHR Consultation Services.

Rieth, H. J., & Frick, T. W. (1982). *An analysis of academic learning time in special education service delivery systems: Initial report on classroom process variables* (Technical report). Bloomington, IN: Center for Innovation in Teaching the Handicapped, Indiana University.

Rieth, H. J., Polsgrove, L., Okolo, C., Bahr, C., & Eckert, R. (1987). An analysis of the secondary special education classroom ecology with implications for teacher training. *Teacher Education and Special Education, 10*(3), 113–119.

Ritter, S., & Idol-Maestas, L. (1986). Teaching middle school students to use a test-taking strategy. *Journal of Educational Research, 79*(6), 350–357.

Rivera, B. D., & Rogers-Adkinson, D. (1997). Culturally sensitive interventions: Social skills training with children and parents from culturally and linguistically diverse backgrounds. *Intervention in School and Clinic, 33*(2), 75–80.

Rivera, D. P. (1995). Portfolio assessment. *Diagnostique, 20* (1–4), 207–210.

Rivera, D. P., & Smith, D. D. (1988). Using a demonstration strategy to teach midschool students with learning disabilities how to compute long division. *Journal of Learning Disabilities, 21*(2), 77–81.

Rivera, D. P., & Smith, D. D. (1997). Teaching students with learning and behavior problems. Needham Heights, MA: Allyn & Bacon.

Roberds-Baxter, S. (1984). The parent connection: Enhancing the affective component of parent conferences. *TEACHING Exceptional Children, 17*(1), 55–58.

Roberts, G. H. (1968). The failure strategies of third grade arithmetic pupils. *The Arithmetic Teacher, 15,* 442–446.

Robinson, H. A. (1975). *Teaching reading and study strategies: The content areas.* Needham Heights, MA: Allyn & Bacon.

Roblyer, M. D. (1989). *Making the most of computers in the classroom: Effective models for integrating computer courseware into school instructional programs.* Tallahassee, FL: Florida Department of Education.

Roessler, R. R., Brolin, D. E., & Johnson, J. M. (1990). Factors affecting employment success and quality of life: A one year follow-up of students in special education. *Career Development for Exceptional Individuals, 13*(2), 95–107.

Rooney, K., Polloway, E. A., & Hallahan, D. P. (1985). The use of self-monitoring procedures with low IQ LD students. *Journal of Learning Disabilities, 18,* 384–394.

Rosenberg, M. S. (1986). Maximizing the effectiveness of structured classroom management programs: Implementing rule-review procedures with disruptive and distractible students. *Behavioral Disorders, 11*(4), 239–248.

Rosenfield, P., Lambert, N., & Black, A. (1985). Desk arrangement effects on pupil classroom behavior. *Journal of Educational Psychology, 77,* 101–108.

Rosenshine, B. (1980). How time is spent in elementary classrooms. In C. Denharm & A. Lieberman (Eds.), *Time to learn.* Washington, DC: National Institute of Education.

Rosenshine, B. (1983). Teaching functions in instructional programs. *Elementary School Journal, 83,* 335–351.

Rosenshine, B. (1990). How time is spent in elementary classrooms. In C. Denharm & A. Lieberman (Eds.), *Time to learn.* Washington, DC: National Institute of Education.

Rosenshine, B. (1997, March). *The case for explicit, teacher-led, cognitive strategy instruction.* Paper presented at the annual meeting of the American Educational Research Association, Chicago.

Rosenshine, B., & Stevens, R. (1986). Teaching functions. In M. Wittrock (Ed.), *Third handbook of re-*

search on teaching (pp. 376–391). New York: Macmillan.

Rosenthal-Malek, A. L. (1997). STOP and THINK: Using metacognitive strategies to teach students social skills. *TEACHING Exceptional Children, 29*(3), 29–31.

Roser, N. L., Hoffman, J. V., & Farest, C. (1990). Language, literature, and at-risk children. *Reading Teacher, 43*(8), 554–561.

Rounds, K. A., Weil, M., & Bishop, K. K. (1994), Practice with culturally diverse families of young children with disabilities. *Families and Society: The Journal of Contemporary Human Services, 75*(1), 3–14.

Rowe, M. B. (1974). Wait time and rewards as instructional variables, their influence on language, logic, and rate control: Part 1: Wait time. *Journal of Research in Science Teaching, 11,* 81–94.

Rowe, M. B. (1987). Wait-time: Slowing down may be a way of speeding up. *American Educator, 11*(1), 38–47.

Rozenholtz, S., Basler, O., & Hoover-Dempsey. (1985). *Organizational conditions of teacher learning* (NIE-G-83-0041). Urbana, IL: University of Illinois.

Rueda, R., & Garcia, E. (1997). Do portfolios make a difference for diverse students? The influence of type of data on making instructional decisions. *Learning Disabilities Research & Practice, 12*(2), 114–122.

Ruhl, K. L., Hughes, C. A., & Gajar. (1990). Efficiency of the pause procedure for enhancing learning disabled and nondisabled college students' long- and short-term recall of facts presented through lecture. *Learning Disability Quarterly, 13*(2), pp. 55–64.

Ruiz, N. T. (1989). An optimal learning environment for Rosemary. *Exceptional Child, 56*(2), 130–144.

Rutherford, R., Chipman, J., DiGangi, S., & Anderson, K. (1992). *Teaching social skill: A practical instructional approach.* Reston, VA: Council for Exceptional Children.

Ryan, E. B., Weed, K. A., & Short, E. J. (1986). Cognitive behavior modification: Promoting active, self-regulatory learning styles. In J. K. Torgesen & B. Y. L. Wong (Eds.), *Psychological and educational perspectives on learning disabilities* (pp. 367–397). New York: Academic Press.

Sailor, W. (1991). Special education in the restructured school. *Remedial and Special Education, 12*(6), 8–22.

Sainato, D. M., Strain, P. S., & Lyon, S. L. (1987). Increasing academic responding of handicapped preschool children during group instruction. *Journal of the Division of Early Childhood Special Education, 12,* 23–30.

Salembier, G., & Furney, K. S. (1997). Facilitating participation: Parents' perceptions of their involvement in the IEP/transition planning process. *Career Development for Exceptional Individuals, 20,* 29–42.

Salend, S. J. (1995). *Effective mainstreaming: Creating inclusive classrooms* (2nd ed.). New York: Macmillan.

Salend, S. J. (1995). Using videocassette recorder technology in special education classrooms. *TEACHING Exceptional Children, 27*(3), 4–9.

Salend, S. J., & Allen, E. M. (1985). A comparison of self-managed and externally managed response cost systems on learning disabled children. *Journal of School Psychology, 23,* 59–67.

Salend, S. J., Jantzen, N. R., & Giek, K. (1992). Using a peer confrontation system in a group setting. *Behavioral Disorders, 17*(3), 211–218.

Salvia, J., & Hughes, C. (1990). *Curriculum-based assessment: Testing what is taught.* New York: Macmillan.

Salvia, J., & Ysseldyke, J. E. (1988). *Assessment in special and remedial education* (4th ed.). Boston: Houghton-Mifflin.

Sapon-Shevin, M. (1986). Teaching cooperation. In G. Cartledge & J. F. Milburn (Eds.), *Teaching social skills to children: Innovative approaches* (3rd ed.). Elmsford, NY: Pergamon.

Sargent, L. R. (1981). Resource teacher time utilization: An observational study. *Exceptional Children, 47*(6), 420–426.

Sargent, L. R. (1991). *Social skills in the school and community.* Reston, VA: Council for Exceptional Children.

Saski, J., Swicegood, P., & Carter, J. (1983). Notetaking formats for learning disabled adolescents. *Learning Disability Quarterly, 6*(3), 265–272.

Saville-Troike, M. (1976). *Foundations for teaching English as a second language: Theory and method for multicultural education.* Upper Saddle River, NJ: Prentice Hall.

Sawyer, R., Graham, S., & Harris, K. R. (1992). Direct teaching, strategy instruction, and strategy instruction with explicit self-regulation: Effects on learning disabled students' compositions and self-efficacy. *Journal of Educational Psychology, 84,* 340–352.

Scanlon, D., Deshler, D. D., & Schumaker, J. B. (1996). Can a strategy be taught and learned in secondary inclusive classrooms? *Learning Disabilities Research and Practice, 11*(1), 41–57.

Schloss, P. J., & Schloss, C. N. (1987). A critical review of social skills research in mental retardation. In R. P. Barrett & J. L. Matson (Eds.), *Advances in developmental disorders* (pp. 107–151). Greenwich, CT: JAI Press.

Schloss, P. J., Schloss, C. N., & Harris, L. (1984). A multiple baseline analysis of an interpersonal skills training program for depressed youth. *Behavior Disorders, 9,* 182–188.

Schloss, P. J., & Sedlak, R. A. (1986). *Instructional methods for students with learning and behavior problems.* Needham Heights, MA: Allyn & Bacon.

Schloss, P. J., Smith, M. A., & Schloss, C. N. (1995). *Instructional methods for adolescents with learning and behavior problems* (2nd ed.). Needham Heights, MA: Allyn & Bacon.

Schmidt, J. L. (1983). *The effects of four generalization conditions on learning disabled adolescents' written language performance in the regular classroom.* Unpublished doctoral dissertation, University of Kansas, Lawrence.

Schneider, W. (1985). Developmental trends in metamemory-memory relationships: An integrative review. In D. Forrest-Pressley, G. E. McKinnnon, & T. G. Waller (Eds.), *Metacognition, cognition, and human performance* (pp. 57–109). New York: Academic Press.

Schniedewind, N., & Salend, S. J. (1987). Cooperative learning works. *TEACHING Exceptional Children, 19*(2), 22–25.

Schuler, L., Ogulthorpe, R. T., & Eiserman, W. D. (1987). The effects of reverse-role tutoring on the social acceptance of students with behavioral disorders. *Behavioral Disorders, 13*(1), 35–44.

Schumaker, J. B. (1989). The heart of strategy instruction. *Strategram: Strategies intervention model, 1*(4). Kansas City, KS: The University of Kansas Institute for Research in Learning Disabilities, pp. 1–5.

Schumaker, J. B., & Deshler, D. D. (1988). Implementing the regular education initiative in secondary schools: A different ball game. *Journal of Learning Disabilities, 21*(1), 36–42.

Schumaker, J. B., Deshler, D. D., & McKnight, P. (1989). *Teaching routines to enhance the mainstream performance of adolescents with learning disabilities.* Final report submitted to U.S. Department of Education, Special Education Services.

Schumaker, J. B., Nolan, S. M., & Deshler, D. D. (1985). *The error monitoring strategy.* Lawrence, KA: The University of Kansas.

Schumaker, J. B., & Sheldon, J. (1985). *Learning strategies curriculum: The sentence writing strategy, instructor's manual.* Lawrence, KA: The University of Kansas.

Schutt, P. W., & McCabe, V. M. (1994). Portfolio assessment for students with learning disabilities. *Learning Disabilities, 5*(2), 81–85.

Scruggs, T. E., & Mastropieri, M. A. (1984). Improving memory for facts: The "keyword" method. *Academic Therapy, 20*(2), 159–166.

Scruggs, T. E., & Mastropieri, M. A. (1986). Academic characteristics of behaviorally disordered and learning-disabled students. *Behavioral Disorders, 11*(3), 184–190.

Scruggs, T. E., & Mastropieri, M. A. (1993). Current approaches to science education: Implications for mainstreaming instruction to students with disabilities. *Remedial and Special Education, 14,* 15–24.

Scruggs, T. E., Mastropieri, M. A., Levin, J. R., & Gaffney, J. S. (1985). Facilitating the acquisition of science facts in learning-disabled students. *American Educational Research Journal, 22,* 575–586.

Scruggs, T. E., Mastropieri, M. A., & Richter, L. (1985). Peer tutoring with behaviorally disordered students: Social and academic benefits. *Behavioral Disorders, 10*(4), 283–294.

Scruggs, T. E., & Wong, B. Y. L. (1990). *Intervention research in learning disabilities.* New York: Springer-Verlag.

Secretary's Commission on Achieving Necessary Skills (SCANS). (1991). *What work requires of schools.* Washington, DC: U.S. Department of Labor.

Senate Subcommittee. (1986). *Report to the U.S. Senate: President's committee on employment of the handicapped.* Washington, DC: U.S. Department of Education.

Serna, L. A. & Lau-Smith, J. (1995). *Learning with PURPOSE: An instructor's manual for teaching self-determination skills to students who are at-risk for failure.* Albuquerque: University of New Mexico.

Shanahan, T., Robinson, B., & Schneider, M. (1995). Integrating curriculum: Avoiding some of the pitfalls of thematic units. *The Reading Teacher, 48*(8), 718–719.

Shields, J. M., & Heron, T. E. (1989). Teaching organizational skills to students with learning disabilities. *TEACHING Exceptional Children, 21*(2), 8–13.

Shinn, M. (Ed.). (1989). *Curriculum-based measurement: Assessing special children.* New York: The Guilford Press.

Shinn, M., & Marston, D. (1985). Differentiating mildly handicapped, low achieving, and regular education students: A curriculum-based approach. *RASE, 6*(2), 31–38.

Showers, B. (1985). Teachers coaching teachers. *Educational Leadership, 42*(7), 43–48.

Showers, B. (1990). Aiming for superior classroom instruction for all children: A comprehensive staff development model. *Remedial and Special Education, 11*(3), 50–53.

Shute, A. P., Haynes, H., & Choate, S. A. (1986). *Applying mathematics in daily living.* Sacramento, CA: Laidlaw Brothers Publishers.

Silbert, J., Carnine, D., & Stein, M. (1990). *Direct instruction mathematics* (2nd ed.). Upper Saddle River, NJ: Merrill/Prentice Hall.

Silver Burdett Spelling Teacher Resource Book 4, Unit 6 (developed by J. D'Andrea Hunt). (1986). Morristown, NJ: Silver Burdett Co.

Simmonds, E. P. M., Luchow, J. P., Kaminsky, S., & Cottone, V. (1989). Applying cognitive learning strategies in the classroom: A collaborative training institute. *Learning Disabilities Focus, 4,* 96–105.

Simpson, R. L. (1982). *Conferencing parents of exceptional children.* Rockville, MD: Aspen.

Sinclair, R. L., & Ghory, W. J. (1987). *Reaching marginal students: A primary concern for school renewal.* Chicago: McCutchan.

Sindelar, P. T., Bursuck, W. D., & Halle, J. W. (1986). The effects of two variations of teacher questioning on student performance. *Education and Treatment of Children, 9*(1), 56–66.

Sindelar, P. T., Griffin, C. C., Smith, S. W., & Watanabe, A. K. (1992). Prereferral intervention: Encouraging notes on preliminary findings. *The Elementary School Journal, 92*(3), 245–259.

Sindelar, P. T., Smith, M., Harriman, N., Hale, R., & Wilson, R. (1986). Teacher effectiveness in special education programs. *Journal of Special Education, 20*(2), 195–207.

Sitlington, P. L., Frank, A. R., & Carson, R. (1993). Adult adjustment among high school graduates with mild disabilities. *Exceptional Children, 59*(3), 221–233.

Slavin, R. E. (1984). Team-assisted individualization: Cooperative learning and individualized instruction in the mainstreamed classroom. *Remedial and Special Education, 5*(6), 33–42.

Slavin, R. E. (1985). Cooperative learning: Applying contact theory in desegregated schools. *Journal of Social Issues, 41*(3), 45–62.

Slavin, R. E. (1988a). Cooperative learning and student achievement. *Educational Leadership, 46*(2), 31–33.

Slavin, R. E. (1988b). *Student team learning: An overview and practical guide* (2nd ed.). Washington, DC: National Education Association.

Slavin, R. E., Leavey, M., & Madden, N. A. (1984). Combining cooperative learning and individualized instruction: Effects on student mathematics achievement, attitudes, and behaviors. *Elementary School Journal, 84,* 409–422.

Slavin, R. E., Stevens, R. J., & Madden, N. A. (1988). Accommodating student diversity in reading and writing instruction: A cooperative learning approach. *Remedial and Special Education, 9*(1), 60–66.

Smith, D. D. (1998). *Introduction to Special Education: Teaching in an Age of Challenge* (3rd ed.). Needham Heights, MA: Allyn and Bacon.

Smith, J. O. (1995). Getting to the bottom of social skills deficits. *LD Forum, 21*(1), 23–26.

Smith, S., Boone, R., & Higgins, K. (1998). Expanding the writing process to the web. *TEACHING Exceptional Children, 30*(5), 22–26.

Snider, V. E. (1992). Learning styles and learning to read: A critique. *Remedial and Special Education, 13*(1), 6–18.

Soldier, L. L. (1989). Language learning of Native American students. *Educational Leadership, 46*(5), 74–75.

Sonnenschein, P. (1981). Parents and professionals: An uneasy relationship. *TEACHING Exceptional Children, 14*(2), 62–65.

Spache, G. D., & Spache, E. B. (1977). *Reading in the elementary school.* Needham Heights, MA: Allyn & Bacon.

Speece, D. L., MacDonald, V., Kilsheimer, L., & Krist, J. (1997). Research to practice: Preservice teachers reflect on reciprocal teaching. *Learning Disabilities Practice, 12*(3), 177–187.

Sprick, R. S. (1981). *The solution book: A guide to classroom discipline.* Chicago: Science Research Associates.

Sprick, R. S. (1985). *Discipline in the secondary classroom: A problem-by-problem survival guide.* West Nyack, NY: The Center for Applied Research in Education.

Squires, D. A., Huitt, W. G., & Segars, J. K. (1983). *Effective schools and classrooms: A research-based perspective.* Alexandria, VA: Association for Supervision and Curriculum Development.

Stahl, S., McKenna, M., & Pagnucco, J. (1994). The effects of whole-language instruction: An update and a reappraisal. *Educational Psychologist, 29*(4), 175–185.

Stainback, W., & Stainback, S. (1984). A rationale for the merger of special and regular education. *Exceptional Children, 51*, 102–111.

Stainback, W., & Stainback, S. (1991). Rationale for integration and restructuring: A synopsis. In J. W. Lloyd, A. C. Repp, & N. N. Singh (Eds.), *The Regular Education Initiative: Alternative perspectives on concepts, issues, and models* (pp. 225–239). Sycamore, IL: Sycamore.

Stainback, W., Stainback, S., & Stefanich, G. (1996). Learning together in inclusive classrooms. *TEACHING Exceptional Children, 28*(3), 14–19.

Stallings, J. (1980). Allocated academic learning time revisited, or beyond time on-task. *Educational Researcher, 9*, 11–16.

Stamm, J. M. (1980). Teacher competencies: Recommendations for personnel preparation. *Teacher Education and Special Education, 3*(1), 52–57.

Stanciak, L. A. (1997). Curriculum integration and brain-based learning. *Connections, 2*(1), 2.

Standal, T. (1978). Readabiliity formulas: What's out, what's in? *The Reading Teacher, 21*, 642–646.

Stanley, S. O., & Greenwood, C. R. (1983). How much "opportunity to respond" does the minority disadvantaged student receive in school? *Exceptional Children, 49*, 370–373.

Stanovich, K. (1994). Constructivism in reading education. *The Journal of Special Education, 28*(3), 259–274.

State of Florida. (1993). *Transition the IDEA way.* Tallahassee, FL: Florida Department of Education, Bureau of Education for Exceptional Students.

Stein, C. L'E., & Goldman, J. (1980). Beginning reading instruction for children with minimal brain dysfunction. *Journal of Learning Disability, 13*(4), 52–55.

Stein, M., Carnine, D., & Dixon, R. (1998). Direct instruction: Integrating curriculum design and effective teaching practice. *Intervention in School and Clinic, 33*(4), 227–234.

Stemmer, P., Brown, B., & Smith., C. (1992). The employability skills portfolio. *Educational Leadership, 49*(6), 32–35.

Stephens, T. M., Blackhurst, A. E., & Magliocca, L. A. (1988). *Teaching mainstreamed students* (2nd ed.). New York: Pergamon.

Steptoe, J. (1987). *Mufaro's beautiful daughters.* New York: Lothrop, Lee, & Shepard.

Stevens, R. J., & Slavin, R. E. (1991). When cooperative learning improves the achievement of students with mild disabilities: A response to Tateyama-Sniezek. *Exceptional Children, 57*(3), 276–280.

Strichart, S. S., & Mangrum, C. T. (1993). *Teaching study strategies to students with learning disabilities.* Needham Heights, MA: Allyn & Bacon.

Sugai, G., Maheady, L., & Skouge, J. (1989). Best assessment practices for students with behavioral disorders: Accommodation to cultural diversity and individual differences. *Behavioral Disorders, 14*(4), 263–278.

Suritsky, S. K., and Hughes, C. A. (1996). Notetaking strategy instruction. In D. D. Deshler, E. S. Ellis, & B. K. Lenz (Eds.), *Adolescents with learning disabilities: Strategies and methods* (2nd ed.). Denver, CO: Love.

Swaggert, B. L. (1998). Implementing a cognitive behavior management program. *Intervention School and Clinic, 33*(4), 235–238.

Swanson, H. L. (1989). Strategy instruction: Overview of principles and procedures. *Learning Disability Quarterly, 12*(1), 3–15.

Swicegood, P. R., & Parsons, J. L. (1991). The thematic unit approach: Content and process instruction for secondary learning disabled students. *Learning Disabilities Research & Practice, 6*(2), 112–116.

Tarver, S. G. (1986). Cognitive behavior modification, direct instruction and holistic approaches to the education of students with learning disabilities. *Journal of Learning Disabilities, 19*(6), 368–375.

Tateyama-Sniezek, K. M. (1990). Cooperative learning: Does it improve the academic achievement of students with handicaps? *Exceptional Children, 56*(5), 426–437.

Taylor, B. M., & Beach, R. W. (1984). The effects of text structure instruction on middle-grade students' comprehension and production of expository text. *Reading Research Quarterly, 19*, 134–146.

Taylor, S. E. (1964). *Listening.* Washington, DC: National Education Association.

Tharp, R. G. (1975). The triadic model of consultation. In C. Parker (Ed.), *Psychological consultation in the schools: Helping teachers meet special needs* (pp. 133–151). Reston, VA: The Council for Exceptional Children.

Tharp, R. G., & Wetzel, R. J. (1969). *Behavior modification in the natural environment.* New York: Academic Press.

Thurlow, M., Christenson, S., & Ysseldyke, J. (1987). *School effectiveness: Implications of effective construction for handicapped students* (Monograph B. 3). Minneapolis, MN: Instructional Alternative Project, University of Minnesota.

Thurston, L. P. (1987). *Survival skills for women: Facilitator manual.* Manhattan, KS: Survival Skills and Development.

Tiedt, P. L., & Tiedt, I. M. (1986). *Multicultural teaching.* Needham Heights, MA: Allyn & Bacon.

Tindal, G. A., & Marston, D. B. (1990). *Classroom-based assessment: Evaluating instructional outcomes.* Upper Saddle River, NJ: Merrill/Prentice Hall.

Tindal, G. A., Shinn, M. R., & Rodden-Nord, K. (1990). Contextually based school consultation: Influential variables. *Exceptional Children, 56*(4), 324–336.

Tobin, K. (1987). The role of wait time in higher cognitive level learning. *Review of Educational Research, 57*(1), 69–95.

Tolan, S. S. (1978). *Grandpa and me.* New York: Charles Scribner's Sons.

Torgesen, J. K. (1977). Memorization processes in reading disabled children. *Journal of Educational Psychology, 69,* 571–578.

Torgesen, J. K. (1982). The learning disabled child as an inactive learner: Educational implications. *Topics in Learning and Learning Disabilities, 2*(1), 45–52.

Trammel, D. L., Schloss, P. T., & Alper, S. (1994). Using self-recording, evaluation, and graphing to increase completion of homework assignments. *Journal of Learning Disabilities, 27*(2), 75–81.

Turnbull, A. P., Strickland, B. B., & Brantley, J. C. (1982). *Developing and implementing individualized education programs.* Upper Saddle River, NJ: Merrill/Prentice Hall.

Turnbull, A. P., & Turnbull, H. R. (1986). *Families, professionals, and exceptionality: A special partnership.* Upper Saddle River, NJ: Merrill/Prentice Hall.

Udvari-Solner, A. (1997). Effective accommodations for students with exceptionalities. *CEC Today, 4*(3), 1, 9–15.

U.S. Department of Education (1996). *Eighteenth annual report to Congress on the implementation of the Education for Handicapped Act.* Washington, DC: U.S. Government Printing Office.

Uthe-Reyno, M. G., & McKinnon, D. L. J. (1989). Teacher's modeling encourages learning in Indian students. *Education Horizons, 67*(4), 163–165.

Utley, C. A., Mortsweet, S. L., & Greenwood, C. R. (1997). Peer-mediated instruction and interventions. *Focus on Exceptional Children, 29*(5), 1–23.

Valencia, S. (1990). A portfolio approach to classroom reading assessment: The whys, whats, and hows. *The Reading Teacher, 43*(4), 338–340.

VanReusen, A. K., & Bos, C. S. (1994). Facilitating student participation in individualized education programs through motivation strategy instruction. *Exceptional Children, 60*(5), 466–475.

VanReusen, A. K., Bos, C. S., Schumaker, J. B., & Deshler, D. (1987). *The education planning strategy: A motivation strategy.* Lawrence, KS: Edge Enterprises, Inc.

VanReusen, A. K., Bos, C. S., Schumaker, J. B., & Deshler, D. D. (1994). *The self-advocacy strategy for education and transition planning.* Lawrence, KS: Edge Enterprises.

Vaughn, S., & Schumm, J. S., (1995). Responsible inclusion for students with learning disabilities. *Journal of Learning Disabilities, 28*(5), 264–270, 290.

Veit, D. T., Scruggs, T. E., & Mastropieri, M. A. (1986). Extended mnemonic instruction with learning disabled students. *Journal of Educational Psychology, 78,* 300–308.

Viorst, J. (1972). *Alexander and the terrible, horrible, no-good, very bad day.* New York: Atheneum.

Voltz, D. L., & Elliot, R. N. (1997). Collaborative teacher roles in facilitating inclusion: Preservice preparation for general and special educators. *The Teacher Educator, 33*(1), 44–60.

Voltz, D. L., Elliot, R. N., & Cobb, H. (1994). Collaborative teacher roles: Special and general educators. *Journal of Learning Disabilities, 27*(8), 527–535.

Vygotsky, L. S. (1962). *Thought and language.* New York: Wiley.

Wagner, M. M., & Blackorby, J. (1996, Spring). Transition from high school to work or college: How special education students fare. *The Future of Children,* 103–120.

Wagner, M. M., Blackorby, J., Cameto, R., & Newman, L. (1993). *What makes a difference? Influences on postschool outcomes of youth with disabilities.* Menlo Park, CA: SRI International.

Wagner, M. M., Blackorby, J., & Hebbler, K. (1993). *Beyond the report card: The multiple dimensions of secondary school performance for students with disabilities.* Menlo Park, CA: SRI International.

Walker, B. L. (1988). *Basic English grammar* (2nd ed.) Baltimore, MD: Media Materials.

Walker, D. M., Schwarz, I. E., Nippold, M. S., Irvin, L. K., & Noell, J. W. (1994). Social skills in school-age children and youth: Issues and best practices in assessment and intervention. *Topics in Language Disorders, 14*(3), 70–82.

Walker, J. L. (1987). Language and curriculum development for American Indian handicapped children. In M. J. Johnson & B. A. Ramirez (Eds.), *American Indian exceptional children and youth* (pp. 17–23). Reston, VA: The Council for Exceptional Children.

Walker, J. L. (1988). Young American Indian children. *TEACHING Exceptional Children, 20*(4), 50–51.

Walker, S. (1981). *Structuring the learning environment for minority handicapped students.* Washington, DC: National Alliance of Black School Educators, Special Education Programs.

Wallace, G., & Kauffman, J. M. (1986). *Teaching students with learning and behavior problems* (3rd ed.). Upper Saddle River, NJ: Merrill/Prentice Hall.

Wang, M. C., & Reynolds, M. (1985). Avoiding the "catch-22" in special education reform. *Exceptional Children, 51,* 497–502.

Warger, C. L. (1990). *Can social skills for employment be taught using cognitive-behavioral procedures with adolescents with mild disabilities?* (Research and Resources on Special Education, No. 28). Reston, VA: Council for Exceptional Children.

Washington, V. M., & Miller-Jones, D. (1989). Teacher interactions with nonstandard English speakers during reading instruction. *Contemporary Educational Psychology, 14,* 280–312.

Watson, D. L., Northcutt, L., & Rydele, L. (1989). Teaching bilingual students successfully. *Educational Leadership, 46*(5), 59–61.

Watson, O. M. (1970). Proxemic behavior: A cross-cultural study. *The Hague.* The Hague: Mouton.

Weaver, C., Chaston, J., & Peterson, S. (1993). *Theme exploration: A voyage of discovery.* Portsmouth, NH: Heinemann.

Wehman, P. (1993). *Life beyond the classroom: Transition services for youth with disabilities.* Baltimore, MD: Paul H. Brookes.

Wehmeyer, M. L. (1995). *Whose future is it anyway? Student-directed transition planning process.* Arlington, TX: Arc National Headquarters.

Wei, T. T. D. (1980). *Vietnamese refugee students: A handbook for school personnel* (2nd ed.). (ERIC Document Reproduction Service No. ED 208 109)

Weinstein, C. S. (1981). Classroom design as an external condition for learning. *Educational Technology, 21*(8), 12–19.

Welch, M., Judge, T., Anderson, J., Bray, J., Child, B., & Franke, L. (1990). COOP: A tool for implementing prereferral consultation. *TEACHING Exceptional Children, 22*(2), 30–31.

Wells, G. (1981). *Learning through interaction.* Cambridge, MA: Cambridge University Press.

Wesson, C. L. (1987). Increasing efficiency. *Teaching Exceptional Children, 20*(1), 46.

Wesson, C. L., & King, R. P. (1996). Portfolio assessment and special education students. *TEACHING Exceptional Children, 28*(2), 44–48.

West, J. F., & Cannon, G. S. (1988). Essential collaborative consultation competencies for regular and special educators. *Journal of Learning Disabilities, 21*(1), 56–63.

West, J. F., Idol, L., & Cannon, G. (1989). *Collaboration in the schools: An inservice and preservice curriculum for teacher, support staff, and administrators.* Austin, TX: PRO-ED.

West, R. P., West, J. F., & Idol, L. (1990). Collaborative consultation in the education of mildly handicapped and at-risk students. *Remedial & Special Education, 11,* 22–31.

West, R. P., Young, K. R., & Spooner, F. (1990). Precision teaching: An introduction. *TEACHING Exceptional Children, 22*(3), 4–9.

West, R. P., Young, K. R., West, W. J., Johnson, J. I., & Freston, C. W. (1985). *AC-CEL: An artificial intelligence system for student performance evaluation and instructional decision making.* Sarasota, FL: Precision Teaching Materials and Associates.

White, A. E., & White, L. L. (1992). A collaborative model for students with mild disabilities in middle schools. *Focus on Exceptional Children, 24*(9), 1–10.

White, O. R. (1980). *Precision teaching workshop.* Orlando, FL.

White, O. R., & Haring, N. G. (1976). *Exceptional teaching.* Upper Saddle River, NJ: Merrill/Prentice Hall.

White, O. R., & Haring, N. G. (1980). *Exceptional teaching* (2nd ed.). Upper Saddle River, NJ: Merrill/Prentice Hall.

White, O. R., & Liberty, K. A. (1976). Evaluation and measurement. In N. G. Haring & R. Schiefelbusch (Eds.), *Teaching special children* (pp. 31–71). New York: McGraw-Hill.

Wiig, E., & Semel, E. (1984). *Language assessment and intervention for the learning disabled.* (2nd ed.). Upper Saddle River, NJ: Merrill/Prentice Hall.

Will, M. C. (1986). Educating children with learning problems: A shared responsibility. *Exceptional Children, 51*(5), 411–416.

Williams, R. M., & Rooney, K. J. (1986). *A handbook of cognitive behavior modification procedures for teachers.* Charlottesville: University of Virginia Learning Disabilities Research Institute.

Wilson, A. B. (1989). Theory into practice: An effective program for urban youth. *Educational Horizons, 67,* 136–144.

Wilson, L., Cone, T., Bradley, C., & Reese, J. (1986). The characteristics of learning disabled and other handicapped students referred for evaluation in the state of Iowa. *Journal of Learning Disabilities, 19*(9), 553–557.

Wilson, R. (1987). Direct observation of academic learning time. *TEACHING Exceptional Children, 19*(2), 13–17.

Winograd, P., & Hare, V. C. (1988). Direct instruction of reading comprehension strategies: The nature of teacher explanation. In E. T., Goetz, P. Alexander, & C. Weinstein (Eds.), *Learning and study strategies: Assessment, instruction, and evaluation* (pp. 25–56). New York: Academic Press.

Winzer, M. A., & Mazurek, K. (1998). *Special education in multicultural contexts.* Upper Saddle River, NJ: Merrill/Prentice Hall.

Wise, W. E., & Matthews, C. L. (1987). *A study of the relationship of education and transition factors to the job status of mildly and moderately handicapped students* (Report #95–01/87/06/04). Dover, DE: Delaware State Department of Public Instruction.

Wissick, C. A., & Gardner, J. E. (1998). A learner's permit to the World Wide Web. *TEACHING Exceptional Children, 30*(5), 8–15.

Wohlge, N. (1983). Keeping communication clear. In O. Miramontes (Ed.), Application of research and theory in the classroom (p. 538). *Learning Disability Quarterly, 6*(4), 535–542.

Wolf, D. P. (1989). Portfolio assessment: Sampling student work. *Educational Leadership, 46*(7), 35–39.

Wong, B. Y. L. (1986). Metacognition and special education: A review of a view. *The Journal of Special Education, 20*(1), 9–29.

Wong, B. Y. L. (1992). On cognitive process-based instruction. *Journal of Learning Disabilities, 25,* 150–152.

Wong, B. Y. L. (1993). Pursuing an elusive goal: Molding strategic teachers and learners. *Journal of Learning Disabilities, 26,* 354–357.

Wong, B. Y. L., & Jones, W. (1982). Increasing metacomprehension in learning-disabled and normally-achieving students through self-questioning training. *Learning Disability Quarterly, 5,* 228–240.

Wong, B. Y. L., Wong, R., & LaMare, L. (1982). The effects of knowledge of criterion-task on comprehension and recall in normally achieving and learning-disabled children. *Journal of Educational Research, 76,* 119–126.

Wood, J. W., & Wooley, J. A. (1986). Adapting textbooks. *Clearing House, 59*(7), 332–335.

Woodward, J., & Gersten, R. (1993). Innovative technology for secondary students with learning disabilities. In E. L. Meyen, G. A. Vergason, & R. J. Whelan (Eds.), *Challenges facing special education* (pp. 141–161). Denver: Love.

Working Forum on Inclusive Schools. (1994). *Creating schools for all our students: What 12 schools have to say.* Reston, VA: The Council for Exceptional Children. (ERIC Document Reproduction Service No. ED 377 633).

Yasutake, D., Bryan, T., & Dohrn, E. (1996). The effects of combining peer tutoring and attribution training on students' perceived self-competence. *Remedial and Special Education, 17*(2), 83–91.

Yell, M. L., & Shriner, J. G. (1997). The IDEA amendments of 1997: Implications for special and general education teachers, administrators, and teacher trainers. *Focus on Exceptional Children, 30*(1), 1–19.

Zaragoza, N. (1987). Process writing for high-risk and learning-disabled students. *Reading Research and Instruction, 26*(4), 290–301.

Zigmond, N., Jenkins, J., Fuchs, L., Deno, S., Fuchs, D., Baker, J. N., Jenkins, L., & Coutinho, M. (1995). Special education in restructured schools. *Phi Delta Kappan, 76*(7), 531–540.

Zigmond, N., Levin, E., & Laurie, T. (1985). Managing the mainstream: An analysis of teacher attitudes and student performance in mainstream high school programs. *Journal of Learning Disabilities, 18,* 535–541.

Zigmond, N., Sansone, J., Miller, S.E., Donahoe, K. R., & Kohnke, R. (1986). *Teaching learning disabled students at the secondary school level.* Reston, VA: The Council for Exceptional Children.

Zirpoli, T. J., & Melloy, K. J. (1993). *Behavior management: Applications for teachers and parents.* New York: Macmillan Publishing Co.

Name Index

Subject Index